FOURTH EDITION

Qualitative Inquiry
& Research Design

John dedicates this book to Uncle Jim (James W. Marshall, MD, 1915–1997),
who provided love, support, and inspiration.

Cheryl dedicates this book to her dad (Richard F. Poth, MBA, 1944–2016), who instilled
confidence for trying new things, lessons for guiding life choices, and encouragement for pursuing bold dreams.

SAGE was founded in 1965 by Sara Miller McCune to support the dissemination of usable knowledge by publishing innovative and high-quality research and teaching content. Today, we publish over 900 journals, including those of more than 400 learned societies, more than 800 new books per year, and a growing range of library products including archives, data, case studies, reports, and video. SAGE remains majority-owned by our founder, and after Sara's lifetime will become owned by a charitable trust that secures our continued independence.

Los Angeles | London | New Delhi | Singapore | Washington DC | Melbourne

FOURTH EDITION

Qualitative Inquiry & Research Design
Choosing Among Five Approaches

John W. Creswell
University of Michigan

Cheryl N. Poth
University of Alberta

Los Angeles | London | New Delhi
Singapore | Washington DC | Melbourne

FOR INFORMATION:

SAGE Publications, Inc.
2455 Teller Road
Thousand Oaks, California 91320
E-mail: order@sagepub.com

SAGE Publications Ltd.
1 Oliver's Yard
55 City Road
London EC1Y 1SP
United Kingdom

SAGE Publications India Pvt. Ltd.
B 1/I 1 Mohan Cooperative Industrial Area
Mathura Road, New Delhi 110 044
India

SAGE Publications Asia-Pacific Pte. Ltd.
3 Church Street
#10-04 Samsung Hub
Singapore 049483

Acquisitions Editor: Helen Salmon
eLearning Editor: John Scappini
Editorial Assistant: Chelsea Pearson
Production Editor: Libby Larson
Copy Editor: Megan Markanich
Typesetter: C&M Digitals (P) Ltd.
Proofreader: Alison Syring
Indexer: Molly Hall
Cover Designer: Glenn Vogel
Marketing Manager: Susannah Goldes

Printed in the United States of America

Library of Congress Cataloging-in-Publication Data

ISBN 978-1-5063-3020-4

This book is printed on acid-free paper.

19 20 21 10 9 8 7 6 5 4 3

• Brief Contents •

• Detailed Contents •

• About the Authors •

John W. Creswell, PhD, is an adjunct professor of family medicine at the University of Michigan. He has authored numerous articles and 26 books (including new editions) on mixed methods research, qualitative research, and research design. While at the University of Nebraska–Lincoln, he held the Clifton Endowed Professor Chair; served as director of a mixed methods center; founded the SAGE journal, the *Journal of Mixed Methods Research*; and was an adjunct professor of family medicine at the University of Michigan and a consultant to the Veterans Administration health services research center, Ann Arbor, Michigan. He was a Senior Fulbright Scholar to South Africa in 2008 and to Thailand in 2012. In 2011, he led a national working group that advanced mixed methods practices in the health sciences at the National Institutes of Health (NIH). He also served as a visiting professor at the Harvard School of Public Health in 2013 and received an honorary doctorate from the University of Pretoria, South Africa in 2014. In 2014, he became the first president of the Mixed Methods International Research Association (MMIRA). In 2015, he assumed the role of the co-director of the Michigan Mixed Methods Research and Scholarship Program at the University of Michigan. He currently serves as a consultant and co-investigator on several national projects.

Cheryl N. Poth, PhD, has been a faculty member of the Centre for Research and Applied Measurement and Evaluation within the Department of Educational Psychology in the Faculty of Education at the University of Alberta since 2008. In this role, she has developed and taught graduate-level research methods and program evaluation courses in addition to supervising and mentoring students, faculty, and community members in qualitative, quantitative, and mixed methods research. Dr. Poth has an adjunct appointment in the Faculty of Medicine and Dentistry and serves as the methodologist on several cross-disciplinary research teams. She has been principal investigator for projects and grants funded federally (e.g., Social Sciences and Humanities Research Council and Physiotherapy Foundation of Canada), provincially (e.g., Alberta Education and Alberta Centre for Child, Family and Community Research and Alberta Advisory Committee for Educational Studies), and locally (e.g., University of Alberta and School Boards). She has authored over 30 peer reviewed journal articles and served as guest co-editor of two special issues of the *International Journal of Qualitative Methods*. In 2016, she was elected as the fourth president of the Mixed Methods International Research Association. (MMIRA). In addition to more than 100 conference and 25 workshop presentations, she served as co-chair of the 2013

Advances in Qualitative Methods (AQM) Conference. She has led research methods workshops with diverse audiences—for example, at the International Institute of Qualitative Methods' Thinking Qualitatively Series. She is a current associate editor of the Journal of Mixed Methods Research and editorial board member of the International Journal of Qualitative Inquiry.

• Acknowledgments •

John is most thankful to the many students in his qualitative research methods classes at the University of Nebraska–Lincoln who helped to shape this book over the years. They offered suggestions, provided examples, and discussed the material in this book. Also, he benefited from capable scholars who helped to shape and form this book in the first edition: Paul Turner, Ken Robson, Dana Miller, Diane Gillespie, Gregory Schraw, Sharon Hudson, Karen Eifler, Neilida Aguilar, and Harry Wolcott. Ben Crabtree and Rich Hofmann helped form the first edition text significantly and encouraged him to proceed, and they diligently and timely responded to the SAGE request to be first edition external reviewers. In addition, Keith Pezzoli, Kathy O'Byrne, Joanne Cooper, and Phyllis Langton served as first edition reviewers for SAGE and added insight into content and structure that he could not see because of his closeness to the material.

To the reviewers for this fourth edition, we appreciate your time and effort reviewing the draft of our book. As always, John is indebted to C. Deborah Laughton, who served as his acquisition editor for the first edition; to Lisa Cuevas Shaw, who served as editor for the second edition; to Vicki Knight, who served as editor for the third edition and who lined up Helen Salmon as acquisition editor for this fourth edition. Also for all of the previous editions, members of the Office of Qualitative and Mixed Methods Research (OQMMR) all provided valuable input. John especially singles out Dr. Vicki Plano Clark and Dr. Ron Shope, who have been instrumental in refining and shaping his ideas about qualitative research through the editions.

Cheryl is grateful to John and also Vicki Knight for presenting the opportunity to contribute to the current edition. John has been an influential mentor for her thinking and writing about qualitative research. She has especially appreciated John's willingness to consider new content ideas and ways of presenting material. Also, we are both grateful to our Department of Educational Psychology, University of Alberta and the Department of Family Medicine, University of Michigan, and colleagues.

Finally, to members of our families (for John—Karen, David, Kasey, Johanna, and Bonny; for Cheryl—Damian, Avery, and Jasper), thanks for providing us with time to spend long hours writing and revising this book. Thank you all.

• Analytic Table of Contents by Approach •

Narrative Research

Phenomenology

Grounded Theory

Ethnography

Case Study

• List of Tables and Figures •

Tables

Figures

Introduction

The work on this book began during a 1994 summer qualitative seminar in Vail, Colorado, sponsored by the University of Denver under the able guidance of Edith King of the College of Education. At that seminar, while discussing qualitative data analysis, John began on a personal note, introducing one of his recently completed qualitative studies—a case study of a campus response to a student gun incident (Asmussen & Creswell, 1995). John knew this case might provoke some discussion and present some complex analysis issues. It involved a Midwestern university's reaction to a gunman who entered an actuarial science undergraduate class with a semiautomatic rifle and attempted to fire on students in his class. The rifle jammed and did not discharge, and the gunman fled and was captured a few miles away. Standing before the group, John chronicled the events of the case, the themes, and the lessons we learned about a university reaction to a near tragic event. Then, unplanned, Harry Wolcott of the University of Oregon, another resource person for this seminar, raised his hand and asked for the podium. He explained how *he* would approach the study as a cultural anthropologist. To John's surprise, Harry had "turned" his case study into ethnography, framing the study in an entirely new way. After Harry had concluded, Les Goodchild, then of Denver University, discussed how he would examine the gunman case from a historical perspective. Together the three had, then, multiple renderings of the incident, surprising "turns" of the initial case study using different qualitative approaches. It was this event that sparked an idea that John had long harbored— that the design of a qualitative study related to the specific *approach* taken to *qualitative research* (see the glossary in Appendix A for definitions of bold italics terms). John began to write the first edition of this book, guided by a single, compelling question: How does the type or approach of qualitative inquiry shape the design or procedures of a study?

Purpose and Rationale for the Book

This book is now in its fourth edition, and we are still formulating an answer to this question. For this new edition, John sought to include another perspective to the conversation. Our primary intent in this book is to examine five different approaches to qualitative inquiry—narrative, phenomenology, grounded theory, ethnography, and case studies—and put them side by side so that we can see their differences. These differences can be most vividly displayed by exploring their use throughout the process of research, including the introduction to a study through its purpose and research questions, data collection, data analysis, report writing, and standards of validation and evaluation. For example, by studying qualitative articles in journals, we can see that research questions framed from grounded theory look different than questions framed from a phenomenological study.

This combination of the different approaches and how their distinctiveness plays out in the process of research is what distinguishes this book from others on qualitative research that you may have read. Most qualitative researchers focus on only one approach—say ethnography or grounded theory—and try to convince their readers of the value of that approach. This makes sense in our highly specialized world of academia. However, students and beginning qualitative researchers need choices that fit their research problems and that suit their own interests in conducting research. Hopefully, this book opens up the expanse of qualitative research and invites readers to examine multiple ways of engaging in the process of research. It provides qualitative researchers with options for conducting qualitative inquiry and helps them with decisions about what approach is best to use in studying their research problems. With so many books on qualitative research in general and on the various approaches of inquiry, qualitative research students are often at a loss for understanding what options (i.e., approaches) exist and how one makes an informed choice of an option for research.

By reading this book, we hope that you will gain a better understanding of the steps in the process of research, learn five qualitative approaches to inquiry, and understand the differences and similarities among the five *approaches to inquiry*.

What Is New in This Edition

Since John wrote the first, second, and third editions of this book, the content of the book has both remained the same and changed. In this edition, we introduce several new ideas:

- We have updated the key book readings introduced in Chapter 1 to reflect advances within each approach in narrative research (Clandinin, 2013), in phenomenology (van Manen, 2014), in grounded theory (Charmaz, 2014; Corbin & Strauss, 2015), and in case study (Yin, 2014).
- Based on reviewers' feedback, we have revised Chapter 2 on the philosophical assumptions and the interpretive frameworks used by qualitative researchers and expanded our use of studies to illustrate differences among interpretive frameworks.
- Across all the chapters, we have responded to reviewers' comments about the need for further inclusivity and diversity in our examples and references. We have added descriptions of each of the further readings at the end of the chapter to help readers to decide which readings are most appropriate for their needs.
- In Chapter 3, we have expanded the section on ethical issues that traces the types of qualitative ethical dilemmas likely to arise at different phases of the research process that are developed in subsequent chapters. In this way, we are continuing to expand the ethical coverage in this book in response to reviewer feedback.
- We have added two sections in Chapter 3 for guiding qualitative researchers' thinking about their own study by describing features of a good qualitative study and design considerations for engaging readers. We have added two visuals summarizing when to use qualitative research and describing phases of research, and revised the section on writing structures for a proposal.
- In discussing each of the five approaches in this book in Chapter 4, we have added visuals and enhanced descriptions related to "defining characteristics" of the approach. Readers will have our best assessment of the key features of the approach summarized in one place in the end of chapter tables. Also in Chapter 4, we have incorporated new visuals, updated key book readings, and added recent literature for each approach.
- We have updated the illustrative articles used in the book in Chapter 5 and replaced some outdated references with new examples. Consequently, we have added two new articles: one in ethnographic research (Mac an Ghaill & Haywood, 2015) and one in case study research (Frelin, 2015).
- In Chapter 6, we have provided additional purpose statement examples to include an alternative to the "scriptlike" purpose. In the discussion about subresearch questions, we have provided examples for each type of approach to guide subdivision of the central question into several parts.
- In the area of data collection in Chapter 7, we needed to better integrate issues of data management (e.g., data storage and security) as well as articles reflective of developments in data collection (e.g., computer-mediated, visual methods) to keep pace with new ways of gathering qualitative data.
- We also expanded the coverage of ethical considerations in earlier editions of this book and added two new visuals summarizing the procedures for preparing and conducting interviews and observations.

- In data analysis, in Chapter 8, we have expanded our discussion of new techniques that are being discussed for analyzing the data in each of the five approaches, cited recent references inclusive of audiovisual materials, and revised the visual representation of data analysis spiral. We also have updated the discussion about the use of memoing, developing interpretations, and representing data. In the description of qualitative computer software analysis packages, we have updated resources and added a section related to "how to decide whether to use a computer program."
- In the writing of qualitative research, as presented in Chapter 9, we have added more information about ethical considerations and reflexivity as well as their importance and guidance for incorporating into a qualitative study.
- We have updated the descriptions of validation and reliability perspectives and strategies in Chapter 10, including new visual summaries and greater detail in comparing standards of quality across the five approaches.
- At the end of each chapter, you will find a "check-in" section to practice specific skills introduced in the chapter. Many of these exercises have been rewritten in this new edition to reflect our growing understanding of the specific skills that a qualitative researcher needs to know.
- In the final chapter, we have added the text of the initial qualitative gunman case study and have not only "turned" the case study into a narrative project, a phenomenology, a grounded theory study, and an ethnography but we have also made more explicit what changes actually occurred in this reworking.
- As with all new editions, we have updated the references to include recent books on qualitative research methods as well as select journal articles that illustrate these methods.

Many areas have also remained the same as in the third edition. These include the following:

- The core characteristics of qualitative research have remained essentially the same.
- An emphasis on social justice as one of the primary features of qualitative research is continued in this edition. While a social justice orientation may not be for everyone, it has again been given primacy in the recent edition of the *SAGE Handbook of Qualitative Research* (Denzin & Lincoln, 2011).
- The need for considering ethical issues both in advance and responding as issues emerge throughout the research process.
- A healthy respect exists for variations within each of the five approaches. We have come to understand that there is no single way to approach an ethnography, a grounded theory study, and so forth. We have selectively chosen what we believe to be the most popular approaches within each approach and to highlight books that emphasize them.

- On a similar note, we have continued to use the five approaches that have now stood the test of time since the first edition. This is not to say that we have not considered additional approaches. Participatory action research, for example, could certainly be a sixth approach, but we include some discussion of it in the interpretive framework passages in Chapter 2 (Kemmis & Wilkinson, 1998). Also, discourse analysis and conversational analysis could certainly have been included as an additional approach (Cheek, 2004), but we have added some thoughts about conversational approaches in narrative approaches. Mixed methods, too, is sometimes so closely associated with qualitative research that it is considered one of the genres (see Saldaña, 2011). However, we see mixed methods as a distinct methodology from qualitative inquiry and one that bridges qualitative and quantitative research. Further, it has its own distinct literature (see Creswell & Plano Clark, 2011); thus, we wanted to limit the scope of this book to qualitative approaches. Accordingly, we have chosen to keep the initial five approaches and to expand within these five approaches.

- We have continued to provide resources throughout the book for the qualitative researcher. We have included a detailed glossary of terms (and have added terms from the last edition), an analytic table of contents that organizes the material in this book according to the five approaches, and complete journal articles that model designing and writing a study within each of the five approaches. For both inexperienced and experienced researchers, we highlighted key resources at the ends of chapters for further reading that can extend the material in this book.

- The term used in the first edition, *traditions*, has now been replaced by *approaches*, and we have continued this use of terms in subsequent editions. This approach signals that we not only want to respect past approaches but we also want to encourage current practices in qualitative research. Other writers have referred to the approaches as "strategies of inquiry" (Denzin & Lincoln, 2005), "varieties" (Tesch, 1990), or "methods" (Morse & Richards, 2002). By ***research design***, we refer to the entire process of research from conceptualizing a problem to writing research questions and on to data collection, analysis, interpretation, and report writing (Bogdan & Taylor, 1975). Yin (2009) commented, "The design is the logical sequence that connects the empirical data to a study's initial research questions and, ultimately, to its conclusions" (p. 29). Hence, we included in the specific design features from the broad philosophical and theoretical perspectives to the quality and validation of a study.

Positioning Ourselves

You need to know some information about our backgrounds in order to understand the approach adopted in this book. John was trained as a quantitative researcher about 40 years ago. By the mid-1980s, John was asked to teach the first qualitative research course at my university, and he volunteered to do so. This was followed a few years later with the writing of the first edition of this book. While John has expanded his repertoire to mixed methods as well as qualitative research, he continually returns to a strong interest in qualitative research. Over the years, John has evolved into an applied research methodologist with a specialization in research design, qualitative research, and mixed methods research. Interestingly, Cheryl was also trained as a quantitative researcher within the biological natural sciences. When working as a high school science teacher, she began to question the limitations of the quantitative evidence test scores for assessing and reporting student learning. Instead, she began to draw upon more qualitative evidence to inform her communication with students and parents. This was followed by a return to graduate school to gain expertise in qualitative research methods and eventually to engage in the emerging field of mixed methods research. As an applied researcher and program evaluator, she is committed to building research capacity through mentoring her students and collaborators in rigorous methods across a variety of organizational settings.

This background explains why we write from the standpoint of conveying an understanding of the process of qualitative research (whether you want to call it the scientific method or something else), a focus on strong methods features such as extensive qualitative data collection, rigorous data analysis through multiple steps, and the use of computer programs. Moreover, John has developed a fascination with the structure of writing, whether the writing is a qualitative study, a poem, or creative nonfiction. An enduring interest of John's has been the *composition* of qualitative research. This compositional interest flows into how to best structure qualitative inquiry and to visualize how the structure shifts and changes given different approaches to research. For Cheryl, a persistent research interest in promoting use of findings and processes has lead to her focus on providing enhanced *access* to what findings are generated and seeking diverse *formats* for how research and evaluation is communicated.

John's interest in structured features has often placed him in the camp of post-positivist writers in qualitative inquiry (see Denzin & Lincoln, 2005), but like most researchers, he defies easy categorization. In an article in *Qualitative Inquiry* about a homeless shelter (Miller, Creswell, & Olander, 1998), John's ethnography assumed a realist, a confessional, and an advocacy stance. Also, he is not advocating the acceptance of qualitative research in a "quantitative" world (Ely, Anzul, Friedman, Garner, & Steinmetz, 1991). Qualitative inquiry represents a legitimate mode of social and human science exploration, without apology or comparisons to quantitative research. In the same way, Cheryl draws on her experiences as a quantitative and mixed methods researcher in her qualitative work but is careful to maintain the essential characteristics of qualitative research that we discuss in Chapter 3.

John also tends to be oriented toward citing numerous ideas to document articles; to incorporate the latest writings from the ever-growing, vast literature of qualitative inquiry; and to advance an applied, practical form of conducting research. For example, it was not enough for John to convey philosophical assumptions of qualitative inquiry in Chapter 2; he also had to construct a discussion around how these philosophical ideas are applied in the design and writing of a qualitative study. John concurs with Agger (1991), who says that readers and writers can understand methodology in less technical ways, thereby affording greater access to scholars and democraticizing science. We continue to seek and be influenced by our interactions with beginning and more experienced researchers who are expanding their methodological expertise in our courses, workshops, and conferences. Always before us as we write is the picture of a beginning master's or doctoral student who is learning qualitative research for the first time. Because this picture remains central in our thinking, some may say that we oversimplify the craft of research. This picture may well blur the image for a more seasoned qualitative writer—and especially one who seeks more advanced discussions and who looks for problematizing the process of research. It is important to both of us that, in this book, we provide access to learning about five qualitative research approaches in a way that stimulates the beginning of a qualitative inquiry journey.

Definition of Qualitative Research

We typically begin a book about qualitative research by posing a definition for it. This seemingly uncomplicated approach has become more difficult in recent years. We note that some extremely useful introductory books to qualitative research these days do not contain a definition that can be easily located (Morse & Richards, 2002; Weis & Fine, 2000). Perhaps this has less to do with the authors' decision to convey the nature of this inquiry and more to do with a concern about advancing a "fixed" definition. Other authors advance a definition. The evolving definition by Denzin and Lincoln (1994, 2000, 2005, 2011) in their *SAGE Handbook of Qualitative Research* conveys the ever-changing nature of qualitative inquiry from social construction, to interpretivism, and then on to social justice in the world. We include their latest definition here:

> Qualitative research is a situated activity that locates the observer in the world. Qualitative research consists of a set of interpretive, material practices that make the world visible. These practices transform the world. They turn the world into a series of representations, including field notes, interviews, conversations, photographs, recordings, and memos to the self. At this level, qualitative research involves an interpretive, naturalistic approach to the world. This means that qualitative researchers study things in their natural settings, attempting to make sense of, or interpret, phenomena in terms of the meanings people bring to them. (Denzin & Lincoln, 2011, p. 3)

Although some of the traditional approaches to qualitative research, such as the "interpretive, naturalistic approach" and "meanings," are evident in this definition, the definition also has a strong orientation toward the impact of qualitative research and its ability to transform the world.

As applied research methodologists, our working definitions of qualitative research incorporate many of the Denzin and Lincoln elements, but it provides greater emphasis on the design of research and the use of distinct approaches to inquiry (e.g., ethnography, narrative). We adopt the following definition:

> Qualitative research begins with assumptions and the use of interpretive/theoretical frameworks that inform the study of research problems addressing the meaning individuals or groups ascribe to a social or human problem. To study this problem, qualitative researchers use an emerging qualitative approach to inquiry, the collection of data in a natural setting sensitive to the people and places under study, and data analysis that is both inductive and deductive and establishes patterns or themes. The final written report or presentation includes the voices of participants, the reflexivity of the researcher, a complex description and interpretation of the problem, and its contribution to the literature or a call for change. (Creswell, 2013, p. 44)

Selection of the Five Approaches

Those undertaking qualitative studies have a baffling number of choices of approaches. One can gain a sense of this diversity by examining several classifications or typologies. Tesch (1990) provided a classification consisting of 28 approaches organized into four branches of a flowchart, sorting out these approaches based on the central interest of the investigator. Wolcott (1992) classified approaches in a "tree" diagram with branches of the tree designating strategies for data collection. Miller and Crabtree (1992) organized 18 types according to the "domain" of human life of primary concern to the researcher, such as a focus on the individual, the social world, or the culture. In the field of education, Jacob (1987) categorized all qualitative research into "traditions" such as ecological psychology, symbolic interactionism, and holistic ethnography. Jacob's categorization provided a key framework for the first edition of this book. Lancy (1993) organized qualitative inquiry into discipline perspectives, such as anthropology, sociology, biology, cognitive psychology, and history. Denzin and Lincoln (2011) have organized and reorganized their types of qualitative strategies over the years.

Table 1.1 provides these and other various classifications of qualitative approaches that have surfaced over the years. This list is not meant to be exhaustive of the possibilities; it is intended to illustrate the diversity of approaches recommended by different authors and how the disciplines might emphasize some approaches over others.

Looking closely at these classifications, we can discern that some approaches appear consistently over the years, such as ethnography, grounded theory, phenomenology, and case studies. Also, a number of narrative-related approaches have

TABLE 1.1 ● Qualitative Approaches Mentioned by Authors and Their Disciplines/Fields

Authors	Qualitative Approaches			Disciplines
Jacob (1987)	• Ecological psychology • Ethnography of communication	• Holistic ethnography • Symbolic interactionism	• Cognitive anthropology	Education
Munhall and Oiler (1986)	• Phenomenology • Historical research	• Grounded theory	• Ethnography	Nursing
Lancy (1993)	• Anthropological perspectives • Case studies	• Sociological perspectives • Personal accounts	• Biological perspectives • Cognitive studies • Historical inquiries	Education
Strauss and Corbin (1990)	• Grounded theory • Life histories	• Ethnography • Conversational analysis	• Phenomenology	Sociology, nursing
Morse (1994)	• Phenomenology • Grounded theory	• Ethnography	• Ethnoscience	Nursing
Moustakas (1994)	• Ethnography • Empirical phenomenological research	• Grounded theory • Heuristic research	• Hermeneutics • Transcendental • Phenomenology	Psychology
Denzin and Lincoln (1994)	• Case studies • Ethnomethodology • Biographical	• Ethnography • Interpretative practices • Historical	• Phenomenology • Grounded theory • Clinical research	Social sciences
Miles and Huberman (1994)	Approaches to Qualitative Data Analysis: • Interpretivism	• Social anthropology	• Collaborative social research	Social sciences
Slife and Williams (1995)	Categories of Qualitative Methods: • Ethnography	• Phenomenology	• Studies of artifacts	Psychology
Denzin and Lincoln (2005)	• Performance, critical, and public ethnography • Grounded theory	• Interpretive practices • Life history • Clinical research	• Case studies • Narrative authority • Participatory action research	Social sciences
Marshall and Rossman (2015)	• Ethnographic approaches	• Phenomenological approaches	• Sociolinguistic approaches (e.g., critical genres)	Education

(Continued)

TABLE 1.1 ● (Continued)

Authors	Qualitative Approaches			Disciplines
Saldaña (2011)	• Ethnography • Case study • Narrative inquiry • Evaluation research • Critical inquiry	• Grounded theory • Content analysis • Arts-based research • Action research • Autoethnography	• Phenomenology • Mixed methods research • Investigative journalism	Arts (theater)
Denzin and Lincoln (2011)	Research Strategies: • Design • Ethnography • Ethnomethodology • Historical method • Clinical research	• Case study • Phenomenology • Grounded theory • Action and applied research	• Ethnography, participant observation, performance • Life history, testimonio	
Mertens (2015)	Types of Qualitative Research: • Ethnographic research • Grounded theory	• Case study • Participatory action research	• Phenomenological research	Education, psychology

been discussed, such as life history, autoethnography, and biography. With so many possibilities, how was the selection decision made to focus on the five approaches presented in this book?

The choice of the five approaches resulted from reflecting on personal interests, selecting different approaches popular in the social science and health science literature, and electing to choose representative discipline orientations. Each of us have had personal experience with each of the five and have advised students and participated on research teams using these qualitative approaches. Beyond these personal experiences, our reading the qualitative literature has been ongoing and our learning continues. The five approaches discussed in this book reflect the types of qualitative research that we most frequently see in the social, behavioral, and health science literature. It is not unusual, too, for authors to state that certain approaches are most important in their fields (e.g., Morse & Field, 1995). Also, we prefer approaches with systematic procedures for inquiry. The books we have chosen to illustrate each approach tend to have procedures of rigorous data collection and analysis methods that are attractive to beginning researchers. The primary books chosen for each approach also represent different discipline perspectives in the social, behavioral, and health sciences. This is an attractive feature to broaden the audience for the book and to recognize the diverse disciplines that have embraced qualitative research. For example, narrative originates from the humanities and social sciences, phenomenology from psychology and philosophy, grounded theory from sociology, ethnography from anthropology and sociology, and case studies from the human and social sciences and applied areas such as evaluation research.

Key Book Readings

The primary ideas that we use to discuss each approach come from select books. More specifically, we will rely heavily on two books on each approach. These are the books that we highly recommend for you to get started in learning a specific approach to qualitative inquiry. These books reflect classics often cited by authors as well as new works. They also reflect diverse disciplines and perspectives. Please see the essential readings for each chapter listed under the Further Readings heading appearing after each chapter summary.

Narrative Research

Clandinin, D. J. (2013). *Engaging in narrative inquiry.* Walnut Creek, CA: Left Coast Press.

In this book, Jean Clandinin articulates her intention to "return to the question of what it is that narrative inquirers do" (p. 18). Chapter 2 is noteworthy for her practical guidance using detailed descriptions and examples of educational research what it means to think and act narratively.

Riessman, C. K. (2008). *Narrative methods for the human sciences.* Thousand Oaks, CA: Sage.

Catherine Riessman uses cross-disciplinary exemplars alongside detailed descriptions for four specific methods of narrative analysis (thematic, structural, dialogic/performance, and visual). A unique contribution is the discussion of visual analysis and how images can be used within qualitative research.

Phenomenology

Moustakas, C. (1994). *Phenomenological research methods.* Thousand Oaks, CA: Sage.

Clark Moustakas contributes a description of a heuristic process in phenomenological analysis. His practical instructions in the systematic interpretation of interview transcripts is helpful for extracting themes common across interviews or unique to an interview and then creating a conceptual link.

van Manen, M. (2014). *Phenomenology of practice: Meaning-giving methods in phenomenological research and writing.* Walnut Creek, CA: Left Coast Press.

Max van Manen describes the evolution of key phenomenological ideas, presents a range of methods, and discusses current issues. Among the key contributions is his summary of seven criteria for appraising phenomenological reporting (see p. 355).

Grounded Theory

Charmaz, K. (2014). *Constructing grounded theory* (2nd ed.). Thousand Oaks, CA: Sage.

In this new edition, Kathy Charmaz provides additional examples from varied disciplines and professions as well as reflections from scholars about using grounded theory. Features of the second edition include further details related to the coding and writing processes including guidelines and examples.

Corbin, J., & Strauss, A. (2015). *Basics of qualitative research: Techniques and procedures for developing grounded theory* (4th ed.). Thousand Oaks, CA: Sage.

A new pedagogical feature of the fourth edition by Julie Corbin and Anselm Strauss called Insider Insights provides viewpoints from former students and colleagues to enrich the reading experience. Of particular note is a summary of analyses processes (see pp. 216–219).

Ethnography

Fetterman, D. M. (2010). *Ethnography: Step-by-step* (3rd ed.). Thousand Oaks, CA: Sage.

David Fetterman offers discussions about the basic features of ethnography and the use of theory. The chapter on anthropological concepts provides a useful connection between the cyclical processes of acquiring ethnographic knowledge and human life. This, along with the analytical strategies described in Chapter 5, make this resource required reading.

Wolcott, H. F. (2008). *Ethnography: A way of seeing* (2nd ed.). Lanham, MD: AltaMira.

A good understanding of the nature of ethnography, the study of groups, and the development of an understanding of culture is provided by Harry Wolcott. In particular, his emphasis on both the artistic and common sense elements involved in fieldwork provides a unique perspective.

Case Study

Stake, R. (1995). *The art of case study research.* Thousand Oaks, CA: Sage.

Through his personable style, Robert Stake offers insights gained from experience along with illustrative examples. The book reads differently than a typical text, emphasizing the "art" involved in conducting a case study and the role of researcher's intuition.

Yin, R. K. (2014). *Case study research: Design and method* (5th ed.). Thousand Oaks, CA: Sage.

Robert Yin adds breadth and depth to this new edition with end-of-chapter tutorials. His emphasis on systems and procedures for generating reliable findings and valid interpretations is particularly noted in designs (see Chapter 2), data collection (see Chapter 4), and analysis (see Chapter 5).

Audience

Although multiple audiences, both known and unknown, exist for any text (Fetterman, 2010), we direct this book toward academics and scholars affiliated with the social, human, and health sciences. Examples throughout the book illustrate the diversity of disciplines and fields of study including sociology, psychology, education, nursing, family medicine, allied health, urban studies, marketing, communication and journalism, educational psychology, family science and therapy, and other social and human science areas.

Our aim is to provide a useful text for those who produce scholarly qualitative research in the form of journal articles, theses, or dissertations. We have pitched the level of discussion to be suitable for upper-division students and beyond into graduate school. For graduate students writing master's theses or doctoral dissertations, we compare and contrast the five approaches in the hope that such analysis helps in establishing a rationale for the choice of a type to use. For beginning qualitative researchers, we introduce the philosophical and interpretive frameworks that shape qualitative research followed by the basic elements in designing a qualitative study. We feel that understanding the basics of qualitative research is essential before venturing out into the specifics of one of the qualitative approaches. We begin each chapter with an overview of the topic of the chapter and then go into how the topic might be addressed within each of the five approaches. While discussing the basic elements, we suggest several books aimed at the beginning qualitative researcher that can provide a more extensive review of the basics of qualitative research. Such basics are necessary before delving into the five approaches. A focus on comparing the five approaches throughout this book provides an introduction for experienced researchers to approaches that build on their training and research experiences.

Organization

Following this introduction and the list of key book resources, in Chapter 2 we provide an introduction to the philosophical assumptions and interpretive frameworks that inform qualitative research. We emphasize how they might be written into a qualitative study. In Chapter 3, we review the basic elements for designing a qualitative study. These elements begin with a definition of *qualitative research*, the reasons for using this approach, and the phases in the process of research. In Chapter 4, we provide an introduction to each of the five approaches of inquiry: narrative research, phenomenology, grounded theory, ethnography, and case study research. The chapter includes an overview of the elements of each of the five approaches. Chapter 5 continues this discussion by presenting five published journal articles (one on each approach with the complete articles in Appendices B–F), which provide good illustrations of each of the approaches. By reading our overview in Chapter 4 and then reviewing a journal article that illustrates the approach, you can develop a working knowledge of an approach. Choosing one of the books we recommend for the approach in this chapter and beginning a mastery of it for your research study can then expand this knowledge.

These five preliminary chapters form an introduction to the five approaches and an overview of the process of research design. They set the stage for the remaining chapters, which take up in turn each step in the research process: writing introductions to studies (Chapter 6), collecting data (Chapter 7), analyzing and representing data (Chapter 8), writing qualitative studies (Chapter 9), and validating and evaluating a qualitative study (Chapter 10). Throughout these design chapters, we start with the basics of qualitative research and then expand the discussion to advance and compare the five types.

As a final experience to sharpen distinctions made among the five approaches, we present Chapter 11, in which we present a gunman case study (Asmussen & Creswell, 1995), and "turn" the story from a case study into a narrative biography, a phenomenology, a grounded theory study, and an ethnography. This culminating chapter brings the reader full circle to examining the gunman case in several ways, an extension of John's 1994 Vail seminar experience in looking at the same problem from diverse qualitative perspectives.

Philosophical Assumptions and Interpretive Frameworks

Whether we are aware of it or not, we always bring certain beliefs and *philosophical assumptions* to our research. Sometimes these are deeply ingrained views about the types of problems that we need to study, what research questions to ask, or how we go about gathering data. These beliefs are instilled in us during our educational training through journal articles and books, through advice dispensed by our advisors, and through the scholarly communities we engage at our conferences and scholarly meetings. The difficulty lies first in becoming aware of these assumptions and beliefs and second in deciding whether we will actively incorporate them into our qualitative studies. Often, at a less abstract level, these philosophical assumptions inform our choice of theories that guide our research. Theories are more apparent in our qualitative studies than are philosophical assumptions, and researchers, often trained in the use of theories, typically make them explicit in research studies.

Qualitative researchers have underscored the importance of not only understanding the beliefs and theories that inform our research but also actively writing about them in our reports and studies. This chapter highlights various philosophical assumptions that have occupied the minds of qualitative researchers for some years and the various theoretical and *interpretive frameworks* that enact these beliefs.

A close tie does exist between the philosophy that one brings to the research act and how one proceeds to use a framework to shroud his or her inquiry.

This chapter will help you begin to explore your philosophical assumptions and inform decisions about the influence of theories in your qualitative research. We do this by presenting a framework for understanding how both philosophy and theory fit into the large schema of the research process. Then we present details about philosophical assumptions common to qualitative researchers, consider the types of philosophical assumptions, and explore how they are often used or made explicit in qualitative studies. Finally, various interpretive frameworks are suggested that link back to philosophical assumptions with embedded commentary related to how these frameworks play out in the actual practice of research.

Questions for Discussion

- Where do philosophy and interpretive frameworks (theory) fit into the overall process of research?
- Why is it important to understand the philosophical assumptions?
- What four philosophical assumptions exist when you choose qualitative research?
- How are these philosophical assumptions used and written into a qualitative study?
- What types of interpretive frameworks are used in qualitative research?
- How are interpretive frameworks written into a qualitative study?
- How are philosophical assumptions and interpretive frameworks linked in a qualitative study?

Situating Philosophy and Interpretive Frameworks Within the Research Process

An understanding of the philosophical assumptions behind qualitative research begins with assessing where it fits within the overall process of research, noting its importance as an element of research, and considering how to actively write it into a study. To help in this process, we use a framework to guide understanding of how philosophical assumptions and interpretive frameworks (paradigm perspectives and theoretical orientations) are situated within and influential to the research process. *Philosophy* means the use of abstract ideas and beliefs that inform our research. We know that philosophical assumptions are typically the first ideas in developing a study, but how

FIGURE 2.1 ● Situating Philosophy and Interpretive Frameworks Within the Research Process

Phase 1: The Researcher as a Multicultural Subject

- History and research tradition
- Conceptions of self and the other
- The ethics and politics of research

> What perspectives and experiences do you bring to your research?

Phase 2: Philosophical Assumptions and Interpretive Frameworks

- Ontological
- Epistemological
- Axiological
- Methodological

- Postpositivism
- Social constructivism
- Transformative frameworks
- Postmodern perspectives
- Pragmatism

- Feminist theories
- Critical theory and critical race theory
- Queer theory
- Disabilities theories

> How do your beliefs guide your actions as a researcher?

Phase 3: Research Strategies and Approaches

- Design
- Case study
- Ethnography, participant observation, performance ethnography
- Phenomenology, ethnomethodology

- Grounded theory
- Life history, testimonio
- Historical method
- Action and applied research
- Clinical research

> How do your philosophical and theoretical frameworks inform your choice of research approaches?

Phase 4: Methods of Collection and Analysis

- Observing
- Interviewing
- Artifacts, documents, and records
- Visual methods
- Autoethnography
- Oral history

- Data management methods
- Computer-assisted analysis
- Textual analysis
- Focus groups
- Applied ethnography

> In what ways does your research approach influence the methods used for data collection and analysis?

Phase 5: The Art, Practice, and Politics of Interpretation and Evaluation

- Criteria for judging adequacy
- Practices and politics of interpretation
- Writing as interpretation

- Evaluation traditions
- Policy analysis
- Applied research

> What contributes to your decisions related to rigor, inferences, and use of findings?

Source: Adapted from Denzin and Lincoln (2011, p. 12). Used with permission, SAGE.

they relate to the overall process of research remains a mystery. It is here that adapting an overview of the process of research compiled by Denzin and Lincoln (2011, p. 12), as shown in Figure 2.1, helps us to situate philosophy and interpretative frameworks into perspective in the research process. The questions embedded within each phase help you begin to explore the philosophical assumptions you bring to research.

This conceptualization of the research process begins in Phase 1 with the researchers considering what they bring to the inquiry, such as their personal history, views of themselves and others, and ethical and political issues. Inquirers often overlook this phase, so it is helpful to have it highlighted and positioned first in the levels of the research process. In Phase 2 the researcher brings to the inquiry certain philosophical assumptions. These are stances taken by the researcher that provide direction for the study, such as the researcher's view of reality (ontology), how the researcher knows reality (epistemology), the value-stance taken by the inquirer (axiology), and the procedures used in the study (*methodology*). These assumptions, in turn, are often applied in research through the use of *paradigms* and theories (or, as we call them, interpretive frameworks). Paradigms are a "basic set of beliefs that guides action" (Guba, 1990, p. 17). These beliefs are brought to the process of research by the investigator and they may be called worldviews (Creswell & Plano Clark, 2011). *Theories or theoretical orientations*, on the other hand, are found in the literature and they provide a general explanation as to what the researcher hopes to find in a study or a lens through which to view the needs of participants and communities in a study. Granted, the difference between the philosophical assumptions, paradigms, and theoretical orientation is not always clear, but sorting out what exists at a broad philosophical level (assumptions) and what operates at a more practical level (interpretive frameworks) is a helpful heuristic.

In Phase 2, we find the philosophical and paradigm/theoretical interpretative frameworks addressed in this chapter. The following chapters in this book are devoted, then, to the Phase 3 research strategies, called approaches in this book, that will be enumerated as they relate to the research process. Finally, the inquirer engages in Phase 4 methods of data collection and analysis, followed by Phase 5, the interpretation and evaluation of the data. Taking Figure 2.1 in its entirety, we see that research involves differing levels of abstraction from the broad assessment of individual characteristics brought by the researcher on through the researcher's philosophy and theory that lay the foundation for more specific approaches and methods of data collection, analysis, and interpretation. Also implicit in Figure 2.1 is the importance of having an understanding of philosophy and interpretative frameworks that inform a qualitative study.

Philosophical Assumptions

Why Philosophy Is Important

We can begin by thinking about why it is important to understand the philosophical assumptions that underlie qualitative research and to be able to articulate them in a research study or present them to an audience. Huff (2009) is helpful in articulating the importance of philosophy in research.

- *Direction of research goals and outcomes.* How we formulate our problem and research questions to study is shaped by our assumptions and, in turn, influences how we seek information to answer the questions. A cause-and-effect type of question in which certain variables are predicted to explain an outcome is different from an exploration of a single phenomenon as found in qualitative research.

- *Scope of training and research experiences.* These assumptions are deeply rooted in our training and reinforced by the scholarly community in which we work. Granted, some communities are more eclectic and borrow from many disciplines (e.g., education), while others are more narrowly focused on studying specific research problems, using particular methods, and adding certain research knowledge.

- *Basis of evaluative criteria for research-related decisions.* Unquestionably, reviewers make philosophical assumptions about a study when they evaluate it. Knowing how reviewers stand on issues of epistemology is helpful to author–researchers. When the assumptions between the author and the reviewer diverge, the author's work may not receive a fair hearing, and conclusions may be drawn that it does not make a contribution to the literature. This unfair hearing may occur within the context of a graduate student presenting to a committee, an author submitting to a scholarly journal, or an investigator presenting a proposal to a funding agency. On the reverse side, understanding the differences used by a reviewer may enable a researcher to resolve points of difference before they become a focal point for critique.

The question as to whether key assumptions can change and/or whether multiple philosophical assumptions can be used in a given study needs to be addressed. Our stance is that assumptions can change over time and over a career, and they often do, especially after a scholar leaves the enclave of his or her discipline and begins to work in more of a trans- or multidisciplinary way. Whether multiple assumptions can be taken in a given study is open to debate, and again, it may be related to research experiences of the investigator, his or her openness to exploring using differing assumptions, and the acceptability of ideas taken in the larger scientific community of which he or she is a part. Looking across the four philosophical assumptions described next can be helpful for monitoring individual changes over time.

Four Philosophical Assumptions

What are the philosophical assumptions made by researchers when they undertake a qualitative study? These assumptions have been articulated throughout the past 20 years in the various editions of the *SAGE Handbook of Qualitative Research* (Denzin & Lincoln, 1994, 2000, 2005, 2011) and as the "axiomatic" issues advanced by Guba and Lincoln (1988) as the guiding philosophy behind qualitative research. These beliefs have been called philosophical assumptions, epistemologies, and ontologies (Crotty, 1998); broadly conceived research methodologies (Neuman, 2000); and alternative knowledge claims (Creswell, 2009). They are beliefs about ontology (the nature of reality), epistemology (what counts as knowledge and how knowledge claims are justified), axiology (the role of values in research), and methodology (the process of research). In this discussion, we will first discuss each of these philosophical assumptions, detail how they might be used and written into qualitative research, and then link them to different interpretive frameworks that operate at a more specific level in the process of research (see Table 2.1).

The ***ontological*** issue relates to the nature of reality and its characteristics. When researchers conduct qualitative research, they are embracing the idea of multiple realities. Different researchers embrace different realities, as do the individuals being studied and the readers of a qualitative study. When studying individuals, qualitative researchers conduct a study with the intent of reporting these multiple realities. Evidence of multiple realities includes the use of multiple forms of evidence in themes using the actual words of different individuals and presenting different perspectives. For example, when writers compile a phenomenology, they report how individuals participating in the study view their experiences differently (Moustakas, 1994).

TABLE 2.1 ● Philosophical Assumptions With Implications for Practice

Assumption	Questions	Characteristics	Implications for Practice (Examples)
Ontological	What is the nature of reality?	Reality is multiple as seen through many views.	The researcher reports different perspectives as themes develop in the findings.
Epistemological	What counts as knowledge? How are knowledge claims justified? What is the relationship between the researcher and that being researched?	Subjective evidence is obtained from participants; the researcher attempts to lessen the distance between himself or herself and that being researched.	The researcher relies on quotes as evidence from the participant as well as collaborates, spends time in field with participants, and becomes an "insider."
Axiological	What is the role of values?	The researcher acknowledges that research is value-laden and that biases are present in relation to their role in the study context.	The researcher openly discusses values that shape the narrative and includes his or her own interpretation in conjunction with those of participants.
Methodological	What is the process of research? What is the language of research?	The researcher uses inductive logic, studies the topic within its context, and uses an emerging design.	The researcher works with particulars (details) before generalizations, describes in detail the context of the study, and continually revises questions from experiences in the field.

With the *epistemological* assumption, conducting a qualitative study means that researchers try to get as close as possible to the participants being studied. Therefore, subjective evidence is assembled based on individual views. This is how knowledge is known—through the subjective experiences of people. It becomes important, then, to conduct studies in the "field," where the participants live and work—these are important contexts for understanding what the participants are saying. The longer researchers stay in the field or get to know the participants, the more they "know what they know" from firsthand information. For example, a good ethnography requires prolonged stay at the research site (Wolcott, 2008a). In short, the qualitative researcher tries to minimize the "distance" or "objective separateness" (Guba & Lincoln, 1988, p. 94) between himself or herself and those being researched.

All researchers bring values to a study, but qualitative researchers make their values known in a study. This is the *axiological* assumption that characterizes qualitative research. In a qualitative study, the inquirers admit the value-laden nature of the study and actively report their values and biases as well as the value-laden nature of information gathered from the field. We say that researchers "position themselves" by identifying their "positionality" in relation to the context and setting of the research. Among the aspects described are researcher's social position (e.g., gender, age, race, immigration status), personal experiences, and political and professional beliefs (Berger, 2015). In an interpretive biography, for example, the researcher's presence is apparent in the text, and the author admits that the stories voiced represent an interpretation of the author as much as the subject of the study (Denzin, 1989).

The procedures of qualitative research, or its **methodology**, are characterized as inductive, emerging, and shaped by the researcher's experience in collecting and analyzing the data. The logic that the qualitative researcher follows is inductive, from the ground up, rather than handed down entirely from a theory or from the perspectives of the inquirer. Sometimes the research questions change in the middle of the study to reflect better the types of questions needed to understand the research problem. In response, the data collection strategy, planned before the study, needs to be modified to accompany the new questions. During the data analysis, the researcher follows a path of analyzing the data to develop an increasingly detailed knowledge of the topic being studied.

Writing Philosophical Assumptions Into Qualitative Studies

One further thought is important about philosophical assumptions. In some qualitative studies they remain hidden from view; they can be deduced, however, by the discerning reader who sees the multiple views that appear in the themes, the detailed rendering of the subjective quotes of participants, the carefully laid-out biases of the researcher, or the emerging design that evolves in ever-expanding levels of abstraction from description to themes to broad generalizations. In other studies, the philosophy is made explicit by a special section in the study—typically in the description of the characteristics of qualitative inquiry often found in the methods section. Here, the inquirer talks about ontology, epistemology, and other assumptions explicitly and details how they are exemplified in the study. The form of this discussion is to convey the assumptions, to provide definitions for them, and to discuss how they are illustrated in the study. References to the literature about the philosophy of qualitative research round out the discussion. Sections of this nature are often found in doctoral dissertations, in journal articles reported in major qualitative journals, and in conference paper presentations where the audience may ask about the underlying philosophy of the study. While there are infinite ways for an author to go about describing their philosophical assumptions and implications for research practice, we offer three examples from journal articles to complement the examples provided.

EXAMPLE 2.1

JOURNAL ARTICLE EXAMPLES OF DESCRIPTIONS OF UNDERLYING PHILOSOPHICAL ASSUMPTIONS

Notice how the philosophical assumptions are made explicit in each of the following journal articles:

a) Alongside the phenomenological approach description for the study examining the meaning that people with liver failure ascribe to the experience of waiting for a liver transplant (Brown, Sorrell, McClaren, & Creswell, 2006, p. 122)

b) Integrated within the description of the Piliriqatigiinniq Partnership Community Health Research model guiding the study within the methods section (Healey, 2014, p. e134–135)

c) Embedded within researcher positionality description under the heading of Positioning the Mobile Ethnographer (Jungnickel, 2014, p. 642)

Interpretive Frameworks

In Figure 2.1, the philosophical assumptions are often applied within interpretive frameworks that qualitative researchers use when they conduct a study. Thus, Denzin and Lincoln (2011) consider the philosophical assumptions (ontology, epistemology, axiology, and methodology) as key premises that are folded into interpretive frameworks used in qualitative research. What are these interpretive frameworks? They may be paradigms, or beliefs that the researcher brings to the process of research, or they may be theories or theoretical orientations that guide the practice of research. Paradigm interpretative frameworks may be ***postpositivism***, ***social constructivism***, transformation, and postmodern. Theories may be ***social science theories*** to frame their theoretical lens in studies, such as the use of these theories in ethnography (see Chapter 4). Social science theories may be theories of leadership, attribution, political influence and control, and hundreds of other possibilities that are taught in the social science disciplines. On the other hand, the theories may be ***social justice theories*** or advocacy/participatory theories seeking to bring about change or address social justice issues in our societies. As Denzin and Lincoln (2011) state, "We want a social science committed up front to issues of social justice, equity, nonviolence, peace, and universal human rights" (p. 11).

The interpretive frameworks seem to be ever expanding, and the list in Figure 2.1 does not account for all that are popularly used in qualitative research. Another approach that has been extensively discussed elsewhere is the realist perspective that combines a realist ontology (the belief that a real world exists independently of our beliefs and constructions) and a constructivist epistemology (knowledge of the world is inevitably our own construction; see Maxwell, 2012). Consequently, any discussion (including this one) can only be a partial description of possibilities, but a review of several major interpretive frameworks can provide a sense of options. The participants in these interpretive, theoretically oriented projects often represent under-represented or marginalized groups, whether those differences take the form of gender, race, class, religion, sexuality, or geography (Ladson-Billings & Donnor, 2005) or some intersection of these differences.

Postpositivism

Those who engage in qualitative research using a belief system grounded in postpositivism will take a scientific approach to research. They will employ a social science theoretical lens. We will use the term *postpositivism* rather than *positivism* to denote this approach because postpositivists do not believe in strict cause and effect but rather recognize that all cause and effect is a probability that may or may not occur. Postpositivism has the elements of being reductionistic, logical, empirical, cause-and-effect oriented, and deterministic based on a priori theories. We can see this approach at work among individuals with prior quantitative research training and in fields such as the health sciences in which qualitative research often plays a supportive role to quantitative research and must be couched in terms acceptable to quantitative researchers and funding agents (e.g., the a priori use of theory; see Barbour, 2000). A good overview of postpositivist approaches is available in Phillips and Burbules (2000) and Churchill, Plano Clark, Prochaska-Cue, Creswell, and Onta-Grzebik (2007).

In practice, postpositivist researchers view inquiry as a series of logically related steps, believe in multiple perspectives from participants rather than a single reality, and espouse rigorous methods of qualitative data collection and analysis. They use multiple levels of data analysis for rigor, employ computer programs to assist in their analysis, encourage the use of validity approaches, and write their qualitative studies in the form of scientific reports, with a structure resembling quantitative articles (e.g., problem, questions, data collection, results, conclusions). Our approaches to qualitative research have been identified as belonging to postpositivism (Denzin & Lincoln, 2005), as have the approaches of others (e.g., Taylor & Bogdan, 1998). We do tend to use this belief system, although neither of us would not characterize all of our research as framed within a postpositivist qualitative orientation (e.g., see the constructivist approach in McVea, Harter, McEntarffer, & Creswell, 1999; the social justice perspective in Miller, Creswell, & Olander, 1998; and the pragmatic approach in Henderson, 2011). This postpositivist interpretive framework is exemplified in the systematic procedures of grounded theory found in Strauss and Corbin (1990, 1998) and Corbin and Strauss (2007, 2015), the analytic data analysis steps in phenomenology (Moustakas, 1994), and the data analysis strategies of case comparisons of Yin (2014).

Social Constructivism

Social constructivism (which is often described as interpretivism; see Denzin & Lincoln, 2011; Mertens, 2015) is another paradigm or worldview. In social constructivism, individuals seek understanding of the world in which they live and work. They develop subjective meanings of their experiences—meanings directed toward certain objects or things. These meanings are varied and multiple, leading the researcher to look for the complexity of views rather than narrow the meanings into a few categories or ideas. The goal of research, then, is to rely as much as possible on the participants' views of the situation. Often these subjective meanings are negotiated socially and historically. In other words, they are not simply imprinted on individuals but are formed through interaction with others (hence social construction) and through historical and cultural norms that operate in individuals' lives. Rather than starting with a theory (as in postpositivism), inquirers generate or inductively develop a theory or pattern of meaning. Examples of writers who have summarized this position are Burr (2015), Crotty (1998), Lincoln and Guba (2000), and Schwandt (2007).

In terms of practice, the questions become broad and general so that the participants can construct the meaning of a situation, a meaning typically forged in discussions or interactions with other persons. The more open-ended the questioning, the better, as the researcher listens carefully to what people say or do in their life setting. Thus, constructivist researchers often address the "processes" of interaction among individuals. They also focus on the specific contexts in which people live and work in order to understand the historical and cultural settings of the participants. Researchers recognize that their own background shapes their interpretation, and they "position themselves" in the research to acknowledge how their interpretation flows from their own personal, cultural, and historical experiences. Thus the researchers make an interpretation of what they find, an interpretation shaped by their own experiences and background; for example, see study impetus described by Brown et al. (2006). The researcher's intent, then, is to make sense of (or interpret) the meanings others have about the world. This is why qualitative research is often called interpretive research.

We see the constructivist worldview manifest in phenomenological studies, in which individuals describe their experiences (Moustakas, 1994), and in the grounded theory perspective of Charmaz (2014), in which she grounds her theoretical orientation in the views or perspectives of individuals.

Transformative Frameworks

Researchers might use an alternative framework, a ***transformative framework***, because the postpositivists impose structural laws and theories that do not fit marginalized individuals or groups and the constructivists do not go far enough in advocating action to help individuals. The basic tenet of this transformative framework is that knowledge is not neutral and it reflects the power and social relationships within society; thus, the purpose of knowledge construction is to aid people to improve society (Mertens, 2003). These individuals include marginalized groups such as indigenous groups, lesbians, gays, bisexuals, transgender persons, queers, and societies that need a more hopeful, positive psychology and resilience (Mertens, 2009, 2015).

Qualitative research, then, should contain an action agenda for reform that may change the lives of participants, the institutions in which they live and work, or even the researchers' lives. The issues facing these marginalized groups are of paramount importance to study—issues such as oppression, domination, suppression, alienation, and hegemony. As these issues are studied and exposed, the researchers provide a voice for these participants, raising their consciousness and improving their lives (for an educational example, see Job et al., 2013). Describing it as participatory action research, Kemmis and Wilkinson (1998) embrace features of this transformative framework:

- Participatory action is recursive or dialectical and is focused on bringing about change in practices. Thus, in participatory action research studies, inquirers advance an action agenda for change.
- It is focused on helping individuals free themselves from constraints found in the media, in language, in work procedures, and in the relationships of power in educational settings. Participatory studies often begin with an important issue or stance about the problems in society, such as the need for empowerment.
- It is emancipatory in that it helps unshackle people from the constraints of irrational and unjust structures that limit self-development and self-determination. The aim of this approach is to create a political debate and discussion so that change will occur.
- It is practical and collaborative because it is inquiry completed "with" others rather than "on" or "to" others. In this spirit, participatory authors engage the participants as active collaborators in their inquiries.

Other researchers who embrace this worldview are Fay (1987) and Heron and Reason (1997). In practice, this framework has shaped several approaches to inquiry. Specific social issues (e.g., domination, oppression, inequity) help organize the research questions. Not wanting to further marginalize the individuals participating in the research, transformative inquirers collaborate with research participants. They may ask participants to help with designing the questions, collecting the data, analyzing it, and shaping the final report of the research. In this way, the "voice" of the participants becomes heard throughout the research process and the research products meaningful for all involved. It is encouraging to see guiding research resources emerge from the perspectives of marginalized groups (e.g., Lovern & Locust, 2013; Mertens, Cram, & Chilisa, 2013). The research also contains an action agenda for reform, a specific plan for addressing the injustices of the marginalized group. These practices will be seen in the ethnographic approaches to research with a social justice agenda found in Denzin and Lincoln (2011) and in the change-oriented forms of narrative research (Daiute & Lightfoot, 2004).

Postmodern Perspectives

Thomas (1993) calls postmodernists "armchair radicals" (p. 23) who focus their critiques on changing ways of thinking rather than on calling for action based on these changes. ***Postmodernism*** might be considered a family of theories and perspectives that have something in common (Slife & Williams, 1995). The basic concept is that knowledge claims must be set within the conditions of the world today and in the multiple perspectives of class, race, gender, and other group affiliations. These conditions are well articulated by individuals such as Foucault, Derrida, Lyotard, Giroux, and Freire (Bloland, 1995). These are negative conditions, and they show themselves in the presence of hierarchies, power and control by individuals, and the multiple meanings of language. The conditions include the importance of different discourses, the importance of marginalized people and groups (the "other"), and the presence of "metanarratives" or universals that hold true regardless of the social conditions. Also included is the need to "deconstruct" texts in terms of language, their reading and their writing, and the examining and bringing to the surface of concealed hierarchies as well as dominations, oppositions, inconsistencies, and contradictions (Bloland, 1995; Clarke, 2005; Stringer, 1993). Denzin's (1989) approach to "interpretive" biography, Clandinin and Connelly's (2000) approach to narrative research, and Clarke's (2005) perspective on grounded theory draw on postmodernism in that researchers study turning points, or problematic situations in which people find themselves during transition periods (Borgatta & Borgatta, 1992). Regarding a "postmodern-influenced ethnography," Thomas (1993) writes that such a study might "confront the centrality of media-created realities and the influence of information technologies" (p. 25). Thomas also comments that narrative texts need to be challenged (and written), according to the postmodernists, for their "subtexts" of dominant meanings.

Pragmatism

There are many forms of ***pragmatism***. Individuals holding an interpretive framework based on pragmatism focus on the outcomes of the research—the actions, situations, and consequences of inquiry—rather than antecedent conditions (as in postpositivism).

There is a concern with applications—"what works"—and solutions to problems (Patton, 1990). Thus, instead of a focus on methods, the important aspect of research is the problem being studied and the questions asked about this problem (see Rossman & Wilson, 1985). Cherryholmes (1992) and Murphy (1990) provide direction for the basic ideas:

- Pragmatism is not committed to any one system of philosophy and reality.
- Individual researchers have a freedom of choice. They are "free" to choose the methods, techniques, and procedures of research that best meet their needs and purposes.
- Pragmatists do not see the world as an absolute unity. In a similar way, researchers look to many approaches to collecting and analyzing data rather than subscribing to only one way (e.g., multiple qualitative approaches).
- Truth is what works at the time; it is not based in a dualism between reality independent of the mind or within the mind.
- Pragmatist researchers look to the "what" and "how" of research based on its intended consequences—where they want to go with it.
- Pragmatists agree that research always occurs in social, historical, political, and other contexts.
- Pragmatists have believed in an external world independent of the mind as well as those lodged in the mind. They believe (Cherryholmes, 1992) that we need to stop asking questions about reality and the laws of nature. "They would simply like to change the subject" (Rorty, 1983, p. xiv).
- Recent writers embracing this worldview include Rorty (1990), Murphy (1990), Patton (1990), Cherryholmes (1992), and Tashakkori and Teddlie (2003).

In practice, the individual using this worldview will use multiple methods of data collection to best answer the research question, will employ multiple sources of data collection, will focus on the practical implications of the research, and will emphasize the importance of conducting research that best addresses the research problem. In the discussion here of the five approaches to research, you will see this framework at work when ethnographers employ both quantitative (e.g., surveys) and qualitative data collection (LeCompte & Schensul, 1999) and when case study researchers use both quantitative and qualitative data (Luck, Jackson, & Usher, 2006; Yin, 2014).

Feminist Theories

Feminism draws on different theoretical and pragmatic orientations, different international contexts, and different dynamic developments (Olesen, 2011). *Feminist research approaches* center on and make problematic women's diverse situations and the institutions that frame those situations. Research topics may include a postcolonial thought related to forms of feminism depending on the context of nationalism, globalization and diverse international contexts (e.g., sex workers, domestic servants), and work by or about specific groups of women, such as standpoint theories about lesbians, women with disabilities, and women of color (Olesen, 2011). The theme of domination prevails in the feminist literature as well, but the subject matter is often gender domination within a patriarchal society. Feminist research also embraces many of the tenets of postmodern and poststructuralist critiques as a challenge to the injustices of current society. In feminist research approaches, the goals are to establish collaborative and nonexploitative relationships, to place the researcher within the study so as to avoid objectification, and to conduct research that is transformative. Reinharz (1992) concludes that the use of diverse research methods during the previous two decades has greatly benefited feminist scholarship. Recent critical trends address protecting indigenous knowledge and the intersectionality of feminist research (e.g., the intersection of race, class, gender, sexuality, able-bodiedness, and age; Olesen, 2011). Noteworthy among these emerging conversations about intersectionality of feminist theory is the application of a transformative paradigm with social justice (Thornton Dill & Kohlman, 2012) and with ***critical race theory*** (Chepp, 2015).

One of the leading scholars of this approach, Lather (1991), comments on the essential perspectives of this framework. Feminist researchers see gender as a basic organizing principle that shapes the conditions of their lives. It is "a lens that brings into focus particular questions" (Fox-Keller, 1985, p. 6). The questions feminists pose relate to the centrality of gender in the shaping of our consciousness. The aim of this ideological research is to "correct both the invisibility and distortion of female experience in ways relevant to ending women's unequal social position" (Lather, 1991, p. 71). Another writer, Stewart (1994), translates feminist critiques and methodology into procedural guides. She suggests that researchers need to look for what has been left out in social science writing, and to study women's lives and issues such as identities, sex roles, domestic violence, abortion activism, comparable worth, affirmative action, and the way in which women struggle with their social devaluation and powerlessness within their families. Also, researchers need to consciously and systematically include their own roles or positions and assess how they impact their understandings of a woman's life. In addition, Stewart (1994) views women as having agency, the ability to make choices and resist oppression, and she suggests that researchers need to inquire into how a woman understands her gender, acknowledging that gender is a social construct that differs for each individual. An example of such a study that was undertaken by Therberge (1997) focused on the place of physicality in the practice of women's hockey. Stewart (1994) highlights the importance of studying power relationships and individuals' social position and how they impact women. Finally, she sees each woman as different and recommends that scholars avoid the search for a unified or coherent self or voice.

Recent discussions indicate that the approach of finding appropriate methods for feminist research has given way to the thought that any method can be made feminist (Deem, 2002; Moss, 2007). Olesen (2011) summarizes the current state of feminist research under a number of transformative developments (e.g., globalization, transnational feminism), critical trends (e.g., endarkened, decolonizing research and intersectionality), continuing issues (e.g., bias, troubling traditional concepts), enduring concerns (e.g., participants' voices, ethics), influences on feminist work (e.g., the academy and publishing), and challenges of the future (e.g., the interplay of multiple factors in women's lives, hidden oppressions). Recent discussions about emergent practices integrate international perspectives (e.g., Brisolara, Seigart, & SenGupta, 2014) and new research technologies (e.g., Hesse-Biber, 2012).

Critical Theory and Critical Race Theory

Critical theory perspectives are concerned with empowering human beings to transcend the constraints placed on them by race, class, and gender (Fay, 1987). Researchers need to acknowledge their own power, engage in dialogues, and use theory to interpret or illuminate social action (Madison, 2011). Central themes that a critical researcher might explore include the scientific study of social institutions and their transformations through interpreting the meanings of social life; the historical problems of domination, alienation, and social struggles; and a critique of society and the envisioning of new possibilities (Fay, 1987; Morrow & Brown, 1994).

In research, critical theory can be defined by the particular configuration of methodological postures it embraces. The critical researcher might design, for example, an ethnographic study to include changes in how people think; encourage people to interact, form networks, become activists, and form action-oriented groups; and help individuals examine the conditions of their existence (Madison, 2011; Thomas, 1993). The end goal of the study might be social theorizing, which Morrow and Brown (1994) define as "the desire to comprehend and, in some cases, transform (through praxis) the underlying orders of social life—those social and systemic relations that constitute society" (p. 211). The investigator accomplishes this, for example, through an intensive case study or across a small number of historically comparable cases of specific actors (biographies), mediations, or systems and through "ethnographic accounts (interpretive social psychology), componential taxonomies (cognitive anthropology), and formal models (mathematical sociology)" (p. 212). In critical action research in teacher education, for example, Kincheloe (1991) recommends that the "critical teacher" exposes the assumptions of existing research orientations; critiques the knowledge base; and through these critiques reveals ideological effects on teachers, schools, and the culture's view of education. The design of research within a critical theory approach, according to sociologist Agger (1991), falls into two broad categories: *methodological*, in that it affects the ways in which people write and read, and *substantive*, in the theories and topics of the investigator (e.g., theorizing about the role of state and culture in advanced capitalism). An often-cited classic of critical theory is the ethnography from Willis (1977) of the "lads" who participated in behavior as opposition to authority, as informal groups "having a laff" (p. 29) as a form of resistance to their school. As a study of the manifestations of resistance and state regulation, it highlights ways in which actors come to terms with and struggle against cultural forms that dominate them (Morrow & Brown, 1994). Resistance is also the theme addressed in an ethnography of a subcultural group of youths (Haenfler, 2004).

Critical race theory focuses theoretical attention on "studying and transforming the relationship between race, racism, and power" (Delgado & Stefancic, 2012, p. 3). Race and racism is deeply embedded within the framework of American society (Parker & Lynn, 2002) and has directly shaped the U.S. legal system and the ways people think about the law, racial categories, and privilege (Harris, 1993). According to Parker and Lynn (2002), critical race theory has three main goals. Its first goal is to present stories about discrimination from the perspective of people of color. These may be qualitative case studies of descriptions and interviews. These cases may then be drawn together to build cases against racially biased officials or discriminatory practices. Since many stories advance White privilege through "majoritarian" master narratives, counterstories by people of color can help to shatter the complacency that may accompany such privilege and challenge the dominant discourses that serve to suppress people on the margins of society (Solorzano & Yosso, 2002). As a second goal, critical race theory argues for the eradication of racial subjugation while simultaneously recognizing that race is a social construct (Parker & Lynn, 2002). In this view, *race* is not a fixed term but one that is fluid and continually shaped by political pressures and informed by individual lived experiences. Finally, the third goal of critical race theory addresses other areas of difference, such as gender, class, and any inequities experienced by individuals. As Parker and Lynn (2002) comment, "In the case of Black women, race does not exist outside of gender and gender does not exist outside of race" (p. 12). In research, the use of critical race theory methodology means that the researcher foregrounds race and racism in all aspects of the research process; challenges the traditional research paradigms, texts, and theories used to explain the experiences of people of color; and offers transformative solutions to racial, gender, and class subordination in our societal and institutional structures. Researchers sometimes use critical race theory in concert with other frameworks—for example, disability studies (Watts & Erevelles, 2004) or feminist theories (Chepp, 2015).

Queer Theory

Queer theory is characterized by a variety of methods and strategies relating to individual identity (Plummer, 2011a; Watson, 2005). As a body of literature continuing to evolve, it explores the myriad complexities of the construct, identity, and how identities reproduce and "perform" in social forums. Writers also use a postmodern or poststructural orientation to critique and deconstruct dominant theories related to identity (Plummer, 2011a, 2011b; Watson, 2005). They focus on how it is culturally and historically constituted, is linked to discourse, and overlaps gender and sexuality. The term itself—*queer theory*, rather than *gay, lesbian*, or *homosexual theory*—allows for keeping open to question the elements of race, class, age, and anything else (Turner, 2000), and it is a term that has changed in meaning over the years and differs across cultures and languages (Plummer, 2011b). Most queer theorists work to challenge and undercut identity as singular, fixed, or normal (Watson, 2005). They also seek to challenge categorization processes and their deconstructions, rather than focus on specific populations. The historical binary distinctions are inadequate to describe sexual identity. Plummer (2011a) provides a concise overview of the queer theory stance:

- Both the heterosexual/homosexual binary and the sex/gender split are challenged.
- There is a decentering of identity.
- All sexual categories (lesbian, gay, bisexual, transgender, heterosexual) are open, fluid, and nonfixed.
- Mainstream homosexuality is critiqued.
- Power is embodied discursively.
- All normalizing strategies are shunned.
- Academic work may become ironic and often comic and paradoxical.
- Versions of homosexual subject positions are inscribed everywhere.
- Deviance is abandoned, and interest lies in insider and outsider perspectives and transgressions.
- Common objects of study are films, videos, novels, poetry, and visual images.
- The most frequent interests include the social worlds of the so-called radical sexual fringe (e.g., drag kings and queens, sexual playfulness). (p. 201)

Although queer theory is less a methodology and more a focus of inquiry, queer methods often find expression in a rereading of cultural texts (e.g., films, literature); ethnographies and case studies of sexual worlds that challenge assumptions; data sources that contain multiple texts; documentaries that include performances; and projects that focus on individuals (Plummer, 2011a). Queer theorists have engaged in research and/or political activities such as the AIDS Coalition to Unleash Power (ACT UP) and Queer Nation around HIV/AIDS awareness, as well as artistic and cultural representations of art and theater aimed at disrupting or rendering unnatural and strange practices that are taken for granted. These representations convey the voices and experiences of individuals who have been suppressed (Gamson, 2000) and provide important insights for informing policies and practices (e.g., Adams, Braun, & McCreanor, 2014). Useful readings about queer theory are found in the journal article overview provided by Watson (2005) and the chapter by Plummer (2011a, 2011b) and also in key books, such as the book by Tierney (1997).

Disability Theories

Disability inquiry addresses the meaning of inclusion in schools and encompasses administrators, teachers, and parents who have children with disabilities (Mertens, 2009, 2015). Mertens (2003) recounts how disability research has moved through stages of development, from the medical model of disability (sickness and the role of the medical community in threatening it) to an environmental response to individuals with a disability. Now, researchers using a ***disability interpretive lens*** focus on disability as a dimension of human difference and not as a defect. As a human difference, its meaning is derived from social construction (i.e., society's response to individuals), and it is simply one dimension of human difference (Mertens, 2003). Viewing individuals with disabilities as different is reflected in the research process, such as in the types of questions asked, the labels applied to these individuals, considerations of how the data collection will benefit the community, the appropriateness of communication methods, and how the data are reported in a way that is respectful of power relationships. Mertens, Sullivan, and Stace (2011) have also linked critical disability theory with transformative frameworks because of its use as an intersection for many sources of discrimination. Resources for guiding research informed by disabilities theories are available (e.g., Barnes, Oliver, & Barton, 2002; Kroll, Barbour, & Harris, 2007).

The Practice of Using Interpretive Frameworks in Qualitative Research

The practice of using interpretive frameworks in a qualitative study varies, and it depends on the framework being used and the particular researcher's approach. Each of the descriptions of the interpretive frameworks highlighted unique researcher influences, goals, and practices. Qualitative researchers have found it helpful to distinguish among the interpretive frameworks to see at this point an overall summary (Table 2.2). Once researchers can distinguish among the interpretive frameworks then it is easier to see how they are applied in practice. At the most fundamental level, there are differences and commonalities in which they are trying to accomplish—their goals. Seeking an understanding of the world is different from generating solutions to real-world problems. Potential similarities among the goals should be noted. Feminist theories, critical theory and critical race theory, queer theories, and disability theories share a general intent for researchers to base calls for action on documented struggles. Some common elements to how the interpretive framework will be practiced can be identified:

- Research focuses on understanding specific issues or topics. The problems and the research questions explored aim to allow the researcher an understanding of specific issues or topics—the conditions that serve to disadvantage and exclude individuals or cultures, such as hierarchy, hegemony, racism, sexism, unequal power relations, identity, or inequities in our society.

- Research procedures are sensitive to participants and context. The procedures of research, such as data collection, data analysis, representing the material to audiences, and standards of evaluation and ethics, emphasize an interpretive stance. During data collection, the researcher does not further marginalize the participants but respects the participants and the sites for research. Further, researchers provide reciprocity by giving or paying back those who participate in research, and they focus on the multiple-perspective stories of individuals and who tells the stories. Researchers are also sensitive to power imbalances during all facets of the research process. They respect individual differences rather than employing the traditional aggregation of categories such as men and women, or Hispanics or African Americans.

- Researchers are respectful co-constructors of knowledge. Ethical practices of the researchers recognize the importance of the subjectivity of their own lens, acknowledge the powerful position they have in the research, and admit that the participants or the co-construction of the account between the researchers and the participants are the true owners of the information collected.

- Research is reported in diverse formats and calls for societal change. The research may be presented in traditional ways, such as journal articles, or in experimental approaches, such as theater or poetry. Using an interpretive lens may also lead to the call for action and transformation—the aims of social justice—in which the qualitative project ends with distinct steps of reform and an incitement to action.

Linking Philosophy and Interpretive Frameworks in Qualitative Research

Although the philosophical assumptions are not always stated, the interpretive frameworks do convey different philosophical assumptions, and qualitative researchers need to be aware of this connection. A thoughtful chapter by Lincoln, Lynham, and Guba (2011) makes this connection explicit. We have taken their overview of this connection and adapted it to fit the interpretive communities discussed in this chapter. As shown in Table 2.3, the philosophical assumptions of ontology, epistemology, axiology, and methodology take different forms given the interpretive framework used by the inquirer.

The use of information from Table 2.3 in a qualitative study would be to discuss the interpretive framework used in a project by weaving together the framework used by discussing its central tenets, how it informs the problem to a study, the research questions, the data collection and analysis, and the interpretation. A section of this discussion would also mention the philosophical assumptions (ontology, epistemology, axiology, methodology) associated with the interpretive framework. Thus, there would be two ways to discuss the interpretive framework: its nature and use in the study, and its philosophical assumptions. As we proceed ahead and examine the five qualitative approaches in this book, recognize that each one might use any of the interpretive frameworks. For example, if a grounded theory study were presented as a scientific paper, with a major emphasis on objectivity, with a focus on the theoretical model that results, without reporting biases of the researcher, and with a systematic

TABLE 2.2 ● Comparing Major Interpretive Frameworks			
Interpretive Frameworks	**Possible Researcher Goals**	**Potential Researcher Influences**	**Examples of Researcher Practices**
Postpositivism	To discover contributors to probability within situations of cause and effect	Prior quantitative research training	Reports systematic data collection and analysis procedures followed to ensure rigor
Social constructivism	To understand the world in which they live and work	Recognition of background as shaping interpretation	Interprets participants constructions of meaning in his/her account
Transformative frameworks	To act for societal improvements	Knowledge of power and social relationships within society	Adopts an action agenda for addressing the injustices of marginalized groups
Postmodern perspectives	To change ways of thinking	Understandings of the conditions of the world today	Situates research to highlight multiplicity of perspectives
Pragmatism	To find solutions to real-world problems	Appreciation for diverse approaches to collecting and analyzing and the contexts in which research takes place	Uses the most appropriate methods for addressing the research question
Feminist theories	To conduct research that is transformative for women	Perspectives of power relationships and individuals' social position and how they impact women	Poses questions that relate to the centrality of gender in the shaping of our consciousness
Critical theory and critical race theory	To address areas of inequities and empower humans	Acknowledgment of own power, engagement in dialogues, and use of theory to interpret social actions	Designs research in such a way that transforms the underlying orders of social life
Queer theory	To convey the voices and experiences of individuals who have been suppressed	Understandings of need for thinking about sexual categories as open, fluid, and nonfixed	Engages in inquiry with a focus on exploring the myriad complexities of individual identity
Disability theories	To address the meaning of inclusion	Recognition of disability as a dimension of human difference and not as a defect	Employs a disability interpretive lens for informing the research process

TABLE 2.3 ● Interpretive Frameworks and Associated Philosophical Beliefs				
Interpretive Frameworks	**Ontological Beliefs (the nature of reality)**	**Epistemological Beliefs (how reality is known)**	**Axiological Beliefs (role of values)**	**Methodological Beliefs (approach to inquiry)**
Postpositivism	A single reality exists beyond ourselves, "out there." The researcher may not be able to understand it or get to it because of lack of absolutes.	Reality can only be approximated, but it is constructed through research and statistics. Interaction with research subjects is kept to a minimum. Validity comes from peers, not participants.	The researcher's biases need to be controlled and not expressed in a study.	Scientific method and writing is used. Object of research is to create new knowledge. Method is important. Deductive methods are important, such as testing of theories, specifying important variables, and making comparisons among groups.
Social constructivism	Multiple realities are constructed through our lived experiences and interactions with others.	Reality is co-constructed between the researcher and the researched and shaped by individual experiences.	Individual values are honored and are negotiated among individuals.	More of a literary style of writing is used. Use of an inductive method of emergent ideas (through consensus) is obtained through methods such as interviewing, observing, and analyzing texts.
Transformative/ postmodern	Participation between researcher and communities or individuals is being studied. Often a subjective–objective reality emerges.	There are co-created findings with multiple ways of knowing.	There is respect for indigenous values; values need to be problematized and interrogated.	Methods consist of using collaborative processes of research, encouraging political participation, questioning of methods, and highlighting issues and concerns.
Pragmatism	Reality is what is useful, is practical, and "works."	Reality is known through using many tools of research that reflect both deductive (objective) evidence and inductive (subjective) evidence.	Values are discussed because of the way that knowledge reflects both the researchers' and the participants' views.	The research process involves both quantitative and qualitative approaches to data collection and analysis.

(Continued)

TABLE 2.3 ● (Continued)				
Interpretive Frameworks	Ontological Beliefs (the nature of reality)	Epistemological Beliefs (how reality is known)	Axiological Beliefs (role of values)	Methodological Beliefs (approach to inquiry)
Critical, race, feminist, queer, disability	Reality is based on power and identity struggles. Privilege or oppression based on race or ethnicity, class, gender, mental abilities, sexual preference.	Reality is known through the study of social structures, freedom and oppression, power, and control. Reality can be changed through research.	Diversity of values is emphasized within the standpoint of various communities.	Start with assumptions of power and identity struggles, document them, and call for action and change.

Source: Adapted from Lincoln et al. (2011).

rendering of data analysis, a postpositivist interpretive framework would be used. On the other hand, if the intent of the qualitative narrative study was to examine a marginalized group of disabled learners with attention to their struggles for identity about prostheses that they wear, and with utmost respect for their views and values, and in the end of the study to call for changes in how the disabled group is perceived, then a strong disability interpretive framework would be in use. We could see using any of the interpretive frameworks with any of the five approaches advanced in this book.

Chapter Check-In

1. Do you understand the differences among the four major philosophical assumptions used in qualitative research: ontology (what is reality?), epistemology (how is reality known?), axiology (how are values of the research expressed?), and methodology (how is the research conducted?)?

   Examine a qualitative journal article, such as the qualitative study by Brown et al. (2006) or Healey (2014) or Jungnickel (2014). Begin with identifying the specific ways in which the four philosophical assumptions are evident in the study. List examples using Table 2.1 in this chapter as a guide.

   Brown, J., Sorrell, J. H., McClaren, J., & Creswell, J. W. (2006). Waiting for a liver transplant. *Qualitative Health Research, 16*(1), 119–136. doi:10.1177/1049732305284011

   Healey, G. K. (2014). Inuit family understandings of sexual health and relationships in Nunavut. *Canadian Journal of Public Health, 105*(2), e133–e137. doi:10.17269/cjph.105.4189

Jungnickel, K. (2014). Getting there ... and back: How ethnographic commuting (by bicycle) shaped a study of Australian backyard technologists. *Qualitative Research*, *14*(6), 640–655. doi:10.1177/1468794113481792

2. Do you understand the differences among the associated philosophical beliefs among interpretive frameworks (postpositivism, social constructivism, transformative frameworks, postmodern perspectives, pragmatism, feminist theories, critical theory and critical race theory, queer theory, and disability theories)? Read qualitative journal articles that adopt different interpretive lens, such as Adams et al. (2014) from a queer theory framework, Brown et al. (2006) from social constructivist framework, Churchill et al. (2007) from a postpositivist framework, or Job et al. (2013) from a transformative framework. Identify how these articles differ in their interpretive frameworks. List examples using Table 2.3 in this chapter as a guide.

Adams, J., Braun, V., & McCreanor, T. (2014). "Aren't labels for pickle jars, not people?" Negotiating identity and community in talk about "being gay." *American Journal of Men's Health*, *8*(6), 457–469. doi:0.1177/1557988313518800

Brown, J., Sorrell, J. H., McClaren, J., & Creswell, J. W. (2006). Waiting for a liver transplant. *Qualitative Health Research*, *16*(1), 119–136. doi:10.1177/1049732305284011

Churchill, S. L., Plano Clark, V. L., Prochaska-Cue, M. K., Creswell, J. W., & Onta-Grzebik, L. (2007). How rural low-income families have fun: A grounded theory study. *Journal of Leisure Research*, *39*(2), 271–294.

Job, J., Poth, C., Pei, J., Carter-Pasula, B., Brandell, D., & MacNab, J. (2013). Toward better collaboration in the education of

students with fetal alcohol spectrum disorders: Voices of teachers, administrators, caregivers, and allied professionals. *Qualitative Research in Education*, *2*, 38–64. doi:10.4471/qre.2013.15

3. What are the unique elements within particular interpretive frameworks? Examine qualitative journal articles that adopt different interpretive lens, such as Therberge (1997) from a feminist interpretive framework, and identify such as elements as the feminist issue(s), the directional question, the advocacy orientation of the aim of the study, the methods of data collection, and the call for action.

Therberge, N. (1997). "It's part of the game": Physicality and the production of gender in women's hockey. *Gender & Society*, *11*(1), 69–87. doi:10.1177/089124397011001005

4. Do you understand the differences among interpretive frameworks when used in combinations? Examine qualitative journal articles that adopt a combination of different interpretive lenses, such as Chepp (2015) from feminist and critical race theories frameworks and from Watts and Erevelles (2004) disabilities and critical race theory frameworks. Identify examples of influenced from each interpretive framework using Table 2.2 in this chapter as a guide.

Chepp, V. (2015). Black feminist theory and the politics of irreverence: The case of women's rap. *Feminist Theory*, *16*(2), 207–226. doi:10.1177/1464700115585705

Watts, I. E., & Erevelles, N. (2004). These deadly times: Reconceptualizing school violence by using critical race theory and disability studies. *American Journal of Educational Research*, *41*, 271–299. doi:10.3102/00028312041002271

Summary

This chapter began with an overview of the research process so that philosophical assumptions and interpretive frameworks could be seen as positioned at the beginning of the process and informing the procedures that follow, including the selection and use of one of the five approaches in this book. Then the philosophical assumptions of ontology, epistemology, axiology, and methodology were discussed, as were the key question being asked for each assumption, its major characteristics, and the implication for the practice of writing a qualitative study. Furthermore, the popular interpretive frameworks (paradigm perspectives and theoretical orientations) used in qualitative research were advanced. How these interpretive frameworks are used in a qualitative study was suggested. Finally, a link was made between the philosophical assumptions and the interpretive frameworks, and a discussion followed about how to connect the two in a qualitative project.

Further Readings

The following resources are offered as foundational references for this chapter. The list should not be considered exhaustive, and readers are encouraged to seek out additional readings in the end-of-book reference list.

Brisolara, S., Seigart, D., & SenGupta, S. (2014). *Feminist evaluation and research: Theory and practice.* New York, NY: Guilford Press.

Sharon Brisolara, Denise Seigart, and Saumitra SenGupta bring together illustrative examples exploring the processes involved in feminist research. The authors uniquely situate feminist research within disciplines and international contexts.

Denzin, N. K., & Lincoln, Y. S. (Eds.) (2011). *The SAGE handbook of qualitative research.* Thousand Oaks, CA: Sage.

Handbooks are often a logical starting place for researchers, and Norm Denzin and Yvonna Lincoln offer foundation ideas for contemporary discussions about the role of guiding philosophy behind qualitative research. Specifically, we found the chapters on feminist research by Virginia Olesen; queer theory by Ken Plummer; and transformative research by Donna Mertens, Martin Sullivan, and Hilary Stace to be noteworthy.

Guba, E., & Lincoln, Y. S. (1988). Do inquiry paradigms imply inquiry methodologies? In D. M. Fetterman (Ed.), *Qualitative approaches to evaluation in education* (pp. 89–115). New York, NY: Praeger.

Egon Guba and Yvonna Lincoln, in offering their perspective of the relationship between paradigms and methodologies, contribute seminal work to these discussions.

Hesse-Biber, S. N. (2012). *Handbook of feminist research: Theory and praxis* (2nd ed.). Thousand Oaks, CA: Sage

Sharlene Nagy Hesse-Biber provides a grounding in feminist research through discussions of current perspectives on its influence on social change and transformation as well as the new technologies that are influencing methodological approaches within the field.

Lovern, L. L. & Locust, C. (2013). *Native American communities on health and disability: Borderland dialogues.* New York, NY: Palgrave Macmillan.

Lavonna Lovern and Carol Locust provide a foundational resource for researchers interested in how to begin a genuine dialogue with indigenous communities. The authors experiences are particularly noted in the sections focused on "wellness" concepts that are respectful of disability and indigeneity.

Mertens, D. M. (2009). *Transformative research and evaluation.* New York, NY: Guilford.

In this book, Donna Mertens provides a step-by-step guide to conducting research using a transformative lens in a way that clearly connects theory to practice.

Mertens, D. M. (2015). *Research and evaluation in education and psychology: Integrating diversity with quantitative, qualitative, and mixed methods* (4th ed.). Thousand Oaks, CA: Sage.

Donna Mertens presents a brief history and then focuses on the philosophical underpinnings of four research paradigms: postpositivism, constructivist, transformative, and pragmatic. Of particular note is her useful description of the transformative paradigm including a rationale for its emergence and description of its philosophical and theoretical basis.

Mertens, D. M., Cram, F., & Chilisa, B. (Eds.) (2013). *Indigenous pathways into social research.* Walnut Creek, CA: Left Coast Press.

Through life stories of over 30 indigenous researchers from six continents representing diverse disciplines, editors Donna Mertens, Fiona Cram and Bagele Chilisa provide a powerful conduit for researchers to learn about challenges experienced and effective strategies for producing meaningful work.

Phillips, D. C., & Burbules, N. C. (2000). *Postpositivism and educational research.* Lanham, MD: Rowman & Littlefield.

Dennis Phillips and Nicholas Burbules offer an excellent description of postpositivism in practice that is a foundational read for researchers.

Slife, B. D., & Williams, R. N. (1995). *What's behind the research? Discovering hidden assumptions in the behavioral sciences.* Thousand Oaks, CA: Sage.

Brent Slife and Richard Williams explore the assumptions underpinning major theoretical approaches in the behavioral sciences. This seminal work has been widely cited across disciplines (e.g., psychology, education) as useful for encouraging critical thinking of theories.

(Continued)

(Continued)

Schwandt, T. A. (2003). Three epistemological stances for qualitative inquiry: Interpretativism, hermeneutics and social constructionism. In N. Denzin & Y. Lincoln (Eds.), *The landscape of qualitative research: Theories and issues* (pp. 292–331). Thousand Oaks, CA: Sage.

In his useful comparisons, Thomas Schwandt draws both commonalities and distinctions. For example, he views a shared focus of social constructionists and interpretivists on the process by which meanings are developed, negotiated, sustained, and adapted. Yet how the theory is applied in practice highlights differences.

Tierney, W. G. (1997). *Academic outlaws: Queer theory and cultural studies in the academy*. Thousand Oaks, CA: Sage.

William Tierney situates the theoretical intersection of cultural studies and queer theory in this book. He provides an important historical look backward and an interesting look forward.

Designing a Qualitative Study

We think metaphorically of qualitative research as an intricate fabric comprising minute threads, many colors, different textures, and various blends of material. This fabric is not explained easily or simply. Like the loom on which fabric is woven, general assumptions and interpretive frameworks hold qualitative research together. To describe these frameworks, qualitative researchers use these terms—*constructivist, interpretivist, feminist, postmodernist,* and so forth. Within these assumptions and through these frameworks are approaches (or designs) to qualitative inquiry, such as narrative research, phenomenology, grounded theory, ethnography, and case studies. This field has many different individuals with different perspectives who are on their own looms creating the fabric of qualitative research. Aside from these differences, the creative artists have the common task of making a fabric. In other words, there are characteristics common to all forms of qualitative research, and the different characteristics will receive different emphases depending on the qualitative project. Not all characteristics are present in all qualitative projects, but many are.

The intent of this chapter is to provide an overview of and introduction to qualitative research so that we can see the common characteristics of qualitative research before we explore the different threads of it (through specific approaches such as narrative, phenomenology, and others). We begin with a general definition of *qualitative research* and highlight the essential characteristics of conducting this form of inquiry. We then discuss the types of research problems and issues best suited for a qualitative study. We emphasize the requirements needed to conduct this rigorous, time-consuming research as well as criteria for assessing its quality. Given that you have the essentials (the problem, the time, the criteria) to engage in this inquiry, we then sketch out the overall process involved in designing and planning a study. This process entails preliminary considerations, phases in the process, and overall elements to consider throughout the process. Within these aspects, qualitative researchers need to anticipate and plan for potential ethical issues because these issues arise during many phases of the research process. We end by suggesting design structures including considerations for engaging readers and an outline that you might use to guide the overall structure for planning or proposing a qualitative research study. The chapters to follow will then address the different types of inquiry approaches. The general design features, outlined here, will be refined for the five approaches discussed in the remainder of the book.

Questions for Discussion

- What are the key characteristics of qualitative research?
- What types of problems are best suited for qualitative inquiry?
- What research skills are required to undertake this type of research?
- What are the features of a "good" qualitative study?
- How do researchers design a qualitative study?
- What types of ethical issues need to be anticipated during the process of qualitative research?
- What design structures are useful for a qualitative study plan or proposal?

The Characteristics of Qualitative Research

Our rationale underlying our working definition of qualitative research emphasizes the design of research and the use of distinct approaches to inquiry (e.g., ethnography, narrative). To build upon the definition of qualitative research presented in the introductory chapter for the purpose of discussing the characteristics of qualitative research, we restate our working definition here:

Qualitative research begins with assumptions and the use of interpretive/theoretical frameworks that inform the study of research problems addressing the meaning individuals or groups ascribe to a social or human problem. To study this problem, qualitative researchers use an emerging qualitative approach to inquiry, the collection of data in a natural setting sensitive to the people and places under study, and data analysis that is both inductive and deductive and establishes patterns or themes. The final written report or presentation includes the voices of participants, the reflexivity of the researcher, a complex description and interpretation of the problem, and its contribution to the literature or a call for change. (Creswell, 2013, p. 44)

Notice in this definition that the *process* of research is described as flowing from philosophical assumptions, to interpretive lens, and on to the procedures involved in studying social or human problems. Then, a framework exists for the procedures—the approach to inquiry, such as grounded theory, or case study research, or others.

It is helpful to move from a more general definition to specific characteristics found in qualitative research. We believe that the characteristics have evolved over time, and they certainly do not present a definitive set of elements. But a close examination of the characteristics mentioned in major books in the field shows some common threads. Examine Table 3.1 for four introductory qualitative research books and the characteristics they espouse for doing a qualitative study. As compared to a similar table in the first edition of this book almost 15 years ago (drawing on other authors), qualitative research today involves closer attention to the interpretive nature of inquiry and situating the study within the political, social, and cultural context of the researchers, and the reflexivity or "presence" of the researchers in the accounts they present. By examining Table 3.1, one can arrive at several common characteristics of qualitative research. These are presented in no specific order of importance:

- *Natural setting.* Qualitative researchers often collect data in the field at the site where participants experience the issue or problem under study. They do not bring individuals into a lab (a contrived situation), nor do they typically send out instruments for individuals to complete, such as in survey research. Instead, qualitative researchers gather up-close information by talking directly to people and seeing them behave within their context. These face-to-face interactions might occur over time.
- *Researcher as key instrument.* The qualitative researchers collect data themselves through examining documents, observing behavior, and interviewing participants. They may use an instrument, but it is one designed by the researcher using open-ended questions. They do not tend to use or rely on questionnaires or instruments developed by other researchers.
- *Multiple methods.* Qualitative researchers typically gather multiple forms of data, such as interviews, observations, and documents, rather than rely on a single data source. Then they review all of the data and make sense of it, organizing it into categories or themes that cut across all of the data sources.
- *Complex reasoning through inductive and deductive logic.* Qualitative researchers build their patterns, categories, and themes from the "bottom up" by organizing the data inductively into increasingly more abstract units of information. This inductive process involves researchers working back and forth between the themes and the database until they establish a comprehensive set of themes. It may also involve collaborating with the participants interactively so that they have a chance to

shape the themes or abstractions that emerge from the process. Researchers also use deductive thinking in that they build themes that are constantly being checked against the data. The inductive–deductive logic process means that the qualitative researcher uses complex reasoning skills throughout the process of research.

- *Participants' multiple perspectives and meanings.* In the entire qualitative research process, the researchers keep a focus on learning the meaning that the participants hold about the problem or issue, not the meaning that the researchers bring to the research or writers from the literature. The participant meanings further suggest multiple perspectives on a topic and diverse views. This is why a theme developed in a qualitative report should reflect multiple perspectives of the participants in the study.

- *Context-dependent.* The research is situated within the context or setting of participants or sites. In order to report the setting in which the problem is being studied, the researcher must seek an understanding of contextual features and their influence on participants' experiences (e.g., social, political, and historical). This is essential because the particular contexts allow researchers to "understand how events, actions, and meaning are shaped by the unique circumstances in which these occur" (Maxwell, 2013, p. 30).

- *Emergent design.* The research process for qualitative researchers is emergent. This means that the initial plan for research cannot be tightly prescribed and that all phases of the process may change or shift after the researchers enter the field and begin to collect data. For example, the questions may change, the forms of data collection may be altered, and the individuals studied and the sites visited may be modified during the process of conducting the study. The key idea behind qualitative research is to learn about the problem or issue from participants and engage in the best practices to obtain that information.

- *Reflexivity.* Researchers "position themselves" in a qualitative research study. This means that researchers convey (i.e., in a method section, in an introduction, or in other places in a study) their background (e.g., work experiences, cultural experiences, history), how it informs their interpretation of the information in a study, and what they have to gain from the study. Wolcott (2010) said the following:

> Our readers have a right to know about us. And they do not want to know whether we played in the high school band. They want to know what prompts our interest in the topics we investigate, to whom we are reporting, and what we personally stand to gain from our study. (p. 36)

- *Holistic account.* Qualitative researchers try to develop a complex picture of the problem or issue under study. This involves reporting multiple perspectives, identifying the many factors involved in a situation, and generally sketching the larger picture that emerges. Researchers are bound not by cause-and-effect relationships among factors but rather by describing the complex interactions of factors in any situation.

TABLE 3.1 ● Characteristics of Qualitative Research

Characteristics	LeCompte and Schensul (1999)	Hatch (2002)	Marshall and Rossman (2015)	Ravitch and Mittenfelner Carl (2016)
Is conducted in a natural setting (the field)	Yes	Yes	Yes	Yes
Relies on the researcher as key instrument in data collection		Yes		Yes
Involves using multiple methods	Yes		Yes	
Involves complex reasoning going between inductive and deductive	Yes	Yes	Yes	Yes
Focuses on participants' multiple perspectives and meanings	Yes	Yes		Yes
Is situated within the context or setting of participants or sites	Yes		Yes	Yes
Involves an emergent and evolving design		Yes	Yes	Yes
Is reflective and interpretive of researcher's background influences			Yes	Yes
Presents a holistic, complex picture		Yes	Yes	Yes

When to Use Qualitative Research

When is it appropriate to use qualitative research? We conduct qualitative research because a problem or issue needs to be explored. This exploration is needed, in turn, because of a need to study a group or population, identify variables that cannot be easily measured, or hear silenced voices. These are all good reasons to explore a problem rather than to use predetermined information from the literature or rely on results from other research studies. We also conduct qualitative research because we need a complex, detailed understanding of the issue. This detail can only be established by talking directly with people, going to their homes or places of work, and allowing them to tell the stories unencumbered by what we expect to find or what we have read in the literature.

We conduct qualitative research when we want to empower individuals to share their stories, hear their voices, and minimize the power relationships that often exist between a researcher and the participants in a study. To further deemphasize a power relationship, we may collaborate directly with participants by having them review our research questions, or by having them collaborate with us during the data analysis and interpretation phases of research. We conduct qualitative research when we want to write in a literary, flexible style that conveys stories, or theater, or poems, without the restrictions of formal academic structures of writing. We conduct qualitative research because we want to understand the contexts or settings in which participants in a study address a problem or issue. We cannot always separate what people say from the place where they say it—whether this context is their home, family, or work. We use qualitative research to follow up quantitative research and help explain the mechanisms or linkages in causal theories or models. These theories provide a general picture of trends, associations, and relationships, but they do not tell us about the processes that people experience, why they responded as they did, the context in which they responded, and their deeper thoughts and behaviors that governed their responses.

We use qualitative research to develop theories when partial or inadequate theories exist for certain populations and samples or existing theories do not adequately capture the complexity of the problem we are examining. We also use qualitative research because quantitative measures and the statistical analyses simply do not fit the problem. Interactions among people, for example, are difficult to capture with existing measures, and these measures may not be sensitive to issues such as gender differences, race, economic status, and individual differences. To level all individuals to a statistical mean overlooks the uniqueness of individuals in our studies. Examine Figure 3.1 for a summary description of when qualitative approaches are simply a better fit for our research problem.

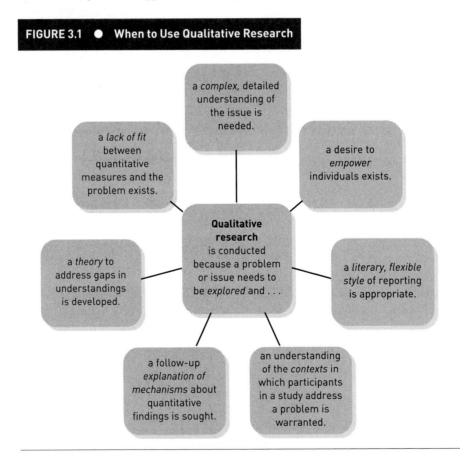

FIGURE 3.1 ● When to Use Qualitative Research

What a Qualitative Study Requires From Us

What does it take to engage in this form of research? To undertake qualitative research requires a strong commitment to study a problem and its demands of time and resources. Qualitative research keeps good company with the most rigorous quantitative approaches, and it should not be viewed as an easy substitute for a "statistical" or quantitative study. Qualitative inquiry is for the researcher who is willing to do the following:

- *Commit to extensive time in the field.* The investigator spends many hours in the field, collects extensive data, and labors over field issues of trying to gain access and establish rapport. Collaborating with participants takes time yet is important for developing an "insider" perspective.
- *Engage in the complex, time-consuming process of data analysis.* The investigator undertakes the ambitious task of sorting through large amounts of data and reducing them to a few themes or categories. For a multidisciplinary team of qualitative researchers, this task can be shared; for most researchers, it is a lonely, isolated time of pondering and making sense of the data.
- *Write lengthy and descriptive passages.* The investigator presents the evidence in a way that the claims are substantiated and reflective of multiple perspectives. The incorporation of quotes to provide participants' perspectives also lengthens the study.
- *Embrace dynamic and emergent procedures.* The investigator participates in a form of social and human science research that does not follow specific procedures and is constantly changing. This might complicate telling others about study plans and how others judge the study when completed.
- *Attend to anticipated and developing ethical issues.* The investigator considers what ethical issues might surface during the study and to plan how these issues need to be addressed. Additionally, new issues might emerge, which require attention, while undertaking the study.

The Features of a "Good" Qualitative Study

In the end, individuals such as readers, participants, graduate committees, editorial board members for journals, and reviewers of proposals for funding will apply some criteria to assess the quality of a study. Standards for assessing the quality of qualitative research are available (Howe & Eisenhardt, 1990; Lincoln, 1995; Marshall & Rossman, 2015). Here is our short list describing the features of a "good" qualitative study. You will see an emphasis on rigorous methods present in this list.

- The researcher frames the study within the assumptions and characteristics of the qualitative approach to research. This includes fundamental characteristics such as an evolving design, the presentation of multiple realities, the researcher as an instrument of data collection, and a focus on participants' views—in short, all of the characteristics mentioned in Table 3.1.

- The researcher conducts an ethical study. This involves more than simply the researcher seeking and obtaining the permission of institutional review committees or boards. It means that the researcher considers and addresses all anticipated and emergent ethical issues in the study.

- The researcher uses an approach to qualitative inquiry such as one of the five approaches (or others) addressed in this book. Use of a recognized approach to research enhances the rigor and sophistication of the research design. It also provides some means to evaluate the qualitative study. Use of an approach means that the researcher identifies and defines the approach, cites studies that employ it, and follows the procedures outlined in the approach. Certainly, the approach taken in the study may not exhaustively cover all of the elements of the approach. However, for the beginning student of qualitative research, we recommend staying within one approach, becoming comfortable with it, learning it, and keeping a study concise and straightforward. Later, especially in long and complex studies, features from several approaches may be useful.

- The researcher begins with a single focus or concept being explored. Although examples of qualitative research show a comparison of groups or of factors or themes, as in case study projects or in ethnographies, we like to begin a qualitative study focused on understanding a single concept or idea (e.g., What does it mean to be a professional? A teacher? A painter? A single mother? A homeless person?). As the study progresses, it can begin incorporating the comparison (e.g., How does the case of a professional teacher differ from that of a professional administrator?) or relating factors (e.g., What explains why painting evokes feelings?). All too often qualitative researchers advance to the comparison or the relationship analysis without first understanding their core concept or idea.

- The researcher employs rigorous data collection procedures. This means that the researcher collects multiple forms of data, creates a summary—perhaps in tabled form—of the forms of data and detail about them and spends adequate time in the field. It is not unusual for qualitative studies to include information about the specific amount of time in the field (e.g., 25 hours observing). We especially like to see unusual forms of qualitative data collection, such as using photographs to elicit responses, sounds, visual materials, or digital text messages.

- The researcher includes detailed methods describing a rigorous approach to data collection, data analysis, and report writing. Rigor is seen, for example, when extensive data collection in the field occurs or when the researcher conducts multiple levels of data analysis from the narrow codes or themes to broader interrelated themes to more abstract dimensions. Rigor means, too, that the researcher validates the accuracy of the account using one or more of the procedures for validation, such as member checking, triangulating sources of data, or using a peer or external auditor of the account.

- The researcher analyzes data using multiple levels of abstraction. We like to see the active work of the researcher as he or she moves from particulars to general levels of abstraction. Often, writers present their studies in stages (e.g., the multiple themes that can be combined into larger themes or perspectives) or layer their analysis from the particular to the general. The codes and themes derived from the data might show mundane, expected, and surprising ideas. Often the best qualitative studies present themes analyzed in terms of exploring the shadow side or unusual angles. In one class project, the student examined how students in a distance learning class reacted to the camera focused on the class. Rather than looking at the students' reaction when the camera was on them, the researcher sought to understand what happened when the camera was *off* them. This approach led to the author taking an unusual angle—one not expected by the readers.
- The researcher writes persuasively so that the reader experiences "being there." The concept of *verisimilitude*, a literary term, captures our thinking (Richardson, 1994, p. 521). The writing is clear, engaging, and full of unexpected ideas. The story and findings become believable and realistic, accurately reflecting all the complexities that exist in real life and engaging the reader.
- The researcher situates himself or herself within the study to reflect his or her history, culture, and personal experiences. This is more than simply an **autobiography**, with the writer or the researcher telling about his or her background. It focuses on how individuals' culture, gender, history, and experiences shape all aspects of the qualitative project, from their choice of a question to address, to how they collect data, to how they make an interpretation of the situation, and to what they expect to obtain from conducting the research. In some way—such as discussing their role, interweaving themselves into the text, or reflecting on the questions they have about the study—individuals position themselves in the qualitative study.

The Process of Designing a Qualitative Study

There is no agreed upon structure for how to design a qualitative study. Although books on qualitative research vary in their suggestions for design, the process is very much shaped by the particular approach adopted by the researcher. You may recall from the introduction that *research design* means the plan for conducting the study. Some authors believe that by reading a study, discussing the procedures, and pointing out issues that emerge, the aspiring qualitative researcher will have a sense of how to conduct this form of inquiry (see Weis & Fine, 2000). That may be true for some individuals. For others, understanding the broader issues may suffice to help design a study (see Richards & Morse, 2012) or to seek guidance from a how-to book (see Hatch, 2002). Rather than offering a how-to perspective, we consider our approach as more in line with creating options for qualitative researchers (hence, the five approaches), weighing the options given our experiences, and then letting readers make informed choices for themselves.

We can share, however, how we think about designing a qualitative study that is logically consistent across its research elements. It can be conveyed in three components: preliminary considerations that we think through prior to beginning a study, the steps we engage in during the conduct of the study, and the elements that flow through all phases of the process of research.

Preliminary Considerations

There are certain design principles that we work from when designing qualitative research studies. We find that qualitative research generally falls within the process of the scientific method, with common phases whether one is writing qualitatively or quantitatively. The scientific method can be described as including the problem, the hypotheses (or questions), the data collection, the results, and the discussion. All researchers seem to start with an issue or problem, examine the literature in some way related to the problem, pose questions, gather data and then analyze them, and write up their reports. Qualitative research fits within this structure, and we have accordingly organized the chapters in this book to reflect this process. We like the concept of **_methodological congruence_** advanced by Morse and Richards (2002) and revisited in Richards and Morse (2012)—that the purposes, questions, and methods of research are all interconnected and interrelated so that the study appears as a cohesive whole rather than as fragmented, isolated parts. With a similar goal for creating coherent and workable relationships among the key components of a research design, Maxwell (2013) advances an interactive approach to research design. When engaging in the process of designing a qualitative study, we believe that the inquirer must be mindful of the interconnectedness of the parts and interactiveness of the design processes.

Several aspects of a qualitative project vary from study to study, and from initial discussions, we make preliminary decisions about what will be emphasized. For example, stances on the use of the literature vary widely, as does the emphasis on using an a priori theory. The literature may be fully reviewed and used to inform the questions actually asked, it may be reviewed late in the process of research, or it may be used solely to help document the importance of the research problem. Other options may also exist, but these possibilities point to the varied uses of literature in qualitative research. Similarly, the use of theory varies in qualitative research. For example, cultural theories form the basic building blocks of a good qualitative ethnography (LeCompte & Schensul, 1999), whereas in grounded theory, the theories are developed or generated during the process of research (Strauss & Corbin, 1990). In health science research, we find the use of a priori theories common practice and a key element that must be included in rigorous qualitative investigations (Barbour, 2000). Another consideration in qualitative research is the writing or reporting format for the qualitative project. It varies considerably from scientific-oriented approaches; to literary storytelling; and on to performances, such as theater, plays, or poems. There is no one standard or accepted structure as one typically finds in quantitative research.

Finally, we also consider background and interests and what each of us brings to research. Researchers have a personal history that situates them as inquirers. They also have an orientation to research and a sense of personal ethics and political stances that inform their research. Denzin and Lincoln (2011) refer to the researchers as a "multicultural subject" (p. 12) and view the history, traditions, and conceptions of self, ethics, and politics as a starting point for inquiry.

Phases in the Research Process

With these preliminary considerations in place, we engage in an eight-phase research process summarized in Figure 3.2. We begin by acknowledging the broad assumptions that bring us to qualitative inquiry, and the interpretive lens that we will use. In addition, we bring a topic or a substantive area of investigation, and have reviewed the literature about the topic and can confidently say that a problem or issue exists that needs to be studied. This problem may be one in the real world, or it may be a

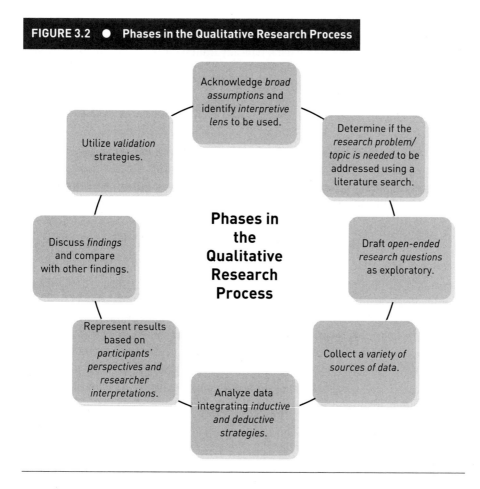

FIGURE 3.2 ● Phases in the Qualitative Research Process

deficiency or gap in the literature or past investigations on a topic, or both. Problems in qualitative research span the topics in the social and human sciences, and a hallmark of qualitative research today is the deep involvement in issues of gender, culture, and marginalized groups. The topics about which we write are emotion laden, close to people, and practical.

To study these topics, we will ask open-ended research questions, wanting to listen to the participants we are studying and shape the questions after we "explore" by talking with a few individuals. We refrain from assuming the role of the expert researcher with the "best" questions. Our questions will change and become more refined during the process of research to reflect an increased understanding of the problem. Furthermore, we will collect a variety of sources of data, including information in the form of "words" or "images." We tend to think in terms of four basic sources of qualitative information: interviews (i.e., data generated through direct interactions), observations (i.e., data generated through passive interactions), documents (i.e., data generated from existing materials), and artifacts (i.e., data generated from audio and visual methods). Certainly, new and emergent sources (e.g., social networking interactions) have challenged this traditional categorization. Unquestionably, the backbone of qualitative research is extensive collection of data, typically from multiple sources of information. Further, we collect data using these sources based on open-ended questions without much structure and by observing and collecting documents (and artifacts) without an agenda of what we hope to find. After organizing and storing data, we analyze them by carefully masking the names of respondents, and engage in the perplexing (and "lonely" if we are the sole researcher) exercise of trying to make sense of the data.

To engage in meaning-making of the data, we analyze the qualitative data working inductively from particulars to more general perspectives, whether these perspectives are called codes, categories, themes, or dimensions. We then work deductively to gather evidence to support the themes and the interpretations. One helpful way to see this process is to recognize it as working through multiple levels of abstraction, starting with the raw data and forming broader and broader categories. Recognizing the highly interrelated set of activities of data collection, analysis, and report writing, we intermingle these stages and find ourselves collecting data, analyzing another set of data, and beginning to write the qualitative report. For example, during a case study, we find ourselves engaging in the interconnectedness processes involved in interviewing, analyzing, and writing the case study—not distinct phases in the process. Also, as we write, we experiment with many forms of narrative, such as making metaphors and analogies, developing matrices and tables, and using visuals to convey simultaneously breaking down the data and reconfiguring them into new forms. Next, we might layer the analysis into increasing levels of abstractions from codes, to themes, to the interrelationship of themes, to larger conceptual models. We will (re)present these data, partly based on participants' perspectives and partly based on my own interpretation, never clearly escaping a personal stamp on a study. In the end, we discuss the findings by comparing my findings with my personal views, with extant literature, and with emerging models that seem to adequately convey the essence of the findings.

At some point we ask ourselves, "Did we (I) get the story 'right'?" (Stake, 1995), knowing that there are no right stories, only multiple stories. Perhaps qualitative studies have no endings, only questions (Wolcott, 1994). We also seek to have the account resonate with the participants, to be an accurate reflection of what they said. So we engage in validation strategies, often multiple strategies, which include confirming or triangulating data from several sources, having our studies reviewed and corrected by the participants, and employing other researchers to review my procedures.

Elements in All Phases of the Research

Throughout the slow process of collecting data and analyzing them, the narrative is being shaped—a narrative that assumes different forms from project to project. We tell a story that unfolds over time and, in some cases, present the study following the traditional approach to scientific research (i.e., problem, question, method, findings). Throughout the different forms, we find it important to talk about our background and experiences and how they have shaped our interpretation of the findings. This might be best described by letting the voices of participants speak and carry the story through dialogue, perhaps dialogue presented in Spanish with English subtitles.

Throughout all phases of the research process, we strive to be sensitive to ethical considerations. Different ethical considerations are especially important at different times during the research process—for example, as we negotiate entry to the field site of the research; involve participants in the study; gather personal, emotional data that reveal the details of life; and ask participants to give considerable time to the projects. Hatch (2002) does a good job of summarizing some of the major ethical issues that researchers need to anticipate and often address in their studies. Key among those is giving back to participants for their time and efforts in our projects—*reciprocity*, and we need to review how participants will benefit from our studies and how they will be protected from harm.

Most often our research is done within the context of a college or university setting where we need to provide evidence to institutional review boards or committees that our study design follows their guidelines for conducting ethical research. Thus, learning about and then engaging in thinking and writing about potential ethical issues specific to the study is an important component of a design process (Israel & Hay, 2006; Sieber & Tolich, 2013). Further, researchers must be prepared for addressing ethical issues as they arise during the research process. To reflect a necessary emphasis on research ethics, we devote the following section to introducing research ethics within qualitative studies.

Ethics in Qualitative Research

During the process of planning and designing a qualitative study, researchers need to consider what ethical issues might surface during the study and to plan how these issues need to be addressed. A common misconception is that these issues only surface during data collection. They arise, however, during several phases of the research process, and they are ever expanding in scope as inquirers become more sensitive to the needs of participants, sites, stakeholders, and publishers of research. One way to examine these issues is to consider the catalogue of possibilities such as provided by Weis and Fine (2000). They ask us to consider ethical considerations involving our roles as insiders/outsiders to the participants; assess issues that we may be fearful of disclosing; establish supportive, respectful relationships without stereotyping and using labels that participants do not embrace; acknowledge whose voices will be represented in our final study; and write ourselves into the study by reflecting on who we are and the people we study. In addition, as summarized by Hatch (2002), we need to be sensitive to vulnerable populations, imbalanced power relations, and placing participants at risk.

Our preferred approach in thinking about ethical issues in qualitative research is to examine them as they apply to different phases of the research process. Important recent books provide useful insight into how they array by phases, such as found in writings by Lincoln (2009), Creswell (2014), Mertens and Ginsberg (2009), Ravitch and Mittenfelner Carl (2016), and the American Psychological Association (APA; 2010). As shown in Table 3.2, ethical issues in qualitative research can be described as occurring prior to conducting the study, at the beginning of the study, during data collection, in conducting data analysis, in reporting the data, and in publishing a study. In this table, we also present some possible solutions to the ethical issues so that these can be actively written into a research design or plan. This table should not be considered exhaustive but rather as a way of starting the conversation about different types of ethical issues that need addressing in qualitative research and will be further developed throughout the chapters.

Prior to conducting a study, it is necessary to gather college or university approval from the institutional review board for the study. The approval processes of many institutional review boards are guided by policies requiring evidence of awareness of relevant ethical issues for the study and plans for addressing ethical issues related to three principles: respect for persons, concern for welfare, and justice. Respect for persons encompasses the treatment of persons and their data involved in the research process and this means that we must provide evidence of measures for respecting the privacy of participants and ensuring the consent process is clearly communicated including the right of participants to withdraw from the study. Concern for welfare involves researchers ensuring adequate protection of participants, and this means we must provide evidence that we do not place participants at risk. Justice refers to the need to treat people fairly and equitably, and this means we must carefully consider recruitment and justifications for sampling strategies as well as site selection and criteria guiding site choice. Completion of the review by institutional review boards or committees is required prior to accessing the study site and participants and, in some cases, for access to funding. Equally important is to examine standards for ethical conduct of research available from professional organizations, such as the American Historical Association, the American Sociological Association, the International Communication Association,

TABLE 3.2 ● Ethical Issues in Qualitative Research

Timing During Research Process	Type of Ethical Issue	How to Address the Issue
Prior to conducting the study	<ul><li>Seek college or university approval.</li><li>Examine professional association standards.</li><li>Gain local access permissions.</li><li>Select a site without a vested interest in the outcome of the study.</li><li>Negotiate authorship for publication.</li><li>Seek permission for use of unpublished instruments or procedures that other researchers might consider to be theirs.</li></ul>	<ul><li>Submit for institutional review board approval.</li><li>Consult types of professional ethical standards.</li><li>Identify and go through local approvals for the site and participants; find a gatekeeper to help.</li><li>Select a site that will not raise power issues with researchers.</li><li>Give credit for work done on the project; decide on author order.</li><li>Obtain permission for use of any material that may be considered proprietary and give credit.</li></ul>
Beginning to conduct the study	<ul><li>Disclose the purpose of the study.</li><li>Refrain from pressure for participants into signing consent forms.</li><li>Respect norms and charters of indigenous societies.</li><li>Have sensitivity to the needs of vulnerable populations (e.g., children).</li></ul>	<ul><li>Contact participants, and inform them of the general purpose of the study.</li><li>Assure participants that their participation is voluntary.</li><li>Find out about cultural, religious, gender, and other differences that need to be respected.</li><li>Obtain appropriate consent (e.g., parents as well as children).</li></ul>
Collecting data	<ul><li>Respect the study site and minimize disruptions.</li><li>Avoid deceiving participants.</li><li>Respect potential power imbalances and exploitation of participants.</li><li>Do not "use" participants by gathering data and leaving the site without giving back.</li><li>Store data and materials (e.g., raw data and protocols) using appropriate security measures.</li></ul>	<ul><li>Build trust and convey the extent of anticipated disruption in gaining access.</li><li>Discuss the purpose and use of the study data.</li><li>Avoid leading questions, withhold sharing personal impressions, and avoid disclosing sensitive information.</li><li>Provide rewards for participating, and attend to opportunities for reciprocity.</li><li>Store data and materials in secure locations for 5 years (APA, 2010).</li></ul>
Analyzing data	<ul><li>Avoid siding with participants and disclosing only positive results.</li><li>Respect the privacy of participants.</li></ul>	<ul><li>Report multiple perspectives, and also report contrary findings.</li><li>Assign fictitious names or aliases; develop composite profiles.</li></ul>

(Continued)

TABLE 3.2 ● (Continued)

Timing During Research Process	Type of Ethical Issue	How to Address the Issue
Reporting data	• Avoid falsifying authorship, evidence, data, findings, and conclusions. • Avoid disclosing information that would harm participants. • Communicate in clear, straightforward, appropriate language. • Do not plagiarize.	• Report honestly. • Use composite stories so that individuals cannot be identified. • Use language appropriate for audiences of the research. • See APA (2010) guidelines for permissions needed to reprint or adapt the work of others.
Publishing study	• Share reports with others. • Tailor the reporting to diverse audience(s). • Do not duplicate or piecemeal publications. • Complete proof of compliance with ethical issues and lack of conflict of interest.	• Provide copies of the report to participants and stakeholders. • Share practical results, consider website distribution, and consider publishing in different languages. • Refrain from using the same material for more than one publication. • Disclose funders for research and who will profit from the research.

Sources: Adapted from APA (2010); Creswell (2013, 2016); Lincoln (2009); Mertens and Ginsberg (2009).

the American Evaluation Association, the Canadian Evaluation Society, the Australasian Evaluation Society, and the American Educational Research Association (Lincoln, 2009). Local permissions to gather data from individuals and sites also need to be obtained at an early stage in the research, and interested parties and gatekeepers can assist in their endeavor. Sites should not be chosen that have a vested interest in the outcomes of the study. Also, at this early stage, authorship should be negotiated among researchers involved in the qualitative study, if more than one individual undertakes the research. The APA (2010) has useful guidelines for negotiating authorship and how it might be accomplished.

Beginning the study involves initial contact with the site and with individuals. It is important to disclose the purpose of the study to the participants. This is often stated on an informed consent form completed for college or university institutional review board purposes. This form should indicate that participating in the study is voluntary and that it would not place the participants at undue risk. Special provisions are needed (e.g., child and parent consent forms) for sensitive populations. Further, at this stage, the researcher needs to anticipate any cultural, religious, gender, or other differences in the participants and the sites that need to be respected. Qualitative writings have made us aware of this respect, especially for indigenous populations

(LaFrance & Crazy Bull, 2009). For example, as American Indian tribes take over the delivery of services to their members, they have reclaimed their right to determine what research will be done and how it will be reported in a sensitive way to tribal cultures and charters.

We have also become more sensitive to potential issues that may arise in collecting data, especially through interviews and observations. Researchers need to seek permission to conduct research on-site and convey to gatekeepers or individuals in authority how their research will provide the least disruption to the activities at the site. The participants should not be deceived about the nature of the research and, in the process of providing data (e.g., through interviews, documents, and so forth), should be appraised on the general nature of the inquiry. We are more sensitive today about the nature of the interview process and how it creates a power imbalance through a hierarchical relationship often established between the researcher and the participant. This potential power imbalance needs to be respected, and building trust and avoiding leading questions help to remove some of this imbalance. Also, the simple act of collecting data may contribute to "using" the participants and the site for the personal gain of the researcher, and strategies such as reward might be used to create reciprocity with participants and sites.

In analyzing the data, certain ethical issues also surface. Because qualitative inquirers often spend considerable time at research sites, they may lose track of the need to present multiple perspectives and a complex picture of the central phenomenon. They may actually side with the participants on issues, and only disclose positive results that create a Pollyanna portrait of the issues. This "going native" may occur during the data collection process, and reporting multiple perspectives needs to be kept in mind for the final report. Also, the research results may unwittingly present a harmful picture of the participants or the site, and qualitative researchers need to be mindful of protecting the participants' privacy through masking names and developing composite profiles or cases.

In recent APA (2010) standards on ethics, discussions report on authorship and the proper disclosure of information. For example, honesty—and how authors should not falsify authorship, the evidence provided in a report, the actual data, the findings, and the conclusions of a study—is stressed. Reports should also not disclose information that will potentially harm participants in the present or in the future. The form of report writing should communicate in clear, appropriate language for the intended audiences of the report. Finally, plagiarism should be avoided by knowing about the types of permissions needed to cite the works by others in a study.

Another area of emerging interest in the APA (2010) standards on ethics resides in the publication of a study. It is important to share information from a research study with participants and stakeholders. This may include sharing practical information, posting information on websites, and publishing in languages that can be understood by a wide audience. There is also concern today about multiple publications from the same research sources and the piecemeal division of studies into parts and their separate publication. Finally, publishers often ask authors to sign letters of compliance with ethical practices, disclose sources of funding, and to state that they do not have a conflict of interest in the results and publications of the studies.

The Design Structures of a Plan or Proposal

Researchers are tasked with the responsibility of clearly outlining their research in a plan or a proposal. The audiences for these plans and proposals are varied from supervisory committee members to funding review panels. A review of final written products for qualitative research points to great diversity. No set format exists yet there exists some design elements for *engaging* your reader, and several writers suggest general topics to be included in a written plan or *proposal* for a qualitative study. In the following section, we describe six design elements that might make the study plan or proposal attractive to a reader.

Design Considerations Useful for Engaging Readers

In many cases, it is advantageous for research to be distinctive. In our experience, benefits from such types of research have ranged from securing funding to publishing opportunities. The following list provides some ideas for study elements to consider when thinking about your study design and these are further expanded in Creswell (2016).

- *Study a unique sample.* Is there a sample or population that has not yet been studied? By studying an unusual group of people, researchers may gain new insights into well-established research areas.
- *Assume an unconventional perspective.* Are there angles or perspectives that may not be expected in your area of study? It might well be the reverse side (the shadow side) of what *is* expected.
- *Observe an uncommon field site.* Is an unusual group of people or an unusual location that could be accessed? It may be that access is now available in cases where it was not previously.
- *Collect atypical forms of data.* Are the data sources that are appropriate yet not typically expected in social science research (e.g., collect sounds, have participants take pictures)? As new media emerges (see Halfpenny & Procter, 2015), researchers have opportunities for contributing new methods.
- *Present findings in an unusual way.* Are there ways of presenting my findings that are influenced by the data I collect? There diverse options exist such as through the creation of analogies (see Wolcott, 2010) or maps or other types of figures and tables.
- *Focus on a timely topic.* Is there a topic warranting research that is drawing a lot of attention? When many individuals are discussing topics, often these topics are also being covered by the news media. In some cases, funding priorities may also shift toward those topics.

General Writing Structures

Comparing across the differing formats of writing qualitative studies (e.g., Creswell, 2014; Marshall & Rossman, 2015; Ravitch & Mittenfelner Carl, 2016), we see common structures for guiding the writing process of a proposal. Next, we describe each of the six parts and highlight the topics where there might be variation due to the inherent nature of different perspectives adopted in qualitative studies. For each section, we provide examples that list the arguments to be advanced in a qualitative proposal (adapted from Creswell, 2014; Maxwell, 2013). These structures and resources, in addition to the *Essentials of a Qualitative Doctorate* (Holloway & Brown, 2012), are especially helpful for the student who has never written a thesis or dissertation project. Greater details for composing each of the six parts of the proposal are addressed in subsequent chapters in this book.

1. Introduce the problem to be studied. The introduction generally includes three sections: statement of the problem, purpose of the study, and research questions. The sections within the study introduction may vary across studies adopting different perspectives; for example, whereas a separate section reviewing literature may be optional in a study adopting a constructivist/interpretivist perspective, the identification of a specific transformative issues being explored is expected in studies adopting a transformative perspective. Researchers may find the following questions useful for guiding their introductory arguments: What do readers need to better understand your topic? What do readers need to know about your topic? What do you propose to study?

2. Describe the procedures guiding the study. The description of the study procedures generally includes eight sections: philosophical assumptions or worldview, qualitative research approach used, role of the researcher, data collection procedures, data analysis procedures, strategies for validating findings, proposed narrative structure of the study, and anticipated ethical issues. Variation in how the procedures are described may occur across studies adopting different perspectives; for example, a collaborative form in data collection is emphasized in studies adopting a transformative perspective and trustworthiness is emphasized in place of what we have been calling validation. Researchers may find the following questions useful for guiding their procedural arguments: What is the setting, and who are the people you will study? What methods do you plan to use to collect data? How will you analyze the data? How will you validate your findings? What ethical issues will your study present?

3. Report the preliminary study findings (if available). The reporting of the preliminary study findings may be available if a pilot study was completed or may be omitted completely. Researchers may find the following question useful for guiding their findings arguments: What do preliminary results (if available) indicate about the practicability and value of the proposed study?

4. Outline the anticipated study implications. This section generally involves specifying the significance of the study. The descriptions of anticipated outcomes are expected to vary across studies adopting different perspectives; for example, whereas a study adopting a constructivist or interpretivist perspective may describe expected impacts, a study adopting a transformative perspective mentions or advocates for the anticipated changes that the research study will likely bring. Researchers may find the following question useful for guiding their implications arguments: What significance does the study intend to have?

5. List the references cited in the study. This section involves listing the references cited in the proposal. It is important that only references that have been cited within the text are included in this list and not those references that were simply consulted during the writing process.

6. Include essential documents as appendices. The focus and quantity of the appendices will differ by study and audience for the proposal. Most common is the inclusion of entry letters, methods protocols (e.g., interview questions, observation forms), and proposed timelines. Less common is the inclusion of informational documents such as a proposed budget and a summary of the proposed content of each chapter in the final study.

These six arguments represent the most important points to include in a qualitative proposal and, in our experience if adequately addressed and used as an organizing structure, create a well-written proposal. It is important to note that these structures speak only to designing a plan or proposal for a qualitative study. In addition to the topics of these proposal formats, the complete study will include additional data findings, interpretations, and a discussion of the overall results, limitations of the study, and future research needs.

Chapter Check-In

1. Do you see how authors incorporate the characteristics of qualitative research into their published studies? Select one of the qualitative articles presented in Appendices B through F. Begin with identifying each of the characteristics advanced in this chapter (summarized in Table 3.1) as they have been applied in the journal article. Note which characteristics are easy and which are more difficult to identify.

2. What structures describe the flow of activities from a published qualitative study? Select one of the articles in Appendices B through F. Begin with listing the activities described in the article. Then indicate the "larger ideas" using boxes or circles and the sequence of ideas using arrows. For example, one study may start with a discussion about the problem and then move on to a theoretical model

and then on to the purpose, and so forth.

3. What ethical issues do you recognize, and what options are available for addressing? Choose one of the ethical issues that arise during the process of qualitative research from Table 3.2. Consider a situation that would give rise to this ethical issue within a research study you would like to conduct and then describe as many

options as possible about how you might address it in the design of your study.

4. What design considerations can you use to begin designing your qualitative study plan or proposal? Consider which (one or more) of the design considerations for engaging readers fit your project and discuss how they relate to your study and then develop a general outline for how you might organize and present the topics in your own study.

Summary

In this chapter, we provided an overview of and introduction to qualitative research. We began with our definition of qualitative research as an approach to inquiry that begins with assumptions, an interpretive or theoretical lens, and the study of research problems exploring the meaning individuals or groups ascribe to a social or human problem. Nine common characteristics for qualitative research were described, including collecting data in natural settings with a sensitivity to the people under study, using inductive and deductive analysis strategies to establish patterns or themes, and developing a complex description and interpretation of the problem that provides for the voices of participants and a reflexivity of the researchers. Recent introductory textbooks underscore the characteristics embedded in this definition. Given this definition, a qualitative approach is appropriate for exploring a research problem; when a complex, detailed understanding is needed; when the researcher wants to write in a literary, flexible style; and when the researcher seeks to understand the context or settings of participants. Qualitative research takes time and expertise as it involves ambitious data collection and analysis and results in extensive reports. Although qualitative research does not have firm guidelines, consensus exists as to the criteria for a good study: rigorous data collection and analysis; the use of a qualitative approach (e.g., narrative, phenomenology, grounded theory, ethnography, case study); a single focus; a persuasive account; a reflection on the researcher's own history, culture, personal experiences, and politics; and ethical practices.

The process of designing a qualitative study emerges during inquiry, but it generally follows the pattern of scientific research. It starts with broad assumptions central to qualitative inquiry, and an interpretive or theoretical lens and a topic of inquiry. After stating a research problem or issue about this topic, the inquirer asks several open-ended research questions, gathers multiple forms of data to answer these questions, and makes sense of the data by grouping information into codes, themes or categories, and larger dimensions. The final narrative the researcher composes will have diverse formats—from a scientific type of study to narrative stories.

(Continued)

(Continued)

Ethical issues need to be anticipated and planned for in designing a qualitative study. These issues arise in many phases of the research process. They develop prior to conducting the study when researchers seek approval for the inquiry. They arise at the beginning of the study when the researchers first contact the participants; gain consent to participate in the study; and acknowledge the customs, culture, and charters of the research site. The ethical issues especially arise during data collection with respect for the site and the participants and gathering data in ways that will not create power imbalances and "use" the participants. They also come during the data analysis phase when researchers do not side with participants, shape findings in a particular direction, and respect the privacy of individuals as their information is reported. In the reporting phase of research, inquirers need to be honest, not plagiarize the work of others; refrain from presenting information that potentially harms participants; and communicate in a useful, clear way to stakeholders. In publishing research studies, inquirers need to openly share data with others, avoid duplicating their studies, and comply with procedures asked by publishers.

Finally, the structure of a plan or proposal for a qualitative study will vary, and considering ways to engage readers is useful. We describe each of the six common parts, highlight the topics where there might be variation due to the inherent nature of different perspectives adopted in qualitative studies, and focus on the essential arguments that researchers need to address in proposals.

Further Readings

The following resources are offered as foundational references for designing a qualitative study. The list should not be considered exhaustive and readers are encouraged to seek out additional readings in the end-of-book reference list.

American Psychological Association. (2010). *Publication manual of the American Psychological Association* (6th ed.). Washington, DC: Author.

A must-have resource for guiding effective communication with words and data, each new edition reflects the latest guidelines—for example, referencing electronic and online sources in the 6th edition.

Creswell, J. W. (2014). *Research design: Qualitative, quantitative, and mixed methods approaches* (4th ed.). Thousand Oaks, CA: Sage.

John W. Creswell presents an excellent resource across three approaches to research. Using the research process as the organizing structure allows the reader to see how each approach are operationalized in a study.

Hatch, J. A. (2002). *Doing qualitative research in education settings*. Albany: State University of New York Press.

J. Amos Hatch adopts a step-by-step approach to study development emphasizing learning the craft of doing qualitative research. He uses data from real studies to elucidate analyses processes, which is useful for any researcher.

Holloway, I., & Brown, L. (2012). *Essentials of a qualitative doctorate*. Walnut Creek, CA: Left Coast Press.

Immy Holloway and Lorraine Brown provide a useful guide for navigating the proposal, writing, and defending doctoral research. In particular, we found the chapters on proposal writing and importance of ethical issues helpful.

Maxwell, J. (2013). *Qualitative research design: An interactive approach* (3rd ed.). Thousand Oaks, CA: Sage.

Joe Maxwell describes a stepwise approach to planning qualitative research emphasizing how the research design components interact with one another. A noteworthy aspect of this book is the embedded comments within two examples of qualitative dissertation proposals.

Mertens, D. M., & Ginsberg, P. E. (2009). *The handbook of social research ethics*. Thousand Oaks, CA: Sage.

Handbooks provide a foundation, and editors Donna Mertens and Pauline Ginsberg deliver a useful starting point for research ethics. Of particular note is Chapter 10 by Yvonna Lincoln, which is related to ethical practices in qualitative research.

Sieber, J. E., & Tolich, M. B. (2013). *Planning ethically responsible research* (2nd ed.). Thousand Oaks, CA: Sage.

Joan Sieber and Martin Tolich provide a user-friendly introduction to research ethics. A unique aspect of this book is the revisit of ethically controversial studies of the past, which provides a fresh perspective to the conversation about what would be required for current institutional review boards.

Five Qualitative Approaches to Inquiry

We want to present a couple of scenarios. In the first, the qualitative researcher does not identify any specific approach to qualitative research he or she is using. Perhaps the methods discussion is short and simply limited to the collection of face-to-face interviews. The findings of the study are presented as a thematic workup of major categories of information collected during the interviews. Contrast this with a second scenario. The researcher adopts a specific approach to qualitative research, such as a ***narrative research*** approach. Now the methods section is detailed describing the meaning of such an approach, why it was used, and how it informed the procedures of the study. The findings in this study convey the specific story of an individual, and it is told chronologically, highlighting some of the tensions in the story. Details about the specific organization in which the individual's story takes place provide important contextual information. Which approach would you find to be the most scholarly? The most inviting? The most sophisticated? We think that you would opt for the second approach.

We need to identify our approach to qualitative inquiry in order to present it as a sophisticated study; to offer it as a specific type so that reviewers can properly assess it; and, for the beginning researcher, who can profit from having a writing ***structure*** to follow, to offer some way of organizing ideas that can be grounded in the scholarly literature of qualitative research. Of course, this beginning researcher could choose several qualitative approaches, such as narrative research *and* phenomenological research, but we would leave this more advanced methodological approach to more experienced researchers. We often say that the beginning researcher needs to first understand one approach thoroughly and then venture out and try another approach before combining different ways of conducting qualitative research.

This chapter will help you begin the mastery of one of the qualitative approaches to inquiry as well as to distinguish among the five approaches. We take each approach, one by one, and provide a definition, discuss its origin, identify the key defining features of it, explore the various types of ways to use it, and provide procedures involved in conducting a study within the approach. Then we consider challenges that you will likely incur as you proceed and outline the emerging directions associated with the approach. Finally, a comparison of the five approaches across foundational considerations, data procedures, and research reporting is followed.

Questions for Discussion

- What is the focus and definition for each approach (narrative research, phenomenological research, ground theory research, ethnographic research, and case study research)?
- What are the origin and background influences for each approach?
- What are the defining features of each approach?
- What various forms can a study take within each approach?
- What are the procedures for using the approach?
- What challenges and emerging directions are associated with each approach?
- What are some similarities and differences among the five approaches?

Deciding Among the Five Approaches

After the need for identifying an approach is established, the next pressing concern is deciding *which* among the five approaches is best suited for addressing your **research focus** (see Figure 4.1). Examining the **research problem** for each of the five approaches is essential for guiding the choice of which approach to further explore. A research focus represents a more general area of study interest such as a study objective or goal and is disguisable from a more specific research problem, referring to the issue or concern that leads to a need to conduct the study. Of course, gaining foundational knowledge about each approach is recommended, and the sections about each of the approaches can be read in any order. A researcher seeking to study a **single individual** may decide that learning about the approaches where the unit of analysis can be focused on the individual is advantageous and so may begin with the separate descriptions of narrative research, ***ethnography***, and ***case study research*** and then use the final chapter section to help differentiate among them. Similarly, a researcher seeking to study groups of participants may explore the chapter sections differently. In sum, read the chapter in the order in which best fits your qualitative research learning needs.

Narrative Research

Definition of Narrative Research

Narrative research has many forms, uses a variety of analytic practices, and is rooted in different social and humanities disciplines (Daiute & Lightfoot, 2004). "Narrative" might be the ***phenomenon*** being studied, such as a narrative of illness, or it might be the method used in a study, such as the procedures of analyzing stories told (Chase, 2005; Clandinin & Connolly, 2000; Pinnegar & Daynes, 2007). As a method, it begins with the experiences as expressed in lived and told stories of individuals. Clandinin (2013) makes the case for the need for attending to the context in which the narrative is embedded, advising, "the focus of narrative inquiry is not only valorizing individuals'

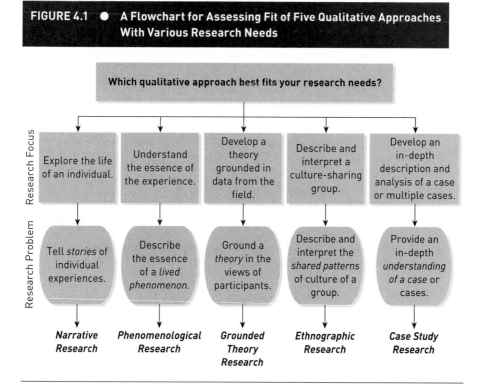

FIGURE 4.1 ● A Flowchart for Assessing Fit of Five Qualitative Approaches With Various Research Needs

Which qualitative approach best fits your research needs?

Research Focus

| Explore the life of an individual. | Understand the essence of the experience. | Develop a theory grounded in data from the field. | Describe and interpret a culture-sharing group. | Develop an in-depth description and analysis of a case or multiple cases. |

Research Problem

| Tell *stories* of individual experiences. | Describe the essence of a *lived phenomenon*. | Ground a *theory* in the views of participants. | Describe and interpret the *shared patterns* of culture of a group. | Provide an in-depth *understanding of a case* or cases. |

| *Narrative Research* | *Phenomenological Research* | *Grounded Theory Research* | *Ethnographic Research* | *Case Study Research* |

experience but is also an exploration of the social, cultural, familial, linguistic, and institutional narratives within which individuals experiences were, and are, constituted, shaped, expressed and enacted" (p. 18). Writers have provided ways for analyzing and understanding the stories lived and told. Czarniawska (2004) defines it here as a specific type of qualitative design in which "narrative is understood as a spoken or written text giving an account of an event/action or series of events/actions, chronologically connected" (p. 17). The procedures for implementing this research consist of focusing on studying one or two individuals, gathering data through the collection of their stories, reporting individual experiences, and chronologically ordering the meaning of those experiences (or using *life course stages*). In the discussion of narrative research, we rely on an accessible book called *Engaging in Narrative Inquiry* (Clandinin, 2013) that revisits "what is it that narrative researchers do" (p. 18). We also bring into the data collection procedures and varied analytic strategies of Riessman (2008) and the seminal work written for social scientists called *Narrative Inquiry* (Clandinin & Connelly, 2000).

Origin of Narrative Research

Narrative research originated from literature, history, anthropology, sociology, sociolinguistics, and education, yet different fields of study have adopted their own approaches (Chase, 2005). We find a postmodern, organizational orientation in Czarniawska (2004); a human developmental perspective in Daiute and Lightfoot (2004); a psychological approach in Lieblich, Tuval-Mashiach, and Zilber (1998); sociological approaches in Cortazzi (1993) and Riessman (1993, 2008); and quantitative (e.g., statistical stories in event history modeling) and qualitative approaches in Elliott (2005). Interdisciplinary efforts at narrative research have also been encouraged by the *Narrative Study of Lives* annual series that began in 1993 (see, e.g., Josselson & Lieblich, 1993), the *Handbook of Narrative Inquiry* (Clandinin, 2007), and the journal *Narrative Inquiry*. Narrative inquiry is distinctive with its own definitions and a well-established view as both a methodology and phenomena (Clandinin, 2007). With many recent books on narrative research, it continues to be a popular "field in the making" (Chase, 2005, p. 651).

Defining Features of Narrative Studies

Reading through a number of narrative articles published in journals and reviewing major books on narrative inquiry, a specific set of features emerged that define its boundaries. Not all narrative projects contain these elements, but many do, and the list is not exhaustive of possibilities.

- Narrative researchers collect *stories* from individuals (and documents, and group conversations) about individuals' lived and told experiences. These stories may emerge from a story told to the researcher, a story that is co-constructed between the researcher and the participant, and a story intended as a performance to convey some message or point (Riessman, 2008). Thus, there may be a strong collaborative feature of narrative research as the story emerges through the interaction or dialogue of the researcher and the participant(s).

- Narrative stories tell of individual experiences, and they may shed light on the identities of individuals and how they see themselves.

- Narrative stories occur within specific places or situations. Temporality becomes important for the researcher's telling of the story within a place. Such contextual details may include descriptions of the physical, emotional, and social situations.

- Narrative stories are gathered through many different forms of data, such as through interviews that may be the primary form of data collection but also through observations, documents, pictures, and other sources of qualitative data.

- Narrative stories are analyzed using varied ***strategies***. An analysis can be made about what was said (thematically), the nature of the telling of the story (structural), who the story is directed toward (dialogic/performance), or using visual analysis of images or interpreting images alongside words (Riessman, 2008). Other options for analysis involve foci on values, plot, significance, or character mapping and time (Daiute, 2014).

- Narrative stories often are heard and shaped by the researchers into a *chronology,* although they may not be told that way by the participant(s). There is a temporal change that is conveyed when individuals talk about their experiences and their lives. They may talk about their past, their present, or their future (Clandinin & Connelly, 2000).

- Narrative stories often contain turning points (Denzin, 1989) or specific tensions or transitions or interruptions that are highlighted by the researchers in the telling of the stories. Such incidents can serve as organizing structures for recounting the story including the lead-up and ***consequences***. Daiute (2014) identifies four types of patterns (across narratives of one individual or two or more) for meaning-making related to similarities, differences, change, or coherence.

Types of Narratives

Narrative studies can be differentiated along two different lines. One line is to consider the data analysis strategy used by the narrative researcher, whereas the other is to consider the types of narratives. We see the choice between the two types of approaches, although up to the individual researcher, might be influenced (among other factors) by the nature of the experiences, the story-generating process, and the audience for the narrative. For example, if the experiences span much of a life, then it might make sense for the researcher to consider guiding the collection as part of a ***life history*** whereas the same story could also be analyzed using a thematic approach. The best guidance is finding a fit for the particular story function; Riessman (2008) outlines the variety of functions a narrative can serve from telling stories for individual and/or group identity formation to claiming a point aimed at mobilizing marginalized groups and initiate political action.

With a focus on the data analysis strategy, Polkinghorne (1995) discusses narrative in which the researcher extracts themes that hold across stories or taxonomies of types of stories, and a more storytelling mode in which the narrative researcher shapes the stories based on a plotline, or a literary approach to analysis. Polkinghorne (1995) goes on to emphasize the second form in his writings. More recently, Chase (2005) suggests analytic strategies based on parsing constraints on narratives—narratives that are composed interactively between researchers and participants and the interpretations developed by various narrators. Combining both of these approaches, we see an insightful analysis of strategies for analyzing narratives in Riessman (2008). She conveys three types of approaches used to analyze narrative stories: a thematic analysis in which the researcher identifies the themes "told" by a participant; a structural analysis in which the meaning shifts to the "telling" and the story can be cast during a conversation in comic terms, tragedy, satire, romance, or other forms; and a dialogic or performance analysis in which the focus turns to how the story is produced (i.e., interactively between the researcher and the participant) and performed (i.e., meant to convey some message or point).

Narrative researchers can select from various types of narratives for guiding the collection of stories. (see, e.g., Casey, 1995/1996). Here is a brief description of some popular approaches and an example for further reading.

- A ***biographical study*** is a form of narrative study in which the researcher writes and records the experiences of another person's life. An example of a biographical study is Ruohotie-Lyhty's (2013) exploration of professional identity of two newly qualified language teachers in Finland. Through contrasting experiences (a painful and an easy beginning), the stories offer insights into the role of reflection on life experiences as a useful means of supporting identity development.

- ***Autoethnography*** is written and recorded by the individuals who are the subject of the study (Ellis, 2004; Muncey, 2010). Muncey (2010) defines *autoethnography* as the idea of multiple layers of consciousness, the vulnerable self, the coherent self, critiquing the self in social contexts, the subversion of dominant discourses, and the evocative potential. They contain the personal story of the author as well as the larger cultural meaning for the individual's story. An example of autoethnography is Ellis' (1993) personal exploration of the family drama enacted in the aftermath of the author's brother's death in an airplane crash. Her story about childhood interactions with her brother, the crash, and the context for which he was traveling—to visit the author—their adulthood relationship, and the experience of going to the family home for the funeral followed by her return to her home as well as other issues shed light on her personal and professional life.

- A life history portrays an individual's entire life, while a personal experience story is a narrative study of an individual's personal experience found in single or multiple episodes, private situations, or communal folklore (Denzin, 1989). An exploration of the life history of a Danish academic's position and perspectives illustrates the complexity of internationalization (Fabricius, 2014).

- An ***oral history*** consists of gathering personal reflections of events and their causes and effects from one individual or several individuals (Plummer, 1983). Narrative studies may have a specific contextual focus, such as stories told by teachers or children in classrooms (Ollerenshaw & Creswell, 2002) or the stories told about organizations (Czarniawska, 2004). Oral history may draw upon diverse research methods and be guided by interpretive framework such as social justice (Janesick, 2013). The framework may advocate for Latin Americans through using *testimonios* (Beverly, 2005), or report stories of women using feminist interpretations (see, e.g., Personal Narratives Group, 1989), a lens that shows how women's voices are muted, multiple, and contradictory (Chase, 2005). It may be told to disrupt the dominant discourse around teenage pregnancy (Muncey, 2010) or to highlight the isolation and limited access to maternal care in a rural community (Orkin & Newberry, 2014).

Procedures for Conducting Narrative Research

Using the approach taken by Clandinin and Connelly (2000) as a general procedural guide, the methods of conducting a narrative study do not follow a lockstep approach but instead represent an informal collection of topics. Clandinin (2013) recently reiterated her stance by saying, "I highlight narrative inquiry as a fluid inquiry, not as set of procedures or linear steps to be followed" (p. 33). Riessman (2008) adds useful information about the data collection process and the strategies for analyzing data. See also Daiute (2014) for a set of practical techniques for conducting narrative research. See Figure 4.2.

- *Determine if the research problem or question best fits narrative research.* Narrative research is best for capturing the detailed stories or life experiences of a single individual or the lives of a small number of individuals.

- *Select one or more individuals who have stories or life experiences to tell, and spend considerable time with them gathering their stories through multiples types of information.* Clandinin and Connelly (2000) refer to the stories as "field texts." Research participants may record their stories in a journal or diary, or the researcher might observe the individuals and record field notes. Researchers may also collect letters sent by the individuals; assemble stories about the individuals from family members; gather documents such as memos or official correspondence about the individuals; or obtain photographs, memory boxes (collection of items that trigger memories), and other personal–family–social ***artifacts***.

- *Consider how the collection of the data and their recording can take different shapes.* Riessman (2008) illustrates different ways that researchers can transcribe interviews to develop different types of stories. The transcription can highlight the researcher as a listener or a questioner, emphasize the interaction between the researcher and the participant, convey a conversation that moves through time or include shifting meanings that may emerge through translated material.

- *Embed information about the context of these stories into data collection, analysis, and writing.* Narrative researchers situate individual stories within participants' personal experiences (their jobs, their homes), their **culture** (racial or ethnic), and their **historical contexts** (time and place). Being context-sensitive is considered essential to narrative inquiry (Czarniawska, 2004).

- *Analyze the participants' stories using the process of reorganizing the stories into some general type of framework called **restorying**.* The researcher may take an active role and "restory" the stories into a framework that makes sense. This framework may consist of gathering stories, analyzing them for key elements of the story (e.g., time, place, plot, and scene) and then rewriting the stories to place them within a chronological sequence (Ollerenshaw & Creswell, 2002). Cortazzi (1993) suggests that the chronology of narrative research, with an emphasis on sequence, sets narrative apart from other genres of research. One aspect of the chronology is that the stories have a beginning, a middle, and an end. Similar to basic elements found in good novels, these aspects involve a predicament, conflict, or struggle; a protagonist, or main character; and a sequence with implied causality (i.e., a plot) during which the predicament is resolved in some fashion (Carter, 1993). Further, the story might include other elements typically found in novels, such as time, place, and scene (Connelly & Clandinin, 1990). The plot, or story line, may also include Clandinin and Connelly's (2000) three-dimensional narrative inquiry space: the personal and social (the interaction); the past, present, and future (continuity); and the place (situation). This story line may include information about the setting or context of the participants' experiences. Beyond the chronology, researchers might detail themes that arise from the story to provide a more detailed discussion of the meaning of the story (Huber & Whelan, 1999). Thus, the qualitative data analysis may be a description of both the story and themes that emerge from it. A postmodern narrative writer, such as Czarniawska (2004), adds another element to the analysis: a deconstruction of the stories, an unmaking of them by such analytic strategies as exposing dichotomies, examining silences, and attending to disruptions and contradictions. Finally, the analysis process consists of the researcher looking for themes or categories; the researcher using a microlinguistic approach and probing for the meaning of words, phrases, and larger units of discourse such as is often done in conversational analysis (see Gee, 1991); or the researcher examining the stories for how they are produced interactively between the researcher and the participant or performed by the participant to convey a specific agenda or message (Riessman, 2008).

- *Embed a collaborative approach in the collection and telling of stories.* Clandinin & Connelly (2000) describe active involvement of participants as central to their work that is, "Narrative inquiry is a way of understanding experience; it is collaboration between research and participants, over time, in a place or series of places, and in social interactions with milieus" (p. 17). As researchers collect stories, they negotiate relationships, smooth transitions, and provide ways to be useful to the participants. In narrative research, a key theme has been the turn toward the relationship between the researcher and the researched in which both parties will learn and change in the encounter (Pinnegar & Daynes, 2007). In this process, the parties negotiate the meaning of the stories, adding a validation check to the analysis (Creswell & Miller, 2000). Within the participant's story may also be an interwoven story of the researcher gaining insight into her or his own life (see Huber & Whelan, 1999). Also, within the story may be *epiphanies*, turning points, or disruptions in which the story line changes direction dramatically. In the end, the narrative study tells the story of individuals unfolding in a chronology of their experiences, set within their personal, social, and historical context, and including the important themes in those *lived experiences*. "Narrative inquiry is stories lived and told," said Clandinin and Connolly (2000, p. 20).

- *Present the narrative in written form.* Adapt the following general reporting structure as appropriate: an introduction to familiarize the reader with the participant(s) and the intended purpose for the story; research procedures to provide a rationale for use of a narrative and details about data collection and analysis; telling of the story to theorize about participant lives, with narrative segments; and patterns of meaning articulated around events, processes, epiphanies, or themes; and a final interpretation of the meaning of the story. It is not uncommon for researchers to find this process challenging "because it is at this point that we make our texts visible to public audiences, unknown audiences who may be far removed from the lived and told experiences of participants" (Clandinin, 2013, p. 50).

Challenges in Narrative Research

Given these procedures and the characteristics of narrative research, narrative research is a challenging approach to use. The researcher needs to collect extensive information about the participant and needs to have a clear understanding of the context of the individual's life. It takes a keen eye to identify in the source material that gathers the particular stories to capture the individual's experiences. As Edel (1984) comments, it is important to uncover the "figure under the carpet" that explains the multilayered context of a life. Active collaboration with the participant is necessary, and researchers need to discuss the participant's stories as well as be reflective about their own personal and political background, which shapes how they "restory" the account. The issue of power relations is of principal concern in narrative inquiry (Clandinin & Connelly, 2000). Multiple issues arise in the collecting, analyzing, and telling of individual stories and building awareness of this responsibility is crucial (Czarniawska, 2004). Pinnegar and Daynes (2007) raise these important questions: Who owns the story? Who can tell it? Who can change it? Whose version is convincing? What happens when narratives compete? As a community, what do stories do among us?

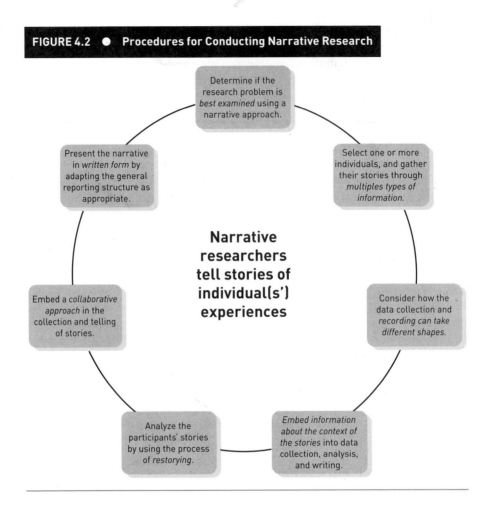

FIGURE 4.2 ● Procedures for Conducting Narrative Research

Narrative researchers tell stories of individual(s') experiences

- Determine if the research problem is *best examined* using a narrative approach.
- Select one or more individuals, and gather their stories through *multiples types of information.*
- Consider how the data collection and *recording can take different shapes.*
- Embed information *about the context of the stories* into data collection, analysis, and writing.
- Analyze the participants' stories by using the process of *restorying.*
- Embed a *collaborative approach* in the collection and telling of stories.
- Present the narrative in *written form* by adapting the general reporting structure as appropriate.

Reflecting the embedded nature of these stories within the larger social, cultural, familial, linguistic, and institutional dimensions allows a more complex understanding to be attended to (Clandinin, 2013), yet is difficult to realize. An emerging area of promise for attaining more complex understandings is visual narrative inquiry whereby images are analyzed alongside textual data (Riessman, 2008). There are several ways that visuals are being integrated; key among them are telling the story with images, telling the story about the images, and using images to inform the story telling (whether they are found or made within the process). In addition, bridges will need to be considered with established visual-based methodologies; for example, the use of photovoice within narrative inquiry in research involving sensitive topics such as gender-based research with South African schoolgirls (see Simmonds, Roux, & ter Avest, 2015).

Phenomenological Research

Definition of Phenomenological Research

Whereas a narrative study reports the stories of experiences of a single individual or several individuals, a ***phenomenological study*** describes the common meaning for several individuals of their lived experiences of a concept or a phenomenon. Phenomenologists focus on describing what all participants have in common as they experience a phenomenon (e.g., grief is universally experienced). The basic purpose of phenomenology is to reduce individual experiences with a phenomenon to a description of the universal essence (a "grasp of the very nature of the thing," van Manen, 1990, p. 177). To this end, qualitative researchers identify a phenomenon, an "object" of human experience (van Manen, 1990, p. 163). Recently van Manen (2014) describes phenomenological research as beginning "with wonder at what gives itself and how something gives itself. It can only be pursued while surrounding to a state of wonder" (p. 27). This human experience may be a phenomenon such as insomnia, being left out, anger, grief, or undergoing coronary artery bypass surgery (Moustakas, 1994). The inquirer then collects data from persons who have experienced the phenomenon and develops a composite description of the essence of the experience for all of the individuals. This description consists of "what" they experienced and "how" they experienced it (Moustakas, 1994).

Origins of Phenomenological Research

Phenomenology has a strong philosophical component to it. It draws heavily on the writings of the German mathematician Edmund Husserl (1859–1938; 1970) and those who expanded on his views, such as Heidegger, Sartre, and Merleau-Ponty (Spiegelberg, 1982). Phenomenology is popular in the social and health sciences, especially in sociology (Borgatta & Borgatta, 1992; Swingewood, 1991), psychology (Giorgi, 1985, 2009; Polkinghorne, 1989; Wertz, 2005), nursing and the health sciences (Nieswiadomy, 1993; Oiler, 1986), and education (Tesch, 1988; van Manen, 1990, 2014). Husserl's ideas are abstract, and Merleau-Ponty (1962) raised this question: "What is phenomenology?" In fact, Husserl was known to call any project currently under way "phenomenology" (Natanson, 1973). van Manen (2014) adopted the phrase ***phenomenology of practice*** to describe the meaning-giving methods of phenomenology based on the primary literature of these scholars.

   Writers following in the footsteps of Husserl also seem to point to different philosophical arguments for the use of phenomenology today (contrast, e.g., the philosophical basis stated in Moustakas, 1994; in Stewart and Mickunas, 1990; and in van Manen, 1990). Looking across all of these perspectives, however, we see that the philosophical assumptions rest on some common grounds: the study of the lived experiences of persons, the view that these experiences are conscious ones (van Manen, 2014), and the development of descriptions of the essences of these experiences, not explanations or analyses (Moustakas, 1994). At a broader level, Stewart and Mickunas (1990) emphasize four ***philosophical perspectives*** in phenomenology:

- *A return to the traditional tasks of philosophy.* By the end of the 19th century, philosophy had become limited to exploring a world by empirical means, which was called scientism. The return to the traditional tasks of philosophy that existed before philosophy became enamored with empirical science is a return to the Greek conception of philosophy as a search for wisdom.
- *A philosophy without presuppositions.* Phenomenology's approach is to suspend all judgments about what is real—the "natural attitude"—until they are founded on a more certain basis. This suspension is called epoche by Husserl.
- *The **intentionality of consciousness**.* This idea is that consciousness is always directed toward an object. Reality of an object, then, is inextricably related to one's consciousness of it. Thus, reality, according to Husserl, is divided not into subjects and objects but into the dual Cartesian nature of both subjects and objects as they appear in consciousness.
- *The refusal of the subject–object dichotomy.* This theme flows naturally from the intentionality of consciousness. The reality of an object is only perceived within the meaning of the experience of an individual.

An individual writing a phenomenology would be remiss to not include some discussion about the philosophical presuppositions of phenomenology along with the methods in this form of inquiry. Moustakas (1994) devotes over 100 pages to the philosophical assumptions before he turns to the methods. We rely on two books for our primary information about phenomenology: van Manen (2014), based on a human science orientation, and Moustakas (1994), taken from a psychological perspective. We also return to the seminal work of van Manen (1990) in our descriptions of methods and traditions within phenomenological

Defining Features of Phenomenology

There are several features that are typically included in all phenomenological studies:

- An emphasis on a phenomenon to be explored, phrased in terms of a single concept or idea, such as the educational idea of "professional growth," the psychological concept of "grief," or the health idea of a "caring relationship."
- The exploration of this phenomenon with a group of individuals who have all experienced the phenomenon. Thus, a heterogeneous group is identified that may vary in size from 3 to 4 individuals to 10 to 15.
- A philosophical discussion about the basic ideas involved in conducting a phenomenology. This turns on the lived experiences of individuals and how they have both subjective experiences of the phenomenon and objective experiences of something in common with other people. Thus, there is a refusal of the subjective–objective perspective, and for these reasons, phenomenology lies somewhere on a continuum between qualitative and quantitative research.

- In some forms of phenomenology, the researcher brackets himself or herself out of the study by discussing personal experiences with the phenomenon. This does not take the researcher completely out of the study, but it does serve to identify personal experiences with the phenomenon and to partly set them aside so that the researcher can focus on the experiences of the participants in the study. This is an ideal, but readers learn about the researcher's experiences and can judge for themselves whether the researcher focused solely on the participants' experiences in the description without bringing himself or herself into the picture. Giorgi (2009) sees this bracketing as a matter not of forgetting what has been experienced but of not letting past knowledge be engaged while determining experiences. He then cites other aspects of life where this same demand holds. A juror in a criminal trial may hear a judge say that a piece of evidence is not admissible; a scientific researcher may hope that a pet hypothesis will be supported but then note that the results do not support it van Manen describes the processes of bracketing and reduction as ***phenomenological reflection***.

- A data collection procedures that typically involves interviewing individuals who have experienced the phenomenon. This is not a universal trait, however, as some phenomenological studies involve varied sources of data, such as poems, observations, and documents.

- A data analysis that can follow systematic procedures that move from the narrow units of analysis (e.g., significant statements), and on to broader units (e.g., meaning units), and on to detailed descriptions that summarize two elements: "what" the individuals have experienced and "how" they have experienced it (Moustakas, 1994).

- An ending for phenomenology with a descriptive passage that discusses the essence of the experience for individuals incorporating "what" they have experienced and "how" they experienced it. The "essence" is the culminating aspect of a phenomenological study.

Types of Phenomenology

Two approaches to phenomenology are highlighted in this discussion: hermeneutic phenomenology (van Manen, 1990, 2014) and empirical, transcendental, or psychological phenomenology (Moustakas, 1994). van Manen (1990, 2014) is widely cited in the health literature (Morse & Field, 1995). An educator, van Manen (1990) has written an instructive book on ***hermeneutical phenomenology*** in which he describes research as oriented toward lived experience (phenomenology) and interpreting the "texts" of life (hermeneutics; p. 4). Although van Manen does not approach phenomenology with a set of rules or methods, he discusses it as a dynamic interplay among six research activities. Researchers first turn to a phenomenon, an "abiding concern" (van Manen, 1990, p. 31), which seriously interests them (e.g., reading, running, driving, mothering). In the process, they reflect on essential themes, what constitutes the nature of this lived experience. They write a description of the phenomenon, maintaining a strong relation to the topic of inquiry and balancing the parts of the writing to the whole. Phenomenology is not only a description but it is also an interpretive process in which the researcher makes an interpretation of the meaning of the lived experiences.

Icelandic researchers offer an example of a hermeneutical phenomenology in their examination of the experience of spirituality and its influence on the lives of ten persons receiving palliative care and their well-being (Asgeirsdottir et al., 2013). Both the religious and nonreligious aspects were emphasized and implications for the function of a theological approach in palliative care are discussed.

Moustakas's (1994) transcendental or psychological phenomenology is focused less on the interpretations of the researcher and more on a description of the experiences of participants. In addition, Moustakas focuses on one of Husserl's concepts, *epoche, or bracketing*, in which investigators set aside their experiences, as much as possible, to take a fresh perspective toward the phenomenon under examination. Hence, *transcendental* means "in which everything is perceived freshly, as if for the first time" (Moustakas, 1994, p. 34). Moustakas admits that this state is seldom perfectly achieved. However, we see researchers who embrace this idea when they begin a project by describing their own experiences with the phenomenon and bracketing out their views before proceeding with the experiences of others.

Besides bracketing, empirical, *transcendental phenomenology* draws on the *Duquesne Studies in Phenomenological Psychology* (e.g., Giorgi, 1985, 2009) and the data analysis procedures of Van Kaam (1966) and Colaizzi (1978). The procedures, illustrated by Moustakas (1994), consist of identifying a phenomenon to study, bracketing out one's experiences, and collecting data from several persons who have experienced the phenomenon. The researcher then analyzes the data by reducing the information to significant statements or quotes and combines the statements into themes. Following that, the researcher develops a *textural description* of the experiences of the persons (what participants experienced), a *structural description* of their experiences (how they experienced it in terms of the conditions, situations, or context), and a combination of the textural and structural descriptions to convey an overall essence of the experience. Transcendental phenomenology was used in the dissertation work to examine the experiences and perceptions of 13 developmental math students (Cordes, 2014). The essence of the participant experience involved descriptions of isolation, self-doubt, and clouding of success.

Procedures for Conducting Phenomenological Research

We use the psychologist Moustakas's (1994) approach because it has systematic steps in the data analysis procedure and guidelines for assembling the textual and structural descriptions. The conduct of psychological phenomenology has been addressed in a number of writings, including Dukes (1984), Tesch (1990), Giorgi (1985, 1994, 2009), Polkinghorne (1989), and, most recently, Moustakas (1994). Pereira (2012) offers reflections on the rigour in phenomenological research from the perspective of a novice researcher. The major procedural steps in the process would be as follows (see Figure 4.3):

• *Determine if the research problem is best examined by using a phenomenological approach.* The type of problem best suited for this form of research is one in which it is important to understand several individuals' common or shared experiences of a phenomenon. It would be important to understand these common experiences in order to develop practices or policies, or to develop a deeper understanding about the features of the phenomenon.

• *Identify a phenomenon of interest to study, and describe it.* Examples of a phenomenon include emotional states such as anger and social constructs such as professionalism. A phenomenon can also involve gaining understandings of a clinical descriptor—for example, what it means to be underweight or a professional descriptor like what it means to be a wrestler. Moustakas (1994) provides numerous examples of phenomena that have been studied. van Manen (1990) identifies the phenomena such as the experience of learning, the beginning of fatherhood, and riding a bicycle.

• *Distinguish and specify the broad philosophical assumptions of phenomenology.* For example, one could write about the combination of objective reality and individual experiences. These lived experiences are furthermore "conscious" and directed toward an object. To fully describe how participants view the phenomenon, researchers must bracket out, as much as possible, their own experiences.

• *Collect data from the individuals who have experienced the phenomenon by using in-depth and multiple interviews.* Polkinghorne (1989) recommends that researchers interview from 5 to 25 individuals who have all experienced the phenomenon. The participants are asked two broad, general questions (Moustakas, 1994): What have you experienced in terms of the phenomenon? What contexts or situations have typically influenced or affected your experiences of the phenomenon? Other open-ended questions may also be asked, but these two, especially, focus attention on gathering data that will lead to a textual and structural description of the experiences, and ultimately provide an understanding of the common experiences of the participants. Other forms of data may also be collected, such as observations, journals, poetry, music, and other forms of art. van Manen (1990) mentions taped conversations; formally written responses; and accounts of vicarious experiences of drama, films, poetry, and novels.

• *Generate themes from the analysis of significant statements.* **Phenomenological data analysis** steps are generally similar for all psychological phenomenologists who discuss the methods (Moustakas, 1994; Polkinghorne, 1989). Building on the data from the first and second research questions, data analysts go through the data (e.g., interview transcriptions) and highlight "significant statements," sentences, or quotes that provide an understanding of how the participants experienced the phenomenon. Moustakas (1994) calls this step **horizonalization**. Next, the researcher develops **clusters of meaning** from these significant statements into themes.

• *Develop textural and structural descriptions.* The significant statements and themes are then used to write a description of what the participants experienced (textural description). They are also used to write a description of the context or setting that influenced how the participants experienced the phenomenon, called structural description or imaginative variation. Moustakas (1994) adds a further step: Researchers also write about their own experiences and the context and situations that have influenced their experiences. We like to shorten Moustakas's procedures and reflect these personal statements at the beginning of the phenomenology or include them in a methods discussion of the role of the researcher (Marshall & Rossman, 2015).

- *Report the "essence" of the phenomenon by using a composite description.* From the structural and textural descriptions, the researcher then writes a composite description that presents the "essence" of the phenomenon, called the ***essential, invariant structure (or essence)***. Primarily this passage focuses on the common experiences of the participants. For example, it means that all experiences have an underlying structure (grief is the same whether the loved one is a puppy, a parakeet, or a child).

- *Present the understanding of the essence of the experience in written form.* The practice of phenomenological inquiry is considered by Max van Manen (2014) to be inseparable from the practice of writing. He goes on to explain that one of the challenges with writing is that "one must bring into presence a phenomenon that cannot be represented in plain words" (p. 370). There are numerous "ways" for communicating phenomenological research including by systematic exploration, meaning the phenomenon is placed in the context of existential (e.g., temporality or spatiality) or by organizing the account reflective of an ever-deepening understanding of the phenomenon experienced. A general reporting structure includes an introduction to familiarize the reader with the phenomenon and in some cases, a personal statement of experiences from the researcher (Moustakas, 1994); research procedures to provide a rationale for the use of phenomenology, and philosophical assumptions and details about data collection and analysis; a report of how the phenomenon was experienced with significant statements; and a conclusion with a composite description of the essence of the phenomenon.

Challenges in Phenomenology

A phenomenology provides a deep understanding of a phenomenon as experienced by several individuals. Knowing some common experiences can be valuable for groups such as therapists, teachers, health personnel, and policy makers. Phenomenology can involve a streamlined form of data collection by including only single or multiple interviews with participants. Using the Moustakas (1994) approach for analyzing the data helps provide a structured approach for novice researchers. It may be too structured for some qualitative researchers. On the other hand, phenomenology requires at least some understanding of the broader philosophical assumptions, and researchers should identify these assumptions in their studies. These philosophical

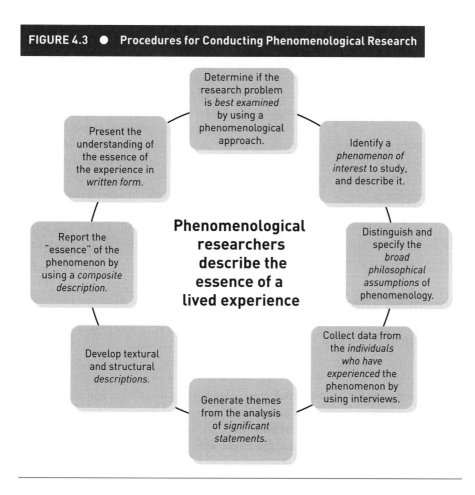

FIGURE 4.3 ● Procedures for Conducting Phenomenological Research

Determine if the research problem is *best examined* by using a phenomenological approach.

Identify a *phenomenon of interest* to study, and describe it.

Distinguish and specify the *broad philosophical assumptions* of phenomenology.

Collect data from the *individuals who have experienced* the phenomenon by using interviews.

Generate themes from the analysis of *significant statements*.

Develop textural and structural *descriptions*.

Report the "essence" of the phenomenon by using a *composite description*.

Present the understanding of the essence of the experience in *written form*.

Phenomenological researchers describe the essence of a lived experience

ideas are abstract concepts and not easily seen in a written phenomenological study. In addition, the participants in the study need to be carefully chosen to be individuals who have all experienced the phenomenon in question, so that the researcher, in the end, can forge a common understanding. Finding individuals who have all experienced the phenomenon may be difficult given a research topic.

Bracketing personal experiences may be difficult for the researcher to implement because interpretations of the data always incorporate the assumptions that the researcher brings to the topic (van Manen, 1990, 2014). Perhaps we need a new definition of *epoche* or *bracketing*, such as suspending our understandings in a reflective move that cultivates curiosity (LeVasseur, 2003). Thus, the researcher needs to decide how and in what way his or her personal understandings will be introduced into the study. Indeed, the practice of engaging in phenomenological research has the potential for lasting effects on the researcher which merit further study as a phenomenon itself. van Manen (1990) describes the potential impact on the researcher, saying,

"Phenomenology projects and their methods often have transformative effect on the researcher himself or herself. Indeed, phenomenological research is often itself a form of deep learning, leading to a transformation of consciousness, heightened perceptiveness, increased thoughtfulness" (p. 163).

A final challenge for phenomenological researchers is how (or for many *if*) a newer approach, interpretive phenomenology, fits within phenomenology. Smith, Flowers, and Larkin (2009) have led the development of interpretive phenomenological analysis as a qualitative research framework grounded in psychology and influenced by phenomenology and hermeneutics, as well as idiography. With a focus on the particular, a thorough and systematic approach to analysis examines "how a particular phenomena has been understood from the perspective of particular people, in a particular context" (Smith et al., 2009, p. 51). Interpretive phenomenological analysis involves a double hermeneutic as it integrates not only the participant's sense of their lived experience but also the researchers' attempt in understanding how the participant makes sense of their personal and social world (Smith et al., 2009).

Grounded Theory Research

Definition of Grounded Theory Research

While narrative research focuses on individual stories told by participants and phenomenology emphasizes the common experiences for a number of individuals, the intent of a ***grounded theory study*** is to move beyond description and to ***generate or discover a theory***, a "unified theoretical explanation" (Corbin & Strauss, 2007, p. 107) for a process or an action. Participants in the study would all have experienced the process, and the development of the theory might help explain practice or provide a framework for further research. A key idea is that this theory development does not come "off the shelf" but rather is generated or "grounded" in data from participants who have experienced the process (Strauss & Corbin, 1998). Thus, grounded theory is a qualitative research design in which the inquirer generates a general explanation (a theory) of a process, an action, or an interaction shaped by the views of a large number of participants.

Origins of Grounded Theory Research

This qualitative design was developed in sociology in 1967 by two researchers, Barney Glaser and Anselm Strauss, who felt that theories used in research were often inappropriate and ill-suited for participants under study. They elaborated on their ideas through several books (Corbin & Strauss, 2007, 2015; Glaser, 1978; Glaser & Strauss, 1967; Strauss, 1987; Strauss & Corbin, 1990, 1998). In contrast to the a priori, theoretical orientations in sociology, grounded theorists held that theories should be "grounded" in data from the field, especially in the actions, interactions, and social processes of people. Thus, grounded theory provided for the generation of a theory (complete with a diagram and hypotheses) of actions, interactions, or processes through interrelating categories of information based on data collected from individuals.

Despite the initial collaboration of Glaser and Strauss that produced such works as *Awareness of Dying* (Glaser & Strauss, 1965) and *Time for Dying* (Glaser & Strauss, 1968), the two authors ultimately disagreed about the meaning and procedures of grounded theory. Glaser has criticized Strauss's approach to grounded theory as too prescribed and structured (Glaser, 1992). More recently, Charmaz (2006, 2014) has advocated for a ***constructivist grounded theory***, thus introducing yet another perspective into the conversation about procedures. Through these different interpretations and publications such as the *SAGE Handbook of Grounded Theory* (Bryant & Charmaz, 2007), grounded theory has gained popularity in fields such as sociology, nursing, education, and psychology, as well as in other social science fields. For a concise historical account, see also Kenny and Fourie (2014) and Bryant and Charmaz (2007).

Another recent grounded theory perspective is that of Clarke (Clarke, 2005; Clarke, Friese, & Washburn, 2015) who, along with Charmaz, seeks to reclaim grounded theory from its "positivist underpinnings" (p. xxiii). Clarke, however, goes further than Charmaz, suggesting that social "situations" should form our unit of analysis in grounded theory and that three sociological modes can be useful in analyzing these situations—situational, social world/arenas, and positional cartographic maps for collecting and analyzing qualitative data. She further expands grounded theory "after the postmodern turn" (Clarke, 2005, p. xxiv) and relies on postmodern perspectives (i.e., the political nature of research and interpretation, reflexivity on the part of researchers, a recognition of problems of representing information, questions of legitimacy and authority, and repositioning the researcher away from the "all knowing analyst" to the "acknowledged participant" (Clarke, 2005, pp. xxvii, xxviii). Clarke frequently turns to the postmodern, poststructural writer Michel Foucault (1972) to base the grounded theory discourse. In our discussion of grounded theory, we will be relying on Corbin and Strauss (2015), who provide a structured approach to grounded theory, and Charmaz (2014), who offers a constructivist and interpretive perspective on grounded theory.

Defining Features of Grounded Theory

There are several major characteristics of grounded theory that might be incorporated into a research study:

- Grounded theory research focuses on a process or an action that has distinct steps or phases that occur over time. Thus, a grounded theory study has "movement" or some action that the researcher is attempting to explain. A process might be "developing a general education program" or the process of "supporting faculty to become good researchers."
- In a grounded theory study, the researcher seeks, in the end, to develop a theory of this process or action. There are many definitions of a theory available in

the literature, but in general, a theory is an explanation of something or an understanding that the researcher develops. This explanation or understanding is a drawing together, in grounded theory, of theoretical categories that are arrayed to show how the theory works. For example, a theory of support for faculty may show how faculty are supported over time, by specific resources, by specific actions taken by individuals, with individual outcomes that enhance the research performance of a faculty member (Creswell & Brown, 1992).

- The process of ***memoing*** becomes part of developing the theory as the researcher writes down ideas as data are collected and analyzed. In these memos, the ideas attempt to formulate the process that is being seen by the researcher and to sketch out the flow of this process.

- The data and analysis procedures are considered to undertaken simultaneously and iteratively. The primary form of data collection is often interviewing in which the grounded theory researcher is constantly comparing data gleaned from participants with ideas about the emerging theory. The process consists of going back and forth between the participants, gathering new interviews, and then returning to the evolving theory to fill in the gaps and to elaborate on how it works.

- The inductive procedures involved in data analysis are described in relation to the type of grounded theory approach. The procedures can be structured and follow the pattern of developing open categories, selecting one ***category*** to be the focus of the theory, and then detailing additional categories (***axial coding***) to form a theoretical model. The intersection of the categories becomes the theory (called ***selective coding***). This theory can be presented as a diagram, as ***propositions*** (or hypotheses), or as a discussion (Strauss & Corbin, 1998). Data analysis can also be less structured and based on developing a theory by piecing together implicit meanings about a category (Charmaz, 2006).

Types of Grounded Theory Studies

The two popular approaches to grounded theory are the systematic procedures of Anselm Strauss and Juliet Corbin (Strauss & Corbin, 1990, 1998; Corbin & Strauss, 2007, 2015) and the constructivist approach of Charmaz (2005, 2006, 2014). Important concepts of the approach associated with Strauss and Corbin involve the categories, codes, and codings and the systematic procedures guided by the constant comparison of data from the field with emerging categories. In contrast, in the constructivist approach, Charmaz emphasizes theory development resulting from a co-construction process dependent upon researcher interactions with participants and field.

In the more systematic, analytic procedures of Strauss and Corbin (Strauss & Corbin, 1990, 1998; Corbin & Strauss, 2007, 2015), the investigator seeks to systematically develop a theory that explains process, action, or interaction on a topic (e.g., the process of developing a curriculum, the therapeutic benefits of sharing psychological test results with clients). The researcher typically conducts 20 to 30 interviews based on several visits "to the field" to collect interview data to saturate the categories (or find information that continues to add to them until no more can be found). A category represents a unit of information that comprises events, happenings, and instances (Strauss & Corbin, 1990). The researcher also collects and analyzes observations and documents, but these data forms are often not used. While the researcher collects data, she or he begins analysis. Our image for data collection in a grounded theory study is a zigzag process: out to the field to gather information, into the office to analyze the data, back to the field to gather more information, into the office, and so forth. The participants interviewed are theoretically chosen (called **theoretical sampling**) to help the researcher best form the theory. How many passes one makes to the field depends on whether the categories of information become saturated—usually considered to be reached when no new ideas are emerging—and whether the theory is elaborated in all of its complexity. This process of taking information from data collection and comparing it to emerging categories is called the **constant comparative** method of data analysis.

The researcher begins with **open coding**, coding the data for its major categories of information. Coding involves a data aggregating and meaning-making process described as "doing analysis and denoting concepts to stand for data" (Corbin & Strauss, 2015, p. 216). From this coding, axial coding emerges in which the researcher identifies one open coding category to focus on (called the "core" phenomenon) and then goes back to the data and creates categories around this core phenomenon. Strauss and Corbin (1990) prescribe the types of categories identified around the core phenomenon. They consist of **causal conditions** (what factors caused the core phenomenon), strategies (actions taken in response to the core phenomenon), contextual and **intervening conditions** (broad and specific situational factors that influence the strategies), and consequences (outcomes from using the strategies). These categories relate to and surround the core phenomenon in a visual model called the axial coding paradigm. The final step, then, is selective coding, in which the researcher takes the model and develops propositions (or hypotheses) that interrelate the categories in the model or assembles a story that describes the interrelationship of categories in the model. This theory, developed by the researcher, is articulated toward the end of a study and can assume several forms, such as a narrative statement (Strauss & Corbin, 1990), a visual picture (Morrow & Smith, 1995), or a series of hypotheses or propositions (Creswell & Brown, 1992).

In their discussion of grounded theory, Corbin and Strauss (2015) take the model one step further to develop a **conditional or consequential matrix**. They advance the conditional matrix as an analysis strategy to help the researcher make connections between the macro and micro conditions influencing the phenomenon and in turn identify the range of consequences that result from the interactions. This matrix is a set of expanding concentric circles with labels that build outward from the individual, group, and organization to the community, region, nation, and global world.

In my experience, this matrix is seldom used in grounded theory research, and researchers typically end their studies with a theory developed in selective coding, a theory that might be viewed as a substantive, low-level theory rather than an abstract, grand theory (e.g., see Creswell & Brown, 1992). Although making connections between the substantive theory and its larger implications for the community, nation, and world in the conditional matrix is important (e.g., a model of work flow in a hospital, the shortage of gloves, and the national guidelines on AIDS may all be connected; see this example provided by Strauss & Corbin, 1998), grounded theorists seldom have the data, time, or resources to employ the conditional matrix. A further example explores the larger historical, social, political, cultural, and environmental conditions in which the Vietnam war combat experience took place and was survived by U.S. soldiers includes use of a consequential matrix (Corbin & Strauss, 2015).

A second variant of grounded theory is found in the constructivist writing of Charmaz (2005, 2006, 2014). Instead of embracing the study of a single process or core category as in the Strauss and Corbin (1998) approach, Charmaz advocates for a social constructivist perspective that includes emphasizing diverse local worlds, multiple realities, and the complexities of particular worlds, views, and actions. Constructivist grounded theory, according to Charmaz (2006, 2014), lies squarely within the interpretive approach to qualitative research with flexible guidelines, a focus on theory developed that depends on the researcher's view, learning about the experience within embedded, hidden networks, situations, and relationships as well as making visible hierarchies of power, communication, and opportunity. Charmaz places more emphasis on the views, values, beliefs, feelings, assumptions, and ideologies of individuals than on the methods of research, although she does describe the practices of gathering rich data, coding the data, memoing, and using theoretical sampling (Charmaz, 2006, 2014). She suggests that complex terms or jargon, diagrams, conceptual maps, and systematic approaches (such as Strauss & Corbin, 1990) detract from grounded theory and represent an attempt to gain power in their use. She advocates using active codes, such as gerund-based phrases like *recasting life*. Moreover, for Charmaz, a grounded theory procedure does not minimize the role of the researcher in the process. The researcher makes decisions about the categories throughout the process, brings questions to the data, and advances personal values, experiences, and priorities. Any conclusions developed by grounded theorists are, according to Charmaz (2005), suggestive, incomplete, and inconclusive.

Procedures for Conducting Grounded Theory Research

In this discussion, we include Charmaz's interpretive approach (e.g., reflexivity, being flexible in structure, as discussed in Chapter 2), and we rely on Strauss and Corbin (1990, 1998) and Corbin and Strauss (2008, 2015) to illustrate grounded theory procedures because their systematic approach is helpful to individuals learning about and applying grounded theory research. In so doing, we adopt the advice offered by Charmaz (2014): "Grounded theory guidelines describe steps of the research process

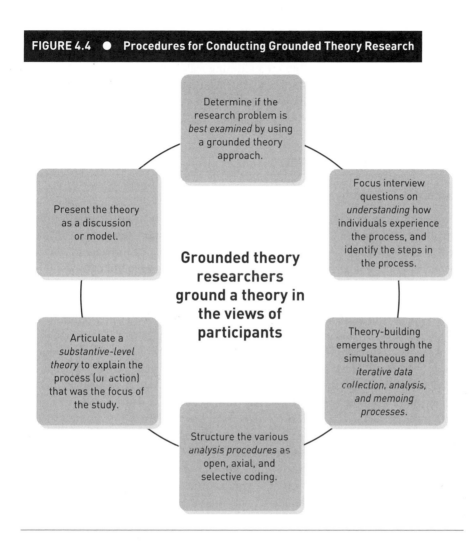

FIGURE 4.4 ● Procedures for Conducting Grounded Theory Research

Determine if the research problem is *best examined* by using a grounded theory approach.

Focus interview questions on *understanding* how individuals experience the process, and identify the steps in the process.

Grounded theory researchers ground a theory in the views of participants

Present the theory as a discussion or model.

Articulate a *substantive-level theory* to explain the process (or action) that was the focus of the study.

Theory-building emerges through the simultaneous and *iterative data collection, analysis, and memoing processes.*

Structure the various *analysis procedures* as open, axial, and selective coding.

sampling, in which the researcher gathers additional information from individuals different from those people initially interviewed to determine if the theory holds true for these additional participants. The researcher needs to recognize that the primary outcome of this study is a theory with specific components: a central phenomenon, causal conditions, strategies, conditions and context, and consequences. These are prescribed categories of information in the theory, so the Strauss and Corbin (1990, 1998) or Corbin and Strauss (2008, 2015) approach may not have the flexibility desired by some qualitative researchers. In this case, the Charmaz (2006, 2014) approach, which is less structured and more adaptable, may be used.

Grounded theory research continues to be applied across varied disciplines and to be influential across professions as diverse as health, engineering, education, and business (Charmaz, 2003). While some benefits for conducting grounded theory research are well established, including generating theory relevant to the context of the study and providing flexibility for addressing real-world issues (Corbin & Strauss, 2015), others may still need to be articulated. Wide adoption of grounded theory has resulted in greater attention and the emergence of guidance for researchers for some of the more abstract concepts—for example, memoing (Lempert, 2007).

Ethnographic Research

Definition of Ethnographic Research

Although a grounded theory researcher develops a theory from examining many individuals who share in the same process, action, or interaction, the study participants are not likely to be located in the same place or interacting on a frequent basis that they develop shared patterns of behavior, beliefs, and *language*. An ethnographer is interested in examining these shared patterns, and the unit of analysis is typically larger than the 20 or so individuals involved in a grounded theory study. An ethnography focuses on an entire *culture-sharing group*. Granted, sometimes this cultural group may be small (a few teachers, a few social workers), but typically it is large, involving many people who interact over time (teachers in an entire school, a community social work group). Thus, ethnography is a qualitative design in which the researcher describes and interprets the shared and learned patterns of values, *behaviors*, beliefs, and language of a culture-sharing group (Harris, 1968). As both a process and an outcome of research (Agar, 1980), ethnography is a way of studying a culture-sharing group as well as the final, written product of that research. As a process, ethnography involves extended observations of the group, most often through *participant observation*, in which the researcher is *immersed* in the day-to-day lives of the people and observes and interviews the group participants. Ethnographers study the meaning of the behavior, the language, and the interaction among members of the culture-sharing group.

Origins of Ethnographic Research

Ethnography had its beginning in comparative cultural anthropology conducted by early 20th-century anthropologists, such as Boas, Malinowski, Radcliffe-Brown, and Mead. Although these researchers initially took the natural sciences as a model for research, they differed from those using traditional scientific approaches through the first-hand collection of data concerning existing "primitive" cultures (Atkinson & Hammersley, 1994). In the 1920s and 1930s, sociologists such as Park, Dewey, and Mead adapted anthropological field methods to the study of cultural groups in the United States (Bogdan & Biklen, 1992). Scientific approaches to ethnography have expanded to include "schools" or subtypes of ethnography with different theoretical orientations and aims, such as structural functionalism, symbolic interactionism, cultural and cognitive anthropology, feminism, Marxism, ethnomethodology, critical theory, cultural studies, and postmodernism (Atkinson & Hammersley, 1994). This has led to a lack of orthodoxy in ethnography and has resulted in pluralistic approaches.

Many excellent books are available on ethnography, including Van Maanen (1988, 2011) on the many forms of ethnography; LeCompte and Schensul (1999) on procedures of ethnography presented in a tool kit of short books; Atkinson, Coffey, and Delamont (2003) on the practices of ethnography; Atkinson (2015) on ethnographic **fieldwork**; and Madison (2011) on **critical ethnography**. Major ideas about ethnography developed in this discussion will draw on Fetterman's (2010) and Wolcott's (2008a) approaches in addition to Wolcott's (2010) companion "primer" on ethnographic lessons.

Defining Features of Ethnographies

From a review of published ethnographies, a brief list of defining characteristics of ethnographies can be assembled.

- Ethnographies focus on developing a complex, complete description of the culture of a group—the entire culture-sharing group or a subset of a group. The culture-sharing group must have been intact and interacting for long enough to develop social behaviors of an identifiable group that can be studied. Key to ethnographic research is the focus on these discernible working patterns, not the study of a culture (Wolcott, 2008a).

- In an ethnography, the researcher looks for patterns (also described as rituals, customary social behaviors, or regularities) of the group's mental activities, such as their ideas and beliefs expressed through language, or material activities, such as how they behave within the group as expressed through their actions observed by the researcher (Fetterman, 2010). Said in another way, the researcher looks for patterns of social organization (e.g., social networks) and ideational systems (e.g., worldview, ideas; Wolcott, 2008a).

- In addition, theory plays an important role in focusing the researcher's attention when conducting an ethnography. For example, ethnographers start with a theory—a broad explanation as to what they hope to find—drawn from cognitive science to understand ideas and beliefs, or from materialist theories, such as techno-environmentalism, Marxism, acculturation, or innovation, to observe how individuals in the culture-sharing group behave and talk (Fetterman, 2010).

- Using the theory and looking for patterns of a culture-sharing group involves engaging in extensive fieldwork, collecting data primarily through interviews, observations, symbols, artifacts, and many diverse sources of data (Atkinson, 2015; Fetterman, 2010).

- In an analysis of this data, the researcher relies on the participants' views as an insider emic perspective and reports them in verbatim quotes and then synthesizes the data filtering it through the researchers' etic scientific perspective to develop an overall cultural interpretation. This cultural interpretation is a description of the group and themes related to the theoretical concepts being explored in the study. Typically, in good ethnographies, not much is known about how the group functions (e.g., how a gang operates), and the reader develops a new, and novel, understanding of the group.

- This analysis results in an understanding of how the culture-sharing group works—how it functions, the group's way of life. Wolcott (2010) provides two helpful questions that, in the end, must be answered in an ethnography: "What do people in this setting have to know and do to make this system work?" and "If culture, sometimes defined simply as shared knowledge, is mostly caught rather than taught, how do those being inducted into the group find their 'way in' so that an adequate level of sharing is achieved?" (p. 74).

Types of Ethnographies

There are many forms of ethnography, such as a confessional ethnography, life history, autoethnography, feminist ethnography, ethnographic novels as well as the visual ethnography found in photography, video, and electronic media (Denzin, 1989; Fetterman, 2010; LeCompte, Millroy, & Preissle, 1992; Pink, 2001; Van Maanen, 1988). Two popular forms of ethnography will be emphasized here: the ***realist ethnography*** and the critical ethnography.

The realist ethnography is a traditional approach used by cultural anthropologists. Characterized by Van Maanen (1988, 2011), it reflects a particular stance taken by the researcher toward the individuals being studied. Realist ethnography is an objective account of the situation, typically written in the third-person point of view and reporting objectively on the information learned from participants at a site. In this ethnographic approach, the realist ethnographer narrates the study in a third-person dispassionate voice and reports on what is observed or heard from participants. The ethnographer remains in the background as an omniscient reporter of the "facts." The realist also reports objective data in a measured style uncontaminated by personal bias, political goals, and judgment. The researcher may provide mundane details of everyday life among the people studied. The ethnographer also uses standard categories for cultural description (e.g., family life, communication networks, work life, social networks, status systems). The ethnographer produces the participants' views through closely edited quotations and has the final word on how the culture is to be interpreted and presented.

Alternatively, for many researchers, ethnography today employs a "critical" approach (Carspecken & Apple, 1992; Madison, 2011; Thomas, 1993) by including in the research an advocacy perspective. This approach is in response to current society, in which the systems of power, prestige, privilege, and authority serve to marginalize individuals who are from different classes, races, and genders. The critical ethnography is a type of ethnographic research in which the authors advocate for the emancipation of groups marginalized in society (Thomas, 1993). Critical researchers typically are politically minded individuals who seek, through their research, to speak out against inequality and domination (Carspecken & Apple, 1992). For example, critical ethnographers might study schools that provide privileges to certain types of students, or counseling practices that serve to overlook the needs of underrepresented groups. The major components of a critical ethnography include a value-laden orientation, empowering people by giving them more authority, challenging the status quo, and addressing concerns about power and control. A critical ethnographer will study issues of power, empowerment, inequality, inequity, dominance, repression, hegemony, and victimization.

Procedures for Conducting an Ethnography

As with all qualitative inquiry, there is no single way to conduct ethnographic research. Although current writings provide more guidance to this approach than ever (e.g., see the excellent overview found in Wolcott, 2008a; and for a concise description, see Jachyra, Atkinson, & Washiya, 2015), the approach taken here includes elements of both realist ethnography and critical approaches (see Figure 4.5). The steps we would use to conduct an ethnography are as follows:

- *Determine if ethnography is the most appropriate design for studying the research problem.* Ethnography is appropriate if the needs are to describe how a cultural group works and to explore the beliefs, language, behaviors, and issues facing the group, such as power, resistance, and dominance. The literature may be deficient in actually knowing how the group works because the group is not in the mainstream, people may not be familiar with the group, or its ways are so different that readers may not identify with the group.

- *Identify and locate a culture-sharing group to study.* Typically, this group is one whose members have been together for an extended period of time so that their shared language, patterns of behavior, and attitudes have merged into discernable patterns. This may also be a group that has been marginalized by society. Because ethnographers spend time talking with and observing this group, access may require finding one or more individuals in the group who will allow the researcher in—a **gatekeeper** or **key informants (or participants)**.

- *Select cultural themes, issues, or theories to study about the group.* These themes, issues, and theories provide an orienting framework for the study of the culture-sharing group. It also informs the **analysis of the culture-sharing group**. The themes may include such topics as enculturation, socialization, learning, cognition, domination, inequality, or child and adult development (LeCompte et al., 1992). As discussed by Hammersley and Atkinson (1995), Wolcott (1987, 1994, 2008a), and Fetterman (2010), the ethnographer begins the study by examining people in interaction in ordinary settings and discerns pervasive patterns such as life cycles, events, and cultural themes.

- *Determine which type of ethnography to use to study cultural concepts.* Perhaps how the group works needs to be described, or a critical ethnography can expose issues such as power, hegemony, and advocacy for certain groups. A critical ethnographer, for example, might address an inequity in society or some part of it; use the research to advocate and call for changes; and specify an issue to explore, such as inequality, dominance, oppression, or empowerment.

- *Gather information in the context or setting where the group works or lives.* This is called fieldwork (Wolcott, 2008a). Gathering the types of information typically needed in an ethnography involves going to the research site, respecting the daily lives of individuals at the site, and collecting a wide variety of materials. Field issues of respect, reciprocity, deciding who owns the data, and others are central to ethnography. Ethnographers bring a sensitivity to fieldwork issues (Hammersley & Atkinson, 1995), such as attending to how they gain access, give back or reciprocate with the participants, and engage in ethical research, such as presenting themselves honestly and describing the purpose of the study. LeCompte and Schensul (1999) organize types of ethnographic data into observations, tests and measures, surveys, interviews, content analysis, elicitation methods, audiovisual methods, spatial mapping, and network research.

- *Generate an overall cultural interpretation of the group from the analysis of patterns across many sources of data.* The researcher begins by compiling a detailed **description of the culture-sharing group**, focusing on a single event, on several activities, or on the group over a prolonged period of time. The ethnographer moves into a theme analysis of patterns or topics that signifies how the cultural group works and lives, and ends with an "overall picture of how a system works" (Fetterman, 2010, p. 10). Fetterman (2010) describes the function of thick description for the reader, stating "ideally the ethnographer shares the participant's understanding of the situation with the reader. Thick description is a written record of cultural interpretation" (p. 125). This description includes verbatim quotes reflective of cultural concepts such as the social structure, kinship, political structure, and the social relations or function among members incorporating the views of the participants (**emic**) as well as the views of the researcher (**etic**).

- *Present the patterns of the culture-sharing group in written or performance formats.* This is often accomplished by describing a working set of rules or generalizations as to how the culture-sharing group functions. This may also be referred to as a holistic **cultural portrait**. Writing ethnographies involves an interactive analysis and writing process often begun during fieldwork. A general reporting structure includes an introduction to familiarize the reader with the culture-sharing group, research procedures to provide a rationale for use of an ethnography, and details about data collection and analysis, providing a cultural interpretation using a variety of ways describing the patterns that emerge from an analysis of cultural. The final product is a holistic cultural portrait of the group from both the participants and the interpretation of the researcher that

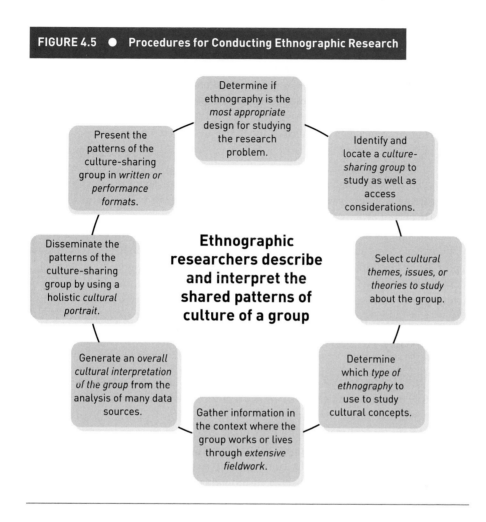

FIGURE 4.5 ●   Procedures for Conducting Ethnographic Research

Determine if ethnography is the *most appropriate* design for studying the research problem.

Identify and locate a *culture-sharing group* to study as well as access considerations.

Select *cultural themes, issues, or theories to study* about the group.

Determine which *type of ethnography* to use to study cultural concepts.

Gather information in the context where the group works or lives through *extensive fieldwork*.

Generate an *overall cultural interpretation of the group* from the analysis of many data sources.

Disseminate the patterns of the culture-sharing group by using a holistic *cultural portrait*.

Present the patterns of the culture-sharing group in *written or performance formats*.

Ethnographic researchers describe and interpret the shared patterns of culture of a group

might also advocate for the needs of the group or suggest changes in society. Other products may be more performance based, such as theater productions, plays, or poems.

Challenges in Ethnographic Research

Ethnography is challenging to use for the following reasons. The researcher needs to have an understanding of cultural anthropology, the meaning of a social–cultural system, and the concepts typically explored by those studying cultures. Culture is an amorphous term, not something "lying about" (Wolcott, 1987, p. 41), but something researchers attribute to a group when looking for patterns of its social world. It is inferred from the words and actions of members of the group, and it is assigned to this group by the researcher. It consists of what people do (behaviors), what they say (language), the potential tension between what they do and ought to do, and what they make and use, such as artifacts (Spradley, 1980). Such themes are diverse, as illustrated in Winthrop's (1991) *Dictionary of Concepts in Cultural Anthropology*. Fetterman (2010) discusses how ethnographers describe a **holistic** perspective of the group's history, religion, politics, economy, and environment.

The time to collect data is extensive, involving prolonged time in the field. In much ethnography, the narratives are written in a literary, almost storytelling approach, an approach that may limit the audience for the work and may be challenging for authors accustomed to traditional approaches to scientific writing. There is a possibility that the researcher will "go native" and be unable to complete or be compromised in the study. This is but one issue in the complex array of fieldwork issues facing ethnographers who venture into an unfamiliar cultural group or system. Sensitivity to the needs of individuals being studied is especially important, and the researcher must access and report his or her impact in conducting the study on the people and the places being explored. Discussions abound about how funding often limits time for ethnographic fieldwork and how data shapes the generation of an ethnographic study.

Case Study Research

Definition of Case Study Research

The entire culture-sharing group in ethnography may be considered a **case**, but the intent in ethnography is to determine how the culture works rather than to either develop an in-depth understanding of a single case or explore an issue or problem using the case as a specific illustration. Thus, case study research involves the study of a case (or cases) within a real-life, contemporary context or setting (Yin, 2014). This case may be a concrete entity, such as an individual, a small group, an organization, or a partnership. At a less concrete level, it may be a community, a relationship, a decision process, or a specific project (see Yin, 2014). Stake (2005) states that case study research is not a methodology but a choice of what is to be studied (i.e., a case within a **bounded system**, bounded by time and place) whereas others present it as a strategy of inquiry, a methodology, or a comprehensive research strategy (Denzin & Lincoln, 2005; Merriam & Tisdell, 2015; Yin, 2014). Similar to Stake (2005), Thomas (2015) argues, "Your case study is defined not so much by the methods that you are using to do the study, but the edges you put around the case" (p. 21).

We choose to view case study research as a methodology: a type of design in qualitative research that may be an object of study as well as a product of the inquiry. Case study research is defined as a qualitative approach in which the investigator explores a real-life, contemporary bounded system (a case) or multiple bounded systems (cases) over time, through detailed, in-depth data collection involving **multiple sources of information** (e.g., observations, interviews, audiovisual material, and documents and reports), and reports a **case description** and **case themes**. The unit of analysis in the case study might be multiple cases (a **multisite** study) or a single case (a **within-site** study).

Origins of Case Study Research

The case study approach is familiar to social scientists because of its popularity in psychology (Freud), medicine (case analysis of a problem), law (case law), and political science (case reports). Case study research has a long, distinguished history across many disciplines. Hamel, Dufour, and Fortin (1993) trace the origin of modern social science case studies through anthropology and sociology. They cite anthropologist Malinowski's study of the Trobriand Islands, French sociologist LePlay's study of families, and the case studies of the University of Chicago Department of Sociology from the 1920s and 1930s through the 1950s (e.g., Thomas and Znaniecki's 1958 study of Polish peasants in Europe and America) as antecedents of qualitative case study research. Today, the case study writer has a large array of texts and approaches from which to choose. Yin (2014), for example, espouses both quantitative and qualitative approaches to case study development and discusses explanatory, exploratory, and descriptive qualitative case studies. Merriam and Tisdell (2015) advocate a general approach to qualitative case studies in the field of education. Stake (1995) systematically establishes procedures for case study research and cites them extensively in his example of "Harper School." Stake's (2006) most recent book on multiple case study analysis presents a step-by-step approach and provides rich illustrations of multiple case studies in Ukraine, Slovakia, and Romania. In discussing the case study approach, we will rely on Stake (1995) and Yin (2014) to form the distinctive features of this approach.

Defining Features of Case Studies

A review of many qualitative case studies reported in the literature yields several defining characteristics of most of them:

- Case study research begins with the identification of a specific case that will be described and analyzed. Examples of a case for study are an individual, a community, a decision process, or an event. A single case can be selected or multiple cases identified so that they can be compared. Typically, case study researchers study current, real-life cases that are in progress so that they can gather accurate information not lost by time.
- The key to the case identification is that it is bounded, meaning that it can be defined or described within certain parameters. Examples of parameters for bounding a case study are such the specific place where the case is located and timeframe in which the case is studied. On occasion, certain people involved in the case may also be defined as a parameter.

- The intent of conducting the case study is also important to focus the procedures for the particular type. A qualitative case study can be composed to illustrate a unique case, a case that has unusual interest in and of itself and needs to be described and detailed. This is called an *intrinsic case* (Stake, 1995). Alternatively, the intent of the case study may be to understand a specific issue, problem, or concern (e.g., teenage pregnancy) and a case or cases selected to best understand the problem. This is called an *instrumental case* (Stake, 1995).
- A hallmark of a good qualitative case study is that it presents an in-depth understanding of the case. In order to accomplish this, the researcher collects and integrates many forms of qualitative data, ranging from interviews, to observations, to documents, to audiovisual materials. Relying on one source of data is typically not enough to develop this in-depth understanding.
- The selection of how to approach the data analysis in a case study will differ. Some case studies involve the analysis of multiple units within the case (e.g., the school, the school district) while others report on the entire case (e.g., the school district). Also, in some studies, the researcher selects multiple cases to analyze and compare while, in other case studies, a single case is analyzed.
- A key to generating the description of the case involves identifying case themes. These themes may also represent issues or specific situations to study in each case. A complete findings section of a case study would then involve both a description of the case and themes or issues that the researcher has uncovered in studying the case. Examples of how the case themes might be organized by the researcher include a chronology, analyzed across cases for similarities and differences among the cases, or presented as a theoretical model.
- Case studies often end with conclusions formed by the researcher about the overall meaning delivering from the case(s). These are called **assertions** by Stake (1995) or building "patterns" or "explanations" by Yin (2009). I think about these as general lessons learned from studying the case(s).

Types of Case Studies

The types of qualitative case studies are distinguished by the focus of analysis for the bounded case, such as whether the case involves studying one individual, several individuals, a group, an entire program, or an activity. They may also be distinguished in terms of the intent of the case analysis. Three variations exist in terms of intent: the single **instrumental case study**, the collective or multiple case study, and the **intrinsic case study**.

In a single instrumental case study, the researcher focuses on an issue or concern and then selects one bounded case to illustrate this issue. Stake (1995) describes his use of an instrumental case study as having "a research question, a puzzlement, a need for general understanding, and feel that we may get insight into the question by studying a particular case" (p. 3). Asmussen and Creswell (1995) used an instrumental case study to explore the issue of campus violence and using the single case of one institution to illustrate the reaction of the campus to a potentially violent incident. The findings from multiple sources of information advanced five themes (denial, fear, safety, retriggering, and campus planning) and assertions in terms of two overriding responses of the campus community to the gunman incident (mentioned briefly in Chapter 1 and explored further in Chapter 11): organizational and social–psychological. This case study should not be seen as an intrinsic case study because campus gun violence has occurred, unfortunately, on several higher education campuses.

In a ***collective case study*** (or multiple case study), the one issue or concern is again selected, but the inquirer selects multiple case studies to illustrate the issue. The researcher might select for study several programs from several research sites or multiple programs within a single site. Often the inquirer purposefully selects multiple cases to show different perspectives on the issue. Some researchers, like Lieberson (2000), argue for the use of a small group of comparison cases because of the potential to draw otherwise inaccessible conclusions. Yin (2009) suggests that the multiple case study design uses the logic of replication, in which the inquirer replicates the procedures for each case. As a general rule, qualitative researchers are reluctant to generalize from one case to another because the contexts of cases differ. To best generalize, however, the inquirer needs to select representative cases for inclusion in the qualitative study. A multiple case study focused on the relationship patterns and management practices across four UK nursing homes involving 406 managers and staff over 6 months (Anderson, Toles, Corazzini, McDaniel, & Colón-Emeric, 2014). The findings suggested the capacity for delivering better resident care resulted from positive interactions strategies and pointed to the need for positive staff engagement with one another as a prerequisite for care quality.

The final type of case study design is an intrinsic case study in which the focus is on the case itself (e.g., evaluating a program, or studying a student having difficulty; see Stake, 1995) because the case presents an unusual or unique situation. This resembles the focus of narrative research, but the case study analytic procedures of a detailed description of the case, set within its context or surroundings, still hold true. An intrinsic case study of Silk Road as an online drug marketplace explored an individual user's "motives for online drug purchasing, experiences of accessing and using the website, drug information sourcing, decision making and purchasing, outcomes and settings for use and perspectives around security" (Van Hout & Bingham, 2013, p. 383). The findings point to differences in relationships, participation, and feelings of safety compared with more traditional online and street sources of drug supply and shed light on the utility of Silk Road to maximize consumer decision making and harm reduction.

Procedures for Conducting a Case Study

Several procedures are available for conducting case studies (see Merriam & Tisdell, 2015; Stake, 1995; Yin, 2009, 2014). This discussion will rely primarily on Stake's

(1995) and Yin's (2014) approaches to conducting a case study (see Figure 4.6). For a concise description from a novice perspective, see also Baxter and Jack (2008).

- *Determine if a case study approach is appropriate for studying the research problem.* A case study is a good approach when the inquirer has clearly identifiable cases with boundaries and seeks to provide an in-depth understanding of the cases or a comparison of several cases.

- *Identify the intent of the study and select the case (or cases).* In conducting case study research, we recommend that investigators consider the intent and type of case study—single or collective, multisite or within-site, and focused on a case or on an issue (intrinsic, instrumental)—is most promising and useful. The case(s) selected may involve an individual, several individuals, a program, an event, or an activity (Stake, 1995; Yin, 2009) with an array of possibilities for ***purposeful sampling*** is available. Often we have found selecting cases that show different perspectives on the problem, process, or event preferable (called purposeful maximal sampling; see Creswell, 2012), but ordinary cases, accessible cases, or unusual cases are also desirable options.

- *Develop procedures for conducting the extensive data collection drawing on multiple data sources.* Among the common sources of information are observations, interviews, documents, and audiovisual materials. For example, Yin (2014) recommends six types of information to collect: documents, archival records, interviews, direct observations, participant observation, and physical artifacts.

- *Specify the analysis approach on which the case description integrates analysis themes and contextual information.* The type of analysis of these data can be a ***holistic analysis*** of the entire case or an ***embedded analysis*** of a specific aspect of the case (Yin, 2009). Through data collecting and analysis, a detailed description of the case (Stake, 1995) emerges in which the researcher details such aspects as the history of the case, the chronology of events, or a day-by-day rendering of the activities of the case. For example, the gunman case study in Chapter 11 involved tracing the campus response to a gunman for 2 weeks immediately following the near-tragedy on campus. Then the researcher might focus on a few key issues (or ***analysis of themes***, or case themes), not for generalizing beyond the case but for understanding the complexity of the case. One analytic strategy would be to identify issues within each case and then look for common themes that transcend the cases (Yin, 2009). This analysis is rich in the ***context of the case*** or setting in which the case presents itself (Merriam, 1988). When multiple cases are chosen, a typical format is to provide first a detailed description of each case and themes within the case, called a ***within-case analysis***, followed by a thematic analysis across the cases, called a ***cross-case analysis***, as well as assertions or an interpretation of the meaning of the case. Whether that meaning comes from learning about the issue of the case (an instrumental case) or learning about an unusual situation (an intrinsic case). As Lincoln and Guba (1985) mention, this phase constitutes the lessons learned from the case, and Stake (1995)

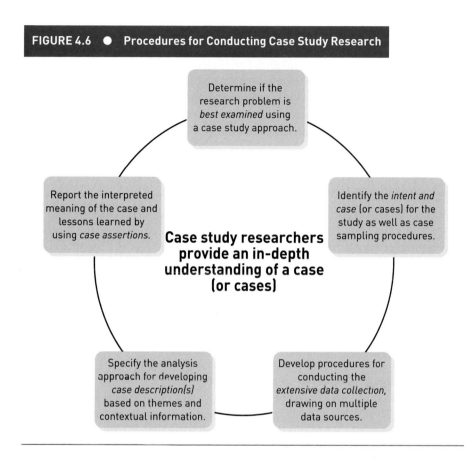

FIGURE 4.6 ● Procedures for Conducting Case Study Research

Determine if the research problem is *best examined* using a case study approach.

Identify the *intent and case* (or cases) for the study as well as case sampling procedures.

Case study researchers provide an in-depth understanding of a case (or cases)

Develop procedures for conducting the *extensive data collection*, drawing on multiple data sources.

Specify the analysis approach for developing *case description(s)* based on themes and contextual information.

Report the interpreted meaning of the case and lessons learned by using *case assertions*.

describes them as assertions. Stake (1995) focuses some of the assertions on lessons learned about the case stating, "Having presented a body of relatively uninterpreted observations, I will summarize what I feel I understand about the case and how my generalizations about he case have changed conceptually or in level of confidence" (Stake, 1995, p. 123).

• *Report the case study and lessons learned by using case assertions in written form.* Writing case descriptions involves a reflective process, and the sooner you begin, our experiences tell us, the easier it is to finish. Certainly the architecture for what works best for individual studies will emerge and be shaped differently by the study assertions. We adopt the advice forwarded by Stake (1995), "The report needs to be organized with readers in mind" (p. 122). A general reporting structure includes an entry vignette to provide the reader with an inviting introduction to the feel of the context in which the case takes place, an introduction to familiarize the reader with the central features including rationale and research procedures, an extensive narrative description of the case or cases and its or their context, which may include historical and organizational information important for understanding the case. Then the issue description draws from additional data sources and integrates with researcher's own interpretations of the issues and both confirming and disproving evidence are presented followed by the presentation of overall case assertions. Finally, a closing vignette provides the reader with a final experience. Stake (1995) portrays the purpose of the closing vignette as way of cautioning the reader to the specific case context saying, "I like to close on an experiential note, reminding the reader that the report is just one person's encounter with a complex case" (p. 123).

Challenges in Case Study Research

One of the challenges inherent in qualitative case study development is that the researcher must identify the case. The case selected may be broad in scope (e.g., the Boy Scout organization) or narrow in scope (e.g., a decision-making process at a specific college). The case study researcher must decide which bounded system to study, recognizing that several might be possible candidates for this selection and realizing that either the case itself or an issue, which a case or cases are selected to illustrate, is worthy of study. The researcher must consider whether to study a single case or multiple cases. As the use of multiple case studies increases, it is important to consider three issues: resource limitations, case selection, and cross-case analysis. First, it is not surprising given resource limitations (i.e., both time and financial) that the study of more than one case dilutes the overall analysis; the more cases an individual studies, the less the depth in any single case can be. Second, when a researcher chooses multiple cases, the issue becomes, "How many cases?" There is no one answer to this question. However, researchers typically choose no more than four or five cases. What motivates the researcher to consider a large number of cases is the idea of *generalizability,* a term that holds little meaning for most qualitative researchers (Glesne & Peshkin, 1992; Lincoln & Guba, 2000). Finally, "What guides the cross-case analysis?" In the analysis of single case studies we are guided by instrumental or intrinsic purposes; in multiple case studies, such explicit purpose identification upfront is not always made. Stake (2006) offers important guidance in this respect through the introduction of the term *quitain.* Stake (2006) describes the quitain as the "object or phenomenon to be studied" (p. 4) across the cases and argues the importance of its identification upfront to guide case selection.

Selecting the case requires that the researcher establish a rationale for his or her purposeful sampling strategy for selecting the case and for gathering information about the case. Having enough information to present an in-depth picture of the case limits the value of some case studies. In planning a case study, we have individuals develop a data collection matrix in which they specify the amount of information they are likely to collect about the case. Deciding the "boundaries" of a case—how it might be constrained in terms of time, events, and processes—may be challenging. Some case studies may not have clean beginning and ending points, and the researcher will need to set boundaries that adequately surround the case.

Among the concerns that have historically plagued case study research are focused on the rigor; certainly evidence of poor quality case study research exist, and it is with providing illustrative examples that we can continue to curtail such practices. Case study research has experienced growing recognition during the past 30 years, evidenced by its more frequent application in published research and increased availability of reference works (e.g., Thomas, 2015; Yin, 2014). Encouraging the use of case study research is an expressed goal of the editors of the recent *Encyclopedia of Case Study Research* (Mills, Durepos, & Wiebe, 2010). Engaging researchers are a focus of a number of publications aimed at guiding those new to the approach (e.g., Baxter & Jack, 2008; Flyvbjerg, 2006).

Comparing the Five Approaches

All five approaches have in common the general process of research that begins with a research problem and proceeds to the questions, the data, the data analysis and interpretations, and the research report. Qualitative researchers have found it helpful to see at this point an overall sketch for each of the five approaches. From these sketches of the five approaches, we can identify fundamental differences among these types of qualitative research. Finally, we compare the five approaches relating the dimensions of foundational considerations (Table 4.1), data procedures (Table 4.2), and research reporting (Table 4.3).

In Table 4.1, we present four dimensions for distinguishing among the foundational considerations for the five approaches. At a most fundamental level, the five differ in what they are trying to accomplish—their foci or the primary objectives of the studies. Exploring a life is different from generating a theory or describing the behavior of a cultural group. A couple of potential similarities among the designs should be noted. Narrative research, ethnography, and case study research may seem similar when the unit of analysis is a single individual. True, one may approach the study of a single individual from any of these three approaches; however, the types of data one would collect and analyze would differ considerably. In *narrative research*, the inquirer focuses on the stories told from the individual and arranges these stories often in chronological order; in *ethnography*, the focus is on setting the individuals' stories within the context of their culture and culture-sharing group; in *case study research*, the single case is typically selected to illustrate an issue, and the researcher compiles a detailed description of the setting for the case. Our approach is to recommend—if the researcher wants to study a single individual—the narrative approach or a single case study because ethnography is a much broader picture of the culture. Then when comparing a narrative study and a single case to study a single individual, we feel that the narrative approach is seen as more appropriate because narrative studies *tend* to focus on a single individual whereas case studies often involve more than one case. The process of developing research question(s) can often be helpful for determining the suitability of the research problem for a specific approach. Moreover, although overlaps exist in discipline origin, some approaches have single-disciplinary traditions (e.g., grounded theory originating in sociology, ethnography founded in anthropology or sociology), and others have broad interdisciplinary backgrounds (e.g., narrative, case study).

TABLE 4.1 ● Contrasting Foundational Considerations of Five Qualitative Approaches

Foundational Considerations	Narrative Research	Phenomenology	Grounded Theory	Ethnography	Case Study
Research focus of approach	Exploring the life of an individual	Understanding the essence of the experience	Developing a theory grounded in data from the field	Describing and interpreting a culture-sharing group	Developing an in-depth description and analysis of a case or multiple cases
Unit of analysis	Studying one or more individuals	Studying several individuals who have shared the experience	Studying a process, an action, or an interaction involving many individuals	Studying a group that shares the same culture	Studying an event, a program, an activity, or more than one individual
Type of research problem best suited for approach	Needing to tell stories of individual experiences	Needing to describe the essence of a lived phenomenon	Grounding a theory in the views of participants	Describing and interpreting the shared patterns of culture of a group	Providing an in-depth understanding of a case or cases
Nature of disciplinary origins	Drawing from the humanities including anthropology, literature, history, psychology, and sociology	Drawing from philosophy, psychology, and education	Drawing from sociology	Drawing from anthropology and sociology	Drawing from psychology, law, political science, and medicine

The approaches employ similar data collection processes, including, in varying degrees, interviews, observations, documents, and audiovisual materials (see Table 4.2). The differences are apparent in terms of emphasis (e.g., more observations in ethnography, more interviews in grounded theory) and extent of data collection (e.g., only interviews in phenomenology, multiple forms in case study research to provide the in-depth case picture). At the data analysis stage, the differences are most pronounced. Not only is the distinction one of specificity of the analysis phase (e.g., grounded theory most specific, narrative research less defined) but the number of steps to be undertaken can vary (e.g., extensive steps in phenomenology, fewer steps in ethnography).

The research reporting of each approach, the written report, takes shape from all the processes before it (see Table 4.3). Stories about an individual's life comprise

TABLE 4.2 ● Contrasting Data Procedures of the Five Qualitative Approaches					
Data Procedures	**Narrative Research**	**Phenomenology**	**Grounded Theory**	**Ethnography**	**Case Study**
Forms of data collection	Using primarily interviews and documents	Using primarily interviews with individuals, although documents, observations, and art may also be considered	Using primarily interviews with 20 to 60 individuals	Using primarily observations and interviews but perhaps collecting other sources during extended time in field	Using multiple sources, such as interviews, observations, documents, and artifacts
Strategies of data analysis	Analyzing data for stories, "restorying" stories, and developing themes, often using a chronology	Analyzing data for significant statements, meaning units, textual and structural description, and description of the "essence"	Analyzing data through open coding, axial coding, and selective coding	Analyzing data through description of the culture-sharing group and themes about the group	Analyzing data through description of the case and themes of the case as well as cross-case themes

narrative research. A description of the essence of the experience of the phenomenon becomes a phenomenology. A theory, often portrayed in a visual model, emerges in grounded theory, and a holistic view of how a culture-sharing group works results in an ethnography. An in-depth study of a bounded system or a case (or several cases) becomes a case study. The general structures of the written report may be used in designing a journal-article-length study. However, because of the numerous steps in each, they also have applicability as chapters of a dissertation or a book-length work. We discuss the differences here because the reader, with an introductory knowledge of each approach, now can sketch the general "architecture" of a study within each approach. Certainly, this architecture will emerge and be shaped differently by the conclusion of the study, but it provides a framework for the design issues to follow. For each approach, the introduction describes the particular focus of the research and common across the approaches, the introduction tends to familiarize the reader to the research problem and research question(s). The research procedures are subsequently outlined, often including a rationale for use of the approach and details related to the data procedures for the study.

Note the unique organizing framework related to each approach and specifically the variations in how the research outcomes can be presented. Providing in-depth

TABLE 4.3 ● Contrasting Research Reporting of Five Qualitative Approaches					
Research Reporting	Narrative Research	Phenomenology	Grounded Theory	Ethnography	Case Study
Introduction of written report	Focusing on participant(s) and nature of the story	Focusing on explaining the phenomenon	Focusing on the process (or action) that the theory is intended to explain	Focusing on the culture-sharing group being studied	Using entry vignette and then focusing on central features of the case
Description of research procedures	Stating the rationale, significance of individual to experiences, and data procedures	Stating the rationale, philosophical assumptions, and data procedures	Stating the rationale and data procedures	Stating the rationale, type, and data procedures	Stating the rationale, type, and data procedures
Organization of research outcomes	Telling stories using a variety of ways involving restorying, theorizing, and narrative segments	Reporting how the phenomenon was experienced using significant statements and discussing meaning of themes	Developing theory involving open coding categories, axial coding, selective coding, theoretical propositions, and a model	Describing the culture and analyzing patterns of cultural themes with verbatim quotes	Providing first extensive description of the case followed by key issues (themes or issues) in the case
Concluding format	Interpreting patterns of meaning	Describing the "essence" of the experience	Advancing a theory and	Describing how a culture-sharing group works using a cultural portrait	Making case study assertions and advancing a closing vignette

descriptions is common across all the approaches, but how the descriptions are organized varies; whereas narrative research might use a chronology for telling stories, a phenomenology may use significant statements as the organizing structure for reporting how the phenomenon was experienced. Similarly, how a research report concludes also varies by the approach; whereas it is common practice for a closing vignette in a case study, a cultural portrait is commonly used in an ethnography referring to overall interpretations, lessons learned, and questions raised representing the essence. These structures should be considered as general templates at this time. In Chapter 5, we will examine five published journal articles, with each study illustrating one of the five approaches, and further explore the writing structure of each.

Chapter Check-In

1. What research problems are appropriate for each of the approaches?

   • List three different research problems that are of interest to you. Begin with identifying the research foci, and identify which approaches might be appropriate. Draft a research question that would be appropriate for each possible approach related to the research problem. Can you identify the subtle differences among the research questions?

2. What defining features can you identity in each of the five approaches within a qualitative journal article?

   • Examine a qualitative journal article that identifies its use of one of the five approaches, such as Huber and Whelan (1999) as a narrative study; Doyle, Pooley, and Breen (2012) as a phenomenology; Leipert and Reutter (2005) as a grounded theory; Miller, Creswell, and Olander (1998) as an ethnography; or Chirgwin (2015) as a multiple case study. Using the elements of "defining features" advanced in this chapter, review the article and locate where each defining feature of the particular approach appears in the article. Can you identify the absence of any defining features or the presence of any new defining features for any of the approaches?

   Chirgwin, S. K. (2015). Burdens too difficult to carry? A case study of three academically able Indigenous Australian Masters students who had to withdraw. *International Journal of Qualitative Studies in Education, 28*, 594–609. doi:10.1080/09518398.2014.916014

   Doyle, J., Pooley, J. A., & Breen, L. (2012). A phenomenological exploration of the childfree choice in a sample of Australian women. *Journal of Health Psychology, 18*, 397–407. doi:10.1177/1359105312444647

   Huber, J., & Whelan, K. (1999). A marginal story as a place of possibility: Negotiating self on the professional knowledge landscape. *Teaching and Teacher Education, 15*, 381–396. doi:10.1016/S0742-051X(98)00048-1

   Leipert, B. D., & Reutter, L. (2005). Developing resilience: How women maintain their health in northern geographically isolated settings. *Qualitative Health Research, 15*, 49–65. doi:10.1177/1049732304269671

   Miller, D. L., Creswell, J. W., & Olander, L. S. (1998). Writing and retelling multiple ethnographic tales of a soup kitchen for the homeless. *Qualitative Inquiry, 4*(4), 469–491. doi:10.1177/107780049800400404

3. What resources of one of the five approaches can you use to begin creating your study proposal?

   • Select one of the five approaches, and write a brief description of the approach, including a definition and the procedures associated with the approach. Include at least five references to the literature to ground your proposal. Can you include at least two new references?

4. Do you understand how to transform the study focus, procedures, and writing structure into each of the five approaches?

(Continued)

(Continued)

- Access a proposed qualitative study that you would like to conduct. Begin with presenting it as a narrative study, and then shape it into a phenomenology, a grounded theory, an ethnography, and finally a case study. Compare differences across each approach related to the focus of the study and the data collection and analysis procedures. Can you discuss how the written report would be differently structured across the approaches?

Summary

In this chapter, we introduced each of the five approaches to qualitative research—narrative studies, phenomenology, grounded theory, ethnography, and case study. In each description we provided a focus and definition, some history of the development of the approach, defining features, and the major forms it has assumed as well as detailed the major procedures for conducting each approach. Finally, we discussed some of the major challenges in conducting each approach, emerging directions, and key resources. To highlight some of the differences among the approaches, we provided overview tables that contrast dimensions related to foundational dimensions of foundational considerations (research focus, unit of analysis, type of research problem, nature of disciplinary origins), data procedures (forms of data collection and strategies of data analysis), and research reporting (research outcomes and structure of written report). In the next chapter, we will examine five studies that illustrate each approach and look more closely at the compositional structure of each type of approach.

Further Readings

Several readings extend this brief overview of each of the five approaches of inquiry. In Chapter 1, we presented the key books that were used to craft discussions about each approach. Here we expand this list for each of the qualitative approaches in the chapter. The list should not be considered exhaustive, and readers are encouraged to seek out additional readings in the end-of-book reference list.

Narrative Research

Clandinin, D. J., & Connelly, F. M. (2000). *Narrative inquiry: Experience and story in qualitative research.* San Francisco, CA: Jossey-Bass.

Jean Clandinin and Michael Connelly weave helpful references throughout the text, describing their own journey of becoming narrative researchers. Of particular help to the beginning narrative researcher is the final chapter on persistent concerns and the comprehensive discussion of ethics within narrative inquiry.

Czarniawska, B. (2004). *Narratives in social science research*. Thousand Oaks, CA: Sage.

Barbara Czarniawska explores the various uses of narrative and its analysis in this important resource. Especially helpful is the use of her own research examples to illustrate concepts from conceptualization to telling of the stories.

Daiute, C. (2014). *Narrative inquiry: A dynamic approach*. Thousand Oaks, CA: Sage.

Colette Daiute provides essential scaffolding for undertaking what she calls dynamic narrative inquiry using examples, activities, and tips. Of particular note is how she builds on practices of daily life and makes connections to narrative research.

Phenomenological Research

Giorgi, A. (2009). *A descriptive phenomenological method in psychology: A modified Husserlian approach*. Pittsburgh, PA: Duquesne University Press.

Amedeo Giorgi uses illustrative research examples to offer practical steps for applying the descriptive phenomenological method. This is essential reading for those working in the psychology field.

Stewart, D., & Mickunas, A. (1990). *Exploring phenomenology: A guide to the field and its literature* (2nd ed.). Athens: Ohio University Press.

In this important work, David Stewart and Algis Mickunas provide an essential introduction to Husserl, Heidegger, and the various strands of phenomenology through the first half of the 20th century. Particularly helpful is the discussion about traditional challenges inherent to phenomenology.

Van Manen, M. (1990). *Researching lived experience: Human science for an action sensitive pedagogy*. Albany: State University of New York Press.

Max Van Manen describes the phenomenological tradition as well as presents methods and processes for engaging in phenomenological research. Among the key contributions is Chapter 5 focused on writing phenomenology.

Grounded Theory Research

Birks, M., & Mills, J. (2015). *Grounded theory: A practical guide* (2nd ed.). Thousand Oaks, CA: Sage.

Melanie Birks and Jane Mills use of figures and pedagogical features throughout helps the reader to make sense of the text. In particular, the critical thinking questions guide the reader in self-assessment of the material and the "window into grounded theory" feature provides important insights.

Bryant, A., & Charmaz, K. (Eds.). (2007). *The SAGE handbook of grounded theory*. Thousand Oaks, CA: Sage.

(Continued)

(Continued)

Handbooks are often a logical starting place for researchers new to an approach, and Alan Bryant and Kathy Charmaz provide useful guiding practices for conducting grounded theory. Specifically, we found the chapters on historical development by the editors and memo-writing by Lora Lempert to be noteworthy.

Clarke, A. E. (2005). *Situational analysis: Grounded theory after the postmodern turn*. Thousand Oaks, CA: Sage.

Adele Clarke represents her thinking using illustrative maps to enhance visibility of complexity. A unique aspect is her conceptualization of a situation as including the missing data (e.g., environmental factors) in addition to what has typically been considered as context.

Ethnographic Research

Atkinson, P. (2015). *For ethnography*. Thousand Oaks, CA: Sage.

At the heart of Paul Atkinson's book is the use of field research in ethnographic studies. He provides easy-to-follow guiding principles for engaging in ethnographic fieldwork.

Madison, D. S. (2011). *Critical ethnography: Method, ethics, and performance* (2nd ed). Thousand Oaks, CA: Sage.

D. Soyini Madison provides important insights about the role of theory in planning processes in a critical ethnography through the use of three case studies.

Wolcott, H. F. (2010). *Ethnography lessons: A primer.* Walnut Creek, CA: Left Coast Press.

Harry Wolcott presents challenges and successes through his five-decade ethnographic career sprinkled with personal interactions with notable anthropologists. An important contribution is the ethical dilemmas experienced by himself and his students and lessons relevant for all qualitative researchers.

Case Study Research

Gomm, R., Hammersley, M., & Foster, P. (2000). *Case study method*. Thousand Oaks, CA: Sage.

Robert Gomm, Martyn Hammersley, and Peter Foster have brought together authors to discuss practices and challenges in cases study research. Specifically, we found the chapters on generalizability by the Yvonna Lincoln and Egon Guba and case comparison by Stanley Lieberson to be noteworthy.

Stake, R. E. (2006). *Multiple case study analysis*. New York, NY: Guilford Press.

This book offers a rare focus on multiple case studies, yet Robert Stake also includes a chapter on single cases. The book leads the reader through conducting an example of a multiple case study (and provides worksheets)—the multinational Step by Step Case Study Project.

Thomas, G. (2015). *How to do your case study* (2nd ed.). Thousand Oaks, CA: Sage.

Gary Thomas provides an easy-to-follow guide on how to read, design, and conduct case study research. Of particular note is his use of examples to illustrate how to focus the purpose of a case study.

Five Different
Qualitative Studies

We have always felt that the best way to learn how to write a qualitative study is to view a number of published qualitative journal articles and to look closely at the way they were composed. If an individual plans on undertaking, for example, a grounded theory study, we would suggest that he or she collect about 20 grounded theory published journal articles, study each one carefully, select the most complete one that advances *all* of the defining characteristics of grounded theory, and then model his or her own project after that one. This same process would hold true for an individual conducting any of the other approaches to qualitative inquiry, such as a narrative study, a phenomenology, an ethnography, or a case study. Short of this ideal, we want to get you started toward building this collection by suggesting an exemplar of each approach as discussed in this chapter.

Each of these five published studies represents one of the types of qualitative approaches being discussed in this book. They are found in Appendices B, C, D, E, and F. The best way to proceed, we believe, is to first read the entire article in the appendix and then return to our summary of the article to compare your understanding with ours. Next, read our analysis of how the article illustrates a good model of the approach to research and incorporates the defining characteristics we introduced in Chapter 4. At the conclusion of this chapter, we reflect on why one might choose one approach over another when conducting a qualitative study and we include further examples for you to read in the end of chapter check in.

The first study, by Chan (2010), as found in Appendix B, illustrates a good narrative study of a single Chinese immigrant student, Ai Mei Zhang, as she participates in a Canadian middle school and as she interacts with her family. The second article, a phenomenological study by Anderson and Spencer (2002), located in Appendix C, is a study about individuals who have experienced AIDS and the images and ways they think about their disease. The third article is a grounded theory study by Harley et al. (2009) as found in Appendix D. It presents a study of the behavioral process among African American women to integrate physical activity into their lifestyle. It incorporates, appropriately, a theoretical framework that explains the pathways linking these key factors in the process together. The fourth article is an ethnographic study by Mac an Ghaill and Haywood (2015), as presented in Appendix E, about the changing cultural condition of British born, working-class Pakistani and Bangladeshi young Muslim men during the late 2000s. The identity formulation of the young Muslim men as members of a broader social community was influenced by the local experiences of growing up in a rapidly changing Britain. The final article is a qualitative case study by Frelin (2015), as shown in Appendix F. It describes and suggests three themes (e.g., trusting relationships, human relationships, and the students' self-images) related to the relational practices of a teacher who negotiates educational relationships with students who have a history of school failure. These exemplars were chosen for their usefulness as a model of the defining features for each approach discussed in Chapter 4 as well as for their disciplinary, geographical, and participant diversity.

Questions for Discussion

- What stories are told in the sample narrative study?
- What experience is examined in the sample phenomenological study?
- What theory emerges in the grounded theory study?
- What culture-sharing group is studied in the sample ethnographic study?
- What is the case being examined in the case study?
- How do the central features of the five approaches differ?
- How does a researcher choose among the five approaches for a particular study?

A Narrative Study (Chan, 2010; see Appendix B)

Chan, E. (2010). Living in the space between participant and researcher as a narrative inquirer: Examining ethnic identity of Chinese Canadian students as conflicting stories to live by. *The Journal of Educational Research*, *103*, 113–122. doi:10.1080/00220670903323792

This is the story of a Chinese immigrant student, Ai Mei Zhang, a seventh- and eighth-grade student at Bay Street School in Toronto, Canada. Ai Mei was chosen for study by the researcher because she could inform how ethnic identity is shaped by expectations from school and her teacher, her peers at school, and her home. Ai Mei told stories about specific incidents in her life, and the author based her narrative article on these stories as well as observations in her classroom. The researcher also conducted interviews with Ai Mei and other students, took extensive field notes, and sought active participation in Ai Mei's school activities (e.g., Multicultural Night), a family dinner, and classroom conversations between Ai Mei and her classmates. The author's overriding interest was in exploring the conflicting stories that emerged during this data collection.

The author introduced the study citing changing school demographics and the need for greater understanding of the lived experiences of immigrant and minority students' daily transitions between home and school. The author identified Dewey's (1938) philosophy of the interconnectedness between experience and education as the theoretical foundation for the study of a three-dimensional narrative inquiry space (Clandinin & Connelly, 2000). In this study, the author followed procedures by Clandinin and colleagues (2006) for describing the interwoven lives of children and teachers.

From a thematic analysis of these data, the author presented several conflicting stories: tensions in friendship because Ai Mei hid her home language at school because it was seen as a hindrance to accepted English, pressure to use the school Chinese language and to use her maternal language at home with her family, multiple conflicting influences of parental expectations for behavior and expectations from peers at school, and conflicts between family needs to help in the family business and teacher expectations to complete homework and prepare for tests and assignments. As a final element of the findings, the author reflected on her experiences in conducting the study, such as how the different events she participated in shaped her understanding, how opportunities arose to build trust, how her relationship with Ai Mei was negotiated, and how she developed a sense of advocacy for this young student. In the end, the study contributed to understanding the challenges of immigrant or minority students; the intersecting expectations of students, teachers, peers, and parents; and how the values of individuals in ethnic communities are shaped by these interactions. In a larger sense, this study informed the work of teachers and administrators working with diverse student populations, and serves as an example of a "life-based literary narrative" (Chan, 2010, p. 121).

This article presents well the defining features of a narrative study as introduced in Chapter 4 (Clandinin, 2013; Riessman, 2008):

- The researcher collected stories from a single individual, a Chinese immigrant student, Ai Mei Zhang.
- The researcher made explicit the collaborative nature of how the stories were collected and the relationship that built over time between the researcher and the participant in the study.
- The researcher chose to focus on the experiences of this one individual and, more specifically, on the cultural identity of this student and how parents, peers, and teachers helped to shape this identity.
- The researcher discussed the place or the physical and social context of Bay Street School where most of the incidents occurred that were reported in the narrative.
- The researcher established an evidence base of information to explore this cultural identity through different forms of data such as personal observations, interviews, field notes, and attendance at events.
- The researcher used a thematic analysis of reporting "what happened" to this individual student, her parents, and her school.
- The researcher collected data over time from the fall of 2001 to June 2003, so there was ample opportunity to examine the unfolding events over time. The narrative, however, was not constructed to report a chronology of themes, and, in reading this account, it is difficult to determine whether one theme (e.g., hiding language in the new student orientation) occurred before or after another theme (e.g., mealtime conversation involving the school Mandarin language and the home Fujianese language).
- The researcher highlighted specific tensions that arose in each of the themes (e.g., the tension between using Mandarin and Fujianese at home). The overall narrative, however, did not convey a specific turning point or epiphany in the story line.

A Phenomenological Study (Anderson & Spencer, 2002; see Appendix C)

Anderson, E. H., & Spencer, M. H. (2002). Cognitive representations of AIDS: A phenomenological study. *Qualitative Health Research, 12*, 1338–1352. doi:10.1177/1049732302238747

This study discusses the images or cognitive representations that AIDS patients held about their disease. The researchers explored this topic because understanding how individuals represented AIDS and their emotional response to it influenced their therapy, reduced high-risk behaviors, and enhanced their quality of life. Thus, the purpose of this study was "to explore patients' experience and cognitive representations of AIDS within the context of phenomenology" (Anderson & Spencer, 2002, p. 1339).

The authors introduced the study by referring to the millions of individuals infected with HIV. They advanced a framework, the Self-Regulation Model of Illness Representations, which suggested that patients were active problem solvers whose behavior was a product of their cognitive and emotional responses to a health threat. Patients formed illness representations that shaped their understanding of their diseases. It was these illness representations (e.g., images) that the researchers needed to understand more thoroughly to help patients with their therapy, behaviors, and quality of life. The authors turned to the literature on patients' experiences with AIDS. They reviewed the literature on qualitative research, noting that several phenomenological studies on such topics as coping and living with HIV had already been examined. However, how patients represented AIDS in images had not been studied.

Their design involved the study of 58 men and women with a diagnosis of AIDS. To study these individuals, the authors used phenomenology and the procedures advanced by Colaizzi (1978), which were later modified by Moustakas (1994). For over 18 months, they conducted interviews with these 58 patients and asked them the following: "What is your experience with AIDS? Do you have a mental image of HIV/AIDS, or how would you describe HIV/AIDS? What feeling comes to mind? What meaning does it have in your life?" (Anderson & Spencer, 2002, pp. 1341–1342). They also asked patients to draw pictures of their disease. Although only 8 of the 58 drew pictures, the authors integrated these pictures into the data analysis. The phenomenological components of this data analysis included the following:

- Reading through the written transcripts several times to obtain an overall feeling for them
- Identifying significant phrases or sentences that pertained directly to the experience
- Formulating meanings and clustering them into themes common to all of the participants' transcripts
- Integrating the results into an in-depth, exhaustive description of the phenomenon
- Validating the findings with the participants, and including participants' remarks in the final description

This analysis led to 11 major themes based on 175 significant statements. "Dreaded bodily destruction" and "devouring life" illustrated two of the themes. The results section of this study reported each of the 11 themes and provided ample quotes and perspectives to illustrate the multiple perspectives on each theme.

The study ended with a discussion in which the authors described the essence (i.e., the exhaustive description) of the patients' experiences and the coping strategies (i.e., the contexts or conditions surrounding the experience) patients used to regulate mood and disease. Finally, the authors compared their 11 themes with results reported by other authors in the literature, and they discussed the implications for nursing and questions for future research.

This study illustrated several aspects of a phenomenological study mentioned earlier in Chapter 4 by Moustakas (1994) and van Manen (1990, 2014):

- A phenomenon—the "cognitive representations or images" of AIDS by patients—was examined in the study.
- Rigorous data collection with a group of individuals through 58 interviews and incorporation of patients' drawings were used.
- The authors only briefly mentioned the philosophical ideas behind phenomenology. They referred to bracketing their personal experiences and their need to explore lived experiences rather than to obtain theoretical explanations.
- The researchers talked about bracketing in the study. Specifically, they stated that the interviewer was a health care provider for and a researcher of persons with HIV/AIDS; thus, it was necessary for the interviewer to acknowledge and attempt to bracket those experiences.
- The data collection consisted of 58 interviews conducted over 18 months at three sites dedicated to persons with HIV/AIDS, a hospital-based clinic, a long-term care facility, and a residence.
- The use of systematic data analysis procedures of significant statements, meanings, themes, and a description of the essence of the phenomenon followed the procedures recommended by Moustakas (1994). The inclusion of tables illustrating the significant statements, meanings, and theme clusters showed how the authors worked from the raw data to the exhaustive description of the essence of the study in the final discussion section.
- The study ended by describing the essence of the experience for the 58 patients and the context in which they experienced AIDS (e.g., coping mechanisms).

A Grounded Theory Study (Harley et al., 2009; see Appendix D)

Harley, A. E., Buckworth, J., Katz, M. L., Willis, S. K., Odoms-Young, A., & Heaney, C. A. (2009). Developing long-term physical activity participation: A grounded theory study with African American women. *Health Education & Behavior, 36*(1), 97–112. doi:10.1177/1090198107306434

This grounded theory study sought to develop a theory of the behavioral process of African American women that explains the pathways linking key factors together in the integration of physical activity into their lifestyles. It was premised on the problem that physical activity is of concern for particular subgroups, such as African American women who remain particularly sedentary. To this end, the researchers chose grounded theory because of the lack of knowledge regarding the specific factors and relationships that compose the process of physical activity behavioral evolution. The authors studied 15 women who met the criterion sampling of being between 25 and 45 years of age, completing at least some college or technical school beyond high school, and holding a commitment to physical activity. Participants were recruited through two local African American sorority alumni associations, and initial data were collected through face-to-face in-depth interviews guided by Spradley (1979). The data collection and preliminary analysis procedures can be considered as undertaken simultaneously as the researchers refined the interview questions that "were not eliciting the intended information and to reflect the categories and concepts that required further development" (p. 100). The purpose for the follow-up focus groups was to disseminate preliminary findings and gather feedback to inform refinement of the framework.

The data were analyzed using the Strauss and Corbin (1998) approach to grounded theory consisting of coding, concept development, constant comparisons between the data and the emerging concepts, and the formulation of a theoretical model. The authors then presented the theoretical model as a figure, and this model consisted of three phases in the behavioral process of integrating physical activity into lifestyle: an initiation phase, a transition phase, and an integration phase. The researchers advanced categories within each of these phases and also specified the context (i.e., African American social and cultural contexts) and the conditions influencing the physical activity integration. The authors then took one of the conditions, the planning practices for physical activity, and elaborated on these possibilities in a figure of the taxonomy of planning methods. This elaboration enabled the researchers to draw specific results for practice, such as the ideal number of physical activity sessions per week, and the maximum number of sessions per week. In conclusion, this grounded theory study advanced important lessons for future efforts at program design for physical activity for African American women.

This study met many of the defining features of a grounded theory study as discussed earlier in Chapter 4 by Charmaz (2014) and Corbin and Strauss (2015):

- Its central focus was to understand a behavior process, and the theoretical model advanced three major phases in this process.
- A theory emerged to suggest the framework of physical activity evolution for the African American women in the study.
- The researchers did not specifically mention memoing or writing down their ideas as they interviewed the women and analyzed the data.
- Their form of data collection and analysis was consistent with many grounded theory studies: the simultaneous collection and analysis of face-to-face interview data was followed by focus groups for validation and refinement purposes.
- The researchers engaged in a structured approach to grounded theory of coding categories and developing a theoretical model that included context and conditions and used qualitative software. The authors mentioned few details of analytical and integration strategies informing the framework development (e.g., of open, axial, and selective coding and memoing).
- The researchers provided a detailed description of the phases of the theoretical model and compared their model with existing theoretical models in the literature.

An Ethnographic Study (Mac an Ghaill & Haywood, 2015; see Appendix E)

Mac an Ghaill, M., & Haywood, C. (2015). British-born Pakistani and Bangladeshi young men: Exploring unstable concepts of Muslim, Islamophobia and racialization. *Critical Sociology*, *41*, 97–114. doi:10.1177/0896920513518947

This ethnography study described the changing cultural conditions of a group of British born, working-class Pakistani and Bangladeshi young men over 3 years. The study involved Birmingham, England–born young men residing in an area representing the highest number of self-identified Muslims for a local authority in the United Kingdom. The authors focused on the group's cultural reductive representations of Islam, the Muslim community and being a young Muslim man within the "urgent need to critically interrogate the assumed social separateness, cultural fixity and boundedness of religious, ethnic and national categories of difference that they [the group under study] claim are imputed to them" (p. 98). The participants were young men who were not only friends but also part of a broader social community described as attending the same youth and community organizations and colleges, sharing the same employers, and participating together in leisure activities. The study explored the group of 25 young men's "geographically-specific local experiences of growing up in a rapidly changing Britain" (p. 99). The researchers described how access to the group was enabled by an established reputation for social commitment to the area and by previous work with families in the local community.

Ethnographic data collection methods provided insights into the young men's growing up, family, schooling, social life, and local community through the use of in-depth group and life history interviews over a 3-year period. Further understandings were gleaned from observations, informal conversations, and interviews with parents and community representatives through snowballing sampling. Braun and Clarke's (2006) thematic analysis guided the data analysis of each of the methods. From the integration of data sources, the authors described group members' generational-specific experiences in relation to the racialization of their ethnicities and changes in terms of how they negotiated the meanings attached to being Muslim. The authors ended with a broad level of abstraction beyond the themes to suggest how the group made sense of the range of social and cultural exclusions they experienced during a time of rapid change within their city. In short, the authors identified a complex situation related to the group of Bangladeshi and Pakistani young men in terms of how they interacted and experienced ethnicity and demarcation of religion and cultural belonging. The authors cautioned readers to carefully consider ways to understand the young men's own participation and the influence of local contexts and broader social and economic processes in identity formation.

Mac an Ghaill and Haywood's ethnography nicely illustrates both core elements of an ethnographic study as mentioned in Chapter 4 (Fetterman, 2010; Wolcott, 2010) and aspects of a critical ethnography (Madison, 2011) as they call for further studies of marginalized groups (e.g., Goffman, 2014):

- This ethnography was the study of a culture-sharing group and its members' changing cultural condition as British-born, working-class Pakistani and Bangladeshi young men. This group had been intact for some time as a community.
- The authors described the group in terms of its 25 members' ideas of their generational-specific experiences. By looking for patterns in this group, the study provided an alternative representational space for critically exploring "debates about the racialization of religion, the central role that religion plays in the process of racialization, and Islamophobia as a contemporary form of the racialization of Muslims" (p. 110).
- Consistent with critical ethnography, the author used a combination of materialist and postcolonial theoretical frameworks and young men's accounts to explain the groups' changing cultural condition.
- The authors positioned themselves by describing their involvement in the broader social community and their role as participant observers of the group for 3 years. The author also engaged in fieldwork by conducting in-depth group and life history interviews with the young men. Further understandings were gleaned from observations, informal conversations, and interviews with parents and community representatives from snowball sampling.
- From the participant (emic) data and the researcher's field notes (etic data), a cultural interpretation was formed into thematic analysis. The group was described first in relation to the racialization of their ethnicities and changes in terms of how they negotiated the meanings attached to being Muslim. The description concluded with a broad level of abstraction beyond the themes to suggest how the group made sense of the range of social and cultural exclusions they experienced during a time of rapid change within their city.
- Unlike other critical approaches, the study did not end with a call for social transformation. Instead, it called for further efforts to validate the findings such as member checking with group members. This is because the cultural interpretation constructed by the group members was primarily intended for themselves. We leave this study with a complex view of how the group of Bangladeshi and Pakistani young men interacted and experienced ethnicity, religion, and cultural belonging as dynamic.

A Case Study (Frelin, 2015; see Appendix F)

Frelin, A. (2015). Relational underpinnings and professionality—A case study of a teacher's practices involving students with experiences of school failure. *School Psychology International, 36*, 589–604. doi:10.1177/0143034315607412

This qualitative case study described the practices of a teacher who negotiates educational relationships with students who have a history of school failure. The author provided a rationale for the use of a case study to "illustrate the complexities of building and sustaining educational relationships with upper secondary students who have experienced school failure" (p. 590). The author situated the need for the study within literature related to relational professionality and, more specifically, the influence of positive teacher–student relationships and challenges associated for students experiencing school failure. The case study procedures were guided by Stake (1995) and began with a detailed description of the relatively unstructured interviews and contextual observation of 11 teachers, preliminary data analysis and selection of "Gunilla," a secondary schoolteacher working in the Swedish "Introduction Programme." She was identified using purposeful sampling because of her ability to form positive relationships with students as well as having extensive teaching experiences of students who have not been accepted in the national upper secondary school program. The author described how the interviews were "focused on eliciting stories of practice and practical arguments whereas the observations served to highlight the context in which the teacher worked and to elicit new questions" (p. 593). The data analysis was guided by means of a cross-case analysis and constant comparisons (Charmaz, 2006); the qualitative software program, ATLAS.ti, aided the analysis.

Following a description of the teacher's context for instruction, the results from the data analysis described Gunilla's negotiations of relationships with students organized into three themes: trusting relationships, humane relationships, and the students' own self-images. The case assertion related to the importance of connecting to students with experiences of school failure and the study conclusions advanced practical implications for school psychologists to support teachers in negotiating these student–teacher relationships.

This study met many of the defining features of a case study as discussed earlier in Chapter 4 by Stake (1995), Yin (2014), and Flyvbjerg (2006):

- The case issue for the study was identified as one teachers' practices of negotiating relationships with students who have a history of school failure.
- The case described in this study was a bounded system, delimited by the participant (Gunilla), by time (limited to data collection), and by place (situated at an institution offering the Swedish Introduction Programme).
- The intent was to report an instrumental case study. Thus, the focus was on exploring the issue of relational practices of a teacher to illustrate the complexity of negotiating educational relationships with students who have a history of school failure.
- The data collection involved the use of interviews and observations to provide a detailed in-depth understanding of teacher practices. This is one area where the author could have drawn on more extensive, multiple sources of information.
- Few details were provided about the data analysis other than it was guided by a constant comparison method (Charmaz, 2006).
- The case context description reflected considerable effort as well as the presentation of the three themes. The authors presented some evidence of a chronology

(i.e., establishing and then sustaining) to describe the negotiations of relationships with students.

- The study concluded with the presentation of a cross-case assertion about the importance of connecting to students with experiences of school failure and advanced practical implications for school psychologists to support teachers in negotiating these student–teacher relationships. However, since this study presented a single case (Gunilla, the teacher) rather than multiple cases, an actual cross-case analysis of several teachers was not presented by the author.

Differences Among the Approaches

A useful perspective to begin the process of differentiating among the five approaches is to assess the central purpose or focus of each approach. As shown in Figure 5.1, the focus of a narrative is on the life of an individual, and the focus of a phenomenology is on a concept or phenomenon and the essence of the lived experiences of persons about that phenomenon. In grounded theory, the aim is to develop a theory, whereas in ethnography, it is to describe a culture-sharing group. In a case study, a specific case is examined, often with the intent of examining an issue with the case illustrating the complexity of the issue. Turning to the five studies, the foci of the approaches to qualitative research become more evident.

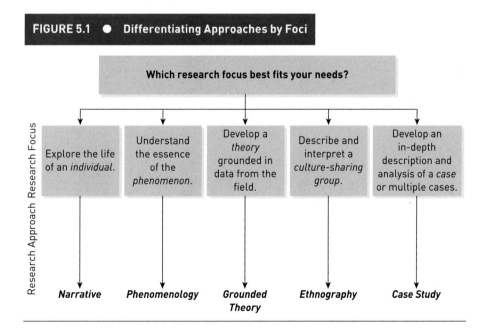

FIGURE 5.1 ● Differentiating Approaches by Foci

Central Features of Each Approach

The story of Ai Mei Zhang, the Chinese immigrant student in a Canadian middle school, is a case in point—one decides to write a narrative when a single individual needs to be studied as the research focus, and that individual can illustrate with experiences the issue of being an immigrant student and the conflicting concerns that she faced (Chan, 2010). Furthermore, the researcher needs to make a case for the need to study this particular individual—someone who illustrates a problem, someone who has had a distinguished career, someone in the national spotlight, or someone who lives an ordinary life (Clandinin, 2013). The process of data collection and analysis involves gathering material about the person, such as from conversations or observations to stories of individual experiences.

The phenomenological study, on the other hand, focuses not on the life of an individual but rather on understanding the lived experiences of individuals around a phenomenon, such as how individuals represent their illnesses (Anderson & Spencer, 2002). Furthermore, individuals are selected who have experienced the phenomenon, and they are asked to provide data, often through interviews (van Manen, 2014). The researcher takes these data and, through several steps of reducing the data, ultimately develops a description of the experiences about the phenomenon that all individuals have in common—the essence of the lived experience.

Whereas the phenomenological project focuses on the meaning of people's experience toward a phenomenon, researchers in grounded theory have a different objective—to generate a substantive theory, such as the theory about how African American women integrate physical activity into their lifestyles (Harley et al., 2009). Thus, grounded theorists undertake research to develop theory about a process or action. The data collection method involves primarily interviewing and the collecting and analyzing processes are considered to be undertaken simultaneously and iteratively. Researchers use systematic procedures for analyzing and developing this theory, procedures such as generating categories of data, relating the categories in a theoretical model, and specifying the context and conditions under which the theory operated (Corbin & Strauss, 2015). The theory is then presented as a discussion or model generating an overall tone of a grounded theory study as one of rigor and scientific credibility.

An ethnographic design is chosen when one wants to study the behaviors of a culture-sharing group, such as the British-born, working-class Pakistani and Bangladeshi young Muslim men (Mac an Ghaill & Haywood, 2015). In an ethnography, the researcher studies an intact culture-sharing group that has been interacting long enough to have shared or regular patterns of language and behavior (Fetterman, 2010). A detailed description of the culture-sharing group is essential at the beginning, and then the author may turn to identifying patterns of the group around some cultural concept such as acculturation, politics, or economy and the like. The ethnography ends with summary statements about how the group functions and works in everyday life. In this way, a reader understands a group that may be unfamiliar, such as the young Muslim men that Mac an Ghaill and Haywood (2015) studied.

Finally, a case study is chosen to study a case with clear boundaries, such as the relational practices of a teacher who negotiates educational relationships with students who have a history of school failure (Frelin, 2015). In this type of instrumental case study, the researcher explores an issue, and a detailed understanding emerges from examining a case or several cases. It is important, too, for the researcher to have contextual material available to describe the setting for the case and draw upon multiple sources of information about the case to provide an in-depth picture of it. Central to writing a case study, the researcher describes the case in detail, and mentions several issues or focuses on a single issue that emerged when examining the case (Stake, 1995). Explanations that can be learned from studying this case or cases end a case study report.

Selecting Your Approach

Based now on a more thorough understanding of the five approaches, how do you choose one approach over the other? We recommend that you start with the outcome—what the approach is attempting to accomplish (e.g., the study of an individual, the examination of the meaning of experiences toward a phenomenon, the generation of a theory, the description and interpretation of a culture-sharing group, the in-depth study of a single case). In addition, other factors need also to be considered:

- *The audience question*: What approach is frequently used by gatekeepers in your field (e.g., committee members, advisors, editorial boards of journals)?
- *The background question*: What training do you have in the inquiry approach (e.g., courses completed, books read)? Or what resources are accessible to guide you in your work (e.g., committee members, books, workshops)?
- *The scholarly literature question*: What is needed most as contributing to the scholarly literature in your field (e.g., a study of an individual, an exploration of the meaning of a concept, a theory, a portrait of a culture-sharing group, an in-depth case study)?
- *The personal approach question*: Are you more comfortable with a more structured approach to research or with a storytelling approach (e.g., narrative research, ethnography)? Or are you more comfortable with a firmer, more well-defined approach to research or with a flexible approach (e.g., grounded theory, case study, phenomenology)?

Chapter Check-In

1. What defining features of one of the five approaches can you use to begin designing your qualitative study? Answer the following questions that apply to the approach you are considering.

    -   For a narrative study: What individual do you plan to study? And do you have access to information about this individual's life experiences?

    -   For a phenomenology: What is the phenomenon of interest that you plan to study? And do you have access to people who have experienced it?

    -   For a grounded theory: What social science concept, action, or process do you plan to explore as the basis for your theory? Can you interview individuals who have experienced the process?

    -   For an ethnography: What cultural group of people do you plan to study? Has the culture-sharing group been together long enough for patterns of behavior, language, and beliefs to form?

    -   For a case study: What is the case you plan to examine? Will the case be described because it is a unique case, or will the case be used to illustrate (and illuminate) an issue or a problem?

2. Do you understand the key differences among the five approaches?

    -   Read qualitative journal articles that adopt different approaches across diverse fields, such as the narrative studies of Geiger (1986) and Nelson (1990), phenomenologies of Edwards (2006) and Padilla (2003), grounded theory studies of Brimhall and Engblom-Deglmann (2011) and Creswell and Brown (1992), ethnographies of Haenfler (2004) and Rhoads (1995), and case studies of Brickhouse and Bodner (1992) and Asmussen and Creswell (1995). Determine the defining features of the approach being used by the author(s), and discuss why the author(s) may have used the approach.

Asmussen, K. J., & Creswell, J. W. (1995). Campus response to a student gunman. *Journal of Higher Education*, *66*(5), 575–591. doi:10.2307/2943937

Brickhouse, N., & Bodner, G. M. (1992). The beginning science teacher: Classroom narratives of convictions and constraints. *Journal of Research in Science Teaching*, *29*, 471–485.

Brimhall, A. C., & Engblom-Deglmann, M. L. (2011). Starting over: A tentative theory exploring the effects of past relationships on postbereavement remarried couples. *Family Process*, *50*(1), 47–62. doi:10.1111/j.1545-5300.2010.01345.x

Creswell, J. W., & Brown, M. L. (1992). How chairpersons enhance faculty research: A grounded theory study. *Review of Higher Education*, *16*(1), 41–62. Retrieved from https://www.press.jhu.edu/journals/review_of_higher_education

Edwards, L. V. (2006). Perceived social support and HIV/AIDS medication adherence among African American women. *Qualitative Health Research*, *16*, 679–691. doi:10.1177/1049732305281597

Geiger, S. N. G. (1986). Women's life histories: Method and content. *Signs: Journal of Women in Culture and Society*, *11*, 334–351. Retrieved from http://www.jstor.org/stable/3174056

Haenfler, R. (2004). Rethinking subcultural resistance: Core values of the straight edge movement. *Journal of Contemporary Ethnography*, *33*, 406–436. doi:10.1177/0891241603259809

Nelson, L. W. (1990). Code-switching in the oral life narratives of African-American women: Challenges to linguistic hegemony. *The Journal of Education, 172(3)*, 142–155.

Padilla, R. (2003). Clara: A phenomenology of disability. *The American Journal of Occupational Therapy, 57(4)*, 413–423. doi:10.5014/ajot.57.4.413

Rhoads, R. A. (1995). Whales tales, dog piles, and beer goggles: An ethnographic case study of fraternity life. *Anthropology and Education Quarterly, 26*, 306–323. Retrieved from http://www.jstor.org/stable/3195675

Summary

This chapter examined five different short articles to illustrate good models for writing a narrative study, a phenomenology, a grounded theory study, an ethnography, and a case study. These articles reflect many of the defining characteristics of each approach and should enable readers to see differences in composing and writing varieties of qualitative studies. Choose a narrative study to examine the life experiences of a single individual when material is available and accessible and the individual is willing (assuming that he or she is living) to share stories. Choose a phenomenology to examine a phenomenon and the meaning it holds for individuals. Be prepared to interview the individuals, ground the study in philosophical tenets of phenomenology, follow set procedures, and end with the essence of the meaning. Choose a grounded theory study to generate or develop a theory. Gather information through interviews (primarily), and use systematic procedures of data gathering and analysis built on procedures such as open, axial, and selective coding. Although the final report will be scientific, it can still address sensitive and emotional issues. Choose an ethnography to study the behavior of a culture-sharing group (or individual). Be prepared to observe and interview, and develop a description of the group and explore themes that emerge from studying human behaviors. Choose a case study to examine a case, bounded in time or place, and look for contextual material about the setting of the case. Gather extensive material from multiple sources of information to provide an in-depth picture of the case.

These are important distinctions among the five approaches to qualitative inquiry. By studying each approach in detail, we can learn more about how to proceed and how to narrow our choice of which approach to use. In the next chapter, we will see how to incorporate each of the five approaches into a scholarly introduction in a qualitative project.

Further Readings

Several readings extend this brief overview and comparison of articles for each of the five approaches. Here we continue to expand the list of books about each approach (see also

(Continued)

(Continued)

Chapters 1 and 4). The list should not be considered exhaustive, and readers are encouraged to seek out additional readings in the end-of-book reference list.

Clandinin, D. J., Huber, J., Huber, M., Murphy, M. S., Murray Orr, A., Pearce, M., & Steeves, P. (2006). *Composing diverse identities: Narrative inquiries into the interwoven lives of children and teachers.* New York, NY: Routledge.

Through this book, the authors illustrate the usefulness of narrative research for capturing the complex interactions among children, families, teachers, and administrators within the school environment. This should be required reading for anyone engaging in narrative research with children.

Colaizzi, P. F. (1978). Psychological research as the phenomenologist views it. In R. Valle & M. King (Eds.), *Existential phenomenological alternatives for psychology* (pp. 48–71). New York, NY: Oxford University Press.

This key resource introduces existential phenomenology as a philosophical and methodological approach within the field of psychology. Within this chapter, Paul Colaizzi advances procedures for conducting phenomenological analysis that remain relevant to this day.

Denzin, N. K., & Lincoln, Y. S. (2013). *Strategies of qualitative inquiry.* Thousand Oaks, CA: Sage.

Norman Denzin and Yvonna Lincoln take a new approach in this accessible version of a handbook on qualitative research. In particular, we find the case study chapter by Flyvberg to be helpful in delineating case study research from the other approaches.

Goffman, A. (2014). *On the run: Fugitive life in an American city (fieldwork encounters and discoveries).* Chicago IL: Chicago University Press.

Alice Goffman contributes an ethnography study of a group of young Black men in a poor community in West Philadelphia over 6 years. She also introduces a number of ethical issues that are worthy of further exploration for those engaging in ethnographic research.

Spradley, J. P. (1979). *The ethnographic interview.* New York, NY: Holt, Rinehart & Winston.

This book by James Spradley has enduring influence for how to conduct open-ended interviews useful across qualitative approaches. In addition to suggestions about how to phrases research questions he offers the reader useful guidance for comparing data during analyses.

6

Introducing and Focusing the Study

T
he beginning of a study, as was mentioned earlier, is the most important part of a research project. If the purpose of the study is unclear, if the research questions are vague, and if the research problem or issue is not clearly identified, then a reader has difficulty following the remainder of the study. Consider a qualitative research journal article that you have recently read. Did it read quickly? If so, that is usually an indication that the study is well tied together: The problem leads to certain research questions, and the data collection naturally follows, and then the data analysis and interpretation relate closely to the questions, which, in turn, help the reader to understand the research problem. The author uses transitions to bridge from one part to the other. Often the logic is back and forth between these components in an integrated, consistent manner so that all parts interrelate (Morse & Richards, 2002) and are considered to be interactive (Maxwell, 2013). This integration of all parts of a good qualitative introduction begins with the identification of a clear problem that needs to be studied. It then advances the primary intent of the study, called the purpose or study aim of the study. Of all parts of a research project, the ***purpose statement*** is most important. It sets the stage for the entire article and conveys what the author hopes to accomplish in the study. It is so important, we believe, that we have scripted a purpose statement that you might use in your qualitative project. All you need to do is insert several components into this statement to have a clear, short, and concise qualitative purpose statement that

will be easy for readers to follow. Then, the qualitative research questions extend and often narrow the purpose statement into questions that will be answered during the course of the study. In this chapter, we will discuss how to compose a good problem statement for a qualitative study, how to compose a clear purpose statement, and how to further specify the research through qualitative research questions. Moreover, we will suggest how these sections of an introduction can be adjusted to fit all five of the approaches to qualitative inquiry addressed in this book.

Questions for Discussion

- What does evidence of interrelationship across the research problem, purpose, and questions look like?
- How can the problem statement be best written to reflect one of the approaches to qualitative research?
- How can the purpose statement be best written to convey the orientation of an approach to research?
- How can a central question be written so that it encodes and foreshadows an approach to qualitative research?
- How can subquestions be presented so that they subdivide the central question into several parts?

Interrelating the Study Problem, Purpose, and Questions Within Research

Demonstrating *methodological congruence* (see Chapter 3 for initial description) begins with identifying a clear problem in need of investigation, advancing the primary purpose of the study, and specifying the questions guiding the study design. This is because these decisions (i.e., problem, purpose, and questions) provide the foundation on which to base subsequent decisions related to the research methods. To help this process, we provide a guiding framework in Figure 6.1. First, the researcher identifies a problem and creates a research problem statement; this problem is then focused on a primary study purpose. Second, the researcher creates a research purpose statement (hereafter, we will call this statement the purpose statement, recognizing that some researchers call it study aim) to advance this primary study goal that is ultimately operationalized by the drafting of specific research questions. These sub- and central research questions subsequently guide the study design. We consider this to be a narrowing process that is similar across the five approaches; yet some distinguishing features will be discussed within the sections that follow. Also implicit in Figure 6.1 is the importance of interrelationship for informing the selection of data collection

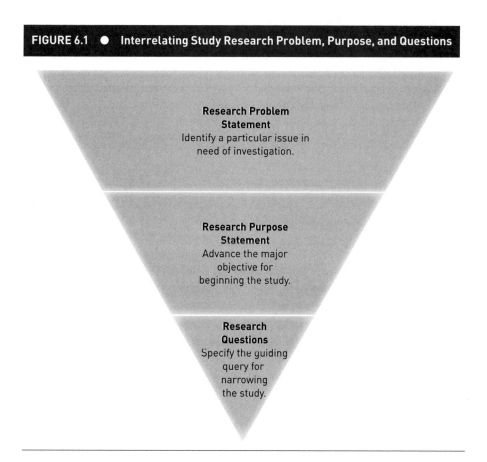

FIGURE 6.1 ● Interrelating Study Research Problem, Purpose, and Questions

**Research Problem
Statement**
Identify a particular issue in
need of investigation.

**Research Purpose
Statement**
Advance the major
objective for
beginning the study.

**Research
Questions**
Specify the guiding
query for
narrowing
the study.

methods and data analysis strategies where the outcome addresses the specified research questions, contributes to the primary study purpose, and investigates the identified research problem.

The Research Problem Statement

How does one begin a qualitative study? Have you realized that all good research begins with an issue or problem that needs to be resolved? Qualitative studies begin with an introduction advancing the research problem or issue in a study. The term *problem* may be a misnomer, and individuals unfamiliar with writing research may struggle with this writing passage. Rather than calling this passage the problem, it might be clearer if we call it the need for the study or creating a rationale for the need for the study. The intent of a research problem in qualitative research is to provide a rationale or need for studying a particular issue or problem. A discussion of this research problem begins a qualitative study. But the actual research problem is framed within several other components in an opening paragraph in a good qualitative study. Here, we want to analyze what these opening paragraphs might look like and to illustrate how they might be tailored to fit one of the five approaches.

Consider designing an introduction to a qualitative study. First examine the model designed for a multiple case study of teen smoking in high schools represented in Figure 6.2. The initial idea for structuring a good introduction came from early study of opening passages in good research articles (see Creswell, 2014). As this article suggests, implicit within good introductions is a model or template that authors use. This model was called a "deficiencies model of an introduction" (Creswell, 2014, p. 111), and it was referred to by this name because it centered on deficiencies in the current literature and how studies were crafted to add to a body of literature. We know now that qualitative studies not only add to the literature but they can also give voice to underrepresented groups; probe a deep understanding of a central phenomenon; and lead to specific outcomes such as stories, the essence of a phenomenon, the generation of theory, the cultural life of a group, and an in-depth analysis of a case. In Figure 6.2, you will see the five elements of a good introduction: the topic, the research problem, the evidence from the literature about the problem, the deficiencies in the evidence, and the importance of the problem for select audiences. Added as a final sixth element in this statement would be the purpose statement, a topic to be covered later in this chapter.

These components of a good introduction are as follows:

1. *Advance the topic or general subject matter of the research study by creating reader interest in a few beginning sentences or a paragraph.* A good first sentence—called a narrative hook in literature composition—would create reader interest through the use of stating timely topics, advancing a key controversy, using numbers, or citing a leading study. We suggest staying away from quotes for the first sentence because they not only often require the reader to focus in on the key idea of the quote but they also need appropriate lead-in and lead-out features. Proceed beyond the first sentence to advance a general discussion about the topic being addressed in the study (see Creswell, 2016, for further discussion).

2. *Discuss the research problem or issue that leads to a need for the study.* Readers simply need to be told about the issue or concern that you plan on addressing in your qualitative project. Another way to frame the research problem is to view it as an argument as to why the topic you wish to study matters. In this way, you can present to the reader the study's importance (Ravitch & Riggan, 2012). Qualitative research methods books (e.g., Creswell, 2012; Marshall & Rossman, 2015; Ravitch & Mittenfelner Carl, 2016) advance several sources for locating research problems. Research problems are found in personal experience with an issue, a job-related problem, an advisor's research agenda, or the scholarly literature (Creswell, 2014). We like to think about the research problem as coming from real-life issues or from a gap in the literature, or both. Real-life problems might be that students struggle with their ethnic identity given the demands of friends, family, and schools, such as in Chan's (2010) study (see Appendix B). Individuals struggle to make sense of the disease of AIDS/HIV (Anderson & Spencer, 2002; see

Appendix C). The need for a study also comes from certain deficiencies or gaps in the existing scholarly literature. Authors mention these gaps in future research sections or in introductions of their published studies. As suggested by Barritt (1986), the rationale is not the discovery of new elements, as in natural scientific study but rather the heightening of awareness for experiences, which has been forgotten and overlooked. By heightening awareness and creating dialogue, it is hoped research can lead to better understanding of the way things appear to someone else and through that insight lead to improvements in practice (Barritt, 1986). Besides dialogue and understanding, a qualitative study may lead to an in-depth understanding, fill a void in existing literature, establish a new line of thinking, lift up the voices of individuals who have been marginalized in our society, or assess an issue with an understudied group or population.

3. *Summarize the scholarly literature.* Briefly discuss the recent evidence that has addressed this research problem. Has anyone directly studied this problem? Or has anyone studied this problem in a general sense or discussed a closely related topic? Although opinions differ about the extent of literature review needed before a study begins, qualitative research authors (e.g., Creswell, 2012; Marshall & Rossman, 2015; Ravitch & Mittenfelner Carl, 2016) refer to the need to review the literature so that one can provide the rationale for the problem and position one's study within the ongoing literature about the topic. We have found it helpful to visually depict where our study can be positioned into the larger literature. For example, one might develop a visual or figure—a research map (Creswell, 2014)—of existing literature and show in this figure the topics addressed in the literature and how one's proposed research fits into or extends the existing literature. We also see this section as not providing detail about any one study, such as what one finds in a complete literature review, but as a statement about the general literature—the groups of literature, if you will—that have addressed the problem. If no groups of literature have addressed the problem, then discuss the extant literature that is closest to the topic. Hopefully, a good qualitative study has not already been done, and no or few studies directly address the topic being proposed in the present study.

4. *Point to deficiencies in evidence using the current literature or discussions.* Indicate in what ways gaps exist in the understanding the problem. Mention several reasons, such as inadequate methods of data collection, a need for research, or inadequate research. It is here, in the deficiencies section of an introduction, that information can be inserted that relates to one of the five qualitative approaches. In a problem statement for a narrative study, for example, writers can mention how individual stories need to be told to gain personal experiences about the research problem. In a phenomenological study, the researcher makes the case that a need exists to know more about a particular phenomenon and the common experiences of individuals with the phenomenon. For a grounded theory study, authors state that we need a theory that explains a process because existing theories are inadequate, are nonexistent for the population under study, or need to be modified for an existing population. In an ethnographic study, the problem statement advances why it is important to describe and to interpret the

cultural behavior of a certain group of people or how a group is marginalized and kept silent by others. For a case study, the researcher might discuss how the study of a case or cases can help inform the issue or concern. In all of these illustrations, the researcher presents the research problem as relating to the particular approach to qualitative research taken in the study.

5. *Argue importance of the study for audiences.* Present how audiences or stakeholders will profit from your study that addresses the problem. Consider different types of audiences and point out, for each one, the ways they will benefit from the study. These audiences could be other researchers, policy makers, practitioners in the field, or students.

The introduction then proceeds on to the purpose statement because, at this point, a reader has a clear understanding of the problem leading to a need for the study, and is encouraged enough to read on to see what the overall intent of the study might be (purpose) as well as the types of questions (research questions) that will be answered in the study.

The Purpose Statement

This interrelationship between design and approach continues with the purpose statement, a statement that provides the major objective or intent, or "road map," to the study. As the most important statement in an entire qualitative study, the purpose statement needs to be carefully constructed and written in clear and concise language. Unfortunately, all too many writers leave this statement implicit, causing readers extra work in interpreting and following a study. This need not be the case, so we have created the following "script" for a purpose statement containing several sentences and blanks that an individual fills in (see also Creswell, 1994, 2009, 2012, 2014):

> The purpose of this _____ (narrative, phenomenological, grounded theory, ethnographic, case) study is (was? will be?) to _____ (understand? describe? develop? discover?) the _____ (central phenomenon of the study) for _____ (the participants) at _____ (the site). At this stage in the research, the _____ (central phenomenon) will be generally defined as _____ (a general definition of the central phenomenon).

As this script shows, several terms can be used to encode a passage for a specific approach to qualitative research. The following occurs in the purpose statement:

- The writer identifies the specific qualitative approach used in the study by mentioning the type. The name of the approach comes first in the passage, thus foreshadowing the inquiry approach for data collection, analysis, and report writing.
- The writer encodes the passage with words that indicate the action of the researcher and the focus of the approach to research. For example, certain words

FIGURE 6.2 ● Sample Research Problem Section (Introduction) to a Study

1. Advance topic

- Exploring the conceptions and misconceptions of teen smoking in high schools

2. Discuss research problem

- Tobacco use is a leading cause of cancer in American society (McGinnis & Foege, 1993). Although smoking among adults has declined in recent years, it has actually increased for adolescents. The Center for Disease Control and Prevention reported that smoking among high school students had risen from 27.5 percent in 1991 to 34.8 percent in 1995 (USDHHS, 1996). Unless this trend is dramatically reversed, an estimated 5 million of our nation's children will ultimately die a premature death (CDC, 1996).

3. Summarize scholarly literature

- Previous research on adolescent tobacco use has focused on four primary topics. Several studies have examined the question of the initiation of smoking by young people, noting that tobacco use initiation begins as early as junior high school (e.g., Heishman, et al., 1997). Other studies have focused on the prevention of smoking and tobacco use in schools. This research has led to numerous school-based prevention programs and interventions (e.g., Sussman et al., 1995). Fewer studies have examined "quit attempts" or cessation of smoking behaviors among adolescents, a distinct contrast to the extensive investigations into adult cessation (Heishman et al., 1997). Of interest as well to researchers studying adolescent tobacco use has been the social context and social influence of smoking (Fearnow et al., 1998). For example, adolescent smoking may occur in work-related situations, at home where one or more parents or caretakers smoke, at teen social events, or at areas designated as "safe" smoking places near high schools (McVea et al., in press).

4. Point to deficiencies in evidence

- Minimal research attention has been directed towards the social context of high schools as a site for examining adolescent tobacco use. During high school students form peer groups which may contribute to adolescent smoking. Often peers become a strong social influence for behavior in general, and belonging to an athletic team, a music group, or the "grunge" crowds can impact thinking about smoking (McVea et al., in press). Schools are also places where teachers and administrators need to be role models for abstaining from tobacco use and enforcing policies about tobacco use (O'Hara et al., 1999). Existing studies of adolescent tobacco use are primarily quantitative with a focus on outcomes and transtheoretical models (Pallonen, 1998). Qualitative investigations, however, provide detailed views of students in their own words, complex analyses of multiple perspectives, and specific school contexts of different high schools that shape student experiences with tobacco (Creswell, in press). Moreover, qualitative inquiry offers the opportunity to involve high school students as co-researchers, a data collection procedure that can enhance the "validity" of students' views uncontaminated by adult perspectives.

5. Argue importance of study for audiences

- By examining these multiple school contexts, using qualitative approaches and involving students as co-researchers, we can better understand the conceptions and misconceptions adolescents hold about tobacco use in high schools. With this understanding, researchers can better isolate variables and develop models about smoking behavior. Administrators and teachers can plan interventions to prevent or change attitudes toward smoking, and school officials can assist with smoking cessation or intervention programs.

Source: Adapted from McVea, Harter, McEntarffer, and Creswell (1999).

encode the qualitative research, such as *understand experiences* (useful in narrative studies), *describe* (useful in case studies, ethnographies, and phenomenologies), *ascribe meaning* (associated with phenomenologies), *develop* or *generate* (useful in grounded theory), and *discover* (useful in all approaches)—several words that a researcher would include in a purpose statement to encode the purpose statement for the approach chosen (see Table 6.1). These words indicate not only researchers' actions but also the foci and outcomes of the studies.

- The writer identifies the central phenomenon. The central phenomenon is the one central concept being explored or examined in the research study. Qualitative researchers focus on only one concept (e.g., relational practices of a teacher who negotiates educational relationships with students who have a history of school failure, or the behaviors of a culture-sharing group, such as the British-born, working-class Pakistani and Bangladeshi young Muslim men) at the beginning of a study. Comparing groups or looking for linkages can be included in the study as one gains experiences in the field and one proceeds on with analysis after initial exploration of the central phenomenon.

- The writer foreshadows the participants and the site for the study, whether the participants are one individual (i.e., narrative or case study), several individuals (i.e., grounded theory or phenomenology), a group (i.e., ethnography), or a site (i.e., program, event, activity, or place in a case study).

We also suggest including a *general definition* for the central phenomenon. This definition is a tentative, preliminary definition that the researcher intends to use at the outset of the study (Clandinin, 2013). The definition may be difficult to determine with any specificity in advance. But, for example, in a narrative study, a writer might define the types of stories to be collected such as life stages, childhood memories, the transition from adolescence to adulthood, attendance at an Alcoholics Anonymous meeting, or even the family drama enacted in the aftermath of death of a sibling (Ellis, 1993). In a phenomenology, the central phenomenon to be explored is clearly specified (van Manen, 2014). For example, the phenomenon might be specified as the meaning of grief, anger, or even chess playing (Aanstoos, 1985). In grounded theory, the central phenomenon might be identified as a concept central to the process being examined (Corbin & Strauss, 2015)—for example, the effect of past relationships on postbereavement remarried couples (Brimhall & Englom-Deglmann, 2011). In an ethnography, the writer might identify the key cultural concepts (often drawn from cultural concepts in anthropology) being examined, such as roles, behaviors, acculturation, communication, myths, stories, or other concepts that the researcher plans to take into the field at the beginning of the study (Wolcott, 2008a). Finally, in a case study such as an "intrinsic" case study (Stake, 1995), the writer might define the boundaries of the case, specifying how the case is bounded in time and place. If an "instrumental" case study is being examined, then the researcher might specify and define generally the issue being examined in the case.

Several examples of purpose statements follow that illustrate the ***encoding*** and foreshadowing of the five approaches to research (see also Creswell, 2012, 2016):

TABLE 6.1 ● Words to Use in Encoding the Purpose Statement				
Narrative	**Phenomenology**	**Grounded Theory**	**Ethnography**	**Case Study**
• Narrative study • Stories • Epiphanies • Lived experiences • Chronology	• Phenomenology • Describe • Experiences • Meaning • Essence	• Grounded theory • Generate • Develop • Propositions • Process • Substantive theory	• Ethnography • Culture-sharing group • Cultural behavior and language • Cultural portrait • Cultural themes	• Case study • Bounded • Single or collective case • Event, process, program, individual

EXAMPLE 6.1

NARRATIVE RESEARCH PURPOSE STATEMENTS

Notice how the lived experience is emphasized in each of the following examples:

a. A single individual and the life history of the individual:

The author describes and analyzes the process of eliciting the life history of a man with mental retardation. (Angrosino, 1994, p. 14)

b. The family and friends of a crash victim and the reactions of these individuals:

The story I tell here describes the aftermath of the crash as my family and friends in Lurary, the town where I was born and where Rex lived, react to and cope with this unanticipated tragedy. (Ellis, 1993, p. 712)

EXAMPLE 6.2

PHENOMENOLOGICAL RESEARCH PURPOSE STATEMENTS

See in the following examples how the phenomenon is clearly described as the following:

a. The role of a group of individuals as fathers:

The present study was designed to explore the beliefs, attitudes, and needs that current and expectant adolescent fathers and young men who are fathers of children born to adolescent mothers have regarding their role as a father. (Lemay, Cashman, Elfenbein, & Felice, 2010, p. 222)

b. The meaning individuals attributed to a health care experience:

The purpose of our phenomenological study was to explore what meaning people with liver failure ascribe to the experience of waiting for a transplant at a major midwestern transplant center. (Brown, Sorrell, McClaren, & Creswell, 2006, p. 120)

EXAMPLE 6.3
GROUNDED THEORY RESEARCH PURPOSE STATEMENTS

In the following examples, the researchers advance a theory by studying a process around:

a. Leadership identity of an individual:

   The purpose of this study was to understand the processes a person experiences in creating a leadership identity. (Komives, Owen, Longerbeam, Mainella, & Osteen, 2005, p. 594)

b. Resilience development by a group of women in an isolated setting:

   The purpose of this study was to explore how women maintain their health in geographical, social, political, economic, and historical contexts. (Leipert & Reutter, 2005, p. 50)

EXAMPLE 6.4
ETHNOGRAPHIC RESEARCH PURPOSE STATEMENTS

A portrait of a culture-sharing group was sought in each of the following examples:

a. The "ballpark" culture of the employees:

   This article examines how the work and the talk of stadium employees reinforce certain meanings of baseball in society, and it reveals how the work and the talk create and maintain ballpark culture. (Trujillo, 1992, p. 351)

b. The core values of the straight edge (sXe) movement:

   This article fills a gap in the literature by giving an empirical account of the sXe movement centered on a description of the group's core values. (Haenfler, 2004, p. 410)

EXAMPLE 6.5
CASE STUDY RESEARCH PURPOSE STATEMENTS

The focus on understanding the bounded system is evident in each of the following:

a. A multiple case study of the integration of technology:

   The purpose of this study was to describe the ways in which three urban elementary schools, in partnership with a local, publicly funded multipurpose university, used a similar array of material and human resources to improve their integration of technology. (Staples, Pugach, & Himes, 2005, p. 287)

> b. As intrinsic case study of the campus reaction to a gunman event:
>
> The study presented in this article is a qualitative case analysis that describes and interprets a campus response to a gun incident. (Asmussen & Creswell, 1995, p. 576)

The Research Questions

The intent of qualitative research questions is to narrow the purpose to several questions that will be addressed in the study. We distinguish between the purpose statement and research questions so that we can clearly see how they are conceptualized and composed; other authors may combine them or more typically state only a purpose statement in a journal article and leave out the research questions. However, in many types of qualitative studies, such as dissertations and theses, the research questions are distinct and stated separately from the purpose statement. Once again, we find that these questions provide an opportunity to encode and foreshadow an approach to inquiry.

The Central Question

Some writers offer suggestions for writing qualitative research questions (e.g., Creswell, 2014, 2016; Marshall & Rossman, 2015). Qualitative research questions are open-ended, evolving, and nondirectional. They restate the purpose of the study in more specific terms and typically start with a word such as *what* or *how* rather than *why* in order to explore a central phenomenon. This is because *why* suggests possible cause-and-effect directional language, not open-ended language that is more apparent with the use of *what* or *how*. Questions are few in number (five to seven) and posed in various forms, from the "grand tour" (Spradley, 1979, 1980) that asks, "Tell me about yourself," to more specific questions.

We recommend that a researcher reduce her or his entire study to a single, overarching **central question** and several **subquestions**. Drafting this central question often takes considerable work because of its breadth and the tendency of some to form specific questions based on traditional training. To reach the overarching central question, we ask qualitative researchers to state the broadest question they could possibly pose to address their research problem.

This central question can be encoded with the language of each of the five approaches to inquiry. Morse (1994) speaks directly to this issue as she reviews the types of research questions. Although she does not refer to narratives or case studies, she mentions that one finds descriptive questions of cultures in ethnographies, process questions in grounded theory studies, and meaning questions in phenomenological studies. For example, we searched through the five studies presented in Chapter 5 to see if we could find or imagine their central research questions. We recognized immediately that the authors of these journal articles typically did not provide central questions but instead presented purpose statements, as is often the case in journal article reports. Still, it is helpful to consider what their central questions, if asked, might have been. In the following examples, we present our versions of the research questions (or the author's version) guiding the studies included in the appendices. Additional examples, based on studies in Chapter 5, are provided to also illustrate research questions for each approach.

EXAMPLE 6.6
NARRATIVE STUDY RESEARCH QUESTIONS

Notice how the focus on the lived experience is emphasized in each of the following narrative research question examples:

a. Gathering stories from Ai Mei, the Chinese immigrant student, might have been written by Chan (2010; see Appendix B):

What are the conflicting stories of ethnic identity that Ai Mei experienced in her school, with her peers, and with her family?

b. Eliciting life narratives, the comparison of code-switching patterns of two African American women, might have been written by Nelson (1990):

What are the patterns and significance of code-switching and other contextualization cues that the African American women experienced as participants in American culture during the latter part of the 20th century?

EXAMPLE 6.7
PHENOMENOLOGY RESEARCH QUESTIONS

See how the focus on describing the phenomenon is articulated in the following examples of phenomenological research questions:

a. Capturing how persons living with AIDS represent and imagine their disease might have proposed by Anderson and Spencer (2002; see Appendix C):

What meaning do men and women with a diagnosis of AIDS ascribe to their illness?

b. Describing the meaning a woman attributed to the lived experience of a long-term disability was stated by Padilla (2003, p. 415):

"What is the lived experience of disability for a woman who sustained a head injury many years ago?"

EXAMPLE 6.8
GROUNDED THEORY RESEARCH QUESTIONS

In the following grounded theory research question examples, the focus on advancing a theory is clearly represented for the purpose of the following:

a. Explaining the process of integrating physical activity into the lifestyle of African American women might have been expressed by Harley and colleagues (2009; see Appendix D) as follows:

What behavioral process theory explains the integration of physical activity into the lifestyle of 15 African American women?

b. Generating an understanding of what the process of remarrying involves between postbereavement couples might have been represented by Brimhall and Engblom-Deglmann (2011) as follows:

What relational process theory describes the effects of past relationships on post postbereavement remarried couples?

EXAMPLE 6.9
ETHNOGRAPHY RESEARCH QUESTIONS

Note how the portrait of a culture-sharing group was sought in each of the following research question examples for ethnography:

a. Representing the changing cultural condition inhabited by a group of British born, working-class Pakistani and Bangladeshi young men over 3 years might have been expressed by Mac an Ghaill and Haywood (2015; see Appendix E) as follows:

What are the core beliefs related to ethnicity, religion, and cultural belonging of the group of British born, working-class Pakistani and Bangladeshi young men, and how do the young men construct and understand their geographically specific experiences of family, schooling, social life as well as both growing up and interacting within their local community in a rapidly changing Britain?

b. Describing the core values of the members of the sXe movement might have been advanced by Haenfler (2004) as follows:

What are the core values of the sXe movement, and how do the members construct and understand their subjective experiences of being a part of the subculture?

EXAMPLE 6.10

CASE STUDY RESEARCH QUESTIONS

The focus on understanding the bounded system is evident in each of the following examples of case study research questions:

a. Tracing one teacher's practices of negotiating relationships with students who have a history of school failure within a particular school program might have been proposed by Frelin (2015; see Appendix F) as follows:

What are the relational and professional practices that can help teachers and other school staff to assist students to overcome obstacles and be more successful at school?

b. Describing and interpreting the campus response to a gun incident was asked by Asmussen and Creswell (1995) using five central guiding questions in the introduction:

'What happened? Who was involved in response to the incident? What themes of response emerged during the eight-month period that followed this incident? What theoretical constructs helped us understand the campus response, and what constructs were unique to this case?' (p. 576)

Example 6.10 illustrates describing individuals' experiences and then in developing themes that represented responses of individuals on the campuses. As these examples show, authors may or may not pose a central question, although one lies implicit if not explicit in all studies. For writing journal articles, central questions may be used less than purpose statements to guide the research. However, for individuals' graduate research, such as theses or dissertations, the trend is toward writing both purpose statements and central questions.

Subquestions

An author typically presents a small number of subquestions that further specify the central question into some areas for inquiry. For example, a central question such as "What does it mean to be a college professor?" would be analyzed in subquestions on topics like "What does it mean to be a college professor in the classroom? As a researcher? As a thesis supervisor? As a colleague in a department?" In this example, the subquestions focus on the roles or responsibilities this particular college professor undertakes as an instructor, researcher, supervisor of students, and colleague within a department. The subquestions essentially take the central question and break it down into its constituent parts. The subquestions will vary if the college professor has different roles assigned—for example, as administrator or practicum supervisor.

Subquestions are useful for informing core questions asked during the data collection, such as in the interviews or in the observations.

Here are some suggestions for writing these subquestions:

- State a small number of subquestions to further refine the central question. We generally recommend five to seven subquestions. New questions may arise during data collection, and, as with all qualitative research questions, they may change or evolve into new questions as the research proceeds.
- Consider the subquestions as a means of subdividing the central question into several parts. Ask yourself, "If the central question were divided into some areas that I would like to explore, what would the areas or parts be?" A good illustration comes from ethnography. Wolcott (2008a) said that the grand tour or central question such as "What is going on here?" can only be addressed when fleshed out with detail: "In terms of what?" (p. 74).
- Create open-ended subquestions that begin with *how* or *what*. These words should reflect a similar manner as the central question.

You can write the subquestions focused on further analyzing the central phenomenon that relates to the type of qualitative research being used. In a narrative study, these questions may further probe the meaning of stories. In a phenomenology, it will help to establish the components of the essence of the study. In a grounded theory, it will help to detail the emerging theory, and in an ethnography, it will detail the aspects of the culture-sharing group you plan to study, such as members' rituals, their communication, their economic way of life, and so forth. In a case study, the subquestions will address the elements of the case or the issue that you seek to understand. The following examples we present our versions of the research subquestions guiding the studies included in the appendices.

EXAMPLE 6.11
NARRATIVE RESEARCH SUBQUESTIONS

Subquestions for gathering stories from Ai Mei, the Chinese immigrant student, might have been written by Chan (2010; see Appendix B) as the following:

What and how did school experiences contribute to Ai Mei's ethnic identity?

How might peer experiences have contributed to Ai Mei's ethnic identity?

What family experiences does Ai Mei describe as influential to her ethnic identity?

EXAMPLE 6.12
PHENOMENOLOGICAL RESEARCH SUBQUESTIONS

Subquestions for understanding how persons living with AIDS represent and image their disease might have stated by Anderson and Spencer (2002; see Appendix C) as the following:

What does receiving an AIDS diagnosis represent?

What is difficult or easy about being diagnosed with AIDS?

How did the patient first become aware of their diagnosis or illness?

EXAMPLE 6.13
GROUNDED THEORY RESEARCH SUBQUESTIONS

Subquestions for explaining the process of integrating physical activity into the lifestyle of African American women might have been written by Harley and colleagues (2009; see Appendix D) as the following:

How do the women go about integrating physical activity into their lifestyle?

What are the greatest challenges for women to integrate physical activity into their lifestyle?

What has motivated the women to integrate physical activity into their lifestyle?

EXAMPLE 6.14
ETHNOGRAPHIC RESEARCH SUBQUESTIONS

Subquestions for documenting the changing cultural condition inhabited by a group of British born, working-class Pakistani and Bangladeshi young men over 3 years might have been expressed by Mac an Ghaill and Haywood (2015; see Appendix E) as the following:

What core beliefs do group members describe related to ethnic identity?

What experiences do group members attribute as influencing their cultural identity?

What social experiences do group members describe as contributing to core beliefs?

EXAMPLE 6.15
CASE STUDY RESEARCH SUBQUESTIONS

Subquestions for tracing one teacher's practices of negotiating relationships with students who have a history of school failure within a particular school program might have been expressed by Frelin (2015; see Appendix F) as the following:

What relational practices does the teacher describe as helpful for students to overcome school obstacles?

What relational practices does the teacher perceive as helping student success?

What professional teacher practices are attributable to school success?

In Chapter 7, we will examine the phases of data collection common to all approaches and then discuss how it differs among the five approaches.

Chapter Check-In

1. Do you "see" how authors focus and introduce their published qualitative studies? Select one of the qualitative articles presented in Appendices B through F.

   a. Begin by identifying the five elements of a research problem statement (summarized in Figure 6.2) as they have been applied in the journal article. Note which elements are easy and which are more difficult to identify.

   b. Then locate the purpose statement as stated in the journal article. Note what (if any) encoding words are used and what (if any) information is provided about the qualitative approach, the central phenomenon, participants, and the site.

   c. Finally, use the script provided in this chapter to rewrite the purpose statement, and compare it with what was stated in the journal article. Note the similarities and differences between the two statements.

2. Can you apply the scripts presented in this chapter for writing a purpose statement?

   a. Use the problem statement outlined in Figure 6.1 for McVea et al. (1999) as the basis for writing a purpose statement for a phenomenological study. Then adopt a different approach, and write the purpose statement using a second approach.

   McVea, K., Harter, L., McEntarffer, R., & Creswell, J. W. (1999). Phenomenological study of student experiences with tobacco use at City High School. *High School Journal, 82*(4), 209–222.

(Continued)

(Continued)

3. Can you identify evidence of an introduction with interrelated parts being used by the author(s)? Read qualitative journal articles that adopt different approaches across diverse fields, such as the narrative study of Ellis (1993), phenomenology of Lemay et al. (2010), grounded theory study of Komives et al. (2005), ethnography of Trujillo (1992), and case study of Staples et al. (2005).

   a. Begin with identifying the research problem investigated in the study, the research purpose for the study, and the research questions guiding the study. Note which topics are easy and which are more difficult to identify. To what extent is there methodological congruence across the three?

   b. Then review the study introduction for how the research problem is introduced. Assess to what extent have the five elements of a research problem statement (summarized in Figure 6.2) been applied in the journal article. Note which elements are easy and which are more difficult to locate.

   c. Next, review the study introduction for how the research purpose is stated. Assess to what extent encoded words are used and information is provided about the qualitative approach, the central phenomenon, participants, and site.

   d. Finally, review the article for evidence of research questions. Assess to what extent a central research question and subquestions are articulated.

Ellis, C. (1993). "There are survivors": Telling a story of sudden death. *The Sociological Quarterly*, *34*, 711–730. doi:10.1111/j.1533-8525.1993.tb00114.x

Komives, S. R., Owen, J. E., Longerbeam, S. D., Mainella, F. C., & Osteen, L. (2005). Developing a leadership identity: A grounded theory. *Journal of College Student Development*, *46*(6), 593–611. doi:10.1353/csd.2005.0061

Lemay, C. A., Cashman, S. B., Elfenbein, D. S., & Felice, M. E. (2010). A qualitative study of the meaning of fatherhood among young urban fathers. *Public Health Nursing*, *27*(3), 221–231. doi:10.1111/j.1525-1446.2010.00847.x

Staples, A., Pugach, M. C., & Himes, D. J. (2005). Rethinking the technology integration challenge: Cases from three urban elementary schools. *Journal of Research on Technology in Education*, *37*(3), 285–311. doi:10.1080/15391523.2005.10782438

Trujillo, N. (1992). Interpreting (the work and the talk of) baseball. *Western Journal of Communication*, *56*, 350–371. doi:10.1353/csd.2005.0061

4. Can you begin to sketch an introduction with interrelated parts for a qualitative study? Follow these steps:

   a. State the research problem or issue that is the focus of your study in a couple of sentences.

   b. Discuss the research literature that will provide evidence for a need for studying the problem.

   c. Present the rationale, within the context of one of the five approaches to research, for studying the problem that reflects your approach to research.

   d. Review the draft, and use the five elements of a research problem statement (summarized in

Figure 6.2) to guide your revisions. Note which elements were easy and which are more difficult to include.

e. Use the script presented in this chapter for writing a purpose statement. Note which elements were "easy" and which were more difficult to identify.

f. Apply the suggestions presented in this chapter for composing research questions. Specifically, write the first draft of your central question, starting with *how* or *what*. Then consider whether you have addressed four key elements of a central question: the central phenomenon, the participants, the site, and the approach to inquiry. Put *what is* before the central phenomenon, and examine what you have written to determine whether it will be a satisfactory central question written as the broadest and most succinct question that you could ask in your study. Subdivide your central question into several subtopics. Then consider these subtopics the types of questions that you would ask a participant. Use these questions to guide the writing of subquestions.

5. Look across the three topics in your introduction for evidence of integration across them.

Summary

In this chapter, we addressed three topics related to introducing and focusing a qualitative study: the problem statement, the purpose statement, and the research questions. We began with describing the need for the parts to be interrelated and a guiding framework for implementation. Although we discussed general features of designing each section in a qualitative study, we related the topics to the five approaches advanced in this book. The problem statement should advance the topic, discuss the research problem, summarize the literature about the problem, point to the deficiencies in this literature, and argue the importance for the audience who will profit from learning about the problem. It is in the deficiencies section that an author can insert specific information related to his or her approach. For example, authors can advance the need for stories to be told, the need to find the "essence" of the experience, the need to develop a theory, the need to portray the life of a culture-sharing group, and the need to use a case to explore a specific issue. A script may be used to construct the purpose statement. This script should include the type of qualitative approach being used and incorporate words that signal the use of one of the five approaches. The research questions divide into one central question and about five to seven subquestions that subdivide the central questions into several parts of inquiry. The central question can be encoded to accomplish the intent of one of the approaches, such as the development of stories in narrative projects or the generation of a theory in grounded theory. Subquestions also can be used in the data collection process as the key questions asked during an interview or to guide an observation.

Further Readings

Several readings extend this brief overview and comparison of articles for each of the five approaches. Here we continue to expand the list of books about each approach (see also from Chapters 1 and 4). The list should not be considered exhaustive, and readers are encouraged to seek out additional readings in the end-of-book reference list.

Creswell, J. W. (2016). *30 essential skills for the qualitative researcher*. Thousand Oaks, CA: Sage.

John W. Creswell's most recent book offers an innovative way for guiding the qualitative researcher by its organization by skills. In so doing, researchers can easily access specific skills information. This resource may be particularly helpful for those new to qualitative research.

Richards, L., & Morse, J. M. (2012). *README FIRST for a users guide to qualitative methods* (3rd ed.). Thousand Oaks, CA: Sage.

Lyn Richards and Janice Morse offer an accessible resource for informing thinking about, planning for, and conducting of qualitative research. We found the chapter about research questions across approaches particularly helpful for delineating differences in how these questions are composed.

Marshall, C., & Rossman, G. B. (2015). *Designing qualitative research* (6th ed.). Thousand Oaks, CA: Sage.

Catherine Marshall and Gretchen Rossman enhance their practical resource in this latest edition by expanding the scope of contemporary issues and designs in qualitative research. The interwoven vignettes providing access to potential questions, which are helpful for defending the proposal, afford a unique perspective.

Ravitch, S. M., & Mittenfelner Carl, N. (2016). *Qualitative research: Bridging the conceptual, theoretical, and methodological*. Thousand Oaks, CA: Sage.

Sharon Ravitch and Nicole Mittenfelner Carl offer an accessible resource to the processes involved in qualitative research. An innovative contribution of this book is Chapter 11, which provides important guidance for thinking about qualitative research ethics and the relational quality of research.

7

Data Collection

A typical reaction to thinking about qualitative data collection is to focus in on the actual types of data and the procedures for gathering them. Data collection, however, involves much more. It means anticipating ethical issues involved in gaining permissions, conducting a good qualitative sampling strategy, developing means for recording information, responding to issues as they arise in the field, and storing the data securely. Also, in the actual forms of data collection, researchers often opt for only conducting interviews and observations. As will be seen in this chapter, the array of qualitative sources of data are ever expanding, and we encourage researchers to use newer, innovative methods in addition to the standard interviews and observations. In addition, these new forms of data and the steps in the process of collecting qualitative data need to be sensitive to the outcomes expected for each of the five different approaches to qualitative research.

We find it useful to visualize the phases of data collection common to all approaches. A "circle" of interrelated activities best displays this process, a process of engaging in activities that include but go beyond collecting data. We begin this chapter by presenting this circle of activities, briefly introducing each activity. These activities are locating a site or an individual, gaining access and making rapport, sampling purposefully, collecting data, recording information, exploring field issues, and storing data. Then we explore how these activities differ in the five approaches to inquiry, and we end with a few summary comments about comparing the data collection activities across the five approaches.

Questions for Discussion

- What are the steps in the overall data collection process of qualitative research?
- What are the key ethical considerations when collecting data?
- How does a researcher find people or places to study?
- What are typical access and rapport issues?
- What decisions influence the selection of a purposeful sampling strategy?
- What type of information typically is collected?
- How is information recorded?
- What are common issues in collecting data?
- How is information typically stored?
- How are the five approaches both similar and different during data collection?

The Data Collection Circle

We visualize data collection as a series of interrelated activities aimed at gathering good information to answer emerging research questions. As shown in Figure 7.1, a qualitative researcher engages in a series of activities in the process of collecting data. Although we start with locating a site or an individual to study, an investigator may begin at another entry point in the circle. Most importantly, we want the researcher to consider the multiple activities often involved in in collecting data—activities that extend beyond the typical reference point of conducting interviews or making observations. By placing ethics at the intersection of the data collection circle, we emphasize the need to attend to ethical considerations across the phases.

An important step in the process is to find people or places to study and to gain access to and establish rapport with participants so that they will provide good data. A closely interrelated step in the process involves determining a strategy for the **_purposeful sampling_** of individuals or sites. This is not a probability sample that will enable a researcher to determine statistical inferences to a population; rather, it is a purposeful sample that will intentionally sample a group of people that can best inform the researcher about the research problem under examination. Thus, the researcher needs to determine which type of purposeful sampling will be best to use.

Once the inquirer selects the sites or people, decisions need to be made about the most appropriate data collection approaches. Increasingly, a qualitative researcher has more choices regarding forms of data and modes of collection and recording—for example, the various types of interviews generate different interactions and subsequently influence the information recorded. Typically, the qualitative researcher will collect data from more than one source. To guide data collection, the researcher develops

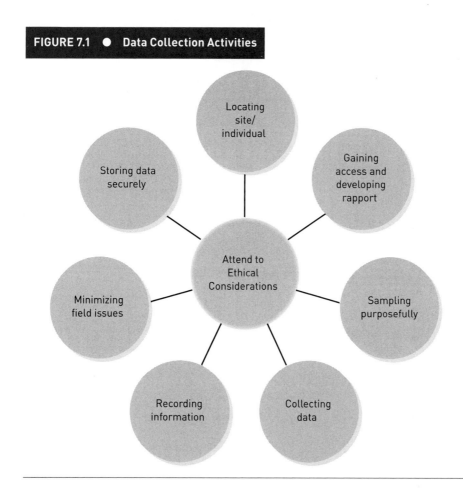

FIGURE 7.1 ● Data Collection Activities

protocols for recording the information and needs to pilot the forms for recording the data, such as interview or observational protocols. Also, the researcher needs to anticipate issues of data collection, called field issues, which may be a problem, such as having inadequate data, needing to prematurely leave the field or site, or contributing to lost information. Finally, a qualitative researcher must decide how he or she will store data so that they can easily be found and protected from damage or loss.

We now turn to each of these seven data collection activities, and we address each for general procedures and within each approach to inquiry. As shown in Table 7.1, these activities are both different and similar across the five approaches to inquiry.

Ethical Considerations for Data Collection

Regardless of the approach to qualitative inquiry, a qualitative researcher faces many ethical issues that surface during data collection in the field and in analysis and

TABLE 7.1 ● Data Collection Activities by Five Approaches

Data Collection Activity	Narrative	Phenomenology	Grounded Theory	Ethnography	Case Study
What is traditionally studied (sites or individuals)?	Single individual, accessible, and distinctive by their stories of experience	Multiple individuals who have experienced the phenomenon	Multiple individuals who have responded to an action or participated in a process about a central phenomenon	Members of a culture-sharing group or individuals representative of the group	A bounded system, such as a process, an activity, an event, a program, or multiple individuals
What are typical access and rapport procedures (access and rapport)?	Gaining permission from individuals, obtaining access to information in archives	Finding people who have experienced the phenomenon	Locating a homogeneous sample	Gaining access through the gatekeeper, gaining the confidence of informants	Gaining access through the gatekeeper, gaining the confidence of participants
How does one select a site or individuals to study (purposeful sampling strategies)?	Several strategies, depending on the person (e.g., convenient, politically important, typical, a critical case)	Finding individuals who have experienced the phenomenon, a "criterion" sample	Finding a homogeneous sample, a "theory-based" sample, a "theoretical" sample	Finding a cultural group to which one is a "stranger," a "representative" sample	Finding a "case" or "cases," an "atypical" case, or a "maximum variation" or "extreme" case
What type of information typically is collected (forms of data)?	Documents and archival material, open-ended interviews, subject journaling, participant observation, casual chatting; typically a single individual	Interviews with a range of people (e.g., 5 to 25)	Primarily interviews with 20 to 30 people to achieve detail in the theory	Participant observations, interviews, artifacts, and documents of a single culture-sharing group	Extensive forms, such as documents and records, interviews, observation, and physical artifacts for 1 to 4 cases
How is information recorded (recording information)?	Notes, interview protocol	Interviews, often multiple interviews with the same individuals	Interview protocol, field notes, memoing	Field notes, interview and observational protocols	Field notes, interview and observational protocols
What are common data collection issues (field issues)?	Access to materials, authenticity of account and materials	Bracketing one's experiences, logistics of interviewing	Interviewing issues (e.g., logistics, openness)	Field issues (e.g., reflexivity, reactivity, reciprocality, "going native," divulging private information, deception)	Interviewing and observing issues
How is information typically stored (storing data)?	File folders, digital files	Transcriptions, digital files	Transcriptions, digital files	Field notes, transcriptions, digital files	Field notes, transcriptions, digital files

dissemination of qualitative reports. In Chapter 3, we visited some of these issues, but ethical issues loom large in the data collection phase of qualitative research (see Table 3.2 for summary of ethical issues in qualitative research). Planning and conducting an ethical study means that the researcher considers and addresses all anticipated and emergent ethical issues in the study. Typically these ethical issues relate to three principles guiding ethical research: respect for persons (i.e., privacy and consent), concern for welfare (i.e., minimize harm and augment reciprocity), and justice (i.e., equitable treatment and enhance inclusivity). A researcher protects the anonymity of the participants, for example, by assigning numbers or aliases to individuals. To gain support from participants, a qualitative researcher conveys to them that they are participating in a study, explains the purpose of the study, and does not engage in ***deception*** about the nature of the study. What if the study is on a sensitive topic and the participants decline to be involved if they are aware of the topic? Another issue likely to develop is when participants share information off the record. Although in most instances this information is deleted from analysis by the researcher, the issue becomes problematic when the information, if reported, harms individuals. We are reminded of a researcher who studied incarcerated Native Americans and learned about a potential "breakout" during one of the interviews. This researcher concluded that it would be a breach of faith with the participants if she reported the matter, and she kept quiet. Fortunately, the breakout did not occur. Finally, we point to the increased focus on how we elicit and record information in appropriate ways for participants. In so doing, it is the responsibility of the researcher to become familiar with the research context and participants and to respect different knowledge systems and ways of interacting. Many excellent resources exist for situating research in diverse contexts and/or with marginalized populations (e.g., Chilisa, 2012; Clandinin et al., 2006; Stanfield, 2011).

Institutional Review Boards   Prior to beginning data collection, a key activity involves the researcher seeking and obtaining the permission of institutional review boards (Creswell, 2012; Hatch, 2002; Sieber & Tolich, 2013). The purpose of this activity is to provide evidence to the review boards that our study design follows their guidelines for conducting ethical research. Most qualitative studies are exempt from a lengthy review (e.g., the expedited or full review), but studies involving individuals as minors (i.e., 18 years or under) or studies of high-risk, sensitive populations (e.g., HIV-positive individuals) require a thorough review; a process involving detailed, lengthy applications; and an extended time for review. The review process involves submitting a proposal that details the procedures in the project related to how selection, access, and permissions for site and individuals will be sought; how selection, sampling, and collection strategies for data will be implemented; and how recording, storage, and use of information will be managed. Table 7.2 summarizes the ethical issues by the data collection activities where each of these procedures will be further described.

TABLE 7.2 ● **Examples of Ethical Issues and Details to Describe by Data Collection Activity**

Data Collection Activity	Examples of Ethics Issues to Anticipate and Address	Examples of Details to Describe
The site or individual	Situations where site selection might raise power issues with researchers (e.g., research within own work context). Consider alternatives free of power concerns	Site or individual selection rationale and procedures
Access and rapport	Sites requiring local approvals for access. Identify additional review processes and gatekeeper for help	Site access and permission rationale and procedures
	Participants' informed of study procedures and their rights. Seek consent from appropriate individuals for participation	Individual consent procedures
	Become familiar with research context and population. Find out about cultural, religious, gender, and other differences that need to be respected	Rapport building rationale and procedures
Sampling strategy	Participants aware of why they are invited to participate with reference to the study purpose	Sample selection rationale and recruitment procedures
Forms of data	Situations where data collection might disrupt the site and be appropriate for the participants	Data source selection rationale
	Consider how the researcher goes about eliciting information with participants, provides appropriate rewards for participating, and attends to opportunities for reciprocity	Data procedures
Recording procedures	Situations when recording might be intrusive and participants informed of measures taken for maintaining confidentiality	Data recording rationale and procedures
Field issues	Consider various issues as entry and access, appropriateness of data forms, and procedures for information collection	Varies
Data storage	Store data and materials in secure locations and be attentive to intended use of data	Data management procedures and use

The Site or Individual

We are often asked how a researcher locates a site or an individual to study, and our answer typically refers to the approach we have decided to use. In a narrative study, one needs to find one or more individuals to study—individuals who are accessible, willing to provide information, and distinctive for their accomplishments and ordinariness or who shed light on a specific phenomenon or issue being explored. Plummer (1983) recommends two sources of individuals to study. The pragmatic approach is where individuals are met on a chance encounter, emerge from a wider study, or are volunteers. Alternatively, one might identify a "marginal person" who lives in conflicting cultures, a "great person" who impacts the age in which he or she lives, or an "ordinary person" who provides an example of a large population. An alternative perspective is available from Gergen (1994), who suggests that narratives "come into existence" (p. 280) not as a product of an individual but as a facet of relationships, as a part of culture, as reflected in social roles such as gender and age. Thus, to ask which individuals will participate is not to focus on the right question. Instead, narrative researchers need to focus on the stories to emerge, recognizing that all people have stories to tell. Yet Daiute (2014) suggests that sensemaking of the narratives begins with sampling relevant time and space dimensions. Also instructive in considering the individual in narrative research is to consider whether first-order or second-order narratives are the focus of inquiry (Elliott, 2005). In first-order narratives, individuals tell stories about themselves and their own experiences, while in second-order narratives, researchers construct a narrative about other people's experiences (e.g., biography) or present a collective story that represents the lives of many.

In a phenomenological study, the participants may be located at a single site, although they need not be. Most importantly, they must be individuals who have all experienced the phenomenon being explored and can articulate their lived experiences (van Manen, 2014). The more diverse the characteristics of the individuals, the more difficult it will be for the researcher to find common experiences, themes, and the overall essence of the experience for all participants. In a grounded theory study, the individuals may not be located at a single site; in fact, if they are dispersed, they can provide important contextual information useful in developing categories in the axial coding phase of research. They need to be individuals who have participated in the process or action the researcher is studying in the grounded theory study. For example, Creswell and Brown (1992) interviewed 32 department chairpersons located across the United States who had mentored faculty in their departments. In an ethnographic study, a single site, in which an intact culture-sharing group has developed shared values, beliefs, and assumptions, is often important (Fetterman, 2010). The researcher needs to identify a group (or an individual or individuals representative of a group) to study, preferably one to which the inquirer is a "stranger" (Agar, 1986) and can gain access. For a case study, the researcher needs to select a site or sites to study, such as programs, events, processes, activities, individuals, or several individuals. Although Stake (1995) refers to an individual as an appropriate "case," we turn to the narrative biographical approach or the life history approach in studying a single individual. However, the study of multiple individuals, each defined as a case and considered a collective case study, is acceptable practice.

A question that students often ask is whether they can study their own organization, place of work, or themselves. Such a study may raise issues of power and risk to the researcher, the participants, and the site. To study one's own workplace, for example, raises questions about whether good data can be collected when the act of data collection may introduce a power imbalance between the researcher and the individuals being studied. Although studying one's own "backyard" is often convenient and eliminates many obstacles to collecting data, researchers can jeopardize their jobs if they report unfavorable data or if participants disclose private information that might negatively influence the organization or workplace. A hallmark of all good qualitative research is the report of multiple perspectives that range over the entire spectrum of perspectives (see the section in Chapter 3 on the characteristics of qualitative research). We are not alone in sounding this cautionary note about studying one's own organization or workplace. Glesne and Peshkin (1992) question research that examines "your own *backyard*—within your own institution or agency, or among friends or colleagues" (p. 21), and they suggest that such information is "dangerous knowledge" that is political and risky for an "inside" investigator. When it becomes important to study one's own organization or workplace, we typically recommend that multiple strategies of validation (see Chapter 10) be used to ensure that the account is accurate and insightful.

Studying yourself can be a different matter. As mentioned in Chapter 4, autoethnography provides an approach or method for studying yourself. Several helpful books are available on autoethnography that discuss how personal stories are blended with larger cultural issues (see Ellis, 2004; Muncey, 2010). Ellis's (1993) story of the experiences of her brother's sudden death illustrates the power of personal emotion and the use of cultural perspectives around one's own experiences. We recommend that individuals wanting to study themselves and their own experiences turn to autoethnography or biographical memoir for scholarly procedures in how to conduct their studies.

Access and Rapport

Qualitative research involves the study of a research site(s) and gaining permission to study the site in a way that will enable the easy collection of data. Gaining access to sites and individuals also involves several steps. Regardless of the approach to inquiry, permissions need to be sought from a human subjects review board, especially in the United States. This means obtaining approval from university or college institutional review boards as well as individuals at the research site—and in some cases from an organizational body such as a school board or hospital-based research review committee. Evidence of having gained approval should be stated in a research report or proposal (if applicable). For example, "The study was approved by the Institutional Review Board of The Ohio State University" (Harley et al., 2009, p. 99; see Appendix D) or "After approval from the university's Institutional Review Board and a city hospital's Human Subject Review Committee, persons who met inclusion criteria were approached and asked to participate" (Anderson & Spencer, 2002, p. 1340; see Appendix C).

As part of the review process application, researchers include examples of materials that will be used in their study. It is helpful to examine a sample consent form that participants need to review and sign in a qualitative study. An example is shown in Figure 7.2.

FIGURE 7.2 ● Sample Human Subjects Consent-to-Participate Form

"Experiences in Learning Qualitative Research: A Qualitative Case Study"

Dear Participant,

The following information is provided for you to decide whether you wish to participate in the present study. You should be aware that you are free to decide not to participate or to withdraw at any time without affecting your relationship with this department, the instructor, or the University of Nebraska–Lincoln.

The purpose of this study is to understand the process of learning qualitative research in a doctoral-level college course. The procedure will be a single, holistic case study design. At this stage in the research, process will be generally defined as perceptions of the course and making sense out of qualitative research at different phases in the course.

Data will be collected at three points—at the beginning of the course, at the midpoint, and at the end of the course. Data collection will involve documents (journal entries made by students and the instructor, student evaluations of the class and the research procedure), audiovisual material (a videotape of the class), interviews (transcripts of interviews between students), and classroom observation field notes (made by students and the instructor). Individuals involved in the data collection will be the instructor and the students in the class.

Do not hesitate to ask any questions about the study either before participating or during the time that you are participating. We would be happy to share our findings with you after the research is completed. However, your name will not be associated with the research findings in any way, and only the researchers will know your identity as a participant.

There are no known risks and/or discomforts associated with this study. The expected benefits associated with your participation are the information about the experiences in learning qualitative research, the opportunity to participate in a qualitative research study, and coauthorship for those students who participate in the detailed analysis of the data. If submitted for publication, a byline will indicate the participation of all students in the class.

Please sign your consent with full knowledge of the nature and purpose of the procedures. A copy of this consent form will be given to you to keep.

Date

Signature of Participant
John W. Creswell, PhD, University of Michigan, Principal Investigator

This consent form often requires that specific elements be included, such as the following:

- The right of participants to voluntarily withdraw from the study at any time
- The central purpose of the study and the procedures to be used in data collection
- The protection of the confidentiality of the respondents
- The known risks associated with participation in the study
- The expected benefits to accrue to the participants in the study
- The signature of the participant as well as the researcher

Gaining access also means finding individuals who can provide access to the research site and facilitate the collection of data. The permissions and building of rapport will differ depending on the type of qualitative approach being used and the participants sought. For a narrative study, inquirers gain information from individuals by obtaining their permission to participate in the study. Study participants should be apprised of the motivation of the researcher for their selection, granted anonymity (if they desire it), and told by the researcher about the purpose of the study. This disclosure helps build rapport. Access to biographical documents and archives requires permission and, in some cases, travel—for example, libraries to access paper-based documents.

In a phenomenological study in which the sample includes individuals who have experienced the phenomenon, it is also important to obtain participants' written permission to be studied. In the Anderson and Spencer (2002; see Appendix C) study of the patients' images of AIDS, 58 men and women participated in the project at three sites dedicated to persons with HIV/AIDS: a hospital clinic, a long-term care facility, and a residence. These were all individuals with a diagnosis of AIDS, 18 years of age or older, able to communicate in English, and with a mini-mental state exam score above 22. In such a study, it was important to obtain permission to have access to the vulnerable individuals participating in the study.

In a grounded theory study, the participants need to provide permission to be studied, while the researcher should have established rapport with the participants so that they will disclose detailed perspectives about responding to an action or a process. The grounded theorist starts with a homogeneous sample and individuals who have commonly experienced the action or process. In the grounded theory study of physical activity participation, Harley and colleagues (2009; see Appendix D) met with contacts at two local African American sorority alumni associations to access meetings where recruitment could take place. In an ethnography, access typically begins with a "gatekeeper," an individual who is a member of or has insider status with a cultural group. This gatekeeper is the initial contact for the researcher and leads the researcher to other participants (Atkinson, 2015). An example of such a gatekeeper are the two young men who provided the initial access point to the group studied in the ethnography described by Mac an Ghaill and Haywood (2015; see Appendix E).

A gatekeeper can be especially important when seeking access to marginalized groups because of the trust, culture, and language concerns identified by Creswell (2016). Approaching this gatekeeper and the cultural system slowly is wise advice for "strangers" studying the culture. For both ethnographies and case studies, gatekeepers require information about the studies that often includes answers from the researchers to the following questions, as Bogdan and Biklen (1992) suggest:

- Why was the site chosen for study?
- What will be done at the site during the research study? How much time will be spent at the site by the researchers?
- Will the researcher's presence be disruptive?
- How will the results be reported?
- What will the gatekeeper, the participants, and the site gain from the study (reciprocity)?

Purposeful Sampling Strategy

Three considerations go into the purposeful sampling approach in qualitative research, and these considerations vary depending on the specific approach. They are the decision as to whom to select as participants (or sites) for the study, the specific type of sampling strategy, and the size of the sample to be studied.

Participants in the Sample In a narrative study, the researcher reflects more on whom to sample—the individual may be convenient to study because she or he is available; a politically important individual who attracts attention or is marginalized; or a typical, ordinary person. All of the individuals need to have stories to tell about their lived experiences. Inquirers may select several options, depending on whether the person is marginal, great, or ordinary (Plummer, 1983). The schoolgirls, who consented to participate and provided insightful information about gender-based violence, poverty, and HIV/AIDS (Simmonds, Roux, & ter Avest, 2015), were convenient to study but also provided a critical illustration of the types of challenges surrounding broader issues of gender within an African society. Ai Mei Zhang was a Chinese immigrant student in Canada who could inform an understanding of the ethnic identity through student, teacher, and parent narratives (Chan, 2010; see Appendix B).

We have found, however, a much more narrow range of sampling strategies for phenomenological studies. It is essential that all participants have experience of the phenomenon being studied. Criterion sampling works well when all individuals studied represent people who have experienced the phenomenon. In a grounded theory study, the researcher chooses participants who can contribute to the development of the theory. Corbin and Strauss (2015) refer to theoretical sampling, which is a process of sampling individuals that can contribute to building the opening and axial coding of the theory. This begins with selecting and studying a homogeneous sample of individuals (e.g., all women who have experienced childhood abuse) and then, after initially developing the theory, selecting and studying a heterogeneous sample (e.g., types of support groups other than women who have experienced childhood abuse). The rationale for studying this heterogeneous sample is to confirm or disconfirm the conditions, both contextual and intervening, under which the model holds.

In ethnography, once the investigator selects a site with a cultural group, the next decision is who and what will be studied. Thus, within-culture sampling proceeds, and several authors offer suggestions for this procedure. Fetterman (2010) recommends proceeding with the big net approach, where at first the researcher mingles with everyone. Ethnographers rely on their judgment to select members of the subculture or unit based on their research questions. They take advantage of opportunities (i.e., opportunistic sampling; Miles & Huberman, 1994) or establish criteria for studying select individuals (criterion sampling). The criteria for selecting who and what to study, according to Hammersley and Atkinson (1995), are based on gaining some perspective on chronological time in the social life of the group, people representative of the culture-sharing group in terms of demographics, and the contexts that lead to different forms of behavior.

In a case study, we prefer to select unusual cases in collective case studies and employ maximum variation as a sampling strategy to represent diverse cases and to fully describe multiple perspectives about the cases. Extreme and deviant cases may comprise a collective case study, such as the study of the unusual user experience of Silk Road, the virtual drug marketplace (Van Hout & Bingham, 2013).

Types of Sampling Strategies   The concept of purposeful sampling is used in qualitative research. This means that the inquirer selects individuals and sites for study because they can purposefully inform an understanding of the research problem and central phenomenon in the study. Decisions need to be made about who or what should be sampled, what form the sampling will take, and how many people or sites need to be sampled. Further, the researchers need to decide if the sampling will be consistent with the information within one of the five approaches to inquiry.

We will begin with some general remarks about sampling and then turn to sampling within each of the five approaches. The decision about who or what should be sampled can benefit from the conceptualization of Marshall and Rossman (2015), who provide an example of sampling four aspects: people, actions, events, and/or processes. They also note that sampling can change during a study and that researchers need to be flexible, but despite this, researchers need to plan ahead as much as possible for their sampling strategy. We like to think as well in terms of levels of sampling in qualitative research. Researchers can sample at the site level, at the event or process level, and at the participant level. In a good plan for a qualitative study, one or more of these levels might be present, and each one needs to be identified.

On the question of what form the sampling will take, we need to note that there are several qualitative sampling strategies available (see Table 7.3 for a list of possibilities). These strategies have names and definitions, and they can be described in research reports. Also, researchers might use one or more of the strategies in a single study. Looking down the list, ***maximum variation sampling*** is listed first because it is a popular approach in qualitative studies. This approach consists of determining in advance some criteria that differentiate the sites or participants and then selecting sites or participants that are quite different on the criteria. This approach is often selected because when a researcher maximizes differences at the beginning of the study, it increases the likelihood that the findings will reflect differences or different perspectives—an ideal in qualitative research. Other sampling strategies frequently used are critical cases, which provide specific information about a problem, and convenience cases, which represent sites or individuals from which the researcher can access and easily collect data.

Sample Size   The size question is an equally important decision to sampling strategy in the data collection process. One general guideline for ***sample size*** in qualitative research is not only to study a few sites or individuals but also to collect extensive detail about each site or individual studied. The intent in qualitative research is not to generalize the information (except in some forms of case study research) but to elucidate the particular, the specific (Pinnegar & Daynes, 2007). Beyond these general suggestions, each of the five approaches to research raises specific sample size considerations. See also Guest, Namey, and Mitchell (2013) for their discussion of sampling considerations across data forms.

Type of Sampling	Purpose
Maximum variation	Documents diverse variations of individuals or sites based on specific characteristics
Homogeneous	Focuses, reduces, simplifies, and facilitates group interviewing
Critical case	Permits logical generalization and maximum application of information to other cases
Theory based	Elaborates on and examines a construct of a theory or the entire theory
Confirming and disconfirming cases	Elaborates on initial analysis, seeks exceptions, and looks for variation
Snowball or chain	Identifies cases of interest from people who know people who know what cases are information-rich
Extreme or deviant case	Learns from highly unusual manifestations of the phenomenon of interest
Typical case	Highlights what is normal or average
Intensity	Seeks information-rich cases that manifest the phenomenon intensely but not extremely
Politically important	Attracts desired attention or avoids attracting undesired attention
Random purposeful	Adds credibility to sample when potential purposeful sample is too large
Stratified purposeful	Illustrates subgroups and facilitates comparisons
Criterion	Seeks cases that meet some criterion; useful for quality assurance
Opportunistic	Follows new leads; taking advantage of the unexpected
Combination or mixed	Meets multiple interests and needs through triangulation, flexibility
Convenience	Saves time, money, and effort, but at the expense of information and credibility

TABLE 7.3 ● Typology of Sampling Strategies in Qualitative Inquiry

Source: Miles and Huberman (1994, p. 28). Reprinted with permission from SAGE.

In narrative research, we have found many examples with one or two individuals, unless a larger pool of participants is used to develop a collective story (Huber & Whelan, 1999). In phenomenology, we have seen the number of participants range from 1 (Padilla, 2003) up to 325 (Polkinghorne, 1989). Dukes (1984) recommends studying 3 to 10 participants, and one phenomenology, Edwards (2006), studied 33 individuals. In grounded theory, we recommend including 20 to 30 individuals in order to develop a well-saturated theory, but this number may be much larger (Charmaz, 2014). In ethnography, we like well-defined studies of single culture-sharing groups, with numerous artifacts, interviews, and observations collected until the workings of the cultural group are clear. For case study research, we would not include more than four or five case studies in a single study (Yin, 2014). This number should provide ample opportunity to identify themes of the cases as well as conduct cross-case theme analysis. Wolcott (2008a) has recommended that any case over 1 dilutes the level of detail that a researcher can provide.

Forms of Data

New forms of qualitative data continually emerge in the literature (see Creswell, 2012; Merriam & Tisdell, 2015; Warren & Xavia Karner, 2015), but all forms might be grouped into four basic types of information: interviews (ranging from one-on-one, in person interactions to group, web-based interactions), observations (ranging from nonparticipant to participant), documents (ranging from private to public), and audiovisual materials (ranging from photographs to participant-created artifacts). Over the years, a compendium with an evolving list of data types, as shown in Figure 7.3.

We organize the list into the four basic types, although some forms may not be easily placed into one category or the other. In recent years, new forms of data have emerged, such as journaling in narrative story writing, using e-mail messages, and observing through examining videos and photographs. Particularly noteworthy have been the emergence of procedures for qualitative research using visual, sound, and digital methods (Bauer & Gaskell, 2007; Mitchell, 2011). Common formats of computer-mediated data collection for qualitative research include virtual focus groups and web-based interviews via e-mail or text-based chat rooms, weblogs and life journals (such as open-ended diaries online), Internet message boards, and social media (Halfpenny & Procter, 2015; Markham & Baym, 2009; Warren & Xavia Karner, 2015). Some ethnographic researchers have conducted advanced qualitative studies online, collecting data through e-mail, chat room interactions, instant messaging, videoconferencing, and the images and sound of the websites (Garcia, Standlee, Bechkoff, & Cui, 2009). Qualitative data collection via web-based platforms has the advantages of cost and time efficiency in terms of reduced costs for travel and data transcription. It also provides participants with time and space flexibility that allows them more time to consider and respond to requests for information. Thus, they can provide a deeper reflection on the discussed topics and help to create a nonthreatening and comfortable environment, providing greater ease for participants discussing sensitive issues (Nicholas et al., 2010). More importantly, online data collection offers an alternative for hard-to-reach groups (due to practical constraints, disability, or language or communication barriers) who may be marginalized from qualitative research (James & Busher, 2009).

There are, however, increased ethical concerns with online data collection, such as participants' privacy protection, new power differentials, ownership of the data, authenticity, and trust in the data collected (James & Busher, 2009; Marshall & Rossman, 2015; Nicholas et al., 2010). This is particularly noteworthy when working with children such as the ethnographic study conducted by Jachyra, Atkinson, and Washiya (2015) with adolescent boys using social media. Moreover, web-based research brings new requirements to both participants and researchers. For instance, participants are required to have some technical skills, access to the Internet, and necessary reading and writing proficiency. In using online information, researchers have to adapt to a new way of observation by watching texts on a screen, by strengthening their skills in interpreting textual data, and in improving online interview skills (Garcia et al., 2009; Nicholas et al., 2010).

Despite problems in innovative data collection such as these, we encourage individuals designing qualitative projects to include new and creative data collection methods that will encourage readers and editors to examine their studies. An illustrative example by van der Hoorn (2015) uses an arts-based research method (musical improvisation on a xylophone and/or glockenspiel) to access the participant's perception of their experience of managing a project. A follow-up interview asks participants to explain their improvisation and thus accessing their experience. Researchers need to consider visual ethnography (Marion & Crowder, 2013; Pink, 2001) or the possibilities of narrative research to include living stories, metaphorical visual narratives, and digital archives (see Clandinin, 2007). We like the technique of "photo elicitation" in which participants are shown pictures (their own or those taken by the researcher) and asked by the inquirer to discuss the contents of the pictures as in photovoice. Guell and Ogilvie (2015), for example, collected over 500 photos of pictures of commuting work journey from 19 participants in Cambridge, England.

The particular approach to research often directs a qualitative researcher's attention toward preferred approaches to data collection, although these preferred approaches cannot be seen as rigid guidelines. For a narrative study, Czarniawska (2004) mentions three ways to collect data for stories: recording spontaneous incidents of storytelling, eliciting stories through interviews, and asking for stories through such mediums as the Internet. Clandinin and Connelly (2000) suggest collecting field texts through a wide array of sources—autobiographies, journals, researcher field notes, letters, conversations, interviews, stories of families, documents, photographs, and personal–family–social artifacts. The conflicting stories of Ai Mei's ethnic identity were generated personal observations, interviews, field notes, and attendance at events (Chan, 2010; see Appendix B). For a phenomenological study, the process of collecting information involves primarily in-depth interviews (e.g., the discussion about the long interview in McCracken, 1988) with as many as 10 individuals. The important point is to describe the meaning of the phenomenon for a small number of individuals who have experienced it. Often multiple interviews are conducted with the each of the research participants. This was the case for Anderson & Spencer (2002; see Appendix C) whose phenomenological study examined the "cognitive representations or images" of AIDS by patients involved 58 interviews conducted over 18 months. Besides interviewing and self-reflection, Polkinghorne (1989) advocates gathering information from depictions of the experience outside the context of the research projects, such as descriptions drawn from novelists, poets, painters, and choreographers. We recommend Lauterbach (1993), the study of wished-for babies from mothers, as an especially rich example of phenomenological research using diverse forms of data collection.

Interviews play a central role in the data collection in a grounded theory study. In one study, each interview with 33 academic chairpersons lasted approximately an hour

(Creswell & Brown, 1992). Other data forms besides interviewing, such as participant observation, researcher reflection or journaling (memoing), participant journaling, and focus groups, may be used to help develop the theory (Birks & Mills, 2015; Corbin & Strauss, 2015). Adolph, Kruchten, and Hall (2012) drew on interviews, participant observation, and documents to explain the process of software development. However, in our experience, these multiple data forms often play a secondary role to interviewing in grounded theory studies. In an ethnographic study, the investigator collects descriptions of behavior through observations, interviews, documents, and artifacts (Atkinson, 2015; Fetterman, 2010; Spradley, 1980), although observing and interviewing appear to be the most popular forms of ethnographic data collection. A detailed description of the core values of the straight edge (sXe) movement was generated from participating in the movement for 14 years and attending more than 250 music shows, interviewing 28 men and women, and gathering documents from sources such as newspaper stories, music lyrics, World Wide Web pages, and sXe magazines (Haenfler, 2004). Ethnography has the distinction among the five approaches, we believe, of advocating the use of quantitative surveys and tests and measures as part of data collection. For example, examine the wide array of forms of data in ethnography as advanced by LeCompte and Schensul (1999). They reviewed ethnographic data collection techniques of observation, tests and repeated measures, sample surveys, interviews, content analysis of secondary or visual data, elicitation methods, audiovisual information, spatial mapping, and network research.

Like ethnography, case study data collection involves a wide array of procedures as the researcher builds an in-depth picture of the case. We are reminded of the multiple forms of data collection recommended by Yin (2014) in his book about case studies. He referred to six forms: documents, archival records, interviews, direct observation, participant observation, and physical artifacts. To represent the extensive data collection involved in a campus gun incident case study, Asmussen and Creswell (1995) used a matrix of information of the four types of data (interviews, observations, documents, and audiovisual materials) in the columns and the specific forms of information (e.g., students at large, central administration) in the rows. The use of a matrix, which is especially applicable in an information-rich case study, might serve the inquirer equally well in all approaches of inquiry to convey the depth and multiple forms of data collection.

Of the four data collection forms in Figure 7.3, documents and audiovisual materials are typically used to supplement interviews and observations. Yet it is important to recognize the important historical and contextual information generated by a review of existing individual and organizational documents and artefacts (Prior, 2003). Bogdan and Biklen (2006) categorize existing data into three types: personal documents (i.e., individually produced websites, e-mails, blogs), official documents (i.e., organizationally produced websites, handbooks, reports), and popular culture documents (i.e., those that are publicly accessible photographs, magazines). To mitigate many of the challenges of reviewing documents and audiovisual materials, we recommend negotiating access to materials ahead of time, defining clear inclusion or

FIGURE 7.3 ● A Compendium of Data Collection Approaches in Qualitative Research

Interviews

- Conduct one-on-one interview in the same room, virtually via web-based or e-mail platforms.
- Conduct a focus group interview in the same room, virtually via web-based or e-mail platforms.

Observations

- Conduct an observation as a participant or as an observer.
- Conduct an observation shifting position from participant to observer (and vice versa).

Documents

- Keep a research journal during the study, or have a participant keep a journal or diary.
- Examine personal documents (e.g., letters, e-mails, private blogs).
- Analyze organizational documents (e.g., reports, strategic plans, charts, medical records).
- Analyze public documents (e.g., official memos, blogs, records, archival information).
- Examine autobiographies and biographies.

Audiovisual Materials

- Have participants take photographs or record videos (i.e., photo elicitation).
- Use video or film in a social situation or an individual.
- Examine photographs or videos.
- Examine website, tweets, Facebook messages.
- Collect sounds (e.g., musical sounds, a child's laughter, car horns honking).
- Gather phone or computer-based messages.
- Examine possessions or ritual objects.

Source: Adapted from Creswell (2016).

exclusion criteria based on the purpose for the data, and allocating adequate time for review and synthesis.

Interviewing and observing deserve special attention because they are frequently used in all five of the approaches to research. Entire books are available on these two topics (e.g., on interviewing: Brinkmann & Kvale, 2015; Rubin & Rubin, 2012; on observing: Angrosino, 2007; Bernard, 2011); thus, we highlight basic procedures that we recommend to prospective interviewers and observers.

Interviewing An interview is considered to be a social interaction based on a conversation (Rubin & Rubin, 2012; Warren & Xavia Karner, 2015). According to Brinkmann and Kvale (2015), an interview is where "knowledge is constructed in the interaction between the interviewer and the interviewee" (p. 4). The qualitative research interview is further described as "attempts to understand the world from the subjects' point of view, to unfold the meaning of their experience, to uncover their lived world" (p. 3). Who is interviewed and what questions are asked depends on the purpose for the study and research questions guiding the study. Interview questions are often the subquestions in the research study, phrased in a way that interviewees can understand. These might be seen as the core of the **_interview protocol_**, bounded on the front end by questions to invite the interviewee to open up and talk and located at the end by questions about "Whom should I talk to in order to learn more?" or comments thanking the participants for their time for the interview. It is not surprising given the complex skills necessary for conducting a good interview, that interviewing is often referred to as a "craft" that is developed through practice (Brinkmann & Kvale, 2015; Rubin & Rubin, 2012).

How the interactions take place depends on the choice of interview type of which there is great variety. A variation for a one-on-one interview is for both the interviewee and interviewer being physically located in the same room, talking face-to-face using technology, or talking over the phone. An alternative to talking is to interact in writing using text messaging or an online chat function. Focus groups are advantageous when the interaction among interviewees will likely yield the best information, when interviewees are similar and cooperative with each other, when time to collect information is limited, and when individuals interviewed one-on-one may be hesitant to provide information (Krueger & Casey, 2014; Morgan, 1997). Krueger and Casey (2014) discuss the use of focus groups on the Internet, including chat room focus groups and bulletin board groups. They discuss how to manage the Internet groups as well as how to develop questions for the groups. Stewart and Williams (2005) reviewed both synchronous (real-time) and asynchronous (non–real-time) applications of online focus groups for social research. They highlighted the advantages of new developments such as virtual reality applications because participants can be questioned over long periods of time, larger numbers can be managed, and more heated and open exchanges occur. Problems arise with online focus groups, such as obtaining complete informed consent, recruiting individuals to participate, and choosing times to convene given different international time zones. It is important to carefully weigh the drawbacks for some types with the benefits of increased access; for example, some forms lack visual communication, and most require individuals who are not hesitant to speak and share ideas or who are technology-savvy (James & Busher, 2009). The less articulate, shy interviewee may present the researcher with a challenge and less than adequate data. Regardless of interview mode, care must be taken to create an environment as comfortable as possible and, in group settings, to encourage all participants to talk and to monitor individuals who may dominate the conversation.

One might view interviewing as a series of steps in a procedure. Several authors have advanced the steps necessary in conducting qualitative interviews, such as Brinkmann and Kvale (2015) and Rubin and Rubin (2012). The Brinkmann and Kvale (2015) seven stages of an interview inquiry report a logical sequence of stages from thematizing the inquiry; to designing the study; to interviewing; to transcribing the interview;

to analyzing the data; to verifying the validity, to reliability, and generalizability of the findings; and finally to reporting the study. The seven steps described by Rubin and Rubin (2012), called the responsive interviewing model, are similar in scope to Brinkmann and Kvale (2015), but they view the sequence as not fixed, allowing the researcher to change questions asked, the sites chosen, and the situations to study. Both approaches to the stages of interviewing sweep across the many phases of research from deciding on a topic to the actual writing of the study. In the approach presented here, we focus on the data collection process in some detail, recognizing that this process is embedded within a larger sequence of research. The procedures for preparing and conducting interviews are summarized in Figure 7.4:

- *Determine the research questions that will be answered by interviews.* These questions are open-ended, general, and focused on understanding your central phenomenon in the study.
- *Identify interviewees who can best answer these questions based on one of the purposeful sampling procedures mentioned in the preceding discussion* (see Table 7.3).
- *Distinguish the type of interview by determining what mode is practical and what interactions will net the most useful information to answer research questions.* We recommend assessing the types available and deciding the best fit for the particular context.
- *Collect data using adequate recording procedures when conducting one-on-one or focus group interviews.* We recommend microphone equipment that is sensitive to the acoustics of the room from its location, such as the use of lapel microphones or headsets. We also recommend using more than one recording device placed at different locations in a group environment.
- *Design and use an interview protocol, or interview guide* (Brinkmann & Kvale, 2015). Use approximately five to seven open-ended questions and ample space between the questions to write responses to the interviewee's comments (see the sample protocol in Figure 7.5).
- *Refine the interview questions and the procedures through pilot testing.* In an ethnography of boat pilots aboard cargo vessels, Sampson (2004) used pilot testing to refine and develop research instruments, assess the degrees of observer bias, frame questions, collect background information, and adapt research procedures. In case study research, Yin (2014) recommends a pilot test to refine data collection plans and develop relevant lines of questions. These pilot cases are selected on the basis of convenience, access, and geographic proximity.
- *Locate a distraction-free place for conducting the interview.* Find, if possible, a physical setting where a private conversation can be held that lends itself to audiotaping.
- *Obtain consent from the interviewee to participate in the study by completing a consent form approved by the human relations review board.* At the beginning of the interview, review the purpose of the study, the amount of time that will be needed to complete the interview, their right to withdraw from the study, and plans for

using the results from the interview (offer a copy of the report or an abstract of it to the interviewee).

- *As an interviewer, follow good interview procedures.* Stay within the study boundaries you have reviewed, use the protocol to guide your questions, complete the interview within the time specified, be respectful and courteous, and offer few questions and advice. This last point is an important reminder of how a good interviewer is a good listener rather than a frequent speaker during an interview.
- *Decide transcription logistics ahead of time.* For example, what will be transcribed if needed? If software will be used, then how will it be checked? Decisions here need to be made about verbal cues and extraneous words and utterances (e.g., "hmms"). Analysis will be limited if you don't include certain things.

Observing Observation is one of the key tools for collecting data in qualitative research. It is the act of noting a phenomenon in the field setting through the five senses of the observer, often with a note-taking instrument, and recording it for scientific purposes (Angrosino, 2007). The observations are based on the research purpose and questions. You

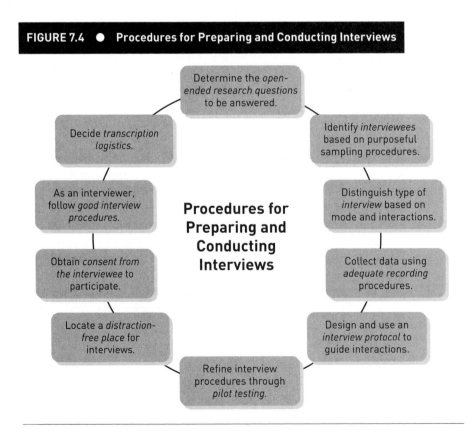

FIGURE 7.4 ● **Procedures for Preparing and Conducting Interviews**

Determine the *open-ended research questions* to be answered.

Identify *interviewees* based on purposeful sampling procedures.

Decide *transcription logistics.*

As an interviewer, follow *good interview procedures.*

Procedures for Preparing and Conducting Interviews

Distinguish type of *interview* based on mode and interactions.

Obtain *consent from the interviewee* to participate.

Collect data using *adequate recording* procedures.

Locate a *distraction-free place* for interviews.

Design and use an *interview protocol* to guide interactions.

Refine interview procedures through *pilot testing.*

FIGURE 7.5 ● Sample Interview Protocol or Guide

Interview Protocol Project: University Reaction to a Terrorist Incident

Time of interview:

Date:

Place:

Interviewer:

Interviewee:

Position of interviewee:

(Briefly describe the project)

Questions:

1. What has been your role in the incident?

2. What has happened since the event that you have been involved in?

3. What has been the impact on the university community of this incident?

4. What larger ramifications, if any, exist from the incident?

5. To whom should we talk to find out more about campus reaction to the incident?

Thank the individual for participating in this interview. Assure him or her of confidentiality of responses and potential future interviews.

---

may watch physical setting, participants, activities, interactions, conversations, and your own behaviors during the observation. Use your senses, including sight, sound, touch, smell, and taste. You should realize that writing down everything is impossible. Thus, you may start the observation broadly and then concentrate on research questions. To one degree or another, the observer is usually involved in that which he or she is observing.

The extent to which the observer is engaged in terms of participating and observing is usually distinguished into four observation *types:*

- **Complete participant.** The researcher is fully engaged with the people he or she is observing. This may help him or her establish greater rapport with the people being observed (Angrosino, 2007).
- **Participant as observer.** The researcher is participating in the activity at the site. The participant role is more salient than the researcher role. This may help the researcher gain insider views and subjective data. However, it may be distracting for the researcher to record data when he or she is integrated into the activity (Bogdewic, 1999).

- ***Nonparticipant or observer as participant.*** The researcher is an outsider of the group under study, watching and taking field notes from a distance. He or she can record data without direct involvement with activity or people (Bernard, 2011).
- ***Complete observer.*** The researcher is neither seen nor noticed by the people under study.

As a good qualitative observer, you may change your role during an observation, such as starting as a nonparticipant and then moving into the participant role, or vice versa. Participant observation, for example, offers possibilities for the researcher on a continuum from being a complete outsider to being a complete insider (Jorgensen, 1989). The approach of changing one's role from that of an outsider to that of an insider through the course of the ethnographic study is well documented in field research (Bernard, 2011; Jorgensen, 1989). Wolcott's (1994) study of the Principal Selection Committee illustrates an outsider perspective, as he observed and recorded events in the process of selecting a principal for a school without becoming an active participant in the committee's conversations and activities.

Observing in a setting is a special skill that requires addressing issues such as the potential deception of the people being interviewed, impression management, and the potential marginality of the researcher in a strange setting (Atkinson, 2015). Like interviewing, we also see observing as a series of procedural steps for preparing and conducting observations summarized in Figure 7.6:

- *Select a site to be observed.* Obtain the required permissions needed to gain access to the site.
- *At the site, identify who or what to observe, when, and for how long.* A gatekeeper helps in this process.
- *Distinguish type of observation based, initially, on a role to be assumed as an observer.* This role can range from that of a complete participant (going native) to that of a complete observer. We especially like the procedure of being an outsider initially, followed by becoming an insider over time.
- *Design and use an **observational protocol** as a method for recording notes in the field.* Include in this protocol both descriptive and reflective notes (i.e., notes about your experiences, hunches, and learnings). Make sure this is headed by the date, place, and time of observation (Angrosino, 2007).
- *Record aspects such as portraits of the participant, the physical setting, particular events and activities, and your own reactions* (Bogdan & Biklen, 1992). Describe what happened and also reflect on these aspects, including personal reflections, insights, ideas, confusions, hunches, initial interpretations, and breakthroughs.
- *Build initial rapport by having someone introduce you if you are an outsider, being passive and friendly, and starting with limited objectives in the first few sessions of observation.* The early observational sessions may be times in which to take few notes and simply observe.

FIGURE 7.6 ● Procedures for Preparing and Conducting Observations

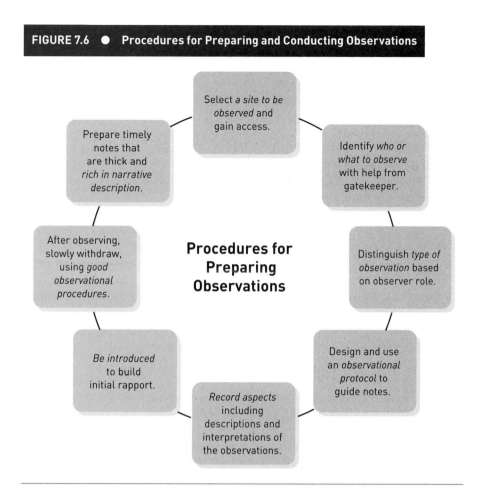

Select *a site to be observed* and gain access.

Identify *who or what to observe* with help from gatekeeper.

Distinguish *type of observation* based on observer role.

Design and use an *observational protocol* to guide notes.

Record aspects including descriptions and interpretations of the observations.

Be introduced to build initial rapport.

After observing, slowly withdraw, using *good observational procedures*.

Prepare timely notes that are thick and *rich in narrative description*.

Procedures for Preparing Observations

- *As an observer, follow good observational procedures.* After observing, slowly withdraw from the site, thanking the participants and informing them of the use of the data and their accessibility to the study.
- *Prepare timely notes that are thick and rich in narrative description after the observation.* Give full description of the people and events under observation (Emerson, Fretz, & Shaw, 2011).

Recording Procedures

In discussing interviewing and observing procedures, we mention the use of a protocol, a predesigned form used to record information collected during an interview or observation. The interview protocol enables a person to take notes during the interview about the responses of the interviewee. It also helps a researcher organize thoughts on items such as headings, information about starting the interview, concluding ideas, information on ending the interview, and thanking the respondent. In Figure 7.5, the authors provided the interview protocol used in the gunman case study (Asmussen & Creswell, 1995).

Besides the five open-ended questions in the study, this form contains several features we recommend. The instructions for using the interview protocol are as follows:

- Use a header to record essential information about the project and as a reminder to go over the purpose of the study with the interviewee. This heading might also include information about confidentiality and address aspects included in the consent form.
- Place space between the questions in the protocol form. Recognize that an individual may not always respond directly to the questions being asked. For example, a researcher may ask Question 2, but the interviewee's response may be to Question 4. Be prepared to write notes on all of the questions as the interviewee speaks.
- Memorize the questions and their order to minimize losing eye contact with the participant. Provide appropriate verbal transitions from one question to the next.
- Write out the closing comments that thank the individual for the interview and request follow-up information, if needed, from him or her.

During an observation, use an observational protocol to record information. As shown in Figure 7.7 this protocol contains notes taken by one a student on a class visit by the late Professor Harry Wolcott. We provide only one page of the protocol, but this is sufficient for one to see what it includes. It has a header giving information about the observational session and then includes a "descriptive notes" section for recording a description of activities. The section with a box around it in the "descriptive notes" column indicates the observer's attempt to summarize, in chronological fashion, the flow of activities in the classroom. This can be useful information for developing a chronology of the ways the activities unfolded during the class session. There is also a "reflective notes" section for notes about the process, reflections on activities, and summary conclusions about activities for later theme development. A line down the center of the page divides descriptive notes from reflective notes. A visual sketch of the setting and a label for it provide additional useful information.

Whether a researcher uses an observational or interview protocol, the essential process is recording information or, as Lofland and Lofland (1995) state, "logging data" (p. 66). This process involves recording information through various forms, such as observational field notes, interview write-ups, and documents as well as mapping, census taking, photographing, and sound recording. An informal process may occur in recording information comprising initial "jottings" (Emerson et al., 2011), daily logs or summaries, and descriptive summaries (for examples of field notes, see Marshall & Rossman, 2015; Sanjek, 1990). These forms of recording information are popular in narrative research, ethnographies, and case studies.

FIGURE 7.7 ● Sample Observational Protocol

Length of Activity: 90 Minutes	
Descriptive Notes	*Reflective Notes*
General: What are the experiences of graduate students as they learn qualitative research in the classroom?	
See classroom layout and comments about physical setting at the bottom of this page.	*Overhead with details: I wonder if the back of the room was able to read it.*
Approximately 5:17 p.m., Dr. Creswell enters the filled room, introduces Dr. Wolcott. Class members seem relieved.	Overhead projector not plugged in at the beginning of the class: I wonder if this was a distraction (when it took extra time to plug it in).
Dr. Creswell gives brief background of guest, concentrating on his international experiences; features a comment about the educational ethnography "The Man in the Principal's Office."	*Lateness of the arrival of Drs. Creswell and Wolcott: Students seemed a bit anxious. Maybe it had to do with the change in starting time to 5 p.m. (some may have had 6:30 classes or appointments to get to).*
Descriptive Notes	*Reflective Notes*
Dr. Wolcott begins by telling the class he now writes out educational ethnography and highlights this primary occupation by mentioning two books: *Transferring Qualitative Data* and *The Art of Fieldwork*.	*Drs. Creswell and Wolcott seem to have a good rapport between them, judging from many short exchanges that they had.*
While Dr. Wolcott begins his presentation by apologizing for his weary voice (due to talking all day, apparently), Dr. Creswell leaves the classroom to retrieve the guest's overhead transparencies. Seemed to be three parts to this activity: (1) the speaker's challenge to the class of detecting pure ethnographical methodologies, (2) the speaker's presentation of the "tree" that portrays various strategies and substrategies for qualitative research in education, and (3) the relaxed "elder statesman" fielding class questions, primarily about students' potential research projects and prior studies Dr. Wolcott had written.	 SKETCH OF CLASSROOM
The first question was "How do you look at qualitative research?" followed by "How does ethnography fit in?"	

Field Issues

Researchers engaged in studies within all five approaches face issues in the field when gathering data that need to be anticipated. During the past several years, the number of books and articles on field issues has expanded considerably as interpretive frameworks (see Chapter 2) have been widely discussed. Beginning researchers are often overwhelmed by the amount of time needed to collect qualitative data and the richness of the data encountered. As a practical recommendation, we suggest that beginners start with limited data collection and engage in a pilot project to gain some initial experiences (Sampson, 2004). This limited data collection might consist of one or two interviews or observations so that researchers can estimate the time needed to collect data.

One way to think about and anticipate the types of issues that may arise during data collection is to view the issues as they relate to several aspects of data collection, such as entry and organizational access, procedures for observations, dynamics between interviewer and interviewee, and availability of documents and audiovisual materials.

Entry and Organizational Access Gaining access to organizations, sites, and individuals to study has its own challenges. Convincing individuals to participate in the study, building trust and credibility at the field site, and getting people from a site to respond are all important access challenges. Factors related to considering the appropriateness of a site need to be considered as well (see Weis & Fine, 2000). For example, researchers may choose a site that is one in which they have a vested interest (e.g., employed at the site, a study of superiors or subordinates at the site) that would limit ability to develop diverse perspectives on coding data or developing themes. A researcher's own particular "stance" within the group may keep him or her from acknowledging all dimensions of the experiences. The researchers may hear or see something uncomfortable when they collect data. In addition, participants may be fearful that their issues will be exposed to people outside their community, and this may make them unwilling to accept the researcher's interpretation of the situation.

Also related to access is the issue of working with an institutional review board that may not be familiar with unstructured interviews in qualitative research and the risks associated with these interviews (Corbin & Morse, 2003). Weis and Fine (2000) raised the important question of whether the response of the institutional review board to a project influences the researcher's telling of the narrative story.

Procedures for Observations The types of challenges experienced during observations will closely relate to the role of the inquirer in observation, such as whether the researcher assumes a participant, nonparticipant, or middle-ground position. There are challenges as well with the mechanics of observing, such as remembering to take field notes, recording quotes accurately for inclusion in field notes, determining the best timing for moving from a nonparticipant to a participant (if this role change is desired), keeping from being overwhelmed at the site with information, and learning how to funnel the observations from the broad picture to a narrower one in time. Participant observation has attracted several commentaries by writers (Ezeh, 2003; Labaree, 2002). Labaree (2002), who was a participant in an academic senate on a campus, notes the advantages of this role but also discusses the dilemmas of entering the field, disclosing oneself to the participants, sharing relationships with other individuals, and attempting to disengage from the site. Ezeh (2003), a Nigerian, studied the Orring, a little-known minority ethnic group in Nigeria. Although his initial contact with the group was supportive, the more the researcher became integrated into the host community, the more he experienced human relations problems, such as being accused of spying, pressured to be more generous in his material gifts, and suspected of trysts with women. Ezeh concluded that being of the same nationality was no guarantee of a lack of challenges at the site.

Dynamics Between Interviewer and Interviewee Challenges in qualitative interviewing often focus on the mechanics of conducting the interview. Roulston, deMarrais, and Lewis (2003) chronicle the challenges in interviewing by postgraduate students during a 15-day intensive course. These challenges related to unexpected participant behaviors and students' ability to create good instructions, phrase and negotiate questions, deal with sensitive issues, and develop transcriptions. Suoninen and Jokinen (2005), from the field of social work, ask whether the phrasing of our interview questions leads to subtle persuasive questions, responses, or explanations.

Undoubtedly, conducting interviews is taxing, especially for inexperienced researchers engaged in studies that require extensive interviewing, such as phenomenology, grounded theory, and case study research. Equipment issues loom large as a problem in interviewing, and both recording and transcribing equipment need to be organized in advance of the interview. The process of questioning during an interview (e.g., saying little, handling emotional outbursts, using icebreakers) includes problems that an interviewer must address. Many inexperienced researchers express surprise at the difficulty of conducting interviews and the lengthy process involved in transcribing audiotapes from the interviews. In addition, in phenomenological interviews, asking appropriate questions and relying on participants to discuss the meaning of their experiences require patience and skill on the part of the researcher.

Recent discussions about qualitative interviewing highlight the importance of reflecting about the relationship that exists between the interviewer and the interviewee (Brinkmann & Kvale, 2015; Nunkoosing, 2005; Weis & Fine, 2000). Brinkmann and Kvale (2015), for example, discuss the power asymmetry in which the research interview should not be regarded as a completely open and free dialogue between egalitarian partners. Instead, the nature of an interview sets up an unequal power dynamic between the interviewer and the interviewee. In this dynamic, the interview is "ruled" by the interviewer. The interview is dialogue that is conducted one-way, provides information for the researcher, is based on the researcher's agenda, leads to the researcher's interpretations, and contains "counter control" elements by the interviewee who withholds information. To correct for this asymmetry, Brinkmann and Kvale (2015) suggest more collaborative interviewing, where the researcher and the participant approach equality in questioning, interpreting, and reporting.

An extension to the discussion is provided by the reflections of Nunkoosing (2005) on the problems of power and resistance, distinguishing truth from authenticity, the impossibility of consent, and projection of the interviewers' own self (their status, race, culture, and gender). Weis and Fine (2000) raise additional questions for consideration: Are your interviewees able to articulate the forces that interrupt, suppress, or oppress them? Do they erase their history, approaches, and cultural identity? Do they choose not to expose their history or go on record about the difficult aspects of their lives? These questions and the points raised about the nature of the interviewer–interviewee relationship cannot be easily answered with pragmatic decisions that encompass all interview situations. They do, however, sensitize us to important challenges in qualitative interviewing that need to be anticipated.

A final issue is whether the researcher shares personal experiences with participants in an interview setting such as in a case study, a phenomenology, or an ethnography. This sharing minimizes the "bracketing" that is essential to construct the meaning of participants in a phenomenology and reduces information shared by participants in case studies and ethnographies.

Availability of Documents and Audiovisual Materials In document research, many issues involve locating materials, often at sites far away or assessing how publically these materials are, and obtaining permission to use the materials (Marshall & Rossman, 2015). For biographers, the primary form of data collection might be archival research from documents; some of these may be online. The increasing use and evolving forms of data generated by Internet-based technologies continue to raise important ethical considerations (Davidson & di Gregorio, 2011).

When researchers ask participants in a study to keep journals or to create audiovisual materials and documents during the process of research, additional field issues emerge. Journaling is a popular data collection process in case studies and narrative research. What instructions should be given to individuals prior to writing in their journals? Are all participants equally comfortable with journaling? Is it appropriate, for example, with small children who express themselves well verbally but have limited writing skills? The researcher also may have difficulty reading the handwriting of participants who journal. Recording on videotape raises issues for the qualitative researcher such as keeping disturbing room sounds to a minimum, deciding on the best location for the camera, and determining whether to provide close-up shots or distant shots.

Data Storage and Security We are surprised at how little attention is given in books and articles to managing data storage of qualitative data. The approach to storage will reflect the type of information collected, which varies by approach to inquiry. In writing a narrative life history, the researcher needs to develop a filing system for the "wad of handwritten notes or a tape" (Plummer, 1983, p. 98)—and more recently to digital recordings and files. Davidson's (1996) suggestion about backing up information collected and noting changes made to the database is sound advice for all types of research studies. With extensive use of computers in qualitative research, more attention will likely be given to how qualitative data are organized and stored, whether the data are field notes, transcripts, or rough jottings. With extremely large databases being used by some qualitative researchers, this aspect assumes major importance. In his discussion of data management, Lambert (2015) highlights the vast data available through the Understanding Society survey in the United Kingdom that were unwieldy without the use of digital-based storage methods. Specifically, he describes the data set as "involving repeated extended interviews with more than a hundred thousand responses, collecting detailed and extensive health and social information . . . . [and as] one of several major government sponsored surveys of a similar scale" (Lambert, 2015, p. 105). Lambert concludes that the key challenges for e-research platforms is for researchers to employ new methods of data management in qualitative research that facilitate access and whose analysis has strong potential for societal implications.

Some principles about data storage and handling that are especially well suited for qualitative research include the following:

- Always develop backup copies of computer files (Davidson, 1996).
- Use high-quality tapes or recording devices for audio recording information during interviews. Also, make sure that the size of the tapes fits the transcriber's machine.
- Develop a master list of types of information gathered.
- Protect the anonymity of participants by masking their names in the data, and if a master list is needed, be sure to store it separately.
- Develop a data collection matrix as a visual means of locating and identifying information for a study.

Five Approaches Compared

Returning again to Table 7.1, there are both differences and similarities among the activities of data collection for the five approaches to inquiry. Turning to differences, certain approaches seem more directed toward specific types of data collection than others. For case and narrative studies, the researcher uses multiple forms of data to build the in-depth case or the storied experiences. For grounded theory studies and phenomenological projects, inquirers rely primarily on interviews as data. Ethnographers highlight the importance of participant observation and interviews, but as noted earlier, they may use many different sources of information. Unquestionably, some mixing of forms occurs, but in general these patterns of collection by approach hold true. Case study writers employ multiple forms of data collection.

Second, the unit of analysis for data collection varies among the five approaches. Narrative researchers, phenomenologists, and ground theorists study individuals; case study researchers examine groups of individuals participating in an event or activity or an organization; and ethnographers study entire cultural systems or some subcultures of the systems.

Third, we found the amount of discussion about field issues to vary among the five approaches. Ethnographers have written extensively about field issues (e.g., Atkinson, 2015; Hammersley & Atkinson, 1995). This may reflect historical concerns about imbalanced power relationships, imposing objective, external standards on participants, and failures to be sensitive to marginalized groups. Narrative researchers are less specific about field issues, although their concerns have been voiced about how to conduct the interview (Elliott, 2005). Across all approaches, ethical issues are widely discussed.

Fourth, the approaches vary in their intrusiveness of data collection. Conducting interviews seems less intrusive in phenomenological projects and grounded theory studies than in the high level of access needed in personal narratives, the prolonged stays in the field in ethnographies, and the immersion into programs or events in case studies.

These differences do not lessen some important similarities that need to be observed. All qualitative studies sponsored by public institutions need to be approved by a human subjects review board, at least in the United States and in other countries. Also, the use of interviews and observations is central to many of the approaches. Furthermore, the recording devices, such as observational and interview protocols, can be similar regardless of approach (although specific questions on each protocol will reflect the language of the approach). Finally, the issue of data storage of information is closely related to the form of data collection, and the basic objective of researchers, regardless of approach, is to develop some management system for organized retrieval of information and secure storage. In Chapter 8, we build upon the data collection circle to examine the features of the data analysis spiral common to all approaches with the analyses and representations compared across the five approaches.

Chapter Check-In

1. Do you see the similarities and differences in how the authors describe the data collection activities within their published qualitative studies? Select two of the qualitative articles presented in Appendices B through F.

   a. Begin with identifying evidence of the seven data collection activities (summarized in Figure 7.1) as they have been applied in each of the journal articles. Note which elements are easy and which are more difficult to identify.

   b. Then compare the descriptions for each of the data collection activities across the articles. Note which elements are similar and which are different.

2. Can you identify evidence of integration between the study purpose and data being collected by the author(s)? Read qualitative journal articles that adopt different approaches across diverse fields, such as the narrative study of Ellis (1993), phenomenology of Lemay, Cashman, Elfenbein, and Felice (2010), grounded theory study of Komives, Owen, Longerbeam, Mainella, and Osteen (2005), ethnography of Trujillo (1992), and case study of Staples, Pugach, and Himes (2005).

   a. Begin by identifying the forms of data collected in the study. What rationales are presented for their use?

   b. Then review the study introduction, and note the research purpose (and research questions if present) and qualitative approach adopted.

   c. Next, assess to what extent the forms of data collection are appropriate for the approach and purpose for conducting the study. In brief, can the data collected address the articulated purpose? Why or why not?

Ellis, C. (1993). "There are survivors": Telling a story of sudden death. *The Sociological Quarterly, 34*, 711–730. doi:10.1111/j.1533-8525.1993.tb00114.x

Komives, S. R., Owen, J. E., Longerbeam, S. D., Mainella, F. C., & Osteen, L. (2005). Developing a leadership identity: A grounded theory. *Journal of College Student Development, 46*(6), 593–611. doi:10.1353/csd.2005.0061

Lemay, C. A., Cashman, S. B., Elfenbein, D. S., & Felice, M. E. (2010). A qualitative study of the meaning of fatherhood among young urban fathers. *Public Health Nursing, 27*(3), 221–231. doi:10.1111/j.1525-1446.2010.00847.x

Staples, A., Pugach, M. C., & Himes, D. J. (2005). Rethinking the technology integration challenge: Cases from three urban elementary schools. *Journal of Research on Technology in Education, 37*(3), 285–311. doi:10.1080/15391523 .2005.10782438

Trujillo, N. (1992). Interpreting (the work and the talk of) baseball. *Western Journal of Communication, 56*, 350–371. doi:10.1353/ csd.2005.0061

3. Can you begin to sketch the data collection circle for a qualitative study? Examine Figure 7.1 for the seven activities. Develop a matrix that describes data collection for all seven activities for your project. Provide detail in this matrix for each of the seven activities. Follow these steps:

   a. State the site and/or individuals that are the focus of your study and rationale for their choice in a couple of sentences.

   b. Discuss the processes by which you will gain access and develop a rapport with individuals and/or gatekeepers (if applicable).

   c. Present the strategy for purposeful sampling and rationale that reflects your approach to research.

   d. Describe the forms of data you will collect, and provide a rationale for the appropriateness of their use referring to the approach you chose.

   e. Outline the procedures you will develop for recording information.

(Continued)

(Continued)

f. Consider the issues that may emerge as you begin fieldwork. Present a plan for resolving each of them.

g. Apply the suggestions presented in this chapter for storing data securely, and draft the procedures you will follow.

h. Look across the descriptions of the activities within the data collection circle for any ethical issues that have not been attended to.

4. Can you apply your understandings to a practical experience in collecting data for your project?

5. Design an interview or an observational protocol for your study. Conduct either an interview or an observation, and record the information on the protocol you have developed. After this experience, identify issues that posed challenges during this data collection.

Summary

In this chapter, we addressed several components of the data collection process. The researcher attends to ethical considerations across the activities in addition to locating a site or person to study; gaining access to and building rapport at the site or with the individual; sampling purposefully using one or more of the many approaches to sampling in qualitative research; collecting information through many forms, such as interviews, observations, documents, and audiovisual materials and newer forms emerging in the literature; establishing approaches for recording information such as the use of interview or observational protocols; anticipating and addressing field issues ranging from access to ethical concerns; and developing a system for storing and securely handling the databases. The five approaches to inquiry differ in the diversity of information collected, the unit of study being examined, the extent of field issues discussed in the literature, and the intrusiveness of the data collection effort. An essential aspect for researchers, regardless of approach, is the collection and management of data in an ethical manner. This typically involves gaining institutional approvals—and in some cases, organizational approvals—from review boards prior to beginning the research and then following the consent, recording, and storage protocols that are described in the application.

Further Readings

Several readings extend this brief overview introduction to data collection beginning with general resources and then by specific data forms. The list should not be considered exhaustive, and readers are encouraged to seek out additional readings in the end-of-book reference list.

Creswell, J. W. (2012). *Educational research: Planning, conducting, and evaluating quantitative and qualitative research* (4th ed.). Upper Saddle River, NJ: Pearson.

John W. Creswell introduces the steps of conducting qualitative research alongside those of conducting quantitative research. This approach can be especially helpful for the researcher who has some existing research expertise or experience and finds the discussions about sampling and data collection to be essential reading.

Chilisa, B. (2012). *Indigenous research methodologies*. Thousand Oaks, CA: Sage.

Bagele Chilisa describes diverse indigenous research methodologies and provides illustrative case studies from around the globe. She also provides practical guidance for researchers within indigenous contexts.

Guest, G., Namey, E. E., & Mitchell, M. L. (2013). *Collecting qualitative data: A field manual for applied research*. Thousand Oaks, CA: Sage.

Greg Guest, Emily Namey, and Marilyn Mitchell offer detailed procedures related to participant observation, in-depth interviews, and focus groups. In particular, we found their discussion of document analysis as well as sampling size across data forms to be helpful guidance.

Stanfield, J. H., II (Ed.) (2011). *Rethinking race and ethnicity in research methods*. Walnut Creek, CA: Left Coast Press.

In this work, John Stanfield draws on the personal and professional lives of contributing authors to highlight their uses of methods and the practical issues that emerged.

For Guidance Related to Interviewing

Brinkmann, S., & Kvale, S. (2015). *InterViews: Learning the craft of qualitative research interviewing* (3rd ed.). Thousand Oaks, CA: Sage.

Svend Brinkmann and Steinar Kvale describe seven stages of an interview investigation to structure their comprehensive guidance for conducting interviews, which provide the organizing structure for the book.

James, N., & Busher, H. (2009). *Online interviewing*. Thousand Oaks, CA: Sage.

Nalita James and Hugh Busher discuss the methodological and epistemological challenges associated with computer-mediated interviews. Of particular note is the discussion about ethical considerations in conducting online interviews within a virtual environment.

Krueger, R. A., & Casey, M. A. (2014). *Focus groups: A practical guide for applied research* (5th ed.). Thousand Oaks, CA: Sage.

A good overview for planning and conducting focus groups, this new edition expands guidance on developing questions. Particularly useful is the discussion on moderating skills in different contexts (e.g., young participants, cross-cultural settings).

Rubin, H. J., & Rubin, I. S. (2012). *Qualitative interviewing: The art of hearing data* (3rd ed.). Thousand Oaks, CA: Sage.

Herbert Rubin and Irene Rubin describe their seven-step responsive interviewing approach. The writing is accessible and provides access to the lessons learned from their extensive interview experiences.

(Continued)

(Continued)

For Discussions About Making Observations and Taking Field Notes

Angrosino, M. V. (2007). *Doing ethnographic and observational research*. Thousand Oaks, CA: Sage.

Michael Angrosino provides a comprehensive guide to the process of conducting ethnographic research. Of particular note is his discussion of ethical considerations and descriptions of a variety of data collection techniques for participant observer field researchers.

Bernard, H. R. (2011). *Research methods in anthropology: Qualitative and quantitative approaches* (5th ed.). Walnut Creek, CA: AltaMira.

In this comprehensive resource, Russ Bernard outlines procedures for sampling, collecting, and analyzing data. We find his guidance for observational procedures to be particularly helpful.

Emerson, R. M., Fretz, R. I., & Shaw, L. L. (2011). *Writing ethnographic fieldnotes* (2nd ed.). Chicago, IL: University of Chicago Press.

Robert Emerson, Rachel Fretz, and Linda Shaw outline practical guidance for creating and interpreting field notes. Through embedding illustrative examples, they make accessible a difficult process to describe.

For Information About Issues and Use of Documents and Audiovisual Materials

Bauer, W. M., & Gaskell, G. D. (Eds.). (2007). *Qualitative research with text, image and sound: A practical handbook*. Thousand Oaks, CA: Sage.

Noteworthy within this handbook are chapters related to use of video, film, and photographs (Chapter 6) and analysis guidance of conversations (Chapter 11), images (Chapters 13 and 14), and music (Chapter 15).

Merriam, S. B., & Tisdell, E. J. (2015). *Qualitative research: A guide to design and implementation* (4th ed.). San Fransisco, CA: Jossey-Bass.

This is a useful resource for designing, conducting, and reporting qualitative research. Of particular note is their description of documents including popular culture documents (e.g., cartoons, movies), visual (e.g., video, web-based media), physical material, and artifacts (e.g., tools, electronics).

Warren, C. A., & Xavia Karner, T. (2015). *Discovering qualitative methods: Ethnography, interviews, documents, and images* (3rd ed.). New York, NY: Oxford University Press.

Carol Warren and Tracey Xavia Karner describe the decisions and processes involved in sampling, collecting, and analyzing a variety of types of documents and images.

Data Analysis and Representation

Analyzing text and multiple other forms of data presents a challenging task for qualitative researchers. Deciding how to **represent the data** in tables, matrices, and narrative form adds to the challenge. Often qualitative researchers equate data analysis with approaches for analyzing text and image data. The process of analysis is much more. It also involves organizing the data, conducting a preliminary read-through of the database, **coding** and organizing **themes**, representing the data, and forming an **interpretation** of them. These steps are interconnected and form a spiral of activities all related to the analysis and representation of the data. Computers can assist in qualitative data analysis because the programs facilitate tasks—usually making them easier and faster to complete over time, but they are not necessary for completion. Patton (2015) notes the role of software in the process of analysis, saying while "many swear by it because it can offer leaps in productivity for those adept at it, using software is not a requisite for qualitative analysis. Whether you do or do not use software, the real analytical work takes place in your head" (p. 530–531).

In this chapter, we begin with a review of key ethical issues to anticipate during data analysis and representation processes followed by a summary of three general approaches to analysis so that we can see how leading authors follow similar processes as well as different ones. We then present a visual model—a data analysis spiral—that we find useful to conceptualize a larger picture of all steps in the data analysis process in qualitative research. We use this spiral as a conceptualization to further explore each of the five approaches to inquiry, and we examine specific data analysis procedures within each approach and compare these procedures. We then discuss the use of computers in qualitative analysis—including weighing the advantages with the disadvantages. Finally, we introduce four software programs—MAXQDA, ATLAS.ti, NVivo, and HyperRESEARCH—and discuss the common features of using software programs in data analysis as well as templates for coding data within each of the five approaches.

Questions for Discussion

- What ethical issues may arise during data analysis?
- What are common data analysis strategies used in qualitative research?
- How might the overall data analysis process be conceptualized in qualitative research?
- What are specific data analysis procedures used within each of the approaches to inquiry, and how do they differ?
- What are the procedures available in qualitative computer analysis programs, and how would these procedures differ by approach to qualitative inquiry?

Ethical Considerations for Data Analysis

Among the challenges researchers encounter during the data analysis and representation process are ethical issues related to participant protection from harm and disclosure of comprehensive findings (see Table 8.1). This review, positioned in advance of specific analysis strategies, reminds us to carefully consider ethical issues across all approaches to inquiry (see initial discussion in Chapter 3). For the protection of participants, it is essential that researchers mask participant names as soon as possible to avoid inclusion of identifiable information in the analysis files. Researchers may also create composite profiles to avoid situations where participants might be identifiable in the reporting documents. During the disclosure of findings, it is researchers who embed member-checking strategies to enhance confidence in the data interpretations, a procedure to be discussed in Chapter 10 as a key validation step in research. Engaging participants in the data analysis may foster collaboration in how the data is interpreted and ultimately represented.

TABLE 8.1 ● Examples of Ethical Issues to Attend to During Data Analysis		
Type of Ethical Issue	**Examples of Ethics Issues to Anticipate and Address**	**Examples of How to Minimize**
Protection of participants from harm	Avoidance of disclosing information that would harm participants	Mask names or assign aliases
	Situations where data might be identifiable to a particular source	Create composite participant profiles
Disclosure of comprehensive findings	Limited access to analysis procedures and lack of agreement about how findings are represented	Embed member-checking strategies and opportunities for sharing procedures and results
	Siding with participants and disclosure of only positive results	Present multiple perspectives reflective of a complex picture

Three Analysis Strategies

Data analysis in qualitative research consists of preparing and organizing the data (i.e., text data as in transcripts, or image data as in photographs) for analysis; then reducing the data into themes through a process of coding and condensing the codes; and finally representing the data in figures, tables, or a discussion. Across many books on qualitative research, this is the general process that researchers use. Undoubtedly, there will be some variations in this approach. An important point to note is that beyond these steps, the five approaches to inquiry have additional analysis steps. Before examining the specific analysis steps in the five approaches, it is helpful to have in mind the general analysis procedures that are fundamental to all forms of qualitative research.

Table 8.2 presents typical general analysis procedures as illustrated through the writings of three qualitative researchers. We have chosen these three authors because they represent different perspectives. Madison (2005, 2011) presents an interpretive framework taken from critical ethnography, Huberman and Miles (1994) adopt a systematic approach to analysis that has a long history of use in qualitative inquiry, and Wolcott (1994) uses a more traditional approach to research from ethnography and case study analysis. These three influential sources advocate many similar processes, as well as a few different approaches to the analytic phase of qualitative research.

All of these authors comment on the central steps of coding the data (reducing the data into meaningful segments and assigning names for the segments), combining

TABLE 8.2 ● General Data Analysis Strategies Advanced by Select Authors			
Analytic Strategy	**Madison (2005, 2011)**	**Huberman and Miles (1994)**	**Wolcott (1994)**
Taking notes while reading		Write margin notes in field notes.	Highlight certain information in description.
Sketching reflective thinking		Write reflective passages in notes.	
Summarizing field notes		Draft a summary sheet on field notes.	
Working with words		Make metaphors.	
Identifying codes	Use abstract coding or concrete coding.	Write codes and memos.	
Reducing codes to themes	Identify salient themes or patterns.	Note patterns and themes.	Identify patterned regularities.
Counting frequency of codes		Count frequency of codes.	
Relating categories		Note relations among variables, and build a logical chain of evidence.	
Relating categories to analytic framework in literature			Contextualize with the framework from literature.
Creating a point of view	Create a point of view for scenes, audience, and readers.		
Displaying and reporting the data	Create a graph or picture of the framework.	Make contrasts and comparisons.	Display findings in tables, charts, diagrams, and figures; compare cases; compare with a standard case.

the codes into broader categories or themes, and displaying and making comparisons in the data graphs, tables, and charts. These are the core elements of qualitative data analysis.

Beyond these elements, the authors present different phases in the data analysis process. Huberman and Miles (1994), for example, provide more detailed steps in the process, such as writing marginal notes, drafting summaries of field notes, and noting relationships among the categories. The practical application of many of these strategies were recently described and in some cases expanded upon by Bazeley (2013)—for example, how participants can be involved, the use of visuals, and the role of software. Madison (2011), however, introduces the need to create a point of view—a stance that signals the interpretive framework (e.g., critical, feminist) taken in the study. This point of view is central to the analysis in critical, theoretically oriented qualitative studies. Wolcott (1994), on the other hand, discusses the importance of forming a description from the data, as well as relating the description to the literature and cultural themes in cultural anthropology.

The Data Analysis Spiral

Data analysis is not off-the-shelf; rather, it is custom-built, revised, and "choreographed" (Huberman & Miles, 1994). The processes of data collection, data analysis, and report writing are not distinct steps in the process—they are interrelated and often go on simultaneously in a research project. Bazeley (2013) attributes success in data analysis to early preparation, cautioning "from the time of its [your research project] conception you will take steps that will facilitate or hinder your interpretation and explanation of the phenomena you observe" (p. 1). One of the challenges is making the data analysis process explicit because qualitative researchers often "learn by doing" (Dey, 1993, p. 6). This leads critics to claim that qualitative research is largely intuitive, soft, and relativistic or that qualitative data analysts fall back on the three I's—"insight, intuition, and impression" (Dey, 1995, p. 78). Undeniably, qualitative researchers preserve the unusual and serendipitous, and writers craft studies differently, using analytic procedures that often evolve while they are in the field. Despite this uniqueness, we believe that the analysis process conforms to a general contour.

The contour is best represented in a spiral image, a data analysis spiral. As shown in Figure 8.1, to analyze qualitative data, the researcher engages in the process of moving in analytic circles rather than using a fixed linear approach. One enters with data of text or audiovisual materials (e.g., images, sound recordings) and exits with an account or a narrative. In between, the researcher touches on several facets of analysis and circles around and around. Within each spiral, the researcher uses analytic strategies for the goal of generating specific analytic outcomes—all of which will be further described in the following sections (see Table 8.3 for summary).

Managing and Organizing the Data

Data management, the first loop in the spiral, begins the process. At an early stage in the analysis process, researchers typically organize their data into digital files and create a file naming system. The consistent application of a file naming system ensures materials can be easily located in large databases of text (or images or recordings) for analysis either by hand or by computer (Bazeley, 2013). A searchable spreadsheet or

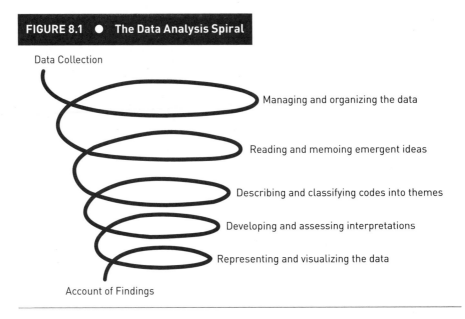

FIGURE 8.1 ● The Data Analysis Spiral

Data Collection

Managing and organizing the data

Reading and memoing emergent ideas

Describing and classifying codes into themes

Developing and assessing interpretations

Representing and visualizing the data

Account of Findings

database by data form, participant, date of collection (among other features) is critical for locating files efficiently. Patton (1980) says the following:

> The data generated by qualitative methods are voluminous. I have found no way of preparing students for the sheer massive volumes of information with which they will find themselves confronted when data collection has ended. Sitting down to make sense out of pages of interviews and whole files of field notes can be overwhelming. (p. 297)

Besides organizing files, researchers convert data and make plans for long-term secure file storage. Data conversion requires the researcher to make decisions about appropriate text units of the data (e.g., a word, a sentence, an entire story) and digital representations of the audiovisual materials. Grbich (2013) advises representing audiovisual materials digitally using a JPEG or pdf file of an image (e.g., photo, newspaper advertisement) or artifact (e.g., clay sculpture, clothing). It is important for researchers to carefully consider these early organizational decisions because of the potential impact on future analysis—for example, if the researcher intends to compare files, then how the individual files are initially set up and (if applicable) uploaded to a software program matter. For example, comparisons over chronological time or across multiple participants or across particular forms of data (e.g., interviews, focus groups, documents) are enabled or hindered by initial file organization. Computer programs help with file management and analysis tasks, and their role in this process will be addressed later in this chapter.

TABLE 8.3 ● The Data Analysis Spiral Activities, Strategies, and Outcomes

Data Analysis Spiral Activities	Analytic Strategies	Analytic Outcomes
Managing and organizing the data	Preparing files and units	File naming system and organizing database of files and units of text, images, and recordings
	Ensuring ongoing secure storage of files	Creation of long-term file storage plan
	Selecting mode of analysis	Use of software, by hand or hybrid
Reading and memoing emergent ideas	Taking notes while reading	Written memos leading to code development, reflections over time, and/or summaries across files or questions or project
	Sketching reflective thinking	
	Summarizing field notes	
Describing and classifying codes into themes	Working with words	Naming of initial codes
	Identifying codes	List of code categories and descriptions
	Applying codes	Assign the codes to units of text, images, and recordings
	Reducing codes to themes	Finalized codebook
Developing and assessing interpretations	Relating categories/themes/families	Contextual understandings and diagrams
	Relating categories/themes/families to analytic framework in literature	Theories and propositions
Representing and visualizing the data	Creating a point of view	Matrix, trees, and models
	Displaying and reporting the data	Account of the findings

Reading and Memoing Emergent Ideas

Following the organization of the data, researchers continue analysis by getting a sense of the whole database. Agar (1980), for example, suggests that researchers "read the transcripts in their entirety several times. Immerse yourself in the details, trying to get a sense of the interview as a whole before breaking it into parts" (p. 103). Similarly, Bazeley (2013) describes her read, reflect, play, and explore strategies as an "initial foray as into new data" (p. 101). Writing notes or memos in the margins of field notes or transcripts or under images helps in this initial process of exploring a database.

Scanning the text allows the researcher to build a sense of the data as a whole without getting caught up in the details of coding. Rapid reading has the benefits of approaching the text in a new light "as if they had been written by a stranger" (Emerson, Fretz, & Shaw, 2011, p. 145).

Memos are short phrases, ideas, or key concepts that occur to the reader. The role of the memoing process is described by the Miles, Huberman, and Saldaña (2014) definition. Memos are "not just descriptive summaries of data but attempts to synthesize in them into higher level analytic meanings." (p. 95). Similarly, when examining digital representations of audiovisual materials, write memos of emergent ideas either on the digital representation or in an accompanying text file. Grbich (2013) suggests guiding the examination of the content and context of the material using the following questions: What is it? Why, when, how, and by whom was it produced? What meanings does the material convey? Guidance for the analysis of audiovisual data is available from general resources (e.g., Rose, 2012) in addition to specific forms of audiovisual data—for example, for images, see Banks, (2014); for film and video, see Mikos (2014); Knoblauch, Tuma, and Schnettler (2014); for sounds, see Maeder (2014); and for virtual data, see Marotzki, Holze, and Vertständig (2014).

Memoing procedures were used in the gunman case study (Asmussen & Creswell, 1995); first, the authors scanned all of the databases to identify major organizing ideas. Then, looking over his field notes from observations, interview transcriptions, physical trace evidence, and audio and visual images, the authors disregarded predetermined questions so they could "see" what interviewees said. They then reflected on the larger thoughts presented in the data and formed initial categories. These categories were few in number (about 10), and they looked for multiple forms of evidence to support each. Moreover, they found evidence that portrayed multiple perspectives about each category (Stake, 1995). Common to both of our analysis experiences, we have found memoing to be a worthy investment of our time as a means of creating a digital ***audit trail*** that can be retrieved and examined (Silver & Lewins, 2014). Using an audit trail as a validation strategy for documenting thinking processes that clarify understandings over time will be discussed in Chapter 10.

Here are some recommendations that guide our memoing practice (see also Corbin & Strauss, 2015; Miles et al., 2014; Ravitch & Mittenfelner Carl, 2016).

- Prioritize memoing throughout the analysis process. Begin memoing during the initial read of your data and continue all the way to the writing of the conclusions. For example, we recommend memoing during each and every analytic session and often return to the memos written during the early analysis as a way of tracking the evolution of codes and theme development. Miles et al. (2014) describes the urgency of memoing as "when an idea strikes, *stop* whatever else you are doing and write the memo. . . . Include your musings of all sorts, even the fuzzy and foggy ones" (p. 99; emphasis in original).
- Individualize a system for memo organization. Memos can quickly become unwieldy unless they are developed with an organizational system in mind. At

the same time researchers tout the usefulness of memoing, there is a lack of consensus about guiding procedures for memoing. We approach memoing so that the process meets our individualized needs. For example, we use a system based on the unit of text associated with the memo and creates captions reflective of content to assist in sorting. Three levels can be used in analysis:

- ○ Segment memos capture ideas from reading particular phrases in the data. This type of memo is helpful for identifying initial codes and is similar to a precoding memo described by Ravitch and Mittenfelner Carl (2016).
- ○ Document memos capture concepts developed from reviewing an individual file or as a way of documenting evolving ideas from the review across multiple files. This type of memo is helpful for summarizing and identifying code categories for themes and/or comparisons across questions or data forms.
- ○ Project memos capture the integration of ideas across one concept or as a way of documenting how multiple concepts might fit together across the project. This type of memo is similar a summary memo described by Corbin and Strauss (2015) as useful for helping to move the research along because all the major ideas of the research are accessible.

- • Embed sorting strategies for memo retrieval. Memos need to be easily retrievable and sortable across time, content, data form, or participant. To that end, dating and creating identifiable captions become very important when writing memos. Corbin and Strauss (2015) forward the use of conceptual headings as a feature for enhanced memo retrieval.

To conclude this section, we emphasize the complementary role memoing plays to systematic analysis because memoing helps track development of ideas through the process. This, in turn, lends credibility to the qualitative data analysis process and outcomes because "the qualitative researcher should expect to uncover some information through informed hunches, intuition, and serendipitous occurrences that, in turn, will lead to a richer and more powerful explanation of the setting, context, and participants in any given study" (Janesick, 2011, p. 148).

Describing and Classifying Codes Into Themes

The next step consists of moving from the reading and memoing in the spiral to describing, classifying, and interpreting the data. In this loop, forming *codes* or *categories* (and these two terms will be used interchangeably) represents the heart of qualitative data analysis. Here, researchers build detailed descriptions, apply codes, develop themes or dimensions, and provide an interpretation in light of their own views or views of perspectives in the literature. *Detailed description* means that authors describe what they see. This detail is provided *in situ*—that is, within the context of the setting of the person, place, or event. Description becomes a good place to start in a qualitative study (after reading and managing data), and it plays a central role in ethnographic and case studies.

The process of coding is central to qualitative research and involves making sense of the text collected from interviews, observations, and documents. Coding involves aggregating the text or visual data into small categories of information, seeking evidence for the code from different databases being used in a study, and then assigning a label to the code. We think about "winnowing" the data here; not all information is used in a qualitative study, and some may be discarded (Wolcott, 1994). Researchers develop a short list of tentative codes (e.g., 25–30 or so) that match text segments, regardless of the length of the database.

Beginning researchers tend to develop elaborate lists of codes when they review their databases. We recommend proceeding differently with a short list—only expanding the list of initial codes as necessary. This approach is called lean coding because it begins with five or six categories with shorthand labels or codes and then it expands as review and re-review of the database continues. Typically, regardless of the size of the database, we recommend a final code list of no more than 25 to 30 categories of information, and we find ourselves working to reduce and combine them into the five or six themes that we will use in the end to write a narrative. Those researchers who end up with 100 or 200 categories—and it is easy to find this many in a complex database—struggle to reduce the picture to the five or six themes that they must end with for most publications. For audiovisual materials, identify codes and classify codes into themes by relating the material to other aspects of phenomenon of interest. Grbich (2013) suggests a guide for the coding process of audiovisual materials using the following questions: What codes would be expected to fit? What new codes are emergent? What themes relate to other data sources?

Figure 8.2 illustrates the coding process used to describe one of three themes (i.e., fostering relationships) from the analysis of 11 focus groups and three interviews with teachers, administrators, caregivers, and allied professionals for the purpose of supporting the educational success of students with fetal alcohol spectrum disorders (Job et al., 2013). This illustration shows the development of the theme beginning with the naming of three initial codes (i.e., attitudes, behavior, and strategies), the expansion from three to a total of six codes followed by the reduction to two final code categories (i.e., respectful interactions and candid communication). The description of the theme is organized in the published paper by the two final code categories (sometimes called subthemes) and the methodology includes a general description of the coding process without examples. This is not unusual practice for articles yet some dissertations include such examples in an appendix (for an example of a case study, see Poth, 2008).

Finalizing a list of codes and creating descriptions provides the foundation for a **_codebook_** (see Table 8.4 for an example). The codebook articulates the distinctive boundaries for each code and plays an important role in assessing inter-rater reliability among multiple coders (discussed in Chapter 10). A codebook should contain the following information (adapted from Bazeley, 2013; Bernard & Ryan, 2009):

- Name for the code and, if necessary, a shortened label suitable to apply in a margin

FIGURE 8.2 ● Example of Coding Procedures for Theme "Fostering Relationships"

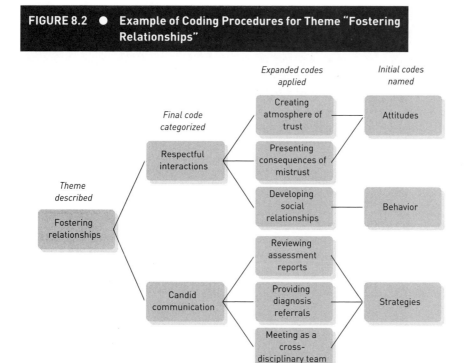

Source: Job et al. (2013).

- Description of the code defining boundaries through use of inclusion and exclusion criteria
- Example(s) of the code using data from the study to illustrate

Table 8.4 illustrates the codebook used to guide the development of the theme, fostering relationships. This illustration provides a description of the boundaries for each of the two code categories (i.e., respectful interactions with one another, candid communication among stakeholders) using a definition, criteria guiding use, and example of a segment of text from the study. What we have found particularly helpful is criteria guiding use that refers to other codes; for example, in this instance, actions and preparation are codes for the second theme, reframing practices, and awareness and availability are codes for the third theme, accessing supports. The methodology of the published paper includes a general description of the inter-rater coding assessment procedures and outcomes without the guiding codebook. This is not unusual, as published papers do not typically include code lists, yet our experience as supervisors, members of supervisory committees, and examiners tells us that qualitative researchers often use a codebook and provide an example of it in an appendix.

TABLE 8.4 ● Example of Codebook Entry for Theme "Fostering Relationships"					
Theme	Code Name (shortened name)	Definition	When to use	When not to use	Example of a segment of text from study
Fostering relationships	Respectful interactions with one another (Respect)	Any evidence recognizing individual contributions as "mattering" or efforts that are valued	Use when interaction led to or hindered student success or trust/mistrust	When referring to outcomes—use actions or training—that is preparation	"This is their turf and I don't [want to] go in there and impose my will on [them]." Job et al. (2013).
	Candid communications among stakeholders (Communication)	Any evidence referring to communication relevant for informing student success	Descriptions of timing, quality, and frequency of information sharing—reports, referrals, team meetings	When referring to supports—use awareness or availability	". . . we have to have [an] openness and . . . willingness to listen without being judgmental. And I think when that comes, everything else will . . . come too. But for right now, there are still too many people that are willing to judge. . ."

Several issues are important to address in this coding process. The first is whether qualitative researchers should count codes. Huberman and Miles (1994), for example, suggest that investigators make preliminary counts of data codes and determine how frequently codes appear in the database. This issue remains contentious as Hays and Singh (2012) declare, "quite a debated topic!" (p. 21) as some (but not all) qualitative researchers feel comfortable counting and reporting the number of times the codes appear in their databases. It does provide an indicator of frequency of occurrence, something typically associated with quantitative research or systematic approaches to qualitative research. In our own work, we may look at the number of passages associated with each code as an indicator of participant interest in a code, but we do not report counts in articles. This is because we, along with others (e.g., Bazeley, 2013; Hays & Singh, 2012), consider counting as conveying a quantitative orientation of magnitude and frequency contrary to qualitative research. In addition, a count conveys that all codes should be given equal emphasis, and it disregards that the passages coded may actually represent contradictory views.

Another issue is the use of preexisting or a priori codes that guide our coding process. Again, we have a mixed reaction to the use of this procedure. Crabtree and Miller (1992) discuss a continuum of coding strategies that range from "prefigured" categories to "emergent" categories (p. 151). Using prefigured codes or categories (often from a theoretical model or the literature) is popular in the health sciences (Crabtree & Miller, 1992), but use of these codes does serve to limit the analysis to the prefigured codes rather than opening up the codes to reflect the views of participants in a traditional qualitative way. If a prefigured coding scheme is used in analysis, we typically encourage the researchers to be open to additional codes emerging during the analysis.

Another issue is the question as to the origin of the code names or labels. Code labels emerge from several sources. They might be *in vivo codes*, names that are the exact words used by participants. They might also be code names drawn from the social or health sciences (e.g., coping strategies), names the researcher composes that seem to best describe the information, or from metaphors we associate with the codes (Bazeley, 2013). In the process of data analysis, we encourage qualitative researchers to look for code segments that can be used to describe information and develop themes. These codes can represent the following:

- Expected information that researchers hope to find
- Surprising information that researchers did not expect to find
- Conceptually interesting or unusual information for the researcher, the participants, or the audiences that is conceptually interesting or unusual to researchers (and potentially participants and audiences)

A final issue is the types of information a qualitative researcher codes. The researcher might look for stories (as in narrative research); individual experiences and the context of those experiences (in phenomenology); processes, actions, or interactions (in grounded theory); cultural themes and how the culture-sharing group works that can be described or categorized (in ethnography); or a detailed description of the particular case or cases (in case study research). Another way of thinking about the types of information would be to use a deconstructive stance, a stance focused on issues of desire and power (Czarniawska, 2004). Czarniawska (2004) identifies the data analysis strategies used in deconstruction, adapted from Martin (1990, p. 355), that help focus attention on types of information to analyze from qualitative data in all approaches:

- Dismantling a dichotomy, exposing it as a false distinction (e.g., public/private, nature/culture)
- Examining silences—what is not said (e.g., noting who or what is excluded by the use of pronouns such as *we*)

- Attending to disruptions and contradictions; places where a text fails to make sense or does not continue
- Focusing on the element that is most alien or peculiar in the text—to find the limits of what is conceivable or permissible
- Interpreting metaphors as a rich source of multiple meanings
- Analyzing double entendres that may point to an unconscious subtext, often sexual in content
- Separating group-specific and more general sources of bias by "reconstructing" the text with substitution of its main elements

Moving beyond coding, classifying pertains to taking the text or qualitative information apart and looking for categories, themes, or dimensions of information. As a popular form of analysis, classification involves identifying five to seven general themes. Themes in qualitative research (also called categories) are broad units of information that consist of several codes aggregated to form a common idea. These themes, in turn, we view as a family of themes with children, or subthemes, and even grandchildren represented by segments of data. It is difficult, especially in a large database, to reduce the information down into five or seven "families," but our process involves winnowing the data, reducing them to a small, manageable set of themes to write into a final narrative. Among the key challenges for beginning qualitative researchers is the leap from codes to themes. We forward the following strategies for exploring and developing themes (inspired by ideas from Bazeley, 2013):

- Use memoing to capture emerging thematic ideas. As you work with the data, write memos and include details about relevant codes. For example, an early project memo identified relationships as important in the study of educational success and it was not until later that how and what relationships needed to be fostered became clear from the coding process (Job et al., 2013).
- Highlight noteworthy quotes as you code. In addition to its identification, include a description of why this quote was noteworthy. For example, include an initial code called noteworthy quotes simply for the purpose of keeping track of the quotes deemed as noteworthy. These "noteworthy quotes" can also inform the development of themes. Researchers can assign interesting quotes to use in a qualitative report into this code label and easily retrieve them for a report.
- Create diagrams representing relationships among codes or emerging concepts. Visual representations are helpful for seeing overlap among codes. For example, use a network diagram of codes in ATLAS.ti (i.e., a qualitative software program) to visualize the relationships among codes and the concurrence tool to review possible overlaps among codes.
- Draft summary statements reflective of recurring or striking aspects of the data. Noting recurrences or outliers in the data may help to see **patterns** between conditions and consequences.

- Prior to transitioning to focus on the process of interpreting, it is important to recognize that some present thematic analysis as an alternative to coding. In our work, we emphasize the integral role of coding in the development of themes. This view is eloquently described by Bazeley (2013): "The consensus among those who seek to interpret, analyse, and theorise qualitative data, however, is that the development of themes depends on data having been coded already" (p. 191).

Developing and Assessing Interpretations

Researchers engage in interpreting the data when they conduct qualitative research. Interpretation involves making sense of the data, the "lessons learned," as described by Lincoln and Guba (1985). Patton (2015) describes this interpretative process as requiring both creative and critical faculties in making carefully considered judgments about what is meaningful in the patterns, themes, and categories generated by analysis. Interpretation in qualitative research involves abstracting out beyond the codes and themes to the larger meaning of the data. It is a process that begins with the development of the codes, the formation of themes from the codes, and then the organization of themes into larger units of abstraction to make sense of the data. Several forms exist, such as interpretation based on hunches, insights, and intuition (for further details about strategies for relating codes and connecting concepts, see the following: Bazeley, 2013; Ravitch & Mittenfelner Carl, 2016). Interpretation also might be within a social science construct or idea or a combination of personal views as contrasted with a social science construct or idea. Thus, the researcher would link his or her interpretation to the larger research literature developed by others. For postmodern and interpretive researchers, these interpretations are seen as tentative, inconclusive, and questioning.

As part of the iterative interpretative process, Marshall and Rossman (2015) encourage "scrupulous qualitative researchers to be on guard" (p. 228) for alternative understandings using such strategies as challenging ones' own interpretations through comparisons with existing data, relevant literature, or initial hypotheses. Specific to audiovisual materials, develop and assess interpretations of the materials using strategies to locate patterns and develop stories, summaries, or statements. Grbich (2013) suggests guiding the interpretation using the following questions: What surprising information did you not expect to find? What information is conceptually interesting or unusual to participants and audiences? What are the dominant interpretations and what are the alternate notions?

The researcher might obtain peer feedback on early data interpretations or on their audit trail (discussed further in Chapter 10) and procedures. This can be helpful for assessing "how do I know what I know or think I know?" because it requires the researcher to clearly articulate the patterns they see in the data categories. A researcher might use diagramming as a way of representing the relationships among concepts visually at this point, and in some cases, these representations are used in the final reporting.

Representing and Visualizing the Data

In the final phase of the spiral, researchers represent the data, a packaging of what was found in text, tabular, or figure form. For example, creating a visual image of the information, a researcher may present a comparison table (see Spradley, 1980) or a matrix—for example, a 2×2 table that compares men and women in terms of one of the themes or categories in the study or a 6×6 effects matrix that displays assistance location and types (see Miles & Huberman, 1994; Miles et al., 2014). The cells contain text, not numbers, and depending on the content, researchers use matrices to compare and cross-reference categories to establish a picture of data patterns or ranges (Marshall & Rossman, 2015). A hierarchical tree diagram represents another form of presentation (Angrosino, 2007). This shows different levels of abstraction, with the boxes in the top of the tree representing the most abstract information and those at the bottom representing the least abstract themes. Figure 8.3 illustrates the levels of abstraction from the gunman case (Asmussen & Creswell, 1995). This illustration shows inductive analysis that begins with the raw data consisting of multiple sources of information and then broadens to several specific themes (e.g., safety, denial) and on to the most general themes represented by the two perspectives of social–psychological and psychological factors.

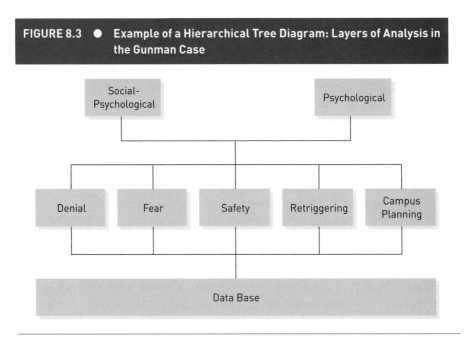

FIGURE 8.3 ● Example of a Hierarchical Tree Diagram: Layers of Analysis in the Gunman Case

Source: Asmussen and Creswell (1995).

Given the variety of displays available to researchers, it can be difficult to decide which one works best. We forward the following guidance for creating and using matrix displays; we believe these strategies to be iterative and as useful for data displays beyond matrices (adapted from Miles et al., 2014):

- Search data and select level and type of data to be displayed. Begin by revisiting the research question and available data. Decide what forms and types of data will appear; for example, direct quotes or paraphrases or researcher explanations or any combination. Hand search data or use search functions within software to locate potential material. Maintain a log of inclusion/exclusion criteria as a way of keeping "an explicit record of the 'decision rules'" (Miles et al., 2014, p. 116).
- Sketch and seek feedback on initial formatting ideas. Select labels for row and column headings as part of the initial sketching process. Be sure to balance amount and type of information because "more information is better than less" (Miles et al., 2014, p. 116). Ask colleagues to review your initial sketches and provide feedback about suggestions for alternative ways of displaying data.
- Assess completeness and readability and modify as needed. Look for areas of missing or ambiguous data, and if warranted, show this explicitly in the display. Reduce the number of rows or columns if possible—ideally no more than five or six is considered manageable—create groups within rows or columns or multiple displays as appropriate. Do not feel restricted by the formats you see, rather "**Think display**. Adapt and invent formats that will serve you best" (*emphasis in original*, Miles et al., 2014, p. 114).
- Note patterns and possible comparisons and clusters in the display. Examine the display using various strategies and summarize initial interpretations. The process of writing is essential for refining and clarifying ideas. Displays always need accompanying text as they "never speak for themselves" (Miles et al., 2014, p. 117).
- Revisit accompanying text and verify conclusions. Check that the text goes beyond a descriptive summary of the data presented and instead offers explanations and conclusions. Then verify the conclusions against raw data or data summaries because "if a conclusion does not ring true at the 'ground level' when you try it out there, it needs revision" (Miles et al., 2014, p. 117).

Hypotheses or propositions that specify the relationship among categories of information also represent qualitative data. In grounded theory, for example, investigators advance propositions that interrelate the causes of a phenomenon with its context and strategies. Finally, authors present metaphors to analyze the data, literary devices in which something borrowed from one domain applies to another (Hammersley & Atkinson, 1995). Qualitative writers may compose entire studies shaped by analyses of metaphors. For additional ideas of innovative styles of data displays and guidance about how to best represent data from the analysis of audiovisual materials, see also Grbich (2013).

At this point, the researcher might obtain feedback on the initial summaries and data displays by taking information back to informants, a procedure to be discussed in Chapter 10 as a key validation step in research.

Analysis Within Approaches to Inquiry

Think about the process of qualitative data analysis as having two layers. The first layer is to cover the processes we have described in the general spiral analysis. The second layer is to build on this general analysis by using specific procedures advanced for each of the five approaches to inquiry. These procedures will take your data analysis beyond a "generic" approach to analysis and into a sophisticated, more advanced set of procedures. Our organizing framework for this discussion is found in Table 8.5. We address each approach and discuss specific analysis and representing characteristics. At the end of this discussion, we return to significant differences and similarities among the five approaches.

Narrative Research Analysis and Representation

We think that Riessman (2008) says it best when she comments that narrative analysis "refers to a family of methods for interpreting texts that have in common a storied form" (p. 11). The data collected in a narrative study need to be analyzed for the story they have to tell, a *chronology* of unfolding events, and turning points or epiphanies. Within this broad sketch of analysis, several options exist for the narrative researcher.

A narrative researcher can take a literary orientation to his or her analysis. For example, using a story in science education told by four fourth graders in one elementary school included several approaches to narrative analysis (Ollerenshaw & Creswell, 2002). One approach is a process advanced by Yussen and Ozcan (1997) that involves analyzing text data for five elements of plot structure (i.e., characters, setting, problem, actions, and resolution). A narrative researcher could use an approach that incorporates different elements that go into the story. The three-dimensional space approach of Clandinin and Connelly (2000) includes analyzing the data for three elements: interaction (personal and social), continuity (past, present, and future), and situation (physical places or the storyteller's places). In the Ollerenshaw and Creswell (2002) narrative, we see common elements of narrative analysis: collecting stories of personal experiences in the form of field texts such as conducting interviews or having conversations, retelling the stories based on narrative elements (e.g., three-dimensional space approach and the five elements of plot), rewriting the stories into a chronological sequence, and incorporating the setting or place of the participants' experiences.

A chronological approach can also be taken in the analysis of the narratives. Denzin (1989) suggests that a researcher begin biographical analysis by identifying an objective set of experiences in the subject's life. Having the individual journal a sketch of his or her life may be a good beginning point for analysis. In this sketch, the researcher looks for life-course stages or experiences (e.g., childhood, marriage, employment) to develop

Data Analysis and Representation	Narrative	Phenomenology	Grounded Theory Study	Ethnography	Case Study
Managing and organizing the data	• Create and organize data files.	• Create and organize data files.	• Create and organize data files.	• Create and organize data files.	• Create and organize data files.
Reading and memoing emergent ideas	• Read through text, make margin notes, and form initial codes.	• Read through text, make margin notes, and form initial codes.	• Read through text, make margin notes, and form initial codes.	• Read through text, make margin notes, and form initial codes.	• Read through text, make margin notes, and form initial codes.
Describing and classifying codes into themes	• Describe the patterns across the objective set of experiences. • Identify and describe the stories into a chronology.	• Describe personal experiences through epoche. • Describe the essence of the phenomenon.	• Describe open coding categories. • Select one open coding category to build toward central phenomenon in process.	• Describe the social setting, actors, and events; draw a picture of the setting.	• Describe the case and its context.
Developing and assessing interpretations	• Locate epiphanies within stories. • Identify contextual materials.	• Develop significant statements. • Group statements into meaning units.	• Engage in axial coding—causal condition, context, intervening conditions, strategies, and consequences. • Develop the theory.	• Analyze data for themes and patterned regularities.	• Use categorical aggregation to establish themes or patterns.
Representing and visualizing the data	• Restory and interpret the larger meaning of the story.	• Develop a textural description—"what happened." • Develop a structural description—"how the phenomenon was experienced." • Develop the "essence," using a composite description.	• Engage in selective coding and interrelate the categories to develop a "story" or propositions or matrix.	• Interpret and make sense of the findings—how the culture "works."	• Use direct interpretation. • Develop naturalistic generalizations of what was "learned."

a chronology of the individual's life. Stories and epiphanies will emerge from the individual's journal or from interviews. The researcher looks in the database (typically interviews or documents) for concrete, contextual biographical materials. During the interview, the researcher prompts the participant to expand on various sections of the stories and asks the interviewee to theorize about his or her life. These theories may relate to career models, processes in the life course, models of the social world, relational models of biography, and natural history models of the life course. Then, the researcher organizes larger patterns and meaning from the narrative segments and categories. Daiute (2014) identifies four types of patterns for meaning-making related to similarities, differences, change, or coherence. Finally, the individual's biography is reconstructed, and the researcher identifies factors that have shaped the life. This leads to the writing of an analytic abstraction of the case that highlights (a) the processes in the individual's life, (b) the different theories that relate to these life experiences, and (c) the unique and general features of the life. Embedded within narrative analysis and representation processes is a collaborative approach whereby participants are actively involved (Clandinin 2013; Clandinin & Connelly, 2000).

Another approach to narrative analysis turns on how the narrative report is composed. Riessman (2008) suggests a typology of four analytic strategies that reflect this diversity in composing the stories. Riessman calls it thematic analysis when the researcher analyzes "what" is spoken or written during data collection. She comments that this approach is the most popular form of narrative studies, and we see it in the Chan (2010) narrative project reported in Appendix B. A second form in Riessman's (2008) typology is called the structural form, and it emphasizes "how" a story is told. This brings in linguistic analysis in which the individual telling the story uses form and language to achieve a particular effect. Discourse analysis, based on Gee's (1991) method, would examine the storytellers' narrative for such elements as the sequence of utterances, the pitch of the voice, and the intonation. A third form for Riessman (2008) is the dialogic or performance analysis, in which the talk is interactively produced by the researcher and the participant or actively performed by the participant through such activities as poetry or a play. The fourth form is an emerging area of using visual analysis of images or interpreting images alongside words. It could also be a story told about the production of an image or how different audiences view an image.

In the narrative study of Ai Mei Zhang, the Chinese immigrant student presented by Chan (2010) in Appendix B, the analytic approach begins with a thematic analysis similar to Riessman's (2008) approach. After briefly mentioning a description of Ai Mei's school, Chan then discusses several themes, all of which have to do with conflict (e.g., home language conflicts with school language). That Chan saw conflict introduces the idea that she analyzed the data for this phenomenon and rendered the theme development from a postmodern type of interpretive lens. Chan then goes on to analyze the data beyond the themes to explore her role as a narrative researcher learning about Ai Mei's experiences. Thus, while overall the analysis is based on a thematic approach, the introduction of conflict and the researcher's experiences adds a thoughtful conceptual analysis to the study.

Phenomenological Analysis and Representation

The suggestions for narrative analysis present a general template for qualitative researchers. In contrast, in phenomenology, there have been specific, structured methods of analysis advanced, especially by Moustakas (1994). Moustakas reviews several approaches in his book, but we see his modification of the Stevick–Colaizzi–Keen method as providing the most practical, useful approach. Our approach, a simplified version of this method discussed by Moustakas (1994), is as follows:

- Describe personal experiences with the phenomenon under study. The researcher begins with a full description of his or her own experience of the phenomenon. This is an attempt to set aside the researcher's personal experiences (which cannot be done entirely) so that the focus can be directed to the participants in the study.
- Develop a list of significant statements. The researcher then finds statements (in the interviews or other data sources) about how individuals are experiencing the topic; lists these significant statements (horizonalization of the data) and treats each statement as having equal worth; and works to develop a list of nonrepetitive, nonoverlapping statements.
- Group the significant statements into broader units of information. These larger units, also called meaning units or themes, provide the foundation for interpretation because it creates clusters and removes repetition.
- Create a description of "what" the participants in the study experienced with the phenomenon. This is called a textural description of the experience—what happened—and includes verbatim examples.
- Draft a description of "how" the experience happened. This is called structural description, and the inquirer reflects on the setting and context in which the phenomenon was experienced. For example, in a phenomenological study of the smoking behavior of high school students (McVea, Harter, McEntarffer, & Creswell, 1999), the authors provided a structural description about where the phenomenon of smoking occurs, such as in the parking lot, outside the school, by student lockers, in remote locations at the school, and so forth.
- Write a composite description of the phenomenon. A composite description incorporates both the textural and structural descriptions. This passage is the "essence" of the experience and represents the culminating aspect of a phenomenological study. It is typically a long paragraph that tells the reader "what" the participants experienced with the phenomenon and "how" they experienced it (i.e., the context).

Moustakas (1994) is a psychologist, and the essence typically is of a phenomenon in psychology, such as grief or loss. Giorgi (2009), also a psychologist, provides an analytic approach similar to that of Stevick, Colaizzi, and Keen. Giorgi discusses how researchers read for a sense of the whole, determine meaning units, transform the participants' expressions into psychologically sensitive expressions, and then write a description of the essence. Most helpful in Giorgi's discussion is the example he provides of describing jealousy as analyzed by himself and another researcher.

The phenomenological study by Riemen (1986) tends to follow a structured analytic approach. In Riemen's study of caring by patients and their nurses, she presents significant statements of caring and noncaring interactions for both males and females. Furthermore, Riemen formulates meaning statements from these significant statements and presents them in tables. Finally, Riemen advances two "exhaustive" descriptions for the essence of the experience—two short paragraphs—and sets them apart by enclosing them in tables. In the phenomenological study of individuals with AIDS by Anderson and Spencer (2002; see Appendix C) reviewed in Chapter 5, the authors use Colaizzi's (1978) method of analysis, one of the approaches mentioned by Moustakas (1994). This approach follows the general guideline of analyzing the data for significant phrases, developing meanings and clustering them into themes, and presenting an exhaustive description of the phenomenon.

A less structured approach is found in van Manen (1990, 2014) for use when two conditions for the possibility of doing phenomenological analysis are met with an appropriate question and data. First, the phenomenological question guiding the study is critical because "if the question lacks heuristic clarity, point, and power, then analysis will fail for the lack of reflective focus" (van Manen, 2014, p. 297). Second, the experiential quality of the data is necessary because "if the material lacks experiential detail, concreteness, vividness, and lived-thoroughness, then the analysis will fail for lack of substance" (van Manen, 2014, p. 297). He begins discussing data analysis by calling it "phenomenological reflection" (van Manen, 1990, p. 77). The basic idea of this reflection is to grasp the essential meaning of something. The wide array of data sources of expressions or forms that we would reflect on might be transcribed taped conversations, interview materials, daily accounts or stories, suppertime talk, formally written responses, diaries, other people's writings, film, drama, poetry, novels, and so forth. van Manen (1990) places emphasis on gaining an understanding of themes by asking, "What is this example an example of?" (p. 86). These themes should have certain qualities such as focus, a simplification of ideas, and a description of the structure of the lived experience (van Manen, 1990, 2014). The process involved attending to the entire text (holistic reading approach), looking for statements or phrases (selective reading or highlighting approach), and examining every sentence (the detailed reading or line-by-line approach). Attending to four guides for reflection was also important: the space felt by individuals (e.g., the modern bank), physical or bodily presence (e.g., what does a person in love look like?), time (e.g., the dimensions of past, present, and future), and the relationships with others (e.g., expressed through a handshake). In the end, analyzing the data for themes, using different approaches to examine the information, and considering the guides for reflection should yield an explicit structure of the meaning of the lived experience.

Grounded Theory Analysis and Representation

Similar to phenomenology, grounded theory uses detailed procedures for analysis. It consists of three phases of coding—open, axial, and selective—as advanced by Strauss and Corbin (1990, 1998) and Corbin and Strauss (2007, 2015). Grounded theory provides a procedure for developing categories of information (open coding), interconnecting the categories (axial coding), building a "story" that connects the categories (selective coding), and ending with a discursive set of theoretical propositions (Strauss & Corbin, 1990).

In the open coding phase, the researcher examines the text (e.g., transcripts, field notes, documents) for salient categories of information supported by the text. Using the constant comparative approach, the researcher attempts to "saturate" the categories— to look for instances that represent the category and to continue looking (and interviewing) until the new information obtained does not provide further insight into the category. These categories comprise subcategories, called properties, that represent multiple perspectives about the categories. Properties, in turn, are ***dimensionalized*** and presented on a continuum. Overall, this is the process of reducing the database to a small set of themes or categories that characterize the process or action being explored in the grounded theory study.

Once an initial set of categories has been developed, the researcher identifies a single category from the open coding list as the central phenomenon of interest. The open coding category selected for this purpose is typically one that is extensively discussed by the participants or one of particular conceptual interest because it seems central to the process being studied in the grounded theory project. The inquirer selects this one open coding category (a central phenomenon), positions it as the central feature of the theory, and then returns to the database (or collects additional data) to understand the categories that relate to this central phenomenon. Specifically, the researcher engages in the coding process called axial coding in which the database is reviewed (or new data are collected) to provide insight into specific coding categories that relate to or explain the central phenomenon. These are causal conditions that influence the central phenomenon, the strategies for addressing the phenomenon, the context and intervening conditions that shape the strategies, and the consequences of undertaking the strategies. Information from this coding phase is then organized into a figure, a coding paradigm, that presents a theoretical model of the process under study. In this way, a theory is built or generated. From this theory, the inquirer generates propositions (or hypotheses) or statements that interrelate the categories in the coding paradigm. This is called selective coding. Finally, at the broadest level of analysis, the researcher can create a conditional matrix. This matrix is an analytical aid—a diagram—that helps the researcher visualize the wide range of conditions and consequences (e.g., society, world) related to the central phenomenon (Corbin & Strauss, 2015; Strauss & Corbin, 1990). Seldom have we found the conditional matrix actually used in studies.

A key to understanding the difference that Charmaz brings to grounded theory data analysis is to hear her say, "Avoid imposing a forced framework" (Charmaz,

2006, p. 66). Her approach emphasized an emerging process of forming the theory. Her analytic steps began with an initial phase of coding each word, line, or segment of data. At this early stage, she was interested in having the initial codes treated analytically to understand a process and larger theoretical categories. This initial phase was followed by focused coding, using the initial codes to sift through large amounts of data, analyzing for syntheses and larger explanations. She did not support the Strauss and Corbin (1998) formal procedures of axial coding that organized the data into conditions, actions/interactions, consequences, and so forth. However, Charmaz (2006, 2014) did examine the categories and begins to develop links among them. She also believed in using theoretical coding, first developed by Glaser (1978). This step involved specifying possible relationships between categories based on a priori theoretical coding families (e.g., causes, context, ordering). However, Charmaz (2006, 2014) goes on to say that these theoretical codes needed to earn their way into the grounded theory that emerges. The theory that emerged for Charmaz emphasizes understanding rather than explanation. It assumes emergent, multiple realities; the link of facts and values; provisional information; and a narrative about social life as a process. It might be presented as a figure or as a narrative that pulls together experiences and shows the range of meanings.

The specific form for presenting the theory differs. In a study of department chairs, theory is presented as hypotheses (Creswell & Brown, 1992), and in their study of the process of the evolution of physical activity for African American women (see Appendix D), Harley et al. (2009) present a discussion of a theoretical model as displayed in a figure with three phases. In the Harley et al. study, the analysis consists of citing Strauss and Corbin (1998) and then creating codes, grouping these codes into concepts, and forming a theoretical framework. The specific steps of open coding were not reported; however, the results section focused on the theoretical model's phases, and the axial coding steps of context, conditions, and an elaboration on the condition most integral to the women's movement through the process and the planning methods.

Ethnographic Analysis and Representation

For ethnographic research, we recommend the three aspects of data analysis advanced by Wolcott (1994): description, analysis, and ***interpretation of the culture-sharing group***. Wolcott (1990) believes that a good starting point for writing an ethnography is to describe the culture-sharing group and setting:

> Description is the foundation upon which qualitative research is built. . . . Here you become the storyteller, inviting the reader to see through your eyes what you have seen. . . . Start by presenting a straightforward description of the setting and events. No footnotes, no intrusive analysis—just the facts, carefully presented and interestingly related at an appropriate level of detail. (p. 28)

From an interpretive perspective, the researcher may present only one set of facts; other facts and interpretations await the reading of the ethnography by the participants and others. But this description may be analyzed by presenting information in chronological order. The writer describes through progressively focusing the description or chronicling a "day in the life" of the group or individual. Finally, other techniques involve focusing on a critical or key event, developing a "story" complete with a plot and characters, writing it as a "mystery," examining groups in interaction, following an analytical framework, or showing different perspectives through the views of participants.

Analysis for Wolcott (1994) is a sorting procedure—"the quantitative side of qualitative research" (p. 26). This involves highlighting specific material introduced in the descriptive phase or displaying findings through tables, charts, diagrams, and figures. The researcher also analyzes through using systematic procedures such as those advanced by Spradley (1979, 1980), who called for building taxonomies, generating comparison tables, and developing semantic tables. Perhaps the most popular analysis procedure, also mentioned by Wolcott (1994), is the search for patterned regularities in the data. Other forms of analysis consist of comparing the cultural group to others, evaluating the group in terms of standards, and drawing connections between the culture-sharing group and larger theoretical frameworks. Other analysis steps include critiquing the research process and proposing a redesign for the study.

Making an ethnographic interpretation of the culture-sharing group is a data transformation step as well. Here the researcher goes beyond the database and probes "what is to be made of them" (Wolcott, 1994, p. 36). The researcher speculates outrageous, comparative interpretations that raise doubts or questions for the reader. The researcher draws inferences from the data or turns to theory to provide structure for his or her interpretations. The researcher also personalizes the interpretation: "This is what I make of it" or "This is how the research experience affected me" (p. 44). Finally, the investigator forges an interpretation through expressions such as poetry, fiction, or performance.

Multiple forms of analysis represent Fetterman's (2010) approach to ethnography. He did not have a lockstep procedure but recommended triangulating the data by testing one source of data against another, looking for patterns of thought and behavior, and focusing in on key events that the ethnography can use to analyze an entire culture (e.g., ritual observance of the Sabbath). Ethnographers also draw maps of the setting, develop charts, design matrices, and sometimes employ statistical analysis to examine frequency and magnitude. They might also crystallize their thoughts to provide "a mundane conclusion, a novel insight, or an earth-shattering epiphany" (Fetterman, 2010, p. 109).

The ethnography presented in Appendix E by Mac an Ghaill and Haywood (2015) was guided by Braun and Clarke's (2006) thematic analysis. The authors describe the group of Bangladeshi and Pakistani young men's generational-specific experiences in relation to the racialization of their ethnicities and changes in terms of how they negotiated the meanings attached to being Muslim. The final section offered a broad level of abstraction beyond the themes to suggest how the group made sense of the range of social and cultural exclusions they experienced during a time of rapid change within their city. The authors situate their conclusions within their own experiences of listening to the group's narratives over 3 years and resisting representing their identities "using popular and academic explanations" (p. 111). Instead, they chose to emphasis the need for careful consideration and facilitation of ways for understanding the young men's own participation and the influence of local contexts and broader social and economic processes in identity formation. Another example of an ethnography applied a critical perspective to the analytic procedures of ethnography (Haenfler, 2004). Haenfler provides a detailed description of the straight edge core values of resistance to other cultures and then discussed five themes related to these core values (e.g., positive, clean living). Then, the conclusion to the article includes broad interpretations of the group's core values, such as the individualized and collective meanings for participation in the subculture. However, Haenfler began the methods discussion with a self-disclosing, positioning statement about his background and participation in the straight edge (sXe) movement. This positioning was also presented as a chronology of his experiences from 1989 to 2001.

Case Study Analysis and Representation

For a case study, as in ethnography, analysis consists of making a detailed description of the case and its setting. If the case presents a chronology of events, we then recommend analyzing the multiple sources of data to determine evidence for each step or phase in the evolution of the case. Moreover, the setting is particularly important. For example, in Frelin's (2015) case study (see Appendix F), she analyzed the information to determine what relational practices were successful within a particular school context—in this situation, a program for students who have a history of school failure. Another example, in the gunman case (Asmussen & Creswell, 1995), the authors sought to establish how the incident fit into the setting—in this situation, a tranquil, peaceful Midwestern community.

In addition, Stake (1995) advocates four forms of data analysis and interpretation in case study research. In categorical aggregation, the researcher seeks a collection of instances from the data, hoping that issue-relevant meanings will emerge. In ***direct interpretation***, on the other hand, the case study researcher looks at a single instance and draws meaning from it without looking for multiple instances. It is a process of pulling the data apart and putting them back together in more meaningful ways. Also, the researcher establishes patterns and looks for a correspondence between two or more categories. This correspondence might take the form of a table, possibly a 2x2 table, showing the relationship between two categories. Yin (2014) advances a cross-case synthesis as an analytic technique when the researcher studies two or more cases. He suggests that a word table can be created to display the data from individual cases according to some uniform framework. The implication of this is that the researcher can then look for similarities and differences among the cases. Finally, the researcher develops ***naturalistic generalizations*** from analyzing the data, generalizations that people can learn from the case for themselves, apply learnings to a population of cases, or transfer them to another similar context.

To these analysis steps we would add description of the case, a detailed view of aspects about the case—the "facts." In Frelin's (2015) case study (see Appendix F), the illustrations of relational practices are organized chronologically describing how relationships were negotiated and the qualities trust, humaneness, and students' self-images. The final section discusses the complex and temporal nature of teachers work in light of the literature about the population of students with experiences of school failure and considers the transferability of the findings related to teachers to the roles of school psychologists within similar contexts. To provide another account, in the gunman case study, we have access to greater details about the analytic processes (Asmussen & Creswell, 1995). The case description centers on the events following the gunman incident for 2 weeks and highlights the major players, the sites, and the activities. The data were then aggregated into about 20 categories (categorical aggregation) and collapsed into five themes. The final section of the study presents generalizations about the case in terms of the themes and how they compared and contrasted with published literature on campus violence.

Comparing the Five Approaches

Returning to Table 8.2, data analysis and representation in the five approaches have several common and distinctive features. Across all five approaches, the researcher typically begins by creating and organizing files of information. Next, the process consists of a general reading and memoing of information to develop a sense of the data and to begin the process of making sense of them. Then, all approaches have a phase dedicated to description, with the exception of grounded theory, in which the inquirer also seeks to begin building toward a theory of the action or process.

However, several important differences exist in the five approaches. Grounded theory and phenomenology have the most detailed, explicated procedure for data analysis, depending on the author chosen for guidance on analysis. Ethnography and case studies have analysis procedures that are common, and narrative research represents the least structured procedure. Also, the terms used in the phase of classifying show distinct language among these approaches (see Appendix A for a glossary of terms used in each approach); what is called open coding in grounded theory is similar to the first stage of identifying significant statements in phenomenology and to categorical aggregation in case study research. The researcher needs to become familiar with the definition of these terms of analysis and employ them correctly in the chosen approach to inquiry. Finally, the presentation of the data, in turn, reflects the data analysis steps, and it varies from a narration in narrative to tabled statements, meanings, and description in phenomenology to a visual model or theory in grounded theory.

Computer Use in Qualitative Data Analysis

Qualitative computer programs have been available since the late 1980s, and they have become more refined and helpful in computerizing the process of analyzing text and image data. The process used for qualitative data analysis is the same for hand coding or using a computer: the inquirer identifies a text segment or image segment, assigns a code label, searches through the database for all text segments that have the same code label, and develops a printout of these text segments for the code. In this process the researcher, not the computer program, does the coding and categorizing. Marshall and Rossman (2015) explain the role of software as qualitative analysis tool: "We caution that software is only a tool to help with some of the mechanical and management aspects of analysis; so the hard analytic thinking must be done by the researcher's own internal hard drive!" (p. 228). Over time, the differing options of qualitative data analysis software and types of unique features have expanded considerably, making the selection of a program challenging for novice qualitative researchers. See Davidson and di Gregorio (2011) for a detailed historical description of qualitative data analysis software.

Computers in qualitative data analysis might be worthwhile to consider, yet it is also essential for researchers to be aware of their limitations. Among the key considerations, for those familiar with quantitative computer software programs, is the differences in expectations because in qualitative analysis, "such software . . . cannot do the analysis for you, not in the same sense in which a statistical package such as SPSS or SAS can do, say, multiple regressions" (Weitzman, 2000, p. 805). The following sections will help you to become familiar with the available functions and options in for computer use in qualitative data analysis.

Advantages and Disadvantages

How the researcher intends to use the computer program for organizing, coding, sorting, representing the data interpretations is a key consideration. This is because, in our view, a computer program simply provides the researcher the means for storing the data and easily accessing the coded segments of data. We feel that computer programs are most helpful with large databases, such as 500 or more pages of text, although they can have value for small databases as well. Although using a computer may not be of interest to all qualitative researchers, there are several advantages to using them. A computer program does the following:

- *Provides an organized storage file system for ease of retrieval.* The researcher can easily manage data files, memos, and diagrams stored systematically in one place by creating a vessel in which to contain the project and bound the search. In our experience, this aspect becomes especially important in locating entire cases or cases with specific characteristics.
- *Helps locate material with ease for the purposes of sorting.* The researcher can quickly search and locate materials for sorting—whether this material is an idea, a statement, a phrase, or a word. In our experience, no longer do we need to cut and paste material onto file cards and sort and resort the cards according to themes. No longer do we need to develop an elaborate "color code" system for text related to themes or topics. The search for text can be easily accomplished with a computer program. Once researchers identify categories in grounded theory,

or themes in case studies, the names of the categories can be searched using the computer program for other instances when the names occur in the database.

- *Encourages a researcher to look closely at the data.* By reading line by line and thinking about the meaning of each sentence and idea, the researcher engages in an active reading strategy. In our experience, without a program, the researcher is likely to casually read through the text files or transcripts and not analyze each idea carefully.
- *Produces visual representations for codes and themes.* The concept-mapping feature of computer programs enables the researcher to visualize relationships among codes and themes useful for interpreting. In our experience, interactive modeling features allows for exploring relationships and building theory through a visual representation that was often included in the final reporting.
- *Links memos with codes, themes, or documents for ease of reviewing.* A computer program allows the researcher to easily retrieve memos associated with codes, themes, or documents through the use of **hyperlinks**. In our experience, enabling the researcher to "see" the coded segments within the original document is important for verifying interpretations.
- *Enables collaborative analysis and sharing among team members.* A computer program facilitates access to analysis files and communication among team members who may be geographically dispersed. In our experience, without a program, researchers might complete work independently without a common purpose or use of common codes that are difficult to integrate.

The disadvantages go beyond their cost because using computer programs involves the following:

- *Requires a time investment for learning how to set up and run the program.* The researcher invests time and resources in learning how to run the program. This is sometimes a daunting task that is above and beyond learning required for understanding the procedures of qualitative research. Granted, some people learn computer programs more easily than do others, and prior experience with programs shortens the learning time. Working with different software may require learning different terminology and procedures. In our experience, we could get up and running the basic functions (files import, memoing) quickly across programs but found gaining proficiency in the specific search, retrieval, and diagramming features to be time consuming.
- *Interferes with the analysis by creating distance and hindering creativity.* Some researchers note concerns with positioning a machine between the researcher and actual data to producing an uncomfortable distance or hindering the creative process of analysis (e.g., Bazeley & Jackson, 2013; Gibbs, 2014; Hesse-Biber & Leavy, 2010). To mitigate some of these concerns, in our work with research teams, we have used a hybrid approach using computers for management and

eventually coding, but the initial code development was undertaken through making margin notes on paper transcripts.

- *Makes implementing changes, for some individuals, a hindrance.* Although researchers may see the categories developed during computer analysis as fixed, they can be changed in software programs—called recoding (Kelle, 1995). Some individuals may find changing the categories or moving information around less desirable than others and find that the computer program slows down or inhibits this process. In our experience, we like the ability to make changes efficiently but we aware that some programs changes are difficult to undo.
- *Offers, for the most part, limited guidance for analysis.* Instructions for using computer programs vary in their ease of use and accessibility, although this is a growing area of interest with specific books and videos available to help the new learner. For example, see the discussion about computer applications in grounded theory (Corbin & Strauss, 2015), or with steps in pattern analysis (Bazeley, 2013).
- *Places the onus on the researcher to select appropriate programs for their needs.* The challenge for researchers is learning about the unique features offered by computer programs. In our work, we have found it sometimes difficult to predict what features will be most important. Gilbert, Jackson, and di Gregorio (2014) lament the focus on program choice when researchers are better served by asking, "what analytical tasks will I be engaged in, and what are the different ways I can leverage technology to do them well" (p. 221)?

A particular computer program may not have the features or capability that researchers need, so researchers can shop comparatively to find a program that meets their needs.

How to Decide Whether to Use a Computer Program

The range of software and techniques designed for qualitative analysis (often referred to as CAQDAS, an acronym for Computer Assisted Qualitative Data Analysis Software) offers something for everyone, yet the challenge remains whether to choose to use it. A useful resource is the CAQDAS Networking Project: http://www.surrey.ac.uk/sociology/research/researcjcetmres/caqdas. Basically all processes involved in the data analysis spiral, discussed earlier in this chapter, can be undertaken by hand, using a computer or as a hybrid.

A review of introductory qualitative research texts revealed the majority address (at least cursively) the use of computer programs in qualitative analysis (e.g., Hays & Singh, 2012; Saldaña, 2013; Silverman, 2013). These authors describe the popular use of computer programs in qualitative data analysis. Kuckartz (2014) says, "Computer programs have been developed and are used fairly standardly in qualitative research. For over two decades, the field of computer-assisted analysis of qualitative data has been considered one of the most innovative fields in social science methodology development" (pp. 121–122). The ever-increasing number of available resources (e.g., texts, blogs, and videos) and reported use of a computer program in published papers (Gibbs, 2014) may make the decision easier for some. Resources have been developed specifically for giving an overview of the use of computer software programs in qualitative analysis (e.g., Kuckartz, 2014; Silver & Lewins, 2014). In this way, you can access the views of researchers about uses and experiences using software.

In Figure 8.4, we advance five questions for guiding whether to use a computer program for qualitative analysis: existing expertise in qualitative analysis; current level of proficiency with any programs; complexity of the study database; necessary program features for addressing study purpose; and configuration of the study researchers. These criteria can be used to identify whether using a computer program will meet a researcher's needs.

FIGURE 8.4 ● Five Questions to Guide Whether to Use a Computer Program for Qualitative Analysis

1. What expertise do I bring to qualitative data analysis?
   a. Can I develop, apply, and sort codes into themes?
   b. Can I use themes to develop and verify qualitative data interpretations?
   c. What additional expertise do I need to develop in qualitative analysis?
   d. What additional resources do I need to invest in learning about qualitative analysis?

2. How proficient am I with any computer program in qualitative data analysis?
   a. Is the program I am familiar with optimal for addressing my study purpose?
   b. Can I use the program features for my particular approach?
   c. What additional training do I need to seek?
   d. What additional resources do I need to invest for learning a program?

3. How complex is my study database?
   a. What quantity of files will be included in my analysis?
   b. What types of data file formats will I use in my analysis?

4. What analyses features do I anticipate my study needing for addressing my study purpose?
   a. Will I compare among codes, themes, or files?
   b. Will I seek patterns among codes, themes, or files?
   c. Will I create diagrams or visual representations?
   d. Will I develop theory, stories, or understandings?

5. What is the anticipated researcher configuration for my study?
   a. Will I work as a team on the analysis?
   b. Will we merge analyses from multiple researchers?

A Sampling of Computer Programs and Features

There are many computer programs available for analysis; some have been developed by individuals on campuses, and some are available for commercial purchase. Several texts offer useful resources for reading about available computer programs; for example, Silver and Lewins (2014) describe seven different programs, and Weitzman and Miles (1995) review 24 programs. It is important to compare these programs in light of the differing logistics, functions, and features of the different approaches (see Table 11.1 in Guest, Namey, & Mitchell, 2013). We highlight four commercial programs that are popular and that we have examined closely (see Creswell, 2012; Creswell & Maietta, 2002)—MAXQDA, ATLAS.ti, NVivo, and HyperRESEARCH. We have intentionally left out the version numbers and have presented a general discussion of the programs because the developers are continually upgrading the programs.

MAXQDA (http://www.maxqda.com). MAXQDA is a computer software program that helps the researcher to systematically evaluate and interpret qualitative texts. It is also a powerful tool for developing theories and testing theoretical conclusions. The main menu has four windows: the data, the code or category system, the text being analyzed, and the results of basic and complex searches. It uses a hierarchical code system, and the researcher can attach a weight score to a text segment to indicate the relevance of the segment. Memos can be easily written and stored as different types of memos (e.g., theory memos or methodological memos). It has a visual mapping feature for producing different types of conceptual maps representing theoretical associations, empirical relations, and data dependencies. Data can be exported to statistical programs, such as SPSS or Excel, and the software can import Excel or SPSS programs as well. Multiple coders on a particular project easily use it to collaborate. Images and video segments can also be stored and coded in this program. The mobile companion, MAXApp, allows researchers to use smartphones for data gathering, coding, and memoing, which can be directly transferred for further analysis. MAXQDA is distributed by VERBI Software in Germany. The Corbin and Strauss (2015) book contains an extensive illustration of the use of the software program MAXQDA to discuss grounded theory and a demonstration program is available to learn more about the unique features of this program.

ATLAS.ti (http://www.atlasti.com). This program enables you to organize your text, graphic, audio, and visual data files, along with your coding, memos, and findings, into a project. Further, you can code, annotate, and compare segments of information. You can drag and drop codes within an interactive margin screen. You can rapidly search, retrieve, and browse all data segments and notes relevant to an idea and, importantly, build unique visual networks that allow you to connect visually selected passages, memos, and codes in a concept map. Data can be exported to programs such as SPSS, HTML, XML, and CSV. This program also allows for a group of researchers to work on the same project and make comparisons of how each researcher coded the data. Freise (2014) offers a useful resource specific to the features offered by ATLAS.ti, and a demonstration software package is available to test out this program, which is described by and available from Scientific Software Development in Germany.

NVivo (http://www.qsrinternational.com). NVivo is the latest version of software from QSR International. NVivo combines the features of the popular software program N6 (or NUD*IST 6) and NVivo 2.0. NVivo helps analyze, manage, shape, and analyze qualitative data. Its streamlined look makes it easy to use. It provides security by storing the database and files together in a single file, enables a researcher to use multiple languages, has a merge function for team research, and enables the researcher to easily manipulate the data and conduct searches. Further, it can display graphically the codes and categories. NCapture enables handling of social media data including profile data from Facebook, Twitter, and LinkedIn. A good overview of the evolution of the software from N6 to NVivo is available from Bazeley (2002) and a resource specific to using NVivo (Bazeley & Jackson, 2013). NVivo is distributed by QSR International in Australia. A demonstration copy is available to see and try out the features of this software program.

HyperRESEARCH (http://www.researchware.com). This program is an easy-to-use qualitative software package enabling you to code and retrieve, build theories, and conduct analyses of the data. Now with advanced multimedia and language capabilities, HyperRESEARCH allows the researcher to work with text, graphics, audio, and video sources—making it a valuable research analysis tool. HyperRESEARCH is a solid code-and-retrieve data analysis program, with additional theory-building features provided by the Hypothesis Tester. This program also allows the researcher to draw visual diagrams, and it now has a module that can be added, called HyperTRANSCRIBE that will allow researchers to create a transfer of video and audio data. This program, developed by Researchware, is available in the United States.

Additional programs to consider:

I. Commercial software programs
   - QDA Miner: http://provalisresearch.com
     - QDA Miner, developed by Provalis, was designed as qualitative software for mixed methods research.
   - Qualrus: http://www.qualrus.com
     - Qualrus, developed by Idea Works, designed for managing and analyzing text, multimedia, and webpages.
   - Transana: http://www.transana.org
     - Transana, developed by University of Wisconsin–Madison, for the qualitative analysis of video, audio data, and still images.

II. Open source software programs:
   - Open code: http//www.phmed.umu.se/English/edpidemology/research/open-code
     - Open code, developed by Umea University in Sweden, was intended to follow the first steps of the grounded theory approach.

   III. Web-based software:
- Dedoose: www.dedoose.com
  - Dedoose, developed by SocioCultural Research Consultants, to meet the needs of research teams for working in real time.

Use of Computer Software Programs With the Five Approaches

After reviewing all of these computer programs, we see several ways that they can facilitate qualitative data analysis across the five approaches. Computer programs assist in the following:

- *Storing and organizing diverse forms of qualitative data.* The programs provide a convenient way to store qualitative data. Data are stored in document files (files converted from a word processing program to DOS, ASCII, or RTF files in some programs). These document files consist of information from one discrete unit of information such as a transcript from one interview, one set of observational notes, or one article scanned from a newspaper. For all five of the approaches to qualitative inquiry, the document could be one interview, one observation, or one image document and easily identifiable within the database.

- *Locating and sorting text or image segments associated with a code or theme.* When using a computer program, the researcher goes through the text or images one line or image at a time and asks, "What is the person saying (or doing) in this passage?" Then the researcher assigns a code label using the words of the participant, employing social or human science terms, or composing a term that seems to relate to the situation. After reviewing many pages or images, the researcher can use the search function of the program to locate all the text or image segments that fit a code label. In this way, the researcher can easily see how participants are discussing the code or theme in a similar or different way.

- *Retrieving and reviewing common passages or segments that relate to two or more code labels.* The search process can be extended to include two or more code labels. For example, the code label "two-parent family" might be combined with "females" to yield text segments in which women are discussing a "two-parent family." Alternatively, "two-parent family" might be combined with "males" to generate text segments in which men talk about the "two-parent family." The co-occurrence features highlight the frequency of the double coding. After reviewing the frequency of these code combinations, the researcher can use the search function of the program to search for specific words to see how frequently they occur in the texts. In this way, the researcher can create new codes or possible themes based on the frequency of the use of specific words describing the focus for each of the approaches—for example, patterns among story elements for narrative research, significant statements for phenomenology, properties representing multiple perspectives for grounded theory, group thought and behavior for ethnography, and instances for case study.

- *Comparing and relating among code labels.* If the researcher makes both of these requests about females and males, data then exist for making comparisons among the responses of females and males on their views about the "two-parent family." The computer program thus enables a researcher to interrogate the database about the interrelationship among codes or categories. In this way, the researcher can easily retrieve the relevant data segments associated with these codes and categories during the development of themes, models, and abstractions relevant for each approach.

- *Supporting the researcher to conceptualize different levels of abstraction.* The process of qualitative data analysis, as discussed earlier in this chapter, starts with the researcher analyzing the raw data (e.g., interviews), forming the data into codes, and then combining the codes into broader themes. These themes can be and often are "headings" used in a qualitative study. The software programs provide a means for organizing codes hierarchically so that smaller units, such as codes, can be placed under larger units, such as themes. In NVivo, the concept of children and parent codes illustrates two levels of abstraction. In this way, the computer program helps the researcher to build levels of analysis and see the relationship between the raw data and the broader themes. Thus, contributing to the development of the story for narrative research, the description of the essence in phenomenology, the theory in grounded theory, cultural interpretation in ethnography, and the case assertions in case study.

- *Representing and visualizing codes and themes.* Many computer programs contain the feature of concept mapping, charts, and cluster analyses so that the user can generate a visual diagram of the codes and themes and their interrelationships. In this way, the researcher can continually moved around and reorganize these codes and themes under new categories of information as the project progresses. Also, keeping track of the different versions of the diagrams creates an audit trail comprising of a log of the analytic process that can be revisited as needed (see Chapter 10 for further discussion).

- *Documenting and managing memos into codes.* Computer programs provide the capability to write and store memos associated with different units of data—for example, segments of text or images, codes, files, and the overall project. In this way, the researcher can begin to create the codebook or qualitative report during data analysis or simply record insights as they emerge.

- *Creating and applying templates for coding data within each of the five approaches.* The researcher can establish a preset list of codes that match the data analysis procedure within the approach of choice. Then, as data are reviewed during computer analysis, the researcher can identify information that fits into the codes or write memos that become codes. As shown in Figures 8.5 through 8.9, Creswell (2013) initially created these templates for coding within each approach that fit the general structure in analyzing data within the approach. He developed these codes as a hierarchical picture, but they could be drawn as circles or in a less linear fashion. Hierarchical organization of codes is the approach often used in the concept-mapping feature of software programs.

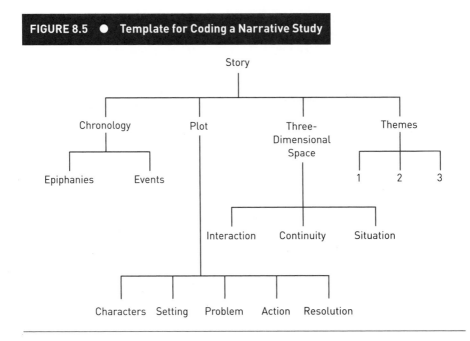

FIGURE 8.5 ● Template for Coding a Narrative Study

In narrative research (see Figure 8.5), we create codes that relate to the story, such as the chronology, the plot or the three-dimensional space model, and the themes that might arise from the story. The analysis might proceed using the plot structure approach or the three-dimensional model, but we placed both in the figure to provide the most options for analysis. The researcher will not know what approach to use until he or she actually starts the data analysis process. The researcher might develop a code, or "story," and begin writing out the story based on the elements analyzed.

In the template for coding a phenomenological study (see Figure 8.6), we used the categories mentioned earlier in data analysis. We placed codes for epoche or bracketing (if this is used), significant statements, meaning units, and textural and structural descriptions (which both might be written as memos). The code at the top, "essence of the phenomenon," is written as a memo about the "essence" that will become the essence description in the final written report. In the template for coding a grounded theory study (see Figure 8.7), we included the three major coding phases: open coding, axial coding, and selective coding. We also included a code for the conditional matrix if that feature is used by the grounded theorist. The researcher can use the code at the top, "theory description or visual model," to create a visual model of the process that is linked to this code.

In the template for coding an ethnography (see Figure 8.8), we included a code that might be a memo or reference to text about the theoretical lens used in the

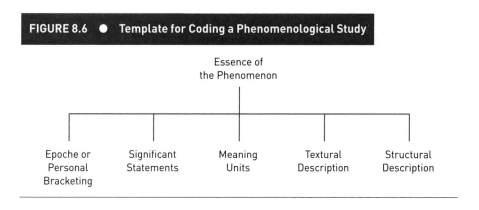

FIGURE 8.6 ● Template for Coding a Phenomenological Study

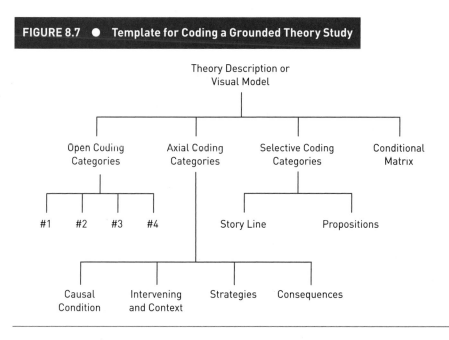

FIGURE 8.7 ● Template for Coding a Grounded Theory Study

ethnography, codes on the description of the culture and an analysis of themes, a code on field issues, and a code on interpretation. The code at the top, "cultural portrait of culture-sharing group—'how it works,'" can be a code in which the ethnographer writes a memo summarizing the major cultural rules that pertain to the group. Finally, in the template for coding a case study (see Figure 8.9), we chose a multiple case study to illustrate the precode specification. For each case, codes exist for the context and description of the case. Also, we advanced codes for themes within each case, and for themes that are similar and different in cross-case analysis. Finally, we included codes for assertions and generalizations across all cases.

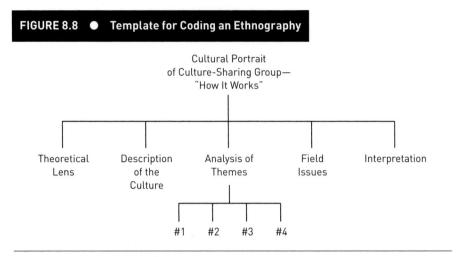

FIGURE 8.8 ● Template for Coding an Ethnography

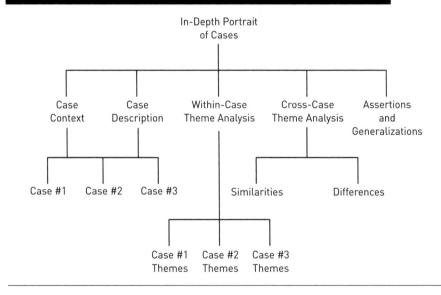

FIGURE 8.9 ● Template for Coding a Case Study (Using a Multiple or Collective Case Approach)

How to Choose Among the Computer Programs

With different programs available, decisions need to be made about the proper choice of a qualitative software program. Basically, all of the programs provide similar features, and some have more features than others. Many of the programs have a demonstration copy available at their websites so that you can examine and try out the program

FIGURE 8.10 ● Nine Features to Consider When Comparing Qualitative Data Analysis Software

1. How easy is the program to integrate into your research?
   a. Is it easy to access in terms of cost and necessary operating system, available support and resources for learning the basics, and opportunities for further learning?
   b. Is it easy to use in getting started and working through an initial document?
   c. Are key features needed for the specific study easy to use?

2. What diversity of data file formats will the program accept?
   a. Will the program handle different types of text and audiovisual data?
   b. Will the program handle different languages (if needed)?
   c. Can the data files be changed once imported?

3. What reading and searching features does the program offer?
   a. Can I highlight data segments?
   b. Can I search for specific data segments?

4. What memo writing and retrieval features does the program offer?
   a. Can I add and access memos associated with data segments?
   b. Can I add and access memos associated with data codes, themes, and files?
   c. Can I add and access memos associated with the overall project?

5. What coding and reviewing features does the program offer?
   a. Can I develop codes?
   b. Can I easily apply codes to text or images?
   c. Can I easily display the data segments associated with individual codes?
   d. Can I easily review and make changes to the codes?

6. What sorting and categorizing features does the program offer?
   a. Can I sort for specific codes?
   b. Can I combine codes in a search?

7. What diagramming features does the program offer?
   a. Can I create a visual display of codes (i.e., network diagram, concept map)?
   b. Can I create a visual representation of a model or theory?

8. What importing or exporting features does the program offer?
   a. Can I important a quantitative database (e.g., SPSS)?
   b. Can I export a word or image qualitative database to a quantitative program?
   c. Can I export a code list with associated codes?
   d. Can I export visual displays and diagrams?

9. What merging, storing, and security features does the program offer?
   a. Can two or more researchers analyze data and then merge these analyses?
   b. Can a backup of the project files be easily created?
   c. What security features are available?

Adapted from Creswell & Maietta (2002), Qualitative Research. In D.C. Miller & N.J. Salkind (Eds.), *Handbook of Research Design and Social Measurement* (pp. 167–168). Thousand Oaks, CA: SAGE.

for ease and fit. Also, guiding resources for specific programs are now available and other researchers can be approached who have used the program. In this way, you can draw upon the views and experiences of other researchers about the software. In 2002, Creswell and Maietta reviewed several computer programs using eight criteria. In Figure 8.10, we present expanded criteria for selecting a program: the ease of use; the diversity of data file formats it accepts; the capability to read and search text; the memo-writing functions; coding and reviewing; sorting and categorization features; diagramming functions, such as concept mapping; importing and exporting files; support for multiple researchers and merging different databases; and storage and security. These criteria can be used to identify a computer program that will meet a researcher's needs.

Chapter Check-In

1. Do you see the similarities and differences in how the authors describe data analysis procedures within their published qualitative studies? Select two of the qualitative articles presented in Appendices B through F.

    a. Begin with identifying evidence of the five data analysis spiral activities (summarized in Table 8.3) as they have been applied in each of the journal articles. Note which elements are easy to identify and which are more difficult to identify.

    b. Then compare the descriptions for each of the data analysis activities across the articles. Note which elements are similar and which are different.

2. What general coding strategies can you use to practice coding text to develop an analysis within one of the five approaches?

    a. To conduct this practice, obtain a short text file, which may be a transcript of an interview, field notes typed from an observation, or a digital file of a document, such as a newspaper article.

    b. Next, read and assign memos by bracketing large text segments and asking yourself the following questions:

        i. What is the content being discussed in the text?

        ii. What would you expect to find in the database?

        iii. What surprising information did you not expect to find?

        iv. What information is conceptually interesting or unusual to participants?

    c. Develop and assign code labels to the text segments using information in this chapter and guided by such questions as the following:

   i. What codes would be expected to fit?

   ii. What new codes are emergent?

   iii. What codes relate to other data sources?

  d. Finally, revisit the segments assigned to each of the codes label and consider which ones might be useful in forming themes in your study.

3. What general coding strategies can you use to practice coding images to develop an analysis within one of the five approaches?

  a. To conduct this practice, obtain pictures from one of your projects or select pictures from magazine articles and prepare a digital file.

  b. Next examine the imagine and assign memos by asking yourself the following questions:

   i. What is in the picture?

   ii. Why, when, how, and by whom was it produced?

   iii. What meanings does the image convey?

  c. Develop and assign code labels to the image using information in this chapter and guided by such questions as the following:

   i. What codes would be expected to fit?

   ii. What new codes are emergent?

   iii. What codes relate to other data sources?

  d. Finally, revisit the image segments assigned to each of the code labels and consider which ones might be useful in forming themes in your study.

4. What considerations should guide your use of qualitative data analysis software?

  a. Using a qualitative study you want to pursue, apply the questions advanced in this chapter to guide whether to use a computer program (see Figure 8.4).

  b. Using the questions to consider when comparing qualitative data analysis software in this chapter (see Figure 8.10), select a computer program or two that best fits your study needs.

  c. Go to the website of the selected computer programs, and find the demonstration program and resources to help you get started.

  d. Try out the program. If possible, input a small database to try out the program features related to memoing, coding, sorting, retrieving, and diagramming.

  e. Now, you might experiment with demonstrations from different software programs. Consider which one has the features that work best for you. Why?

Summary

This chapter presented data analysis and representation. We began by revisiting ethical considerations specific to data analysis followed by a review of procedures advanced by three authors and noted the common features of coding, developing themes, and providing a visual representation of the data. We also noted some of the differences among their approaches. We then advanced a spiral of analysis that captured the general process. This spiral contained aspects of using data management and organization; reading and memoing emergent ideas; describing and classifying codes into themes; developing and assessing interpretations; and representing and visualizing data. We next introduced each of the five approaches to inquiry and discussed how they had unique data analysis steps beyond the "generic" steps of the spiral. Finally, we described how computer programs aid in the analysis and representation of data; discussed criteria guiding how to decide whether to use and features specific to four programs; presented common features of using computer software and templates for coding each of the five approaches to inquiry; and ended with information about criteria for choosing a computer software program.

Further Readings

Several readings extend this brief overview introduction to data analysis, beginning with general resources and then specific for using qualitative data analysis software. The list should not be considered exhaustive, and readers are encouraged to seek out additional readings in the end-of-book reference list.

For Information About Procedures and Issues in Qualitative Data Analysis

Bazeley, P. (2013). *Qualitative data analysis: Practical strategies*. Thousand Oaks, CA: Sage.

Pat Bazeley provides a comprehensive description of analysis including illustrative examples of her practical strategies. This book should be essential reading because of its usefulness for a researcher at any level of expertise.

Flick, U. (Ed.). (2014). *The SAGE handbook of qualitative analysis*. Thousand Oaks, CA: Sage.

Handbooks offer diverse perspectives on a common theme as a starting place. Uwe Flick provides guidance about the basics of qualitative research, analytic strategies, and specific types of data.

Grbich, C. (2013). *Qualitative data analysis: An introduction* (2nd ed.). Thousand Oaks, CA: Sage.

Carol Grbich uses the background a researcher needs, the processes involved in research, and the displays used for presenting findings on which to organize this easy-to-read book. Noteworthy is her practical explanations related to coding (Chapter 21) and theorizing from data (Chapter 23).

Hays, D. G., & Singh, A. A. (2012). *Qualitative inquiry in clinical and educational settings*. New York, NY: Guilford Press.

In this foundational qualitative research text, Danico Hays and Anneliese Singh embed useful pedagogical features such as cautionary notes about possible research pitfalls. In particular, we found the data management and analysis descriptions and examples to be helpful.

Miles, M. B., Huberman, A. M., & Saldaña, J. (2014). *Qualitative data analysis: A sourcebook of new methods* (3rd ed.). Thousand Oaks, CA: Sage.

In this edition, Johnny Saldaña has updated Matthew B. Miles and A. Michael Huberman's seminal resource. In so doing, he has expanded the scope to include (among others) narrative inquiry and autoethnography. This text is a must-read for researchers.

Wolcott, H. F. (1994). *Transforming qualitative data: Description, analysis, and interpretation*. Thousand Oaks, CA: Sage.

In this classical work, Harry Wolcott describes the process of data analysis and representation using nine studies. He makes the case for the need for a good written description as a study outcome.

For Information About Procedures and Issues About the Use of Qualitative Data Analysis Software

Bazeley, P., & Jackson, K. (2013). *Qualitative data analysis with NVivo* (2nd ed.) Thousand Oaks, CA: Sage.

Pat Bazeley and Kristi Jackson provide a comprehensive guide using examples to illustrate the use of NVivo features for getting started, coding, interpreting, and diagramming.

Friese, S. (2014). *Qualitative data analysis with ATLAS.ti* (2nd ed.). Thousand Oaks, CA: Sage.

Susanne Friese provides a step-by-step guide for using ATLAS.ti based on a method for QDAS involving noticing things, collecting things, and thinking about things.

Kuckartz, U. (2014). *Qualitative text analysis: A guide to methods, practice and using software*. Thousand Oaks, CA: Sage.

Udo Kuckartz, developer of MAXQDA, provides a good grounding in three types of qualitative text analysis—thematic, evaluative, and type-building—in addition to how computer analysis software can be embedded in the analysis process.

Silver, C., & Lewins, A. (2014). *Using software in qualitative research: A step-by-step guide* (2nd ed.) Thousand Oaks, CA: Sage.

In this second edition, Christina Silver and Ann Lewins have expanded their excellent overview of how to optimize use of software into qualitative analysis with numerous examples. In particular, we found the summaries comparing seven software program features in Chapter 3 useful.

Writing a Qualitative Study

Writing and composing the narrative report brings the entire study together. Borrowing a term from Strauss and Corbin (1990), we are fascinated by the *architecture* of a study, how it is composed and organized by writers. We also like Strauss and Corbin's (1990) suggestion that writers use a "spatial metaphor" (p. 231) to visualize their full reports or studies. To consider a study spatially, they ask the following questions: Is coming away with an idea like walking slowly around a statue, studying it from a variety of interrelated views? Like walking downhill step by step? Like walking through the rooms of a house? We are intrigued by what Pelias (2011) refers to as *realization* (the writer's process) and *record* (the completed text)—specifically how we might make this progression less obscure. Engaging in the process of writing a qualitative study can be considered ambiguous because "we may not realize what we have or know where we are going" (Charmaz, 2014, p. 290). In short, we may not be able to trace the path our writing process has taken until we complete the written report.

In this chapter, we assess the general architecture of a qualitative study, and then we invite the reader to enter specific rooms of the study to see how they are composed. In this process, we begin with revisiting the key ethical considerations for writing a qualitative study. Then we present four writing strategies for addressing issues in the rendering of a study regardless of approach: **reflexivity** and representation, audience, encoding, and quotes. Then we take each of the five approaches to inquiry and assess two writing structures: the overall structure (i.e., overall organization of the report or study) and the embedded structure (i.e., specific narrative devices and techniques that the writer uses in the report). We return once again to the five examples of studies in Chapter 5 to illustrate overall and embedded structures. Finally, we compare the narrative structures for the five approaches in terms of four dimensions. In this chapter, we will not address the use of grammar and syntax and will refer readers to books that provide a detailed treatment of these subjects (e.g., Creswell, 2014; Strunk & White, 2000; Sword, 2012).

Questions for Discussion

- What ethical issues require attention when writing a qualitative study?
- What are several broad writing strategies associated with crafting a qualitative study?
- What are the larger writing structures used within each of the five approaches of inquiry?
- What are the embedded writing structures within each of the five approaches of inquiry?
- How do the narrative structures for the five approaches differ?

Ethical Considerations for Writing

Before considering the architecture underpinning writing qualitative studies, we carefully consider relevant ethical issues (see initial discussion in Chapter 3). In particular, we must attend to the application of appropriate reporting strategies and compliance with ethical publishing practices (see Table 9.1). For appropriate reporting strategies, it is essential that researchers tailor reports to diverse audiences and use language that is appropriate for target audiences. To comply with ethical publishing practices, researchers must create reports that are honest and trustworthy, seek permissions as needed, ensure same material is not used for more than one publication, and disclose funders and beneficiaries of the research.

Creswell (2016) presents an adapted checklist from the "Ethical Compliance Checklist" (APA, 2010, p. 20) to inform writing. These are questions that should be considered by all qualitative researchers about their study manuscripts and research proposals:

- Have I obtained permission for use of unpublished instruments, procedures, or data that other researchers might consider theirs (proprietary)?
- Have I properly cited other published work presented in portions of the manuscript?
- Am I prepared to answer questions about institutional review of my study or studies?
- Am I prepared to answer editorial questions about the informed consent and debriefing procedures used in the study?
- Have all authors reviewed the manuscript and agreed on the responsibility for its content?

- Have I adequately protected the confidentiality of research participants, clients–patients, organizations, third parties, or others who were the source of information presented in this manuscript?
- Have all authors agreed to the order of the authorship?
- Have I obtained permission for use of any copyrighted material included?

Several Writing Strategies

Unquestionably, the narrative forms are extensive in qualitative research. In reviewing the forms, Glesne (2016) notes that narratives tell stories that blur the lines between fiction, journalism, and scholarly studies. Other qualitative forms engage the reader through a chronological approach as events unfold slowly over time, whether the subject is a study of a culture-sharing group, the narrative story of the life of an individual, or the evolution of a program or an organization. Another form is to narrow and expand the focus, evoking the metaphor of a camera lens that pans out, zooms in, and then zooms out again. Some reports rely heavily on description of events, whereas others advance a small number of "themes" or perspectives. A narrative might capture a "typical day in the life" of an individual or a group. Some reports are heavily oriented toward theory, whereas others, such as Stake's (1995) "Harper School," employ little

TABLE 9.1 ● Examples of Ethical Issues to Attend to During Writing		
Type of Ethical Issue	**Examples of Ethics Issues to Anticipate and Avoid**	**Examples of How to Minimize**
Application of appropriate reporting strategies	Reporting situations that are not appropriate for intended audiences	Tailor reporting to diverse audiences
	Limiting access to reports through use of language that is unclear and convoluted	Use language appropriate for target audiences of the research
Compliance with ethical publishing practices	Falsifying authorship, evidence, data, findings, and conclusions	Create reports that are honest and trustworthy
	Reporting situations where permissions are not sought or plagiarism exists	Follow American Psychological Association (APA; 2010) guidelines for permissions needed to report or adapt work of others
	Duplicating or advancing piecemeal publications	Ensure same material is not used for more than one publication
	Creating conflicts of interest where beneficiaries may not be apparent	Disclose funders for research and who will profit from the research

literature and theory. In addition, since the publication of Clifford and Marcus's (1986) edited volume *Writing Culture* in ethnography, qualitative writing has been shaped by a need for researchers to be self-disclosing about their role in the writing, the impact of it on participants, and how information conveyed is read by audiences. Researcher reflexivity and representations is the first issue to which we turn.

Reflexivity and Representations in Writing

Qualitative researchers today are much more self-disclosing about their qualitative writings than they were a few years ago. Ronald Pelias (2011) describes reflexive writers as "ethically and politically self-aware, make themselves part of their own inquiry" (p. 662). No longer is it acceptable to be the omniscient, distanced qualitative writer. As Laurel Richardson wrote, researchers "do not have to try to play God, writing as disembodied omniscient narrators claiming universal and atemporal general knowledge" (Richardson & St. Pierre, 2005, p. 961). Through these omniscient narrators, postmodern thinkers "deconstruct" the narrative, challenging text as contested terrain that cannot be understood without references to ideas being concealed by the author and contexts within the author's life (Agger, 1991). This theme is espoused by Denzin (2001) in his "interpretive" approach to biographical writing. As a response, qualitative researchers today acknowledge that the writing of a qualitative text cannot be separated from the author, how it is received by readers, and how it impacts the participants and sites under study.

How we write is a reflection of our own interpretation based on the cultural, social, gender, class, and personal politics that we bring to research. All writing is "positioned" and within a stance. All researchers shape the writing that emerges, and qualitative researchers need to accept this interpretation and be open about it in their writings. According to Richardson (1994), the best writing acknowledges its own "undecidability" forthrightly, that all writing has "subtexts" that "situate" or "position" the material within a particular historical and local specific time and place. In this perspective, no writing has "privileged status" (p. 518) or is superior over other writings. Indeed, writings are co-constructions, representations of interactive processes between researchers and the researched (Gilgun, 2005).

Also, there is increased concern about the impact of the writing on the participants. How will they see the write-up? Will they be marginalized because of it? Will they be offended? Will they hide their true feelings and perspectives? Have the participants reviewed the material and interpreted, challenged, and dissented from the interpretation (Weis & Fine, 2000)? Perhaps researchers' writing objectively, in a scientific way, has the impact of silencing the participants and silencing the researchers as well. Czarniawska (2004) and Gilgun (2005) make the point that this silence is contradictory to qualitative research that seeks to hear all voices and perspectives.

Also, the writing has an impact on the reader, who also makes an interpretation of the account and may form an entirely different interpretation than the author or the participants. Should the researcher be afraid that certain people will see the final report? Can the researcher give any kind of definitive account when it is the reader who makes the ultimate interpretation of the events? Indeed, the writing may be a performance, and the standard writing of qualitative research into text has expanded to include split-page writings, theater, poetry, photography, music, collage, drawing, sculpture, quilting, stained glass, and dance (Gilgun, 2005). Language may "kill" whatever it touches, and qualitative researchers understand that it is impossible to truly "say" something (van Manen, 2006).

Weis and Fine (2000) discussed a "set of self-reflective points of critical consciousness around the questions of how to represent responsibility" in qualitative writings (p. 33). There are questions that can be formed from their major points and should be considered by all qualitative researchers about their writings:

- Should I write about what people say or recognize that sometimes they cannot remember or choose not to remember?
- What are my political reflexivities that need to come into my report?
- Has my writing connected the voices and stories of individuals back to the set of historic, structural, and economic relations in which they are situated?
- How far should I go in theorizing the words of participants?
- Have I considered how my words could be used for progressive, conservative, and repressive social policies?
- Have I backed into the passive voice and decoupled my responsibility from my interpretation?
- To what extent has my analysis (and writing) offered an alternative to common sense or the dominant discourse?

Qualitative researchers need to "position" themselves in their writings. This is the concept of reflexivity in which the writer engages in self-understanding about the biases, values, and experiences that he or she brings to a qualitative research study. One characteristic of good qualitative research is that the inquirer makes his or her "position" explicit (Hammersley & Atkinson, 1995). We think about reflexivity as having two parts. The researcher first talks about his or her experiences with the phenomenon being explored. This involves relaying past experiences through work, schooling, family dynamics, and so forth. The second part is to discuss how these past experiences shape the researcher's interpretation of the phenomenon. This is a second important ingredient that is often overlooked or often left out because the process is challenging and the lack of guiding resources (van Manen, 2014).

We suggest writing reflexive comments about what is being experienced as the study progresses—these might be observations during data collection or hunches about what the findings might indicate or reactions from participants during the study. These comments could be easily captured and retrieved using memo functions in qualitative software programs. Reviewing and then discussing how biases, values, and experiences impact emerging understandings is actually the heart of being reflexive in a study, because it is important that the researcher not only detail his or her experiences with the phenomenon but also be self-conscious about how these experiences may potentially have shaped the findings, the conclusions, and the interpretations drawn in a study. Thus, the act of writing a qualitative text cannot be considered separate from the author, the study participants, or the readers. The placement of reflexive comments in a study also needs some consideration.

The reflexive comments may be positioned in one or more positions in a qualitative study. Among the most popular placements involve the opening (or closing) passage of the study, a methods discussion in which the writer talks about his or her role in the study, and personal comments threaded throughout the study. It is not unusual to begin with a personal statement in a phenomenology whereby the authors disclose their backgrounds (see Brown, Sorrell, McClaren, & Creswell, 2006). Similarly, a case study may open with a personal vignette (see Stake, 1995) or end with an epilogue (see Asmussen & Creswell, 1995). As part of a methods description, a phenomenological researcher may disclose his or her experiences as health care provider for and a researcher of persons with HIV/AIDS as necessary for the interviewer to acknowledge and attempt to bracket those experiences (see Anderson & Spencer, 2002; Appendix C). Finally, the researcher may talk about his or her "position" in the introduction, the methods, and the findings or themes as is often the case in an ethnographic study (e.g., see Mac an Ghaill & Haywood, 2015; Appendix E).

Audience for Our Writings

A basic axiom holds that all writers write for an audience. As Clandinin and Connelly (2000) say, "A sense of an audience peering over the writer's shoulder needs to pervade the writing and the written text" (p. 149). Thus, writers consciously think about their audience or multiple audiences for their studies (Richardson, 1990, 1994). Tierney (1995), for example, identifies four potential audiences: colleagues, those involved in the interviews and observations, policy makers, and the general public. More recently Silverman (2013) differentiated the expectations of academic and practitioner colleagues in that the former sought theoretical, factual, or methodological insights from our research, whereas the latter sought practical suggestions for better procedures or reform of existing practices. Identifying target audiences helps inform choices during the writing process. In short, how the report is structured depends on the readers you intend to engage with your writing. For example, because Fischer and Wertz (1979) disseminated information about their phenomenological study at public forums, they produced several expressions of their findings, all responding to different audiences. One form was a general structure, four paragraphs in length, an approach that they admitted lost its richness and concreteness. Another form consisted of case synopses, each reporting the experiences of one individual and each two and a half pages in length. More recently, MacKenzie, Christensen, and Turner (2015) discussed the challenges they experienced while trying to communicate their participatory research results with their indigenous participants.

Ravitch and Mittenfelner Carl (2016) discussed 14 questions related to the purpose and audience of a study. The following are adapted to inform writing decisions and should be considered by all qualitative researchers about their target audiences:

- For what audience(s) is this study being written? What informs these choices?
- What am I hoping to achieve with this report to my audience?
- What writing structures would my audience expect?
- Are there other audiences who could benefit from my learning and knowledge?
- How might I structure my writing to fit other audiences' needs?

Encoding Our Writings

A closely related topic is recognizing the importance of language in shaping our qualitative texts. The words we use encode our report, revealing how we perceive the needs of our audiences. Earlier, in Chapter 6, we presented encoding the problem, purpose, and research questions; now, we consider encoding the entire narrative report. Richardson's (1990) study of women in affairs with married men illustrates how a writer can shape a work differently for a trade audience, an academic audience, or a moral or political audience. For a trade audience, she encoded her work with literary devices such as the following:

> Jazzy titles, attractive covers, lack of specialized jargon, marginalization of methodology, common-world metaphors and images, and book blurbs and prefatory material about the "lay" interest in the material. (Richardson, 1990, p. 32)

For the moral or political audience, she encoded through devices such as the following:

> In-group words in the title, for example, woman/women/feminist in feminist writing; the moral or activist "credentials" of the author, for example, the author's role in particular social movements; references to moral and activist authorities; empowerment metaphors, and book blurbs and prefatory material about how this work relates to real people's lives. (Richardson, 1990, pp. 32–33)

Finally, for the academic audience (e.g., journals, conference papers, academic books), she marked it by the following:

> Prominent display of academic credentials of author, references, footnotes, methodology sections, use of familiar academic metaphors and images (such as "exchange theory," "roles," and "stratification"), and book blurbs and prefatory material about the science or scholarship involved. (Richardson, 1990, p. 32)

Although we emphasize academic writing here, researchers encode qualitative studies for audiences other than academics. For example, in the social and human sciences, policy makers may be a primary audience, and this necessitates writing with minimal methods, more parsimony, and a focus on practice and results.

Richardson's (1990) ideas triggered thoughts about how one might encode a qualitative narrative. Such encoding might include the following:

- An overall structure that does not conform to the standard quantitative introduction, methods, results, and discussion format. Instead, the methods might be called procedures, and the results might be called findings. In fact, the researcher might phrase the headings for themes in the words of participants in the study as they discuss "denial," "retriggering," and so forth, as was done in the gunman case (Asmussen & Creswell, 1995).
- A writing style that is personal, familiar, perhaps "up-close," highly readable, friendly, and applied for a broad audience. Our qualitative writings should strive for a "persuasive" effect (Czarniawska, 2004, p. 124). Readers should find the material interesting and memorable, the "grab" in writing (Gilgun, 2005).
- A level of detail that makes the work come alive—***verisimilitude*** comes to mind (Richardson, 1994, p. 521). This word indicates the presentation of a good literary study in which the writing becomes "real" and "alive," writing that transports the reader directly into the world of the study, whether this world is the cultural setting of youths' resistance to both the counterculture and the dominant culture (Haenfler, 2004) or an immigrant student in a school classroom (Chan, 2010; see Appendix B). Still, we must recognize that the writing is only a representation of what we see or understand.

Quotes in Our Writings

In addition to encoding text with the language of qualitative research, authors bring in the voice of participants in the study. A good rule of thumb is that quotes should be as illustrative as possible and be contextualized, interpreted, and incorporated within the text of the manuscript (Brinkmann & Kvale, 2015). Writers use ample quotes, and we find Richardson's (1990) discussion about three types of quotes most useful. The first consists of short, eye-catching quotations. These are easy to read, take up little space, and stand out from the narrator's text and are indented to signify different perspectives. For example, in the phenomenological study of how persons live with AIDS, Anderson and Spencer (2002; see Appendix C) used paragraph-long quotes from men and women in the study to convey the "magic of not thinking" theme:

> It's a sickness, but in my mind I don't think that I got it. Because if you think about having HIV, it comes down more on you. It's more like a mind game. To try and stay alive is that you don't even think about it. It's not in the mind. (p. 1347)

The second approach consists of embedded quotes, briefly quoted phrases within the analyst's narrative. These quotes, according to Richardson (1990), prepare a reader for a shift in emphasis or display a point and allow the writer (and reader) to move on. Harley et al. (2009; see Appendix D) used short, embedded quotes extensively in their grounded theory study because they consume little space and provide specific concrete evidence, in the participants' words, to support a theme such as the initiation phase:

> Many of the women were juggling careers and family, so time out for themselves was another important benefit of physical activity. One woman explained, "I had a little time for me. I started enjoying it. I started liking it." (p. 103)

A third type of quote is the longer quotation used to convey more complex understandings. These are difficult to use because of space limitations in publications and because longer quotes may contain many ideas, and so the reader needs to be guided both "into" the quote and "out of" the quote to focus his or her attention on the controlling idea that the writer would like the reader to see. Frelin (2015; see Appendix F) used longer quotes to describe the impact of time on the development of teacher-student relationships:

> That you always have the time to spend with a student, and can sit down and talk if you see that something is wrong. You can always have a proper conversation with a student. Always. It is fantastic, but you can't do that at compulsory school when you have a group of 30 and need to rush off to the next lesson. (p. 598)

Overall and Embedded Writing Strategies

In addition to these writing approaches, the qualitative researcher needs to address how he or she is going to compose the overall narrative structure of the report and use embedded structures within the report to provide a narrative within the approach of choice. We offer Table 9.2 as a guide to the discussion to follow, in which we list many overall and embedded structural approaches as they apply to the five approaches of inquiry.

Narrative Writing Structures

As we read about the writing of studies in narrative research, we find authors unwilling to prescribe a tightly structured writing strategy (Clandinin, 2013; Clandinin & Connelly, 2000; Czarniawska, 2004; Riessman, 2008). Instead, we find the authors suggesting maximum flexibility in structure (see Ely, 2007) but emphasizing core elements that might go into the narrative study. In so doing, Clandinin (2013) describes the writer as well positioned for matching the narrative structures to the particular study context:

> As narrative inquirers, we need to hold open and to make visible the ways that participants, and we, struggle for that coherence, sometimes successfully, sometimes not. We must, in the composing, co-composing and negotiation of interim

TABLE 9.2 ● Overall and Embedded Writing Structures Within the Five Approaches

Approach	Overall Writing Structures	Embedded Writing Structures
Narrative	• Flexible and evolving processes (Clandinin, 2013; Clandinin & Connelly, 2000) • Three-dimensional space inquiry model (Clandinin & Connelly, 2000) • Story chronologies (Clandinin & Connelly, 2000) or temporal or episodic ordering of information (Riessman, 2008) • Reporting what participants said (themes), how they said it (order of their story), or how they interacted with others (dialogue and performance; Riessman, 2008)	• Epiphanies (Denzin, 2001) • Key events or plots (Czarniawska, 2004; Smith, 1994) • Metaphors and transitions (Clandinin & Connelly, 2000; Lomask, 1986) • Progressive–regressive methods (Czarniawska, 2004; Denzin, 2001; Ellis, 1993; Huber & Whelan, 1999) • Threads across multiple narrative accounts (Clandinin, 2013; Clandinin & Connelly, 2000) • Themes or categories (Chan, 2010; Riessman, 2008) • Dialogues or conversations (Chan, 2010; Riessman, 2008)
Phenomenology	• Structure of a "research manuscript" (Moustakas, 1994) • The "research report" format (Polkinghorne, 1989) • Themes and analytic analysis start with the essence; engage with other authors; use time, space, and other dimensions (van Manen, 2014)	• Figures or tables reporting essences (Anderson & Spencer, 2002; Grigsby & Megel, 1995) • Philosophical discussions (Harper, 1981) • Creative closings (Moustakas, 1994)
Grounded theory	• Grounded theory study components (May, 1986) • Results of open, axial, and selective coding (Strauss & Corbin, 1990, 1998) • Focus is on theory and arguments that support it (Charmaz, 2014)	• Extent of analysis (Chenitz & Swanson, 1986; Creswell & Brown, 1992; Kus, 1986) • Propositions (Conrad, 1978; Strauss & Corbin, 1990) • Visual diagrams (Harley et al., 2009; Morrow & Smith, 1995) • Emotions, rhythm, rhetorical questions, tone, pacing, stories, evocative writing (Charmaz, 2014)
Ethnography	• Types of tales (Van Maanen, 2011) • Description, analysis, and interpretation (Wolcott, 1994) • "Thematic narrative" (Emerson, Fretz, & Shaw, 2011)	• Tropes (Fetterman, 2010; Hammersley & Atkinson, 2007; Rhoads, 1995) • "Thick" description (Denzin, 2001; Fetterman, 2010) • Verbatim quotations (Fetterman, 2010; Haenfler, 2004; Mac an Ghaill & Haywood, 2015) • Dialogue (Nelson, 1990) or scenes (Emerson et al., 2011) • Literary devices, such as voices of different speakers, metaphors, irony, and similes (Fetterman, 2010)

Approach	Overall Writing Structures	Embedded Writing Structures
Case study	• Format with vignettes (Stake, 1995) • Substantive case report format (Lincoln & Guba, 1985) • Types of cases (Yin, 2014) • Alternative structures based on linear and nonlinear approaches (Yin, 2014)	• Chronological and funnel approaches (Asmussen & Creswell, 1995; Frelin, 2015; Staples, Pugach, & Himes, et al., 2005) • Description (Merriam, 1988; Merriam & Tisdell, 2015)

and final research texts, make visible the multiplicity, as well as the narrative coherence and lack of narrative coherence, of our lives, the lives of participants, and the lives we co-compose in the midst of our narrative inquiries. (p. 49)

Overall Structures Narrative researchers encourage individuals to write narrative studies that experiment with form (Clandinin, 2013; Clandinin & Connelly, 2000). Researchers can come to their narrative form by first looking to their own preferences in reading (e.g., memoirs, novels), reading other narrative dissertations and books, and viewing the narrative study as back-and-forth writing, as a process (Clandinin & Connelly, 2000). Within these general guidelines, Clandinin and Connelly (2000) review two doctoral dissertations that employ narrative research. The two have different narrative structures: One provides narratives of a chronology of the lives of three women; the other adopts a more classical approach to a dissertation including an introduction, a literature review, and a methodology. For this second example, the remaining chapters then go into a discussion that tells the stories of the author's experiences with the participants. Reading through these two examples, we are struck by how they both reflect the three-dimensional inquiry space that Clandinin and Connelly (2000) discuss. This space, as mentioned earlier, is a text that looks backward and forward, looks inward and outward, and situates the experiences within place. For example, the dissertation of He, cited by Clandinin, is a study about the lives of two participants and the author in their past life in China and in their present situation in Canada. The story does the following:

> [It] looks backward to the past for her and her two participants and forward to the puzzle of who they are and who they are becoming in their new land. She looks inward to her personal reasons for doing this study and outward to the social significance of the work. She paints landscapes of China and Canada and the in-between places where she imagines herself to reside. (Clandinin & Connelly, 2000, p. 156)

Later in Clandinin and Connelly (2000), there is a story about Clandinin's advice for students about the narrative form of their studies. This form again relates to the three-dimensional space model:

> When they came to Jean for conversations about their emerging texts, she found herself responding not so much with comments about preestablished and accepted forms but with response that raised questions situated within the three-dimensional narrative inquiry space. (Clandinin & Connelly, 2000, p. 165)

Notice in this passage how Clandinin "raised questions" rather than told the student how to proceed, and how she returned to the larger *rhetorical* structure of the three-dimensional inquiry space model as a framework for thinking about the writing of a narrative study. This framework also suggests a chronology to the narrative report, and this ordering within the chronology might further be organized by time or by specific episodes (Riessman, 2008).

In narrative research, as in all forms of qualitative inquiry, there is a close relationship between the data collection procedures, the analysis, and the form and structure of the writing report. For example, the larger writing structure in a thematic analysis would be the presentation of several themes (Riessman, 2008). In a more structured approach—analyzing how the individual tells a story—the elements presented in the report might follow six elements, what Riessman (2008) calls a "fully formed narrative" (p. 84). These would be the elements of the following:

- A summary and/or the point of the story
- Orientation (the time, place, characters, and situations)
- Complicating action (the event sequence, or plot usually with a crisis or turning point)
- Evaluation (where the narrator comments on meaning or emotions)
- Resolution (the outcome of the plot)
- Coda (ending the story and bringing it back to the present)

In a narrative study focused on the interrogation between speakers (such as the interviewer and the interviewee), the larger writing structure would focus on direct speech and dialogue. Further, the dialogue might contain features of a performance, such as direct speeches, asides to the audience, repetition, expressive sounds, and switches in verb tense. The entire report may be a poem, a play, or another dramatic rendering. In previous chapters, we have described narrative studies that illustrate these narrative elements (see Chan, 2010; Appendix B), and we encourage you to review them for similarities and differences in how the studies are presented.

Embedded Structures   Assuming that the larger writing structure proceeds with experimentation and flexibility, the writing structure at the more micro level relates to several elements of writing strategies that authors might use in composing a narrative study. These are drawn from Clandinin (2013), Clandinin and Connelly (2000), Czarniawska (2004), and Riessman (2008).

The writing of a narrative needs to not silence some of the voices, and it ultimately gives more space to certain voices than others (Czarniawska, 2004). In addition, there can be a spatial element to the writing, such as in the ***progressive–regressive method*** (Denzin, 2001) whereby the biographer begins with a key event in the participant's life and then works forward and backward from that event, such as in Denzin's (2001) study of alcoholics. Alternatively, there can be a "zooming in" and "zooming out," such as describing a large context to a concrete field of study (e.g., a site) and then telescoping out again (Czarniawska, 2004). Huber and Whelan's (1999) retelling of the narrative of a teacher's identity shaping refers to personal background influences as she talks about more current professional experiences. Similarly, Ellis's (1993) personal narrative of a family drama enacted in the aftermath of her brother's death in airplane crash is told by alternating between descriptions of childhood experiences and those surrounding the crash.

The writing may emphasize the "key event" or the epiphany, defined as interactional moments and experiences that mark people's lives (Denzin, 2001). Denzin distinguishes four types: the major event that touches the fabric of the individual's life; the cumulative or representative events or experiences that continue for some time; the minor epiphany, which represents a moment in an individual's life; and episodes or relived epiphanies, which involve reliving the experience. Czarniawska (2004) introduces the key element of the plot or the emplotment, a means of introducing structure that allows for making sense of the events reported.

Themes can be reported in narrative writing. Smith (1994) recommends finding a theme to guide the development of the life to be written. This theme emerges from preliminary knowledge or a review of the entire life, although researchers often experience difficulty in distinguishing the major theme from lesser or minor themes. Clandinin and Connelly (2000) refer to writing research texts at the reductionistic boundary, an approach consisting of a "reduction downward" (p. 143) to themes in which the researcher looks for common threads or elements across participants. Clandinin (2013) describes these threads as important for composing multiple narrative accounts.

Specific narrative writing strategies also include the use of dialogue, such as that between the researcher and the participants (Riessman, 2008). Sometimes in this approach the specific language of the narrator is interrogated and is not taken at face value. The dialogue unfolds in the study, and often it is presented in different languages, including the language of the narrator and an English translation. An example is provided by Chan's (2010; see Appendix B) story of one Chinese immigrant student and the affiliation this student had with other students, her teacher, and her family where dialogue between the researcher and the student provided evidence for each theme. Each dialogue segment was titled to shape the meaning of the conversation, such as "Susan doesn't speak Fujianese" (Chan, 2010, p. 117).

Other narrative rhetorical devices include the use of transitions. Lomask (1986) refers to these as built into the narratives in natural chronological linkages. Writers insert them through words or phrases, questions (which Lomask calls being lazy), and time-and-place shifts moving the action forward or backward. In addition to transitions, narrative researchers employ ***foreshadowing***, the frequent use of narrative hints of things to come or of events or themes to be developed later. Narrative researchers also use metaphors, and Clandinin and Connelly (2000) suggest the metaphor of a soup (i.e., with description of people, places, and things; arguments for understandings; and richly textured narratives of people situated in place, time, scene, and plot) within containers (i.e., dissertation, journal article) to describe their narrative texts.

Phenomenological Writing Structures

Those who write about phenomenology (e.g., Moustakas, 1994; van Manen, 2014) provide more extensive attention to overall writing structures than to embedded ones. However, as in all forms of qualitative research, one can learn much from a careful study of research reports in journal article, monograph, or book form.

Overall Structures The highly structured approach to analysis by Moustakas (1994) presents a detailed form for composing a phenomenological study. The analysis steps—identifying significant statements, creating meaning units, clustering themes, advancing textural and structural descriptions, and ending with a composite description of textural and structural descriptions with an exhaustive description of the essential invariant structure (or essence) of the experience—provide a clearly articulated procedure for organizing a report (Moustakas, 1994). In our experience, individuals are quite surprised to find highly structured approaches to phenomenological studies on sensitive topics (e.g., "being left out," "insomnia," "being criminally victimized," "life's meaning," "voluntarily changing one's career during midlife," "longing," "adults being abused as children"; Moustakas, 1994, p. 153). But the data analysis procedure, we think, guides a researcher in that direction and presents an overall structure for analysis and ultimately the organization of the report.

Consider the overall organization of a report as suggested by Moustakas (1994). He recommends specific chapters in "creating a research manuscript":

Chapter 1: *Introduction and statement of topic and outline.* Topics include an autobiographical statement about experiences of the author leading to the topic, incidents that lead to a puzzlement or curiosity about the topic, the social implications and relevance of the topic, new knowledge and contribution to the profession to emerge from studying the topic, knowledge to be gained by the researcher, the research question, and the terms of the study.

Chapter 2: *Review of the relevant literature.* Topics include a review of databases searched, an introduction to the literature, a procedure for selecting studies, the conduct of these studies and themes that emerged in them, and a summary of core findings and statements as to how the present research differs from prior research (in question, model, methodology, and data collected).

Chapter 3: *Conceptual framework of the model.* Topics include the theory to be used as well as the concepts and processes related to the research design (Chapters 3 and 4 might be combined).

Chapter 4: *Methodology*. Topics include the methods and procedures in preparing to conduct the study; in collecting data; and in organizing, analyzing, and synthesizing the data.

Chapter 5: *Presentation of data*. Topics include verbatim examples of data collection, data analysis, a synthesis of data, horizonalization, meaning units, clustered themes, textural and structural descriptions, and a synthesis of meanings and essences of the experience.

Chapter 6: *Summary, implications, and outcomes*. Sections include a summary of the study, statements about how the findings differ from those in the literature review, recommendations for future studies, the identification of limitations, a discussion about implications, and the inclusion of a creative closure that speaks to the essence of the study and its inspiration for the researcher.

A second model, not as specific, is found in Polkinghorne (1989) where he discusses the "research report." In this model, the researcher describes the procedures to collect data and the steps to move from the raw data to a more general description of the experience. Also, the investigator includes a review of previous research, the theory pertaining to the topic, and implications for psychological theory and application. We especially like Polkinghorne's (1989) comment about the impact of such a report:

> Produce a research report that gives an accurate, clear, and articulate description of an experience. The reader of the report should come away with the feeling that "I understand better what it is like for someone to experience that." (p. 46)

A third model of the overall writing structure of a phenomenological study comes from van Manen (1990, 2014). He begins his discussion of "working the text" (van Manen, 1990, p. 167) with the thought that studies that present and organize transcripts for the final report fall short of being a good phenomenological study. Instead, he recommends several options for writing the study. The study might be organized thematically, examining essential aspects of the phenomenon under study. It might also be presented analytically by reworking the text data into larger ideas (e.g., contrasting ideas), or focused narrowly on the description of a particular life situation. It might begin with the essence description and then present varying examples of how the essence is manifested. Other approaches include engaging one's writing in a dialogue with other phenomenological authors and weaving the description against time, space, the lived body, and relationships to others. In the end, van Manen suggests that authors may invest new ways of reporting their data or combine approaches.

Embedded Structures Turning to embedded rhetorical structures, the literature provides the best evidence. A writer presents the "essence" of the experience for participants in a study through sketching a short paragraph about it in the narrative or by enclosing this paragraph in a figure. This latter approach is used effectively in a study of the caring experiences of nurses who teach (Grigsby & Megel, 1995). Another structural device is to educate the reader through a discussion about phenomenology and its philosophical assumptions. Harper (1981) uses this approach and describes several of Husserl's major tenets as well as the advantages of studying the meaning of "leisure" in a phenomenology.

Finally, we like Moustakas's (1994) suggestion: "Write a brief creative close that speaks to the essence of the study and its inspiration to you in terms of the value of the knowledge and future directions of your professional-personal life" (p. 184). Despite the phenomenologist's inclination to bracket himself or herself out of the narrative, Moustakas introduces the reflexivity that psychological phenomenologists can bring to a study, such as casting an initial problem statement within an autobiographical context. In previous chapters, we have described phenomenologies that follow general outlines (see Anderson & Spencer, 2002; Appendix C), and we encourage you to review them for similarities and differences in how the studies are presented. Specifically, Anderson and Spencer's phenomenology of how persons living with AIDS image their disease represented many of these overall and embedded writing structures. The over-all article has a structured organization, opening with a quote from a 53-year-old man with AIDS, followed by a study introduction, a review of the literature, methods, and results. It followed Colaizzi's (1978) phenomenological methods by reporting a table of significant statements and a table of meaning themes. Anderson and Spencer (2002) ended with an in-depth, exhaustive description of the phenomenon:

> Results were integrated into an essential scheme of AIDS. The lived experience of AIDS was initially frightening, with a dread of body wasting and personal loss. Cognitive representations of AIDS included inescapable death, bodily destruc-tion, fighting a battle, and having a chronic disease. Coping methods included searching for the "right drug," caring for oneself, accepting the diagnosis, wiping AIDS out of their thoughts, turning to God, and using vigilance. With time, most people adjusted to living with AIDS. Feelings ranged from "devastating," "sad," and "angry" to being at "peace" and "not worrying." (p. 1349)

A similar structured approach informed by Moustakas (1994) was taken in Padilla's (2003) phenomenology of the lived experience of a disability of a woman who sus-tained a head injury 21 years ago. Quotes from the woman were used to begin and end the article and are embedded throughout—the only exception being the writer's description of the background of the project.

Grounded Theory Writing Structures

From reviewing grounded theory studies in journal articles, qualitative researchers can deduce a general form (and variations) for composing the narrative. The problem with journal articles is that the authors present truncated versions of the studies to fit within the parameters of the journals. Thus, a reader emerges from a review of a particular study without a full sense of the entire project.

Overall Structures Most importantly, authors need to present the theory in any grounded theory narrative. To do this requires the writer to engage in an iterative process: "It means going back and forth between the sections to rethink, revise, and sometimes recast and rewrite" (Charmaz, 2014, p. 285). As May (1986) comments, "In strict terms, the findings are the theory itself, i.e., a set of concepts and propositions which link them" (p. 148). May (1986) continues to describe the research procedures in grounded theory:

- The research questions are broad. They will change several times during data collection and analysis.
- The literature review "neither provides key concepts nor suggests hypotheses" (p. 149). Instead, the literature review in grounded theory shows gaps or bias in existing knowledge, thus providing a rationale for this type of qualitative study.
- The methodology evolves during the course of the study, so writing it early in a study poses difficulties. However, the researcher begins somewhere, and she or he describes preliminary ideas about the sample, the setting, and the data collection procedures.
- The findings section presents the theoretical scheme. The writer includes references from the literature to show outside support for the theoretical model. Also, segments of actual data in the form of vignettes and quotes provide useful explanatory material. This material helps the reader form a judgment about how well the theory is grounded in the data.
- The final discussion section discusses the relationship of the theory to other existing knowledge and the implications of the theory for future research and practice.

Strauss and Corbin (1990) also provide broad writing parameters for their grounded theory studies. They suggest the following:

- Develop a clear analytic story. This is to be provided in the selective coding phase of the study.
- Write on a conceptual level, with description kept secondary to concepts and the analytic story. This means that one finds little description of the phenomenon being studied and more analytic theory at an abstract level.
- Specify the relationship among categories. This is the theorizing part of grounded theory found in axial coding when the researcher tells the story and advances propositions.
- Specify the variations and the relevant conditions, consequences, and so forth for the relationships among categories. In a good theory, one finds variation and different conditions under which the theory holds. This means that the multiple perspectives or variations in each component of axial coding are developed fully. For example, the consequences in the theory are multiple and detailed.

More specifically, in a structured approach to grounded theory as advanced by Strauss and Corbin (1990, 1998), specific aspects of the final written report contain a section on open coding that identifies the various open codes that the researcher dis-covered in the data, and the axial coding, which includes a diagram of the theory and a discussion about each component in the diagram (i.e., causal conditions, the central phenomenon, the intervening conditions, the context, the strategies, and the conse-quences). Also, the report contains a section on the theory in which the researcher advances theoretical propositions tying together the elements of the categories in the diagram, or discusses the theory interrelating the categories. In previous chapters, we have described grounded theory studies that follow this general outline (see Harley et al., 2009; Appendix D), and we encourage you to review them for similarities and dif-ferences in how the studies are presented.

For Charmaz (2006, 2014), a less-structured approach flows into her suggestions for writing the draft of the grounded theory study. She emphasizes the importance of allowing the ideas to emerge as the theory develops, revising early drafts, asking yourself questions about the theory (e.g., have you raised major categories to concepts in the theory?), constructing an argument about the importance of the theory, and closely examining the categories in the theory. Thus, Charmaz does not have a tem-plate for writing a grounded theory study but focuses our attention on the importance of the argument in the theory and the nature of the theory.

Embedded Structures In grounded theory studies, the researcher varies the narrative report based on the extent of data analysis. Chenitz and Swanson (1986), for example, present six grounded theory studies that vary in the types of analysis reported in the narrative. In a preface to these examples, they mention that the analysis (and narra-tive) might address one or more of the following: description; the generation of catego-ries through open coding; linking categories around a core category in axial coding, thus developing a substantive, low-level theory; and/or a substantive theory linked to a formal theory.

We have seen grounded theory studies that include one or more of these analyses. For example, in a study of gays and their "coming out" process, Kus (1986) uses only open coding in the analysis and identifies four stages in the process of coming out: iden-tification, in which a gay person undergoes a radical identity transformation; cognitive changes, in which the individual changes negative views about gays into positive ideas; acceptance, a stage in which the individual accepts being gay as a positive life force; and action, the process of the individual's engaging in behavior that results from accepting being gay, such as self-disclosure, expanding the circle of friends to include gays, becom-ing politically involved in gay causes, and volunteering for gay groups. Set in contrast to this focus on the process, Creswell and Brown (1992) follow the coding steps in Strauss and Corbin (1990). First, they examined the faculty development practices of chairper-sons who enhance the research productivity of their faculties. They begin with open coding, move to axial coding complete with a logic diagram, and state a series of explicit propositions in directional (as opposed to the null) form.

Another embedded narrative feature is to examine the form for stating propositions or theoretical relationships in grounded theory studies. Sometimes, these are presented in "discursive" form, or describing the theory in narrative form. Strauss and Corbin (1990) present such a model in their theory of "protective governing" (p. 134) in the health care setting. Another example is seen in Conrad's (1978) formal propositions about academic change in the academy.

Another embedded structure is the presentation of the "logic diagram," the "mini-framework," or the "integrative" diagram, where the researcher presents the actual theory in the form of a visual model. The researcher identifies elements of this structure in the axial coding phase, and then tells the "story" in axial coding as a narrative version of it. How is this visual model presented? A good example of this diagram is found in the Morrow and Smith (1995) study of women who have survived childhood sexual abuse. Their diagram shows a theoretical model that contains the axial coding categories of causal conditions, the central phenomenon, the context, intervening conditions, strategies, and consequences. It is presented with directional arrows indicating the flow of causality from left to right, from causal conditions to consequences. Arrows also show that the context and intervening conditions directly impact the strategies. Presented near the end of the study, this visual form represents the culminating theory for the study. Harley et al. (2009; see Appendix D) advance a visual of the theory about the evolution of physical activity involving a main progression of three phases (initiation, transition and integration) along with two alternatives described as the modification loop and the cessation loop.

Charmaz (2006, 2014) provides an array of embedded writing strategies useful in grounded theory reports including a centering of the analytical frameworks. Examples of grounded theory studies illustrate imparting mood or emotions into a theoretical discussion, straightforward language, and ways that writing can be accessible to readers such as the use of rhythm and time [e.g., "Days slip by" (Charmaz, 2006, p. 173)]. Charmaz also invites the use of unexpected definitions and assertions by the grounded theory author. Rhetorical questions are also useful, and the writing includes pacing and a tone that leads a reader into the topic. Stories can be told in grounded theory studies, and overall the writing brings evocative language to persuade the reader of the theory.

Ethnographic Writing Structures

Ethnographers write extensively about narrative construction, from how the nature of the text shapes the subject matter to the "literary" conventions and devices used by authors (Atkinson & Hammersley, 1994). The general shapes of ethnographies and embedded structures are well detailed in the literature.

Overall Structures   The overall writing structure of ethnographies varies. For example, Van Maanen (1988; 2011) provides the alternative forms of ethnography. Some ethnographies are written as realist tales, reports that provide direct, matter-of-fact portraits of studied cultures without much information about how the ethnographers produced the portraits. In this type of tale, a writer uses an impersonal point of view, conveying a "scientific" and "objective" perspective. A confessional tale takes the opposite approach, and the researcher focuses more on his or her fieldwork experiences than on the culture. The final type, the impressionistic tale, is a personalized account of "the fieldwork case in dramatic form" (Van Maanen, 1988, p. 7). It has elements of both realist and confessional writing and, in our opinion, presents a compelling and persuasive story. In both confessional and impressionistic tales, the first-person point of view is used, conveying a personal style of writing. Van Maanen states that other, less frequently written tales also exist—critical tales focusing on large social, political, symbolic, or economic issues; formalist tales that build, test, generalize, and exhibit theory; literary tales in which the ethnographers write like journalists, borrowing fiction-writing techniques from novelists; and jointly told tales in which the production of the studies is jointly authored by the fieldworkers and the participants, opening up shared and discursive narratives.

On a slightly different note but yet related to the larger rhetorical structure, Wolcott (1994) provides three components of a good qualitative inquiry that are a centerpiece of good ethnographic writing as well as steps in data analysis. First, an ethnographer writes a "description" of the culture that answers this question: "What is going on here?" (Wolcott, 1994, p. 12). Wolcott offers useful techniques for writing this description: chronological order, the researcher or narrator order, a progressive focusing, a critical or key event, plots and characters, groups in interaction, an analytical framework, and a story told through several perspectives. Second, after describing the culture using one of these approaches, the researcher "analyzes" the data. Analysis includes highlighting findings, displaying findings, reporting fieldwork procedures, identifying patterned regularities in the data, comparing the case with a known case, evaluating the information, contextualizing the information within a broader analytic framework, critiquing the research process, and proposing a redesign of the study. Of all these analytic techniques, the identification of "patterns" or themes is central to ethnographic writing. Third, interpretation is involved in the rhetorical structure. This means that the researcher can extend the analysis, make inferences from the information, do as directed or as suggested by gatekeepers, turn to theory, refocus the interpretation itself, connect with personal experience, analyze or interpret the interpretive process, or explore alternative formats. Of these interpretive strategies, we like the approach of interpreting the findings both within the context of the researcher's experiences and within the larger body of scholarly research on the topic.

A more detailed, structured outline for ethnography was found in Emerson, Fretz, and Shaw (2011). They discuss developing an ethnographic study as a "thematic narrative," a story "analytically thematized, but often in relatively loose ways . . . constructed out of a series of thematically organized units of fieldnote excerpts and analytic commentary" (p. 202). This thematic narrative builds inductively from a main idea or thesis that incorporates several specific analytic themes and is elaborated throughout the study. It is structured as follows:

- First is an introduction that engages the reader's attention and focuses the study, and then the researcher proceeds to link his or her interpretation to wider issues of scholarly interest in the discipline.

- After this, the researcher introduces the setting and the methods for learning about it. In this section, too, the ethnographer relates details about entry into and participation in the setting as well as advantages and constraints of the ethnographer's research role.
- The researcher presents analytic claims next. Emerson and colleagues (2011) indicate the utility of "excerpt commentary" units, whereby an author incorporates an analytic point, provides orientation information about the point, presents the excerpt or direct quote, and then advances analytic commentary about the quote as it relates to the analytic point.
- In the conclusion, the researcher reflects and elaborates on the thesis advanced at the beginning. This interpretation may extend or modify the thesis in light of the materials examined; relate the thesis to general theory or a current issue; or offer a metacommentary on the thesis, methods, or assumptions of the study.

In previous chapters, we have described ethnographies that follow this general outline (see Mac an Ghaill & Haywood, 2015; Appendix E), and we encourage you to review them for similarities and differences in how the studies are presented.

Embedded Structures Ethnographers use embedded rhetorical devices such as figures of speech or "tropes" (Fetterman, 2010; Hammersley & Atkinson, 2007). Metaphors, for example, provide visual and spatial images or dramaturgical characterizations of social actions as theater. Another trope is the synecdoche, in which ethnographers present examples, illustrations, cases, and/or vignettes that form a part but stand for the whole. See Rhoads (1995) for an example of an effective opening vignette in an ethnography of fraternity life on campus. Ethnographers present storytelling tropes examining cause and sequence that follow grand narratives to smaller parables. A final trope is irony, in which researchers bring to light contrasts of competing frames of reference and rationality.

More specific rhetorical devices depict scenes in ethnography (Emerson et al., 2011). Writers can incorporate details or "write lushly" (Goffman, 1989, p. 131) or "thickly" a description that creates verisimilitude and produces for readers the feeling that they experience, or perhaps could experience, the events described (Denzin, 2001; Fetterman, 2010). The ethnographic study of the core values of the straight edge (sXe) movement illustrated many of these writing conventions (Haenfler, 2004). He told a persuasive story, with colorful elements (e.g., T-shirt slogans), "thick" description, and extensive quotes. Denzin (2001) talks about the importance of using "thick description" in writing qualitative research. By this, he means that the narrative "presents detail, context, emotion, and the webs of social relationships . . . [and] evokes emotionality and self-feelings. . . . The voices, feelings, actions, and meanings of interacting individuals are heard" (Denzin, 2001, p. 100). As an example, Denzin (2001) first refers to an illustration of thick description from Sudnow (1978) and then provides his own version as if it were a thin description.

"Sitting at the piano and moving into the production of a chord, the chord as a whole was prepared for as the hand moved toward the keyboard, and the terrain was seen as a field relative to the task. . . . There was chord A and chord B, separated from one another. . . . A's production entailed a tightly compressed hand, and B's . . . an open and extended spread. . . . The beginner gets from A to B disjointly." (Sudnow, 1978, pp. 9–10)

"I had trouble learning the piano keyboard." (Denzin, 2001, p. 102)

Also, ethnographers present dialogue, and the dialogue becomes especially vivid when written in the dialect and natural language of the culture (see, e.g., the articles on Black English vernacular or "code switching" in Nelson, 1990). Writers also rely on characterization in which human beings are shown talking, acting, and relating to others. Longer scenes take the form of sketches, a "slice of life" (Emerson et al., 2011, p. 75), or larger episodes and tales.

Ethnographic writers tell "a good story" (Richardson, 1990). Thus, one of the forms of "evocative" experimental qualitative writing for Richardson (1990) is the fictional representation form in which writers draw on the literary devices such as flashback, flash-forward, alternative points of view, deep characterization, tone shifts, synecdoche, dialogue, interior monologue, and sometimes the omniscient narrator. Similarly, Wolcott (2008a) emphasizes the use of techniques for telling the story as a travelogue, life history, or organized around specific themes.

Case Study Writing Structures

Turning to case studies, we are reminded by Merriam (1988) that "there is no standard format for reporting case study research" (p. 193). Unquestionably, some case studies generate theory, some are simply descriptions of cases, and others are more analytical in nature and display cross-case or inter-site comparisons. The overall intent of the case study undoubtedly shapes the larger structure of the written narrative. Still, we find it useful to conceptualize a general form, and we turn to key texts on case studies to receive guidance.

Overall Structures   One can open and close the case study narrative with vignettes to draw the reader into the case. This approach is suggested by Stake (1995), who provides an outline of topics that might be included in a qualitative case study. We feel that this is a helpful way to stage the topics in a good case study:

- The writer opens with a vignette. This is so the reader can develop a vicarious experience to get a feel for the time and place of the study.
- Next, the researcher identifies the issue, the purpose, and the method of the study so that the reader learns about how the study came to be, the background of the writer, and the issues surrounding the case.

- This is followed by an extensive description of the case and its context—a body of relatively uncontested data. This is a description the reader might make if he or she had been there.
- Issues are presented next, a few key issues, so that the reader can understand the complexity of the case. This complexity builds through references to other research or the writer's understanding of other cases.
- Next, several of the issues are probed further. At this point, too, the writer brings in both confirming and disconfirming evidence.
- Assertions are presented. These are a summary of what the writer understands about the case and whether the initial naturalistic generalizations, conclusions arrived at through personal experience or offered as vicarious experiences for the reader, have been changed conceptually or challenged.
- Finally, the writer ends with a closing vignette, an experiential note. It is to remind the reader that this report is one person's encounter with a complex case.

We like this general outline because it provides a description of the case; presents themes, assertions, or interpretations of the researcher; and begins and ends with realistic scenarios. In previous chapters, we have referred to case studies that follow this general outline (see Frelin, 2015; Appendix F), and we encourage you to review them for similarities and differences in how the cases are presented.

A similar model is found in Lincoln and Guba's (1985) substantive case report. They describe a need for the explication of the problem, a thorough description of the context or setting, a description of the transactions or processes observed in that context, saliences at the site (elements studied in depth), and outcomes of the inquiry ("lessons learned").

At a more general level yet, we find Yin's (2014) 2x2 table of types of case studies helpful. Case studies can be either single-case or multiple-case designs and either holistic (single unit of analysis) or embedded (multiple units of analysis). Yin comments further that a single case is best when a need exists to study a critical case, an extreme or unique case, or a revelatory case. Whether the case is single or multiple, the researcher decides to study the entire case, a holistic design, or multiple subunits within the case (the embedded design). Although the holistic design may be more abstract, it captures the entire case better than the embedded design does. However, the embedded design starts with an examination of subunits and allows for the detailed perspective should the questions begin to shift and change during fieldwork.

Yin (2014) also presents several possible structures for composing a case study report. In a linear-analytic approach, a standard approach according to Yin, the researcher discusses the problem, the methods, the findings, and the conclusions. An alternative structure repeats the same case study several times and compares alternative descriptions or explanations of the same case. A chronological structure presents the case study in a sequence, such as sections or chapters that address the early, middle, and late phase of a case history. Theories are also used as a framework, and the case studies can debate various hypotheses or propositions. In a suspense structure, the "answer" or outcome of a case study and its significance is presented in an initial chapter or section. The remaining sections are then devoted to the development of an explanation for this outcome. In a final structure, the unsequenced structure, the author describes a case with no particular order to the sections or chapter.

Embedded Structures What specific narrative devices, embedded structures, do case study writers use to "mark" their studies? One might approach the description of the context and setting for the case in a chronology from a broader picture to a narrower one. The gunman case (Asmussen & Creswell, 1995) begins with a description of the actual campus incident in terms of the city in which the situation developed, followed by the campus and, more narrow yet, the actual classroom on campus. This represents a funneling approach that narrowed the setting from a calm city environment to a potentially volatile campus classroom, and this approach seemed to launch the study into a chronology of events that occurred. Another example is provided by the multiple case study of technology integration across three schools (Staples, Pugach, & Himes, 2005). Each case description begins with the technology context that existed prior to the study, the changes that occurred during the study, and concludes with future projections. The chronological approach seemed to work best when events unfolded and followed a process; case studies often are bounded by time and cover events over time (Yin, 2014).

The case study describing the relational practices of a teacher who negotiates educational relationships with students who have a history of school failure (Frelin, 2015; see Appendix F) also represented a single-case study (Yin, 2014), with a single narrative about the case, its themes, and its interpretation. In other studies (e.g., Chirgwin, 2015; Staples et al., 2005), the case presentations are of multiple cases, with each case discussed separately with no separate discussions of each case but followed by an overall cross-case analysis (Yin, 2014). Another Yin (2014) narrative format is to pose a series of questions and answers based on the case study database.

Finally, researchers need to be cognizant of the amount of description in their case studies versus the amount of analysis and interpretation or assertions (Merriam & Tisdell, 2015). In comparing description and analysis, Merriam (1988) suggests that the proper balance might be 60% to 40% or 70% to 30% in favor of description. An examination of the gunman case revealed a balancing of elements in equal thirds (33% to 33% to 33%)—a concrete description of the setting and the actual events (and those that occurred within 2 weeks after the incident); the five themes; and our interpretation, the lessons learned, reported in the discussion section. Writers must make these decisions, and it is conceivable that a case study might contain mainly descriptive material, especially if the bounded system, the case, is quite large and complex.

A Comparison of Writing Structures Across Approaches

Looking back over Table 9.1, we see many diverse structures for writing the qualitative report. What major differences exist in the structures depending on one's choice of approach?

First, we are struck by the diversity of discussions about narrative structures. We found little crossover or sharing of structures among the five approaches, although, in practice, this undoubtedly occurs. The narrative tropes and the literary devices, discussed by ethnographers and narrative researchers, have applicability regardless of approach. Second, the writing structures are highly related to data analysis procedures. A phenomenological study and a grounded theory study follow closely their data analysis steps. In short, we are reminded once again that it is difficult to separate the activities of data collection, analysis, and report writing in a qualitative study. Third, the emphasis given to writing the narrative, especially the embedded narrative structures, varies among the approaches. Ethnographers lead the group in their extensive discussions about narrative and text construction. Phenomenologists and grounded theory writers spend less time discussing this topic. Fourth, the overall narrative structure is clearly specified in some approaches (e.g., a grounded theory study, a phenomenological study, and perhaps a case study), whereas it is flexible and evolving in others (e.g., a narrative, an ethnography). Perhaps this conclusion reflects the more structured approach versus the less structured approach, overall, among the five approaches of inquiry.

Chapter Check-In

1. Do you see how authors use several broad writing strategies in their published qualitative studies? Select one of the qualitative articles presented in Appendices B through F.

   a. Begin with identifying the four strategies described (i.e., reflexivity and representations, audience, encoding, and quotes) as they have been applied in the journal article. Note the influence of which strategies are apparent and which are more difficult to identify.

   b. Identify the intended audience for each of the articles. Consider how the other strategies might be adapted if a different audience was targeted.

2. Do you see the overall writing structures within a particular approach to qualitative research and then can you adapt it to guide your own work? Select one of the qualitative articles presented in Appendices B through F that fits your particular approach.

   a. Begin with diagramming its overall structure by identifying the flow within its components. How does the article start? With a personal vignette, a statement of the problem, a literature review? What comes next? How does the article end?

   b. Then look within each component and identify the embedded strategies used—for example, metaphors, quotes, and diagrams.

(Continued)

(Continued)

3. Can you identify the characteristics of "good" writing to develop a deeper understanding of the embedded writing structures in a qualitative study? Read qualitative journal articles or books that adopt different strategies, such as progressive–regressive methods in the narrative study of Ellis (1993), creative closings in the phenomenology of Anderson and Spencer (2002), visual diagrams in the grounded theory study of Morrow and Smith (1995), tropes in in the ethnography of Rhoads (1995), and the funneling approach in the case study of Asmussen and Creswell (1995).

 a. Underline examples of the embedded strategy the authors use, and consider the effectiveness of their strategy.

 b. Could the strategy be used as effectively in other approaches?

 c. How would different audiences impact your use of various embedded writing structures?

4. Can you identify the characteristics of thick description to apply our understandings to a practical experience in writing qualitative research? To do this, turn to novels in which the author provides exquisite detail about an event, a thing, or a person. For example, turn to page 14 in Paul Harding's (2009) award-winning book, *Tinkers*, and read the passage about how George repaired a broken clock at a tag sale.

 a. Write about how Harding incorporates a physical description, includes a description of the steps (or movement), uses strong action verbs, draws on references or quotes, and relies on the five senses to convey detail (sight, hearing, taste, smell, touch).

 b. Use this type of detail in your qualitative descriptions or themes.

Summary

In this chapter, we discussed writing the qualitative report. We began by revisiting ethical considerations and then by discussing several rhetorical issues the writer must address. These rhetorical issues include writing reflexively and with representation, the audience for the writing, the encoding for that audience, and the use of quotes. Then we turned to each of the five approaches of inquiry and presented overall rhetorical structures for organizing the entire study as well as specific embedded structures, writing devices, and techniques that the researcher incorporates into the study. A table of these structures shows the diversity of perspectives about structure that reflects different data analysis procedures and discipline affiliations. We concluded with observations about the differences in writing structures among the five approaches, differences reflected in the variability of approaches, the relationships between data analysis and report writing, the emphasis in the literature of each approach on narrative construction, and the amount of structure in the overall architecture of a study within each approach.

Further Readings

In addition to many of the resources already suggested in earlier chapters, which include strategies and guidance for writing and communicating qualitative research, we highlight a few here focused on information about procedures and issues about writing. The list should not be considered exhaustive, and readers are encouraged to seek out additional readings in the end-of-book reference list.

Denzin, N. K. (2001). *Interpretive interactionism* (2nd ed.). Thousand Oaks, CA: Sage.

In this second edition, Norman Denzin expands his guidance about how "to do" interpretive interactionism—that is to make the lived experiences successfully accessible to a reader.

Gilgun, J. F. (2005). "Grab" and good science: Writing up the results of qualitative research. *Qualitative Health Research, 15*, 256–262. doi:10.1177/1049732304268796

Jane Gilgun presents compelling historical and contemporary arguments for the use of first-person voice and guidance for writing qualitative research.

Richardson, L. (1990). *Writing strategies: Reaching diverse audiences*. Newbury Park, CA: Sage.

Laurel Richardson offers an important resource for guiding qualitative writing and how it needs to be adjusted based on the target audience.

Strunk, W., & White, E. B. (2000). *The elements of style* (4th ed.). Upper Saddle River, NJ: Pearson.

William Strunk and E. B. White convey the principles of English style in an accessible manner with illustrative examples accompanying detailed descriptions. This is essential reading.

Sword, H. (2012). *Stylish academic writing*. Cambridge, MA: Harvard University Press.

Helen Sword describes the elements of stylishness for scholars writing for larger audiences. Of particular note are her chapters on "tempting titles" and "hooks and sinkers."

Van Maanen, J. (2011). *Tales of the field: On writing ethnography* (2nd ed.). Chicago, IL: University of Chicago Press.

John Van Maanen unpacks the styles associated with written representations of culture. In so doing, he offers valuable advice to an ethnographer through illustrative examples and practices.

Weis, L., & Fine, M. (2000). *Speed bumps: A student-friendly guide to qualitative research*. New York, NY: Teachers College Press.

Lois Weis and Michelle Fine provide an excellent resource focused on reflexivity. Specifically, they clearly explain the potential impact of qualitative writing on readers, audiences, and the participants studied.

Wolcott, H. F. (2008b). *Writing up qualitative research* (3rd ed.) Thousand Oaks, CA: Sage.

Harry Wolcott leads the reader through a time-tested process of interpreting and communicating qualitative research. Noteworthy are his guidance with respect to perseverance in writing and tightening the message.

10

Standards of Validation and Evaluation

Q ualitative researchers strive for "understanding," that deep structure of knowledge that comes from visiting personally with participants, spending extensive time in the field, and probing to obtain detailed meanings. During or after a study, qualitative researchers ask, "Did we get it right?" (Stake, 1995, p. 107) or "Did we publish a 'wrong' or inaccurate account?" (Thomas, 1993, p. 39). Is it possible to even have a right answer? To answer these questions, researchers need to look to themselves, to the participants, and to the readers. There are multi- or polyvocal discourses at work here that provide insight into the validation and evaluation of a qualitative narrative.

In this chapter, we address two interrelated questions: Is the account valid, and by whose standards? How do we evaluate the quality of qualitative research? Answers to these questions will take us into the many perspectives on validation to emerge within the qualitative community and the multiple standards for evaluation discussed by authors with procedural, interpretive, and postmodern perspectives.

●

Questions for Discussion

- What are some perspectives on validation within the qualitative community?
- What are some alternative procedures useful in establishing validation in qualitative research?
- How is reliability realized in qualitative research?
- What are some alternative stances on evaluating the quality of qualitative research?
- How do these stances differ by types of approaches to qualitative inquiry?

Validation and Reliability in Qualitative Research

Perspectives on Validation

Many perspectives exist regarding the importance of validation in qualitative research, the definition of it, terms to describe it, and procedures for establishing it. Our view of validation as an evolving construct means that a broad understanding of both traditional and contemporary perspectives is essential for informing the work of qualitative researchers and readers of qualitative research. In Table 10.1, we illustrate several of the perspectives, arranged chronologically, available on validation in the qualitative literature. These perspectives position validation in qualitative research in terms of quantitative equivalents, postmodern and interpretive lenses, and importance of the construct. Most use qualitative terms to describe validation that are distinct from quantitative terms; some combine or synthesize many perspectives or use a metaphor for visualizing it. Evidence of evolving thinking about validation in qualitative research is apparent within as well as across authors and we conclude this section by forwarding our own stance.

Writers have searched for and found qualitative equivalents that parallel traditional quantitative approaches to validation. LeCompte and Goetz (1982) took this approach when they compared the issues of validation and reliability to their counterparts in experimental design and survey research. They contend that qualitative research has garnered much criticism in the scientific ranks for its failure to "adhere to canons of reliability and validation" (LeCompte & Goetz, 1982, p. 31) in the traditional sense. They apply threats to internal validation in experimental research to ethnographic research (e.g., history and maturation, observer effects, selection and regression, mortality, spurious conclusions). They further identify threats to external validation as "effects that obstruct or reduce a study's comparability or translatability" (LeCompte & Goetz, 1982, p. 51).

Some writers argue that authors who use positivist terminology facilitate the acceptance of qualitative research in a traditionally focused quantitative world. Ely and colleagues (Ely, Anzul, Friedman, Garner, & Steinmetz, 1991) assert that using quantitative terms tend to be a defensive measure that muddies the waters and that "the language

TABLE 10.1 ● Perspectives and Terms Used for Validation in Qualitative Research		
Authors	**Perspective**	**Terms**
LeCompte and Goetz (1982)	Use of parallel, qualitative equivalents to their quantitative counterparts in experimental and survey research	Internal validity, external validity, reliability, and objectivity
Lincoln and Guba (1985)	Use of alternative terms that apply more to naturalistic axioms	Credibility, transferability, dependability, and confirmability
Eisner (1991)	Use of alternative terms that provide reasonable standards for judging the credibility of qualitative research	Structural corroboration, consensual validation, and referential adequacy
Lather (1991)	Use of four types for reconceptualizing validity	Triangulation, construct validation, face validation, and catalytic validation
Lather (1993)	Use of four frames of validity	Ironic validity, paralogic validity, rhizomatic validity, and situated or embedded voluptuous validity
Wolcott (1990, 1994)	Use of terms other than *validity* because it neither guides nor informs qualitative research	Understanding is a better word than validity
Angen (2000)	Use of two types of validation within the context of interpretive inquiry	Ethical validation and substantive validation
Whittemore, Chase, and Mandle (2001)	Use of synthesized perspectives of validity to organize key validation criteria into primary and secondary	Primary criteria: credibility, authenticity, criticality, and integrity Secondary criteria: explicitness, vividness, creativity, thoroughness, congruence, and sensitivity
Richardson and St. Pierre (2005)	Use of a metaphorical, reconceptualized form of validity as a crystal	Crystals as growing, changing, altering, reflecting externalities, and refracting within themselves
Lincoln, Lynham, and Guba (2011)	Use of authenticity, transgression, and ethical relationships	Fairness representing views, raised awareness, and action; hidden assumptions and repressions, the crystal that can be turned many ways; relationships with research participants
Creswell and Poth (this book)	Use of a validation process for assessing the accuracy of the findings as best described by the researcher and the participants	Process involves a combination of qualitative research strategies—for example, extensive field time, thick description, and closeness of researcher to participants

of positivistic research is not congruent with or adequate to qualitative work" (p. 95). Lincoln and Guba (1985) offer alternative terms that, they contend, adhere more to naturalistic research. To establish the "trustworthiness" of a study, Lincoln and Guba

(1985) use unique terms, such as *credibility, authenticity, transferability, dependability,* and *confirmability* as "the naturalist's equivalents" for *internal validation, external validation, reliability,* and *objectivity* (p. 300). To operationalize these new terms, they propose techniques such as prolonged engagement in the field and the **triangulation** of data sources, methods, and investigators to establish credibility. To make sure that the findings are transferable between the researcher and those being studied, thick description is necessary. Rather than reliability, one seeks dependability that the results will be subject to change and instability. The naturalistic researcher looks for confirmability rather than objectivity in establishing the value of the data. Both dependability and confirmability are established through an auditing of the research process. We find the Lincoln and Guba criteria still popular today in qualitative reports.

Rather than using the term *validation,* Eisner (1991) constructed standards such as structural corroboration, consensual validation, and referential adequacy as evidence for asserting the credibility of qualitative research. In structural corroboration, the researcher uses multiple types of data to support or contradict the interpretation. As Eisner (1991) states, "We seek a confluence of evidence that breeds credibility, that allows us to feel confident about our observations, interpretations, and conclusions" (p. 110). He further illustrates this point with an analogy drawn from detective work: The researcher compiles bits and pieces of evidence to formulate a "compelling whole." At this stage, the researcher looks for recurring behaviors or actions and considers disconfirming evidence and contrary interpretations. Moreover, Eisner recommends that to demonstrate credibility, the weight of evidence should become persuasive. Consensual validation seeks the opinion of others, and Eisner (1991) refers to "an agreement among competent others that the description, interpretation, evaluation, and thematics of an educational situation are right" (p. 112). Referential adequacy suggests the importance of criticism, and Eisner describes the goal of criticism as illuminating the subject matter and bringing about more complex and sensitive human perception and understanding.

Qualitative researchers also have reconceptualized validation with a postmodern sensibility. Lather (1991) initially identified four types of validation (i.e., triangulation, construct validation, face validation, and catalytic validation) as a "reconceptualization of validation." Lather comments that current "paradigmatic uncertainty in the human sciences is leading to the re-conceptualizing of validation" and calls for "new techniques and concepts for obtaining and defining trustworthy data which avoids the pitfalls of orthodox notions of validation" (p. 66). For Lather, the character of a social science report changes from a closed narrative with a tight argument structure to a more open narrative with holes and questions and an admission of situatedness and partiality. In *Getting Smart,* Lather (1991) describes triangulation as drawing upon multiple data sources, methods, and theoretical schemes, construct validation as recognizing the constructs that exist rather than imposing theories or constructs on informants or the context, face validation citing Kidder (1982) as "a 'click of recognition' and a 'yes, of course,' instead of 'yes, but' experience" (p. 56) and catalytic validation as energizing participants toward knowing reality to transform it.

In a later article, Lather's (1993) terms became more unique and closely relate to feminist research in "four frames of validation." The first, *ironic* validation, is where the researcher presents truth as a problem. The second, *paralogic* validation, is concerned with undecidables, limits, paradoxes, and complexities, a movement away from theorizing things and toward providing direct exposure to other voices in an almost unmediated way. The third, *rhizomatic* validation, pertains to questioning proliferations, crossings, and overlaps without underlying structures or deeply rooted connections. The researcher also questions taxonomies, constructs, and interconnected networks whereby the reader jumps from one assemblage to another and consequently moves from judgment to understanding. The fourth type is situated, embodied, or *voluptuous* validation, which means that the researcher sets out to understand more than one can know and to write toward what one does not understand.

Other writers, such as Wolcott (1990), have little use for validation, suggesting that "validation neither guides nor informs" his work (p. 136). He does not dismiss validation but rather places it in a broader perspective. Wolcott's (1990) goal is to identify "critical elements" and write "plausible interpretations from them" (p. 146). He ultimately tries to understand rather than convince, and he voices the view that validation distracts from his work of understanding what is really going on. Wolcott (1990, 1994) claims that the term *validation* does not capture the essence of what he seeks, adding that perhaps someone would coin a term appropriate for the naturalistic paradigm. But for now, he says, the term *understanding* seems to encapsulate the idea as well as any other (Wolcott, 1994).

Validation has also been cast within an interpretive approach to qualitative research marked by a focus on the importance of the researcher; a lack of truth in validation; a form of validation based on negotiation and dialogue with participants; and interpretations that are temporal, located, and always open to reinterpretation (Angen, 2000). Angen (2000) suggests that within interpretative research, validation is "a judgment of the trustworthiness or goodness of a piece of research" (p. 387). She espouses an ongoing, open dialogue on the topic of what makes interpretive research worthy of our trust. Considerations of validation are not definitive as the final word on the topic, nor should every study be required to address them. Further, she advances two types of validation: ethical validation and substantive validation. Ethical validation means that all research agendas must question their underlying moral assumptions, their political and ethical implications, and the equitable treatment of diverse voices. It also requires research to provide some practical answers to questions. Angen (2000) also proposes that our interpretive qualitative research should have a "generative promise" (p. 389) and raise new possibilities, open up new questions, stimulate new dialogue, and provide non-dogmatic answers to the questions we pose. In so doing, interpretive qualitative research must have transformative value leading to action and change. Substantive validation means understanding one's own topic, understandings derived from other sources, and the documentation of this process in the written study. Self-reflection contributes to the validation of the work. The interpretive qualitative researcher, as a sociohistorical interpreter, interacts with the subject matter to co-create the interpretations derived. Understandings derived from previous research give substance to the inquiry. Interpretive research also is a chain of interpretations that must be documented for others to judge the trustworthiness of the meanings arrived at in the end. Written accounts must resonate with their intended audiences, and must be compelling, powerful, and convincing.

A synthesis of validation perspectives comes from Whittemore, Chase, and Mandle (2001), who analyze 13 writings about validation and extract key validation criteria from these studies. They organize these criteria into primary and secondary criteria. They find four primary criteria: credibility (Are the results an accurate interpretation of the participants' meaning?); authenticity (Are different voices heard?); criticality (Is there a critical appraisal of all aspects of the research?); and integrity (Are the investigators self-critical?). Secondary criteria relate to explicitness, vividness, creativity, thoroughness, congruence, and sensitivity. In summary, with these criteria, it seems like the validation standard has moved toward the interpretive lens of qualitative research, with an emphasis on researcher reflexivity and on researcher challenges that include raising questions about the ideas developed during a research study.

A postmodern perspective draws on the metaphorical image of a crystal. Richardson (in Richardson & St. Pierre, 2005) describes this image:

> I propose that the central imaginary for "validation" for postmodern texts is not the triangle—a rigid, fixed, two-dimensional object. Rather the central imaginary is the crystal, which combines symmetry and substance with an infinite variety of shapes, substances, transmutations, multidimensionalities, and angles of approach. Crystals grow, change, and are altered, but they are not amorphous. Crystals are prisms that reflect externalities and refract within themselves, creating different colors, patterns, and arrays casting off in different directions. What we see depends on our angle of response—not triangulation but rather crystallization. (p. 963)

A final perspective is that drawn from Lincoln, Lynham, and Guba (2011). They capture the many perspectives developed through the years. They suggest that the question of validity criteria is not whether we should have such criteria or whose criteria the scientific community might adopt but rather how criteria need to be developed within the projected transformations being suggested by social scientists. To this end, they review their focus on establishing authenticity but frame it within the perspectives of a balance of views, raising the level of awareness among participants and other stakeholders, and advancing the ability of inquiry to lead to action on the part of research participants and training those participants to take action. Lincoln and colleagues (2011) also see a role for validity in understanding hidden assumptions through the image (also shared by Richardson and St. Pierre, 2005) of a crystal that reflects and refracts the processes of research, such as discovery, seeing, telling, storying, and representation. Finally, for these authors validity is an ethical relationship with research participants through such standards as positioning themselves, having discourses, encouraging voices, and being self-reflective.

Given these many perspectives, we summarize our own stance. We consider "valida-tion" in qualitative research to be an attempt to assess the "accuracy" of the findings, as best described by the researcher, the participants, and the readers (or reviewers). This view also suggests that any report of research is a representation by the author. We also view validation as a distinct strength of qualitative research in that the account made through extensive time spent in the field, the detailed thick description, and the closeness of the researcher to participants in the study all add to the value or accu-racy of a study. We use the term *validation* to emphasize a process (see Angen, 2000), rather than *verification* (which has quantitative overtones) or historical words such as *trustworthiness* and *authenticity* (recognizing that many qualitative writers do return to these words, suggesting the "staying power" of Lincoln and Guba's, 1985, standards; see Whittemore et al., 2001).

We acknowledge that there are many types of validation in qualitative research and that authors need to choose the types and terms with which they are comfortable. We recommend that writers reference their validation terms and strategies. The subject of validation arises in several of the approaches to qualitative research (e.g., Corbin & Strauss, 2015; Riessman, 2008; Stake, 1995), but we do not think that distinct valida-tion approaches exist for the five approaches to qualitative research. At best, there might be less emphasis on validation in narrative research and more emphasis on it in grounded theory, case study, and ethnography, especially when the authors of these approaches want to employ systematic procedures. We recommend using multiple validation strategies regardless of type of qualitative approach.

Our framework for thinking about validation in qualitative research is to suggest that researchers employ accepted strategies to document the accuracy of their studies. These we call validation strategies.

Validation Strategies

It is not enough to gain perspectives and terms; ultimately, these ideas are translated into practice as strategies or techniques. Whittemore and colleagues (2001) organize the techniques into 29 forms that apply to design consideration, data generating, analysis, and presentation. We describe nine strategies frequently used by qualitative researchers during the process of validation adapted from the work of Creswell and Miller (2000) and provide some general guidance about how we go about implement-ing these strategies (see Figure 10.1).

The strategies are not presented in any specific order of importance but are orga-nized in three groups by the lens the strategy represents: researcher's lens, participant's lens, and reader's or reviewer's lens (Creswell, 2016). Our recommendation that quali-tative researchers engage in *at least two* of the validation strategies in any given study is further discussed next.

Researcher's Lens Among the many roles a researcher undertakes is to check the accuracy of a qualitative account and any of the following validation strategies can assist the researcher in this role:

FIGURE 10.1   ●   Strategies for Validation in Qualitative Research

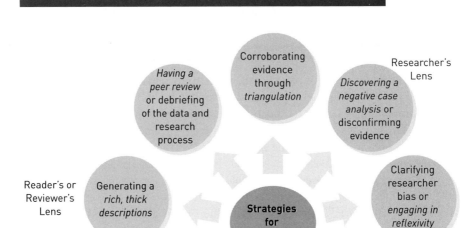

- *Corroborating evidence through triangulation of multiple data sources.* The researcher makes use of multiple and different sources, methods, investigators, and theories to provide corroborating evidence (Bazeley, 2013; Ely et al., 1991; Erlandson, Harris, Skipper, & Allen, 1993; Glesne, 2016; Lincoln & Guba, 1985; Miles & Huberman, 1994; Patton, 1980, 1990, 2015; Yin, 2014). Typically, this process involves corroborating evidence from different sources to shed light on a theme or perspective. When qualitative researchers locate evidence to document a code or theme in different sources of data, they are triangulating information and providing validity to their findings. For this validation strategy, we begin considering how various data sources can be used in tandem when planning the study. Then, as data is collected, we further explore evidence of corroboration and use these insights in our interpretation and writing.

- *Discovering negative case analysis or disconfirming evidence.* The researcher refines working hypotheses as the inquiry advances in light of negative or rival evidence (Ely et al., 1991; Lincoln & Guba, 1985; Miles & Huberman, 1994; Patton, 1980, 1990, 2015; Yin, 2014). Not all evidence will fit the pattern of a code or a theme. It is necessary then to report this negative analysis, and in doing so, the researcher provides a realistic assessment of the phenomenon under study. In real life, not all evidence is either positive or negative; it is some of both. For this validation strategy, we both admit that we tend to be attentive to such evidence and make a point of following what we call "points of intrigue" throughout the study. We find these points are often our key points of discussion in our writing.
- *Clarifying researcher bias or engaging in reflexivity.* The researcher discloses their understandings about the biases, values, and experiences that he or she brings to a qualitative research study from the outset of the study so that the reader understands the position from which researcher undertakes the inquiry (Hammersley & Atkinson, 1995; Merriam & Tisdell, 2015). In this clarification, according to Weiner-Levey and Popper-Giveon (2013), the researcher illuminates what they call the "dark matter" that is often omitted in qualitative research by commenting on past experiences, biases, prejudices, and orientations that have likely shaped the interpretation and approach to the study. For this validation strategy, we embed opportunities throughout a study for writing and discussing connections that emerge with our past experiences and perspectives.

Participant's Lens Participants can play an important role in the following validation strategies:

- *Member checking or seeking participant feedback.* The researcher solicits participants' views of the credibility of the findings and interpretations (Bazeley, 2013; Ely et al., 1991; Erlandson et al., 1993; Glesne, 2016; Lincoln & Guba, 1985; Merriam & Tisdell, 2015; Miles & Huberman, 1994). This technique is considered by Lincoln and Guba (1985) to be "the most critical technique for establishing credibility" (p. 314). This approach, *writ large* in most qualitative studies, involves taking data, analyses, interpretations, and conclusions back to the participants so that they can judge the accuracy and credibility of the account. According to Stake (1995), participants should "play a major role directing as well as acting in case study" research (p. 115). They should be asked to examine rough drafts of the researcher's work and to provide alternative language, "critical observations or interpretations" (Stake, 1995, p. 115). In so doing, participants play a critical role because they are asked "how well the ongoing data analysis represents their experience" (Hays & Singh, 2012, p. 206). For this validation strategy, we convene a focus group made up of participants in the study and ask them to reflect on the accuracy of the account. We do not take back to participants the transcripts or the raw data, but the preliminary analyses consisting of description or themes. We are interested in their views of these written analyses as well as what was missing (see also Richards, 2015, for practical guidance about how to interpret participant feedback).

- *Prolonged engagement and persistent observation in the field.* The researcher makes field-based decisions about what is salient to study, relevant to the purpose of the study, and of interest for focus. Researchers build rapport with participants and gatekeepers, learn the culture and context, and check for misinformation that stems from distortions introduced by themselves or informants (Ely et al., 1991; Erlandson et al., 1993; Glesne, 2016; Lincoln & Guba, 1985; Merriam & Tisdell, 2015). Fetterman (2010) contends that "participant observation requires close, long-term contact with the people under study" (p. 39). For this validation strategy, we spend as much time in the field as is feasible during the study and prior to beginning data collection we familiarize ourselves with the site and participants.

- *Collaborating with participants.* The researcher embeds opportunities for participants to be involved throughout the research process in varying ways and degrees. Among the various ways is involvement in key research decisions such as developing data collection protocols and contributing to data analysis and interpretation. The degree to which participants are involved can vary along a continuum from minimal to extensive. Participant involvement is based on the idea (and ever-growing body of research) that the study is more likely to be supported and findings used when participants are involved (Patton, 2011, 2015). For this validation strategy, we are often guided by community-based participatory research practices that involve participants as co-researchers in the study (see, e.g., Hacker, 2013, for further discussions).

Reader's or Reviewer's Lens Including others beyond the researcher and those involved in the research contribute in the following validation strategies:

- *Enabling external audits.* The researcher facilitates auditing by an external consultant, the auditor, to examine both the process and the product of the account to assess their accuracy (Erlandson et al., 1993; Lincoln & Guba, 1985; Merriam & Tisdell, 2015; Miles & Huberman, 1994). This auditor should have no connection to the study. In assessing the product, the auditor examines whether or not the findings, interpretations, and conclusions are supported by the data. Lincoln and Guba (1985) compare this, metaphorically, with a fiscal audit, and the procedure provides a sense of interrater reliability to a study. This process can be assisted by the creation of documentation, sometimes referred to as an audit trail and described by Silver and Lewins (2014) as "comprising a log of all the processes followed, describing the small analytic leaps contributing to the analysis as a whole" (p. 140). For this validation strategy, we engage in two processes; first, we create a tracking document at the beginning of a study on which we detail our key decisions including rationale and potential consequence. Second, when resources permit, we use an auditor to review our process and findings.

- *Generating a rich, thick description.* The researcher allows readers to make decisions regarding transferability because the writer describes in detail the participants or setting under study (Erlandson et al., 1993; Lincoln & Guba, 1985; Merriam & Tisdell, 2015). With such a detailed description, the researcher enables readers to transfer information to other settings and to determine whether the findings can be transferred "because of shared characteristics" (Erlandson et al., 1993, p. 32). Thick description means that the researcher provides details when describing a case or when writing about a theme. According to Stake (2010), "a description is rich if it provides abundant, interconnected details . . ." (p. 49). Detail can emerge through physical description, movement description, and activity description. It can also involve describing from the general ideas to the narrow, interconnecting the details, using strong action verbs, and quotes. For this validation strategy, we devote time to revisiting our raw data soon after its collection to add further descriptions that might be helpful during the analysis—for example, contextual descriptions like atmosphere.

- *Having a peer review or debriefing of the data and research process.* The researcher seeks an external check by "someone who is familiar with the research or the phenomenon explored" (Creswell & Miller, 2000, p. 129), in much in the same spirit as interrater reliability in quantitative research (Ely et al., 1991; Erlandson et al., 1993; Glesne, 2016; Lincoln & Guba, 1985; Merriam & Tisdell, 2015). Lincoln and Guba (1985) define the role of the peer debriefer as a "devil's advocate," an individual who keeps the researcher honest; asks hard questions about methods, meanings, and interpretations; and provides the researcher with the opportunity for catharsis by sympathetically listening to the researcher's feelings. For this validation strategy, we involve colleagues and students as reviewers (and for our students we play this role) in what Lincoln and Guba (1985) called peer debriefing sessions during which both the reviewers and the researcher keep written accounts of the sessions.

Examining these nine procedures as a whole (just discussed and outlined in Figure 10.1), we advise that researchers engage in at least two of them in any given qualitative study. Unquestionably, procedures such as triangulating among different data sources (assuming that the investigator collects more than one), writing with detailed and thick description, and taking the entire written narrative back to participants in member checking all are reasonably easy procedures to conduct. They also are the most popular and cost-effective procedures. Other procedures, such as peer audits and external audits, are more time consuming in their application and may also involve substantial costs to the researcher. We also point out that differences among the validity lenses (i.e., researchers, participants, readers, and reviewers) can be attributed to the philosophical orientation of the researcher and may therefore impact his or her use of specific validation strategies (see Creswell, 2016, for further discussion).

Reliability Perspectives and Procedures

Reliability can be addressed in qualitative research in several ways (Silverman, 2013). Reliability can be enhanced if the researcher obtains detailed field notes by employing good-quality recording devices and by transcribing the digital files. Also, the recording needs to be transcribed to indicate the trivial, but often crucial, pauses and overlaps. Further coding can be done "blind" with the coding staff and the analysts conducting their research without knowledge of the expectations and questions of the project directors. Silverman also supports the use of computer programs to assist in recording and analyzing the data.

Our focus on reliability here will be on ***intercoder agreement*** based on the use of multiple coders to analyze transcript data. In qualitative research, *reliability* often refers to the stability of responses to multiple coders of data sets. It is important to develop codes and assess the reliability among coders as part of the analysis process (Kuckartz, 2014; Richards & Morse, 2012). We find this practice especially used in qualitative health science research and within the form of qualitative research in which inquirers want an external check on the highly interpretive coding process. What seems to be largely missing in the literature (with the exception of Armstrong, Gosling, Weinman, & Marteau, 1997; Campbell, Quincy, Osserman, & Pederson, 2013; Miles & Huberman, 1994; and Miles, Huberman, & Saldaña, 2014) is a discussion about the procedures of actually conducting intercoder agreement checks. One of the key issues is determining what exactly the coders agree on, whether they seek agreement on code names, the coded passages, or the same passages coded the same way. We also need to decide on whether researchers seek agreement based on codes, themes, or both codes and themes (see Armstrong et al., 1997). Finally, we need to carefully interpret our findings—as Richards (2015) wisely advises that we cannot expect to find complete consistency in coding over time or between coders. Undoubtedly, there is flexibility in the process, and researchers need to fashion an approach consistent with the resources and time to engage in coding.

Drawing upon our experiences working with multiple coders, we propose the following procedures for assessing intercoder agreement in coding of qualitative research (see Figure 10.2):

- *Establish a common platform for coding, and develop a preliminary code list.* The researchers decide which software program or paper-based methods they will use; a common platform is essential to be able to easily share the results of their initial read and preliminary coding efforts. In our recent work, we have often used computer-assisted qualitative data analysis software packages (MAXQDA, ATLAS.ti, or NVivo, depending on familiarity across researchers) and have implemented training sessions at the beginning of the study. Each researcher then reads several transcripts independently and develops a list of preliminary codes. As discussed in Chapter 8, computer software programs have features that facilitate the creation of these lists.

- *Develop and share the initial codebook among coders.* The researchers develop a shared understanding of codes to create a codebook that is stable and represents the coding analysis of four independent coders. To do this, after coding, say, three transcripts (i.e., A, B, and C), we then meet and examine the codes, their names, and the text segments that each researcher codes. We begin developing an initial codebook of the major codes. This codebook contains a definition of each code and the text segments that we assigned to each code. In this initial codebook, we had main codes and subcodes. In this initial codebook, we focus on the main codes we were finding in the database than in an exhaustive list. Additional codes are added as the analyses proceeds.

- *Apply the codebook to additional transcripts, and compare coding across multiple researchers.* The researchers independently apply the shared codebook to additional transcripts and then compare their coding to assess consistency. To do this, the researchers had to agree upon a unit of text to compare (e.g., phrase, sentence, and paragraph), and then each researcher independently codes three additional transcripts (i.e., D, E, and F). With no clear guidance in the literature as to what the appropriate unit should be for coding, consensus can be difficult to reach (Hruschka et al., 2004). To streamline the process in their exploratory study, Campbell and colleagues (2013) suggest having the lead researcher identify the segments of data into coding units. Often in our work we feel it is more important to have agreement on the text segments we were assigning to codes than to have the same, exact passages coded. The decision about the unit of text is crucial because it becomes the basis on which intercoder agreement is defined, and we are ready to actually compare our coding. Thus, often in our work, intercoder agreement means that we agree that when we assign a code word to a passage, we all assign this same code word to the passage. It does not mean that we all code the same passages—an ideal that we believe would be hard to achieve because some people code short passages and others longer passages. Nor does it mean that we all bracket the exact same lines for our code word, another ideal difficult to achieve.

- *Assess and report the intercoder agreement among researchers.* The researchers define individual instances of intercoder agreement before assessing overall intercoder agreement. In our work, we tend to take a realistic stance, look at the passages that are coded across researchers, and ask ourselves whether we all assign the same code word to the passage based on our tentative definitions in the code-book. The decision would be either a yes or a no, and we could calculate the percentage of agreement among all researchers on this passage that we all code. We seek to establish an 80% agreement of coding on these passages informed by Miles and Huberman's (1994) recommendation of an 80% agreement. More recently, Miles and colleagues (2014) suggest achieving 85% to 90% agreement depending on the "size and range of the coding scheme" (p. 85). Many computer-assisted qualitative data analysis software packages include features to facilitate the calculation among multiple coders. Other researchers might actually calculate a kappa reliability statistic on the agreement, but we feel that a percentage is sufficient to report in our published studies (see also Creswell, 2016, for practical guidance about three different approaches to intercoder agreement).

- *Revise and finalize the codebook to inform further coding.* The researchers review and refine the codebook to further differentiate code definitions. In our work, after the process continues through several more transcripts, we then revise the codebook and conduct anew an assessment of passages that all researchers code and determine if we apply the same or different codes. With each phase in the intercoder agreement process, we hope to achieve a higher percentage of agreed upon codes and themes for text segments. Then we can collapse codes into broader themes and can conduct the same process with themes, to see if the passages all coded as themes by the researchers were consistent in the use of the same theme.

Evaluation Criteria

Qualitative Perspectives

In reviewing validation in the qualitative research literature, we are struck by how validation is sometimes used in discussing the quality of a study (e.g., Angen, 2000). Although validation is certainly an aspect of evaluating the quality of a study, other criteria are useful as well. In reviewing the criteria, we find that here, too, the standards vary within the qualitative community (see also Creswell, 2012, for contrast of three approaches to qualitative evaluation). We will first review three general standards and then turn to specific criteria within each of our five approaches to qualitative research.

A methodological perspective comes from Howe and Eisenhardt (1990), who suggest that only broad, abstract standards are possible for qualitative (and quantitative) research. Moreover, to determine, for example, whether a study is a good ethnography cannot be answered apart from whether the study contributes to our understanding of important questions. Silverman (2013) advances four criteria that good research must satisfy. The following five standards are adapted from Howe and Eisenhardt (1990) in question form for researchers to ask:

- Does the research questions drive the data collection and analysis? (That is, rather than the reverse?) Silverman (2013) states similar criteria about good research using "methods which are demonstrably appropriate to the research problem" (p. 322).

- To what extent are the data collection and analysis techniques competently applied? (That is, in a technical sense?) Silverman (2013) states similar criteria about good research developing "empirically sound, reliable, and valid findings" (p. 322).
- Are the researcher's assumptions made explicit? (That is, such as the researcher's own subjectivity?)
- Does the study have overall warrant? (That is, is it robust, does it use respected theoretical explanations, and does it discuss disconfirmed theoretical explanations?) Silverman (2013) states similar criteria about good research thinking "theoretically through and with data" (p. 322).
- Does the study have value both in informing and improving practice and in protecting the confidentiality, privacy, and truth telling of participants conducting in an ethical manner? (That is, does it contribute to the "so what?" question and is it conducted ethically?) Silverman (2013) states similar criteria about good research contributing "where possible, to practice and policy" (p. 322).

A postmodern, interpretive framework forms a second perspective, from Lincoln (1995), who thinks about the quality issue in terms of emerging criteria. She tracks her own thinking (and that of her late colleague, Guba) from early approaches of developing parallel methodological criteria (Lincoln & Guba, 1985) to establishing the criteria of "fairness" (a balance of stakeholder views), sharing knowledge, and

FIGURE 10.2 ● Procedures for Reliability of Intercoder Agreement in Qualitative Research

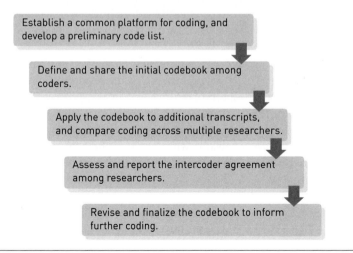

Establish a common platform for coding, and develop a preliminary code list.

Define and share the initial codebook among coders.

Apply the codebook to additional transcripts, and compare coding across multiple researchers.

Assess and report the intercoder agreement among researchers.

Revise and finalize the codebook to inform further coding.

fostering social action (Guba & Lincoln, 1989) to her current stance. The new emerging approach to quality is based on three new commitments: to emergent relations with respondents, to a set of stances, and to a vision of research that enables and promotes justice. Based on these commitments, Lincoln (1995) then proceeds to identify several standards:

- The standard is set in the inquiry community, such as by guidelines for publication. These guidelines admit that within diverse approaches to research, inquiry communities have developed their own traditions of rigor, communication, and ways of working toward consensus. These guidelines, she also maintains, serve to exclude legitimate research knowledge and social science researchers.
- The standard of positionality guides interpretive or qualitative research. Drawing on those concerned about standpoint epistemology, this means that the text should display honesty or authenticity about its own stance and about the position of the author.
- Another standard is under the rubric of community. This standard acknowledges that all research takes place in, is addressed to, and serves the purposes of the community in which it is carried out. Such communities might be feminist thought, Black scholarship, Native American studies, or ecological studies.
- Interpretive or qualitative research must give voice to participants so that their voice is not silenced, disengaged, or marginalized. Moreover, this standard requires that alternative or multiple voices be heard in a text.
- Critical subjectivity as a standard means that the researcher needs to have heightened self-awareness in the research process and create personal and social transformation. This "high-quality awareness" enables the researcher to understand his or her psychological and emotional states before, during, and after the research experience.
- High-quality interpretive or qualitative research involves reciprocity between the researcher and those being researched. This standard requires that intense sharing, trust, and mutuality exist.
- The researcher should respect the sacredness of relationships in the research-to-action continuum. This standard means that the researcher respects the collaborative and egalitarian aspects of research and "make[s] spaces for the lifeways of others" (Lincoln, 1995, p. 284).
- Sharing of the privileges acknowledges that in good qualitative research, researchers share their rewards with persons whose lives they portray. This sharing may be in the form of royalties from books or the sharing of rights to publication.

A final perspective utilizes interpretive standards of conducting qualitative research. Richardson (in Richardson & St. Pierre, 2005) identifies multiple criteria she uses when she reviews papers or monographs submitted for social science publication:

- ***Substantive contribution***. Does this piece contribute to our understanding of social life? Demonstrate a deeply grounded social scientific perspective? Seem "true"?
- ***Aesthetic merit***. Does this piece succeed aesthetically? Does the use of creative analytical practices open up the text and invite interpretive responses? Is the text artistically shaped, satisfying, complex, and not boring?
- ***Reflexivity***. How has the author's subjectivity been both a producer and a product of this text? Is there self-awareness and self-exposure? Does the author hold himself or herself accountable to the standards of knowing and telling of the people he or she has studied?
- ***Impact***. Does this piece affect me emotionally or intellectually? Generate new questions or move me to write? Try new research practices or move me to action? (p. 964)

As applied research methodologists, we prefer the methodological standards of evaluation, but we can also support the postmodern and interpretive perspectives. We also agree with Flick (2014), who states, "the problem of how to assess qualitative research has not yet been solved" (p. 480). What seems to be missing in all of the approaches discussed thus far is their connection to the five approaches of qualitative inquiry. What standards of evaluation, beyond those already mentioned, would signal a high-quality narrative study, a phenomenology, a grounded theory study, an ethnography, and a case study?

Narrative Research

In discussing what makes for a good narrative study, both Riessman (2008) and Clandinin (2013) point to seeking coherence of participants' narratives yet acknowledge that it may not always be possible. To that end, Riessman (2008) proposes questions for assessing coherence (p. 189):

- Do episodes of a life story hang together?
- Are sections of a theoretical argument linked and consistent?
- Are there major gaps and inconsistencies?
- Is the interpreter's analytic account persuasive?

Clandinin (2013) proposes a different way for "judging and responding to narrative inquiries" (p. 211) by describing what she and Vera Caine define as touchstones:

While one meaning directs our attention to a touchstone as a quality of example that is used to test the excellence or genuineness of others, we were also drawn to a touchstone as a hard black stone, such as jasper or basalt, that was used to test the quality of gold or silver by comparing the streak left on the stone by one of these metals with that of a standard alloy. We wondered, if we metaphorically touched or scratched a narrative inquiry, what kinds of streaks or marks would be left. (Clandinin & Caine, 2013, p. 191)

FIGURE 10.3 ● Guiding Aspects for a "Good" Narrative Study

Does the narrative study do the following?

1. Focus on an individual?

   - The author may choose to focus on a single or two or three individuals.

2. Collect stories about a significant issue?

   - The author may focus on the stories told by the individual or individuals.

3. Develop a chronology?

   - The author may use a chronology to connect different phases or aspects of a story.

4. Tell a story?

   - The author may, through the story, report what was said (themes), how it was said (unfolding story), or how speakers interact or perform the narrative.

5. Embed reflexivity?

   - The author may use reflexive thinking and writing to bring himself or herself into the study.

Clandinin (2013) lists twelve touchstones and considers them as evolving (see also Clandinin & Caine, 2013, for in-depth touchstone descriptions). In Figure 10.3, we advance five aspects of what we would look for in a "good" narrative study.

When writing an interpretive biography, Denzin (1989) is primarily interested in the problem of "how to locate and interpret the subject in biographical materials" (p. 26). He advances several guidelines for writing:

The lived experiences of interacting individuals are the proper subject matter of sociology. The meanings of these experiences are best given by the persons who experience them; thus, a preoccupation with method, validation, reliability, generalizability, and theoretical relevance of the biographical method must be set aside in favor of a concern for meaning and interpretation.

Students of the biographical method must learn how to use the strategies and techniques of literary interpretation and criticism (i.e., bring their method in line with the concern about reading and writing of social texts, where texts are seen as "narrative fictions." (Denzin, 1989, p. 26)

When an individual writes a biography, he or she writes himself or herself into the life of the subject about whom the individual is writing; likewise, the reader reads through her or his perspective.

Thus, within a humanistic, interpretive stance, Denzin (2001) identifies "criteria of interpretation" as a standard for judging the quality of a biography. These criteria are based on respecting the researcher's perspective as well as on thick description. Denzin (2001) advocates for the ability of the researcher to illuminate the phenomenon in a thickly contextualized manner (i.e., thick description of developed context) so as to reveal the historical, processual, and interactional features of the experience. Also, the researcher's interpretation must engulf what is learned about the phenomenon and incorporate prior understandings while always remaining incomplete and unfinished.

This focus on interpretation and thick description is in contrast to criteria established within the more traditional approach to biographical writing. For example, Plummer (1983) asserts that three sets of questions related to sampling, the sources, and the validation of the account should guide a researcher to a good life history study:

- Is the individual representative? Edel (1984) asks a similar question: How has the biographer distinguished between reliable and unreliable witnesses?
- What are the sources of bias (about the participant, the researcher, and the participant–researcher interaction)? Or, as Edel (1984) questions, how has the researcher avoided making himself or herself simply the voice of the subject?
- Is the account valid when subjects are asked to read it, when it is compared to official records, and when it is compared to accounts from other participant?

Phenomenological Research

What criteria should be used to judge the quality of a phenomenological study? From the many readings about phenomenology, one can infer criteria from the discussions about steps (Giorgi, 1985) or the "core facets" of transcendental phenomenology (Moustakas, 1994, p. 58). We have found direct discussions of the criteria to be missing, but perhaps Polkinghorne (1989) and van Manen (2014) come the closest in our readings when Polkinghorne discusses whether the findings are "valid" (p. 57) and when van Manen outlines validation and evaluative criteria.

For Polkinghorne, validation refers to the notion that an idea is well grounded and well supported. He asks, "Does the general structural description provide an accurate portrait of the common features and structural connections that are manifest in the examples collected?" (Polkinghorne, 1989, p. 57). He then proceeds to identify five questions that researchers might ask themselves:

- Did the interviewer influence the contents of the participants' descriptions in such a way that the descriptions do not truly reflect the participants' actual experience?
- Is the transcription accurate, and does it convey the meaning of the oral presentation in the interview?

- In the analysis of the transcriptions, were there conclusions other than those offered by the researcher that could have been derived? Has the researcher identified these alternatives?
- Is it possible to go from the general structural description to the transcriptions and to account for the specific contents and connections in the original examples of the experience?
- Is the structural description situation specific, or does it hold in general for the experience in other situations? (Polkinghorne, 1989)

van Manen (2014) points to questions as a way to "test its [a phenomenology's] level of validity" (p. 350).

- Is the study based on a valid phenomenological question? In other words, does the study ask, "What is this human experience like?" "How is this or that phenomenon or event experienced?" A phenomenological question should not be confused with empirical studies of a particular population, person(s), or group of people at a particular time and location. Also, phenomenology cannot deal with causal questions or theoretical explanations. However, a particular individual or group may be studied for the understanding of a phenomenological theme—such as gender phenomenon, a sociopolitical event, or the experience of a human disaster.
- Is the analysis performed on experientially descriptive accounts, transcripts? (Does the analysis avoid empirical material that mostly consists of perceptions, opinions, beliefs, views, and so on?)
- Is the study properly rooted in primary and scholarly phenomenological literature—rather than mostly relying on questionable secondary and tertiary sources?
- Does the study avoid trying to legitimate itself with validation criteria derived from sources that are concerned with other (non-phenomenological) methodologies? (van Manen, 2014, pp. 350–351)

van Manen (2014) also provides criteria for evaluative appraisal of phenomenological studies.

- *Heuristic questioning*: Does the text induce a sense of contemplative wonder and questioning attentiveness—*ti estin* (the wonder what this is) and *hoti estin* (the wonder that something exists at all)?
- *Descriptive richness*: Does the text contain rich and recognizable experiential material?
- *Interpretive depth*: Does the text offer reflective insights that go beyond the taken-for-granted understandings of everyday life?
- *Distinctive rigor*: Does the text remain constantly guided by a self-critical question of distinct meaning of the phenomenon or event?

- *Strong and addressive meaning*: Does the text "speak" to and address our sense of embodied meaning?
- *Experiential awakening*: Does the text awaken prereflective or primal experience through vocative and presentative language?
- *Inceptual epiphany*: Does the study offer us the possibility of deeper and original insight, and perhaps, an intuitive or inspirited grasp of the ethics and ethos of life commitments and practices? (pp. 355–356)

In Figure 10.4, we advance our five standards for assessing the quality of a phenomenology.

Grounded Theory Research

Strauss and Corbin (1990) identified criteria by which one judges the quality of a grounded theory study. They describe seven criteria related to the general research process and six criteria related to the empirical grounding of a study. Corbin and Strauss (2015) advance the term *checkpoint* in place of criteria saying "dislike using the word *criteria* because that makes the evaluative process seem so dogmatic, an "all nothing" approach to evaluation" (p. 350, emphasis in original).

FIGURE 10.4 ● Standards for Assessing the Quality of a Phenomenology

Does the phenomenology do the following?

1. Articulate a clear "phenomenon" to study in a concise way?
    - The author may use a phenomenological question to guide the study.

2. Convey an understanding of the philosophical tenets of phenomenology?
    - The author may ground the study in primary and scholarly phenomenological literature.

3. Use procedures of data analysis in phenomenology?
    - The author may refer to procedures recommended by Moustakas (1994) or van Manen (1990).

4. Communicate the overall essence of the experience of the participants?
    - The author may describe the context in which the experience occurred.

5. Embed reflexivity throughout the study?
    - The author may explain the process and outcomes of reflexive thinking.

Corbin and Strauss (2015) describe 16 checkpoints for guiding researchers and reviewers in evaluating the methodological consistency of a grounded theory study:

1. What was the target sample population? How was the original sample selected?

2. How did sampling proceed? What kinds of data were collected? Were there multiple sources of data and multiple comparative groups?

3. Did data collection alternate with analysis?

4. Were ethical considerations taken into account in both data collection and analysis?

5. Were the concepts driving the data collection arrived at through analysis (based on theoretical sampling), or were concepts derived from the literature and established before the data were collected not true theoretical sampling)?

6. Was theoretical sampling used, and was there a description of how it proceeded?

7. Did the research demonstrate sensitivity to the participants and to the data?

8. Is there evidence or examples of memos?

9. At what point did data collection end or a discussion of saturation end?

10. Is there a description of how coding proceeded along with examples of theoretical sampling, concepts, categories, and statements of relations? What were some of the events, incidents, or actions (indicators) that pointed to some of these major categories?

11. Is there a core category, and is there a description of how that core category was arrived at?

12. Were there changes in design as the research went along based on findings?

13. Did the researcher(s) encounter any problems while doing the research? Is there any mention of a negative case, and how was that data handled?

14. Are methodological decisions made clear so that readers can judge their appropriateness for gathering data (theoretical sampling) and doing analysis?

15. Was there feedback on the findings from other professionals and from participants? And were changes made in the theory based on this feedback?

16. Did the researcher keep a research journal or notebook? (Corbin & Strauss, 2015, pp. 350–351)

They also advance 17 checkpoints for researchers and reviewers to evaluate the quality and applicability of a grounded theory study:

1. What is the core category, and how do the major categories relate to it? Is there a diagram depicting these relationship?

2. Is the core category sufficiently broad so that it can be used to study other populations and similar situations beyond this setting?

3. Are each of the categories developed in terms of their properties and dimensions so that they show depth, breadth, and variation?

4. Is there descriptive data given under each category that brings that theory to life so that it provides understanding and can be used in a variety of situations?

5. Has context been identified and integrated into the theory? Conditions and consequences should be listed merely as background information in a separate section but woven into the actual analysis with explanations of how they impact and flow from action–interaction in the data.

6. Has process been incorporated into the theory in the form of changes in action–interaction in relationship to changes in conditions? Is action–interaction matched to different situations, demonstrating how the theory might vary under different conditions and therefore be applied to different situations?

7. How is saturation explained, and when and how was it determined that categories were saturated?

8. Do the findings resonate or fit with the experience of both the professionals for whom the research ended and the participants who took part in the study? Can participants see themselves in the story even if not every detail applies to them?

9. Are there gaps, or missing links, in the theory, leaving the reader confused and with a sense that something is missing?

10. Is there an account of extremes or negative cases?

11. Is variation built into the theory?

12. Are the findings presented in a creative and innovative manner? Does the research say something new or put old ideas together in new ways?

13. Do findings give insight into situation and provide knowledge that can be applied to develop policy, change practice, and add to the knowledge base of a profession?

14. Do the theoretical findings seem significant, and to what extent? It is entirely possible to complete a theory-generating study, or any research investigation, yet not produce findings that are significant.

15. Do the findings have the potential to become part of the discussion and ideas exchanged among relevant social and professional groups?

16. Are the limitations of the study clearly spelled out?

17. Are there suggestions for practice, policy, teaching, and application of the research? (Corbin & Strauss, 2015, pp. 351–352)

Charmaz (2014) reflects on the quality of the theory developed in a grounded theory study. She suggests that grounded theorists look at their theory and ask themselves the following evaluative questions:

- Are the definitions of major categories complete?
- Have I raised major categories to concepts in my theory?
- How have I increased the scope and depth of the analysis in this draft?
- Have I established strong theoretical links between categories and between categories and their properties, in addition to the data?
- How have I increased understanding of the studied phenomenon?
- How does my grounded theory study make a fresh contribution?
- With which theoretical, substantive, or practical problems is this analysis most closely aligned? Which audiences might be most interested in it? Where shall I go with it?
- What implications does this analysis hold for theoretical each, depth, and breadth? For methods? For substantive knowledge? For actions or interventions? (Charmaz, 2014, pp. 337–338)

See also Charmaz (2014, pp. 337–338) for guiding questions for assessing criteria for grounded theory studies organized by four categories: credibility, originality, resonance, and usefulness. In Figure 10.5, we describe features of the general process and a relationship among the concepts we look for when evaluating a grounded theory study.

Ethnographic Research

Few ethnographic resources identify criteria for quality ethnographies. Instead, the preference, it seems, for ethnographers is to describe the "basics" of ethnographical studies as prolonged fieldwork that generate thick, contextual descriptions reflective of the triangulation of multiple data sources (Fetterman, 2010; Wolcott, 2008a, 2010). Two exceptions are Richardson (2000) and Spindler and Spindler (1987).

Richardson (2000) describes her criteria for evaluating ethnographies:

Substantive contribution: Does this piece contribute to our understanding of social life? Does the writer demonstrate a deeply grounded (if embedded) human world understanding and perspective? How has this perspective informed the construction of the text?

FIGURE 10.5 ● Features for Evaluating a Grounded Theory Study

Does the grounded theory study do the following?

1. Focus on the study of a process, an action, or an interaction as the key element in the theory?

   • The author may focus on the steps that unfold when studying a central phenomenon as a process, action, or interaction among individuals.

2. Integrate a coding process that works from the data to a larger theoretical model?

   • The author may describe the data collection as alternating with data analysis to build a theoretical model.

3. Present the theoretical model in a figure or diagram?

   • The author may use innovative means for presenting the theory in a creative and innovative manner.

4. Advance a story line or proposition connected with the categories in the theoretical model that presents further questions to be answered?

   • The author may refer to the overall picture emerging in the current study as a springboard for future directions of research.

5. Use memoing throughout the process of research?

   • The author may describe the different types of memos or ways of recording ongoing thought in the process of conducting the study.

6. Embed evidence of reflexivity or self-disclosure by the researcher about his or her stance in the study?

   • The author may describe how a research journal or notebook (or other form) documented their reflexive thinking during the study.

Aesthetic merit: Does this piece succeed aesthetically? Does the use of creative analytical practices open up the text and invite interpretive responses? Is the text artistically shaped, satisfying, complex, and not boring?

Reflexivity: How did the author come to write this text? How was the information gathered? Ethical issues? How has the author's subjectivity been both a producer and a product of this text? Is there adequate self-awareness and self-exposure for the reader to make judgments about the point of view? Do authors hold themselves accountable to the standards of knowing and telling of the people they have studied?

Impact: Does this affect me? Emotionally? Intellectually? Generate new questions? Move me to write? Move me to try new research practices? Move me to action.

Expresses a reality: Does this text embody a fleshed out, embodied sense of lived experience? Does it seem "true"—a credible account of a cultural, social, individual, or communal sense of the "real"? (p. 254)

The ethnographers Spindler and Spindler (1987) emphasize that the most important requirement for an ethnographic approach is to explain behavior from the "native's point of view" (p. 20) and to be systematic in recording this information using note taking, tape recorders, and cameras. This requires that the ethnographer be present in the situation and engage in constant interaction between observation and interviews. These points are reinforced in Spindler and Spindler's (1987) nine criteria for a "good ethnography":

Criterion I. Observations are contextualized.

Criterion II. Hypotheses emerge *in situ* as the study goes on.

Criterion III. Observation is prolonged and repetitive.

Criterion IV. Through interviews, observations, and other eliciting procedures, the native view of reality is obtained.

Criterion V. Ethnographers elicit knowledge from informant-participants in a systematic fashion.

Criterion VI. Instruments, codes, schedules, questionnaires, agenda for interviews, and so forth are generated *in situ* as a result of inquiry.

Criterion VII. A transcultural, comparative perspective is frequently an unstated assumption.

Criterion VIII. The ethnographer makes explicit what is implicit and tacit to informants.

Criterion IX. The ethnographic interviewer must not predetermine responses by the kinds of questions asked. (p. 18)

This list, grounded in fieldwork, leads to a strong ethnography. Moreover, as Lofland (1974) contends, the study is located in wide conceptual frameworks; presents the novel but not necessarily new; provides evidence for the framework(s); is endowed with concrete, eventful interactional events, incidents, occurrences, episodes, anecdotes, scenes, and happenings without being "hyper-eventful"; and shows an interplay between the concrete and analytical and the empirical and theoretical. In Figure 10.6, we advance seven criteria we would look for in a "good" ethnography.

FIGURE 10.6 ● Criteria for a "Good" Ethnography

Does the ethnography do the following?

1. Convey evidence of clear identification of a culture-sharing group?

   - The author may describe the group in some detail—how the group was selected, access including gatekeepers, how it interacts and communicates, and so forth.

2. Specify a cultural theme that will be examined in light of this culture-sharing group?

   - The author may identify a cultural theme and the rationale for choosing it.

3. Describe the cultural group in detail?

   - The author may use creative analytical practices to convey these descriptions.

4. Communicate themes derived from an understanding of the cultural group?

   - The author may organize a thematic narrative or tale.

5. Identify issues that arose "in the field" that reflect on the relationship between the researcher and the participants, the interpretive nature of reporting, and sensitivity and reciprocity in the co-creating of the account?

   - The author may present these field issues so that they are a credible account of the challenges in conducting the study.

6. Explain how the culture-sharing group works overall?

   - The author may describe a working set of rules or generalizations as to how the culture-sharing group functions.

7. Integrate self-disclosure and reflexivity by the researcher about her or his position in the research?

   - The author may describe their background experiences with the group and describe their reflections about interactions with the group.

Case Study Research

Evaluative criteria for a case study are provided by Stake's (1995) rather extensive "critique checklist." In so doing, Stake (1995) shares criteria for assessing a good case study report:

- Is the report easy to read?
- Does it fit together, each sentence contributing to the whole?
- Does the report have a conceptual structure (i.e., themes or issues)?

- Are its issues developed in a serious and scholarly way?
- Is the case adequately defined?
- Is there a sense of story to the presentation?
- Is the reader provided some vicarious experience?
- Have quotations been used effectively?
- Are headings, figures, artifacts, appendixes, and indexes used effectively?
- Was it edited well—and then again with a last-minute polish?
- Has the writer made sound assertions, neither over- nor misinterpreting?
- Has adequate attention been paid to various contexts?
- Were sufficient raw data presented?
- Were data sources well chosen and in sufficient number?
- Do observations and interpretations appear to have been triangulated?
- Is the role and point of view of the researcher nicely apparent?
- Is the nature of the intended audience apparent?
- Is empathy shown for all sides?
- Are personal intentions examined?
- Does it appear that individuals were put at risk? (p. 131)

Yin (2014) reflects on the quality of the description presented in a case study. He describes several characteristics for an exemplary case study.

- *Significant.* Has the researcher focused the case(s) "unusual and of general public interest" or underlying issues "nationally important—either in theoretical terms or in policy or practical terms" (p. 201)?
- *Complete.* Has the researcher clearly defined the case(s) boundaries, collected extensive evidence, and conducted the study absent "of certain artefactual conditions" (p. 203)—for example, if a time or resource constraint unwittingly ended the study?
- *Consider alternative perspectives.* Has the researcher considered rival propositions and sought to collect evidence from differing perspectives in the case(s)?
- *Display sufficient evidence.* Has the researcher reported the case(s) in such a way that a reader can "reach an independent judgment regarding the merits" (p. 205)?
- *Composed in an engaging manner.* Has the researcher presented the case(s) in a way that communicates "the results widely"—either in writing or performance (p. 206)?

In Figure 10.7, we describe our six criteria for evaluating a "good" case study.

Comparing the Evaluation Standards of the Five Approaches

The standards discussed for each approach differ slightly depending on the procedures of the approaches. Certainly less is mentioned about narrative research and its standards of quality, and more is available about the other approaches. From within the

---

FIGURE 10.7 ● Evaluative Criteria for a Case Study

Does the case study do the following?

1. Identify the case(s) studied?

   - The author may identify the boundaries and time parameters of a single case or multiple cases.

2. Present a rationale for the case(s) selection?

   - The author may identify rationales for selecting the case, such as to understand a research issue or describe intrinsic merit.

3. Describe the case(s) in detail?

   - The author may begin with a rich description of the case(s) and its setting or context(s).

4. Articulate the themes identified for the case(s)?

   - The author may focus on a few key thematic issues for individual case(s) or across cases.

5. Report assertions or generalizations from the case analysis?

   - The author may interpret how the case(s) provides insight into the issue, or the findings can be generalized to other cases. Sometimes this may take the form of summary statements or a vignette.

6. Embed researcher reflexivity or self-disclosure about his or her position in the study?

   - The author may use reflective thinking and writing throughout the study.

---

major books used for each approach, we have attempted to extract the evaluation standards recommended for their approach to research. To these, we have added our own standards that we use in our qualitative classes when we evaluate a project or study presented within each of the five approaches. We can compare these standards across the five approaches relating five dimensions summarized in Table 10.2. At the most fundamental level, the five differ in the focus of the study. A couple of potential similarities should be noted. Phenomenology, grounded theory, and ethnography typically focus the study on a singular phenomenon, process (or action or interaction), and culture-sharing group respectively. True, one may also focus narrative research or a case study on a single individual or case but it also possible to focus on two or three individuals or multiple cases. The study procedures offer distinguishing features for each approach whereby some research features the collection of stories (i.e., narrative), specification of cultural themes (i.e., ethnography), and selection of cases (i.e., case study)—others such as phenomenology are distinguishable by initial conveyance of an understanding of the philosophical tenets or integration of analysis into data collection activities and use of memoing (i.e., grounded theory). When examining a study, the approach can be identifiable by its presentation and outcomes of a story chronology for narrative research, theoretical diagramming for grounded theory research, explanation of how a culture-sharing group works for ethnography, and the assertions for a case study. Common across all the qualitative approaches is the use of reflexive and self-disclosing practices for embedding what the researcher brings to the study.

TABLE 10.2 ● Comparing the Evaluation Standards Across the Five Qualitative Approaches

Criteria	Narrative Research	Phenomenology	Grounded Theory	Ethnography	Case Study
What is the focus of the study?	Focuses on a single individual (or two or three individuals)	Articulates a "phenomenon" to study in a concise way	Studies a process, an action, or an interaction as the key element in the theory	Identifies a culture-sharing group	Identifies the study case (or multiple cases)
How does the study proceed?	Collects stories about a significant issue related to the individual's life	Conveys an understanding of the philosophical tenets of phenomenology Uses recommended procedures of data analysis in phenomenology	Integrates coding process that works from the data to a larger theoretical model Uses memoing throughout the process of research	Specifies a cultural theme that will be examined in light of this culture-sharing group Identifies issues that arose in the field	Rationalizes case(s) selection in terms of understandings that will be generated Identifies themes for the case (or across cases)
How is the study presented?	Develops a chronology that connects different phases or aspects of a story		Presents the theoretical model in a figure or diagram	Communicates themes derived from an understanding of the cultural group	Reports assertions or generalizations from the case analysis
What is the study outcome?	Tells a story that reports what was said (themes), how it was said, (unfolding story), and how speakers interact or perform	Communicates the overall essence of the experience of the participants including the context	Advances a story line or proposition that connects categories in the theoretical model and presents further questions	Describes the cultural group in detail Explains how the culture-sharing group works overall	Details a description of the case(s)
What does a researcher bring to the study?	Uses reflexive thinking and writing	Embeds reflexivity throughout the study	Self-discloses his or her stance	Integrates reflexivity about her or his position	Uses reflexivity about his or her position

Chapter Check-In

1. Can you identify the characteristics of "thick description" to develop a deeper understanding of how cases, settings, and themes are presented in a qualitative study?

    a. Look for a detailed description in a short story or a novel. If you do not find one, you might use the story about the "Cat 'n' Mouse" as found in Steven Millhauser's book (2008), *Dangerous Laughter.*

    b. Next, identify passages in which Millhauser (2008) creates detail by physical passages, movement, or activity description.

    c. Finally, identify how the author interconnects the details.

2. Can you identify validation strategies for enhancing the accuracy of your study within one of the five approaches? Read qualitative journal articles or books that adopt different strategies.

    a. Underline examples of the strategy in use and consider its effectiveness.

    b. Could the strategy be used as effectively in other approaches?

    c. How would different approaches impact your use of various validation strategies?

3. What intercoder agreement procedures can you use to practice assessing reliability across coders?

    a. To conduct this practice, obtain a short text file, which may be a transcript of an interview; field notes typed from an observation; or a digital file of a document, such as a newspaper article.

    b. Next, have two or more coders go through a transcript and record their codes. Then look at the passages all coders have identified and see whether their codes are similar or match.

    c. Look back at the procedures we propose for intercoder agreement in Figure 10.2 and see which were easy to implement and more challenging.

4. Do you see the key characteristics of each of the five approaches that might be used in evaluating a study? Select one of the approaches, find a journal article that uses the approach, and then see if you can find the key characteristics of evaluation of that approach in the article.

Summary

In this chapter, we discussed validation, reliability, and standards of quality in qualitative research. Validation approaches vary considerably, such as strategies that emphasize using qualitative terms

(Continued)

(Continued)

comparable to quantitative terms, the use of distinct terms, perspectives from postmodern and interpretive lenses, syntheses of different perspectives, descriptions based on metaphorical images, or some combination of these perspectives on validity. Reliability is used in qualitative research in several ways, one of the most popular being the use of intercoder agreements when multiple coders analyze and then compare their code segments to establish the reliability of the data analysis process. A detailed procedure for establishing intercoder agreement is described in this chapter. Also, diverse standards exist for establishing the quality of qualitative research, and these criteria are based on procedural perspectives, postmodern perspectives, and interpretive perspectives. Within each of the five approaches to inquiry, specific standards also exist; these were reviewed in this chapter. Finally, we advanced standards that we use to assess the quality of studies presented in each and compare across the five approaches.

Further Readings

In addition to many of the resources already suggested in earlier chapters that include perspectives and guidance for evaluation, validation, and reliability in qualitative research, we highlight a few key resources here. The list should not be considered exhaustive and readers are encouraged to seek out additional readings in the end-of-book reference list.

Resources Focused on Validation Perspectives

Angen, M. J. (2000). Evaluating interpretive inquiry: Reviewing the validity debate and opening the dialogue. *Qualitative Health Research*, *10*, 378–395. doi:10.1177/104973230001000308

Maureen Jane Angen traces the origins of validity and suggests its application within interpretive approaches. In so doing, she relates validity to terms of trustworthiness and validation strategies.

Lincoln, Y. S., Lynham, S. A., & Guba, E. G. (2011). Paradigmatic controversies, contradictions, and emerging confluences. In N. K. Denzin & Y. S. Lincoln (Eds.), *The SAGE handbook of qualitative research* (4th ed., pp. 97–128). Thousand Oaks, CA: Sage.

In this chapter, the authors revisit many issues from earlier handbook editions and advance their view of the essential role of authenticity within discussions of validity and ethical research.

Lincoln, Y. S., & Guba, E. G. (1985). *Naturalistic inquiry.* Beverly Hills, CA: Sage.

In this classical text, Yvonna Lincoln and Egon Guba describe the alternative terms for validation in qualitative research that remain in use today. This is a must-read for many researchers.

Whittemore, R., Chase, S. K., & Mandle, C. L. (2001). Validity in qualitative research. *Qualitative Health Research*, *11*, 522–537. doi:10.1177/104973201129119299

In their exploration of validity issues in 13 writings of qualitative research, Robin Whittemore and colleagues extract key validation criteria and organize into four primary and six secondary criteria. The article also provides a comprehensive description of historical development of validity issues in qualitative research.

Resources Focused on Reliability Perspectives

Armstrong, D., Gosling, A., Weinman, J., & Marteau, T. (1997). The place of inter-rater reliability in qualitative research: An empirical study. *Sociology, 31,* 597–606. doi:10.1177/0038038597031003015

The authors use the assessment of inter-rater reliability among six researchers as a springboard for discussing procedures of conducting intercoder agreement checks. Noteworthy is their focus on key issues related to what coding agreements specify.

Campbell, J. L., Quincy, C., Osserman, J., & Pederson, O. K. (2013). Coding in-depth semistructured interviews: Problems of unitization and intercoder reliability and agreement. *Sociological Methods & Research, 42,* 294–320. doi:10.1177/0049124113500475

The authors provide practical procedures for reliability of coding in an exploratory study. Of particular interest was the discussion related to the possible impact of coder knowledge of the text being coded.

Richards, L. (2015). *Handling qualitative data: A practical guide* (3rd ed.). Thousand Oaks, CA: Sage.

Lyn Richards provides accessible information for guiding researchers in generating reliable coding and valid interpretations of qualitative data. The text is organized by setting up, handling, and making sense of data.

Silverman, D. (2013). *Doing qualitative research: A practical handbook* (4th ed.). Thousand Oaks, CA: Sage.

David Silverman provides practical guidance for planning and conducting high-quality qualitative research. Of particular note is his discussion on reliability and illustrative examples embedded throughout.

Resources Focused on Qualitative Evaluation Criteria

Howe, K., & Eisenhardt, M. (1990). Standards for qualitative (and quantitative) research: A prolegomenon. *Educational Researcher, 19*(4), 2–9. doi:10.3102/0013189X019004002.

Kenneth Howe and Margaret Eisenhardt contribute important discussions of quality standards related to driver of research, methodological competence, the making researcher assumptions explicit, study warrant, and practical and theoretical implications. An essential read for understanding historical developments.

Lincoln, Y. S. (1995). Emerging criteria for quality in qualitative and interpretive research. *Qualitative Inquiry, 1,* 275–289. doi:10.1177/107780049500100301

(Continued)

(Continued)

In this work, Yvonna Lincoln relates the researcher's relationship with research participants as a measure of quality—for example, meeting ethical standards such as reciprocity would serve as necessary criteria.

Richardson, L., & St. Pierre, E. A. (2005). Writing: A method of inquiry. In N. K. Denzin & Y. S. Lincoln (Eds.), *The SAGE handbook of qualitative research* (3rd ed., pp. 959–978). Thousand Oaks, CA: Sage.

Laurel Richardson and Elizabeth Adams St. Pierre offer two individual yet complementary perspectives on evaluative criteria. A hidden gem is their discussion at the end of the chapter of creative analytical writing practices.

11

"Turning the Story" and Conclusion

How might the story be turned if it was a case study, a narrative project, a phenomenology, a grounded theory, or an ethnography? In this book, we suggest that researchers be cognizant of the procedures of qualitative research and of the differences in approaches of qualitative inquiry. This is not to suggest a preoccupation with method or methodology; indeed, we see two parallel tracks in a study: the substantive content of the study and the methodology. With increased interest in qualitative research, it is important that studies being conducted go forward with rigor and attention to the procedures developed within approaches of inquiry.

The approaches are many, and their procedures for research are well documented within books and articles. A few writers classify the approaches, and some authors mention their favorites. Unquestionably, qualitative research cannot be characterized as of one type, attested to by the multivocal discourse surrounding qualitative research today. Adding to this discourse are perspectives about philosophical, theoretical, and ideological stances. To capture the essence of a good qualitative study, we visualize such a study as comprising three interconnected circles. As shown in Figure 11.1, these circles include the approach of inquiry, research design procedures, and philosophical and theoretical frameworks and assumptions. The interplay of these three factors contributes to a complex, rigorous study.

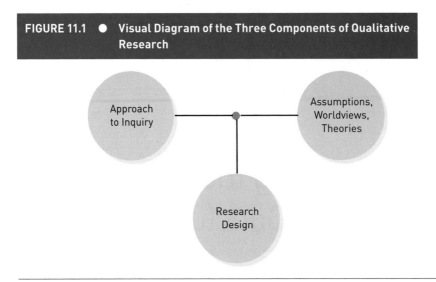

FIGURE 11.1 ● Visual Diagram of the Three Components of Qualitative Research

Turning the Story

In this chapter, we again sharpen the distinctions among the approaches of inquiry, but we depart from our side-by-side approach used in prior chapters. We focus the lens in a new direction and "turn the story" of the gunman case study (Asmussen & Creswell, 1995) into a narrative study, a phenomenology, a grounded theory, and an ethnography.

Turning the story through different approaches of inquiry raises the issue of whether one should match a particular problem to an approach to inquiry. Much emphasis is placed on this relationship in social and human science research. We agree this needs to be done. But for the purposes of this book, our way around this issue is to pose a *general* problem—"How did the campus react?"—and then construct scenarios for specific problems. For instance, the specific problem of studying a single individual's reaction to the gun incident is different from the specific problem of how several students as a culture-sharing group reacted, but both scenarios are reactions to the general issue of a campus response to the incident. The general problem that we address is that we know little about how campuses respond to violence and even less about how different constituent groups on campus respond to a potentially violent incident. Knowing this information would help us devise better plans for reacting to this type of problem as well as add to the literature on violence in educational settings. This was the central problem in the gunman case study presented next in its complete, original form (Asmussen & Creswell, 1995), and then we briefly review the major dimensions of this study before we begin "turning the story."

A CASE STUDY

"Campus Response to a Student Gunman"

Kelly J. Asmussen

John W. Creswell

Source: The material in this chapter is reprinted from the *Journal of Higher Education, 66 (5),* 575–591. doi:10.2307/2943937. Copyright 1995, the Ohio State University Press. Used by permission.

With increasingly frequent incidents of campus violence, a small, growing scholarly literature about the subject is emerging. For instance, authors have reported on racial [12], courtship and sexually coercive [3, 7, 8], and hazing violence [24]. For the American College Personnel Association, Roark [24] and Roark and Roark [25] reviewed the forms of physical, sexual, and psychological violence on college campuses and suggested guidelines for prevention strategies. Roark [23] has also suggested criteria that high-school students might use to assess the level of violence on college campuses they seek to attend. At the national level, President Bush, in November 1989, signed into law the "Student Right-to-Know and Campus Security Act" (P.L. 101-542), which requires colleges and universities to make available to students, employees, and applicants an annual report on security policies and campus crime statistics [13].

One form of escalating campus violence that has received little attention is student gun violence. Recent campus reports indicate that violent crimes from thefts and burglaries to assaults and homicides are on the rise at colleges and universities [13]. College campuses have been shocked by killings such as those at The University of Iowa [16], The University of Florida [13], Concordia University in Montreal, and the University of Montreal-Ecole Polytechnique [22]. Incidents such as these raise critical concerns, such as psychological trauma, campus safety, and disruption of campus life. Aside from an occasional newspaper report, the postsecondary literature is silent on campus reactions to these tragedies; to understand them one must turn to studies about gun violence in the public school literature. This literature addresses strategies for school intervention [21, 23], provides case studies of incidents in individual schools [6, 14, 15], and discusses the problem of students who carry weapons to school [1] and the psychological trauma that results from homicides [32].

A need exists to study campus reactions to violence in order to build conceptual models for future study as well as to identify campus strategies and protocols for reaction. We need to understand better the psychological dimensions and organizational issues of constituents involved in and affected by these incidents. An in-depth qualitative case study exploring the context of an incident can illuminate such conceptual and pragmatic understandings. The study presented in this article is a qualitative case analysis [31] that describes and interprets a campus response to a gun incident.

We asked the following exploratory research questions: What happened? Who was involved in response to the incident? What themes of response emerged during the eight-month period that followed this incident? What theoretical constructs helped us understand the campus response, and what constructs were unique to this case?

The Incident and Response

The incident occurred on the campus of a large public university in a Midwestern city. A decade ago, this city had been designated an "all-American city," but more recently, its normally tranquil environment has been disturbed by an increasing number of assaults and homicides. Some of these violent incidents have involved students at the university.

The incident that provoked this study occurred on a Monday in October. A forty-three-year-old graduate student, enrolled in a senior-level actuarial science class, arrived a few minutes before class, armed with a vintage Korean War military semiautomatic rifle loaded with a thirty-round clip of thirty caliber ammunition. He carried another thirty-round clip in his pocket. Twenty of the thirty-four students in the class had already gathered for class, and most of them were quietly reading the student newspaper. The instructor was en route to class.

The gunman pointed the rifle at the students, swept it across the room, and pulled the trigger. The gun jammed. Trying to unlock the rifle, he hit the butt of it on the instructor's desk and quickly tried firing it again. Again it did not fire. By this time, most students realized what was happening and dropped to the floor, overturned their desks, and tried to hide behind them. After about twenty seconds, one of the students shoved a desk into the gunman, and students ran past him out into the hall and out of the building. The gunman hastily departed the room and went out of the building to his parked car, which he had left running. He was captured by police within the hour in a nearby small town, where he lived. Although he remains incarcerated at this time, awaiting trial, the motivations for his actions are unknown.

Campus police and campus administrators were the first to react to the incident. Campus police arrived within three minutes after they had received a telephone call for help. They spent several anxious minutes outside the building interviewing students to obtain an accurate description of the gunman. Campus administrators responded by calling a news conference for 4:00 P.M. the same day, approximately four hours after the incident. The police chief as well as the vice-chancellor of Student Affairs and two students described the incident at the news conference. That same afternoon, the Student Affairs office contacted Student Health and Employee Assistance Program (EAP) counselors and instructed them to be available for any students or staff requesting assistance. The Student Affairs office also arranged for a new location, where this class could meet for the rest of the semester. The Office of Judicial Affairs suspended the gunman from the university. The next day, the incident was discussed by campus administrators at a regularly scheduled campuswide cabinet meeting. Throughout the week, Student Affairs received several calls from students and from a faculty member about "disturbed" students or unsettling student relations. A counselor of the Employee Assistance Program consulted a psychologist with a specialty in dealing with trauma and responding to educational crises. Only one student immediately set up an appointment with the student health counselors. The campus and local newspapers continued to carry stories about the incident.

When the actuarial science class met for regularly scheduled classes two and four days later, the students and the instructor were visited by two county attorneys, the police chief, and two student mental health counselors who conducted "debriefing" sessions. These sessions focused on keeping students fully informed about the judicial process and having the students and the instructor, one by one, talk about their experiences and explore their feelings about the incident. By one week after the incident, the students in the class had returned to their standard class format. During this time, a few students, women who were concerned about violence in general, saw Student Health Center counselors. These counselors also fielded questions from several dozen parents who inquired about the counseling services and the level of safety on campus. Some parents also called the campus administration to ask about safety procedures.

In the weeks following the incident, the faculty and staff campus newsletter carried articles about post-trauma fears and psychological trauma. The campus administration wrote a letter that provided facts about the incident to the board of the university. The administration also mailed campus staff and students information about crime prevention. At least one college dean sent out a memo to staff about "aberrant student behavior," and one academic department chair requested and held an educational group session with counselors and staff on identifying and dealing with "aberrant behavior" of students.

Three distinctly different staff groups sought counseling services at the Employee Assistance Program, a program for faculty and staff, during the next several weeks. The first group had had some direct involvement with the assailant, either by seeing him the day of the gun incident or because they had known him personally. This group was concerned about securing professional help, either for the students or for those in the group who were personally experiencing effects of the trauma. The second group consisted of the "silent connection," individuals who were indirectly involved and yet emotionally traumatized. This group recognized that their fears were a result of the gunman incident, and they wanted to deal with these fears before they escalated. The third group consisted of staff who had previously experienced a trauma, and this incident had retriggered their fears. Several employees were seen by the EAP throughout the next month, but no new groups or delayed stress cases were reported. The EAP counselors stated that each group's reactions were normal responses. Within a month, although public discussion of the incident had subsided, the EAP and Student Health counselors began expressing the need for a coordinated campus plan to deal with the current as well as any future violent incidents.

The Research Study

We began our study two days after the incident. Our first step was to draft a research protocol for approval by the university administration and the Institutional Review Board. We made explicit that we would not become involved in the investigation of the gunman or in the therapy to students or staff who had sought assistance from counselors.

We also limited our study to the reactions of groups on campus rather than expand it to include off-campus groups (for example, television and newspaper coverage). This bounding of the study was consistent with an exploratory qualitative case study design [31], which was chosen because models and variables were not available for assessing a campus reaction to a gun incident in higher education. In the constructionist tradition, this study incorporated the paradigm assumptions of an emerging design, a context-dependent inquiry, and an inductive data analysis [10]. We also bounded the study by time (eight months) and by a single case (the campus community). Consistent with case study design [17, 31], we identified campus administrators and student newspaper reporters as multiple sources of information for initial interviews. Later we expanded interviews to include a wide array of campus informants, using a semi-structured interview protocol that consisted of five questions: What has been your role in the incident? What has happened since the event that you have been involved in? What has been the impact of this incident on the university community? What larger ramifications, if any, exist from the incident? To whom should we talk to find out more about the campus reaction to the incident? We also gathered observational data, documents, and visual materials (see table 1 for types of information and sources).

The narrative structure was a "realist" tale [28], describing details, incorporating edited quotes from informants, and stating our interpretations of events, especially an interpretation within the framework of organizational and psychological issues. We verified the description and interpretation by taking a preliminary draft of the case to select informants for feedback and later incorporating their comments into the final study [17, 18]. We gathered this feedback in a group interview where we asked: Is our description of the incident and the reaction accurate? Are the themes and constructs we have identified consistent with your experiences? Are there some themes and constructs we have missed? Is a campus plan needed? If so, what form should it take?

Themes

Denial

Several weeks later we returned to the classroom where the incident occurred. Instead of finding the desks overturned, we found them to be neatly in order; the room was ready for a lecture or discussion class. The hallway outside the room was narrow, and we visualized how students, on that Monday in October, had quickly left the building, unaware that the gunman, too, was exiting through this same passageway. Many of the students in the hallway during the incident had seemed unaware of what was going on until they saw or heard that there was a gunman in the building. Ironically though, the students had seemed to ignore or deny their dangerous situation. After exiting the building, instead of seeking a hiding place that would be safe, they had huddled together just outside the building. None of the students had barricaded themselves in classrooms or offices or had exited at a safe distance from the scene in anticipation that the gunman might return. "People wanted to stand their ground and stick around," claimed a campus police officer. Failing to respond to the potential danger, the class members had huddled together outside the building, talking nervously. A few had been openly emotional and crying. When asked about their mood, one of the students had said, "Most of us were kidding about it." Their conversations had led one to believe that they were dismissing the incident as though it were trivial and as though no one had actually been in danger. An investigating campus police officer was not surprised by the students' behavior:

> It is not unusual to see people standing around after one of these types of incidents. The American people want to see excitement and have a morbid curiosity. That is why you see spectators hanging around bad accidents. They do not seem to understand the potential danger they are in and do not want to leave until they are injured.

This description corroborates the response reported by mental health counselors: an initial surrealistic first reaction. In the debriefing by counselors, one female student had commented, "I thought the gunman would shoot out a little flag that would say 'bang.'" For her, the event had been like a dream. In this atmosphere no one from the targeted class had called the campus mental health center in the first twenty-four hours following the incident, although they knew that services were available. Instead, students described how they had visited with friends or had gone to bars; the severity of the situation had dawned on them later. One student commented that he had felt fearful and angry only after he had seen the television newscast with pictures of the classroom the evening of the incident.

Though some parents had expressed concern by phoning counselors, the students' denial may have been reinforced by parent comments. One student reported that his parents had made comments like, "I am not surprised you were involved in this. You are always getting yourself into things like this!" or "You did not get hurt. What is the big deal? Just let it drop!" One student expressed how much more traumatized he had been as a result of his mother's dismissal of the event. He had wanted to have someone whom he trusted willing to sit down and listen to him.

Fear

Our visit to the classroom suggested a second theme: the response of fear. Still posted on the door several weeks after the incident, we saw the sign announcing that the class was being moved to another undisclosed building and that students were to check with a secretary in an adjoining room about the new location. It was in this undisclosed classroom, two days after the incident, that two student mental health counselors, the campus police chief, and two county attorneys had met with students in the class to discuss fears, reactions, and thoughts. Reactions of fear had begun to surface in this first "debriefing" session and continued to emerge in a second session.

The immediate fear for most students centered around the thought that the alleged assailant would be able to make bail. Students felt that the assailant might have

TABLE 1 ● Data Collection Matrix: Type of Information by Source				
Information/ Information Source	Interviews	Observations	Documents	Audio-Visual Materials
Students involved	Yes		Yes	
Students at large	Yes			
Central administration	Yes		Yes	
Campus police	Yes	Yes		
Faculty	Yes	Yes	Yes	
Staff	Yes			
Physical plant		Yes	Yes	
News reporters/papers/ television	Yes		Yes	Yes
Student health counselors	Yes			
Employee Assistance Program counselors	Yes			
Trauma expert	Yes		Yes	Yes
Campus businesses			Yes	
Board members			Yes	

harbored resentment toward certain students and that he would seek retribution if he made bail. "I think I am going to be afraid when I go back to class. They can change the rooms, but there is nothing stopping him from finding out where we are!" said one student. At the first debriefing session the campus police chief was able to dispel some of this fear by announcing that during the initial hearing the judge had denied bail. This announcement helped to reassure some students about their safety. The campus police chief thought it necessary to keep the students informed of the gunman's status, because several students had called his office to say that they feared for their safety if the gunman were released.

During the second debriefing session, another fear surfaced: the possibility that a different assailant could attack the class. One student reacted so severely to this potential threat that, according to one counselor, since the October incident, "he had caught himself walking into class and sitting at a desk with a clear shot to the door. He was beginning to see each classroom as a 'battlefield.'" In this second session students had sounded angry, they expressed feeling violated, and finally [they] began to admit that they felt unsafe. Yet only one female student immediately accessed the available mental health services, even though an announcement had been made that any student could obtain free counseling.

The fear students expressed during the "debriefing" sessions mirrored a more general concern on campus about increasingly frequent violent acts in the metropolitan area. Prior to this gun incident, three young females and a male had been kidnapped and had later been found dead in a nearby city. A university football player who experienced a psychotic episode had severely beaten a woman. He had later suffered a relapse and was shot by police in a scuffle. Just three weeks prior to the October gun incident, a female university student had been abducted and brutally murdered, and several other homicides had occurred in the city. As a student news reporter commented, "This whole semester has been a violent one."

Safety

The violence in the city that involved university students and the subsequent gun incident that occurred in a campus classroom shocked the typically tranquil campus. A counselor aptly summed up the feelings of many: "When the students walked out of that classroom, their world had become very chaotic; it had become very random, something had happened that robbed them of their sense of safety." Concern for safety became a central reaction for many informants.

When the chief student affairs officer described the administration's reaction to the incident, he listed the safety of students in the classroom as his primary goal, followed by the needs of the news media for details about the case, helping all students with psychological stress, and providing public information on safety. As he talked about the safety issue and the presence of guns on campus, he mentioned that a policy was under consideration for the storage of guns used by students for hunting. Within four hours after the incident, a press conference was called during which the press was briefed not only on the details of the incident, but also on the need to ensure the safety of the campus. Soon thereafter the university administration initiated an informational campaign on campus safety. A letter, describing the incident, was sent to the university board members. (One board member asked, "How could such an incident happen at this university?") The Student Affairs Office sent a letter to all students in which it advised them of the various dimensions of the campus security office and of the types of services it provided. The Counseling and Psychological Services of the Student Health Center promoted their services in a colorful brochure, which was mailed to students in the following week. It emphasized that services were "confidential, accessible, and professional." The Student Judiciary Office advised academic departments on various methods of dealing with students who exhibited abnormal behavior in class. The weekly faculty newsletter stressed that staff needed to respond quickly to any post-trauma fears associated with this incident. The campus newspaper quoted a professor as saying, "I'm totally shocked that in this environment, something like this would happen." Responding to the concerns about disruptive students or employees, the campus police department sent plainclothes officers to sit outside offices whenever faculty and staff indicated concerns.

An emergency phone system, Code Blue, was installed on campus only ten days after the incident. These thirty-six ten-foot-tall emergency phones, with bright blue flashing lights, had previously been approved, and specific spots had already been identified from an earlier study. "The phones will be quite an attention getter," the director of the Telecommunications Center commented. "We hope they will also be a big detractor [to crime]." Soon afterwards, in response to calls from concerned students, trees and shrubbery in poorly lit areas of campus were trimmed.

Students and parents also responded to these safety concerns. At least twenty-five parents called the Student Health Center, the university police, and the Student Affairs Office during the first week after the incident to inquire what kind of services were available for their students. Many parents had been traumatized by the news of the event and immediately demanded answers from the university. They wanted assurances that this type of incident would not happen again and that their child[ren were] safe on the campus. Undoubtedly, many parents also called their children during the weeks immediately following the incident. The students on campus responded to these safety concerns by forming groups of volunteers who would escort anyone on campus, male or female, during the evening hours.

Local businesses profited by exploiting the commercial aspects of the safety needs created by this incident. Various advertisements for self-defense classes and protection devices inundated the newspapers for several weeks. Campus and local clubs [that] offered self-defense classes filled quickly, and new classes were formed in response to numerous additional requests. The campus bookstore's supply of pocket mace and whistles was quickly depleted. The campus police received several inquiries by students who wanted to purchase handguns to carry for protection. None [was] approved, but one wonders whether some guns were not purchased by students anyway. The purchase of cellular telephones from local vendors increased sharply. Most of these purchases were made by females; however, some males also sought out these items for their safety and protection. Not unexpectedly, the price of some products was raised as much as 40 percent to capitalize on the newly created demand. Student conversations centered around the purchase of these safety products: how much they cost, how to use them correctly, how accessible they would be if students should need to use them, and whether they were really necessary.

Retriggering

In our original protocol, which we designed to seek approval from the campus administration and the Institutional Review Board, we had outlined a study that would last only three months—a reasonable time, we thought, for this incident to run its course. But during early interviews with counselors, we were referred to a psychologist who specialized in dealing with "trauma" in educational settings. It was this psychologist who mentioned the theme of "retriggering." Now, eight months later, we begin to understand how, through "retriggering," that October incident could have a long-term effect on this campus.

This psychologist explained retriggering as a process by which new incidents of violence would cause individuals to relive the feelings of fear, denial, and threats to personal safety that they had experienced in connection with the original event. The counseling staffs and violence expert also stated that one should expect to see such feelings retriggered at a later point in time, for example, on the anniversary date of the attack or whenever newspapers or television broadcasts mentioned the incident again. They added that a drawn-out judicial process, during which a case were "kept alive" through legal maneuvering, could cause a long period of retriggering and thereby greatly thwart the healing process. The fairness of the judgment of the court as seen by each victim, we were told, would also influence the amount of healing and resolution of feelings that could occur.

As of this writing, it is difficult to detect specific evidence of retriggering from the October incident, but we discovered the potential consequences of this process first-hand by observing the effects of a nearly identical violent gun incident that had happened some eighteen years earlier. A graduate student carrying a rifle had entered a campus building with the intention of shooting the department chairman. The student was seeking revenge, because several years earlier he had flunked a course taught by this professor. This attempted attack followed several years of legal maneuvers to arrest, prosecute, and incarcerate this student, who, on more than one occasion, had tried to carry out his plan but each time had been thwarted by quick-thinking staff members who would not reveal the professor's whereabouts. Fortunately, no shots were ever fired, and the student was finally apprehended and arrested.

The professor who was the target of these threats on his life was seriously traumatized not only during the period of these repeated incidents, but his trauma continued even after the attacker's arrest. The complex processes of the criminal justice system, which, he believed, did not work as it should have, resulted in his feeling further victimized. To this day, the feelings aroused by the original trauma are retriggered each time a gun incident is reported in the news. He was not offered professional help from the university at any time; the counseling services he did receive were secured through his own initiative. Eighteen years later his entire department is still affected in that unwritten rules for dealing with disgruntled students and for protecting this particular professor's schedule have been established.

Campus Planning

The question of campus preparedness surfaced during discussions with the psychologist about the process of "debriefing" individuals who had been involved in the October incident [19]. Considering how many diverse groups and individuals had been affected by this incident, a final theme that emerged from our data was the need for a campuswide plan. A counselor remarked, "We would have been inundated had there been twenty-five to thirty deaths. We need a mobilized plan of communication. It would be a wonderful addition to the campus considering the nature of today's violent world." It became apparent during our interviews that better communication could have occurred among the constituents who responded to this incident. Of course, one campus police officer noted, "We can't have an officer in every building all day long!" But the theme of being prepared across the whole campus was mentioned by several individuals.

The lack of a formal plan to deal with such gun incidents was surprising, given the existence of formal written plans on campus that addressed various other emergencies: bomb threats, chemical spills, fires, earthquakes, explosions, electrical storms, radiation accidents, tornadoes, hazardous material spills, snowstorms, and numerous medical emergencies. Moreover, we found that specific campus units had their own protocols that had actually been used during the October gun incident. For example, the police had a procedure and used that procedure for dealing with the gunman and the students at the scene; the EAP counselors debriefed staff and faculty; the Student Health counselors used a "debriefing" process when they visited the students twice in the classroom following the incident. The question that concerned us was, what would a campuswide plan consist of, and how would it be developed and evaluated?

As shown in table 2, using evidence gathered in our case, we assembled the basic questions to be addressed in a plan and cross-referenced these questions to the literature about post-trauma stress, campus violence, and the disaster literature (for a similar list drawn from the public school literature, see Poland and Pitcher [21]). Basic elements of a campus plan to enhance communication across units should include determining what the rationale for the plan is; who should be involved in its development; how it should be coordinated; how it should be staffed; and what specific procedures should be followed. These procedures might include responding to an immediate crisis, making the campus safe, dealing with external groups, and providing for the psychological welfare of victims.

Discussion

The themes of denial, fear, safety, retriggering, and developing a campuswide plan might further be grouped into two categories, an organizational and a psychological or social-psychological response of the campus community to the gunman incident. Organizationally, the campus units responding to the crisis exhibited both a loose coupling [30] and an interdependent communication. Issues such as leadership, communication, and authority emerged during the case analysis. Also, an environmental response developed, because the campus was transformed into a safer place for students and staff. The need for centralized planning, while allowing for autonomous operation of units in response to a crisis, called for organizational change that would require cooperation and coordination among units.

TABLE 2 ● Evidence From the Case, Questions for a Campus Plan, and References

Evidence From the Case	Question for the Plan	Useful References
Need expressed by counselors	Why should a plan be developed?	Walker (1990); Bird et al. (1991)
Multiple constitutes reacting to incident	Who should be involved in developing the plan?	Roark & Roark (1987); Walker (1990)
Leadership found in units with their own protocols	Should the leadership for coordinating be identified within one office?	Roark & Roark (1987)
Several unit protocols being used in incident	Should campus units be allowed their own protocols?	Roark & Roark (1987)
Questions raised by students reacting to case	What types of violence should be covered in the plan?	Roark (1987); Jones (1990)
Groups/individuals surfaced during our interviews	How are those likely to be affected by the incident to be identified?	Walker (1990); Bromet (1990)
Comments from campus police, central administration	What provisions are made for the immediate safety of those in the incident?	
Campus environment changed after incident	How should the physical environment be made safer?	Roark & Roark (1987)
Comments from central administration	How will the external publics (e.g., press, businesses) be apprised of the incident?	Poland & Pitcher (1990)
Issue raised by counselors and trauma specialist	What are the likely sequelae of psychological events for victims?	Bromet (1990); Mitchell (1983)
Issue raised by trauma specialist	What long-term impact will the incident have on victims?	Zelikoff (1987)
Procedure used by Student Health Center counselors	How will the victims be debriefed?	Mitchell (1983); Walker (1990)

Sherrill [27] provides models of response to campus violence that reinforce as well as depart from the evidence in our case. As mentioned by Sherrill, the disciplinary action taken against a perpetrator, the group counseling of victims, and the use of safety education for the campus community were all factors apparent in our case. However, Sherrill raises issues about responses that were not discussed by our informants, such as developing procedures for individuals who are first to arrive on the scene, dealing with non-students who might be perpetrators or victims, keeping records and documents about incidents, varying responses based on the size and nature of the institution, and relating incidents to substance abuse such as drugs and alcohol.

Also, some of the issues that we had expected after reading the literature about organizational response did not emerge. Aside from occasional newspaper reports (focused mainly on the gunman), there was little campus administrative response to the incident, which was contrary to what we had expected from Roark and Roark [25], for example. No mention was made of establishing a campus unit to manage future incidents—for example, a campus violence resource center—reporting of violent incidents [25], or conducting annual safety audits [20]. Aside from the campus police mentioning that the State Health Department would have been prepared to send a team of trained trauma experts to help emergency personnel cope with the tragedy, no discussion was reported about formal linkages with community agencies that might assist in the event of a tragedy [3]. We also did not hear directly about establishing a "command center" [14] or a crisis coordinator [21], two actions recommended by specialists on crisis situations.

On a psychological and social-psychological level, the campus response was to react to the psychological needs of the students who had been directly involved in the incident as well as to students and staff who had been indirectly affected by the incident. Not only did signs of psychological issues, such as denial, fear, and retriggering, emerge, as expected [15], gender and cultural group issues were also mentioned, though they were not discussed enough to be considered basic themes in our analysis. Contrary to assertions in the literature that violent behavior is often accepted in our culture, we found informants in our study to voice concern and fear about escalating violence on campus and in the community.

Faculty on campus were conspicuously silent on the incident, including the faculty senate, though we had expected this governing body to take up the issue of aberrant student or faculty behavior in their classrooms [25]. Some informants speculated that the faculty might have been passive about this issue because they were unconcerned, but another explanation might be that they were passive because they were unsure of what to do or whom to ask for assistance. From the students we failed to hear that they responded to their post-traumatic stress with "coping" strategies, such as relaxation, physical activity, and the establishment of normal routines [29]. Although the issues of gender and race surfaced in early conversations with informants, we did not find a direct discussion of these issues. As Bromet [5] comments, the sociocultural needs of populations with different mores must be considered when individuals assess reactions to trauma. In regard to the issue of gender, we did hear that females were the first students to seek out counseling at the Student Health Center. Perhaps our "near-miss" case was unique. We do not know what the reaction of the campus might have been had a death (or multiple deaths) occurred, although, according to the trauma psychologist, "the trauma of no deaths is as great as if deaths had occurred." Moreover, as with any exploratory case analysis, this case has limited generalizability [17], although thematic generalizability is certainly a possibility. The fact that our information was self-reported and that we were unable to interview all students who had been directly affected by the incident so as to not intervene in student therapy or the investigation also poses a problem.

Despite these limitations, our research provides a detailed account of a campus reaction to a violent incident with the potential for making a contribution to the literature. Events emerged during the process of reaction that could be "critical incidents" in future studies, such as the victim response, media reporting, the debriefing process, campus changes, and the evolution of a campus plan. With the scarcity of literature on campus violence related to gun incidents, this study breaks new ground by identifying themes and conceptual frameworks that could be examined in future cases. On a practical level, it can benefit campus administrators who are looking for a plan to respond to campus violence, and it focuses attention on questions that need to be addressed in such a plan. The large number of different groups of people who were affected by this particular gunman incident shows the complexity of responding to a campus crisis and should alert college personnel to the need for preparedness.

Epilogue

As we conducted this study, we asked ourselves whether we would have had access to informants if someone had been killed. This "near-miss" incident provided a unique research opportunity, which could, however, only approximate an event in which a fatality had actually occurred. Our involvement in this study was serendipitous, for one of us had been employed by a correctional facility and therefore had direct experience with gunmen such as the individual in our case; the other was a University of Iowa graduate and thus familiar with the setting and circumstances surrounding another violent incident there in 1992. These experiences obviously affected our assessment of this case by drawing our attention to the campus response in the first plan and to psychological reactions like fear and denial. At the time of this writing, campus discussions have been held about adapting the in-place campus emergency preparedness plan to a critical incident management team concept. Counselors have met to discuss coordinating the activities of different units in the event of another incident, and the police are working with faculty members and department staff to help identify potentially violence-prone students. We have the impression that, as a result of this case study, campus personnel see the interrelatedness and the large number of units that may be involved in a single incident. The anniversary date passed without incident or acknowledgment in the campus newspaper. As for the gunman, he is still incarcerated awaiting trial, and we wonder, as do some of the students he threatened, if he will seek retribution against us for writing up this case if he is released. The campus response to the October incident continues.

References

1. Asmussen, K. J. "Weapon Possession in Public High Schools." *School Safety* (Fall 1992), 28–30.

2. Bird, G. W., S. M. Stith, and J. Schladale. "Psychological Resources, Coping Strategies, and Negotiation Styles as Discriminators of Violence in Dating Relationships." *Family Relations*, 40 (1991), 45–50.

3. Bogal-Allbritten, R., and W. Allbritten. "Courtship Violence on Campus: A Nationwide Survey of Student Affairs Professionals." *NASPA Journal,* 28 (1991), 312–18.

4. Boothe, J. W., T. M. Flick, S. P. Kirk, L. H. Bradley, and K. E. Keough. "The Violence at Your Door." *Executive Educator* (February 1993), 16–22.

5. Bromet, E. J. "Methodological Issues in the Assessment of Traumatic Events." *Journal of Applied Psychology,* 20 (1990), 1719–24.

6. Bushweller, K. "Guards with Guns." *American School Board Journal* (January 1993), 34–36.

7. Copenhaver, S., and E. Grauerholz. "Sexual Victimization among Sorority Women." *Sex Roles: A Journal of Research,* 24 (1991), 31–41.

8. Follingstad, D., S. Wright, S. Lloyd, and J. Sebastian. "Sex Differences in Motivations and Effects in Dating Violence." *Family Relations,* 40 (1991), 51–57.

9. Gordon, M. T., and S. Riger. *The Female Fear.* Urbana: University of Illinois Press, 1991.

10. Guba, E., and Y. Lincoln. "Do Inquiry Paradigms Imply Inquiry Methodologies?" In *Qualitative Approaches to Evaluation in Education,* edited by D. M. Fetterman. New York: Praeger, 1988.

11. Johnson, K. "The Tip of the Iceberg." *School Safety* (Fall 1992), 24–26.

12. Jones, D. J. "The College Campus as a Microcosm of U.S. Society: The Issue of Racially Motivated Violence." *Urban League Review,* 13 (1990), 129–39.

13. Legislative Update. "Campuses Must Tell Crime Rates." *School Safety* (Winter 1991), 31.

14. Long, N. J. "Managing a Shooting Incident." *Journal of Emotional and Behavioral Problems,* 1 (1992), 23–26.

15. Lowe, J. A. "What We Learned: Some Generalizations in Dealing with a Traumatic Event at Cokeville." Paper presented at the Annual Meeting of the National School Boards Association, San Francisco, 4–7 April 1987.

16. Mann, J. *Los Angeles Times Magazine,* 2 June 1992, pp. 26–27, 32, 46–47.

17. Merriam, S. B. Case Study Research in Education: A Qualitative Approach. San Francisco: Jossey-Bass, 1988.

18. Miles, M. B., and A. M. Huberman. *Qualitative Data Analysis: A Sourcebook of New Methods.* Beverly Hills, Calif.: Sage, 1984.

19. Mitchell, J. "When Disaster Strikes." *Journal of Emergency Medical Services* (January 1983), 36–39.

20. NSSC Report on School Safety. "Preparing Schools for Terroristic Attacks." *School Safety* (Winter 1991), 18–19.

21. Poland, S., and G. Pitcher. *Crisis Intervention in the Schools.* New York: Guilford, 1992.

22. Quimet, M. "The Polytechnique Incident and Imitative Violence against Women." *SSR,* 76 (1992), 45–47.

23. Roark, M. L. "Helping High School Students Assess Campus Safety." *The School Counselor,* 39 (1992), 251–56.

24. ——. "Preventing Violence on College Campuses." *Journal of Counseling and Development,* 65 (1987), 367–70.

25. Roark, M. L., and E. W. Roark. "Administrative Responses to Campus Violence." Paper presented at the annual meeting of the American College Personnel Association/National Association of Student Personnel Administrators, Chicago, 15–18 March 1987.

26. "School Crisis: Under Control," 1991 [video]. National School Safety Center, a partnership of Pepperdine University and the United States Departments of Justice and Education.

27. Sherill, J. M., and D. G. Seigel (eds.). *Responding to Violence on Campus.* New Directions for Student Services, No. 47. San Francisco: Jossey-Bass, 1989.

28. Van Maanen, J. *Tales of the Field.* Chicago: University of Chicago Press, 1988.

29. Walker, G. "Crisis-Care in Critical Incident Debriefing." *Death Studies,* 14 (1990), 121–33.

30. Weick, K. E. "Educational Organizations as Loosely Coupled Systems." *Administrative Science Quarterly,* 21 (1976), 1–19.

31. Yin, R. K. *Case Study Research, Design and Methods.* Newbury Park, Calif.: Sage, 1989.

32. Zelikoff, W. I., and I. A. Hyman. "Psychological Trauma in the Schools: A Retrospective Study." Paper presented at the annual meeting of the National Association of School Psychologists, New Orleans, La., 4–8 March 1987.

A Case Study

This qualitative case study (Asmussen & Creswell, 1995) presented a campus reaction to a gunman incident in which a student attempted to fire a gun at his classmates. The authors based the composition of this case study on the "substantive case report" format of Lincoln and Guba (1985) and Stake (1995). These formats called for an explication of the problem; a thorough description of the context or setting and the processes observed; a discussion of important themes; and, finally, "lessons to be learned" (Lincoln & Guba, 1985, p. 362). After introducing the case study with the problem of violence on college campuses, the authors turned to a detailed description of the setting and a chronology of events immediately following the incident and events during the following 2 weeks. Then they presented the important themes related to denial, fear, safety, retriggering, and campus planning. In a process of layering of themes, the authors combined the more specific themes into two overarching themes: an organizational theme and a psychological or social–psychological theme. Asmussen and Creswell (1995) gathered data through interviews with participants, observations, documents, and audiovisual materials. From the case emerges a proposed plan for campuses, and the case ends with an implied lesson for the specific Midwestern campus and a specific set of questions this campus or other campuses might use to design a plan for handling future campus terrorist incidents.

Turning to specific research questions in this case, the authors asked the following questions: What happened? Who was involved in response to the incident? What themes of response emerged during an 8-month period? What theoretical constructs helped us understand the campus response, and what constructs developed that were unique to this case? Asmussen and Creswell (1995) entered the field 2 days after the incident and did not use any a priori theoretical lens to guide our questions or the results.

The narrative first described the incident, analyzed it through levels of abstraction, and provided some interpretation by relating the context to larger theoretical frameworks. The authors validated the case analysis by using multiple data sources for the themes and by checking the final account with select participants, or member checking.

A Narrative Study

How might we have approached this same general problem as an interpretive biographical study with a narrative approach? Rather than identifying responses from multiple campus constituents, we would have focused on one individual, such as the instructor of the class involved in the incident. We would have tentatively titled the project, "Confrontation of Brothers: An Interpretive Biography of an African American Professor." This instructor, like the gunman, was African American, and his response to such an incident might be situated within racial and cultural contexts. Hence, as an interpretive biographer, we might have asked the following research question: What are the life experiences of the African American instructor of the class, and how do these experiences form and shape his reaction to the incident? This biographical approach would have relied on studying a single individual and situating this individual within his historic background. We would have examined *life events* or "epiphanies" culled from stories he told me. Our approach would have been to "restory the stories" into an account of his experiences of the gunman that followed a chronology of events. We might have relied on the Clandinin and Connelly (2000) and Clandinin (2013) three-dimensional space model to organize the story into the personal, social, and interactional components. Alternatively, the story might have had a plot to tie it together, such as the theoretical perspective. This plot might have spoken to the issues of race, discrimination, and marginality and how these issues played out both within the African American culture and between Black culture and other cultures. These perspectives may have shaped how the instructor viewed the student gunman in the class. We also might have composed this report by discussing our own situated beliefs followed by those of the instructor and the changes he brought about as a result of his experiences. For instance, did he continue teaching? Did he talk with the class about his feelings? Did he see the situation as a confrontation within his racial group? For validation, our narrative story about this instructor would have contained a detailed description of the context to reveal the historical and interactional features of the experience (Denzin, 2001). We also would have acknowledged that any interpretation of the instructor's reaction would be incomplete, unfinished, and a rendering from our own perspectives as a non–African American and a non–African Canadian.

A Phenomenology

Rather than study a single individual as in a biography, we would have studied several individual students and examined a psychological concept in the tradition of psychological phenomenology (Moustakas, 1994). Our working title might have been "The

Meaning of Fear for Students Caught in a Near Tragedy on Campus." Our assumption would have been that students expressed this concept of fear during the incident, immediately after it, and several weeks later. We might have posed the following questions: What fear did the students experience, and how did they experience it? What meanings did they ascribe to this experience? As a phenomenologist, we assume that human experience makes sense to those who live it and that human experience can be consciously expressed (Dukes, 1984). Thus, we would bring to the study a phenomenon to explore (fear) and a philosophical orientation to use (we want to study the meaning of the students' experiences). We would have engaged in extensive interviews with up to 10 students, and we would have analyzed the interviews using the steps described by Moustakas (1994). We would have begun with a description of our own fears and experiences (*epoche*) with it as a means to position ourselves, recognizing that we could not completely remove ourselves from the situation. Then, after reading through all of the students' statements, we would have located significant statements or quotes about their meanings of fear. These significant statements would then be clustered into broader themes. Our final step would have been to write a long paragraph providing a narrative description of what they experienced (*textural description*) and how they experienced it (*structural description*) and combine these two descriptions into a longer description that conveys the *essence* of their experiences. This would be the endpoint for the discussion.

A Grounded Theory Study

If a theory needed to be developed (or modified) to explain the campus reaction to this incident, we would have used a grounded theory approach. For example, we might have developed a theory around a process—the "surreal" experiences of several students immediately following the incident, experiences resulting in actions and reactions by students. The draft title of our study might have been "A Grounded Theory Explanation of the Surreal Experiences for Students in a Campus Gunman Incident." We might have introduced the study with a specific quote about the surreal experiences:

> In the debriefing by counselors, one female student commented, "I thought the gunman would shoot out a little flag that would say 'bang.'" For her, the event was like a dream.

Our research questions might have been as follows: What theory explains the phenomenon of the "surreal" experiences of the students immediately following the incident? What were these experiences? What caused them? What strategies did the students use to cope with them? What were the consequences of their strategies? What specific interaction issues and larger conditions influenced their strategies? Consistent with a structured approach to grounded theory, we would not bring into the data collection and analysis a specific theoretical orientation other than to see how the students interact and respond to the incident. Instead, our intent would be to develop or generate a theory. In the results section of this study, I would have first identified the open coding categories that I found. Then, I would have described how we narrowed the study to a central category (e.g., the dream element of the process) and made that category the major feature of a theory of the process. This theory would have been presented as a *visual model,* and in the model we would have included *causal conditions* that influenced the central category, intervening and context factors surrounding it, and specific strategies and consequences (axial coding) as a result of it occurring. We would have advanced *theoretical propositions* or hypotheses that explained the dream element of the surreal experiences of the students (selective coding). We would have validated our account by judging the thoroughness of the research process and whether the findings are empirically grounded, two factors mentioned by Corbin and Strauss (1990, 2015).

An Ethnography

In grounded theory, our focus was on generating a theory grounded in the data. In ethnography, we would turn the focus away from theory development to a description and understanding of the workings of the campus community as a *culture-sharing group.* To keep the study manageable, we might have begun by looking at how the incident, although unpredictable, triggered quite predictable responses among members of the campus community. These community members might have responded according to their roles, and thus we could have looked at some recognized campus microcultures. Students constituted one such microculture, and they, in turn, comprised a number of further microcultures or subcultures. Because the students in this class were together for 16 weeks during the semester, they had enough time to develop some shared patterns of behavior and could have been seen as a culture-sharing group. Alternatively, we might have studied the entire campus community, comprising a constellation of groups each reacting differently.

Assuming that the entire campus comprised the culture-sharing group, the title of the study might have been "Getting Back to Normal: An Ethnography of a Campus Response to a Gunman Incident." Notice how this title immediately invites a contrary perspective into the study. We would have asked the following questions: How did this incident produce predictable role performance within affected groups? Using the entire campus as a cultural system or culture-sharing group, in what roles did the individuals and groups participate? One possibility would be that they wanted to get the campus back to normal after the incident by engaging in predictable patterns of behavior. Although no one anticipated the exact moment or nature of the incident itself, its occurrence set in motion rather predictable role performances throughout the campus community. Administrators did not close the campus and start warning, "The sky is falling." Campus police did not offer counseling sessions, although the Counseling Center did. However, the Counseling Center served the student population, not others (who were marginalized), such as the police or groundskeepers, who also felt unsafe on the campus. In short, predictable performances by campus constituencies followed in the wake of this incident.

Indeed, campus administrators routinely held a news conference following the incident. Also, predictably, police carried out their investigation, and students ultimately and reluctantly contacted their parents. The campus slowly returned to normal—an attempt to return to day-to-day business, to a steady state, or to homeostasis, as the systems thinkers say. In these predictable role behaviors, one saw culture at work.

As we entered the field, we would seek to build rapport with the community participants, to not further marginalize them or disturb the environment more than necessary through our presence. It was a sensitive time on campus with people who had nerves on edge. We would have explored the cultural themes of the "organization of diversity" and "maintenance" activities of individuals and groups within the culture-sharing campus. Wallace (1970) defines the "organization of diversity" as "the actual diversity of habits, of motives, of personalities, of customs that do, in fact, coexist within the boundaries of any culturally organized society" (p. 23). Our data collection would have consisted of observations over time of predictable activities, behaviors, and roles in which people engaged that helped the campus return to normal. This data collection would depend heavily on interviews and observations of the classroom where the incident occurred and newspaper accounts. Our ultimate narrative of the culture-sharing campus would be consistent with Wolcott's (1994) three parts: a detailed description of the campus, an analysis of the cultural themes of "organizational diversity" and maintenance (possibly with taxonomies or comparisons; Spradley, 1979, 1980), and interpretation. Our interpretation would be couched not in terms of a dispassionate, objective report of the facts, but rather within our own experiences of not feeling safe in a soup kitchen for the homeless (Miller, Creswell, & Olander, 1998) and our own personal life experiences of having grown up in "safe" small Midwestern towns. For an ending to the study, we might have used the "canoe into the sunset" approach (H. F. Wolcott, personal communication, November 15, 1996) or the more methodologically oriented ending of checking our account with participants. Here is the canoe into the sunset approach:

> The newsworthiness of the event will be long past before the ethnographic study is ready, but the event itself is of rather little consequence if the ethnographer's focus is on campus culture. Still, without such an event, the ethnographer working in his or her own society (and perhaps on his or her own campus as well) might have a difficult time "seeing" people performing in predictable everyday ways simply because that is the way in which we expect them to act. The ethnographer working "at home" has to find ways in which to make the familiar seem strange. An upsetting event can make ordinary role behavior easier to discern as people respond in predictable ways to unpredictable circumstances. Those predictable patterns are the stuff of culture.

Here is the more methodological ending:

Some of our "facts" or hypotheses may need (and be amenable to) checking or testing if we have carried our analysis in that direction. If we have tried to be more interpretive, then perhaps we can "try out" the account on some of the people described, and the cautions and exceptions they express can be included in our final account to suggest that things are even more complex than the way we have presented them.

Conclusion

How have we answered our "compelling" question raised at the outset of this book at the qualitative workshop at Vail, Colorado: How does the approach to inquiry shape the design of a study? First, one of the most pronounced ways is in the focus of the study. As discussed in Chapter 4, a theory differs from the exploration of a phenomenon or concept, from an in-depth case, and from the creation of an individual or group portrait. Please examine again Table 4.1 that establishes differences among the five approaches, especially in terms of foci.

However, this is not as clear-cut as it appears. A single case study of an individual can be approached either as a narrative study or as a case study. A cultural system may be explored as an ethnography, whereas a smaller "bounded" system, such as an event, a program, or an activity, may be studied as a case study. Both are systems, and the problem arises when one undertakes a microethnography, which might be approached either as a case study or as an ethnography. However, when one seeks to study cultural behavior, language, or artifacts, then the study of a system might be undertaken as an ethnography.

Second, an interpretive orientation flows throughout qualitative research. We cannot step aside and be "objective" about what we see and write. Our words flow from our own personal experiences, culture, history, and backgrounds. When we go to the field to collect data, we need to approach the task with care for the participants and sites and to be reflexive about our role and how it shapes what we see, hear, and write. Ultimately, our writing is an interpretation by us of events, people, and activities, and it is only our interpretation. We must recognize that participants in the field, readers, and other individuals reading our accounts will have their own interpretations. Within this perspective, our writing can only be seen as a discourse, one with tentative conclusions, and one that will be constantly changing and evolving. Qualitative research truly has an interpretation element that flows throughout the process of research.

Third, the approach to inquiry shapes the language of the research design procedures in a study, especially the terms used in the introduction to a study, the data collection, and the analysis phases of design. We incorporated these terms into Chapter 6 as we discussed the wording of purpose statements and research questions for different approaches to qualitative research. Our theme continued on in Chapter 9 as we talked about encoding the text within an approach to research. The glossary in Appendix A also reinforces this theme as it presents a useful list of terms within each tradition that researchers might incorporate into the language of their studies.

Fourth, the approach to research includes the participants who are studied, as discussed in Chapter 7. A study may consist of one or two individuals (i.e., narrative study), groups of people (i.e., phenomenology, grounded theory), or an entire culture (i.e., ethnography). A case study might fit into all three of these categories as one explores a single individual, an event, or a large social setting. Also in Chapter 7, we highlighted how the approaches vary in the extent of data collection, from the use of mainly single sources of information (i.e., narrative interviews, grounded theory interviews, phenomenological interviews) to those that involve multiple sources of information (i.e., ethnographies consisting of observations, interviews, and documents; case studies incorporating interviews, observations, documents, archival material, and video). Although these forms of data collection are not fixed, we see a general pattern that differentiates the approaches.

Fifth, the distinctions among the approaches are most pronounced in the data analysis phase, as discussed in Chapter 8. Data analysis ranges from unstructured to structured approaches. Among the less structured approaches, I include ethnographies (with the exception of Spradley, 1979, 1980) and narratives (e.g., as suggested by Clandinin & Connelly, 2000, and interpretive forms advanced by Denzin, 1989). The more structured approaches consist of grounded theory with a systematic procedure and phenomenology (see Colaizzi's 1978 approach and those of Dukes, 1984, and Moustakas, 1994) and case studies (Stake, 1995; Yin, 2014). These procedures provide direction for the overall structure of the data analysis in the qualitative report. Also, the approach shapes the amount of relative weight given to description in the analysis of the data. In ethnographies, case studies, and biographies, researchers employ substantial description; in phenomenologies, investigators use less description; and in grounded theory, researchers seem not to use it at all, choosing to move directly into analysis of the data.

Sixth, the approach to inquiry shapes the final written product as well as the embedded rhetorical structures used in the narrative. This explains why qualitative studies look so different and are composed so differently, as discussed in Chapter 9. Take, for example, the presence of the researcher. Although reflexivity flows into all qualitative projects, the presence of the researcher is found little in the more "objective" accounts provided in grounded theory. Alternatively, the researcher is center stage in ethnographies and possibly in case studies where "interpretation" plays a major role.

Seventh, the criteria for assessing the quality of a study differ among the approaches, as discussed in Chapter 10. Although some overlap exists in the procedures for validation, the criteria for assessing the worth of a study are available for each tradition.

In summary, when designing a qualitative study, we recommend that the author design the study within one of the approaches of qualitative inquiry. This means that components of the design process (e.g., interpretive framework, research purpose and questions, data collection, data analysis, report writing, validation) will reflect the procedures of the selected approach and will be composed with the encoding and features of that approach. This is not to rigidly suggest that one cannot mix approaches and employ—for example, a grounded theory analysis procedure within a case study design. "Purity" is not our aim. But in this book, we suggest that the reader sort out the approaches first before combining them and see each one as a rigorous procedure in its own right.

We find distinctions as well as overlap among the five approaches, but designing a study attuned to procedures found within one of the approaches suggested in this book will enhance the sophistication of the project and convey a level of methodological expertise for readers of qualitative research.

Chapter Check-In

1. Can you "take" a qualitative study that has been written and turn the story into one of the other approaches of qualitative inquiry?

2. Can you identify, define, and describe each part that is labeled in italics within each of the five scenarios of campus response to a gunman incident presented in this chapter?

   a. Take each scenario and define and describe each part that is labeled in italics.

   b. Check the glossary in Appendix A as needed for help in providing a definition.

• Appendices •

• Appendix A •

An Annotated Glossary of Terms

The definitions in this glossary represent key terms as they are used and defined in this book. Many definitions exist for these terms, but the most workable definitions for us (and we hope for the reader) are those that reflect the content and references presented in this book. We group the terms by approach to inquiry (narrative research, phenomenology, grounded theory, ethnography, case study) and alphabetize them within the approach, and at the end of the glossary, we define additional general qualitative terms that cross all of the five different approaches. In addition to the terms defined in this glossary, see also Given (2008) and Schwandt (2007).

Narrative Research

autobiography This form of biographical writing is the narrative account of a person's life that he or she has personally written or otherwise recorded (Angrosino, 1989a).

autoethnography This form of narrative is written and recorded by the individuals who are the subject of the study (Ellis, 2004; Muncey, 2010). Muncey (2010) defines *autoethnography* as the idea of multiple layers of consciousness, the vulnerable self, the coherent self, critiquing the self in social contexts, the subversion of dominant discourses, and the evocative potential.

biographical study This is the study of a single individual and his or her experiences as told to the researcher or as found in documents and archival materials (Denzin, 1989). We use the term to connote the broad genre of narrative writings that includes individual biographies, autobiographies, life histories, and oral histories.

chronology This is a common approach for undertaking a narrative form of writing in which the author presents the life in stages or steps according to the age of the individual (Clandinin & Connelly, 2000; Denzin, 1989).

epiphanies These are special events in an individual's life that represent turning points. They vary in their impact from minor to major epiphanies, and they may be positive or negative (Denzin, 1989).

historical contexts These are the contexts in which the researcher presents the life of the participant. The context may be the participant's family, society, or the historical, social, or political trends of the participant's times (Denzin, 1989).

life course stages These are stages in an individual's life or key events that become the focus for the biographer (Denzin, 1989).

life history This is a form of biographical writing in which the researcher reports an extensive record of a person's life as told to the researcher (see Geiger, 1986). Thus, the individual being studied is alive, and life as lived in the present is influenced by personal, institutional, and social histories. The investigator may use different disciplinary perspectives (Smith, 1994), such as the exploration of an individual's life as representative of a culture, as in an anthropological life history.

narrative research This is an approach to qualitative research that is both a product and a method. It is a study of stories or narrative or descriptions of a series of events that accounts for human experiences (Pinnegar & Daynes, 2007).

oral history In this biographical approach, the researcher gathers personal recollections of events and their causes and effects from an individual or several individuals. This information may be collected through tape recordings or through written works of individuals who have died or are still living. It often is limited to the distinctly "modern" sphere and to accessible people (Plummer, 1983).

progressive-regressive method This is an approach to writing a narrative in which the researcher begins with a key event in the participant's life and then works forward and backward from that event (Denzin, 1989).

restorying This is an approach in narrative data analysis in which the researchers retell the stories of individual experiences, and the new story typically has a beginning, a middle, and an ending (Ollerenshaw & Creswell, 2002).

single individual This is the person studied in a narrative research. This person may be an individual with great distinction or an ordinary person. This person's life may be a lesser life, a great life, a thwarted life, a life cut short, or a life miraculous in its unapplauded achievement (Heilbrun, 1988).

stories These are aspects that surface during an interview in which the participant describes a situation, usually with a beginning, a middle, and an end, so that the researcher can capture a complete idea and integrate it, intact, into the qualitative narrative (Clandinin & Connelly, 2000; Czarniawska, 2004; Denzin, 1989; Riessman, 2008).

Phenomenology

clusters of meaning This is the third step in phenomenological data analysis, in which the researcher clusters the statements into themes or meaning units, removing overlapping and repetitive statements (Moustakas, 1994).

epoche, or bracketing This is the first step in "phenomenological reduction," the process of data analysis in which the researcher sets aside, as far as is humanly possible, all preconceived experiences to best understand the experiences of participants in the study (Moustakas, 1994).

essential, invariant structure (or essence) This is the goal of the phenomenologist, to reduce the textural (*what*) and structural (*how*) meanings of experiences to a brief description that typifies the experiences of all of the participants in a study. All individuals experience it; hence, it is invariant, and it is a reduction to the "essentials" of the experiences (Moustakas, 1994, van Manen, 2014).

hermeneutical phenomenology A form of phenomenology in which research is oriented toward interpreting the "texts" of life (hermeneutical) and lived experiences (van Manen, 1990).

horizonalization This is the second step in the phenomenological data analysis, in which the researcher lists every significant statement relevant to the topic and gives it equal value (Moustakas, 1994).

intentionality of consciousness Being conscious of objects always is intentional. Thus, when perceiving a tree, "my intentional experience is a combination of the outward appearance of the tree and the tree as contained in my consciousness based on memory, image, and meaning" (Moustakas, 1994, p. 55).

lived experiences This term is used in phenomenological studies to emphasize the importance of individual experiences of people as conscious human beings (Moustakakas: Giorgi (2009) Moustakas, 1994).

phenomenology of practice describes the "development and articulation of meaning-giving methods of phenomenology" which are based on what van Manen (2014) considers to be the practical examples from the primary literature of phenomenology.

phenomenological data analysis Several approaches to analyzing phenomenological data are represented in the literature. Moustakas (1994) reviews these approaches and then advances his own. We rely on the Moustakas modification that includes the researcher bringing personal experiences into the study, the recording of significant statements and meaning units, and the development of descriptions to arrive at the essence of the experiences. Giorgi (2009) advances a rigorous yet more open approach in his book.

phenomenological study This type of study describes the common meaning of experiences of a phenomenon (or topic or concept) for several individuals. In this type of qualitative study, the researcher reduces the experiences to a central meaning or the "essence" of the experience.

phenomenon This is the central concept being examined by the phenomenologist. It is the concept being experienced by subjects in a study, which may include psychological concepts such as grief, anger, or love.

philosophical perspectives Specific philosophical perspectives provide the foundation for phenomenological studies. They originated in the 1930s writings of Husserl. These perspectives include the investigator's conducting research with a broader perspective than that of traditional empirical, quantitative science; suspending his or her own preconceptions of experiences; experiencing an object through his or her own senses (i.e., being conscious of an object) as well as seeing it "out there" as real; and reporting the meaning individuals ascribe to an experience in a few statements that capture the "essence" (Stewart & Mickunas, 1990).

phenomenological reflection According to van Manen (2014), this involves two processes of bracketing (withdrawal) and reduction (constitution of meaning)

structural description From the first three steps in phenomenological data analysis, the researcher writes a description of "how" the phenomenon was experienced by individuals in the study (Moustakas, 1994). The researcher writes a "structural" description of an experience, addressing *how* the phenomenon was experienced. It involves seeking all possible meanings, looking for divergent perspectives, and varying the frames of reference about the phenomenon or using imaginative variation (Moustakas, 1994).

textural description From the first three steps in phenomenological data analysis, the researcher writes about *what* was experienced, a description of the meaning individuals have experienced (Moustakas, 1994).

transcendental phenomenology According to Moustakas (1994), Husserl espoused transcendental phenomenology, and it later became a guiding concept for Moustakas as well. In this approach, the researcher sets aside prejudgments regarding the phenomenon being investigated. Also, the researcher relies on intuition, imagination, and universal structures to obtain a picture of the experience, and the inquirer uses systematic methods of analysis as advanced by Moustakas (1994).

Grounded Theory

axial coding This step in the coding process follows open coding. The researcher takes the categories of open coding, identifies one as a central phenomenon, and then returns to the database to identify (a) what caused this phenomenon to occur, (b) what strategies or actions actors employed in response to it, (c) what context (specific context) and intervening conditions (broad context) influenced the strategies, and (d) what consequences resulted from these strategies. The overall process is one of relating categories of information to the central phenomenon category (Strauss & Corbin, 1990, 1998).

category This is a unit of information analyzed in grounded theory research. It comprises events, happenings, and instances of phenomenon (Strauss & Corbin, 1990) and given a short label. When researchers analyze grounded theory data, their analysis leads, initially, to the formation of a number of categories during the process called open coding. Then, in axial coding, the analyst interrelates the categories and forms a visual model.

causal conditions In axial coding, these are the categories of conditions I identify in my database that cause or influence the central phenomenon to occur.

central phenomenon This is an aspect of axial coding and the formation of the visual theory, model, or paradigm. In open coding, the researcher chooses a central category around which to develop the theory by examining his or her open coding categories and selecting one that holds the most conceptual interest, is most frequently discussed by participants in the study, and is most "saturated" with information. The researcher then places it at the center of his or her grounded theory model and labels it *central phenomenon.*

coding paradigm or logic diagram In axial coding, the central phenomenon, causal conditions, context, intervening conditions, strategies, and consequences are portrayed in a visual diagram. This diagram is drawn with boxes and arrows indicating the process or flow of activities. It is helpful to view this diagram as more than axial coding; it is the theoretical model developed in a grounded theory study (see Harley et al., 2009).

conditional or consequential matrix This is a diagram, typically drawn late in a grounded theory study, that presents the conditions and consequences related to the phenomenon under study. It enables the researcher to both distinguish and link levels of conditions and consequences specified in the axial coding model (Strauss & Corbin, 1990). It is a step seldom seen in data analysis in grounded theory studies.

consequences In axial coding, these are the outcomes of strategies taken by participants in the study. These outcomes may be positive, negative, or neutral (Strauss & Corbin, 1990).

constant comparative This was an early term (Conrad, 1978) in grounded theory research that referred to the researcher identifying incidents, events, and activities and constantly comparing them to an emerging category to develop and saturate the category.

constructivist grounded theory This is a form of grounded theory squarely in the interpretive tradition of qualitative research. As such, it is less structured than traditional approaches to grounded theory. The constructivist approach incorporates the researcher's views; uncovers experiences with embedded, hidden networks, situations, and relationships; and makes visible hierarchies of power, communication, and opportunity (Charmaz, 2006).

context In axial coding, this is the particular set of conditions within which the strategies occur (Strauss & Corbin, 1990). These are specific in nature and close to the actions and interactions.

dimensionalized This is the smallest unit of information analyzed in grounded theory research. The researcher takes the properties and places them on a continuum or dimensionalizes them to see the extreme possibilities for the property. The dimensionalized information appears in the "open coding" analysis (Strauss & Corbin, 1990).

discriminant sampling This is a form of sampling that occurs late in a grounded theory project after the researcher has developed a model. The question becomes this: How would the model hold if we gathered more information from people similar to those I initially interviewed? Thus, to verify the model, the researcher chooses sites, persons, and/or documents that "will maximize opportunities for verifying the story line, relationships between categories, and for filling in poorly developed categories" (Strauss & Corbin, 1990, p. 187).

generate or discover a theory Grounded theory research is the process of developing a theory, not testing a theory. Researchers might begin with a tentative theory they want to modify or no theory at all with the intent of "grounding" the study in views of participants. In either case, an inductive model of theory development is at work here, and the process is one of generating or discovering a theory grounded in views from participants in the field.

grounded theory study In this type of study, the researcher generates an abstract analytical schema of a phenomenon, a theory that explains some action, interaction, or process. This is accomplished primarily through collecting interview data, making multiple visits to the field (theoretical sampling), attempting to develop and interrelate categories (constant comparison) of information, and writing a substantive or context-specific theory (Strauss & Corbin, 1990).

in vivo codes In grounded theory research, the investigator uses the exact words of the interviewee to form the names for these codes or categories. The names are catchy and immediately draw the attention of the reader (Strauss & Corbin, 1990, p. 69).

intervening conditions In axial coding, these are the broader conditions—broader than the context—within which the strategies occur. They might be social, economic, and political forces that influence the strategies in response to the central phenomenon (Strauss & Corbin, 1990).

memoing This is the process in grounded theory research of the researcher writing down ideas about the evolving theory. The writing could be in the form of preliminary propositions (hypotheses), ideas about emerging categories, or some aspects of the connection of categories as in axial coding. In general, these are written records of analysis that help with the formulation of theory (Strauss & Corbin, 1990).

open coding This is the first step in the data analysis process for a grounded theorist. It involves taking data (e.g., interview transcriptions) and segmenting them into categories of information (Strauss & Corbin, 1990). I recommend that researchers try to develop a small number of categories, slowly reducing the number to approximately 30 codes that are then combined into major themes in the study.

properties These are other units of information analyzed in grounded theory research. Each category in grounded theory research can be subdivided into properties that provide the broad dimensions for the category. Strauss and Corbin (1990) refer to them as "attributes or characteristics pertaining to a category" (p. 61). They appear in open coding analysis.

propositions These are hypotheses, typically written in a directional form, that relate categories in a study. They are written from the axial coding model or paradigm and might, for example, suggest why a certain cause influences the central phenomenon that, in turn, influences the use of a specific strategy.

saturate, saturated, or saturation In the development of categories and data analysis phase of grounded theory research, researchers seek to find as many incidents, events, or activities as possible to provide support for the categories. In this process, they come to a point at which the categories are saturated, and the inquirer no longer finds new information that adds to an understanding of the category.

selective coding This is the final phase of coding the information. The researcher takes the central phenomenon and systematically relates it to other categories, validating the relationships and filling in categories that need further refinement and development (Strauss & Corbin, 1990). I like to develop a "story" that narrates these categories and shows their interrelationship (see Creswell & Brown, 1992).

strategies In axial coding, these are the specific actions or interactions that occur as a result of the central phenomenon (Strauss & Corbin, 1990).

substantive-level theory This is a low-level theory that is applicable to immediate situations. This theory evolves from the study of a phenomenon situated in "one particular situational context" (Strauss & Corbin, 1990, p. 174). Researchers differentiate this form of theory from theories of greater abstraction and applicability, called midlevel theories, grand theories, or formal theories.

theoretical sampling In data collection for grounded theory research, the investigator selects a sample of individuals to study based on their contribution to the development of the theory. Often, this process begins with a homogeneous sample of individuals who are similar, and as the data collection proceeds and the categories emerge, the researcher turns to a heterogeneous sample to see under what sample conditions the categories hold true.

Ethnography

analysis of the culture-sharing group In this step in ethnography, the ethnographer develops themes—cultural themes—in the data analysis. It is a process of reviewing all of the data and segmenting them into a small set of common themes, well supported by evidence in the data (Wolcott, 1994).

artifacts This is the focus of attention for the ethnographer as he or she determines what people make and use, such as clothes and tools (cultural artifacts; Spradley, 1980).

behaviors These are the focus of attention for the ethnographer as he or she attempts to understand what people do (cultural behavior; Spradley, 1980).

complete observer The researcher is neither seen nor noticed by the people under study.

complete participant The researcher is fully engaged with the people he or she is observing. This may help him or her establish greater rapport with the people being observed (Angrosino, 2007).

critical ethnography This type of ethnography examines cultural systems of power, prestige, privilege, and authority in society. Critical ethnographers study marginalized groups from different classes, races, and genders, with an aim of advocating for the needs of these participants (Madison, 2011; Thomas, 1993).

cultural portrait One key component of ethnographic research is composing a holistic view of the culture-sharing group or individual. The final product of an ethnography should be this larger portrait, or overview of the cultural scene, presented in all of its complexity (Spradley, 1979).

culture This term is an abstraction, something that one cannot study directly. From observing and participating in a culture-sharing group, an ethnographer can see "culture at work" and provide a description and interpretation of it (H. F. Wolcott, personal communication, October 10, 1996; Wolcott, 2010). It can be seen in behaviors, language, and artifacts (Spradley, 1980).

culture-sharing group This is the unit of analysis for the ethnographer as he or she attempts to understand and interpret the behavior, language, and artifacts of people. The ethnographer typically focuses on an entire group—one that shares learned, acquired behaviors—to make explicit how the group "works." Some ethnographers will focus on part of the social-cultural system for analysis and engage in a microethnography.

deception This is a field issue that has become less and less of a problem since the ethical standards were published in 1967 by the American Anthropological Association. It relates to the act of the researcher intentionally deceiving the informants to gain information. This deception may involve masking the purpose of the research, withholding important information about the purpose of the study, or gathering information secretively.

description of the culture-sharing group One of the first tasks of an ethnographer is to simply record a description of the culture-sharing group and incidents and activities that illustrate the culture (Wolcott, 1994). For example, a factual account may be rendered, pictures of the setting may be drawn, or events may be chronicled.

emic This term refers to the type of information being reported and written into an ethnography when the researcher reports the views of the participants. When the researcher reports his or her own personal views, the term used is *etic* (Fetterman, 2010).

ethnography This is the study of an intact cultural or social group (or an individual or individuals within the group) based primarily on observations and a prolonged period of time spent by the researcher in the field. The ethnographer listens and records the voices of informants with the intent of generating a cultural portrait (Thomas, 1993; Wolcott, 1987).

etic This term refers to the type of information being reported and written into an ethnography when the researcher reports his or her own personal views. When the researcher reports the views of the participants, the term used is *emic* (Fetterman, 2010).

fieldwork In ethnographic data collection, the researcher conducts data gathering in the "field" by going to the site or sites where the culture-sharing group can be studied. Often, this involves a prolonged period of time with varying degrees of immersion in activities, events, rituals, and settings of the cultural group (Sanjek, 1990).

gatekeeper This is a data collection term and refers to the individual the researcher must visit before entering a group or cultural site. To gain access, the researcher must receive this individual's approval (Hammersley & Atkinson, 1995).

holistic The ethnographer assumes this outlook in research to gain a comprehensive and complete picture of a social group. It might include the group's history, religion, politics, economy, and/or environment. In this way, the researcher places information about the group into a larger perspective or "contextualizes" the study (Fetterman, 2010).

immersed The ethnographic researcher becomes immersed in the field through a prolonged stay, often as long as 1 year. Whether the individual loses perspective and "goes native" is a field issue much discussed in the ethnographic literature.

interpretation of the culture-sharing group The researcher makes an interpretation of the meaning of the culture-sharing group. The researcher interprets this information through the use of literature, personal experiences, or theoretical perspectives (Wolcott, 1994).

key informants (or participants) These are individuals with whom the researcher begins in data collection because they are well informed, are accessible, and can provide leads about other information (Gilchrist, 1992).

language This is the focus of attention for the ethnographer as he or she discerns what people say (speech messages; Spradley, 1980).

nonparticipant or observer as participant The researcher is an outsider of the group under study, watching and taking field notes from a distance. He or she can record data without direct involvement with activity or people.

participant as observer The researcher is participating in the activity at the site. The participant role is more salient than the researcher role. This may help the researcher gain insider views and subjective data. However, it may be distracting for the researcher to record data when he or she is integrated into the activity.

participant observation The ethnographer gathers information in many ways, but the primary approach is to observe the culture-sharing group and become a participant in the cultural setting (Jorgensen, 1989).

realist ethnography A traditional approach to ethnography taken by cultural anthropologists, this approach involves the researcher as an "objective" observer, recording the facts and narrating the study with a dispassionate, omniscient stance (Van Maanen, 1988).

reflexivity This means that the writer is conscious of the biases, values, and experiences that he or she brings to a qualitative research study. Typically, the writer makes this explicit in the text (Hammersley & Atkinson, 1995).

structure This is a theme or concept about the social–cultural system or group that the ethnographer attempts to learn. It refers to the social structure or configuration of the group, such as the kinship or political structure of the social–cultural group. This structure might be illustrated by an organizational chart (Fetterman, 2010).

Case Study

analysis of themes Following description, the researcher analyzes the data for specific themes, aggregating information into large clusters of ideas and providing details that support the themes. Stake (1995) calls this analysis "development of issues" (p. 123).

assertions This is the last step in the analysis, where the researcher makes sense of the data and provides an interpretation of the data couched in terms of personal views or in terms of theories or constructs in the literature.

bounded system The case selected for study has boundaries, often bounded by time and place. It also has interrelated parts that form a whole. Hence, the proper case to be studied is both "bounded" and a "system" (Stake, 1995).

case This is the unit of analysis in a case study. It involves the study of a specific case within a real-life, contemporary context or setting (Yin, 2009). The case might be an event, a process, a program, or several people (Stake, 1995). The case could be the focus of attention (intrinsic case study) or the issue and the case used to illustrate the case (Stake, 1995).

case description This means simply stating the facts about the case as recorded by the investigator. This is the first step in analysis of data in a qualitative case study, and Stake (1995) calls it narrative description (p. 123).

case study research This type of research involves the study of a case within a real-life, contemporary context or setting (Yin, 2009).

case themes These are one aspect of the major findings in a case study. In Stake's (1995) terms, these would be called categorical aggregations, the larger categories derived during case study data analysis and made up of multiple incidents that are aggregated.

collective case study This type of case study consists of multiple cases. It might be either intrinsic or instrumental, but its defining feature is that the researcher examines several cases (e.g., multiple case studies; Stake, 1995).

context of the case In analyzing and describing a case, the researcher sets the case within its setting. This setting may be broadly conceptualized (e.g., large historical, social, political issues) or narrowly conceptualized (e.g., the immediate family, the physical location, the time period in which the study occurred; Stake, 1995).

cross-case analysis This form of analysis applies to a collective case (Stake, 1995; Yin, 2009) in which the researcher examines more than one case. It involves examining themes across cases to discern themes that are common and different to all cases. It is an analysis step that typically follows within-case analysis when the researcher studies multiple cases.

direct interpretation This is an aspect of interpretation in case study research where the researcher looks at a single instance and draws meaning from it without looking for multiple instances of it. It is a process of pulling the data apart and putting them back together in more meaningful ways (Stake, 1995).

embedded analysis In this approach to data analysis, the researcher selects one analytic aspect of the case for presentation (Yin, 2009).

holistic analysis In this approach to data analysis, the researcher examines the entire case (Yin, 2009) and presents description, themes, and interpretations or assertions related to the whole case.

instrumental case study This is a type of case study with the focus on a specific issue rather than on the case itself. The case then becomes a vehicle to better understand the issue (Stake, 1995). We would consider the gunman case study (Asmussen & Creswell, 1995), mentioned in Chapter 11, to be an example of an instrumental case study.

intrinsic case study This is a type of case study with the focus of the study on the case because it holds intrinsic or unusual interest (Stake, 1995).

multisite When sites are selected for the case, they might be at different geographical locations. This type of study is considered to be multisite. Alternatively, the case might be at a single location and considered a within-site study.

multiple sources of information One aspect that characterizes good case study research is the use of many different sources of information to provide "depth" to the case. Yin (2009), for example, recommends that the researcher use as many as six different types of information in his or her case study.

naturalistic generalizations In the interpretation of a case, an investigator undertakes a case study to make the case understandable. This understanding may be what the reader learns from the case or its application to other cases (Stake, 1995).

patterns This is an aspect of data analysis in case study research where the researcher establishes patterns and looks for a correspondence between two or more categories to establish a small number of categories (Stake, 1995).

purposeful sampling This is a major issue in case study research, and the researcher needs to clearly specify the type of sampling strategy in selecting the case (or cases) and a rationale for it. It applies to both the selection of the case to study and the sampling of information used within the case. We use Huberman and Miles' (1994) list of sampling strategies and apply it in this book to case studies as well as to other approaches of inquiry.

within-case analysis This type of analysis may apply to either a single case or multiple collective case studies. In within-case analysis, the researcher analyzes each case for themes. In the study of multiple cases, the researcher may compare the within-case themes across multiple cases in cross-case analysis.

within-site When a site is selected for the case, it might be located at a single geographical location. This is considered a within-site study. Alternatively, the case might be different locations and considered to be multisite.

General Qualitative Terms

aesthetic merit A piece succeeds aesthetically when the use of creative analytical practices opens up the text and invites interpretive responses. The text is artistically shaped, satisfying, complex, and not boring.

approaches to inquiry This is an approach to qualitative research that has a distinguished history in one of the social science disciplines and that has spawned books, journals, and distinct methodologies. These approaches, as I call them, are known in other books as "strategies of inquiry" (Denzin & Lincoln, 1994) or "varieties" (Tesch, 1990). We refer to narrative research, phenomenology, grounded theory, ethnography, and case studies in this book as approaches to inquiry.

audit trail This is document that allows a researcher to retrace the process by which the researcher arrived at their final findings.

axiological This qualitative assumption holds that all research is value laden and includes the value systems of the inquirer, the theory, the paradigm used, and the social and cultural norms for either the inquirer or the respondents (Creswell, 2009; Guba & Lincoln, 1988). Accordingly, the researcher admits and discusses these values in his or her research.

central question A central question in a study is the broad, overarching question being answered in the research study. It is the most general question that could be asked to address the research problem.

codebook Also called a master code list, this document contains the record of the codes and categories for a study for the purpose of guiding consistent application of codes either by an individual researcher or across a research team.

coding This is the process of aggregating the text or visual data into small categories of information, seeking evidence for the code from different databases being used in a study, and then assigning a label to the code.

critical race theory This is an interpretive lens used in qualitative research that focuses attention on race and how racism is deeply embedded within the framework of American society (Parker & Lynn, 2002).

critical theory This is an interpretive lens used in qualitative research in which a researcher examines the study of social institutions and their transformations through interpreting the meanings of social life; the historical problems of domination, alienation, and social struggles; and a critique of society and the envisioning of new possibilities (Fay, 1987; Madison, 2011; Morrow & Brown, 1994).

disability interpretive lens Disability is focused on as a dimension of human difference and not as a defect. As a human difference, its meaning is derived from social construction (i.e., society's response to individuals), and it is simply one dimension of human difference.

encoding This term means that the writer places certain features in his or her writing to help a reader know what to expect. These features not only help the reader but also aid the writer, who can then draw on the habits of thought and specialized knowledge of the reader (Richardson, 1990). Such features might be the overall organization, code words, images, and other "signposts" for the reader. As applied in this book, the features consist of terms and procedures of an approach that become part of the language of all facets of research design (e.g., purpose statement, research subquestions, methods).

epistemological This is another philosophical assumption for the qualitative researcher. It addresses the relationship between the researcher and that being studied as interrelated, not independent. Rather than "distance," as we call it, a "closeness" follows between the researcher and that being researched. This closeness, for example, is manifest through time in the field, collaboration, and the impact that being researched has on the researcher.

feminist research approaches In feminist research methods, the goals are to establish collaborative and nonexploitative relationships, to place the researcher within the study so as to avoid objectification, and to conduct research that is transformative (Olesen, 2011; Stewart, 1994).

foreshadowing This term refers to the technique that writers use to portend the development of ideas (Hammersley & Atkinson, 1995). The wording of the problem statement, purpose statement, and research subquestions foreshadows the methods—the data collection and data analysis—used in the study.

hyperlinks In qualitative analysis software, a hyperlink allows the electronic cross-referencing between two points link passage within the database for easy retrieval.

impact A piece has an impact when it affects the reader emotionally or intellectually; generates new questions; or moves him or her to write, try new research practices, or move to action.

intercoder agreement This term means that researchers check for reliability of their coding. It involves coding agreements when multiple coders assign and check their code segments to establish the reliability of the data analysis process.

interpretation In qualitative research, this term represents a phase in qualitative data analysis involving abstracting out beyond the codes and themes to the larger meaning of the data.

interpretive framework Beliefs or frameworks that guide the actions of the researcher in conducting a study.

interview protocol The interview protocol is a form in qualitative data collection in which the researcher directs the activities of an interview and records information provided by the interviewee. It consists of a header, the major substantive question (typically five to seven research subquestions phrased in a way that interviewees can answer), and closing instructions.

maximum variation sampling This is a popular form of qualitative sampling. This sampling approach consists of determining in advance some criteria that differentiate the sites or participants and then selecting sites or participants that are quite different on the criteria.

methodological congruence This describes the interconnectedness and interrelatedness of a study purpose, questions, and methods that appears cohesive rather than as fragmented parts (Morse & Richards, 2002; Richards & Morse, 2012).

methodology This assumption holds that a qualitative researcher conceptualizes the research process in a certain way. For example, a qualitative inquirer relies on views of participants and discusses their views within the context in which they occur, to inductively develop ideas in a study from particulars to abstractions (Creswell, 1994, 2009).

observational protocol This is a form used in qualitative data collection for guiding and recording observational data. It typically consists of two columns representing descriptive and reflective notes. The researcher records information from the observation on this form.

ontological This is a philosophical assumption about the nature of reality. It addresses this question: When is something real? The answer provided is that something is real in qualitative research when it is constructed in the minds of the actors involved in the situation (Guba & Lincoln, 1988). Thus, reality is not "out there," apart from the minds of actors.

paradigm This is the philosophical stance taken by the researcher that provides a basic set of beliefs that guides action (Denzin & Lincoln, 1994). It defines, for its holder, "the nature of the world, the individual's place in it, and the range of possible relationships to that world" (Denzin & Lincoln, 1994, p. 107). Denzin and Lincoln (1994) further call this the "net that contains the researcher's epistemological, onto-logical, and methodological premises" (p. 13). In this discussion, I extend this "net" to also include the axiological assumptions.

philosophical assumptions These are stances taken by the researcher that provide direction for the study such as the researcher's view of reality (ontology), how the researcher knows reality (epistemology), the value-stance taken by the inquirer (axiol-ogy), and the procedures used in the study (methodology). These assumptions, in turn, are often applied in research through the use of theories (or, as we call them, interpre-tive frameworks).

postmodernism This interpretive perspective is considered a family of theories and perspectives that have something in common (Slife & Williams, 1995). Postmodernists advance a reaction or critique of the 19th-century Enlightenment and early 20th-century emphasis on technology, rationality, reason, universals, science, and the positivist, scientific method (Bloland, 1995; Stringer, 1993). Postmodernists assert that knowledge claims must be set within the conditions of the world today and in the multiple perspectives of class, race, gender, and other group affiliations.

postpositivism This interpretive perspective has the elements of being reductionistic, logical, empirical, cause-and-effect oriented, and deterministic based on a priori theories.

pragmatism This interpretive lens focuses on the outcomes of the research—the actions, situations, and consequences of inquiry—rather than antecedent conditions. There is a concern with applications—"what works"—and solutions to problems. Thus, instead of a focus on methods, the important aspect of research is the problem being studied and the questions asked about this problem.

purpose statement This is a statement typically found in an introduction to a quali-tative study in which the author sets forth the major objective or intent of the study. It can be considered a "road map" to the entire study.

purposeful sampling This is the primary sampling strategy used in qualitative research. It means that the inquirer selects individuals and sites for study because they can purposefully inform an understanding of the research problem and central phe-nomenon in the study.

qualitative research This is an inquiry process of understanding based on a distinct methodological approach to inquiry that explores a social or human problem. The researcher builds a complex, holistic picture; analyzes words; reports detailed views of participants; and conducts the study in a natural setting.

queer theory This is an interpretive lens that may be used in qualitative research that focuses on gay, lesbian, or homosexual identity and how it is culturally and historically constituted, is linked to discourse, and overlaps gender and sexuality (Watson, 2005).

reciprocity This is an aspect of good data collection in which the author gives back to participants by providing rewards for their participation in the study. These rewards may be money or gifts or other forms of remuneration. The idea is that the researcher gives back to participants rather than taking the data from the participant and leaving without offering something in return.

reflexivity An approach in writing qualitative research in which the writer is conscious of the biases, values, and experiences that he or she brings to a qualitative research study. In writing a reflexive passage, the researcher discusses her or his experiences with the central phenomenon and then how these experiences may potentially shape the interpretation that the researcher provides. This passage can be written into a qualitative project in different places in the final report (e.g., methods, vignette, threaded throughout, at the end).

represent the data This is a step in the data analysis process of packaging findings (codes, themes) into text, tabular, or figure form.

research design We use this term to refer to the entire process of research, from conceptualizing a problem to writing the narrative, not simply the methods such as data collection, analysis, and report writing (Bogdan & Taylor, 1975).

research focus We use this term in reference to a general area of study interest such as a study objective or goal. This area of interest typically leads to the researcher narrowing the focus for the need of the study and the specific research problem.

research problem A research problem typically introduces a qualitative study, and in this opening passage, the author advances the issue or concern that leads to a need to conduct the study. We discuss this problem as framed from a real-life perspective or a deficiency in the literature perspective.

rhetorical This assumption means that the qualitative investigator uses terms and a narrative unique to the qualitative approach. The narrative is personal and literary (Creswell, 1994, 2009). For example, the researcher might use the first-person pronoun *I* instead of the impersonal third-person voice.

sample size Sample size in qualitative research generally follows the guidelines to study a few individuals or sites, but to collect extensive detail about the individuals or sites studied.

social constructivism In this interpretive framework, qualitative researchers seek understanding of the world in which they live and work. They develop subjective meanings of their experiences—meanings directed toward certain objects or things. These meanings are varied and multiple, leading the researcher to look for the complexity of views rather than narrow the meanings into a few categories or ideas. The goal of research, then, is to rely as much as possible on the participants' views of the situation. Often these subjective meanings are negotiated socially and historically.

social justice theories These advocacy/participatory theories seek to bring about change or address social justice issues in our societies.

social science theories These are the theoretical explanations that social scientists use to explain the world (Slife & Williams, 1995). They are based on empirical evidence that has accumulated in social science fields such as sociology, psychology, education, economics, urban studies, and communication. As a set of interrelated concepts, variables, and propositions, they serve to explain, predict, and provide generalizations about phenomena in the world (Kerlinger, 1979). They may have broad applicability (as in grand theories) or narrow applications (as in minor working hypotheses; Flinders & Mills, 1993).

subquestions Subquestions are a form of research questions in a qualitative study in which the researcher subdivides the central question into parts and examines these parts. These subquestions are often used in interview and observational protocols as the major topics.

substantive contribution A piece makes a substantive contribution when it contributes to our understanding of social life, demonstrates a deeply grounded social scientific perspective, and seems "true."

themes In qualitative research, themes (also called categories) are broad units of information that consist of several codes aggregated to form a common idea.

theories or theoretical orientations They are found in literature and provide a general explanation as to what the researcher hopes to find in a study or a lens through which to view the needs of participants and communities in a study.

transformative framework Researchers who use this interpretive framework advocate that knowledge is not neutral and it reflects the power and social relationships within society, and thus the purpose of knowledge construction is to aid people to improve society (Mertens, 2003). These individuals include marginalized groups such as lesbians, gays, bisexuals, transgenders, queers, and societies that need a more hopeful, positive psychology and resilience (Mertens, 2009).

triangulation Researchers make use of multiple and different sources, methods, investigators, and theories to provide corroborating evidence for validating the accuracy of their study.

verisimilitude This is a criterion for a good literary study, in which the writing seems "real" and "alive," transporting the reader directly into the world of the study (Richardson, 1994).

• Appendix B •

A Narrative Research Study—"Living in the Space Between Participant and Researcher as a Narrative Inquirer: Examining Ethnic Identity of Chinese Canadian Students as Conflicting Stories to Live By"

Elaine Chan

Abstract

Schooling experiences of lst-generation Canadians interact with cultural experiences in their immigrant households to shape a sense of ethnic identity both as Canadians and as members of an ethnic community. This long-term, school-based narrative inquiry is an examination of ways in which expectations for academic performance and behavior by teachers and peers at school and immigrant parents at home contributed to shaping the ethnic identity of an immigrant Chinese student as conflicting stories to live by. A narrative approach revealed challenges of supporting immigrant students in North American schools, and contributed to understanding of the nuances of multicultural education.

Keywords

narrative inquiry, ethnic identity, curriculum, multicultural education, student experiences

Author's Note: Address correspondence to Elaine Chan, Department of Teaching, Learning, and Teacher Education, College of Education and Human Sciences, University of Nebraska–Lincoln, 24 Henzlik Hall, Lincoln, NE 68588-0355. (E-mail: echan2@unl.edu)

Source: The material in this appendix originally appeared in *The Journal of Educational Research*, 103, 133–122 (2010). Reprinted with permission of Taylor & Francis Ltd, http://www.tandfonline.com

For children, school has enormous implications for their sense of identity as members of society, of their families, and of their ethnic communities. Each individual brings to their school context experiences shaped by their participation in schools, whether in Canada or in their home country, whether positive or negative, enriching or demoralizing. For a child of immigrant parents, tensions between home and school, the interaction of parent and teacher experiences of schooling, and their own experiences of schooling may be felt especially strongly, to the point of being experienced as conflicting stories to live by (Connelly & Clandinin, 1999). These students have their own ideas of how they should be in their school context, shaped by interaction with peers, exposure to popular culture and media, and prior experiences of schooling, schools, and teachers. At the same time, they are evaluated by teachers and supported by parents whose experiences of schooling may be vastly different, by nature of social and political influences as well as personal circumstances of the societies of which their own childhood schools were a part.

In the present study, I examined the experiences of one Chinese immigrant student, Ai Mei Zhang. I explore her participation in her Canadian middle school curriculum as the interaction of student, teacher, and parent narratives, a story of interwoven lives (Clandinin et al., 2006). I examined ways in which her sense of ethnic identity may be shaped by expectations for her academic performance and her behavior in her school and her home. I focus in particular on ways in which participation in her urban, multicultural school setting may contribute to shaping her sense of affiliation to family members and members of her ethnic and school communities, and contribute to her maternal-language development and maintenance. I also examined ways in which she experienced well-intended school practices and curriculum activities designed to support her academic performance in ways not anticipated by policymakers and educators. I explored these influences as conflicting stories to live by (Connelly & Clandinin, 1999).

I examined experientially the intersection of school and home influences from the perspective of one middle school student as a long-term, school-based narrative inquirer. I explored features of narrative inquiry, such as the critical role of researcher–participant relationships, and the role of temporal and spatial factors (Clandinin & Connelly, 2000) of the research context in contributing to a nuanced understanding of multicultural education in this diverse school context. The present study is holistic, in that I examined the impact of multiple influences in a connected way as they intersected in the life of one student rather than as examples of ways in which an issue or theme may be experienced by different members of the same ethnic group.

Given the increasing diversity of the North American population (Statistics Canada, 2008; U.S. Census Bureau, 2002) that is in turn reflected in North American schools (Chan & Ross, 2002; He, Phillion, Chan, & Xu, 2007), addressing the curricular needs of students of minority background and supporting the professional development of teachers who work with them is essential. The present study contributes to existing research in the area of multicultural education and, in particular, curriculum development for diverse student populations, and student experiences of multicultural education.

To date, research addressing the interaction of culture and curriculum is often presented as an argument for the inclusion of culture in the school curriculum or as documentation for ways in which the inclusion of culture in the curriculum was successful (Ada, 1988; Cummins et al., 2005). There is an abundance of research highlighting the importance of culturally relevant and responsive pedagogy (Gay, 2000; Ladson-Billings, 1995, 2001; Villegas, 1991) and a culturally sensitive curriculum that builds on the experiences and knowledge of immigrant and minority students (Ada; Cummins, 2001; Igoa, 1995; Nieto & Bode, 2008).

Acknowledging the cultural knowledge of minority students in the classroom has been found to have important implications for their well-being outside of school. For example, Banks (1995) highlighted the inclusion of culture in the curriculum as a means of helping students to develop positive racial attitudes. Rodriguez (1982), Wong-Fillmore (1991), and Kouritzin (1999) presented compelling accounts of ways in which the failure to support the maintenance and development of maternal-language proficiency for students of minority background had dire consequences for their sense of ethnic identity and their sense of belonging in their families and ethnic communities. McCaleb (1994), Cummins (2001), and Wong-Fillmore elaborated on some of the dangers, such as increased dropout rates among immigrant and minority youth as well as increased likelihood of gang involvement, or failing to recognize the cultural communities from which students come.

Existing research has been invaluable in highlighting the importance of acknowledging the cultural knowledge that immigrant and minority students bring to a school context, and the work of educators as they develop curricula and teach an increasingly diverse student population (Banks, 1995; Cummins, 2001; Moodley, 1995). Research has also accentuated the need to develop ways of learning about the ethnic, linguistic, and religious backgrounds of students to inform curriculum development and policymaking for students of diverse backgrounds. Cochran-Smith (1995), Ladson-Billings (1995, 2001), and Conle (2000) explored the practice of drawing on the cultural knowledge of preservice teachers as a resource for preparing them to teach in culturally diverse classrooms. It is interesting to note that although there is research that has acknowledged the potential difficulties of moving from home to school for students of a minority background, and the difficulties of moving from school back home when minority students have assimilated to the school and societal expectations that differ from those of their home cultures, the day-to-day transition as minority and immigrant students move from home to school and back home again seems to have been overlooked. In the present study, I examine the nuances that one student lives as she makes this transition on a daily basis.

This work addresses the need for experiential research, focusing specifically on exploring the intersection of home and school influences from the perspective of the students themselves. Presently, there is a surprising lack of research examining ways in which students, in general (Cook-Sather, 2002), and immigrant and minority students, in particular, personally experience their school curriculum and school contexts (He et al., 2007). Bullough's (2007) examination of a Muslim student's response to curriculum and peer interactions in his U.S. school is among the few pieces examining school-curriculum activities from the perspective of a student of ethnic-minority background. Feuerverger's (2001) ethnographic work exploring tensions that Israeli and Palestinian youth experience in their Israeli-Palestinian school is among few studies documenting and exploring student perspectives of their schooling experiences. Sarroub (2005) and Zine's (2001) accounts of Muslim students in American and Canadian schools, respectively, illustrate the complexities of negotiating a sense of identity among peers in a school context when values in the home differ significantly.

Within the relatively limited body of existing research addressing student experiences of schooling and curriculum presented, I present examples of student experiences thematically to address specific issues, topics, or arguments rather than ways that acknowledge multiple facets and tensions interacting at once to shape the experiences of an individual student. Smith-Hefner (1993), in her ethnographic study of female high school Khmer students, presented examples of Puerto Rican female students whose limited academic success was shaped by cultural and sociohistorical influences in their ethnic communities. Rolon-Dow (2004) examined tensions Puerto Rican students and their teachers experience when values supported in their home and in their ethnic communities seem to conflict with those encouraged in school. Lee's (1994, 1996) ethnographic study focused on ways in which Asian high school students' sense of identity and academic achievement was influenced by self-identified labels and membership in specific peer groups. There does not exist a large body of research examining the experiences of one student in the context of their North American school in a way that presents the stories to illustrate ways in which the interaction of multiple influences and issues of relevance may impact on an immigrant or minority student.

This narrative inquiry is intended to provide a glimpse of the intersection of complex influences shaping the life of an immigrant student. I drew on existing narrative and ethnographic accounts of immigrant and minority students attending North American schools to inform this work. Valdes's (1996) work documenting the experiences of a small number of Latino and Mexican American families in their school and community and Li's (2002) ethnographic study with Chinese families as they supported their children's literacy development provide a glimpse of ways in which transitions between home and school may be challenging, and even overwhelming, due to differences in expectations about the school curriculum and the work of teachers. Carger's (1996) long-term narrative account of a Mexican American family's experiences provides an organizational structure for the present study, in that it is an in-depth account of one family's experiences of supporting their child in school, taking into consideration the intersection of multiple influences shaping the child's education. Ross & Chan's (2008) narrative account of an immigrant student, Raj, and his family's academic, financial, and familial difficulties highlighted the many challenges the family encountered in the process of supporting their children's adaptation to their Canadian school and community. This examination of Ai Mei's experiences contributes to the growing but still limited body of research addressing Chinese students in North American schools (Chan, 2004; Kao, 1995; Kim & Chun, 1994; Lee, 1994, 1996, 2001; Li, 2002, 2005).

Theoretical Framework Given the focus on experience in contributing to Ai Mei's sense of ethnic identity, I used Dewey's (1938) philosophy of the interconnectedness between experience and education as the theoretical foundation for this study. I examined, in particular, ways in which the many influences in her home, school, and neighborhood life with family members, peers, teachers, administrators, and school curriculum events intersected to contribute to her overall experience or learning of a sense of ethnic identity as an immigrant student in a Canadian school context. Ai Mei's stories are set into the framework of a three-dimensional narrative inquiry space (Clandinin & Connelly, 2000), with Bay Street School as the spatial dimension, the years 2001–2003 as the temporal dimension, and my interactions with Ai Mei, her classmates, her teachers, her parents, and other members of the Bay Street School community as the sociopersonal dimension. The stories are a means of exploring the interaction of influences contributing to Ai Mei's sense of identity; they highlight the extent to which this intersection of narratives may be interpreted as conflicting stories to live by (Connelly & Clandinin, 1999).

Method

I first met Ai Mei when I began observations in her seventh-grade class as a classroom-based participant observer for a research project exploring the ethnic identity of first-generation Canadian students. The focus on examining the intersection of culture and curriculum as experienced by Chinese Canadian students over the course of their 2 years in middle school was deliberate from the beginning. As I learned about the details of the students' experiences, the complex interaction of factors contributing to Ai Mei's sense of ethnic identity became apparent and merited further analysis.

   Ai Mei's homeroom teacher, William, told me about how she had arrived at Bay Street School from an urban area of Fuchien province in China as a 7-year-old. Although she did not initially speak English at all, she was relatively proficient by the time I met her 4 1/2 years after her arrival. Her English was distinct from that of her native-English-speaking peers by the unusual turns of phrases and unconventional uses of some words, but the animated way in which she spoke about her experiences caught my attention from the beginning. I later appreciated this quality even more as I began to work more closely with her as a research participant. Her dark eyes, partially hidden behind wisps of hair, seemed to flicker and dance as she elaborated on details of interactions with peers and family members, especially when she recounted amusing or troublesome events pertaining to difficulties she had experienced in communicating with others. She also seemed to enjoy telling me about incidents that had occurred at home, at school, or in the community. As I learned about Ai Mei's stories of immigration and settlement, the conflicting influences and expectations of her family members, peers and teachers at school, and members of her ethnic community became more apparent, thus further contributing to my decision to focus on her stories in this study.

As a narrative inquirer, I learned about Ai Mei's stories of experience (Connelly & Clandinin, 1988) using a variety of narrative approaches, including long-term, school-based participant observations, document collection set into the context of ongoing conversational interviews with key participants, and the writing of extensive field notes following each school visit, interview, and interaction with participants (Clandinin & Connelly, 1994, 2000; Clandinin et al., 2006) to explore the interwoven quality of Ai Mei, her teacher, her classmates, and her family members' lives. I observed and interacted with her in the context of regular classroom lessons as I assisted her and her classmates with assignments, accompanied them on field trips, attended their band concerts and performances, and took part in school activities such as Multicultural Night, Curriculum and Hot Dog Night, school assemblies, and festivals. School visits began during the fall of 2001 as Ai Mei and her classmates began seventh grade and continued until June 2003 when they graduated from eighth grade at Bay Street School.

I conducted interviews as well as ongoing informal conversations with Ai Mei over the course of the 2 years I spent in her homeroom classroom. I also collected documents such as school notices, announcements of community and school events, notices from bulletin boards and classroom walls in the school, agendas and minutes from School Council meetings, and samples of student work. Descriptive field notes, interview transcripts, researcher journals, and theoretical memos written following school visits were computerized and filed into an existing research project archival system. I examined field notes pertaining to Ai Mei's experiences numerous times to identify recurring themes. Her stories were set into the context of field notes written about her classroom teacher, her peers, and her school community since I began research at the school in 2000.

Results

Ai Mei's Stories of Home and School: Conflicting Stories to Live By I subsequently present some of Ai Mei's stories of experience to explore challenges and complexities, harmonies and tensions (Clandinin & Connelly, 2002) she lived as she attempted to balance affiliation to her peers while at the same time accommodating for expectations placed on her by her teachers and parents. I explore ways in which parent, teacher, and peer expectations may contribute to shaping her sense of identity, and examine the contribution of narrative methodology in revealing nuances of the intersection of multiple influences in her life.

Bay Street School Context Ai Mei's stories were set in the context of Bay Street School, a school known to consist of a diverse student community from the time of its establishment (Cochrane, 1950; Connelly, He, Phillion, Chan, & Xu, 2004), located in an urban Toronto neighborhood where the ethnic composition of residents is known to reflect Canadian immigration and settlement patterns (Connelly, Phillion, & He, 2003). Accordingly, the student population at the school reflects this diversity. An Every Student Survey administered to students during the 2001–2002 school year (Chan & Ross, 2002) confirmed the ethnic and linguistic diversity of the students. More specifically, 39 countries and 31 languages were represented in the school. This was the context in which Ai Mei's stories played out.

Home Language Conflicting with School Language I subsequently present the story, "I was trying to hide my identity," as a starting point for examining Ai Mei's experiences of her academic program at Bay Street School.
  "I was trying to hide my identity"

Ai Mei: When I first came to Bay Street School, I stayed with the IL (International Language)[1] teacher, Mrs. Lim . . . I stayed with her for the whole week, and she taught me things in English.

Elaine: What did she teach you?

Ai Mei: You know, easy things, like the alphabet, and how to say "Hello." Then I went to Ms. Jenkins' class. I sat with a strange boy.

Elaine: A strange boy?

Ai Mei: Well, he wasn't that strange. My desk was facing his desk, and he did this to me (Ai Mei demonstrates what the boy did), he stuck his tongue out at me. I didn't know what it meant. He had messy orange hair.

Elaine: Did you make any friends?

Ai Mei: No, not for a long time. Some people tried to talk to me but I didn't understand them. Then Chao tried to talk with me in Fujianese and I pretended I didn't understand her. She tried a few times, then gave up. Then one day, my sister said something to me in Fujianese and Chao heard. She looked at me—she was really surprised because she tried to talk with me and I pretended I couldn't understand her. She didn't like me at all.

Elaine: Why did you do that? Why did you pretend you couldn't understand her?

Ai Mei: I don't know. I was trying to hide my identity.

Ai Mei: (calling over to Chao): Chao, remember how I didn't talk with you, how I pretended I didn't understand you?

Chao: Yeah, I remember. (Chao scowls at Ai Mei.) I didn't like you for a long time.

Ai Mei: Yeah, a long time.

(Fieldnotes, April, 2003)

When Ai Mei arrived at Bay Street School, new students coming into the school spent a week or two with the respective International Language (IL) teacher prior to placement into a classroom. The new student orientation provided teachers the opportunity to assess the English and maternal- language proficiency of new students, identify potential learning difficulties, and learn about their previous schooling experiences. The orientation also provided students an opportunity to learn about school routines in their home language while being gradually introduced into their age-appropriate classroom.

Ai Mei's response to the new student orientation, however, was surprising for a number of reasons. From her teachers' perspective, Chao would have seemed like an ideal friend for Ai Mei—both girls were from the same rural province of southern China, grew up speaking Fujianese at home and Mandarin in school, and Chao could help Ai Mei to adapt to Bay Street School because she had arrived two years earlier. However, Ai Mei did not seem to welcome the opportunity to speak with Chao in Fujianese. Her teachers were also likely puzzled that she would try to "hide [her] identity," because, from their perspective, they worked hard to create programs that would acknowledge students' home cultures in a positive way.

In this context, it is possible that Ai Mei, similar to many students featured in research on immigrant and minority students (Cummins, 2001; Kouritzin, 1999), perceived her affiliation to her family's home language as a hindrance to acceptance by English-speaking peers. She seemed to appreciate learning English from her IL teacher and perhaps felt that her inability to speak in English was an obstacle to forming friendships with English-speaking peers. One day, as we were walking back to her homeroom classroom after art class, she has told me about an incident when she felt embarrassed when she attempted to order drinks at a shopping mall and the vendor could not understand her because "[her] English accent was so bad!" Ai Mei may have been attempting to distance herself from those she perceived as non-English-speaking when she said she "tried to hide [her] identity." Wong-Fillmore (1991) elaborated on how a language minority child might abandon the home language when she or he realizes the low status of this language in relation to the English that is used by peers in school. At the same time, in choosing not to respond to her Fujianese-speaking classmate who attempted to befriend her, Ai Mei was giving up the opportunity to make a friend at a time when she did not have the English proficiency to build friendships easily with English-speaking peers.

School Language Conflicting with Home Language In addition to pressure to achieve a higher level of English proficiency, Ai Mei seemed to be under pressure from her IL Mandarin teacher, Mrs. Lim, to maintain and to develop her Mandarin proficiency.

She was in a high level of language within her grade-level Mandarin program,[2] and she was doing well in the class, judging from the grades I saw when she showed me her Mandarin language textbook and workbooks. Her teacher has said that she did well in her assignments and tests, and that she was a strong student in Mandarin. She stated that it was important for Ai Mei to work hard to maintain the advantage she had over her Canadian-born Chinese peers. Mrs. Lim believed that Ai Mei has an easier time learning the characters that many Canadian-born Chinese students have difficulty with, due to her early years of schooling in China before arriving in Canada. She also felt that Ai Mei had an advantage over her Chinese-born peers, in that her schooling prior to leaving China was regular and uninterrupted in a way some of her Chinese-born peers had not experienced.

Maintenance of her Mandarin language proficiency is an achievement her parents support. At the same time, they would like her to maintain fluency in her family's home dialect of Fujianese. For Ai Mei and her parents, maternal language maintenance has important implications for communication within the family. Ai Mei told me about the following mealtime conversation involving her mother and her younger sister, Susan.

"Susan doesn't speak Fujianese"

Ai Mei: We were eating supper and my mother said to my sister, "(phrase in Fujianese)." My sister asked me, "What did she say?" so I told her, "She wants to know if you want more vegetables."

Elaine: Your sister doesn't understand Fujianese?

Ai Mei: She does but not everything.

Elaine: What did your mother say? Is she worried that your sister doesn't understand her?

Ai Mei: She looked at her like this—(Ai Mei showed me how her mother gave her sister a dirty look).

(Fieldnotes, April, 2003)

From the fieldnote, it seems that Ai Mei's parents were beginning to feel the effects of maternal language loss within the family. Fujianese is not easy to develop and maintain because its use in Canada is not widely supported outside the home, with the exception of exposure to the dialect through other recent immigrants from Fuchien Province. Susan's inability to understand basic vocabulary in her home language likely worried her and Ai Mei's parents, but given the limited resources to support it and limited time to encourage her themselves, they might wonder what can be done. Ai Mei spoke about how her parents reminded her often to speak with her sister in Fujianese. Meanwhile, the sisters had long grown into the habit of speaking to one another in English; communication in their home language of Fujianese would have been stifled at that point due to the lack of ease both felt in using it as well as Susan's limited vocabulary. It might be the case that their parents, as they began to realize the extent of their daughter's maternal language loss, might already be too late to stop it. This pressure to develop and to maintain language proficiency interacted with other factors contributing to Ai Mei's sense of identity and affiliation in her school and in her home and ethnic communities.

Parent Values Conflicting with Peer Values In addition to pressure to succeed academically, Ai Mei was also under pressure to behave according to the expectations of her peers, teachers, and parents. Through interaction with Ai Mei at Bay Street School over the course of two full academic years, it became apparent that being included within her peer group was very important to her. Like her peers, Ai Mei was becoming more firmly entrenched into popular movies, music, and fashion trends as she moved into adolescence. These influences were coupled with increasing pressure from peers to scoff at school success and downplay the importance of academic work. During the fall of 2001, there were a number of days when I arrived at Ai Mei's classroom to find her friends trying to console her after a popular and outspoken male classmate, Felix, had made unflattering comments about her appearance. Her homeroom teacher also told me about incidents when she had left school in tears after being excluded from an after school activity that had been planned by classmates. Another day, I overheard Felix mimicking one of the stories from Ai Mei's Mandarin IL text; although he spoke in English, the tone and storyline were along the lines of what might be found in the text. Ai Mei laughed at Felix's attempts and seemed to appreciate that he knew a little about what she did in IL class but I also wondered whether she was embarrassed or annoyed with him.

In addition to concerns about being excluded by her peers and feeling the pull of multiple influences in school to behave in certain ways, Ai Mei also seemed to live the tensions of parental expectations and standards for her behavior and comportment that, at times, conflicted with those of her peers, and ways in which she saw herself. I wrote the following fieldnote after a conversation with Ai Mei in which she complained about her mother's comments about her in relation to her mother's friend during a family outing.

"Dim Sum with her mother's friend"

Ai Mei told me today about going out to dim sum with her mother's friend and her family. She said she was very annoyed at being compared to her mother's friend's daughter who is close in age to Ai Mei but who seems like a perfect daughter in her mother's eyes. Ai Mei told me, "My mother said, 'Look at Ming Ming, so pretty and tall. And so quiet! She helps her mother do the cooking and the cleaning at home.' She said to Ming Ming's mother, 'Look at Ai Mei, 13 years old and so short. And she doesn't help me at home, and she doesn't cook!' She kept comparing us, saying how nice Ming Ming is and how terrible I am." Ai Mei rolled her eyes.

(Fieldnotes, April, 2003)

The interaction between Ai Mei and her mother highlighted the potential for tensions to develop when expressing differences in perspective about the value of certain kinds of behaviors over others. It sounded as if Ai Mei resented that her mother did not think she was quiet or helpful or tall enough when compared with her friend's daughter. Although a generational gap might account for some of the tension about what constituted appropriate behavior and goals for Ai Mei with respect to what she did to contribute to the family, some of this tension might also have been shaped by the very different contexts in which Ai Mei and her mother have spent their childhood. Ai Mei has spent a good portion of her childhood living in different homes in an urban, commercial district of Toronto. Her perception of appropriate behavior and practices has likely been shaped by influences different from what her mother experienced in rural Fuchien province of China where she spent her own childhood.

Teacher Expectations Conflicting with Parent Expectations Moreover, although Ai Mei's parents and her teachers had in common the goal of academic success for her, tensions surfaced about the time commitment needed to fulfill these school and family responsibilities. Ai Mei seemed to be caught between pressures to help in the family business and teacher expectations for completed homework and thorough preparation for tests and assignments.

Ai Mei's family acquired a dumpling restaurant during the fall of her eighth-grade year, and since then, the whole family had devoted much time and energy toward building a successful business. I knew that Ai Mei's family owned a dumpling restaurant because she had told me about what she did to help.

Ai Mei: There's a door that no one can close but me.

Elaine: What's wrong with it?

Ai Mei: It's stuck, so I have to kick it shut. (She demonstrates as she says this, kicking to one side as she leans over.) Then, we go home, me, my mom, and my dad.

Elaine: How about your sister?

Ai Mei: She goes home a little earlier, with my grandmother and grandfather.

(Fieldnotes, October, 2002)

Each day after school, Ai Mei and her sister, Susan, after spending some time with their friends in the classroom or in the school yard, headed to the dumpling restaurant to spend the evening there helping their parents. Ai Mei's sister, Susan, has told me about how she helped their father by standing outside the restaurant where the family sells vegetables and fruits to watch for people who attempted to take food without paying for it. When I asked her whether this often happened, she nodded gravely.

The importance of Ai Mei and Susan's participation in the family business could be denied, but Ai Mei's teachers had questioned the time commitment involved. Late in the fall after the family acquired the dumpling restaurant, Ai Mei's teacher, William, noticed that she had begun to come to school looking very tired, and without her homework done. One day while he was meeting with her to discuss the report card that would soon be sent home to her parents, he told her that she could have done better had she submitted all of her homework and done a better job on recent tests. Ai Mei surprised him by bursting into tears. Little by little, William learned that Ai Mei had little opportunity to do her homework or to study because she was helping out at the restaurant during evenings and weekends. By the time the family had closed up the restaurant, traveled home, and eaten supper, it was past 11:00 pm or 12:00 am, beyond what William thought was appropriate for a 12-year-old. With a sense of professional responsibility to report potentially negligent situations to officials and the support of school board policies guiding his actions, William spoke with his principal about the situation. Both decided it was a borderline case, and with the principal's knowledge, William contacted the Children's Aid Society (CAS) about Ai Mei's family. I wrote the following field note the day William told me about his call to the CAS.

> "I called the CAS"
>
> I was helping William straighten up the textbooks, sort student assignments into piles, and organize pens, pencils, and chalk into appropriate places in the classroom. We have gotten into the habit of talking about events of the day as we tidy up the classroom after the students have left for French class toward the end of the day. Today, William said to me, "I called the CAS about Ai Mei. She doesn't do her homework or have time to study because she's up late working in the family restaurant. She's exhausted." (Fieldnotes, December, 2002)

The dumpling restaurant was tied to Ai Mei's family's dreams of financial success and family reunification. Ai Mei had spoken about how her parents had sponsored her maternal grandparents to come to Toronto from Fuchien province, and were in the process of trying to bring her paternal grandparents over to join the family as well. The importance of helping her family with their business could not be denied from her parents' perspective and, from what Ai Mei has said about the ways in which she helped the family, it could be assumed that she also recognized the importance of her role as well.

At the same time, it was beginning to become apparent that assisting her parents in the family business might have diverted her attention away from fulfilling her parents' desire for her to do well in school, in that time spent in the restaurant helping her family was time that she could have otherwise devoted to her school work. Ai Mei was caught between her parents' dreams of financial and business success, her sense of responsibility, as the oldest daughter in the family, to help them achieve this success, her parents' desire for her to perform well academically to secure her own future economic success, and her teacher's professional responsibility to report potentially negligent situations to officials. She lived the tensions of deciding how best to use her time to assist her parents in the family business as well as to perform well academically.

This situation also needed to be examined in terms of her teacher's professional tensions and ways in which these tensions might have contributed to Ai Mei's sense of identity. Her teacher, William, was aware that the cultural and social narratives guiding his professional practices might have differed from those guiding the practices of the parents of his students, and had expressed a commitment to acknowledging the diversity of his students. The potential for conflict between teacher, student, and parent perspectives pertaining to Ai Mei's use of time in the evenings and on weekends became apparent when William contacted child-protection officials to report that Ai Mei's time in the family's restaurant in the evenings was contributing to her late arrival at school in the mornings, without her assigned homework completed. He did so with the belief in the importance of protecting Ai Mei's time to ensure that she had adequate time and necessary conditions in her home to complete her school work.

William's call to the CAS, however well intentioned, had the potential to cause difficulties in Ai Mei's family as well as a rift in his own relationship with Ai Mei. In fact, he later told me about how Ai Mei, on realizing that he had reported her parents to the CAS, neither came around after school to spend time in his classroom nor did she tell him about what was happening in her life as she was accustomed to doing up until that time. He felt he had lost her trust and believed that his call to the CAS had been the cause. This example highlights some of the tension William felt as he attempted to balance his professional obligation to report potentially negligent situations to child protection officials and his ideal of the role of teacher as an advocate who supported students in ways they would appreciate.

Learning About Ai Mei's Experiences as a Narrative Inquirer These stories highlight some of the complexities of the interaction of multiple influences in contributing to Ai Mei's sense of identity. Underlying these accounts of Ai Mei's experiences with her peers, teachers, and parents in the context of school and community-based events are accounts of my interactions with Ai Mei as a narrative inquirer. The narrative inquiry approach used in this study facilitated the identification of the many nuances of living as an immigrant student in a North American school context, and provided a framework in which to ponder these complexities. To begin, the stories of experience documenting Ai Mei's experiences as an immigrant student at Bay Street School were gathered over a long period of time as I spent 2 full school years in her homeroom classroom with her, her teachers, and her peers as a participant observer. During this time, I became a member of the classroom, joining the class for activities such as field trips, special school events, band concerts, and school assemblies. More importantly, however, I was a part of their class during the uneventful days of lessons and regular school activities. It was during these times that I was able to build a relationship with Ai Mei and her peers and teachers. They grew to see me as an additional teacher in the classroom who was able to help them with assignments, act as an adult supervisor during in-school activities or field trips, and as a listening ear when they had disagreements with friends or with teachers.

I learned about the details of Ai Mei's life as she told me about her classmates, her parents, her family's dumpling restaurant, her sister, and family outings. I heard about her perceptions of how she fit into her peer group, her ethnic community, and her family as she told me about specific interactions, such as the family dinner when her sister did not understand what her mother had said in Fujianese, her mother's criticisms of her in comparison with her mother's friend's daughter, or her impressions of the new student orientation that was in place to ease her transition into the school as a new student from China.

As the students came to realize my interest in learning about their school lives, they began to update me on events I had missed between visits, and to fill me in on what they referred to as "gossip" at school. At one point partway through my second year with Ai Mei's homeroom class, I conducted interviews with the students. As I planned the questions and discussed them with William, I remember wondering whether this shift to a more formal kind of interaction with the students would change the relationship we had established. My concern about negatively impacting the relationship turned out to be unfounded. In fact, I was pleased to realize one day when Ai Mei approached me to tell me about a family dinner (see "Susan doesn't speak Fujianese") that the process had opened up further opportunities to learn about the students' lives. Realizing that I was interested in hearing about their interactions at home and in the community with members of their ethnic groups, the students began to tell me more about them. Our existing relationship had provided a foundation such that I could talk with the students about their experiences with family and members of their ethnic communities, and the interviews provided an opportunity for the students to learn, in a more explicit way, about my interest in hearing about out-of-school aspects of their lives. Our relationship was such that they knew they could trust that I would treat their stories and their perceptions of these stories with interest and respect.

I also saw Ai Mei in the neighborhood with her friends during the after school hours as they moved from house to house visiting one another in the housing project while their parents worked in nearby restaurants and shops, and on weekends as she shopped with her sister and her parents in the stores that lined the commercial area near the school. These brief interactions provided further glimpses of influences interacting in her life to contribute to shaping a sense of identity in ways that would not be possible through formal interviews or a more structured schedule of research observations. In addition, these interactions provided an opportunity for Ai Mei's friends and family to become familiar with my presence and participation in the school.

Tensions of acting as a researcher with a focus on learning about the experiences of my participants became more apparent as my role as researcher became less clear. As I got to know Ai Mei and her family, I felt the tensions she experienced as she balanced the multiple influences in her life and wanted to advocate for her. I felt a sense of responsibility to Ai Mei, to support her learning and to attempt to ease some of the tensions she experienced as she balanced affiliation to her home and school cultures. I understood a little of the betrayal she felt when her parents were reported to child protection officials, and the fear her parents might have felt. When she told me about how her parents would not be able to attend her eighth-grade graduation because they needed to work, I wanted to be sure to attend and to take photos of her with her sister so that she would have a record of the event. The nature of the researcher-participant relationship in contributing to understanding about the nuances of experiences lived by my student participant heightened my understanding of what the events might mean for her.

The role of narrative inquiry, and, more specifically, the role of long-term participation in the day to day school life of an immigrant student that was critical to this narrative inquiry, contributed to the researcher-participant relationship I was able to develop with Ai Mei, her peers, and her teachers. Careful attention to the details of life in classrooms (Jackson, 1990) and within the school, and respect for the ongoing negotiation so critical to building a research relationship from initial negotiation of entry into the school-research site to negotiation of exit towards the completion of school-based narrative inquiries—features foundational to Clandinin & Connelly's (2000) approach—further contributed to the development of a research relationship based on trust and familiarity with Ai Mei. This trust, in turn, engaged me in careful consideration of the potential implications of telling and retelling Ai Mei's stories, and what they might mean for her, as well as other immigrant and minority students who may struggle with similar challenges of balancing tensions of affiliation to home and school cultures in a North American school context. It was also through this commitment to examining these tensions narratively from multiple perspectives of others in Ai Mei's school, as well as in relation to temporal, spatial, and sociopersonal dimensions at play in her school, that enabled me to see some of the nuances and complexities of the conflicting influences in Ai Mei's life. In the process of examining Ai Mei's experiences narratively, I also became a participant, in that my experiences and interpretations of Ai Mei's stories were continually being examined and reflected on as I shared my interpretations with Ai Mei in an ongoing process to better understand the stories she told.

This relationship, in turn, was critical to my learning about the complexities of Ai Mei's experiences. In this way, this long-term, school-based narrative inquiry approach contributes not only to knowledge about the experiences of my participants as I focus on examining nuances of the research phenomenon at hand but it also raises awareness about the intricacies, and the impact, of the work of researchers in the lives of our participants.

Discussion

Conflicting Student, Teacher, and Parent Stories to Live By: Implications for Practice, Research, and Theory This examination of the intersection of home, school, and ethnic community influences in Ai Mei's life provided a glimpse of the challenges immigrant or minority students might encounter as they negotiate a sense of ethnic identity. More specifically, examining Ai Mei's stories reveals ways in which immigrant and minority students may be pulled in many directions, with some of these influences experienced as conflicting stories to live by as teacher, peer, and parent expectations intersect on a school landscape. The stories highlight the potential for conflict when immigrant students have values shaped by interaction with family and members of their ethnic community as well as values shaped by interaction with peers, teachers, and other members of their North American school communities.

As Ai Mei grows up, she needs to determine which aspects of her home and school communities she incorporates into her own set of values. The age-old tension between children and their parents as children move toward adulthood and make decisions pertaining to their education and the kind of life they see themselves leading is exacerbated by differences in perspective that are influenced by differences in culture between their new host society that the children are navigating and the landscape that their immigrant parents experienced as children in their home countries. This tension is further complicated by struggles that their parents have endured in the immigration process as they settle into new countries. Ai Mei's stories revealed the extent to which ideas for innovative curricula and the good intentions of teachers, administrators, researchers, and policymakers may unfold in unexpected ways. Learning about Ai Mei's conflicting stories to live by highlighted the importance of examining ways in which curriculum and school events may contribute to shaping the ethnic identity of immigrant and minority students in ways much more complex than anticipated by their teachers, their parents, and even the students themselves.

This knowledge, in turn, informs the work of teachers and administrators as they attempt to meet the needs of their increasingly diverse student populations. Teachers need to learn to meet the academic and social needs of their immigrant and minority students in a school context with sometimes little knowledge about the cultures and education systems from which they are coming. In this way, knowledge gained from this study has implications for teachers working in diverse school contexts, professional development for in-service and pre-service educators, and decision making pertaining to the development of curriculum policies for multicultural school contexts. Examining Ai Mei's experiences of the intersection of home and school influences informs the development and implementation of programs designed to facilitate the adaptation of immigrant students in North American schools. Ai Mei's stories of experience may be referred to as an example of a life-based literary narrative (Phillion & He, 2004), and contribute to the body of student lore introduced by Schubert and Ayers (1992) and recognized by Jackson (1992) in Pinar, Reynolds, Slattery, and Taubman's book, Understanding Curriculum (1995). Attention to the narratives of students and their families is a reminder not to lose sight of the diversity in student populations and highlights the need for attention to issues of social justice and equity in education. Not only does this research address the dearth of research focused specifically on students' experiences from their perspective, but it also contributes to understanding of the experiences of immigrant and minority students to provide insights into the experiences of a group about which educators and policymakers involved in developing and implementing school curriculum are desperately in need of better understanding.

Conclusion

Teachers and administrators with whom I shared this piece appreciated the acknowledgment of the challenges they encounter in their work with their students. William, as a beginning teacher, recognized the need for further attention to prepare teachers for diverse classrooms and felt that stories such as those presented in this article contributed to raising awareness of difficulties teachers may encounter; he recognized the potential of the stories as a forum to generate discussion among teachers and administrators. His administrators spoke of the challenges inherent to meeting the needs of their student population, and referred to the tensions of needing to abide by existing policies even as they lived the difficulties of implementing some of the policies with their students and teachers.

Exploring the multitude of influences shaping student participation in school curriculum using a narrative inquiry approach to examining student experiences is also a means of acknowledging the complexity of schooling and teacher preparation (Cochran Smith, 2006), and the need for guidance about how best to develop curriculum and pedagogy for students of minority background, and the challenges associated with working with diverse student populations. Given the increasingly diverse North American context, is it essential that educators and policymakers are well informed about the students for whom educational practices and policies are developed.

Notes

1. Students at Bay Street School chose from IL classes in Cantonese or Mandarin Chinese, Vietnamese, Arabic, Swahili/Black History, or Spanish that were integrated into their regular school day.

2. The Mandarin texts used in the IL program were based on a multi-grade format in which each grade level was in turn divided into six levels of difficulty ranging from beginner to advanced to accommodate for differences in language proficiency among students in the same grade level.

References

Ada, A. F. (1988). The Pajaro Valley experience: Working with Spanish-speaking parents to develop children's reading and writing skills in the home through the use of children's literature. In T. Skutnabb-Kangas & J. Cummins (Eds.), *Minority education: From shame to struggle* (pp. 223–237). Clevedon, UK: Multilingual Matters.

Banks, J. A. (1995). Multicultural education: Its effects on students' racial and gender role attitudes. In J. A. Banks & C. A. McGee Banks (Eds.), *Handbook of research on multicultural education* (pp. 617–627). Toronto, Canada: Prentice Hall International.

Bullough, R. V., Jr. (2007). Ali: Becoming a student—A life history. In D. Thiessen & A. Cook-Sather (Eds.), *International handbook of student experience in elementary and secondary school* (pp. 493–516). Dordecht, The Netherlands: Springer.

Carger, C. (1996). *Of borders and dreams: Mexican-American experience of urban education*. New York: Teachers College Press.

Chan, E. (2004). *Narratives of ethnic identity: Experiences of first generation Chinese Canadian students*. Unpublished doctoral dissertation, University of Toronto, Ontario, Canada.

Chan, E., & Ross, V. (2002). *ESL Survey Report. Sponsored by the ESL Work-group in collaboration with the OISE/UT Narrative and Diversity Research Team*. Toronto, Canada: Centre for Teacher Development, Ontario Institute for Studies in Education, University of Toronto, Ontario, Canada.

Clandinin, D. J., & Connelly, F. M. (1994). Personal experience methods. In N. K. Denzin & Y. S. Lincoln (Eds.), *Handbook of qualitative research in the social sciences* (pp. 413–427). Thousand Oaks, CA: Sage.

Clandinin, D. J., & Connelly, F. M. (2000). *Narrative inquiry: Experience and story in qualitative research*. San Francisco: Jossey-Bass.

Clandinin, D. J., & Connelly, F. M. (2002, October). Intersecting narratives: Cultural harmonies and tensions in inner-city urban Canadian schools. Proposal submitted to the Social Sciences and Humanities Research Council of Canada.

Clandinin, D. J., Huber, J., Huber, M., Murphy, M. S., Murray Orr, A., Pearce, M., et al. (2006). *Composing diverse identities: Narrative inquiries into the interwoven lives of children and teachers*. New York: Routledge.

Cochrane, M. (Ed.). (1950). *Centennial story: Board of education for the city of Toronto: 1850–1950*. Toronto, Canada: Thomas Nelson.

Cochran-Smith, M. (1995). Uncertain allies: Understanding the boundaries of race and teaching. *Harvard Educational Review, 65,* 541–570.

Cochran-Smith, M. (2006). Thirty editorials later: Signing off as editor. *Journal of Teacher Education, 57*(2), 95–101.

Conle, C. (2000). The asset of cultural pluralism: an account of cross-cultural learning in pre-service teacher education. *Teaching and Teacher Education, 16,* 365–387.

Connelly, F. M., & Clandinin, D. J. (1988). *Teachers as curriculum planners: Narratives of experience*. New York: Teachers College Press.

Connelly, F. M., & Clandinin, D. J. (1999). Stories to live by: Teacher identities on a changing professional knowledge landscape. In F. M. Connelly & D. J. Clandinin (Eds.), *Shaping a professional identity: Stories of educational practice* (pp. 114–132). London, Canada: Althouse Press.

Connelly, F. M., He, M. F., Phillion, J., Chan, E., & Xu, S. (2004). Bay Street Community School: Where you belong. *Orbit, 34*(3), 39–42.

Connelly, F. M., Phillion, J., & He, M. F. (2003). An exploration of narrative inquiry into multiculturalism in education: Reflecting on two decades of research in an inner-city Canadian community school. *Curriculum Inquiry, 33,* 363–384.

Cook-Sather, A. (2002) Authorizing students' perspectives: toward trust, dialogue, and change in education. *Educational Researcher, 31* (4), 3–14.

Cummins, J. (2001). *Negotiating identities: Education for empowerment in a diverse society* (2nd ed.). Ontario, CA: CABE (California Association for Bilingual Education).

Cummins, J., Bismilla, V., Chow, P., Cohen, S., Giampapa, F., Leoni, L., et al. (2005). Affirming identity in multilingual classrooms. *Educational Leadership, 63*(1), 38–43.

Dewey, J. (1938). *Experience and education*. New York: Simon & Schuster.

Feuerverger, G. (2001). *Oasis of dreams: Teaching and learning peace in a Jewish-Palestinian village in Israel*. New York: Routledge.

Gay, G. (2000). *Culturally responsive teaching: Theory, research, & practice*. New York: Teachers College Press.

He, M. F., Phillion, J., Chan, E., & Xu, S. (2007). Chapter 15—Immigrant students' experience of curriculum. In F. M. Connelly, M. F. He, & J. Phillion (Eds.), *Handbook of curriculum and instruction* (pp. 219–239). Thousand Oaks, CA: Sage.

Igoa, C. (1995). *The inner world of the immigrant child*. New York: St. Martin's Press.

Jackson, P. (1990). *Life in classrooms*. New York: Teachers College Press. Jackson, P. (1992). Conceptions of curriculum specialists. In P. Jackson (Ed.), *Handbook of research on curriculum* (pp. 3–40). New York: Peter Lang.

Kao, G. (1995). Asian Americans as model minorities? A look at their academic performance. *American Journal of Education, 103,* 121–159.

Kim, U., & Chun, M. J. B. (1994). The educational 'success' of Asian Americans: An indigenous perspective. *Journal of Applied Developmental Psychology,* 15, 329–339.

Kouritzin, S. G. (1999). *Face(t)s of first language* loss.Mahwah, NJ: Erlbaum.

Ladson-Billings, G. (1995). Multicultural teacher education: Research, practice, and policy. In J. A. Banks & C. A. McGee Banks (Eds.), *Handbook of research on multicultural education* (pp. 747–759). Toronto, Canada: Prentice Hall International.

Ladson-Billings, G. (2001). *Crossing over to Canaan: The journey of new teachers in diverse classrooms*. San Francisco: Jossey-Bass.

Lee, S. J. (1994). Behind the model-minority stereotype: Voices of high and low-achieving Asian American students. *Anthropology & Education Quarterly,* 25, 413–429.

Lee, S. J. (1996). *Unravelling the "modelminority" stereotype: Listening to Asian American youth*. New York: Teachers College Press.

Lee, S. J. (2001). More than "model minority" or "delinquents": A look at Hmong American high school students. *Harvard Educational Review, 71,* 505–528.

Li, G. (2002). "East is East, West is West"? Home literacy, culture, and schooling. In J. L. Kincheloe & J. A. Jipson (Eds.), *Rethinking childhood book series* (Vol. 28). New York: Peter Lang.

Li, G. (2005). *Culturally contested pedagogy: Battles of literacy and schooling between mainstream teachers and Asian immigrant parents*. Albany, NY: SUNY Press.

McCaleb, S. P. (1994). *Building communities of learners: A collaboration among teachers, students, families and community*. New York: St. Martin's Press.

Moodley, K. A. (1995). Multicultural education in Canada: Historical development and current status. In J. A. Banks & C. A. McGee Banks (Eds.), *Handbook of research on multicultural education* (pp. 801–820). Toronto, Canada: Prentice Hall International.

Nieto, S., & Bode, P. (2008). *Affirming diversity: The sociopolitical context of multicultural education* (5th ed.). New York: Longman.

Phillion, J., & He, M. F. (2004). Using life based literary narratives in multicultural teacher education. *Multicultural Perspectives, 6*(2), 3–9.

Pinar, W. F., Reynolds, W. M., Slattery, P., & Taubman, P. M. (1995). *Understanding curriculum: An introduction to the study of historical and contemporary curriculum discourses*. New York: Peter Lang.

Rodriguez, R. (1982). *Hunger of memory: The education of Richard Rodriguez*. Boston: David R. Godine.

Rolon-Dow, R. (2004). Seduced by images: Identity and schooling in the lives of Puerto Rican girls. *Anthropology & Education Quarterly, 35,* 8–29.

Ross, V., & Chan, E. (2008). Multicultural education: Raj's story using a curricular conceptual lens of the particular. *Teaching and Teacher Education, 24,* 1705–1716.

Sarroub, L. K. (2005). *All-American Yemeni girls: Being Muslim in a public school*. Philadelphia: University of Pennsylvania Press.

Schubert, W., & Ayers, W. (Eds.) *Teacher lore: Learning from our own experience*. New York: Longman.

Smith-Hefner, N. (1993). Education, gender, and generational conflict among Khmer refugees. *Anthropology & Education Quarterly, 24,* 135–158.

Statistics Canada. (2008). *Canada's ethnocultural mosaic, 2006* census. Retrieved July 1, 2008, from http://www12.statcan.ca/english/census06/analysis/ethnicorigin/pdf/97-562-XIE2006001.pdf

U.S. Census Bureau. (2002). *United States Census 2000*. Washington, D.C: U.S. Government Printing Office.

Valdes, G. (1996). *Con respeto: Bridging the distances between culturally diverse families and schools. An ethnographic portrait*. New York: Teachers College Press.

Villegas, A. M. (1991). *Culturally responsive pedagogy for the 1990's and beyond*. Princeton, NJ: Educational Testing Service.

Wong-Fillmore, L. (1991). When learning a second language means losing the first. *Early Childhood Research Quarterly, 6,* 323–346.

Zine, J. (2001). Muslim youth in Canadian schools: Education and the politics of religious identity. *Anthropology & Education Quarterly, 32,* 399–423.

Author Note

Elaine Chan is an assistant professor of Diversity and Curriculum Studies in the Department of Teaching, Learning, and Teacher Education at the College of Education and Human Sciences, the University of Nebraska-Lincoln. Her research and teaching interests are in the areas of: narrative inquiry, culture and curriculum; multicultural education; ethnic identity of first-generation North Americans; student experiences of schooling; and educational equity policies. She has taught and conducted long-term classroom-based research in Canadian, Japanese, and American schools. She is currently co-authoring a book on engaging ELL students in arts education with Margaret Macintyre Latta.

• Appendix C •

A Phenomenological Study—"Cognitive Representations of AIDS"

Elizabeth H. Anderson

Margaret Hull Spencer

Authors' Note: This study was funded in part by a University of Connecticut Intramural Faculty Small Grants and School of Nursing Dean's Fund.

We wish to thank Cheryl Beck, D.N.Sc., and Deborah McDonald, Ph.D., for reading an earlier draft. Special thanks go to Stephanie Lennon, BSN, for her research assistance.

Address reprint requests to Elizabeth H. Anderson, Ph.D., A.P.R.N., Assistant Professor, University of Connecticut School of Nursing, 231 Glenbrook Road, U-2026, Storrs, CT 06269-2026, USA.

Cognitive representations of illness determine behavior. How persons living with AIDS image their disease might be key to understanding medication adherence and other health behaviors. The authors' purpose was to describe AIDS patients' cognitive representations of their illness. A purposive sample of 58 men and women with AIDS were interviewed. Using Colaizzi's (1978) phenomenological method, rigor was established through application of verification, validation, and validity. From 175 significant statements, 11 themes emerged. Cognitive representations included imaging AIDS as death, bodily destruction, and just a disease. Coping focused on wiping AIDS out of the mind, hoping for the right drug, and caring for oneself. Inquiring about a patient's image of AIDS might help nurses assess coping processes and enhance nurse-patient relationships.

A 53-year-old man with a history of intravenous drug use, prison, shelters, and methadone maintenance described AIDS as follows:

> My image of the virus was one of total destruction. It might as well have killed me, because it took just about everything out of my life. It was just as bad as

being locked up. You have everything taken away from you. The only thing to do is to wait for death. I was afraid and I was mad. Mostly I didn't care about myself anymore. I will start thinking about the disease, and I'll start wondering if these meds are really going to do it for me.

To date, 36 million people worldwide (Centers for Disease Control and Prevention [CDC], 2001b) are infected with Human Immunodeficiency Virus (HIV) that develops into end-stage Acquired Immunodeficiency Syndrome (AIDS). In the United States, 448,060 have died of AIDS-related illnesses, and more than 322,000 persons are living with AIDS, the highest number ever reported (CDC, 2001a). With HIV/AIDS, 95% adherence to antiretroviral (ART) drug regimens is necessary for complete viral suppression and prevention of mutant strains (Bartlett & Gallant, 2001). Adherence to ART regimens can slow the disease process but does not cure HIV or AIDS. Persons with AIDS experience numerous side effects associated with ART drugs, which can lead to missed doses, profound weight loss, and decreased quality of life (Douaihy & Singh, 2001). The incidence of HIV/AIDS is reduced through prevention that is dependent on life-long commitment to the reduction of high-risk drug and sexual behaviors. To achieve maximum individual and public health benefits, it might be helpful to explore patients' lived experience of AIDS within the framework of the self-regulation model of illness.

In the Self-Regulation Model of Illness Representations, patients are active problem solvers whose behavior is a product of their cognitive and emotional responses to a health threat (Leventhal, Leventhal, & Cameron, 2001). In an ongoing process, people transform internal (e.g., symptoms) or external (e.g., laboratory results) stimuli into cognitive representations of threat and/or emotional reactions that they attempt to understand and regulate. The meaning placed on a stimulus (internal or external) will influence the selection and performance of one or more coping procedures (Leventhal, Idler, & Leventhal, 1999). Emotions influence the formation of illness representations and can motivate a person to action or dissuade him or her from it. Appraisal of the consequences of coping efforts is the final step in the model and provides feedback for further information processing.

Although very individual, illness representations are the central cognitive constructs that guide coping and appraisal of outcomes. A patient's theory of illness is based on many factors, including bodily experience, previous illness, and external information. An illness representation has five sets of attributes: (a) identity (i.e., label, symptoms), (b) time line (i.e., onset, duration), (c) perceived cause (i.e., germs, stress, genetics), (d) consequences (i.e., death, disability, social loss), and (e) controllability (i.e., cured, controlled) (Leventhal, Idler, et al., 1999; Leventhal, Leventhal, et al., 2001).

Attributes have both abstract and concrete form. For example, the attribute "identity" can have an abstract disease label (e.g., AIDS) and concrete physical symptoms (e.g., nausea and vomiting). Symptoms are convenient and available cues or suggestions that can shape an illness representation and help a person correctly or incorrectly interpret the experience. Although symptoms are not medically associated with hypertension, patients who believed medications reduced their symptoms reported greater adherence and better blood pressure control (Leventhal, Leventhal, et al., 2001).

Understanding how individuals cognitively represent AIDS and their emotional responses can facilitate adherence to therapeutic regimens, reduce high-risk behaviors, and enhance quality of life. Phenomenology provides the richest and most descriptive data (Streubert & Carpenter, 1999) and thus is the ideal research process for eliciting cognitive representations. Consequently, the purpose of this study was to explore patients' experience and cognitive representations of AIDS within the context of phenomenology.

Review of the Literature

Vogl et al. (1999), in a study of 504 ambulatory patients with AIDS who were not taking protease inhibitor (PI) drugs, found the most prevalent symptoms were worry, fatigue, sadness, and pain. Both the number of symptoms and the level of symptom distress were associated with psychological distress and poorer quality of life. Persons with a history of intravenous drug use reported more symptoms and greater symptom distress. In contrast, a telephone survey and chart review of 45 men and women with HIV/AIDS suggested that PI therapy was associated with weight gain, improved CD4 counts, decreased HIV RNA viral loads, fewer opportunistic infections, and better quality of life (Echeverria, Jonnalagadda, Hopkins, & Rosenbloom, 1999).

Reporting on pain from patients' perspective, Holzemer, Henry, and Reilly (1998) noted that 249 AIDS patients reported experiencing a moderate level of pain, but only 80% had effective pain control. A higher level of pain was associated with lower quality of life. In a phenomenological study focusing on pain, persons with HIV/AIDS viewed pain as not only physical but also an experience of loss, not knowing, and social (Laschinger & Fothergill-Bourbonnais, 1999).

Turner (2000), in a hermeneutic study of HIV-infected men and women, found that AIDS-related multiple loss was an intense, repetitive process of grief. Two constitutive patterns emerged: Living with Loss and Living beyond Loss. Likewise, Brauhn (1999), in a phenomenological study of 12 men and 5 women, found that although persons with HIV/AIDS experienced their illness as a chronic disease, their illness had a profound and pervasive impact on their identity. Participants planned for their future with cautious optimism but could identify positive aspects about their illness.

McCain and Gramling (1992), in a phenomenological study on coping with HIV disease, reported three processes: Living with Dying, Fighting the Sickness, and Getting Worn Out. Koopman et al. (2000) found that among 147 HIV-positive persons, those with the greatest level of stress in their daily lives had lower incomes, disengaged behaviorally/emotionally in coping with their illness, and approached interpersonal relationships in a less secure or more anxious manner. With somewhat similar results, Farber, Schwartz, Schaper, Moonen, and McDaniel (2000) noted that adaptation to HIV/AIDS was associated with lower psychological distress, higher quality of life, and more positive personal beliefs related to the world, people, and self-worth. Fryback and Reinert (1999), in a qualitative study of women with cancer and men with HIV/AIDS, found spirituality to be an essential component to health and well-being. Respondents who found meaning in their disease reported a better quality of life than before diagnosis.

Dominguez (1996) summarized the essential structure of living with HIV/AIDS for women of Mexican heritage as struggling in despair to endure a fatal, transmittable, and socially stigmatizing illness that threatens a woman's very self and existence. Women were seen as suffering in silence while experiencing shame, blame, and concern for children. In a phenomenological study of five HIV-infected African American women, 12 themes emerged, ranging from violence, shock, and denial to uncertainty and survival (Russell & Smith, 1999). The researchers concluded that women have complex experiences that need to be better understood before effective health care interventions can be designed.

No studies reported AIDS patients' cognitive representations or images of AIDS. Consequently, this study focused on how persons with AIDS cognitively represented and imaged their disease.

Method

Sample

A purposive sample of 41 men and 17 women with a diagnosis of AIDS participated in this phenomenological study. Participants were predominately Black (40%), White (29%), and Hispanic (28%). Average age was 42 years ($SD = 8.2$). The majority had less than a high school education (52%) and were never married (53%), although many reported being in a relationship. Mean CD4 count was 153.4 ($SD = 162.8$) and mean viral load, 138,113 ($SD = 270,564.9$). Average time from HIV diagnosis to interview was 106.4 months ($SD = 64.2$). Inclusion criteria were (a) diagnosis of AIDS, (b) 18 years of age or older, (c) able to communicate in English, and (d) Mini-Mental Status exam score > 22.

Research Design

In phenomenology, the researcher transcends or suspends past knowledge and experience to understand a phenomenon at a deeper level (Merleau-Ponty, 1956). It is an attempt to approach a lived experience with a sense of "newness" to elicit rich and descriptive data. Bracketing is a process of setting aside one's beliefs, feelings, and perceptions to be more open or faithful to the phenomenon (Colaizzi, 1978; Streubert & Carpenter, 1999). As a health care provider for and researcher with persons with HIV/AIDS, it was necessary for the interviewer to acknowledge and attempt to bracket those experiences. No participant had been a patient of the interviewer.

Colaizzi (1978) held that the success of phenomenological research questions depends on the extent to which the questions touch lived experiences distinct from theoretical explanations. Exploring a person's image of AIDS taps into a personal experience not previously studied or shared clinically with health care providers.

Procedure

After approval from the university's Institutional Review Board and a city hospital's Human Subject Review Committee, persons who met inclusion criteria were approached and asked to participate. Interviews were conducted over 18 months at three sites dedicated to persons with HIV/AIDS: a hospital-based clinic, a long-term care facility, and a residence. All interviews were tape-recorded and transcribed verbatim. Participants were involved in multiple life situations and were unavailable for repeated interviews related to personal plans, discharge, returning to life on the street, or progression of the disease. One participant died within 4 weeks of the interview. Interviews lasted between 10 and 40 minutes and proceeded until no new themes emerged. Persons who reported not thinking about AIDS provided the shortest interviews. Consequently, to obtain greater richness of data and variation of images, we interviewed 58 participants (Morse, 2000). The first researcher conducted all 58 interviews.

After obtaining informed consent, each participant was asked to verbally respond to the following: "What is your experience with AIDS? Do you have a mental image of HIV/AIDS, or how would you describe HIV/AIDS? What feelings come to mind? What meaning does it have in your life?" As the richness of cognitive representations emerged, it became apparent that greater depth could be achieved by asking participants to draw their image of AIDS and provide an explanation of their drawing. Eight participants drew their image of AIDS.

Background information was obtained through a paper-and-pencil questionnaire. Most recent CD4 and Viral Load laboratory values were obtained from patient charts. Based on institution policy, participants at the long-term care facility and residence received a $5.00 movie pass. Clinic participants received $20.00.

Data Analysis

Colaizzi's (1978) phenomenological method was employed in analyzing participants' transcripts. In this method, all written transcripts are read several times to obtain an overall feeling for them. From each transcript, significant phrases or sentences that pertain directly to the lived experience of AIDS are identified. Meanings are then formulated from the significant statements and phrases. The formulated meanings are clustered into themes allowing for the emergence of themes common to all of the participants' transcripts. The results are then integrated into an in-depth, exhaustive description of the phenomenon. Once descriptions and themes have been obtained, the researcher in the final step may approach some participants a second time to validate the findings. If new relevant data emerge, they are included in the final description.

Methodological rigor was attained through the application of verification, validation, and validity (Meadows & Morse, 2001). Verification is the first step in achieving validity of a research project. This standard was fulfilled through literature searches, adhering to the phenomenological method, bracketing past experiences, keeping field notes, using an adequate sample, identification of negative cases, and interviewing until saturation of data was achieved (Frankel, 1999; Meadows & Morse, 2001). Validation, a within-project evaluation, was accomplished by multiple methods of data collection (observations, interviews, and drawings), data analysis and coding by the more experienced researcher, member checks by participants and key informants, and audit trails. Validity is the outcome goal of research and is based on trustworthiness and external reviews. Clinical application is suggested through empathy and assessment of coping status (Kearney, 2001).

Results

From 58 verbatim transcripts, 175 significant statements were extracted. Table 1 includes examples of significant statements with their formulated meanings. Arranging the formulated meanings into clusters resulted in 11 themes. Table 2 contains two examples of theme clusters that emerged from their associated meanings.

Theme 1: Inescapable death. Focusing on negative consequences of their disease was the pervading image for many persons with AIDS. Responding quickly and spontaneously, AIDS was described as "death, just death," "leprosy," "a nightmare," "a curse," a "black cloud," and "an evil force getting back at you." The sense of not being able to escape was evident in descriptions of AIDS as "The blob. It's a big Jell-O thing that comes and swallows you up" and "It's like I'm in a hole and I can't get out." Another stated, "AIDS, it's a killer and it will get you at any God-given time."

A sense of defeat was evident in a Hispanic man's explanation that with AIDS you are a "goner." He stated, "With HIV you still have a chance to fight. Once that word 'AIDS' starts coming up in your records, you bought a ticket [to death]."

TABLE 1 ● Selected Examples of Significant Statements of Persons With AIDS and Related Formulated Meanings	
Significant Statement	*Formulated Meaning*
In the beginning, I had a sense that I did have it, so it wasn't an unexpected thing although it did bother me. I know it was a bad thing to let it traumatize so.	AIDS is such a traumatizing reality that people have difficulty verbalizing the word "AIDS."
[AIDS] a disease that has no cure. Meaning of dread and doom and you got to fight it the best way you can. You got to fight it with everything you can to keep going.	AIDS is a dangerous disease that requires every fiber of your being to fight so you can live.
I see people go from somebody being really healthy to just nothing—to skin and bones and deteriorate. I've lost a lot of friends that way. It's nothing pretty. I used to be a diesel mechanic. I can't even carry groceries up a flight of stairs anymore.	As physical changes are experienced, an image of AIDS wasting dominates thoughts.
First image—death. Right away fear and death. That's because I didn't know any better. Now it's destruction. Pac-man eating all your immune cells up and you have nothing to fight with.	Overwhelming image of AIDS is one of death and destruction, with no hope of winning

TABLE 2 ● Example of Two Theme Clusters With Their Associated Formulated Meanings
Dreaded bodily destruction
Physical changes include dry mouth, weight loss, mental changes
Expects tiredness, loss of vision, marks all over the body
Holocaust victims
Confined to bed with sores all over
Extreme weight loss
Horrible way to die
Changes from being really healthy to skin and bones
Bodily deterioration
Devouring life
Whole perspective on life changed
Never had a chance to have a family
Life has stopped
No longer able to work
Will never have normal relations with women
Uncertain what's going to happen from day to day
Worked hard and lost everything

A 29-year-old woman, diagnosed with HIV and AIDS 9 months before the interview, drew a picture of a grave with delicate red and yellow flowers and wrote on the tomb stone "RIP Devoted Sister and Daughter." Over the grave, she drew a black cloud with the sun peeking around the edge, which she described as symbolizing her family's sadness at her death.

Theme 2: Dreaded bodily destruction. In this cluster, respondents focused on physical changes associated with their illness. AIDS was envisioned as people who were skin and bones, extremely weak, in pain, losing their minds, and lying in bed waiting for the end. Descriptions were physically consistent but drawn from a variety of experiences, such as seeing a family member or friend die from AIDS, or from pictures of holocaust victims. It is an ending that is feared and a thought that causes deep pain. Body image became a marker for level of wellness or approach of death.

One woman described her image of AIDS as a skeleton crying. An extremely tall, thin man awaiting a laryngectomy on the eve of his 44th birthday described his image of AIDS by saying, "Look at me." Another recalled Tom Hanks in the movie *Philadelphia* (Saxon & Demme, 1993): "The guy in the hospital and how he aged and how thin he got. You start worrying about . . . you don't want to end like that. I don't

like the image I see when I see AIDS." A 53-year-old man with a 10-year history of HIV/
AIDS drew his image of AIDS as a devil with multiple ragged horns, bloodshot eyes,
and a mouth with numerous sharp, pointed teeth. He described the mouth as "teeth
with blood dripping down and sucking you dry." Another man drew AIDS as an angry
purple animal with red teeth. He stated the color purple symbolized a "bruise" and the
red teeth "destruction." The extensive physical and emotional devastation of AIDS was
evident in the drawing by a 36-year-old Black woman, who pictured herself lying on a
bed surrounded by her husband and children. She wrote, "Pain from head to toe, no
hair, 75 pounds, can't move, can't eat, lonely and scared. Family loving you and you
can't love them back."

Theme 3: Devouring life. Persons grieved for their past lives. A 41-year-old man
described AIDS as, "It's not like I can walk around the corner or go to the park with
friends because it has devoured your life." Another man noted, "My life has stopped."
A 48-year-old woman stated, "I feel like I have no life. It has changed my whole perspective."

With the diagnosis of AIDS, dreams of marrying, having children, or working were
no longer perceived as possible. The impact on each one's life was measured differently
from loss of ability to work to loss of children, family, possessions, and sense of oneself. The thought of leaving children, family, and friends was extremely difficult but
considered a reality. A woman with four children aged 8 to 12 years stated,

> It's not a disease that you would want to have because it's really bad. I know
> I get upset sometimes because I have it. You know you are going to die and I
> have kids. I really don't want to leave them. I want to see them grow up and
> everything. I know that's not going to happen.

Consistently, participants felt a deep rupture in life as illustrated in the following
statement: "It just took my whole life and turned it upside down. I can't do a lot of the
things I used to. I lost a house because of it. Everything I worked for I lost." A 44-year-
old Hispanic mother of two boys reported with sadness,

> It has affected my life. I have lost my children by not being able to take care of
> them. It has changed my freedom and relationships. Being sick all the time and
> I couldn't take care of my little one, so he was taken away from me.

A Black woman described the far-reaching effect AIDS had on her life as follows:

> Everything is different about me now. The way I look, the way I talk, the way I
> walk, the way I feel on a daily basis. I miss my life before, I really do. I miss it a
> lot. I don't think about it because it makes me sad.

Theme 4: Hoping for the right drug. In this theme, people focused on pharmacological treatment/cure for AIDS. Hope was evident as participants expressed anticipation that a medication recently started would help them or a cure would be found in their lifetime. One person described it as, "You start becoming anxious and you're hoping that you get some kind of good news today about a new pill or something that's going to help you with the disease." Another, diagnosed within the last 3 years, wondered, "With all the new meds and everything, they say you can live a normal life and a long life. Time will tell, I guess."

Some participants had been told that there were no drugs available for them. A 31-year-old woman, diagnosed for 16 years, reported, "They haven't been able to find a medicine that won't keep me from being sick, so I'm not taking any HIV meds." Others spoke of waiting to see how their bodies responded to newly prescribed ART medications. A Hispanic man articulated his search:

> I try not to let it bother me because my viral load and everything is real low. The meds are not working for me. We [health care provider and patient] are still trying to find the right one. As long as I'm still living, that's what I'm happy about.

The hope of finding a cure was on the minds of many. A 53-year-old man diagnosed for 10 years noted, "I'm just happy to be here now and hope to be here when they find something." Another stated, "Just hope [for a cure] and hold on." In contrast, a 41-year-old man diagnosed for 9 years stated, "There is no cure and I don't see any coming either." A 56-year-old man, living 13 years with HIV/AIDS, expressed a similar view: "I don't think there is a cure, not right around the corner anyhow. Not in my lifetime."

Theme 5: Caring for oneself. Persons with AIDS attempted to control the progress of their disease by caring for themselves. This was evident in the following responses: "If I don't take care of myself, I know I can die from it [AIDS]" and "It's a deadly disease if you don't take care of yourself." A Hispanic man explained, "We never know how long we are going to live. I have to take care of myself if I want to live a couple of years." One woman spoke of her fears and efforts to cope:

> I'm scared—losing the weight and losing the mind and whatnot. I'm scared, but I don't let it get me down. I think about it and whatever is going to happen. I can't stop it. I try to take care of myself and go on.

How to take care of oneself was not always articulated. Eating and taking prescribed medications seemed to be a major focus. "When I get up I know that my first priority is to eat and take my medication." This singleness of purpose is further illustrated in the statement, "I can't think of anything else other than keeping myself healthy so that I can live a little longer. Take my medications. Live a little longer."

Theme 6: Just a disease. In this cluster of images, people cognitively represented the cause of AIDS as "an unseen virus," "like any infection," "a common cold," and "a little mini bug the size of a mite." Minimizing the external cause, one participant viewed AIDS as an "inconvenience" and another as having been dealt a "bad card."

Some normalized AIDS by imaging it as a chronic disease. Like people with cancer or diabetes, persons with AIDS felt the need to get on with their lives and not focus on their illness. The supposition was that if medications were taken and treatments followed they could control their illness the same as persons do with cancer or diabetes. The physical or psychological consequences that occur with other chronic diseases were not mentioned. The following two excerpts illustrate the disease image:

> It's just a disease. Since I go to support groups and everything, they tell me to look at it as if it were cancer or diabetes and just do what you have to do. Take your medicine, leave the drugs alone, and you will acquire a long life.

And

> [AIDS is] a controllable disease, not a curse. I'm going to control it for the rest of my life. I feel lucky. There is nothing wrong with me. I'm insisting on seeing it that way. It may not be right, but it keeps me going good.

Sometimes, the explanations for AIDS were scientifically incorrect but presented a means for coping. One man described AIDS: "It's just a disease. It's a form of cancer and that's been going on for years and they just come up with the diagnosis."

Theme 7: Holding a wildcat. In this theme, people focused on hypervigilance during battle. While under permanent siege, every fiber of their being was used to fight "a life-altering disease." A 48-year-old man diagnosed 6 months before the interview stated, "I have to pay attention to it. It's serious enough to put me out of work." Another man, diagnosed for 6 years, was firm in his resolve: "I'm a fighter and I'm never going to give up until they come up with a cure for this." These images were essentially positive as can be seen in the following description of AIDS in which a scratch by a wildcat is not "super serious."

> To me HIV is sort of like you've got a wildcat by the head staring you in the face, snapping and snarling. As long as you are attentive, you can keep it at bay. If you lose your grip or don't maintain the attentiveness, it will reach out and scratch you. Which in most cases is not a super serious thing, but it's something of a concern that it will put you in the hospital or something like that. You got to follow the rules quite regimentally and don't let go. If you let go, it will run you over.

Vigilance was used not only to control one's own disease progression but also to protect others. A woman diagnosed for 3 years noted,

Just being conscious of it because when you got kids and when you got family that you live with, you have to be extremely cautious. You got to realize it at all times. It has to just be stuck in your mind that you have it and don't want to share it. Even attending to one of your children's cuts.

Theme 8: Magic of not thinking. Some made a strong effort to forget their disease and, at times, their need for treatment. A few reported no image of AIDS. Thinking about AIDS caused anger, anxiety, sadness, and depression. Not thinking about AIDS seemed to magically erase the reality, and it provided a means for controlling emotions and the disease. A 41-year-old man who has lived with his disease 10 years described AIDS:

It's a sickness, but in my mind I don't think that I got it. Because if you think about having HIV, it comes down more on you. It's more like a mind game. To try and stay alive is that you don't even think about it. It's not in the mind.

The extent to which some participants tried not to think about AIDS can be seen in the following descriptions in which the word *AIDS* was not spoken and only referred to as "it." A 44-year-old Hispanic woman stated, "It's a painful thing. It's a sad thing. It's an angry thing. I don't think much of it. I try to keep it out of my mind." Another woman asserted, "It's a terrible experience. It's very bad, I can't even explain it. I never think about it. I try not to think about it. I just don't think about it. That's it, just cross it out of my mind."

Theme 9: Accepting AIDS. In this theme, cognitive representations centered on a general acceptance of the diagnosis of AIDS. Accepting the fact of having AIDS was seen as vital to coping well. People with AIDS readily assessed their coping efforts.

A Hispanic woman noted, "I'm not in denial any more." A 39-year-old Hispanic man who has had the disease for 8 years stated, "Like it or not you have to deal with this disease." Another noted, "You have to live with it and deal with it and that's what I'm trying to do." A 56-year-old man who has had the disease for 13 years summarized his coping:

Either you adjust or you don't adjust. What are you going to do? That's life. It's up to you. I'm happy. I eat well and I take care of myself. I go out. I don't let this put me in a box. Sometimes you don't like it, but you have to accept it because you really can't change it.

Individuals diagnosed more recently struggled to accept their disease. A Black man diagnosed for 2 years vacillated in his acceptance: "I hate that word. I'm still trying to accept it, I think. Yes, I am trying to accept it." However, he stated that he avoids conversation about HIV/AIDS and is not as open with his family. Another man diagnosed 3 years prior noted,

I still don't believe that it's happen to me and it's taken all this time to get a grip on it or to deal with it. I still haven't got a grip on it, but I'm trying. It's finally sinking in that I do have it and I'm starting to feel lousy about it.

Neither of these last participants mentioned the word "HIV" or "AIDS."

Theme 10: Turning to a higher power. In this theme, cognitive representations of AIDS were associated with "God," "prayer," "church," and "spirituality." Some saw AIDS as a motivation to change their lives and reach for God. An Hispanic man living with HIV/AIDS for 6 years stated, "If I didn't have AIDS, I'd probably still be out there drinking, drugging, and hurting people. I turned my life around. I gave myself over to the Lord and Jesus Christ." Another noted, "It [AIDS] worries me. What I do is a lot of praying. It really makes me reach for God."

Others saw religion as a means to help them cope with AIDS. One person expressed it as "I know I can make it from the grace of God. My Jesus Christ is my Savior and that's what's keeping me going every day." One man reported how his spirituality not only helped him cope but also made him a better person:

At one point I just wanted to give up. If it wasn't for knowing the love of Jesus I couldn't have the strength to keep going. I feel today that I'm a better person spiritually. Maybe not healthwise, but more understanding of this disease.

In contrast, a man diagnosed in jail attributed AIDS to a punishment from God: "Sometimes God punishes you. It's like I told my wife. I should have cleaned up my act."

Theme 11: Recouping with time. Although the initial fear and shock was overwhelming, time became a healer such that images, feelings, and processes of coping changed. A sense of imminent doom hurled some into constant preoccupation with their illness, despondency, and increased addiction. Living with HIV/AIDS facilitated change. One woman noted, "When I first found out, I wanted to kill myself and just get it over with. But now it's different. I want to live and just live out the rest of my life." Another described her transition as, "At first I thought I was going to be all messed up, all dried up and looking weird and stuff like that, but I don't think of those things anymore. I just keep living life."

As time passed, negative behaviors were replaced with knowledge about their illness, efforts at medication adherence, and a journey of personal growth facilitated by people who believed in them. One man reported that his initial image changed from being in bed with tubes coming out of his nose and Kaposi sarcoma over his body to living a normal life except for not being able to work.

Change was evident in one man's image of AIDS as a time line. He drew a wide vertical line beginning at the top with the first phase, diagnosis, colored red because "it means things are not good, like a red light on a machine." The next phase was shaded blue and labeled "medication, education, and acceptance" to reflect the sky that he could see from his inpatient bed. The final stage was colored bright yellow and labeled "hope."

A 40-year-old Hispanic man drew a chronicle of his life with five addictive substances beginning with alcohol to the injection of heroin. He then sketched four views of himself showing the end stage of his disease: a standing skeleton without face, hair, clothes, or shoes; a sad-faced person without hair lying in a hospital bed; and a grave with flowers. The final picture drawn was of a drug-free person with a well-developed body, smiling face, hair, shoes, shirt, and shorts, symbolizing his readiness for a vacation in Florida. In contrast, a 53-year-old man reported that in 14 years he had no change in his image of AIDS as a "black cloud."

Results were integrated into an essential schema of AIDS. The lived experience of AIDS was initially frightening, with a dread of body wasting and personal loss.

Cognitive representations of AIDS included inescapable death, bodily destruction, fighting a battle, and having a chronic disease. Coping methods included searching for the "right drug," caring for oneself, accepting the diagnosis, wiping AIDS out of their thoughts, turning to God, and using vigilance. With time, most people adjusted to living with AIDS. Feelings ranged from "devastating," "sad," and "angry" to being at "peace" and "not worrying."

Discussion

In this study, persons with AIDS focused on the end stage of wasting, weakness, and mental incapacity as a painful, dreaded, inevitable outcome. An initial response was to ignore the disease, but symptoms pressed in on their reality and forced a seeking of health care. Hope was manifested in waiting for a particular drug to work and holding on until a cure is found. Many participants saw a connection between caring for themselves and the length of their lives.

Some participants focused on the final outcome of death, whereas others spoke of the emotional and social consequences of AIDS in their lives. Efforts were made to regulate mood and disease by increased attentiveness, controlling thoughts, accepting their illness, and turning to spirituality. Some coped by thinking of AIDS as a chronic illness like cancer or diabetes.

As noted earlier, McCain and Gramling (1992) identified three methods of coping with HIV, namely, Living with Dying, Fighting the Sickness, and Getting Worn Out. Images of Dying and Fighting were strong in Themes 1 (Inescapable Death) and 7 (Holding a Wildcat). Participants in this study were well aware of whether they were coping. Many spoke about accepting or dealing with AIDS, whereas others could not stand the word, tried to wipe it out of their minds, or referred to AIDS as "it."

Consistent with Fryback and Reinert's study (1999), Theme 10, Turning to a Higher Power, emerged as a means of coping as participants faced their mortality. Like Turner's (2000) sample, participants in the current study experienced many changes/losses in their lives and reflected on death and dying. Similar to Turner's theme of Lessons Learned, some participants saw AIDS as a turning point in their lives.

Aligned with Brauhn's (1999) study, chronic disease emerged as an image. In contrast to Brauhn's sample, these participants used the nomenclature of chronic illness to minimize the negative aspects of AIDS. It can be posited that the lack of cautious optimism in planning their future was not present in this study because the entire sample had AIDS.

Theoretical Elements

As Diefenbach and Leventhal (1996) noted, cognitive representations were highly individual and not always in accord with medical facts. Consistent with research in other illnesses, persons with AIDS had cognitive representations reflecting attributes of consequences, causes, disease time line, and controllability (Leventhal, Leventhal, et al., 2001). In particular, we identified three themes that centered on anticipated or experienced consequences associated with AIDS. Inescapable Death and Dreaded Bodily Destruction involved negative physical consequences that are understandable at end stage in a disease with no known cure. The theme Devouring Life focused on the far-reaching emotional, social, and economic consequences experienced by participants. The Just a Disease theme reflected cognitive representations of the cause of AIDS and Recouping with Time had elements of a disease time line from diagnosis to burial.

Six themes (Hoping for the Right Drug, Caring for Oneself, Holding a Wildcat, Magic of Not Thinking, Accepting AIDS, and Turning to a Higher Power) were similar to the controllability attribute of illness representations. Previous research centered on controlling a disease or condition through an intervention by the individual or an expert, such as taking a medication or having surgery (Leventhal, Leventhal, et al., 2001). This finding was substantiated in the themes Hoping for the Right Drug and Caring for Oneself. Unique to this study, persons with AIDS attempted to control not only their emotions but also their disease through vigilance, avoidance, acceptance, and spirituality coping methods. This is particularly evident in the statement that "To try and stay alive is that you don't even think about it." This study extends previous research on illness representations to persons with AIDS and contributes to the theory of Self-Regulation by suggesting that in AIDS coping methods function like the attribute controllability. Of note is that eight participants drew and described their dominant image of AIDS. These drawings provide a unique revelation of participants' concerns, fears, and beliefs. Having participants draw images of AIDS provides a new method of assessing a person's dominant illness representation.

Implications for Nursing

Inquiring about a patient's image of AIDS might be an efficient, cost-effective method for nurses to assess a patient's illness representation and coping processes as well as enhance nurse-patient relationships. Patients who respond that AIDS is "death" or "they wipe it out of their minds" might need more psychological support.

Many respondents used their image of AIDS as a starting point to share their illness experiences. As persons with AIDS face their mortality, reminiscing with someone who treasures their stories can be a priceless gift. Asking patients about their image of AIDS might touch feelings not previously shared and facilitate patients' self-discovery and acceptance of their illness.

Future Research

Cognitive representations have been identified with AIDS. From this research, it can be posited that how a person images AIDS might influence medication adherence, high-risk behavior, and quality of life. If persons with AIDS believed that there is no hope for them, would they adhere to a difficult medication regimen or one with noxious side effects? Would a person who experienced emotional and social consequences of AIDS be more likely to protect others from contracting the disease? Would it be reasonable to expect that persons who focus on fighting AIDS or caring for themselves would be more likely to adhere to medication regimens? Do persons who turn to a higher power, accept their diagnosis, or minimize the disease have a better quality of life? Further research combining images of AIDS and objective measures of medication adherence, risk behaviors, and quality of life is needed to determine if there is an association between specific illness representations and adherence, risk behaviors, and/or quality of life.

References

Bartlett, J. G., & Gallant, J. E. (2001). *Medical management of HIV infection, 2001–2002.* Baltimore: Johns Hopkins University, Division of Infectious Diseases.

Brauhn, N. E. H. (1999). Phenomenology of having HIV/AIDS at a time when medical advances are improving prognosis. Unpublished doctoral dissertation, University of Iowa.

Centers for Disease Control and Prevention. (2001a). HIV and AIDS—United States, 1981–2000. *MMWR 2001, 50*(21), 430–434.

Centers for Disease Control and Prevention. (2001b). The global HIV and AIDS epidemic, 2001. *MMWR 2001, 50*(21), 434–439.

Colaizzi, P. F. (1978). Psychological research as the phenomenologist views it. In R. Valle & M. King (Eds.), *Existential phenomenological alternatives in psychology* (pp. 48–71). New York: Oxford University Press.

Diefenbach, M. A., & Leventhal, H. (1996). The common-sense model of illness representation: Theoretical and practical considerations. *Journal of Social Distress and the Homeless, 5*(1), 11–38.

Dominguez, L. M. (1996). *The lived experience of women of Mexican heritage with HIV/AIDS.* Unpublished doctoral dissertation, University of Arizona.

Douaihy, A., & Singh, N. (2001). Factors affecting quality of life in patients with HIV infection. *AIDS Reader, 11*(9), 450–454, 460–461.

Echeverria, P. S., Jonnalagadda, S. S., Hopkins, B. L., & Rosenbloom, C. A. (1999). Perception of quality of life of persons with HIV/AIDS and maintenance of nutritional parameters while on protease inhibitors. *AIDS Patient Care and STDs, 13*(7), 427–433.

Farber, E. W., Schwartz, J. A., Schaper, P. E., Moonen, D. J., & McDaniel, J. S. (2000). Resilience factors associated with adaptation to HIV disease. *Psychosomatics, 41*(2), 140–146.

Frankel, R. M. (1999). Standards of qualitative research. In B. F. Crabtree & W. L. Miller (Eds.), *Doing qualitative research* (2nd ed., pp. 333–346). Thousand Oaks, CA: Sage.

Fryback, P. B., & Reinert, B. R. (1999). Spirituality and people with potentially fatal diagnoses. *Nursing Forum, 34*(1), 13–22.

Holzemer, W. L., Henry, S. B., & Reilly, C. A. (1998). Assessing and managing pain in AIDS care: The patient perspective. *Journal of the Association of Nurses in AIDS Care, 9*(1), 22–30.

Kearney, M. H. (2001). Focus on research methods: Levels and applications of qualitative research evidence. *Research in Nursing & Health, 24,* 145–153.

Koopman, C., Gore, F. C., Marouf, F., Butler, L. D., Field, N., Gill, M., Chen, X., Israelski, D., & Spiegel, D. (2000). Relationships of perceived stress to coping, attachment and social support among HIV positive persons. *AIDS Care, 12*(5), 663–672.

Laschinger, S. J., & Fothergill-Bourbonnais, F. (1999). The experience of pain in persons with HIV/AIDS. *Journal of the Association of Nurses in AIDS Care, 10*(5), 59–67.

Leventhal, H., Idler, E. L., & Leventhal, E. A. (1999). The impact of chronic illness on the self system. In R. J. Contrada & R. D. Ashmore (Eds.), *Self, social identity, and physical health* (pp. 185–208). New York: Oxford University Press.

Leventhal, H., Leventhal, E. A., & Cameron, L. (2001). Representations, procedures, and affect in illness self-regulation: A perceptual-cognitive model. In A. Baum, T. A. Revenson, & J. E. Singer (Eds.), *Handbook of health psychology* (pp. 19–47). Mahwah, NJ: Lawrence Erlbaum.

McCain, N. L., & Gramling, L. F. (1992). Living with dying: Coping with HIV disease. *Issues in Mental Health Nursing, 13*(3), 271–284.

Meadows, L. M., & Morse, J. M. (2001). Constructing evidence within the qualitative project. In J. M. Morse, J. M. Swansen, & A. Kuzel (Eds.), *Nature of qualitative evidence* (pp. 187–200). Thousand Oaks, CA: Sage.

Merleau-Ponty, M. (1956). What is phenomenology? *Cross Currents, 6,* 59–70.

Morse, J. M. (2000). Determining sample size. *Qualitative Health Research, 10*(1), 3–5.

Russell, J. M., & Smith, K. V. (1999). A holistic life view of human immunodeficiency virus-infected African American women. *Journal of Holistic Nursing, 17*(4), 331–345.

Saxon, E. (Producer), & Demme, J. (Producer/Director). (1993). *Philadelphia* [motion picture]. Burbank, CA: Columbia Tristar Home Video.

Streubert, H. J., & Carpenter, D. R. (1999). *Qualitative research in nursing: Advancing the humanistic imperative* (2nd ed.). New York: Lippincott.

Turner, J. A. (2000). The experience of multiple AIDS-related loss in persons with HIV disease: A Heideggerian hermeneutic analysis. Unpublished doctoral dissertation, Georgia State University.

Vogl, D., Rosenfeld, B., Breitbart, W., Thaler, H., Passik, S., McDonald, M., et al. (1999). Symptom prevalence, characteristics, and distress in AIDS outpatients. *Journal of Pain and Symptom Management, 18*(4), 253–262.

• Appendix D •

A Grounded Theory Study—"Developing Long-Term Physical Activity Participation: A Grounded Theory Study With African American Women"

Amy E. Harley

Janet Buckworth

Mira L. Katz

Sharla K. Willis

Angela Odoms-Young

Catherine A. Heaney

Amy E. Harley, Harvard School of Public Health, Boston. Janet Buckworth, The Ohio State University School of Physical Activity and Educational Services, Columbus. Mira L. Katz and Sharla K. Willis, The Ohio State University College of Public Health, Columbus. Angela Odoms-Young, Northern Illinois University College of Health and Human Sciences, DeKalb, Illinois. Catherine A. Heaney, Stanford University Psychology Department, California.

Address correspondence to Amy E. Harley, Harvard School of Public Health, 677 Huntington Avenue, 7th Floor, Boston, MA 02115; phone: (617) 582-8292; e-mail: amy_harley@dfci.harvard.edu.

Health Education & Behavior, Vol. 36 (1): 97–112 (February 2009)
DOI: 10.1177/1090198107306434
© 2009 by SOPHE

Regular physical activity is linked to a reduced risk of obesity and chronic disease. African American women bear a disproportionate burden from these conditions and many do not get the recommended amount of physical activity. Long-term success of interventions to initiate and maintain a physically active lifestyle among African American women has not been realized. By clearly elucidating the process of physical activity adoption and maintenance, effective programming could be implemented to reduce African American women's burden from chronic conditions. In-depth interviews were conducted with physically active African American women. Grounded theory, a rigorous qualitative research method used to develop theoretical explanation of human behavior grounded in data collected from those exhibiting that behavior, was used to guide the data collection and analysis process. Data derived inductively from the interviews and focus groups guided the development of a behavioral framework explaining the process of physical activity evolution.

Keywords

physical activity; African American; women's health; qualitative research

The link between physical activity and health is well established. Not only does lack of participation in physical activity contribute to the rising obesity rates in the United States, but it also directly contributes to the risk for several chronic diseases and leading causes of death in the United States, such as heart disease, hypertension, Type 2 diabetes, and certain cancers (Friedenreich & Orenstein, 2002; U.S. Department of Health and Human Services [USDHHS], 1996). In addition, regular physical activity is linked to a reduction in the risk of dying prematurely in general and improvements in psychological well-being (USDHHS, 1996). Despite the Centers for Disease Control and Prevention (CDC) and American College of Sports Medicine (ACSM) recommendation to engage in at least 30 min of moderate-intensity activity on 5 or more days per week (Pate et al., 1995) and the Healthy People 2010 objective to increase participation in at least 20 min of vigorous-intensity activity on 3 or more days per week (USDHHS, 2000), only 47.2% of U.S. adults were classified as physically active by the Behavioral Risk Factor Surveillance System in 2003 (CDC, 2003). In addition, about 23% of adults get no physical activity at all (CDC, 2003).

Although lack of physical activity is of concern for the entire U.S. population, it is of particular concern for certain subgroups, including African American women, who remain particularly sedentary (CDC, 2003; National Center for Health Statistics, 2004). In a large study comparing four racial/ethnic groups of women (African American, White, Hispanic, Asian; Brownson et al., 2000), the proportion of African American women reporting recommended levels of regular physical activity was 8.4%, the lowest rate of the four groups. A larger proportion of African American women (37.2%) also reported no leisure time physical activity compared to White (31.7%) or Hispanic (32.5%) women. Other studies of racially diverse women also have shown lower participation for African American women in a wide range of activities, including household and occupational physical activity (Ainsworth, Irwin, Addy, Whitt, & Stolarcyzk, 1999; Sternfeld, Ainsworth, & Quesenberry, 1999). Paired with higher cardiovascular disease death rates than other groups of women (Malarcher et al., 2001), higher obesity rates (USDHHS, 2001), and higher rates of Type 2 diabetes (CDC, 2002), lack of physical activity among African American women is an especially important public health issue to address.

Factors influencing participation in physical activity among African American women have been increasingly studied. Important factors identified in previous studies include the social and physical environment, caregiving/family responsibility roles, hair type, time, cost, enjoyment, and embarrassment (Carter-Nolan, Adams-Campbell, & Williams, 1996; Fleury & Lee, 2006). Studies also have found that these factors vary by racial/ethnic group (Henderson & Ainsworth, 2000; King et al., 2002). Although this body of literature provides insight into why African American women do not participate in physical activity, studies are not available that weave these factors together to portray an overall understanding of how African American women become and stay physically active.

Researchers also have drawn on the current knowledge of correlates of participation and application of behavioral theory to implement intervention programs to increase physical activity participation among African American women (Banks-Wallace & Conn, 2002; Wilbur, Miller, Chandler, & McDevitt, 2003). Many of these studies resulted in modest success through reduced body weight or blood pressure or increased physical activity level during the short term, thus indicating that physical activity behavior and/or its related health effects can be affected through intervention activities. However, they do not elucidate the pathways linking the key factors and steps in a behavioral process that result in subsequent physical activity participation.

Many studies have attempted to verify these pathways through the application of existing behavioral frameworks in the physical activity domain. Most of them have been focused on explaining variation in physical activity levels and have only been able to account for a small percentage of that change (King, Stokols, Talen, Brassington, & Killingsworth, 2002). Even those that have found support for existing behavioral theories, including investigations of the Transtheoretical Model (TTM; Prochaska & DiClemente, 1983), have not been focused on illustrating the behavioral process of physical activity adoption and maintenance that would be most effective in informing interventions to enhance physical activity participation.

To thoroughly understand this process, the important factors and their interrelationships must be clearly elucidated through continued behavioral theory refinement. In the physical activity domain, theoretical explanation of behavior has shown promise for certain constructs, such as self-efficacy and self-regulation. However, a behavioral theory or framework is not currently available explaining the full process from behavioral adoption through maintenance in this domain. The purpose of this study was to understand this behavioral process among African American women through the development of a theoretical framework explaining the pathways linking the key factors together that result in subsequent integration of physical activity into the lifestyle.

Method

A grounded theory approach (Strauss & Corbin, 1998) was selected because of the lack of knowledge regarding the specific factors and factor relationships that comprise the process of physical activity behavioral evolution. An iterative process of data collection and analysis was used to develop a theoretical explanation of human behavior grounded in data collected from those exhibiting that behavior. In this study, the grounded theory approach was used to develop a framework of the process by which physical activity is adopted and maintained among African American women. The study was approved by the Institutional Review Board of The Ohio State University.

Sampling

Purposeful sampling methods (Patton, 1990) were used to gather information-rich cases, primarily criterion sampling. Criterion sampling refers to picking cases that meet some prespecified criterion. Inclusion criteria for this study were African American, female, 25 to 45 years of age, completion of at least some college or technical school beyond high school, and commitment to physical activity. Based on the focus of the study, it was crucial to only include physically active women. Women had to be currently active at recommended levels (CDC, 2001) for at least 1 year. Exclusion criteria included having difficulty walking or moving around, recent diagnosis of an eating disorder, diagnosis with a terminal illness, or having participated in varsity athletics in college or on a professional athletic team. Theoretical sampling (Strauss & Corbin, 1998) also was used to ensure that the women who participated in the study had adequately experienced the phenomenon to provide rich description.

Participants were primarily recruited through two local African American sorority alumni associations. The researcher met with contacts at each sorority and identified meetings or other events where study information could be presented. At each event a sign-up sheet was circulated requesting interested women's names and phone numbers. Follow-up phone calls were made after the events using a comprehensive screening tool addressing each factor of the inclusion and exclusion criteria.

Data Collection

Data were collected by conducting face-to-face, in-depth interviews. These interviews were guided by the research questions but were unstructured enough to allow the discovery of new ideas and themes. The guide was modified as data collection proceeded to further refine questions that were not eliciting the intended information and to reflect the categories and concepts that required further development (Spradley, 1979; Strauss & Corbin, 1998).

When the interviews and the preliminary data analysis were complete, two focus groups of the study participants were held. The purpose of these groups was to disseminate the preliminary findings from the study and to gather feedback from the participants to ensure that the findings reflected their experience with physical activity. Data from the focus groups were incorporated into the analysis for further refinement of the framework.

All interviews and focus groups were tape-recorded with the permission of the participants and transcribed verbatim. Transcribed interviews and field notes were entered into the Atlas.TI qualitative data analysis program for analysis (Muhr, 1994). The lead researcher performed all data analysis tasks with regular consultation and feedback from the coinvestigators.

TABLE 1 ● Participant Characteristics

Age (years)	Body Mass Index[a]	Primary Activity	% Active[b]	Time Active	Commit Score[c]
41	29.4	Weights/treadmill	435	1 year	53
35	30.9	Group fitness	465	8 months	
			230	4 months	44
45	21.0	Treadmill	590	10+ years	48
31	26.0	Group fitness	650	2 months	
			280	1+ years	46
42	39.7	Weights/walking	350	3 months	
			158	1+ years	48
26	20.4	Weights/misc. cardio[d]	1,280	5+ years	43
26	19.4	Weights/misc. cardio	150	1 year	40
33	25.8	Dance/volleyball/gym	370	15 years	41
42	23.0	Group fitness	1,305	1 year	49
33	24.8	Tae Bo/lifestyle	165	4 years	41
33	21.1	Exercise videos	575	20+ years	55
31	22.1	Weights/misc. cardio	120	20+ years	41
30	27.7	Weights/misc. cardio	580	3 years	45
45	23.4	Group fitness/running	280	3 years	52
25	21.9	Group fitness/running	490	15+ years	48

a. Body Mass Index calculated from self-reported height and weight.

b. Percentage of minimum eligible physical activity participation criteria as calculated from the adapted Godin Leisure-Time Questionnaire (Godin & Shephard, 1985).

c. Score on the adapted Commitment to Physical Activity Scale (possible range =11 -55; Corbin, Nielsen, Bordsdorf, & Laurie, 1987).

d. Refers to use of miscellaneous cardiovascular fitness equipment, including treadmill, stair stepper, stationary bicycle, and elliptical machine.

Sample Size

In grounded theory, the ultimate criterion for the final sample size is theoretical saturation (Strauss & Corbin, 1998). Theoretical saturation employs the general rule that when building theory, data should be gathered until each category (or theme) is saturated. A sample size of 15 women was used as a baseline (Lincoln & Guba, 1985; Strauss & Corbin, 1998) and theoretical saturation was employed to determine the final sample size.

Thirty women were screened for the study and, of those, 17 women were eligible. Fifteen of the 17 women participated in the interviews. An interview could not be scheduled with 2 women who did not return phone calls from the researcher.

Using theoretical saturation as the desired criterion, interviews were analyzed to determine the need for additional sampling. Based on the depth of the data provided by the 15 women, the scarcity of new information emerging from the last two interviews, and the importance of analyzing the rich experiences of the women in the study in great depth and detail to unearth the structure of a very specific process, sampling for the interviews was completed with 15 women. Characteristics of the participants are presented in Table 1. Nine of the women interviewed also participated in the focus groups.

Data Analysis

The basic principles of grounded theory data analysis (Strauss & Corbin, 1998) guided this study. Microanalysis was used for all of the interviews to ensure that no important ideas or constructs were overlooked. Codes were created for each new idea and themes that were found to be conceptually similar in nature or related in meaning were grouped together as concepts. These concepts were then developed through constant comparison, with the most relevant concepts being integrated to form a theoretical framework. This framework, the final product of the study, explains the central theme of the data as well as accounts for variation.

Results

The Physical Activity Evolution Model

The women's rich and illustrative descriptions provided the basis for the framework explaining the process of physical activity adoption and maintenance. The framework or model, Physical Activity Evolution, presents the psychological and behavioral changes that African American women experienced throughout the process of becoming physically active (see Figure 1). The model indicates a main flow through which women progress as well as two alternative loops. Flow through the process is characterized by three phases: the Initiation Phase, Transition Phase, and Integration Phase. Alternative loops are the Modification Loop and the Cessation Loop. Each pivotal psychological or behavioral change is indicated by a step in the process. Arrows

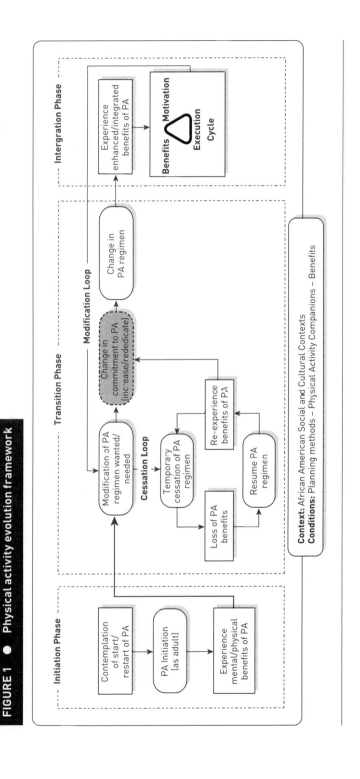

FIGURE 1 ● **Physical activity evolution framework**

371

direct movement from one step to another, into and out of the loops. An important feature of the process is that it exists within the context of the women's lives, in this case African American social and cultural context. Furthermore, certain conditions emerged as important for helping women progress through the physical activity evolution process, including planning methods, physical activity companions, and types of benefits experienced.

Initiation Phase

The first phase of the process, the Initiation Phase, is characterized by the early decision-making and initiation behaviors of the women. The women entered the process by contemplating the start or restart of physical activity. Although not the only reason, many of the women cited body weight as their impetus to begin a program. In this phase, women were experimenting with physical activity and beginning to experience some of the benefits associated with physical activity participation. It was during the Initiation Phase of the process that women began to learn which activities they enjoyed, how well different activities fit into their schedules, and which ones might meet the needs that prompted physical activity participation (e.g., weight management). One woman said of starting her physical activity program,

> It evolved because baby fat does not go away. So the first baby—I retained 10 pounds . . . the 10 pounds though was the issue for me because after the first baby is when I really started working out.

Shortly after engaging in some form of physical activity, the women started experiencing benefits. Women discussed mental benefits such as feeling good, relieving stress, feeling more alert, and feeling like they were taking time for themselves or taking care of themselves. Other benefits were the discovery of activities that brought them enjoyment or enabled them to do other activities during their exercise sessions such as reading or praying. Although mental benefits dominated the discussions of early exercise experiences, some of the women did experience physical benefits early in their physical activity experience, such as initial weight loss, although the majority of these benefits occurred later in the process. Other important benefits experienced during the Initiation Phase included having more energy and sleeping better. One of the women said of the benefits she was experiencing,

> This is something that I need to do because it makes me feel good and it relieves stress . . . even though I'm hot and sweaty and stinky, mentally I feel more alert . . . my body feels more alert . . . I feel more energetic.

Many of the women were juggling careers and family, so time out for themselves was another important benefit of physical activity. One woman explained, "I had a little time for me. I started enjoying it. I started liking it."

Transition Phase

After experiencing the Initiation Phase, women moved into the Transition Phase. The time it took to progress to this phase varied. As women entered the Transition Phase, they became aware that a modification of their regimen was needed. This need arose from a number of situations, including having scheduling problems, not seeing expected benefits, not enjoying chosen routines, or experiencing increased fitness or skill requiring more challenging activities. Women started physical activity and experimented to build experience and knowledge during the Initiation Phase. During the Transition Phase, they then restructured their regimens to fit their lifestyle or desired benefits.

Once the women realized that their regimens needed modification, they needed to commit to their pursuit of a physically active lifestyle and make the necessary changes. For some of the women, this commitment was a reprioritization of physical activity or an increase in their dedication to a physically active lifestyle. For others, it was a reaffirmation of previous commitment. This marks a pivotal point in the process and serves as the bridge through the Transition Phase. This key step in the model is shaded to highlight its importance in the process. Without this conscious commitment to physical activity, the women would not have moved farther along in the process, becoming more experienced with, and dedicated to, a lifetime of physical activity. Some women spoke about this point using words such as "break-through" or "light clicking on." For example, one woman said, "So then the light clicked on that I needed to make a change. It is a lifestyle change." Highlighting that change in commitment, one woman explained, "You know you have to increase your exercise . . . you just have to make that change, increase, rededicate. It's a continual thing."

Women talked about realizing that physical activity was something that they would have to do for the rest of their lives. They finally understood that they could not exercise until they reached a short-term goal and then quit and expect to maintain that success. One of the women who had been sporadically exercising in the past for weight control purposes realized

> I have to keep remembering that all these changes are lifestyle changes so I know I am in it for the long haul . . . it is not when I get to my goal weight I am done working out. I know I have to keep working out forever and so sometimes I am a little disenchanted like I got to get up every morning for the rest of my life, but then sometimes I enjoy it. I like the time by myself on the treadmill at the gym with no kids, no husband, so sometimes it's just like freedom.

This quotation was presented during the focus groups and one woman stated, "I know that's me!" when in fact it was another participant. Clearly, the notion of physical activity as a source of personal time or freedom from other obligations was an important benefit for these busy women.

Integration Phase

The Integration Phase represents the last phase of the main flow of the process. At this point in the process, women began to see some of the enhanced results of their efforts and the results that took longer to realize. Many of these results were the physical benefits that the women started physical activity to achieve, including weight loss, weight maintenance, or muscle toning. Enhanced benefits also included health benefits, such as blood pressure or diabetes control. These benefits were more integrated into life or transcendent of the exercise experience, for example, the formation of a new social network or the opportunity to serve as a role model for other women who were trying to become physically active.

After realizing enhanced or integrated benefits, motivation was reinforced for continuing physical activity. Women wanted to maintain the changes they had achieved. One woman explained,

> But once you actually learn and try to get some benefits from it and it makes you feel better . . . outside of the other health benefits that you know exercise can play. You just want to do it. Sort of like you want to go shopping—you just want to exercise after awhile.

At this point in the process, women entered the Benefits-Motivation-Execution cycle. This cycle indicates that once an appropriate (e.g., frequency and intensity) and successful (e.g., consistent) physical activity regimen was planned and executed, enhanced benefits were noticed and these benefits provided motivation to continue, creating a circular cycle. The reason for the cycle occurring at the end of the process is that long-term, significant benefits from physical activity took time and energy to achieve. Because it took time to achieve these benefits, it took time to experience the Benefits-Motivation-Execution cycle.

Experiencing the cycle led women to feel that physical activity had become integrated into their lives. Although they still had to work on maintaining the behavior, some of the early efforts could be relaxed because physical activity had become part of their usual routine. Women described this feeling of integration in a variety of ways, including, "I think it frustrates me not to go. Like something's missing. I'm at that point" and "It's something that's routine, like you get up in the morning and you brush your teeth."

Modification Loop

Although the Benefits-Motivation-Execution cycle appears as the final box in the process, there was an important dynamic component to even the most successful exercise regimens. The dynamic and flexible nature of women's physical activity regimens was expressed in each of the interviews within the context of each woman's life. After experiencing the cycle and integration, women found themselves having to modify their regimens to fit with changes in lifestyles and goals over time as depicted by the feedback arrows at the top of the main flow labeled Modification Loop.

With experience, women learned to change their regimens as needed for reasons that included change in job or school schedule/responsibilities, dealing with a health problem or injury, or change in child care. The Modification Loop began with the realization that a change to the regimen was wanted or needed and was defined by the decision to continue her commitment to physical activity and make the required changes. By choosing to modify her program and stick with physical activity, she set herself up to continue to see results and to successfully navigate a life change. In doing so, she furthered her experience with the Benefits-Motivation-Execution cycle. For example, one woman describes her work-related modification as follows:

> It used to be up until last week that I got to work at about 10:30 . . . but now [my colleague] is on maternity leave so I am her until the end of the year. In the mornings I used to take my daughter to the bus stop and then I would work out at the Y. But now I have to get up at 6:30, workout, take her to the bus stop, and go straight to [work] so it has been a juggle. We have a gym in our basement so I have been working out in the basement. She has to wake herself up. I set her alarm. I'm working out. By 7:45 I have to be leaving my house—so it has been working.

Alternatively, there were times when women were unwilling or unable to commit to making the necessary changes, resulting in their temporary progression through the Cessation Loop.

Cessation Loop

An important aspect of the dynamic nature of the physical activity regimen was the Cessation Loop. It became apparent in the analysis that there were times when women temporarily could not maintain their physical activity regimens. As the arrows indicate, it is possible to experience the Cessation Loop the first time through the process, after reaching the Benefits-Motivation-Execution cycle (through the Modification Loop), or both.

This loop accommodates the situation revealed in all of the women's lives where regular physical activity had to be temporarily ceased for various reasons. Furthermore, when women fell into this loop early in their experience with physical activity, it was sometimes due to having reached their goals. They thought their mission was accomplished and ceased regular participation. Key to the resumption of physical activity was the loss of benefits from the previous level of involvement. The women knew what they could achieve, so they were aware of what they were missing and wanted to get it back. Thus, even though they were not regularly active at this point in the process, they were different from when they had first adopted the behavior. They now had a frame of reference for what they could achieve through physical activity. This loss served as the motivation to resume physical activity to realize those achievements again. One woman explained,

So that was that thing where you wake up one morning and you can't fit into your jeans— you're just too big. And that actually happened to me. . . . So I hated that so it was a really good incentive for me to get back into my routine of incorporating exercise back into life.

Successfully executing the regimen and reexperiencing benefits led women back to the main flow of the process with a renewed commitment to physical activity.

The number of times women experienced the Cessation Loop as well as the length of time in the loop varied with each woman. However, it was apparent that temporary hiatus from regular physical activity was a normal part of integrating physical activity into daily life and that navigating potential interruptions was something that needed to be learned. Indeed, the experience of overcoming such challenges improved a woman's belief that she could overcome the next challenge, perhaps without falling into the Cessation Loop.

Context and Conditions

The Physical Activity Evolution process occurred within the context and conditions of the women's lives, such as their social network, racial/cultural background, and elements of their personal experience with physical activity, including their conceptualization of planning and benefits realized. The roles of social network for physical activity and African American social and cultural contexts were significant aspects of the study and will be presented in subsequent articles as they are beyond the scope of this article, which focuses on the framework and personal experiences with physical activity.

Planning Methods

One of the conditions most integral to movement through the process model and interwoven into the women's experiences was their planning practices for physical activity. The two main themes that emerged were Scheduling Physical Activity and Planning Alternates for Missed Sessions. The concept of Planning with Flexibility transcended these themes and described the practices of every woman in the study. Regardless of how they scheduled their regimens, the overall plan for the physical activity sessions had to be flexible and remain dynamic in response to interruptions in daily life. A taxonomy of the key concepts related to planning methods is presented in Figure 2. Illustrative quotations for this condition are presented in Table 2.

One of the most compelling concepts that emerged from this condition was the technique of scheduling physical activity using the minimum acceptable-maximum possible criterion. This criterion refers to the successful practice of many of the women of planning an ideal number of sessions for the week, a maximum, but also setting a minimum number of sessions that had to be completed. The minimum acceptable-maximum possible conceptualization allowed women to shoot for their highest goal while ensuring they did not fall below a prespecified minimum. This planning method also provided a technique for dealing with missed sessions. Using this criterion, a missed session could either be made up if time permitted or simply skipped if it would not cause the total number of sessions to fall below the minimum.

Although planning methods seems like a very simple condition associated with integration of physical activity into daily life, the overall concept of planning with flexibility was vital and interwoven throughout both main themes. Furthermore, it defined the method by which women incorporated the sessions into their lives and viewed the role of physical activity within the context of their daily experience. Physical activity was a priority, but for it to remain a reality it could not be viewed as static or prescriptive. It had to be dynamic, ever-changing, and constantly adaptable to the ups and downs of life both in terms of daily and long-term challenges.

Discussion

The data provided by the women supplied the foundation for the development of the Physical Activity Evolution behavioral framework describing the adoption and maintenance of physical activity among African American women. The construction of a framework that identifies both psychological and behavioral steps in the process of developing a long-term, physically active lifestyle fills a gap in the literature and serves to forward the science behind the development and implementation of effective physical activity interventions.

Although the call for investigating physical activity as a process has been made (Dishman, 1987), it is difficult to make overall comparisons of the Physical Activity Evolution framework to other behavioral process frameworks because they are largely unavailable. The TTM (Prochaska & DiClemente, 1983) is one of few process models applied to exercise behavior, and the only one widely implemented. In the absence of a selection of process models through which to study exercise behavior, substantive models or frameworks specific to physical activity have been developed but gone largely unnoticed (Laverie, 1998; Medina, 1996). As such, there is no empirical evidence beyond the founding studies to provide support for the utility of these frameworks.

The most pertinent of these studies was a dissertation that undertook a grounded theory study of the journey from nonexerciser to exerciser (Medina, 1996). The resulting framework identified three phases of identity development with some parallels to the Physical Activity Evolution phases. Medina's framework provides support for four important elements of the Physical Activity Evolution model: personal fit of the physical activity regimen, the dynamic nature of the process itself, physical activity as a reinforcing behavior, and integration of physical activity into the lifestyle. These commonalities arising from two separate studies exemplify the potential for understanding physical activity behavior when considered as a process and studied using a contextual method. Although different populations were investigated and the resulting models reflected these differing viewpoints, several important features of the underlying process emerged from both studies.

When considering conceptualizing participation in physical activity as evolving through separate, dynamic phases, as was elucidated in this study, the TTM provides an obvious comparison. The Physical Activity Evolution framework posits a clear Initiation Phase where women are contemplating and subsequently acting on a need or desire to start a physical activity program. In this phase, women are experimenting with the behavior, building skills, and learning what features work for them related to their goals and lifestyles. Support for this finding can be found in a meta-analysis conducted with 80 study samples measuring one or more of the constructs of the TTM (Marshall & Biddle, 2001). The largest effect size was for the movement from Preparation to Action (Cohen's d = 0.85), as would be expected. An unexpected finding was evidence of small to moderate increases in physical activity from Precontemplation to Contemplation (Cohen's d = 0.34). This finding may provide support for the behavioral experimentation seen in the present study. Even when people have not fully committed to trying to adopt an active lifestyle, they might be testing various aspects of the behavior in preparation for that change in commitment. Without the knowledge and skills gleaned from this phase of the adoption process, the ability to adjust and recommit based on the fit of the regimen would not be possible.

Another key finding of this study was the distinct difference between behavioral acquisition or action and behavioral integration or maintenance. Furthermore, in this study, behavioral integration was elucidated as a dynamic state, one that needed to be periodically evaluated and adjusted via the Modification Loop. Two studies using the TTM provided support for the concept of a dynamic maintenance phase with its own unique characteristics requiring continued use of skills and techniques to maintain the behavior change (Bock, Marcus, Pinto, & Forsyth, 2001; Buckworth & Wallace, 2002). Because long-term behavior change is the primary mechanism by which the health benefits of physical activity can be realized, this aspect of the behavioral framework is an important contribution to the limited work available in the area of understanding of how to maintain this behavior.

The Cessation Loop is another crucial element of the Physical Activity Evolution process. The experience of relapse was universal among the women and not separate from the process of integrating physical activity into daily life. A relapse did not mean she was no longer a physically active woman. More accurately, it meant that she was in a distinct phase of lifestyle integration, which when handled positively, as was the experience of each of the women in this study, would result in further behavioral participation and development of skills in relapse prevention. Women did not revert to the beginning of the process once they overcame relapse because they were different at that point than when they had started; rather, they reentered the process through their renewed commitment (in the Transition Phase). This concept of potentially cycling back through phases while remaining different from when the process began also is reflected in Medina's (1996) finding. The spiral conceptualization of the TTM (Prochaska, DiClemente, & Norcross, 1992) also allows for relapse and recycling through the stages. There is limited evidence available on the application of the TTM in the physical activity domain using a relapse conceptualization. However, one study was found (Bock et al., 2001) that provided support for this phase of the behavioral process. Further support for conceptualizing relapse as a natural phase of

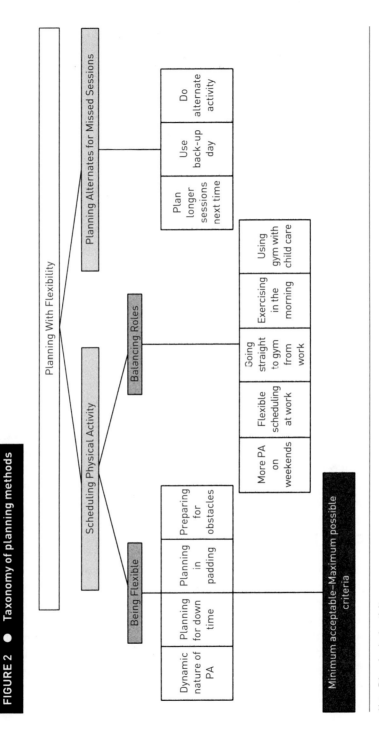

FIGURE 2 ● Taxonomy of planning methods

Planning With Flexibility

Scheduling Physical Activity

Planning Alternates for Missed Sessions

Being Flexible

Balancing Roles

Dynamic nature of PA

Planning for down time

Planning in padding

Preparing for obstacles

More PA on weekends

Flexible scheduling at work

Going straight to gym from work

Exercising in the morning

Using gym with child care

Plan longer sessions next time

Use back-up day

Do alternate activity

Minimum acceptable–Maximum possible criteria

Note: PA = physical activity.

TABLE 2 ● Illustrative Quotes for Selected Conditions	
Condition	**Quotation**
Planning Methods	" . . . missing one or two workouts during the week isn't going to cause me to gain all that weight back. You have to be disciplined and again, a little flexibility. I mean I am not going to get depressed and then go eat a bag of Oreo's—okay I missed this and just go ahead. Perhaps there is something I can do, take a walk around the block or something like that in place of it or take the stairs . . . I try to do at least something."
	(from focus group) "Well a lot of the things I liked that you said that you viewed exercise as being dynamic and I think that is important and I think that people who have integrated physical activity into their lifestyle also find the time to have flexibility even though they are being active, they have managed to add some type of flexibility because life situations change. That was good."

physical activity adoption and maintenance whose successful navigation is crucial to progression through the process can be found from application of the Relapse Prevention Model (RPM; Marlatt & Gordon, 1985) in the physical activity domain (Belisle, Roskies, & Levesque, 1987; King & Frederiksen, 1984).

In general, studies investigating the full process of physical activity adoption through maintenance provide the best comparison to the current theory. It is clear that work is limited in this area. The actual process of behavioral integration in the physical activity domain has remained largely untapped. Medina's (1996) study and some of the work using the TTM and RPM provide support for the present study's conceptualization of this process. There is still much work to be done. Once the full process of behavioral integration is better understood, constructs can be operationalized and pathways postulated and quantified. Until then, further attention is needed to refining, and in some cases integrating, the process models available at this time.

Practical Implications

although the process model proposed in this study is a new framework for understanding physical activity evolution among African American women, the following important lessons can be garnered for future efforts at program design: (a) attention should be paid to learning how to navigate life changes and potential obstacles after the Integration Phase by including techniques for modifying a regimen to fit into daily life, plans for dealing with future challenges, and learning a variety of activity options for different goals and preferences; (b) during the Initiation Phase, programs should focus on the fit of the prescribed regimen to the desired goals of the woman, ensuring that the selected activities fit both her lifestyle and the results important to her; and

(c) programs should guide women in the planning of their physical activity regimens to include flexibility and dynamic qualities, perhaps using the minimum acceptable-maximum possible criteria.

Study Limitations

Limitations of this study stem from two main areas: the chosen methodology and the study population. Grounded theory requires data collection in an environment constructed by the researcher and the participant. Although measures were put in place to maximize credibility and dependability, it is possible that different investigators with different groups of participants would have had different findings. Another factor to consider is selection bias. It is possible that women who desired to participate were somehow different than those who elected not to call or those that decided not to participate after screening.

Although each of these limitations should be considered, many elements of the study design were included to ensure that the study was not weakened by these issues. For example, peer debriefing and member checking were both used to ensure that the conclusions of the researcher were indeed grounded in the data. Transcripts were reviewed by the principal investigator and her coinvestigators to check for appropriate interview style and rich data quality. Careful documentation of each data collection and analysis phase was employed. These methods exemplify only a few of the techniques used to ensure that the data collected were of high quality and that the conclusions inferred from those data were grounded in the women's experiences.

Conclusion

this study has made an important contribution to the knowledge base on the development of physical activity among African American women. Future studies can use the knowledge gained to further theory development in this area and expand theory development to women of other backgrounds and situations. These findings also can be used to inform intervention development and spur further investigation into some of the important practical implications. Furthermore, the concept of investigating health behaviors among people who have successfully incorporated those behaviors into their daily lives should be further used in research studies. By studying women who have successfully adopted a behavior, strategies to overcome known barriers can be elucidated and applied to intervention planning for other women.

References

Ainsworth, B. E., Irwin, M., Addy, C., Whitt, M., & Stolarcyzk, L. (1999). Moderate physical activity patterns of minority women: The cross-cultural activity participation study. *Journal of Women's Health and Gender-Based Medicine, 8*(6), 805–813.

Banks-Wallace, J., & Conn, V. (2002). Intervention to promote physical activity among African American women. *Public Health Nursing*, 19(5), 321–335.

Belisle, M., Roskies, E., & Levesque, J. M. (1987). Improving adherence to physical activity. *Health Psychology*, 6(2), 159–172.

Bock, B. C., Marcus, B. H., Pinto, B. M., & Forsyth, L. H. (2001). Maintenance of physical activity following an individualized motivationally tailored intervention. *Annals of Behavioral Medicine*, 23(2), 79–87.

Brownson, R., Eyler, A., King, A. C., Brown, D., Shyu, Y. -L., & Sallis, J. (2000). Patterns and correlates of physical activity among U.S. women 40 years and older. *American Journal of Public Health*, 90(2), 264–270.

Buckworth, J., & Wallace, L. S. (2002). Application of the Transtheoretical Model to physically active adults. *Journal of Sports Medicine and Physical Fitness*, 42(3), 360–367.

Carter-Nolan, P. L., Adams-Campbell, L. L., & Williams, J. (1996, September). Recruitment strategies for Black women at risk for non-insulin-dependent diabetes mellitus into exercise protocols: A qualitative assessment. *Journal of the National Medical Association*, 88, 558–562.

Centers for Disease Control and Prevention. (2001). Physical activity trends: United States, 1990–1998. *MMWR Weekly*, 50(9), 166–169.

Centers for Disease Control and Prevention. (2002). *Chronic disease overview: U.S. Department of Health and Human Services*. Washington, DC: Author.

Centers for Disease Control and Prevention. (2003). *Behavioral risk factor surveillance system survey data*. Atlanta, GA: Author.

Corbin, C., Nielsen, A., Bordsdorf, L., & Laurie, D. (1987). Commitment to physical activity. *International Journal of Sport Psychology*, 18, 215–222.

Dishman, R. (1987). Exercise adherence and habitual physical activity. In W. P. Morgan & S. G. Goldstein (Eds.), *Exercise and mental health* (pp. 57–83). Washington, DC: Hemisphere.

Fleury, J., & Lee, S. M. (2006). The Social Ecological Model and physical activity in African American women. *American Journal of Community Psychology*, 37, 129–140.

Friedenreich, C., & Orenstein, M. (2002). Physical activity and cancer prevention: Etiologic evidence and biological mechanisms. *Journal of Nutrition*, 132, 3456S–3465S.

Godin, G., & Shephard, R. (1985). A simple method to assess exercise behavior in the community. *Canadian Journal of Applied Sports Science*, 10, 141–146.

Henderson, K., & Ainsworth, B. (2000). Sociocultural perspectives on physical activity in the lives of older African American and American Indian women: A cross-cultural activity participation study. *Women and Health*, 31(1), 1–20.

King, A. C., Castro, C., Wilcox, S., Eyler, A., Sallis, J., & Brownson, R. (2000). Personal and environmental factors associated with physical inactivity among different racial-ethnic groups of U.S. middle-aged and older-aged women. *Health Psychology*, 19(4), 354–364.

King, A. C., & Frederiksen, L. W. (1984). Low-cost strategies for increasing exercise behavior: Relapse preparation training and social support. *Behavior Modification*, 8(1), 3–21.

King, A. C., Stokols, D., Talen, E., Brassington, G. S., & Killingsworth, R. (2002). Theoretical approaches to the promotion of physical activity: Forging a transdisciplinary paradigm. *American Journal of Preventive Medicine*, 23(2S), 15–25.

Laverie, D. A. (1998). Motivations for ongoing participation in a fitness activity. *Leisure Sciences*, 20(4), 277–302.

Lincoln, Y. S., & Guba, E. G. (1985). *Naturalistic inquiry.* Beverly Hills, CA: Sage.

Malarcher, A., Casper, M., Matson-Koffman, D., Brownstein, J., Croft, J., & Mensah, G. (2001). Women and cardiovascular disease: Addressing disparities through prevention research and a national comprehensive state-based program. *Journal of Women's Health and Gender-Based Medicine*, 10(8), 717–724.

Marlatt, G. A., & Gordon, J. R. (1985). *Relapse prevention: Maintenance strategies in the treatment of addictive behaviors.* New York: Guilford.

Marshall, S., & Biddle, S. (2001). The transtheoretical model of behavior change: A metaanalysis of applications to physical activity and exercise. *Annals of Behavioral Medicine*, 23(4), 229–246.

Medina, K. (1996). *The journey from nonexerciser to exerciser: A grounded theory study.* San Diego, CA: University of San Diego Press.

Muhr, T. (1994). *Atlas.TI* (Version 4.2) [Computer software]. Thousand Oaks, CA: Sage.

National Center for Health Statistics. (2004). *Health United States 2004 with chartbook on trends in the health of Americans with special feature on drugs.* Hyattsville, MD: U.S. Department of Health and Human Services, Centers for Disease Control and Prevention.

Pate, R. R., Pratt, M., Blair, S. N., Haskell, W. L., Macera, C. A., Bouchard, C, et al. (1995). Physical activity and public health: A recommendation from the Centers for Disease Control and Prevention and the American College of Sports Medicine. *JAMA*, 273(5), 402–407.

Patton, M. (1990). *Qualitative evaluation and research methods* (2nd ed.). Newbury Park, CA: Sage.

Prochaska, J., & DiClemente, C. C. (1983). Stages and processes of self-change of smoking: Toward an integrative model of change. *Journal of Consulting and Clinical Psychology*, 51, 390–395.

Prochaska, J., DiClemente, C., & Norcross, J. (1992). In search of how people change: Applications to addictive behaviors. *American Psychologist*, 47(9), 1102–1114.

Spradley, J. P. (1979). *The ethnographic interview.* Orlando, FL: Harcourt Brace.

Sternfeld, B., Ainsworth, B. E., & Quesenberry, C. (1999). Physical activity patterns in a diverse population of women. *Preventive Medicine*, 28, 313–323.

Strauss, A., & Corbin, J. (1998). *Basics of qualitative research: Techniques and procedures for developing grounded theory.* Thousand Oaks, CA: Sage.

U.S. Department of Health and Human Services. (1996). *Physical activity and health: A report of the Surgeon General.* Atlanta, GA: Author.

U.S. Department of Health and Human Services. (2000). *Healthy People 2010: Volume II* (2nd ed.). Washington, DC: Government Printing Office.

U.S. Department of Health and Human Services. (2001). *The Surgeon General's call to action to prevent and decrease overweight and obesity.* Rockville, MD: Author.

Wilbur, J., Miller, A. M., Chandler, P., & McDevitt, J. (2003). Determinants of physical activity and adherence to a 24-week home-based walking program in African American and Caucasian women. *Research in Nursing and Health*, 26(3), 213–224.

• Appendix E •

An Ethnography—"British-Born Pakistani and Bangladeshi Young Men: Exploring Unstable Concepts of Muslim, Islamophobia and Racialization"

Mairtin Mac an Ghaill
Newman University, UK

Chris Haywood
Newcastle University, UK

Abstract

Much recent academic work on making sense of the changing public profile of the Muslim community in Britain operates within an explanatory framework that assumes a shift from ethnicity to religion and an accompanying shift from racialization to Islamophobia. A key limitation of this work, often grounded in media representations, is that it tends to be disconnected from contemporary lived social relations. In response, this paper critically engages with these debates, drawing upon qualitative research that explores a changing cultural condition that is inhabited by British born, working-class Pakistani and Bangladeshi young men. It is argued that this emergent cultural condition cannot conceptually be contained within a singular category of religion as the contours of the young men's cultural condition are embedded within a range of intensified and ambivalent rapidly shifting local, national and international geo-political processes. Therefore in contrast to recent theorizing and research on Muslim communities and identities, the young men in this study critically engage with the contextually-based local meanings of Muslim, Islamophobia and racialization to secure complex masculine subjectivities. Alongside this, the article highlights that young men recognize that Islamophobia, displacing a notion of racialization, is a danger for their community because of the attendant invisibility of the current impact of social class within conditions of socio-economic austerity, which for them is a central element of their social and cultural exclusions.

Source: This article originally appeared in *Critical Sociology, 41*, 97–114. Copyright 2015, SAGE Publications, Inc.

Keywords

Britain, gender, Islamophobia, Muslim, racialization, class

Introduction

For young working-class men born in Britain of Pakistani and Bangladeshi heritage, much British political, media and academic commentary on Muslims serves to re-inscribe them as a major social problem (Richardson, 2004; Hussain, 2008). This is occurring at a time of the emergence of an assertive English nationalism involving a forging of a renewed British identity and a European-wide political questioning about state-led multiculturalism (Fekete, 2004; Ibrahim, 2005; Townsend, 2011). A range of discourses have been projected by government, media and popular culture about failed multi-culturalism, parallel communities and self-segregation (Phillips, 2006; Nagle, 2009; Kundnani, 2009). For McGhee (2008: 145):

> In national level debates . . . . Britain has entered an authoritarian and 'anti-multiculturalism' period in which multiple identities, loyalties and allegiances are both problematized and are deployed in order to facilitate 'our' primary identifications as British citizens who must accept British values above all else.

In response, this article argues for engagement with Pakistani and Bangladeshi young men's narratives that focus upon the reductive representations of Islam, the Muslim community and being a young Muslim man. At the same time, there is an urgent need to critically interrogate the assumed social separateness, cultural fixity and boundedness of religious, ethnic and national categories of difference that they claim are imputed to them. Within the context of the institutional regulatory production of these containing categories, it is important to highlight that identity formation is embedded within the temporal and spatial specificity of a community's disasporian history and the accompanying making of identity affiliations through diverse sources of nationhood, ethnicity, religion, culture and tradition (Bauman, 1996; Zaretsky, 1996).

In turn, these resources are highly classed, gendered, generationally and regionally specific within conditions of late modernity (Brah et al., 2000). Yet we continue to know little of the processes that constitute these positions. Therefore, a combination of materialist and post-colonial theoretical frameworks and young men's accounts provides an alternative representational space that critically explores debates about the racialization of religion, the central role that religion plays in the process of racialization, and Islamophobia as a contemporary form of the racialization of Muslims. The paper begins by outlining our methodological position and the search for an alternative representational space in response to much recent social and cultural theorizing on Muslim representation, identity formation and subjectivity that has disconnected from lived relations within institutions, specific local contexts and broader social and economic processes. This is followed by a discussion of the shifting racialized representations of young Muslim men, addressing the need to go beyond a singular category of religion in exploring their lives. A major focus of the paper is an exploration of their discussion of the instability of concepts such as Muslim, Islamophobia and racialization. Finally, we address the students' nuanced understanding of racialization that highlights the invisibility of the stratification of young Pakistani and Bangladeshi men as classed subjects.

Research Methods: Young Men's Narratives

There is a tendency within the academy, government and media to over-generalize about the Muslim diaspora living in Europe and North America. For example, within a North American context the popular representation of the Muslim is often portrayed as Arab; within a British context the popular representation is often portrayed as South Asian (Haddad, 2004). In reality, the global Muslim diaspora is nationally and ethnically a highly diverse population. Feminist and post-colonial theorists have provided a sophisticated map of British Muslim young women in late modernity (Shain, 2003; Brah and Phoenix, 2004). This article draws upon this work in focusing on young Muslim men, as a generationally-specific gendered category that remains an under-researched field of inquiry.

As indicated above, this study is based upon Birmingham-born young men of Pakistan and Bangladesh heritage. It is suggested that 21 per cent (approximately 232,000 people) of the population resident in Birmingham Local Authority identified as Muslim (Birmingham City Council, 2013) compared to 4.8 per cent in the UK population (Office for National Statistics [ONS], 2012). This is the highest number of Muslims for a local authority in the UK. Furthermore, in terms of ethnicity, the electoral ward of Birmingham records 144,627 (13.5%) Pakistani, and 32,532 (3%) Bangladeshi within these communities. Within this context, such communities are highly diverse, and as a qualitative and explorative study, the paper does not seek inductive validity by suggesting that the participants represent the experiences of the broader Muslim male population of the area or the general population. Instead, as Crouch and McKenzie (2006: 493) argue:

> Rather than being systematically selected instances of specific categories of attitudes and responses, here respondents embody and represent meaningful experience-structure links. Put differently, our respondents are 'cases', or instances of states, rather than (just) individuals who are bearers of certain designated properties (or 'variables').

Our work with a younger generation of Pakistani and Bangladeshi young men, in Newcastle, London and Birmingham, makes clear their geographically-specific local experiences of growing up in a rapidly changing Britain (Popoviciu and Mac an Ghaill, 2004; Mac an Ghaill and Haywood, 2005). In other words, the young men in this Birmingham-based study inhabit specific lifestyles within a spatial context of diverse social trajectories among a changing Muslim diaspora in Britain. Therefore, it is the exploration of the young Muslim men's meaningful experiences that was a key objective of the research design.

Drawing upon our own ethnographic work, we set out to enable the research participants to inhabit an alternative representational space that provides insightful narratives about the complexity of inhabiting subject positions across public and private spaces. During a three year period, 2008–11, we have recorded the experiences of 48 Pakistani (30) and Bangladeshi (18) working-class young men, aged 16–21. Twenty-five of the young men's narratives are reported in this paper. The majority of the young men (38) (20 in this paper) attended local secondary schools, sixth-form colleges and further education colleges. However, as suggested in previous work, Bangladeshi and Pakistani young people's participation in education is highly fractured and non-linear (see Bradley and Devadason, 2008). For example, young men stagger their engagement on part-time courses over a number of years, often to accommodate responsibilities within the home and at work.

The interview groups contained a mix of Bangladeshi and Pakistani young men, as indicated by their names, who shared not only intimate friendships but were part of a broader social community that included attending the same youth and community organizations and colleges, sharing the same employers, and participating together in leisure activities. Furthermore, although they were diverse individuals, in terms of ethnicity, age, past experience and social status with different current experiences of being in education, work/training or unemployed, they held a shared critical reflexivity of ethnic majority assumptions of Muslim identities. The latter emerged as of central importance to the main themes of this paper about Islamophobia and the racialization of Muslims.

While carrying out empirical work with young people, we were introduced to two young men who were politically involved in the local area. In turn, they introduced us to other young people that subsequently led to further snowballing of other friends, family and community representatives (Patton, 1990). Access was greatly enabled by our being known for our social commitment to the local area, working with families in the local community. Group and life history interviews provided the framework through which to explore a range of critical incidents experienced by these young men.

The group interviews were carried out at local community centres and the life history interviews were carried out in a variety of places, including at youth and community organizations and local cafes. These interviews lasted around 45 to 90 minutes and provided insight into growing up, family, schooling, social life and local community. These interviews were supplemented by a range of other research strategies that included observations, informal conversations and interviews with parents and local community representatives (Alvesson and Skoldberg, 2000), as part of a wider critical ethnography on the impact of globally-inflected change upon the local formation of diasporic young men's subjectivity and identity (Appadurai, 1991; Harvey, 2003; Ansari, 2004).

The datasets from each of the methods was subject to thematic analysis (Braun and Clarke, 2006) that enabled us to explore 'the underlying ideas, constructions, and discourses that shape or inform the semantic content of the data' (Ussher et al., 2013: 902). The subsequent analysis was taken back to the young people themselves not simply as a form of 'face validity' but also as a way of exploring the practical and political implications of the findings. All interviews throughout the study were both anonymized and the research participants were given pseudonyms to protect their confidentiality (Wetherell, 1998).

Shifting Racialized Representations of Young Muslim Men: 'From Ethnicity to Religion'—Beyond a Singular Category of Religion

The young men, as post-colonial subjects, have an implicit or explicit understanding of earlier racialized representations of their grandparent and parent generations that do not make sense of contemporary social and spatial relations of their lives in Birmingham (Gilroy, 2004). Importantly, they note that state and public institutional figures have little understanding of their community, of inter-generational changes or, perhaps most significantly, the changing morphology of western urban sites, such as Birmingham, in which new identities, both minority and majority ethnic, are being manufactured (Bhattacharyya, 2008). In a group interview below, Abdul begins a discussion about the generational specific experiences of young men in relation to the racialization of their ethnicities:

Abdul: A lot of people would have heard about how are grandparents/parents were treated really bad when they came from Pakistan. But it's different for the kids, for us. Like the stereotypes our parents had are more like what the Somalis, the Yemenis, or even the Poles, cos they've just arrived, with different language and all that.

MM: So, what about your generation?

Abdul: It's different for us because we're born here, so we're British and have a Pakistan heritage. And, anyway probably everything changed round here and everywhere after 9/11.

Azam: It's changed and not changed, white kids will still call you 'Paki' in certain areas but it's also that we're seen as a terrorist or fundamentalist, those kinds of words, those stereotypes.

Majid: When you start thinking about it, it's all mixed up. Like words like Asian, Pakistani, ethnics, what else, and worst of all the BME and all the rest. I don't know, they're not really about us are they? They're about older generations.

Shabbir: Maybe not about them, just white people giving us labels.

Wasim: There is no straight, no straight-forward stereotype of young Muslims because you get all the propaganda stuff about not joining the terrorists. Like you hear government people on telly after some terrorist stuff has taken place, they're saying that we need the most help, so as not to be persuaded to go off to Afghanistan and train to become a terrorist. But the main stereotype of us is that we are terrorists.

Yusuf: Governments and police and even probably a lot of teachers they don't know nothing. They don't really know about us. About people who live around here. They don't even know anything about our white mates who live here and they're white. They talk as if we have just arrived in this country but even I can see in a few years this city has really changed and our parents say it's really changed. It's not just about us, the whole city has changed. Go and talk to the white kids and their parents and they will tell you. But government and people in charge they don't know this. They don't live here. [Group interview]

One of the experiences within these young men's narratives is the lack of identification with available representations and language (Sandhu, 2011). Current attempts by state institutions to contain them within the singular category of religion often oscillates between representations of the responsible, family-orientated hard-working, socially-passive Muslim father and shifting racialized representations that contradictorily position them as both potential terrorists and highly vulnerable to terrorist recruitment. Exploring the experiences of contemporary young Muslim men, we find complex identifications, affiliations, investments and positionings of a highly visible diasporic group, of whom we know little. More specifically, we know little about the complex processes of subjectivity and accompanying processes of subjectivication, inter-subjectivities and social biographies, complex investments/affiliations and the occupying of multiple and diverse identifications. This lack of social knowledge begins with the conceptual ambiguity and confusion of the deployment of the term Muslim in the social science literature, including 'the re-categorisation of various ethnic (Mirpuri, Bangladeshi, Pakistani) groups into religious (Muslim) ones' (Shain, 2011: 15). The young men discussed the suggested shift from ethnicity to religion as the primary official marker of their public (racial) identity. For example, Anthias and Yuval-Davis (1993: 55) have claimed that:

Since the 'Rushdie Affair', the exclusion of minority religions from the national collectivity has started a process of racialization that especially relates to Muslims. People who used to be known for the place of origin, or even as 'people of colour' have become identified by their assumed religion. The racist stereotype of the 'Paki' has become the racist stereotype of the 'Muslim fundamentalist'.

For the young men, their social lives are marked by an intensified global surveillance, cultural pathologization and social and racial exclusion that is more complex than this suggested shifting classification (Said, 1978). Most importantly, as illustrated in the discussion below, notions of ethnicity, religion and cultural belonging are not clearly demarcated, and the separation of these categories is experienced contradictorily:

Amir: You ... I can't get my head around it. I can't even say it.

M.M: Say what?

Amir: You feel you're been watched all the time, here comes the Muslim. But you can't prepare or something for when it happens, or know how to react, cos it's different, it happens in different ways.

M.M: Like how?

Amir: Like Yusuf was saying the other day, the teachers, the police would look at you differently. Then again, different teachers will act out differently.

Kashif: You can't separate these things like that. You can't split people up like that. It don't work that way. It's not like our parents are ethnic or Asian or Bangladeshi or Bengali or whatever and now younger people are just religious. These things are all mixed up for everyone.

Abdul: Like I said to you the other day, when you said why go to the mosque to pray, you can pray anywhere. That's very true. But deep in being a Muslim is looking after your neighbour. So it's important to meet people, to check out they're OK.

Kashif: So you can't choose between calling us ethnics or religious. That's stupid, makes no sense. [Group interview]

With the young men's ambivalence towards generationally specific ways of being Muslim men, based upon culturally infused religious identities and their rejection of masculinities underpinned by violence, identifications have involved the reconfiguration of the meaning of Muslim. From the above discussion, the notion of a singular homogeneous Muslim identity is not experienced by these young men. Furthermore, representational spaces such as those projected by the police or teachers, which are often based on particular religious and/or political differences, appear not to be connecting with their lived experiences:

Farhad: Do you understand? In the past the word 'Paki' was the stereotype. Now people say Muslims are called terrorists but the real stereotype now is to be called a Muslim.

Kashif: That's what's changed. In the past our parents were seen as good for being religious by white people, well like teachers and police and that, even the government. Now we are seen as bad because of our religion, like we are all extremists or something.

Sajid: That is very true. It's like for these people, religion for them is like a big cage that they try and lock us up in. [Group interview]

These institutional representations are dependent upon the instantiation of such difference, which it can be argued can consolidate Muslim identities. For example, Qureshi (2004) found that a group of young Pakistani men in her research made their masculinities through the Othering of young white men. One of the characteristics of the young men in our research was that the process of Othering of whiteness was seen as a characteristic of an older form of Muslim identity; an identification to which these young men held a growing ambivalence. As a consequence, securing masculine subjectivities appears to be generationally more complex. Here we focus on the young men securing their masculine subjectivities through the unstable concepts of being a Muslim young man, Islamophobia and racialization.

The Instability of Concepts: Muslim, Islamophobia and Racialization

During the early 2000s, exploring the forging of ethnic and national identities among young Bangladeshi men and women, we found increasing diversity of masculine formation in relation to assumed ethno-religious identifications and social practices (Mac an Ghaill and Haywood, 2005). We need to hold onto a socio-historical perspective, in order to trace a range of contemporary fragmented male subjectivities, social trajectories, cultural belonging and contested meanings of the concepts of Muslim, Islamophobia and racialization within regional spaces. As suggested above, Pakistani and Bangladeshi young men are experiencing a specific cultural condition that conceptually cannot be contained within the singular identity category of religion. Their narratives serve to critique the dominant culturalist explanation that the state, including institutional sites, such as schooling and policing, ascribes to them (Faas, 2010). The contours of the young men's cultural condition are embedded within intensified and ambivalent rapidly shifting geo-political processes, involving developments in global economic restructuring and its impact on local and global labour markets, advanced technological systems and increased cultural exchange, a series of western-led wars on Muslim societies, shifting patterns of migration, new forms of racial exclusion, the restructuring of a new world order and the apparent reclamation of ethno/religious identities.

At the same time, young men in this study are subjectively experiencing such changes in terms of dynamic dissonances that are (re) constituting their remembering of the past, the living and doing of the present and their imagined futures. This process is demonstrated through the negotiation of the meanings attached to being Muslim:

Asif: It's wrong to talk about the Muslim perspective and the Muslim community and Muslim young men and women act like this and that. There is no such thing. If you look at young people round here, they have, they take up really different styles, different ways. And, definitely you make friends cos you have things in common that are really different to other groups.

M.M: Like what?

Asif: Like what? Like everything. Obvious things, like whether you go to college or uni, or you're not working or those who join gangs, different interests, music, how you dress, where you go with your mates, everything.

Wasim: You go up North or down to London and its really different. We always say it at the weddings. These people are not like us.

Yasin: When you ask about the future, for young Muslim people, yeah everything is mixed together. When people are planning for the future, it's very different futures. Just even in our college, the future thinking is kind of linked to how you think about the past, and whether you want to get away from it or how much you know about the past in this country and Pakistan and everything that's happening now about all the talk about Muslims. But mostly about how you make the future good, same as any younger people. [Group interview]

In discussion with the young men, they explain that the increasing mobilization of the term Muslim as a collective self-referent, that is seen in the research literature as highly significant in terms of their changing self-definition, does not mean that a young generation of Pakistanis and Bangladeshis are becoming more religious (Samad, 1998). They also point out that the contemporary deployment of the term Muslim does not displace the terms Asian and Pakistani/Bangladeshi that have historically served to mark difference, but rather are contextually used across different sites. Importantly, regulatory mechanisms of power and control of a 'suspect community' are differentially experienced within institutionally specific contexts (Pentazis and Pemberton, 2009). Interestingly, the young men make a distinction between their own self-definition as Muslims embedded within a generationally-specific cultural politics and 'white people's' racialized use of the term (Pilkington and Johnson, 2003; Said, 1993):

Wasim: When you asked us were we proper Muslims, we all laughed and said, no. So, things around prayers, fasting and going to the mosque, no, not real Muslims for most of us, for younger people.

Imran: Groups can label themselves, like we label ourselves Muslim. But it's not the same as when white people use the label.

M.M: What do you mean?

Imran: It's hard to explain, we're both using the same word. But they use Muslim and they don't even know us, or they mean something bad. For us it's a definite good thing or just a normal thing.

M.M: And do you know what it means?

Imran: A good question. I think if I'm been honest, then no. I think a lot of the time, we don't know what Muslim means. Like we're saying here, it can mean lots of things. [Group interview]

A key theme to which the students returned over the period of the research was how to make sense of the range of social and cultural exclusions that they experienced at a time of rapid change within the city. Historically, one of the major ways in which the concept of race and social change and the accompanying social and cultural exclusions has been problematized in the literature is through the use of the term racialization. Banton (1977) used the concept of racialization to refer to the use of the idea of race to structure people's perceptions of different populations. During the 1980s and 1990s the notion was used as a key signifier of racial meanings in a range of discourses (Reeves, 1983; Miles, 1993; Troyna, 1993). Small (1994: 32–3) adopts the 'racialization' problematic in order to unravel the relative influence of multiple factors (economics, politics, demography, culture, ideology and myth) in patterns of 'racialized relations'. As Solomos (1993: 1) argues, a main focus here is 'the growth of ideologies which have focused upon race as an important political symbol, the role of anti-racist and black political mobilisation and the impact of social and economic restructuring on racial and national identities in British society'. Changing processes of racialization are operationalized through the impact of changing race imagery in a range of institutional settings as well as processes of deracialization (Husband, 1982; Miles, 1989).

The usefulness of the concept is indicated by the fact that it has been adopted by theorists from a wide range of perspectives, including those from a race-relations problematic, as well as neo- Marxist and post-structuralist positions (Banton, 1977; Reeves, 1983; Miles, 1989; Smith, 1989; Solomos, 1993; Small, 1994; Holdaway, 1996). Theorists have deployed the concept in different ways in order to address the limits of conventional accounts of race and racism. From a materialist perspective, theorists have challenged the notion of distinct races as biologically given and pointed to the need to explore the conditions under which specific processes of racialization result in differential outcomes. This work has been particularly successful in examining the cumulative institutional effects of ascribing reified meanings to minorities, particularly South Asians and African-Caribbeans. As Green and Carter (1988: 23) have argued, processes of racialization in post-war Britain were 'structurally determined, politically organised and ideologically inflected . . . within the relations of domination and subordination'. Miles (1982) provided an early account of this with reference to post-war labour migration to Britain. Keith (1993: 239) has cogently captured a post-structuralist understanding of race and racialization, while not losing sight of relations of domination and subordination. Arguing that race is not an essential characteristic, he suggests that:

> The pervasive practices of racism, however, and the evolution of racial formations over time and space . . . guarantee some correspondence in the harsh reality of the day-to-day world between the ideological fictions of racial divisions between people and the empirical circumscription of specific groups in society. The generation of racial divisions in society is most easily grasped by use of the notion of racialization, which stresses both the reality of the group formation process as well as the social construction of differences between the racial collective identities so formed. The process of racialization is also of particular significance because it is one of the principal means through which subordination is produced and reproduced in an unjust society.

More recently, theorists have suggested that the concept of racialization is productive in capturing the contemporary structural positioning and subjective experiences of Muslims in Britain (Brah and Phoenix, 2004; Mac an Ghaill and Haywood, 2005). However, the last ten years has seen the term Islamophobia emerge as the dominant explanation of Muslim social and cultural exclusions.

Among the students various positions were taken up in relation to different understandings of the deployment of racialization and Islamophobia. For some students, the term Islamophobia was of key strategic importance in highlighting questions of cultural and religious discrimination that they felt earlier notions of racism and racialization did not capture (Halliday, 1999; Kundnani, 2002). Historically, this has been a central argument among sections of the Muslim community in Britain, highlighted in two main issues: their campaign for government recognition and financial support for Muslim schools and their mobilization against the publication of Salman Rushdie's book *The Satanic Verses* (see Asad, 1990; Al-Azmeh, 1993). In other words, anti-Islamophobia mobilization was a response to the under-theorization of the concept of racialization. In the recent past, within the context of anti-racist politics, the latter term remained locked within the reductionist black/white colour paradigm that underplayed key elements of South Asian and black lives, including religion, culture and migration. More specifically, this younger generation emphasize the role that religious identities and identity-making play in the process of racialization at a time of 'faith-hate' (McGhee, 2005: 92–117).

Tahir: When people talked about racism in the past, they meant black people, not us, not Muslims.

Raqib: If you said we were getting racism at school, everyone would think of colour, but what about religion? And Islamophobia is like special to us. It explains about bad things happening to Muslim people, and our culture.

Iftikhar: If you want to talk about racialization stuff today, it has to include what is really important to us and that is about our religion. [Group interview]

Other students addressed what they considered to be some of the limitations of the pervasiveness of the concept of Islamophobia. A key issue was the extent to which the concept served to disconnect the Muslim community from a wider anti-racist movement and the historical benefits of a broader understanding of racialization. For, example, they identified the effects of the shift from a politics of redistribution to a politics of recognition, and the accompanying limited understanding of processes of racialization within conditions of socio-economic austerity (Fraser, 1998) (explored further below). For others, there was much confusion about the meaning of Islamophobia, with some suggesting that it was a contemporary form of racialization (Commission on British Muslims and Islamophobia, 1997). Life history interviews in particular drew out the differing personal (dis)identifications associated with Islamophobia:

Tamim: My father and his uncles were all involved in the anti-racist movement in the past. At that time, they would have big campaigns and demonstrations about things like unemployment and bad housing and crap schooling. As well as all the racist discrimination. It brought lots of different communities together. But now our community leaders, they couldn't get anyone to, or they wouldn't want to, get people to demonstrate about the recession and what it's doing to all people round here. [Life History Interview]

Yasin: It's true. The only thing they will demonstrate about now is something they think is kind of very religious or offends our religion. [Life History Interview]

Asif: Everyone is really confused about the talk of Islamophobia. Like you listen to racist groups and they say Islam is a threat to the British nation. But they seem to be confused, one minute talking about religion and then about nationality and the British state. [Life History Interview]

Shoaib: I think it is best to see Islamophobia as a new way of been racist to Muslims. [Life History Interview]

In response to the suggested limitations of the concept of Islamophobia, for many young men there was a further limitation of the deployment of Islamophobia, which they perceived as circulating in the form of a universal and homogeneous category of exclusion. In contrast, they emphasized the significance of understanding how diverse international changes are mediated at a local (national and regional) level. More specifically, illustrating the demographic diversity within the Muslim faith, the young people emphasize the need to focus on Muslims' differentiated experiences of discrimination and how they differ historically and geographically across the interconnecting categories of generation, class, and gender (for example, see Tehranian, 2008, for discussion of contemporary American Muslims and Mandeville, 2009, for state responses to Muslims across Europe). Their argument resonates with a major limitation of an abstract notion of 'othering' in the academic literature, which has disconnected from empirical work in 'old' institutional sites, such as family life, schooling, and workplace, resulting in the figure of the Muslim male been represented as an over-generalized racial 'other' (Said, 1978; Mac an Ghaill and Haywood, 2007).

Naqeeb: When it's used generally, it kind of means that people, western people, hate Muslims and have always hated them. But that's not true is it? [Life history interview]

Tamim: You hear people saying this is Islamophobic and that is Islamophobic, like everything. It becomes meaningless. One word cannot mean all those things happening in all Muslim countries and everywhere.

Ali: Lots of Muslim countries are going through loads of changes. And on the telly, in the papers, they talk in bad stereotyped ways about Afghanistan, Syria, Pakistan. But they talk bad about them in different ways. [Group interview]

Many of the young men argued for a complex and nuanced understanding of racialization that acknowledged the effect of the contemporary positioning of Muslims, in which they carry the anxieties of the wider society at a time of globally-inflected changes. These anxieties were seen to produce the specificity of current social and cultural exclusions experienced by Birmingham-based Muslims. They identified a series of issues that have a common theme of projecting Birmingham-based Pakistanis and Bangladeshis as marked by social separateness, cultural fixity and boundedness of religious identity. In short, they are projected as figures of 'anti-modernity' in a late modern urban space.

There is a long history that at a time of crisis in dominant public forms of Anglo-ethnicity, national identity and cultural belonging, racial minorities are forced to carry the burden of the national and ethnic majority's sense of moral disorder (Weeks, 1990; Mercer, 1992; McGhee, 2005). The young Muslim men contextualized the specificities of their highly contradictory masculine identity, as indicated above — represented as both potential terrorists and highly vulnerable to terrorist recruitment — emphasizing how dominant British responses combine internal doubt and external anxiety that are projected onto them. They suggested that the starting point for addressing issues of religious identity should not focus on their community but rather address the wider British society's shifting meanings of religion, faith and secularism and the assumed crisis in the role of Christianity in the making of national identity in a modern era (Woodhead, 2012). They felt that current debates on this issue assumed a highly reductionist dualism between the projected threatening significance of the emergence of a *global* Islamic identity and a disappearing *local* allegiance to Christianity. As a recent editorial in *The Guardian* newspaper (2012: 34) suggested in its commentary on the latest census results, we are a society that is:

> . . . . changing very rapidly, in profound and interesting ways, without any clear overall direction. . . . The most obvious sign of this transformation is the decline of notional Christianity and the rise of the 'no religion' category,

or 'nones'. 'No religion', a kind of undogmatic secular humanism, is not the established religion, but it is the source of values for the people who have replaced the old establishment.

Interestingly, the instability of the religious categories held by ethnic majorities is recognized by young Muslim men:

Parvez: I think people concentrate too much on Islam and Muslims when they talk about Islamophobia. I don't know, really. But maybe it's not so much Muslims are the real problem.

Waqar: But maybe the real problem for British, for white British people is religion itself. I think if you studied it, you would see. Like for my grandparents when they came here, Britain was still a Christian country, there was a lot more Christians about but you ask one of your white mates, he wouldn't know anything about religion or being a Christian. Even at Christmas, it's about shopping and drinking for them.

Imtiaz: It's true when you say it. I don't think they are thinking about baby Jesus. And for the old white people, you have to feel sorry for them, cos they see their churches empty and no young people. Then they see all these mosques full of people, everyone and the young kids all going off to pray. They must think, what's going on?

Furooq: It's not just going to church, that they're not doing. It's on a bigger scale. It's the whole culture has changed. You can hear those atheist guys. I think they're saying if you want to live in Britain today, you should be, have to be modern, you have to move with the times.

Yusuf: That is true, when you think of it. So, when they see all the young Muslim kids especially being religious, they think, these people aren't modern, these people aren't British.

Ali: And round here, lots of people are Mir, and a lot of them are religious, so maybe if they say Islamophobia is growing that's a real reason, a deeper reason, not just hating us because we are Muslim but because we are religious and they don't believe in religion any more.

Shoaib: It's pretty mixed up though, because the older white people round here probably think that young Muslims are like what they were when they were young, and for them Britain has lost this and it's a bad thing. [Group interview]

As illustrated above, in contrast to recent theorizing and research on Muslims, the young men in this study critically engage with the contextually-based local meanings of key unstable concepts, including Muslim, Islamophobia and racialization, through which they are securing complex masculine subjectivities in a 'post-secular' society' (McGhee, 2013). An important theme that emerges from this, as they highlight in the next section, is that Islamophobia displacing a notion of racialization is a danger for their community because of the attendant invisibility of the current impact of social class within conditions of socio-economic austerity. For them, class is a central element of their social and cultural exclusions.

The Invisibility of the Stratification of Young Pakistani and Bangladeshi Men as Classed Subjects

In an earlier period, drawing upon sociology, class was the central analytical concept in researching minority ethnic young people's experiences. For example, Anthias and Yuval-Davis (1993: 65), in their critical re-reading of sociological work in the 1970s and 1980s, identify a range of materialist positions that link race to class: 'Rex's underclass thesis, migrant labour theories, racism as an ideology that is relatively autonomous of class, Gilroy's view that class formation is linked to race, and the dual labour market approaches'. This work was politically important in establishing commonalities of racism among Asians and African-Caribbeans and investigated their different institutionalized positioning, across institutional sites, within a multi-racist industrial-based Britain. It was especially significant in critiquing the dominant culturalist approach, with its focus on ethnic attributes. As Mercer and Prescott (1982: 102) argued: 'The most significant feature of the minority experience is not their ethnicity but their place in the class structure. Their relative powerlessness ensures that they remain in a subordinate position politically and culturally'. This class-based analytical work provided explanatory frameworks to make sense of the social and cultural reproduction of racially structured societies. More specifically, it illustrated the productiveness of deploying class analysis in highlighting how racism, which pervasively structured minority ethnic young people's social world, was mediated through the existing institutional frameworks that discriminated against (white) working-class youth *and* through the operation of race-specific mechanisms, such as gender-inflected racist stereotyping of Asian and African-Caribbean students (Mac an Ghaill, 1988; Mirza, 1992; Bourdieu and Passeron, 1977).

Presently, there is much evidence of the historical continuity of class-based structural constraints on working-class Pakistani and Bangladeshi men. Their collective profile includes highest levels of unemployment and over-representation in low-skilled employment, over-representation in prisons, over-representation in poor housing, high levels of poor health and lowest levels of social mobility (Eade and Garbin, 2002; ONS, 2006; Garner and Bhattacharyya, 2011; Barnard and Turner, 2011; Laird et al., 2007; Ahmad at al., 2003). More specifically, reading through the research literature, a main government and academic image of Pakistani and Bangladeshi students is that of underachievement, with Pakistani and Bangladeshi male students, in terms of ethnicity, faith group, class and gender, placed at the bottom of league tables on academic school performance (DfES, 2007). This is a significant shift from earlier representations of an assumed homogeneous Asian community of 'high achievers'. However, several researchers challenged this account, highlighting the complexity and variability of Asian students' school attainment with reference to class, gender and national group origins. For example, most importantly, middle-class Indian students' academic success served to mask the relatively low examination attainment among working-class Pakistani and Bangladeshi boys (Rattansi, 1992; Mac an Ghaill, 1994). More recently, Archer (2003) has made the argument about the continuing impact of socio-economic inequalities on the education of Muslim boys.

Young men in our study articulate a consciousness of the different social logics that are lived out by working- and middle-class people in the city of Birmingham. More particularly, they suggest a generationally-specific identification with local white working-class young people and a (local) place-affiliation around the increasing socio-economic divisions that circumscribe their collective social lives. It is difficult to capture the intense anger that they feel about the cultural demonization and polarization that they suggest all young people experience within the most deprived areas in the city. Of significance are the classed divisions within social minorities that contributes to (dis) identifications within and across ascribed ethnic boundaries:

Farooq: Lots of people talk about the us and them around religion and segregation and tension and everything. But no-one talks about, like in this city, people from around here, even our white mates, we'd never go to a posh area. They'd think we're aliens.

Shoaib: An' the posh areas have got posher and posher and the poor areas are getting really poor every day, more people out of work and kids leave schools and no jobs.

Javed: My uncle, he reckons that Asians, Bangladeshi people are really looked down upon much more now than before when he came here because they are poor. And that's the Asian middle-class people doing that. They're doing it as well.

Parvez: On telly, in the papers, everywhere, poor people are really hated. I think that it's worse for the poor whites. They have special labels for them, rich people have, like they call them chavs. They've made up a word, special word for them. I feel sorry for the white kids around here. No one looks after them, do you know what I mean? [Group interview]

These comments resonate with Farzana Shain's (2011) work. In response to dominant government and academic representations, she provides one of the most sustained critical explanations of contemporary Muslim boys' experiences in England, arguing for a more theoretically sophisticated approach that includes the development of a socio-economic dimension. She adopts a Gramscian analysis emphasizing the articulation of multiple structures of race, gender *and* class with socio-economic and political relations of domination and subordination (Gramsci, 1970). Shain maintains that:

> Gramsci's framework recognises that young people are located within material contexts that structure and limit the structure of possibilities for agency and action. This entails the recognition of the role of historical forces — in this case colonialism and imperialism — in shaping the class locations and settlements of Muslim communities in areas of England that have suffered most from economic decline. These settlement patterns have had a lasting legacy in terms of the types of schooling and educational and employment opportunities available. Pakistani and Bangladeshi communities find themselves located in some of the most materially deprived wards in the country. (2011: 50)

However, as the young men indicated, across government, media, education and popular culture there is an absence of class representation of Pakistani and Bangladeshi young men. Rather, the cumulative effect of the projected representations of social failure that circulates across different sites is, as argued above, to position them within the singular category of religion, i.e. exclusively as Muslims rather than bearers of any other identity. The invisibility of Pakistanis and Bangladeshis *as classed subjects* across the political spectrum is discursively achieved through two major explanatory frameworks: that of the underclass (the political right) and Islamophobia (the political left). Shain (2011: 7) identifies what have become iconic moments in revisiting a notion of underclass. She writes: 'The Gulf War in 1991, the Bradford riots in 1995, the [2011]summer disturbances, 9/11, the London bombings in 2005 and numerous failed bomb plots have all continued to fuel fears about extremist Muslims, and the discourse conflates the issue of violent Asians and Muslim gangs'. More specifically, she notes how European and British political commentators 'conflate educational underachievement, criminality and the Islamification of Europe through the notion of a Muslim underclass. These three issues form a dominant cultural narrative of a Muslim underclass that is responsible for its own marginality' (Shain, 2011: 9). The young men in our study share Shain's analysis that a major effect of this cultural narrative is that class inequalities are displaced, with different sectors of the working class ascribed specific forms of cultural deficit, as government and media discourses serve to blame individual subjects rather than address the structural causes of social and cultural exclusions (Munt, 2000; Bourdieu, 1986).

Parvez: In poor areas like around here, why don't they give us jobs and good education? But no, if you're from this area and you go for a job, they'll tell you to get lost.

Abdul: Somehow the ruling people have turned the world upside down. Nearly everything that Muslim kids are blamed for, the ones that go bad, it could all be sorted if you gave them proper education and jobs and got rid of all the discrimination against us.

Asif: I think the bad thing now is that there is this big image and you can't move it. All the people in charge just see Muslims as one big problem as bombing the world or causing big trouble here.

M.M: How does this affect people in the area?

Asif: Most of these people are just ordinary people. There's a lot of poverty, unemployment and things, and nothing for the kids to do, they're just bored. They've nothing to do with the racist stereotypes about being radicals and all that. They wouldn't even know what any of that means round here. But like all the kids who came out from our year. How many of them got jobs, went to college or anything? My mother thinks there's much less opportunities for our generation. [Group Interview]

A second explanatory framework can be found in recent empirical work within schools that reinscribes the cultural invisibility of young Pakistani and Bangladeshi men as classed subjects by selectively drawing upon a limited range of signifiers, including *umma, hijab, jilbab,* the war on terror, etc. These signifiers, understood exclusively as religious phenomena, are located within an explanatory framework of Islamophobia, which is projected as a mechanism of entrapment in which it is assumed that young men's social practices can simply be read off as defensive strategies of religious survival.

In work using the notion of Islamophobia, subjectivity is under-theorized, reminiscent of early anti-racist accounts of the black and white dualism. One consequence of this is that state institutions are conceptualized as reflecting the possible identities that can be taken up and lived out. A further limitation of this position is that it is unable to realize the significant challenges of new social movements, which are to create theoretical frameworks that can accommodate a range of inequalities, such as those around ethnicity, class, gender, sexuality and disability (Mac an Ghaill and Haywood, 2012). In short, this position produces difficulties in articulating an inclusive account of multiple forms of social power (Anthias, 2008). It could be argued that the young people's narratives enable an understanding that challenges the view of Islamophobia as a monolithic force that can be read off from the assumed responses of individuals — the Muslim-'non-Muslim' dualism. Rather, within particular institutional sites, there are a range of contextually-based (racist) ideologies and discourses that may place subjects in subordinate positions. These racialized processes are temporally and spatially specific, and articulate in complex ways with other categories of social difference, including class.

Conclusion

The social and cultural uncertainties in contemporary England are creating a series of symbolic spaces where national anxieties and promises around race/ethnicity are being projected. Miller (2006) has discussed the emergence of fear as a key feature of the governability of national otherness. In the context of young Muslim men, one dynamic for such fear is the state's claim of an unsuccessful inclusion and identification with 'Britishness'. In previous historical moments, youth culture has been seen in opposition to parent cultures. At present, the institutional conflation of young people with radicalization and fundamentalism appeals to a potential hyperbolic re-instatement of ascribed parental values by young people. The narratives reported in this article suggest a more complex situation, where the older religious and political designations of being Muslim were reworked. At the same time, young Muslim men were concerned with the material basis of their social and economic location, through which cultural difference was being read. The fieldwork undertaken with these young men could be understood as a process, where they were given the opportunity to explore and discuss the contradictions and tensions that were circulating through their attempts to convey their identifications and subjectivities. One of the difficulties when listening to their narratives has been to resist representation of their identities though pre-existing popular and academic explanations. Rather, the focus here is on facilitating ways of understanding how *they* are participating in the production of ideas of being Muslim, racialization and Islamophobia.

Funding

This research received no specific grant from any funding agency in the public, commercial, or not-for-profit sectors.

References

Ahmad F, Modood T and Lissenburgh S (2003) *South Asian Women and Employment in Britain: The Interaction of Gender and Ethnicity.* London: Policy Studies Institute.

Al-Azmeh A (1993) *Islams and Modernities.* London: Verso.

Alvesson M and Skoldberg K (2000) *Reflexive Methodology: New Vistas for Qualitative Research.* London: SAGE.

Ansari H (2004) *'The Infidel Within': Muslims in Britain since 1800.* London: C. Hurst and Co.

Anthias F (2008) Thinking through the lens of translocational positionality: An intersectionality frame for understanding identity and belonging. *Translocations: Migration and Social Change* 4(1): 5–20.

Anthias F and Yuval-Davies N (1993) *Racialized Boundaries: Race, Nation, Gender, Colour and Class and the Anti-racist Struggle.* London: Routledge.

Appadurai A (1991) Global ethnoscapes: Notes and queries for a transnational anthropology. In Fox RG (ed.) *Recapturing Anthropology: Working in the Present.* Santa Fe, CA: School of American Research.

Archer L (2003) *'Race', Masculinity and Schooling: Muslim Boys and Education.* Berkshire: Open University Press.

Asad T (1990) Multiculturalism in the wake of the Rushdie affair. *Politics and Society* 18(4): 455–80.
Banton M (1977) *The Idea of Race.* London: Tavistock.

Bauman Z (1996) From pilgrim to tourist: A short story of identity. In: Hall S and du gay P (eds) *Questions of Cultural Identity*. London: SAGE.

Barnard H and Turner C (2011) *Poverty and Ethnicity: A Review of Evidence*. York: Joseph Rowntree Foundation.

Bhattacharyya G (2008) State racism and Muslim men as a racialised threat. In: Bhattacharyya G, *Dangerous Brown Men: Exploiting Sex, Violence and Feminism in the War on Terror*. London: Zed Books.

Birmingham City Council (2013) Ethnic groups: Population and census. Available (accessed 7 February 2014) at: http://www.birmingham.gov.uk/cs/Satellite?c=Page&childpagename=Planni ng-and-Regeneration%2FPageLayout&cid=1223096353923&pagename=BCC%2FCommon%2FW rapper%2FWrapper

Blackmore J (2000) Warning signals or dangerous opportunities? Globalization, gender, and educational policy shifts. *Education Theory* 50: 467–486.

Bourdieu P (1986) *Distinction: A Social Critique of Judgement*. London: Routledge.

Bourdieu P and Passeron JC (1977) *Reproduction*. London: SAGE.

Bradley H and Devadason R (2008) Fractured transitions: Young adults' pathways into contemporary labour markets. *Sociology* 42(1): 119–135.

Brah A, Hickman MJ and Mac an Ghaill M (eds) (2000) *Global Futures: Migration, Environment and Globalization*. London: Macmillan.

Brah A and Phoenix A (2004) Ain't I a woman? Revisiting intersectionality. *Journal of International Women's Studies* 5(3): 75–86.

Braun V and Clarke V (2006) Using thematic analysis in psychology. *Qualitative Research in Psychology* 3(2): 77–101.

Cainkar L (2009) *Homeland Insecurity: The Arab American and Muslim American Experience after 9/11*. New York, NY: Russell Sage Foundation Publications.

Choudhurry T (2007) The role of Muslim identity politics in radicalisation (a study in progress). London: Department of Communities and Local Government.

Commission on British Muslims and Islamophobia (1997) *Islamophobia: A Challenge for Us All*. London: Runnymede Trust.

Crouch M and McKenzie H (2006) The logic of small samples in interview-based qualitative research. *Social Science Information* 45(4): 483–499.

Department for Education and Skills (2007) *Gender and Education: The Evidence on Pupils in England Research Information*. London: Department for Education and Skills.

Eade J and Garbin D (2002) Changing narratives of violence, struggle and resistance: Bangladeshis and the competition for scarce resources, *Oxford Development Studies* 30(2): 127–44.

Faas D (2010) *Negotiating Political Identities: Multi-ethnic Schools and Youth in Europe*. Farnham: Ashgate. Fekete L (2004) Anti-Muslim racism and the European security state. *Race and Class* 43: 95–103.

Fraser N (1998) From redistribution to recognition? Dilemmas of justice in a post-socialist age. In: Phillips A (ed.) *Feminism and Politics*. Oxford: Oxford University Press.

Garner S and Bhattacharyya G (2011) *Poverty, Ethnicity and Place*. York: Joseph Rowntree Foundation. Gilroy P (2004) *After Empire: Melancholia or Convivial Culture*. London: Routledge.

Gramsci A (1970) *Selections from the Prison Notebooks*. London: Lawrence and Wishart.

Green M and Carter B (1988) 'Races' and 'race-makers': The politics of racialization. *Sage Race Relations Abstracts* 13: 4–30.

Haddad YY (2004) *Not Quite American? The Shaping of Arab and American Identity in the United States*. Waco, TX: Baylor University Press.

Hall S (1992) The question of cultural identity. In: Hall S, Held D and McGrew T (eds) *Modernity and Its Futures*. Cambridge: Polity.

Halliday F (1999) 'Islamophobia' reconsidered. *Ethnic and Racial Studies* 22(5): 892–902. Harvey D (2003) *The New Imperialism*. Oxford: Oxford University Press.

Holdaway S (1996) *The Racialization of British Policing*. London: Macmillan. Husband C (1982) *'Race' in Britain: Community and Change*. London: Hutchinson. Hussain S (2008) *Muslims on the Map*. London: Tauris Academic Studies.

Ibrahim M (2005) The securitization of migration: A racial discourse. *International Migration* 43: 163–87. Jamal A (2008) Civil liberties and the otherization of Arab and Muslim Americans. In: Jamal A and Naber N (eds) *Race and Arab Americans Before and After 9/11: From Invisible Citizens to Visible Subjects*. Syracuse, NY: Syracuse University Press.

Keith M (1993) *Race, Riots and Policing: Lore and Disorder in a Multi-racist Society*. London: UCL Press.

Kundnani A (2002) An unholy alliance? Racism, religion and communalism. *Race and Class* 44: 71–80. Kundnani A (2009) *Spooked! How Not to Prevent Violent Extremism*. London: Institute of Race Relations.

Laird LD, Amer MM, Barnett ED and Barnes LL (2007) Muslim patients and health disparities in the UK and the US. *Archives of Disease in Childhood* 92(10): 922–26.

Mac an Ghaill M (1988) *Young, Gifted and Black: Teacher-Student Relations in the Schooling of Black Youth*. Milton Keynes: Open University Press.

Mac an Ghaill M (1994) *The Making of Men: Masculinities, Sexualities and Schooling*. Buckingham: Open University Press.

Mac an Ghaill M and Haywood C (2005) *Young Bangladeshi People's Experience of Transition to Adulthood*. York: Joseph Rowntree Foundation.

Mac an Ghaill M and Haywood C (2007) *Gender, Culture and Society: Contemporary Femininities and Masculinities*. London: Palgrave Macmillan.

Mac an Ghaill M and Haywood C (2012) Schooling, masculinity and class analysis: Towards an aesthetics of subjectivity. *British Journal of Sociology of Education* 32(5): 729–44.

Mandeville P (2009) Muslim transnational identity and state responses in Europe and the UK after 9/11: Political community, ideology and authority. *Journal of Ethnic and Migration Studies* 35(3): 491–506.

McGhee D (2005) *Intolerant Britain? Hate, Citizenship and Difference*. Berkshire: Open University Press. McGhee D (2008) *The End of Multi-culturalism: Terrorism, Integration and Human Rights*. Berkshire: Open University Press.

McGhee D (2013) Responding to the post 9/11 challenges facing 'post-secular societies': Critical reflections on Habermas's dialogic solutions. *Ethnicities* 13(1): 68–85.

Mercer K (1992) Just looking for trouble: Robert Mapplethorpe and fantasies. In: Segal L and McIntosh M (eds) *Sex Exposed: Sexuality and the Pornography Debate*. London: Virago.

Mercer N and Prescott W (1982) Perspectives on minority experience. In: *Minority Experience* (Open University Studies, Course E254, Block 3, Units 8 and 9). Milton Keynes: Open University Press.

Miles R (1982) *Racism and Labour Migration.* London: Routledge and Kegan Paul. Miles R (1989) *Racism.* London: Routledge.

Miles R (1993) *Racism after Race Relations.* London: Routledge.

Miller B (2006) The globalization of fear. In: Conway D and Heynen N (eds) *Globalization's Dimensions: Forces of Discipline, Destruction and Resistance.* New York, NY: Routledge, 161–177.

Mills M and Keddie A (2010) Cultural reductionism and the media: polarising discourses around schools, violence and masculinity in an age of terror. *Oxford Review of Education* 36(4): 427–44.

Mirza HS (1992) *Young, Female and Black.* London: Routledge.

Munt SR (ed.) (2000) *Cultural Studies and the Working Class: Subject to Change.* London: Cassell.

Nagle J (2009) *Multiculturalism's Double Bind: Creating Inclusivity, Cosmopolitanism and Difference.* Farnham: Ashgate.

Office for National Statistics (2006) *Religion-Labour Market.* London: Office for National Statistics.

Office for National Statistics (2012) 2011 Census: Religion (detailed), local authorities in England and Wales, Table QS210EW. Available (accessed 1 October 2013) at: http://www.ons.gov.uk

Patton M (1990) *Qualitative Evaluation and Research Methods.* Newbury Park, CA: SAGE.

Pentazis C and Pemberton S (2009) From the 'old' to the 'new' suspect community: Examining the impacts of recent UK counter-terrorist legislation. *British Journal of Criminology* 49: 464–66.

Phillips D (2006) Parallel lives? Challenging discourses of British Muslim self-segregation. *Environment and Planning D: Society and Space* 24: 25–40.

Phoenix A (2004) Neoliberalism and masculinity: Racialization and the contradictions of schooling for 11- to 14-year-olds. *Youth & Society* 36(2): 227–246.

Pilkington HA and Johnson R (2003) Peripheral youth: Relations of identity and power in global/local context. *European Journal of Cultural Studies* 6(3): 259–283.

Popoviciu L and Mac an Ghaill M (2004) Racisms, ethnicities and British nation-making. In: Devine F and Walters MC (eds) *Social Identities in Comparative Perspective.* London: Blackwell.

Qureshi K (2004) Respected and respectable: The centrality of 'performance' and 'audiences' in the (re) production and potential revision of gendered ethnicities. *Particip@tions* 1(2).

Rattansi A (1992) Changing the subject: Racism, culture and education. In: Donald J and Rattansi A (eds) *Race, Culture and Difference.* London: SAGE.

Reeves F (1983) *British Racial Discourse: A Study of Political Discourse about Race and Race-Related Matters.* Cambridge: Cambridge University Press.

Richardson JE (2004) *(Mis)representing Islam: The Racism and Rhetoric of British Broadcast Newspapers.* Amsterdam: John Benjamins.

Said EW (1978) *Orientalism.* London: Routledge & Kegan Paul. Said EW (1993) *Culture and Imperialism.* London: Vintage.

Samad Y (1998) Media and Muslim identity: Intersections of generation and gender. *Innovation. European Journal of Social Studies* 11(4): 425–38.

Sandhu S (2011) Stretch out and wait. *The Guardian, Saturday Review* 24 December, p. 15. Shain F (2003) *The Schooling and Identity of Asian Girls.* Stoke on Trent: Trentham Books.

Shain F (2011) *The New Folk Devils: Muslim Boys and Education in England*. Stoke on Trent: Trentham Books.

Small S (1994) *Racialised Boundaries: The Black Experience in the U.S. and England in the 1980s*. London: Routledge.

Smith SJ (1989) *The Politics of 'Race' and Residence*. Cambridge: Policy Press. Solomos J (1993) *Race and Racism in Britain*. 2nd Edition. Basingstoke: Macmillan.

Tehranian J (2008) *Whitewashed: America's Invisible Middle Eastern Minority*. New York, NY: New York University Press.

The Guardian (2012) Diverging into diversity [editorial], 12 December, p. 34.

Townsend M (2011) Poll reveals surge of sympathy for far right. *The Observer*, 27 February, p. 1. Troyna B (1993) *Racism and Education: Research Perspectives*. Buckingham: Open University Press.

UK Government (2009) *The United Kingdom's Strategy for Countering International Terrorism*. London: The Stationery Office.

Ussher JM, Sandoval M, Perz J, Wong WKT and Butow P (2013) The gendered construction and experience of difficulties and rewards in cancer care. *Qualitative Health Research* 23(7): 900–15.

Weeks G (1990) The value of difference. In: Rutherford J (ed.) *Identity: Community, Culture and Difference*. London: Lawrence and Wishart.

Wetherell M (1998) Positioning and interpretative repertoires: Conversation analysis and post-structuralism in dialogue. *Discourse and Society* 9(3): 387–412.

Woodhead L (2012) A British Christmas has lost faith in rituals, but not religion. *The Observer*, 23 December, p. 32.

Zaretsky E (1996) Identity theory, identity politics: Psychoanalysis, Marxism, poststructuralism. In: Calhoun C (ed.) *Social Theory and the Politics of Identity*. Oxford: Blackwell.

• Appendix F •

A Case Study—"Relational Underpinnings and Professionality—A Case Study of a Teacher's Practices Involving Students With Experiences of School Failure"

Anneli Frelin

University of Gävle, Sweden

Abstract

Relational features of the educational environment, such as positive teacher-student relationships, are important for students' academic success. This case study explores the relational practices of a teacher who negotiates educational relationships with students who have a history of school failure. 'Gunilla,' a secondary school teacher working in the Swedish 'Introduction Programme' (for students who have not been accepted in national upper secondary school programmes) and identified as a successful instructor for students who have failed at school, was selected for the study. The data consists of two semi-structured interviews eliciting the informant's stories of practice and the researcher's contextual observation. Results show how relational practices create an emotionally safe school climate. In the initial phase of the teacher-student relationship the main purpose of the activities is to establish trust and repair the students' self-image so that they can view themselves as successful learners. This requires professional closeness and the teacher distancing herself from a stereotypical teaching role, in order to display humaneness and empathy. The findings contribute to understanding how relational features in the everyday school context help students to learn and how school psychologists can be part of this endeavour.

Keywords

at-risk students, professionalism, school failure, teacher-student relationships, teaching

Teachers encountering students with a history of school failure often face difficult challenges. Some teachers are better equipped to deal with them than others. Because positive teacher-student relationships are particularly important for students who risk school failure (e.g. Pianta, 2006), both teachers and students benefit from support in developing such relationships. The purpose of this article is to trace and exemplify relational and professional practices that can help teachers and other school staff to assist students to overcome obstacles and be more successful at school. A qualitative case study approach is used to illustrate the complexities of building and sustaining educational relationships with upper secondary students who have experienced school failure. A case study can illuminate the specific aspects that emerge in the teacher-student interaction and that contribute to successful academic and social outcomes. It can also take into account how everyday interactions contribute to the specific *temporal* character of teacher-student relationships that are established and maintained in the school environment over the school year.

Although this article draws on an educational perspective, it has the potential to contribute to and complement a psychological perspective in valuable ways for teachers, school psychologists, and others working in an educational setting. It provides insights into teachers' work, the kind of challenges that they face and the professionality that supports them. Such insights are valuable for school psychologists who provide consultation to teachers who struggle with challenges in relationships with their students who have experienced school failure. The literature review will cover teacher professionality and teacher-student relationships with special attention to students with experiences of school failure, and the consulting role of school psychologists.

Relational Professionality

Although there are competing definitions of what constitutes a profession, in order to be viewed as a profession the practice has to fulfil certain criteria. It also includes things such as extensive training and autonomous judgements (Bridges, 2001; Freidson, 1994; Hoyle, 1995). Professionalism can be viewed as the result of the collective achievement of a corps of professionals striving together towards the same end, and professionality as the instantiation of this collective effort by a single individual (Evans, 2008). In this article, teachers' relational professionality refers to the dimension of professionality that teachers use to build and sustain educational relationships with students in order to help them learn and grow (Frelin, 2010, 2013).

Teacher-Student Relationships

Quality instruction characterized by positive teacher-student relationships constitutes an important part of student learning along with contextual factors both inside and outside the school (Darling-Hammond, 2014). The quality of teacher-student relationships and the closeness of cooperation has proven especially beneficial for students' well-being, self-confidence, motivation, and academic outcomes (Backman et al., 2011; den Brok, Brekelmans, & Wubbels, 2004; Jennings & Greenberg, 2009; Roorda et al., 2011; Wentzel, Battle, Russell, & Looney, 2010; Wu, Hughes, & Kwok, 2010; Wubbels et al., 2015; Zimmer-Gembeck & Locke, 2007). Informal environments and situations can be of great value for the negotiation of teacher-student relationships (Frelin & Grannäs, 2010, 2014; Hansen, 1998; van Tartwijk, den Brok, Veldman, & Wubbels, 2009). One prominent factor seems to be the closeness of the relationship; the ability to create a personal relationship that goes beyond the roles of teacher and student, as has been shown in various studies (Baker, Grant, & Morlock, 2008; Cornelius-White, 2007; Hattie, 2009; Pianta, 2006; Rudasill, Reio Jr, Stipanovic, & Taylor, 2010). Thus, besides a need to keep a professional distance, there is also a need to create professional closeness (Frelin, 2008). Warm and supportive teacher-student relationships are also part of the wider school climate that connects students to their schools (Raufelder, Sahabandu, Martínez, & Escobar, 2013; Solomon, Watson, Battistich, Schaps, & Delucchi, 1996; Watson & Battistich, 2006; Woolfolk Hoy & Weinstein, 2006).

Relationships and School Failure

Dealing with challenging situations in teacher-student relationships is a struggle that many teachers face. For students with a negative experience of school, positive and close teacher-student relationships are even more important than for their peers (Baker et al., 2008; Hamre & Pianta, 2001; Johnson, 2008; Pianta, 2006; Pomeroy, 1999; Rudasill et al., 2010). In his study on how 'at risk' students' view their teachers, Johnson (2008) argues that by focusing actively on small and repeated actions in order to relate to and connect with students at the micro level, teachers can make a diffierence in the lives of their students. In his study of minority students, Erickson (1987) highlights the importance of a student's trust in the teacher for the creation of a positive relationship (see also Bliding, Holm, & Hägglund, 2002; Raider-Roth, 2005). Studsrød and Bru (2012) connect teachers' socialization practices, such as academic support, with upper secondary students' school adjustment, whereas Davidson (1999) argues that teachers' expressions of confidence in students' capacities despite their poor performance could elicit their students' acceptance for a broader range of teacher behaviour. In her interviews with abused or neglected youths, Benjaminson (2008) points to the significance of schools as places of emotional support.

The Consulting Role of School Psychologists

In the same manner that teachers build educational relationships with their students, psychologists build therapeutic alliances with their clients (Grossman & McDonald, 2008). However, school psychologists also have consulting roles in schools, in relation to teachers who teach students with experiences of school failure. Consultation has been identified as an efficient approach to school psychology (Guiney, Harris, Zusho, & Cancelli, 2014), and its importance has been highlighted by the National Association of School Psychologists (NASP). In their work, teachers are caught within tensions between internal, relational, and external demands that can lead to moral stress (Colnerud, 2015). For school psychologists, the consultant role may bring challenges and resistance from teachers (Knoff, 2013), even if they have a different set of tools to help students (cf. Thuen & Bru, 2000).

Summary

Teachers draw upon their relational professionality to build educational relationships with their students, relationships that are particularly important for students experiencing difficulties. This case study explores the relational practices of a teacher who negotiates educational relationships with students who have a history of school failure. For school psychologists in consulting roles, a deepened insight into the teachers' everyday practice building relationships with students who struggle, and the arguments that they draw upon, may help them overcome resistance from teachers.

Method

Case studies have a naturalistic approach and are sensitive to the complexities and interactions in a particular context (Stake, 1995). They often focus in-depth on relationships and processes and how to disentangle the complexity of a given situation (Denscombe, 1998). The case study presented in this article is derived from a qualitative study (Frelin, 2010) of the relational professionality of teachers.

Procedure

Eleven teachers in different school contexts were identified by experienced teacher educators as having positive relationships with their students. They were each interviewed twice, usually in small meeting rooms in their schools. Interviews were relatively unstructured, but guided by four themes that were deliberately open-ended. Charmaz (2006) argues that a few broad, open-ended, and nonjudgmental questions can encourage narratives to emerge. The themes were to be regarded as starting points for capturing the various features and stories of everyday practices: 1) the informants' backgrounds, education, families, and important influences as a person; 2) their career histories; 3) important professional influences; and 4) practices fostering democratic citizens. The reason for the last theme is that it is an overarching purpose of education in Sweden that is not specifically connected to one subject.

Through a multitude of follow-up questions the interviews allowed for issues that the informants viewed as important and pressing in their work at the time of the interviews. A common follow-up would be: 'Give me an everyday example of this in your teaching'. After the example I would ask: 'Why do you think this is important?', or 'Why do you do this?'. The interviews lasted approximately one hour. One contextual observation was conducted during a lesson that took place after the first interview. The observations were unstructured and aimed at facilitating conversations of description rather than justification during interviews (Eraut, 2007). The second interview followed up the issues raised during the first interview and the observation. The informants were repeatedly asked to describe their practices and reasons for the various actions taken in their everyday situations.

Analysis

The notion of *story* is central within research on teaching. Narrative forms of representation have often been used to report on teachers' knowledge and practice (Rosiek & Atkinson, 2007) The interviews focused on eliciting *stories of practice* (Goodson & Sikes, 2001) and *practical arguments* (Fenstermacher & Richardson, 1993), whereas the observation served to highlight the context in which the teacher worked and to elicit new questions (Kvale, 1997). In the main study (Frelin, 2010), three aspects or themes of relational practices intended to achieve trusting teacher-student relationships were identified by means of cross-case analysis and constant comparisons (Charmaz, 2006). The software AtlasTi aided the analysis. The themes were constructed from qualitative analyses of informants' stories of actions aimed at achieving positive teacher-student relationships. They involved negotiating: 1) trusting relationships; 2) humane relationships; and 3) the students' own self images (the informants' combined use of self-confidence and self-esteem).

In this article, the case study of one informant, here named Gunilla, was selected for presentation using purposeful selection (Stake, 1995) having been identified by teacher educators as both being able to form positive relationships with students as well as having extensive experience of teaching students with previous school failures. The interviews also provided rich descriptions of relational practices with such students. The study is ideographic and the purpose is not to make generalizations but rather to illustrate a case where the reader can judge its use. The study is valuable to the extent that others may gain further insights into the issue at hand. In this article, the illustrations provided in the results are intended to facilitate professional judgement-based analogies rather than evidence-based method applications (cf. Biesta, 2007).

The Case Context

Gunilla, an upper secondary teacher of Swedish and social studies, is in her early 40s and has about ten years of teaching experience. Together with her colleague, here named Lasse, she manages a small municipal school. The school runs an 'Introduction Programme', which is a one-year upper secondary school programme offering individual solutions for students who after nine years of compulsory schooling, at the age of 16, are not eligible for national upper secondary school programmes, the higher education preparatory programme, or vocational preparatory programmes.[1] The reasons for this vary. For example, the students may have special needs, difficult social circumstances, or have recently migrated to the country and as a result have not obtained the necessary pass grades. Regardless of their individual circumstances they all risk some kind of stigmatization, which requires the teachers to have a flexible yet professional approach (cf. Nilholm & Alm, 2010).

Gunilla's school consists of one group of up to 20 students and is located in a house in a residential area. The curriculum is aimed at obtaining pass grades with a special focus on the core subjects of Swedish, English, and mathematics. The students do regular school work for three days and spend the remaining two days at a work-place selected by the student with the aid of a guidance counsellor. Typically, the students attend the programme for one year. If they obtain pass grades they are then eligible to apply for one of the national upper secondary programmes. The upper secondary school is not part of the compulsory school system, which means that students can either choose to participate or drop out of school. This affects the teacher-student relationship, in that the student's participation becomes negotiable.

Results

In her work, Gunilla is in daily contact with students with a history of school failure, or being failed by school, and regards it as her task to turn their negative experiences into more positive ones. Teacher professionality includes negotiating positive teacher-student relationships that help students to learn (Frelin, 2013). Such negotiations can be very subtle, but in Gunilla's work they often take up substantial time and energy, especially so at the beginning. Gunilla's story illustrates the different negotiations that are involved and provides a basis for reflections and analogies that aid judgement in other situations and professions. The first part involves the establishing phase of the relationship, where the negotiations start, and the following parts each represent one of the three themes identified in the main study: negotiating 1) trusting relationships; 2) humane relationships; and 3) the students' own self images.

Establishing Educational Relationships

When students arrive in the autumn term all Gunilla and Lasse know about them is which school subjects they have not yet passed. This enables them to say to the students:

> Welcome! From now on we'll be looking to the future, we don't look back. This is your second chance, take it if you wish. If you want to go forward, and if you want help, we'll do our very best to provide all the help we can.

Such statements communicate the importance of giving the students another chance and discarding the label of truant, argumentative, or silent.

The students first meet a guidance counsellor to talk about career choices and then have in-depth interviews with the teachers. Gunilla asks whether they are motivated. Surprisingly many are honest and answer no to that question. Their motivation is often tied to an extrinsic goal, such as getting pass grades and being accepted into a particular national programme, although in some cases the goal is limited to turning up at school each day. Based on what emerges during the inter- view all the students are helped to set short- and long-term goals. In order to find out whether there are any latent conflicts, Gunilla asks whether they have problems with any other student. Finally she asks whether there is anything else the teachers need to know. The responses to all these questions remain confidential.

In this way the teachers learn about sensitive issues. This kind of knowledge is important in order to approach the student in a positive and caring way:

> If parents are in the process of divorce or quarrel a lot at home you can see whether a student has not slept well or if something happened. You can simply ask: 'Was it tough at home last night?' 'Yes' they say. Okay, then we can be a bit more careful with that student on that day.

The physical school environment facilitates relation building practices. At Gunilla's school this consists of one classroom, one smaller breakout room, an office for the teachers, and a kitchen where the students and teachers have their coffee breaks. The door to the teachers' office is always open and the teachers make a point of always being available for the students as a way of building trusting relationships. The practices of negotiating aspects of educational relationships are illustrated in the following sections.

Negotiating Trusting Relationships

Trust is an important feature of teacher-student relationships (Brookfield, 1991; Jones, 1996). This section illustrates relational practices of building trust, which is one aspect of relational professionality. Gunilla's view is that caring teacher-student relationships are important for students and make them want to come to school. She says that her trust in a student makes a difference too. If students feel trusted by the teachers they are more likely to feel that they have let them down if they miss school and are more likely to come to school if they are trusted. The only thing that the teachers ask of the students is to let them know if they are ill. If they are absent without reason the teachers contact them to find out what is wrong. This sometimes results in the student coming to school.

Gunilla often encounters students who have little trust in adults, especially teachers. Her first task is to try to change this, and she argues that the size and home-like atmosphere of the school helps to facilitate the building of trusting teacher-student relationships, where teachers and students are physically close and meet informally over tea or coffee. Gunilla argues that meeting over coffee during the break makes the transition to the classroom less traumatic. The students and the teachers can thus meet outside the classroom and display other sides of their personalities.

According to Gunilla, having easy access to teachers and the creation of a relaxed atmosphere among students is both deliberate and extremely important. The teachers make use of the days when students are involved in workplace training to plan their lessons and catch up with administrative and other tasks, so that when the students are at school they are constantly on hand.

Sometimes the teachers need to be very straightforward about how they get a message communicated to the students. However, Gunilla says that such straight-forwardness has to wait until the teacher-student relationship is firmly established and they know each other well. At the beginning of the autumn term Gunilla spends a lot of time reading books with the students and encouraging class discussions, which may run relatively free. The purpose of these discussions is to establish a warm and accepting atmosphere that facilitates direct instruction. Gunilla explains that:

> For some students it may take until January to get going, because these are students who, the only thing they're really good at . . . the only thing they know that they *can* do is fail. They are terribly good at that. And they're so disappointed in the adult world and in school. So it's about showing them that adults are actually also human, and especially so teachers.

One of the purposes is to negotiate and re-establish the students' faith in the adult world. According to Gunilla, one of the signs that students know that she cares about them is that they try very hard to do what she asks and that they view her as fair. She makes a habit of explaining her actions and giving arguments for the school rules at the beginning, so that students can make sense of their environment.

Negotiating Humane Relationships

Caring educational relationships have been highlighted by several scholars in education (Noddings, 1988; O'Connor, 2008) as being particularly important for students in difficulty (Davidson, 1999; Pianta, 2006). In this context, Gunilla is conscious of trying to really listen to her students and remember what they say. Some examples are:

> Good morning. Hi Adam. New cap today? Wow, you must have slept a long time, you look very alert. Good job today, bye, have a nice [day]. All those things are important. And remembering to ask whether the cat is okay and whether their sister had a good time.

This practice is a way of recognizing her students as people and not as the (failed) students they are used to identifying themselves with. It also shows them that someone is listening to them and regards what they say as important. Gunilla experiences that students will see through feigned interest and view it as a betrayal of the relationship if she is not authentic. Negotiating humane relationships means accepting fallibility, in that failing is human. Gunilla says that it also means showing our own humanity and imperfections. Moreover, she has to be prepared to negotiate the demands in situations in order to help a student learn. Stretching the rules a little, such as giving a student permission to sit in the breakout room, can mean a lot in the long run, because it makes her appear human and displays her concern for the student. Gunilla says that she jokes a lot and laughs at herself, which in turn helps the students to lighten up. For her, lifting one's spirits with humour is an important piece of the puzzle in her students' conditions for learning. However, humour can also hurt and she makes a clear distinction between laughing with and laughing at someone.

Negotiating the Student's Self-Image

Meta-analyses, such as Hattie's (2009), emphasize the role of the student's self-confidence for learning. This final section illustrates relational practices in which Gunilla attends to her students' self-image. According to Gunilla the students attending her school have very little self-confidence and self-esteem (here combined in the concept of self-image, see the methods section), which is why she finds it important to do what she can to improve these negative images. Gunilla says that as the students' self-images have been damaged in the past by teachers at school she tries to use her practices in school to repair this damage.

One of the ways in which Gunilla does this is to create a totally different setting and atmosphere, both in terms of the physical environment and her approach. For example, as she wants students to read literature, and students are expected to read novels every day in school, she starts the year by saying: 'You will read a lot here, but you will never be asked to write a book report'. This is because students tend to connect reading to the practice of having to write about it. Instead, they talk informally about the books they have read. She also tries to make the students' learning joyful and immediate, so that the knowledge learned can be put to practical use, also outside school. Another prerequisite is that her students feel that the school is a safe and fair place. Gunilla views these two aspects as essential, because without them:

> To put it bluntly, they wouldn't come here, they wouldn't give a damn. Yes. I don't think they'd actually say that, because they are so used to not being listened to. It doesn't matter, they've been to student welfare conference after student welfare conference after student welfare conference throughout compulsory school. And everyone is against them.

As Gunilla's and Lasse's school has a long history of turnaround students, they have been able to defend their ideas and economic resources in the municipality, which according to Gunilla has been important for the running of the school, especially as their students have been more successful in attaining pass grades compared with similar schools in the municipality. She argues that their time cannot just be spent in the classroom, and that they also need to spend time with their students outside the classroom. This is why time in the in-between spaces is essential for her, so that she is accessible to the students and can give them quality time when necessary:

> That you always have the time to spend with a student, and can sit down and talk if you see that something is wrong. You can always have a proper conversation with a student. Always. It is fantastic, but you can't do that at compulsory school when you have a group of 30 and need to rush off to the next lesson.

It is important for Gunilla to develop closeness in the teacher-student relationship. This also helps her to see why students do not want to work and enables her to resolve the situation and thereby improve the educational experience of the student.

Summary

The results have provided illustrations of relational practices aimed at negotiating educational relationships with students who have been labelled as failures. Providing detailed examples of how Gunilla worked to negotiate relationships and the qualities of trust, humaneness and students' self-images, the complex and temporal nature of teachers' work with making relationships educational is highlighted.

Discussion

The results illustrate a teacher's everyday relational practices and intentions to build and maintain educational relationships with students. It is important to keep in mind that although Gunilla has a reputation and record as being successful in her practice, the results do not aim to provide evidence of, 'what works', but rather to inform professionals' judgement in unique situations and deepen our understanding of complex educational practices (cf. Biesta, 2007).

Positive relationships are particularly important for students with a negative experience of school (Baker et al., 2008; Hamre & Pianta, 2001; Johnson, 2008; Pianta, 2006; Pomeroy, 1999; Rudasill et al., 2010). These are briefly discussed from a relational perspective, after which implications for school psychologists are suggested.

Connecting to Students With Experiences of School Failure

Relationships at school are not educational by default. Sometimes, teacher-student relationships may be the opposite, such as when a student views a teacher as inhumane and unfair and refuses to be taught by him or her. In order to connect to their learning, students may need a relational context, or educational community (Frelin, 2013; Solomon et al., 1996), as an important feature of the wider school climate (e.g. Raufelder et al., 2013).

Negative experiences of school also contribute to the creation of a negative student self-image that impedes further learning. Raider-Roth (2005) highlights the connection between students' self-confidence in their work and trust in someone they respect. What Gunilla views as repair work on students' self-images is also a delicate balancing act that requires relational professionality, especially as students tend to guard themselves against vulnerability (Raider-Roth, 2005).

In her dealings with students who have learned to mistrust adults, Gunilla employs a number of strategies in order to negotiate trust, especially at the beginning of the school year, such as appearing humane by displaying care for the student. The establishing phase of an educational relationship may require practices that are different from those in the maintaining phase. For Gunilla, gaining her students' trust is a prerequisite for being able to teach, which highlights the relational underpinnings of education.

Trusting relationships with adults are important in other senses too, e.g. for students' well-being and health (Backman et al., 2011). Raider Roth (2005) argues that students share and suppress knowledge based on their understanding of school relationships and take the consequences of their own vulnerability into account. That is, confiding sensitive information to an adult requires trust in this person and in what the act might result in (Bliding et al., 2002).

Implications for School Psychologists

The establishment of a professional relationship between psychologist and client or teacher and student is critical for its success. In the teaching context, the professional object of a teacher is student learning. Here, Gunilla's story helps to illustrate the relationship building practices that make it possible for education to happen (cf. Frelin, 2013). What she does can be compared with psychologists' practices of building a therapeutic alliance (cf. Grossman & McDonald, 2008), i.e. a relationship that helps to achieve the professional object of mental health. With students who have experienced failure at school and who tend to distrust adults this practice is particularly demanding and may require a high level of relational professionality (see Frelin, 2013). Given their expertise and experience of negotiating therapeutic alliances, school psychologists have much to offer when it comes to the creation of alliances and relationships. They can also provide tools for the creation of a supporting environment (cf. Thuen & Bru, 2000). However, being mindful of the teacher's work situation and sometimes conflicting demands can help them in their consulting role (cf. Knoff, 2013).

As teachers like Gunilla, by means of an educational relationship, are in some instances the only adult with whom a student has a trusting relationship, they may receive information from students that requires some kind of intervention from other professions, such as school psychologists. The trusting teacher-student relationship may then constitute a bridge that enables the student to be helped. Moreover, teachers may need to consult trained professionals, such as psychologists, for such conversations with students.

A teacher's work thus involves coping with the tensions between internal, relational, and external demands. In other words, they need to work towards improving students' self-images and at the same time work within an institutional frame that may result in the opposite. Living in and with this tension can lead to moral stress (Colnerud, 2015). Teachers may therefore need to turn to school psychologists, who are more able to provide tools for coping with such stress.

This article has illustrated the relational practices of one teacher with experience of helping students who have failed at school. It has also suggested points of connection between teachers and school psychologists that could contribute to an improved and more inclusive education for all students, and in particular for those students who have experienced school failure.

Note

1. Please see http://www.skolverket.se/om-skolverket/andra-sprak-och-lattlast/in-english/the-swedish-education-system [Available 2015-06-11] for a more comprehensive description of the Swedish school system.

References

Backman, Y., Alerby, E., Bergmark, U., Gardelli, Å ., Hertting, K., Kostenius, C., . . . Ö hrling, K. (2011). Learning within and beyond the classroom: Compulsory school stu- dents voicing their positive experiences of school. *Scandinavian Journal of Educational Research*, 1–16. doi: 10.1080/00313831.2011.621138.

Baker, J. A., Grant, S., & Morlock, L. (2008). The teacher-student relationship as a devel- opmental context for children with internalizing or externalizing behavior problems. *School Psychology Quarterly, 23*(1), 3–15. doi: 10.1037/1045-3830.23.1.3.

Benjaminson, C. (2008). *Ungdomars erfarenheter av emotionell utsatthet under uppväxten [Young people's experiences of emotional exposure during their childhood and adolescence].* Diss. Stockholm: Stockholms universitet. Retrieved from http://urn.kb.se/resolve?urn¼ urn:nbn:se:su:diva-7313

Biesta, G. (2007). Why 'What works' won't work: Evidence-based practice and the democratic deficit in educational research. *Educational Theory, 57*(1), 1–22. doi: 10.1111/ j.1741-5446.2006.00241.x.

Bliding, M., Holm, A.-S., & Hägglund, S. (2002). Krä nkande handlingar och informella miljö er. *Elevperspektiv på skolans miljö er och sociala klimat [Offending actions and informal environments. A student perspective on the environments and social climate of school].* Stockholm: Statens skolverk.

Bridges, D. (2001). Professionalism, authenticity and action research. *Educational Action Research, 9*(3), 451–464. doi:10.1080/09650790100200160.

Brookfield, S. (1991). *The skillful teacher: On technique, trust, and responsiveness in the classroom* (1st ed.) San Francisco, CA: Jossey-Bass.

Charmaz, K. (2006). *Constructing grounded theory. A practical guide through qualitative analysis.* London: Sage.

Colnerud, G. (2015). Moral stress in teaching practice. *Teachers and Teaching, 21*(3), 346–360. doi: 10.1080/13540602.2014.953820.

Cornelius-White, J. (2007). Learner-centered teacher-student relationships are effective: A meta-analysis. *Review of Educational Research, 77*(1), 113–143. doi: 10.3102/ 003465430298563.

Darling-Hammond, L. (2014). One piece of the whole: Teacher evaluation as part of a comprehensive system for teaching and learning. *American Educator, 38*(1), 4–13.

Davidson, A. L. (1999). Negotiating social differences: Youths' assessments of educators' strategies. *Urban Education, 34*(3), 338–369. doi: 10.1177/0042085999343004.

den Brok, P., Brekelmans, M., & Wubbels, T. (2004). Interpersonal teacher behaviour and student outcomes. *School Effectiveness and School Improvement, 15*(3–4), 407–442. doi: 10.1080/09243450512331383262.

Denscombe, M. (1998). *The good research guide: For small-scale social research projects.* Buckingham, Philadelphia, PA: Open University Press.

Eraut, M. (2007). Learning from other people in the workplace. *Oxford Review of Education, 33*(4), 403–422. doi: 10.1080/03054980701425706.

Erickson, F. (1987). Transformation and school success: The politics and culture of educational achievement. *Anthropology and Education Quarterly, 18*(4), 335–356.

Evans, L. (2008). Professionalism, professionality and the development of education professionals. *British Journal of Educational Studies, 56*(1), 20–38. doi: 10.1111/j.1467-8527.2007.00392.x.

Fenstermacher, G. D., & Richardson, V. (1993). The elicitation and reconstruction of prac-tical arguments in teaching. *Journal of Curriculum Studies, 25*(2), 101–114. doi: 10.1080/0022027930250201.

Freidson, E. (1994). *Professionalism reborn: Theory, prophecy and policy.* Oxford, Chicago, IL: Polity Press; University of Chicago Press.

Frelin, A. (2008). Professionell nä rhet och distans – en dimension av lä rares arbete ur ett genusperspektiv [Professional closeness and distance. A dimension of teachers' work from a gender perspective]. In C. Aili, U. Blossing, & U. Tornberg (Eds.), *Lä raren i blickpunkten. Olika perspektiv på lä rares liv och arbete [Focal point teacher. Theoretical perspectives on teacher education]* (pp. 177–188). Stockholm: Lä rarfö rbundets fö rlag.

Frelin, A. (2010). *Teachers' relational practices and professionality.* Uppsala: Department of Curriculum Studies, Uppsala University.

Frelin, A. (2013). *Exploring teachers' relational professionalism in schools.* Rotterdam: Sense Publishers.

Frelin, A., & Grannä s, J. (2010). Negotiations left behind: In-between spaces of teacher-student negotiation and their significance for education. *Journal of Curriculum Studies, 42*(3), 353–369. doi: 10.1080/00220272.2010.485650.

Frelin, A., & Grannä s, J. (2014). Studying relational spaces in secondary school: Applying a spatial framework for the study of borderlands and relational work in school improvement processes. *Improving Schools, 17*(2), 135–147. doi: 10.1177/1365480214534540.

Goodson, I. F., & Sikes, P. J. (2001). *Life history research in educational settings: Learning from lives.* Buckingham: Open University Press.

Grossman, P., & McDonald, M. (2008). Back to the future: Directions for research in teaching and teacher education. *American Educational Research Journal, 45*(1), 184–205. doi: 10.3102/0002831207312906.

Guiney, M. C., Harris, A., Zusho, A., & Cancelli, A. (2014). School psychologists' sense of self-efficacy for consultation. *Journal of Educational and Psychological Consultation, 24*(1), 28–54. doi: 10.1080/10474412.2014.870486.

Hamre, B. K., & Pianta, R. C. (2001). Early teacher-child relationships and the trajectory of children's school outcomes through eighth grade. *Child Development, 72*(2), 625. doi: 10.1111/1467-8624.00301.

Hansen, D. T. (1998). The moral is in the practice. *Teaching and Teacher Education, 14*(6), 643–655. doi: 10.1016/S0742-051X(98)00014-6.

Hattie, J. (2009). *Visible learning: A synthesis of over 800 meta-analyses relating to achievement.* London: Routledge.

Hoyle, E. (1995). Teachers as professionals. In L. W. Anderson (Ed.), *International encyclopedia of teaching and teacher education* (2nd ed,. pp. 11–15). Oxford: Pergamon.

Jennings, P. A., & Greenberg, M. T. (2009). The prosocial classroom: Teacher social and emotional competence in relation to student and classroom outcomes. *Review of Educational Research, 79*(1), 491–525. doi: 10.3102/0034654308325693.

Johnson, B. (2008). Teacher-student relationships which promote resilience at school: A micro-level analysis of students' views. *British Journal of Guidance and Counselling, 36*(4), 385–398. doi: 10.1080/03069880802364528.

Jones, K. (1996). Trust as an affective attitude. *Ethics, 107*(1), 4–25.

Knoff, H. M. (2013). Changing resistant consultees: Functional assessment leading to strategic intervention. *Journal of Educational and Psychological Consultation, 23*(4), 307–317. doi: 10.1080/10474412.2013.845496.

Kvale, S. (1997). *Den kvalitativa forskningsintervjun* [*InterViews*]. Lund: Studentlitteratur. Nilholm, C., & Alm, B. (2010). An inclusive classroom? A case study of inclusiveness, teacher strategies, and children's experiences. *European Journal of Special Needs Education, 25*(3), 239–252. doi: 10.1080/08856257.2010.492933.

Noddings, N. (1988). An ethic of caring and its implications for instructional arrangements. *American Journal of Education, 96*(2), 215–230.

O'Connor, K. E. (2008). 'You choose to care': Teachers, emotions and professional identity. *Teaching and Teacher Education, 24*(1), 117–126. doi: http://dx.doi.org/10.1016/ j.tate.2006.11.008.

Pianta, R. C. (2006). Classroom management and relationships between children and teachers: Implications for research and practice. In C. M. Evertson, & C. S. Weinstein (Eds.), *Handbook of classroom management: Research, practice, and contemporary issues* (pp. 685–710). Mahwah, NJ: Lawrence Erlbaum Associates.

Pomeroy, E. (1999). The teacher-student relationship in secondary school: Insights from excluded students. *British Journal of Sociology of Education, 20*(4), 465–482. doi: 10.1080/01425699995218.

Raider-Roth, M. B. (2005). Trusting what you know: Negotiating the relational context of classroom life. *Teachers College Record, 107*(4), 587–628. doi: 10.1111/j.1467- 9620.2005.00488.

Raufelder, D., Sahabandu, D., Martı´nez, G. S., & Escobar, V. (2013). The mediating role of social relationships in the association of adolescents' individual school self-concept and their school engagement, belonging and helplessness in school. *Educational Psychology, 35*(2), 1–21. doi: 10.1080/01443410.2013.849327.

Roorda, D. L., Koomen, Helma, M. Y., Spilt, Jantine, L., Oort, Frans, J. (2011). The influence of affective teacher–student relationships on students' school engagement and achievement: A meta-analytic approach. *Review of Educational Research, 81*(4), 493–529. doi: 10.3102/0034654311421793.

Rosiek, J., & Atkinson, B. (2007). The inevitability and importance of genres in narrative research on teaching practice. *Qualitative Inquiry, 13*(4), 499–521. doi: 10.1177/1077800406297669.

Rudasill, K. M., Reio, T. G. Jr, Stipanovic, N., & Taylor, J. E. (2010). A longitudinal study of student–teacher relationship quality, difficult temperament, and risky behavior from childhood to early adolescence. *Journal of School Psychology, 48*(5), 389–412. doi: http:// dx.doi.org/10.1016/j.jsp.2010.05.001.

Solomon, D., Watson, M., Battistich, V., Schaps, E., & Delucchi, K. (1996). Creating classrooms that students experience as communities. *American Journal of Community Psychology, 24*(6), 719–748. doi: 10.1007/BF02511032.

Stake, R. E. (1995). *The art of case study research.* Thousand Oaks, CA: Sage.

Studsrød, I., & Bru, E. (2012). Upper secondary school students' perceptions of teacher socialization practices and reports of school adjustment. *School Psychology International, 33*(3), 308–324. doi: 10.1177/0143034311412841.

Thuen, E., & Bru, E. (2000). Learning environment, meaningfulness of schoolwork and on-task orientation among norwegian 9th grade students. *School Psychology International, 21*(4), 393–413. doi: 10.1177/0143034300214004.

van Tartwijk, J., den Brok, P., Veldman, I., & Wubbels, T. (2009). Teachers' practical knowledge about classroom management in multicultural classrooms. *Teaching and Teacher Education, 25*(3), 453–460. doi: 10.1016/j.tate.2008.09.005.

Watson, M., & Battistich, V. (2006). Building and sustaining caring communities. In C. M. Evertson, & C. S. Weinstein (Eds.), *Handbook of classroom management: Research, practice, and contemporary issues* (pp. 253–279). Mahwah, NJ: Lawrence Erlbaum Associates.

Wentzel, K. R., Battle, A., Russell, S. L., & Looney, L. B. (2010). Social supports from teachers and peers as predictors of academic and social motivation. *Contemporary Educational Psychology, 35*(3), 193–202. doi: 10.1016/j.cedpsych.2010.03.002.

Woolfolk Hoy, A., & Weinstein, C. S. (2006). Student and teacher perspectives on classroom management. In C. M. Evertson, & C. S. Weinstein (Eds.), *Handbook of classroom management: Research, practice, and contemporary issues* (pp. 181–219). Mahwah, NJ: Lawrence Erlbaum Associates.

Wu, J.-Y., Hughes, J. N., & Kwok, O.-M. (2010). Teacher-student relationship quality type in elementary grades: Effects on trajectories for achievement and engagement. *Journal of School Psychology, 48*(5), 357–387. doi: http://dx.doi.org/10.1016/j.jsp.2010.06.004.

Wubbels, T., Brekelmans, M., den Brok, P., Wijsman, L., Mainhard, T., van Tartwijk, J. (2015). Teacher-student relationships and classroom management. In E. Emmer, & E. Sabornie (Eds.), *Handbook of classroom management* (2nd ed.), Abingdon: Routledge.

Zimmer-Gembeck, M. J., & Locke, E. M. (2007). The socialization of adolescent coping behaviours: Relationships with families and teachers. *Journal of Adolescence, 30*(1), 1–16. doi: http:// dx.doi.org/10.1016/j.adolescence.2005.03.001.

Author Biography

Anneli Frelin is an Associate Professor of Curriculum Studies at the University of Gävle, Sweden. Her research focuses on relational work in educational environments (including school climate) with a special interest in how educative teacher-student relationships are negotiated. Dr. Frelin has participated in three research projects financed by the National Research Council and AFA Insurance, in one of them serving as principal investigator. The *Spaces In-between* project investigated a secondary school in which different categories of school staff colla- borated to create a safe environment for students. Frelin's latest book is *Exploring relational professionalism in schools* (Sense Publishers).

• References •

Aanstoos, C. M. (1985). The structure of thinking in chess. In A. Giorgi (Ed.), *Phenomenology and psychological research* (pp. 86–117). Pittsburgh, PA: Duquesne University Press.

Adams, J., Braun, V., & McCreanor, T. (2014). "Aren't labels for pickle jars, not people?" Negotiating identify and community in talk about "being gay." *American Journal of Men's Health, 8*(6), 457–469. doi: 0.1177/1557988313518800.

Adolph, S., Kruchten, P., & Hall, W. (2012). Reconciling perspectives: A grounded theory of how people manage the process of software development. *Journal of Systems and Software, 86*, 1269–1286. doi:10.1016/j.jss.2012.01.059

Agar, M. H. (1980). *The professional stranger: An informal introduction to ethnography.* San Diego, CA: Academic Press.

Agar, M. H. (1986). *Speaking of ethnography.* Beverly Hills, CA: Sage.

Agger, B. (1991). Critical theory, poststructuralism, postmodernism: Their sociological relevance. In W. R. Scott & J. Blake (Eds.), *Annual review of sociology* (Vol. 17, pp. 105–131). Palo Alto, CA: Annual Reviews.

American Psychological Association. (2010). *Publication manual of the American Psychological Association* (6th ed.). Washington, DC: Author.

Anderson, E. H., & Spencer, M. H. (2002). Cognitive representations of AIDS: A phenomenological study. *Qualitative Health Research, 12*, 1338–1352. doi:10.1177/1049732302238747

Anderson, R. A., Toles, M. P., Corazzini, K., McDaniel, R. R., & Colón-Emeric, C. (2014). Local interaction strategies and capacity for better care in nursing homes: a multiple case study. *BMC Health Services Research, 14*, 244–261 doi:10.1186/1472-6963-14-244

Angen, M. J. (2000). Evaluating interpretive inquiry: Reviewing the validity debate and opening the dialogue. *Qualitative Health Research, 10*, 378–395. doi:10.1177/104973230001000308

Angrosino, M. V. (1989). *Documents of interaction: Biography, autobiography, and life history in social science perspective.* Gainesville: University of Florida Press.

Angrosino, M. V. (1994). On the bus with Vonnie Lee. *Journal of Contemporary Ethnography, 23*, 14–28. doi: 10.1177/089124194023001002.

Angrosino, M. V. (2007). *Doing ethnographic and observational research.* Thousand Oaks, CA: Sage.

Armstrong, D., Gosling, A., Weinman, J., & Marteau, T. (1997). The place of inter-rater reliability in qualitative research: An empirical study. *Sociology, 31*, 597–606. doi:10.1177/0038038597031003015

Asgeirsdottir, G. H., Sigurbjörnsson, E., Traustaddottir, R., Sigurdartottir, V., Gunnardottir, S., & Kelly, E. (2013). "To cherish each day as it comes": A qualitative study of spirituality among persons receiving palliative care, *Support Cancer Care, 21*, 1445–1451. doi:10.1007/s00520-012-1690-6

Asmussen, K. J., & Creswell, J. W. (1995). Campus response to a student gunman. *Journal of Higher Education, 66*(5), 575–591. doi:10.2307/2943937

Atkinson, P., Coffey, A., & Delamont, S. (2003). *Key themes in qualitative research: Continuities and changes.* Walnut Creek, CA: AltaMira Press.

Atkinson, P., & Hammersley, M. (1994). Ethnography and participant observation. In N. K. Denzin & Y. S. Lincoln (Eds.), *Handbook of qualitative research* (pp. 248–261). Thousand Oaks, CA: Sage.

Atkinson, P. A. (2015). *For ethnography.* Thousand Oaks, CA: Sage.

Banks, M. (2014). Analysing images. In U. Flick (Ed.), *The SAGE handbook of qualitative data analysis* (pp. 394–408). Thousand Oaks, CA: Sage.

Barbour, R. S. (2000). The role of qualitative research in broadening the "evidence base" for clinical practice. *Journal of Evaluation in Clinical Practice*, 6(2), 155–163. doi:10.1046/j.1365-2753.2000.00213.x

Barnes, C., Oliver, M., & Barton, L. (Eds.). (2002). *Disabilities studies today*. Cambridge, England: Polity.

Barritt, L. S. (1986). Human sciences and the human image. *Phenomenology + Pedagogy*, 4(3), 14–22.

Bauer, W. M., & Gaskell, G. (Eds.). (2007). *Qualitative research with text, image and sound: A practical handbook*. Thousand Oaks, CA: Sage.

Baxter, P., & Jack, S. (2008). Qualitative case study methodology: Study design and implementation for novice researchers. *The Qualitative Report*, 13(2), 544–559.

Bazeley, P. (2002). The evolution of a project involving an integrated analysis of structured qualitative and quantitative data: From N3 to NVivo. *International Journal of Social Research Methodology*, 5, 229–243. doi:10.1080/13645570210146285

Bazeley, P. (2013). *Qualitative data analysis: Practical strategies*. Thousand Oaks, CA: Sage.

Bazeley, P., & Jackson, K. (2013). *Qualitative data analysis with NVivo* (2nd ed.) Thousand Oaks, CA: Sage.

Berger, R. (2015). Now I see it, now I don't: Researcher's position and reflexivity in qualitative research. *Qualitative Research*, 15(2), 219–234. doi:10.1177/1468794112468475.

Bernard, H. R. (2011). *Research methods in anthropology: Qualitative and quantitative approaches* (5th ed.). Walnut Creek, CA: AltaMira Press.

Bernard, H. R., & Ryan, G. W. (2009). *Analyzing qualitative data: Systemic approaches*. Thousand Oaks, CA: Sage.

Beverly, J. (2005). *Testimonio*, subalternity, and narrative authority. In N. K. Denzin & Y. S. Lincoln (Eds.), *The SAGE handbook of qualitative research* (3rd ed., pp. 547–558). Thousand Oaks, CA: Sage.

Birks, M., & Mills, J. (2015). *Grounded theory: A practical guide* (2nd ed.). Thousand Oaks, CA: Sage.

Bloland, H. G. (1995). Postmodernism and higher education. *Journal of Higher Education*, 66, 521–559. doi:10.2307/2943935

Bogdan, R. C., & Biklen, S. K. (1992). *Qualitative research for education: An introduction to theory and methods*. Boston, MA: Allyn & Bacon.

Bogdan, R., & Biklen, S. K. (2006). *Qualitative research for education: an introduction to theories and methods* (5th ed.). Boston, MA: Pearson.

Bogdan, R., & Taylor, S. (1975). *Introduction to qualitative research methods*. New York, NY: John Wiley.

Bogdewic, S. P. (1992). Participant observation. In B. F. Crabtree & W. L. Miller (Eds.), *Doing qualitative research* (pp. 45–69). Newbury Park, CA: Sage.

Bogdewic, S. P. (1999). Participant observation. In B. F. Crabtree & W. Miller (Eds.),

Doing qualitative research (2nd ed., pp. 47–70). Thousand Oaks, CA: Sage

Borgatta, E. F., & Borgatta, M. L. (Eds.). (1992). *Encyclopedia of sociology* (Vol. 4). New York, NY: Macmillan.

Braun, V., & Clarke, V. (2006). Using thematic analysis in psychology. *Qualitative Research in Psychology*, 3(2), 77–101.

Brickhouse, N., & Bodner, G. M. (1992). The beginning science teacher: Classroom narratives of convictions and constraints. *Journal of Research in Science Teaching*, 29, 471–485. doi:10.1002/tea.3660290504

Brimhall, A. C., & Engblom-Deglmann, M. L. (2011). Starting over: A tentative theory exploring the effects of past relationships on postbereavement remarried couples. *Family Process*, 50(1), 47–62. doi:10.1111/j.1545-5300.2010.01345.x

Brinkmann, S., & Kvale, S. (2015). *InterViews: Learning the craft of qualitative research interviewing* (3rd ed.). Thousand Oaks, CA: Sage.

Brisolara, S., Seigart, D., & SenGupta, S. (2014). *Feminist evaluation and research: Theory and practice*. New York, NY: Guilford Press.

Brown, J., Sorrell, J. H., McClaren, J., & Creswell, J. W. (2006). Waiting for a liver transplant. *Qualitative Health Research*, 16(1), 119–136. doi:10.1177/1049732305284011

Bryant, A., & Charmaz, K. (2007). Grounded theory in historical perspective: An epistemological account. In A. Bryant & K. Charmaz (Eds.), *The SAGE* handbook of grounded theory (pp. 31–57). Thousand Oaks, CA: Sage.

Burr, V. (2015). *Social constructionism* (3rd ed.). New York, NY: Routledge.

Campbell, J. L., Quincy, C., Osserman, J., & Pederson, O. K. (2013). Coding in-depth semistructured interviews: Problems of unitization and intercoder reliability and agreement. *Sociological Methods & Research, 42*, 294–320. doi:10.1177/0049124113500475

Carspecken, P. F., & Apple, M. (1992). Critical qualitative research: Theory, methodology, and practice. In M. L. LeCompte, W. L. Millroy, & J. Preissle (Eds.), *The handbook of qualitative research in education* (pp. 507–553). San Diego, CA: Academic Press.

Carter, K. (1993). The place of a story in the study of teaching and teacher education. *Educational Researcher, 22*, 5–12, 18. Retrieved from http://www.jstor .org/stable/1177300

Casey, K. (1995/1996). The new narrative research in education. *Review of Research in Education, 21*, 211–253. Retrieved from http://www.jstor.org/ stable/1167282

Chan, E. (2010). Living in the space between participant and researcher as a narrative inquirer: Examining ethnic identity of Chinese Canadian students as conflicting stories to live by. *The Journal of Educational Research, 103*, 113–122. doi:10.1080/00220670903323792

Charmaz, K. (2003). Grounded theory. In M. S. Lewisbeck, A. E. Bryman, & T. F. Liao (Eds.), *The SAGE encyclopedia of social science research methods*. Thousand Oaks, CA: Sage.

Charmaz, K. (2005). Grounded theory in the 21st century: Applications for advancing social justice studies. In N. K. Denzin & Y. S. Lincoln (Eds.), *The SAGE handbook of qualitative research* (3rd ed., pp. 507–536). Thousand Oaks, CA: Sage.

Charmaz, K. (2006). *Constructing grounded theory.* Thousand Oaks, CA: Sage.

Charmaz, K. (2014). *Constructing grounded theory* (2nd ed.). Thousand Oaks, CA: Sage.

Chase, S. (2005). Narrative inquiry: Multiple lenses, approaches, voices. In N. K. Denzin & Y. S. Lincoln (Eds.), *The SAGE handbook of qualitative research* (3rd ed., pp. 651–680). Thousand Oaks, CA: Sage.

Cheek, J. (2004). At the margins? Discourse analysis and qualitative research. *Qualitative Health Research, 14*, 1140–1150. doi:10.1177/1049732304266820.

Chepp, V. (2015). Black feminist theory and the politics of irreverence: The case of women's rap. *Feminist Theory, 16*(2), 207–226. doi:10.1177/1464700115585705

Chenitz, W. C., & Swanson, J. M. (1986). *From practice to grounded theory: Qualitative research in nursing.* Menlo Park, CA: Addison-Wesley.

Cherryholmes, C. H. (1992). Notes on pragmatism and scientific realism. *Educational Researcher, 14*, 13–17.

Chilisa, B. (2012). *Indigenous research methodologies.* Thousand Oaks, CA: Sage.

Chirgwin, S. K. (2015). Burdens too difficult to carry? A case study of three academically able Indigenous Australian Masters students who had to withdraw. *International Journal of Qualitative Studies in Education, 28*, 594–609. doi:10.1080/ 09518398.2014.916014

Churchill, S. L., Plano Clark, V. L., Prochaska-Cue, M. K., Creswell, J. W., & Onta-Grzebik, L. (2007). How rural low-income families have fun: A grounded theory study. *Journal of Leisure Research, 39*(2), 271–294.

Clandinin, D. J. (Ed.). (2007). *Handbook of narrative inquiry: Mapping a methodology.* Thousand Oaks, CA: Sage.

Clandinin, D. J. (2013). *Engaging in narrative inquiry.* Walnut Creek, CA: Left Coast Press.

Clandinin, D. J., & Caine, V. (2013). Narrative inquiry. In A. Trainor & E. Graue (Eds.), *Reviewing qualitative research in the social sciences* (pp. 188–202). New York, NY: Taylor and Francis/Routledge.

Clandinin, D. J., & Connelly, F. M. (2000). *Narrative inquiry: Experience and story in qualitative research.* San Francisco, CA: Jossey-Bass.

Clandinin, D. J., Huber, J., Huber, M., Murphy, M. S., Murray Orr, A., Pearce, M., & Steeves, P. (2006). *Composing diverse identities: Narrative inquiries into the interwoven lives of children and teachers.* New York, NY: Routledge.

Clarke, A. E. (2005). *Situational analysis: Grounded theory after the postmodern turn.* Thousand Oaks, CA: Sage.

Clarke, A. E., Friese, C., & Washburn, R. (Eds.). (2015). *Situational analysis practice: Mapping research with grounded theory*. London, England: Routledge.

Clifford, J., & Marcus, G. E. (Eds.). (1986). *Writing culture: The poetics and politics of ethnography*. Berkeley: University of California Press.

Colaizzi, P. F. (1978). Psychological research as the phenomenologist views it. In R. Vaile & M. King (Eds.), *Existential phenomenological alternatives for psychology* (pp. 48–71). New York, NY: Oxford University Press.

Connelly, F. M., & Clandinin, D. J. (1990). Stories of experience and narrative inquiry. *Educational Researcher, 19*(5), 2–14. doi:10.3102/0013189X019005002

Conrad, C. F. (1978). A grounded theory of academic change. *Sociology of Education, 51*, 101–112. doi:10.2307/2112242

Corbin, J., & Morse, J. M. (2003). The unstructured interactive interview: Issues of reciprocity and risks when dealing with sensitive topics. *Qualitative Inquiry, 9*, 335–354. doi:10.1177/1077800403009003001

Corbin, J., & Strauss, A. (1990). Grounded theory research: Procedures, canons, and evaluative criteria. *Qualitative Sociology, 13*(1), 3–21. doi:10.1007/BF00988593

Corbin, J., & Strauss, A. (2007). *Basics of qualitative research: Techniques and procedures for developing grounded theory* (3rd ed.). Thousand Oaks, CA: Sage.

Corbin, J., & Strauss, A. (2015). *Basics of qualitative research: Techniques and procedures for developing grounded theory* (4th ed.). Thousand Oaks, CA: Sage.

Cordes, M. (2014). *A transcendental phenomenological study of developmental math students' experiences and perceptions* (Unpublished doctoral dissertation). Liberty University, Lynchburg, Virginia.

Cortazzi, M. (1993). *Narrative analysis*. London, England: Falmer Press.

Crabtree, B. F., & Miller, W. L. (1992). *Doing qualitative research*. Newbury Park, CA: Sage.

Creswell, J. W. (1994). *Research design: Qualitative and quantitative approaches*. Thousand Oaks, CA: Sage.

Creswell, J. W. (2009). *Research design: Qualitative, quantitative, and mixed methods approaches* (3rd ed.). Thousand Oaks, CA: Sage.

Creswell, J. W. (2012). *Educational research: Planning, conducting, and evaluating quantitative and qualitative research* (4th ed.). Upper Saddle River, NJ: Pearson.

Creswell, J. W. (2013). *Qualitative inquiry & research design: Choosing among the five approaches* (3rd ed.). Thousand Oaks, CA: Sage.

Creswell, J. W. (2014). *Research design: Qualitative, quantitative, and mixed methods approaches* (4th ed.). Thousand Oaks, CA: Sage.

Creswell, J. W. (2016). *30 essential skills for the qualitative researcher*. Thousand Oaks, CA: Sage.

Creswell, J. W., & Brown, M. L. (1992). How chairpersons enhance faculty research: A grounded theory study. *Review of Higher Education, 16*(1), 41–62. Retrieved from https://www.press.jhu.edu/journals/review_of_higher_education

Creswell, J. W., & Maietta, R. C. (2002). Qualitative research. In D. C. Miller & N. J. Salkind (Eds.), *Handbook of Research Design and Social Measurement* (pp. 167–168). Thousand Oaks, CA: Sage.

Creswell, J. W., & Miller, D. L. (2000). Determining validity in qualitative inquiry. *Theory Into Practice, 39*, 124–130. doi:10.1207/s15430421tip3903_2

Creswell, J. W., & Plano Clark, V. L. (2011). *Designing and conducting mixed methods research* (2nd ed.). Thousand Oaks, CA: Sage.

Crotty, M. (1998). *The foundations of social research: Meaning and perspective in the research process*. Thousand Oaks, CA: Sage.

Czarniawska, B. (2004). *Narratives in social science research*. Thousand Oaks, CA: Sage.

Daiute, C. (2014). *Narrative inquiry: A dynamic approach*. Thousand Oaks, CA: Sage.

Daiute, C., & Lightfoot, C. (Eds.). (2004). *Narrative analysis: Studying the development of individuals in society*. Thousand Oaks, CA: Sage.

Davidson, F. (1996). *Principles of statistical data handling*. Thousand Oaks, CA: Sage.

Davidson, J., & di Gregorio, S. (2011). Qualitative research and technology: In the midst of a revolution. In N. K. Denzin & Y. S. Lincoln (Eds.), *The SAGE handbook of qualitative research* (4th ed., pp. 627–644). Thousand Oaks, CA: Sage.

Deem, R. (2002). Talking to manager-academics: Methodological dilemmas and feminist research strategies. *Sociology, 36*(4), 835–855. doi:10.1177/003803850203600403.

Delgado, R., & Stefancic, J. (2012). *Critical race theory: An introduction.* New York: New York University Press.

Denzin, N. K. (1989). *Interpretive biography.* Newbury Park, CA: Sage.

Denzin, N. K. (2001). *Interpretive interactionism* (2nd ed.). Thousand Oaks, CA: Sage.

Denzin, N. K., & Lincoln, Y. S. (1994). *The SAGE handbook of qualitative research.* Thousand Oaks, CA: Sage.

Denzin, N. K., & Lincoln, Y. S. (2000). *The SAGE handbook of qualitative research* (2nd ed.). Thousand Oaks, CA: Sage.

Denzin, N. K., & Lincoln, Y. S. (2005). *The SAGE handbook of qualitative research* (3rd ed.). Thousand Oaks, CA: Sage.

Denzin, N. K., & Lincoln, Y. S. (2011). Introduction: The discipline and practice of qualitative research. *The SAGE handbook of qualitative research* (4th ed., pp. 1–19). Thousand Oaks, CA: Sage.

Denzin, N. K., & Lincoln, Y. S. (2013). *Strategies of qualitative inquiry.* Thousand Oaks, CA: Sage.

Dewey, J. (1938). *Experience and education.* New York, NY: Simon & Schuster.

Dey, I. (1993). *Qualitative data analysis: A user-friendly guide for social scientists.* London, England: Routledge.

Dey, I. (1995). Reducing fragmentation in qualitative research. In U. Keele (Ed.), *Computer-aided qualitative data analysis* (pp. 69–79). Thousand Oaks, CA: Sage.

Doyle, J., Pooley, J. A., & Breen, L. (2012). A phenomenological exploration of the childfree choice in a sample of Australian women. *Journal of Health Psychology, 18,* 397–407. doi:10.1177/1359105312444647

Dukes, S. (1984). Phenomenological methodology in the human sciences. *Journal of Religion and Health, 23*(3), 197–203. doi:10.1007/BF00990785

Edel, L. (1984). *Writing lives: Principia biographica.* New York, NY: Norton.

Edwards, L. V. (2006). Perceived social support and HIV/AIDS medication adherence among African American women. *Qualitative Health Research, 16,* 679–691. doi:10.1177/1049732305281597

Eisner, E. W. (1991). *The enlightened eye: Qualitative inquiry and the enhancement of educational practice.* New York, NY: Macmillan.

Elliott, J. (2005). *Using narrative in social research: Qualitative and quantitative approaches.* London, England: Sage.

Ellis, C. (1993). "There are survivors": Telling a story of sudden death. *The Sociological Quarterly, 34,* 711–730. doi:10.1111/j.1533-8525.1993.tb00114.x

Ellis, C. (2004). *The ethnographic it: A methodological novel about autoethnography.* Walnut Creek, CA: AltaMira Press.

Ely, M. (2007). In-forming re-presentations. In D. J. Clandinin (Ed.), *Handbook of narrative inquiry: Mapping a methodology* (pp. 567–598). Thousand Oaks, CA: Sage.

Ely, M., Anzul, M., Friedman, T., Garner, D., & Steinmetz, A. C. (1991). *Doing qualitative research: Circles within circles.* New York, NY: Falmer Press.

Emerson, R. M., Fretz, R. I., & Shaw, L. L. (2011). *Writing ethnographic fieldnotes* (2nd ed.). Chicago, IL: University of Chicago Press.

Erlandson, D. A., Harris, E. L., Skipper, B. L., & Allen, S. D. (1993). *Doing naturalistic inquiry: A guide to methods.* Newbury Park, CA: Sage.

Ezeh, P. J. (2003). Participant observation. *Qualitative Research, 3,* 191–205. doi:10.1177/14687941030032003

Fabricius, A. H. (2014). The transnational and the individual: A life-history narrative in a Danish university context. *Journal of Education for Teaching: International Research and Pedagogy, 40,* 284–299. doi:10.1080/02607476.2014.903027

Fay, B. (1987). *Critical social science.* Ithaca, NY: Cornell University Press.

Ferguson, M., & Wicke, J. (1994). *Feminism and postmodernism.* Durham, NC: Duke University Press.

Fetterman, D. M. (2010). *Ethnography: Step-by-step* (3rd ed.). Thousand Oaks, CA: Sage.

Fischer, C. T., & Wertz, F. J. (1979). An empirical phenomenology study of being criminally victimized. In A.

Giorgi, R. Knowles, & D. Smith (Eds.), *Duquesne studies in phenomenological psychology* (Vol. 3, pp. 135–158). Pittsburgh, PA: Duquesne University Press.

Flick, U. (Ed.). (2014). *The SAGE handbook of qualitative analysis.* Thousand Oaks, CA: Sage.

Flinders, D. J., & Mills, G. E. (1993). *Theory and concepts in qualitative research.* New York, NY: Teachers College Press.

Flyvbjerg, B. (2006). Five misunderstandings about case-study research. *Qualitative Inquiry, 12*(2), 219–245. doi:10.1177/1077800405284363

Foucault, M. (1972). *The archeology of knowledge and the discourse on language* (A. M. Sheridan Smith, Trans.). New York, NY: Harper.

Fox-Keller, E. (1985). *Reflections on gender and science.* New Haven, CT: Yale University Press.

Frelin, A. (2015). Relational underpinnings and professionality—A case study of a teacher's practices involving students with experiences of school failure. *School Psychology International, 36,* 589–604. doi:10.1177/0143034315607412

Friese, S. (2014). *Qualitative data analysis with ATLAS.ti* (2nd ed.). Thousand Oaks, CA: Sage.

Gamson, J. (2000). Sexualities, queer theory and qualitative research. In N. K. Denzin & Y. S. Lincoln (Eds.), *The SAGE handbook of qualitative research* (2nd ed., pp. 347–365). Thousand Oaks, CA: Sage.

Garcia, A. C., Standlee, A. I., Bechkoff, J., & Cui, Y. (2009). Ethnographic approaches to the Internet and computer-mediated communication. *Journal of Contemporary Ethnography, 38*(1), 52–84. doi:10.1177/0891241607310839

Gee, J. P. (1991). A linguistic approach to narrative. *Journal of Narrative and Life History/Narrative Inquiry, 1,* 15–39. Retrieved from http://www2.clarku.edu/~mbamberg/Pages_Journals/journal-narrative.html

Geiger, S. N. G. (1986). Women's life histories: Method and content. *Signs: Journal of Women in Culture and Society, 11,* 334–351. Retrieved from http://www.jstor.org/stable/3174056

Gergen, K. (1994). *Realities and relationships: Soundings in social construction.* Cambridge, MA: Harvard University Press.

Gibbs, G. R. (2014). Using software in qualitative analysis. In U. Flick (Ed.), *The SAGE handbook of qualitative analysis* (pp. 277–294). Thousand Oaks, CA: Sage.

Gilbert, L. S., Jackson, K., & di Gregorio, S. (2014). Tools for analyzing qualitative data: The history and relevance of qualitative data analysis software. In J. M. Spector, M. D. Merrill, J. Elen, & M. J. Bishop (Eds.), *Handbook of research on educational communications and technology* (4th ed., pp. 221–236). New York, NY: Springer Science+Business Media

Gilchrist, V. J. (1992). Key informant interviews. In B. F. Crabtree & W. L. Miller (Eds.), *Doing qualitative research* (pp. 70–89). Newbury Park, CA: Sage.

Gilgun, J. F. (2005). "Grab" and good science: Writing up the results of qualitative research. *Qualitative Health Research, 15,* 256–262. doi:10.1177/1049732304268796

Giorgi, A. (Ed.). (1985). *Phenomenology and psychological research.* Pittsburgh, PA: Duquesne University Press.

Giorgi, A. (1994). A phenomenological perspective on certain qualitative research methods. *Journal of Phenomenological Psychology, 25,* 190–220. doi:10.1163/156916294X00034.

Giorgi, A. (2009). *The descriptive phenomenological method in psychology: A modified Husserlian approach.* Pittsburgh, PA: Duquesne University Press.

Given, L. (Ed.). (2008). *The SAGE encyclopedia of qualitative research methods.* Thousand Oaks, CA: Sage

Glaser, B., & Strauss, A. (1965). *Awareness of dying.* Chicago, IL: Aldine.

Glaser, B., & Strauss, A. (1967). *The discovery of grounded theory.* Chicago, IL: Aldine.

Glaser, B., & Strauss, A. (1968). *Time for dying.* Chicago, IL: Aldine.

Glaser, B. G. (1978). *Theoretical sensitivity.* Mill Valley, CA: Sociology Press.

Glaser, B. G. (1992). *Basics of grounded theory analysis.* Mill Valley, CA: Sociology Press.

Glesne, C. (2016). *Becoming qualitative researchers: An introduction* (5th ed.). Boston, MA: Pearson.

Glesne, C., & Peshkin, A. (1992). *Becoming qualitative researchers: An introduction.* White Plains, NY: Longman

Goffman, A. (2014). *On the run: Fugitive life in an American city (fieldwork encounters and discoveries).* Chicago IL: Chicago University Press.

Goffman. E. (1989). On fieldwork. *Journal of Contemporary Ethnography, 18,* 123–132.

Grbich, C. (2013). *Qualitative data analysis: An introduction* (2nd ed.). Thousand Oaks, CA: Sage.

Grigsby, K. A., & Megel, M. E. (1995). Caring experiences of nurse educators. *Journal of Nursing Research, 34,* 411–418. doi:10.1177/089124189018002001

Guba, E. G. (1990). The alternative paradigm dialog. In E. G. Guba (Ed.), *The paradigm dialog* (pp. 17–30). Newbury Park, CA: Sage.

Guba, E. G., & Lincoln, Y. S. (1988). Do inquiry paradigms imply inquiry methodologies? In D. M. Fetterman (Ed.), *Qualitative approaches to evaluation in education* (pp. 89–115). New York, NY: Praeger.

Guba, E. G., & Lincoln, Y. S. (1989). *Fourth generation evaluation.* Newbury Park, CA: Sage.

Guell, C., & Ogilvie, D. (2015). Picturing commuting: Photovoice and seeking well-being in everyday travel, *Qualitative Research, 15,* 201–218. doi:10.1177/1468794112468472.

Guest, G., Namey, E. E., & Mitchell, M. L. (2013). *Collecting qualitative data: A field manual for applied research.* Thousand Oaks, CA: Sage.

Hacker, K. (2013). *Community-based participatory research.* Thousand Oaks, CA: Sage.

Haenfler, R. (2004). Rethinking subcultural resistance: Core values of the straight edge movement. *Journal of Contemporary*

Ethnography, 33, 406–436. doi:10.1177/0891241603259809

Halfpenny, P., & Procter, R. (2015). *Innovations in digital research methods.* Thousand Oaks, CA: Sage.

Hamel, J., Dufour, S., & Fortin, D. (1993). *Case study methods.* Newbury Park, CA: Sage.

Hammersley, M., & Atkinson, P. (1995). *Ethnography: Principles in practice* (2nd ed.). New York, NY: Routledge.

Hammersley, M., & Atkinson, P. (2007). *Ethnography: Principles in practice* (3rd ed.). New York, NY: Routledge.

Harding, P. (2009). *Tinkers.* New York, NY: Bellevue Literary Press.

Harley, A. E., Buckworth, J., Katz, M. L., Willis, S. K., Odoms-Young, A., & Heaney, C. A. (2009). Developing long-term physical activity participation: A grounded theory study with African American women. *Health Education & Behavior, 36*(1), 97–112. doi:10.1177/1090198107306434

Harper, W. (1981). The experience of leisure. *Leisure Sciences, 4,* 113–126. doi:10.1080/01490408109512955

Harris, C. (1993). Whiteness as property. *Harvard Law Review, 106,* 1701–1791. doi:10.2307/1341787

Harris, M. (1968). *The rise of anthropological theory: A history of theories of culture.* New York, NY: T. Y. Crowell.

Hatch, J. A. (2002). *Doing qualitative research in education settings.* Albany: State University of New York Press.

Hays, D. G., & Singh, A. A. (2012). *Qualitative inquiry in clinical and educational settings.* New York, NY: Guilford Press.

Healey, G. K. (2014). Inuit family understandings of sexual health and relationships in Nunavut. *Canadian Journal of Public Health, 105*(2), e133–e137. doi:10.17269/cjph.105.4189

Heilbrun, C. G. (1988). *Writing a woman's life.* New York, NY: Ballantine.

Henderson, K. A. (2011). Postpositivism and the pragmatics of leisure research. *Leisure Sciences, 33*(4), 341–346. doi:10.1080/01490400.2011.583166

Heron, J., & Reason, P. (1997). A participatory inquiry paradigm. *Qualitative Inquiry, 3,* 274–294. doi:10.1177/107780049700300302

Hesse-Biber, S. N. (2012). *Handbook of feminist research: Theory and praxis* (2nd ed.). Thousand Oaks, CA: Sage

Hesse-Biber, S. N., & Leavy, P. (2010). The practice of qualitative research (2nd ed.). Thousand Oaks, CA: Sage.

Holloway, I., & Brown, L. (2012). *Essentials of a qualitative doctorate.* Walnut Creek, CA: Left Coast Press.

Howe, K., & Eisenhardt, M. (1990). Standards for qualitative (and quantitative) research: A prolegomenon. *Educational Researcher, 19*(4), 2–9. doi:10.3102/0013189X019004002

Hruschka, D., Schwartz, D., Cobb St. John, D., Picone-Decaro, E., Jenkins, R., & Carey, J. (2004). Reliability in coding open-ended data: Lessons learned from HIV behavioral research.

Field Methods, 16, 307–331. doi:10.1177/1525822X04266540

Huber, J., & Whelan, K. (1999). A marginal story as a place of possibility: Negotiating self on the professional knowledge landscape. *Teaching and Teacher Education, 15*, 381–396. doi:10.1016/S0742-051X(98)00048-1

Huberman, A. M., & Miles, M. B. (1994). Data management and analysis methods. In N. K. Denzin & Y. S. Lincoln (Eds.), *Handbook of qualitative research* (pp. 428–444). Thousand Oaks, CA: Sage.

Huff, A. S. (2009). *Designing research for publication.* Thousand Oaks, CA: Sage.

Husserl, E. (1970). *The crisis of European sciences and transcendental phenomenology* (D. Carr, Trans.). Evanston, IL: Northwestern University Press.

Israel, M., & Hay, I. (2006). *Research ethics for social scientists.* Thousand Oaks, CA: Sage.

Jachyra, P., Atkinson, M., & Washiya, Y. (2015). "Who are you, and what are you doing here": Methodological considerations in ethnographic health and education research. *Ethnography and Education, 10*(2), 242–261. doi:10.1080/17457823.2015.1018290

Jacob, E. (1987). Qualitative research traditions: A review. *Review of Educational Research, 57*, 1–50. doi:10.3102/00346543057001001.

James, N., & Busher, H. (2009). *Online interviewing.* Thousand Oaks, CA: Sage.

Janesick, V. J. (2011). *"Stretching" exercises for qualitative researchers* (3rd ed.). Thousand Oaks, CA: Sage.

Janesick, V. J. (2013). Oral history, life history, and biography. In A. A. Trainor & E. Graue (Eds.), *Reviewing qualitative research in the social sciences* (pp. 151–165). New York, NY: Routledge.

Job, J., Poth, C., Pei, J., Carter-Pasula, B., Brandell, D., & MacNab, J. (2013). Toward better collaboration in the education of students with fetal alcohol spectrum disorders: Voices of teachers, administrators, caregivers, and allied professionals. *Qualitative Research in Education, 2*, 38–64. doi:10.4471/qre.2013.15

Jorgensen, D. L. (1989). *Participant observation: A methodology for human studies.* Newbury Park, CA: Sage.

Josselson, R., & Lieblich, A. (Eds.). (1993). *The narrative study of lives* (Vol. 1). Newbury Park, CA: Sage.

Jungnickel, K. (2014). Getting there . . . and back: How ethnographic commuting (by bicycle) shaped a study of Australian backyard technologists. *Qualitative Research, 14*(6), 640–655. doi:10.1177/1468794113481792

Kelle, E. (Ed.). (1995). *Computer-aided qualitative data analysis.* Thousand Oaks, CA: Sage.

Kemmis, S., & Wilkinson, M. (1998). Participatory action research and the study of practice. In B. Atweh, S. Kemmis, & P. Weeks (Eds.), *Action research in practice: Partnerships for social justice in education* (pp. 21–36). New York, NY: Routledge.

Kenny, M., & Fourie, R. (2014). Tracing the history of grounded theory methodology: From formation to fragmentation. *The Qualitative Report, 19*, 1–9. Retrieved from http://www.nova.edu/ssss/QR/QR19/kenny103.pdf

Kerlinger, F. N. (1979). *Behavioral research: A conceptual approach.* New York, NY: Holt, Rinehart & Winston.

Kidder, L. (1982). Face validity from multiple perspectives. In D. Brinberg & L. Kidder (Eds.), *New directions for methodology of social and behavioral science: Forms of validity in research* (pp. 41–57). San Francisco, CA: Jossey-Bass.

Kincheloe, J. L. (1991). *Teachers as researchers: Qualitative inquiry as a path of empowerment.* London, England: Falmer Press.

Knoblauch, H., Tuma, R., & Schnettler, B. (2014). Video analysis and videography. In U. Flick (Ed.), *The SAGE handbook of qualitative data analysis* (pp. 435–449). Thousand Oaks, CA: Sage.

Komives, S. R., Owen, J. E., Longerbeam, S. D., Mainella, F. C., & Osteen, L. (2005). Developing a leadership identity: A grounded theory. *Journal of College Student Development, 46*(6), 593–611. doi:10.1353/csd.2005.0061

Kroll, T., Barbour, R., & Harris, J. (2007). Using focus groups in disability research, *Qualitative Health Research, 17*, 690–698. doi:10.1177/1049732307301488

Krueger, R. A., & Casey, M. A. (2014). *Focus groups: A practical guide for applied research* (5th ed.). Thousand Oaks, CA: Sage.

Kuckartz, U. (2014). *Qualitative text analysis: A guide to methods, practice and using software*. Thousand Oaks, CA: Sage.

Kus, R. J. (1986). From grounded theory to clinical practice: Cases from gay studies research. In W. C. Chenitz & J. M. Swanson (Eds.), *From practice to grounded theory* (pp. 227–240). Menlo Park, CA: Addison-Wesley.

Labaree, R. V. (2002). The risk of "going observationalist": Negotiating the hidden dilemmas of being an insider participant observer. *Qualitative Research, 2*, 97–122. doi:10.1177/1468794102002001641

Ladson-Billings, G., & Donnor, J. (2005). The moral activist role in critical race theory scholarship. In N. K. Denzin & Y. S. Lincoln (Eds.), *The SAGE handbook of qualitative research* (3rd ed., pp. 279–201). Thousand Oaks, CA: Sage.

LaFrance, J., & Crazy Bull, C. (2009). Researching ourselves back to life: Taking control of the research agenda in Indian Country. In D. M. Mertens & P. E. Ginsburg (Eds.), *The handbook of social research ethics* (pp. 135–149). Thousand Oaks, CA: Sage.

Lambert, P. S. (2015). Advances in data management for social survey research. In P. Halfpenny & R. Proctor (Eds.), *Innovations in digital research methods* (pp. 123–142). Thousand Oaks, CA: Sage.

Lancy, D. F. (1993). *Qualitative research in education: An introduction to the major traditions*. New York, NY: Longman.

Lather, P. (1991). *Getting smart: Feminist research and pedagogy with/in the postmodern*. New York, NY: Routledge.

Lather, P. (1993). Fertile obsession: Validity after poststructuralism. *Sociological Quarterly, 34*, 673–693. doi:10.1111/j.1533-8525.1993.tb00112.x

Lauterbach, S. S. (1993). In another world: A phenomenological perspective and discovery of meaning in mothers' experience with death of a wished-for baby: Doing phenomenology. In P. L. Munhall & C. O. Boyd (Eds.), *Nursing research: A qualitative perspective* (pp. 133–179). New York, NY: National League for Nursing Press.

LeCompte, M. D., & Goetz, J. P. (1982). Problems of reliability and validity in ethnographic research. *Review of Educational Research, 51*, 31–60. doi:10.3102/00346543052001031

LeCompte, M. D., Millroy, W. L., & Preissle, J. (1992). *The handbook of qualitative research in education*. San Diego, CA: Academic Press.

LeCompte, M. D., & Schensul, J. J. (1999). *Designing and conducting ethnographic research* (Ethnographer's toolkit, Vol. 1). Walnut Creek, CA: AltaMira Press.

Leipert, B. D., & Reutter, L. (2005). Developing resilience: How women maintain their health in northern geographically isolated settings. *Qualitative Health Research, 15*, 49–65. doi:10.1177/1049732304269671

Lemay, C. A., Cashman, S. B., Elfenbein, D. S., & Felice, M. E. (2010). A qualitative study of the meaning of fatherhood among young urban fathers. *Public Health Nursing, 27*(3), 221–231. doi:10.1111/j.1525-1446.2010.00847.x

Lempert, L. B. (2007). Asking questions of the data: Memo writing in the grounded theory tradition. In A. Bryant & K. Charmaz (Eds.), *The SAGE handbook of grounded theory* (pp. 245–264). Thousand Oaks, CA: Sage.

LeVasseur, J. J. (2003). The problem of bracketing in phenomenology. *Qualitative Health Research, 13*(3), 408–420. doi:10.1177/1049732302250337

Lieberson, S. (2000). Small N's and big conclusions: An examination of the reasoning in comparative studies based on a small number of cases. In R. Gomm, M. Hammersley, & P. Foster (Eds.), *Case study method* (pp. 208–222). Thousand Oaks, CA: Sage.

Lieblich, A., Tuval-Mashiach, R., & Zilber, T. (1998). *Narrative research: Reading, analysis, and interpretation*. Thousand Oaks, CA: Sage.

Lincoln, Y. S. (1995). Emerging criteria for quality in qualitative and interpretive research. *Qualitative Inquiry, 1*, 275–289. doi:10.1177/107780049500100301

Lincoln, Y. S. (2009). Ethical practices in qualitative research. In D. M. Mertens & P. E. Ginsberg (Ed.), *The handbook of social research ethics* (pp. 150–169). Thousand Oaks, CA: Sage.

Lincoln, Y. S., & Guba, E. G. (1985). *Naturalistic inquiry*. Beverly Hills, CA: Sage.

Lincoln, Y. S., & Guba, E. G. (2000). Paradigmatic controversies, contradictions, and emerging confluences. In N. K. Denzin & Y. S. Lincoln (Eds.), *The SAGE handbook of qualitative research* (2nd ed., pp. 163–188). Thousand Oaks, CA: Sage.

Lincoln, Y. S., Lynham, S. A., & Guba, E. G. (2011). Paradigmatic controversies, contradictions, and emerging confluences. In N. K. Denzin & Y. S. Lincoln (Eds.), *The SAGE handbook of qualitative research* (4th ed., pp. 97–128). Thousand Oaks, CA: Sage.

Lofland, J. (1974). Styles of reporting qualitative field research. *American Sociologist, 9,* 101–111. Retrieved from http://www.jstor.org/stable/27702128

Lofland, J., & Lofland, L. H. (1995). *Analyzing social settings: A guide to qualitative observation and analysis* (3rd ed.). Belmont, CA: Wadsworth.

Lomask, M. (1986). *The biographer's craft.* New York, NY: Harper & Row.

Lovern, L. L. & Locust, C. (2013). *Native American communities on health and disability: Borderland dialogues.* New York, NY: Palgrave Macmillan.

Luck, L., Jackson, D., & Usher, K. (2006). Case study: A bridge across the paradigms. *Nursing Inquiry, 13,* 103–109. doi:10.1111/j.1440-1800.2006.00309.x

Mac an Ghaill, M., & Haywood, C. (2015). British-born Pakistani and Bangladeshi young men: Exploring unstable concepts of Muslim, Islamophobia and racialization. *Critical Sociology, 41,* 97–114. doi:10.1177/0896920513518947

MacKenzie, C. A., Christensen, J., & Turner, S. (2015). Advocating beyond the academy: Dilemmas of communicating relevant research results. *Qualitative Research, 15,* 105–121. doi:10.1177/1049732304268796

Madison, D. S. (2005). *Critical ethnography: Methods, ethics, and performance.* Thousand Oaks, CA: Sage.

Madison, D. S. (2011). *Critical ethnography: Methods, ethics, and performance* (2nd ed.). Thousand Oaks, CA: Sage.

Maeder, C. (2014). Analysing sounds. In U. Flick (Ed.), *The SAGE handbook of qualitative data analysis* (pp. 424–434). Thousand Oaks, CA: Sage.

Marion, J. S., & Crowder, J. W. (2013). *Visual research: A concise introduction to thinking visually.* London, England: Bloomsbury.

Markham, A. N., & Baym, N. K. (2009). *Internet inquiry.* Thousand Oaks, CA: Sage

Marotzki, W., Holze, J., & Verständig, D. (2014). Analysing virtual data. In U. Flick (Ed.), *The SAGE handbook of qualitative data analysis* (pp. 450–464). Thousand Oaks, CA: Sage.

Marshall, C., & Rossman, G. B. (2015). *Designing qualitative research* (6th ed.). Thousand Oaks, CA: Sage.

Martin, J. (1990). Deconstructing organizational taboos: The suppression of gender conflict in organizations. *Organization Science, 1,* 339–359. Retrieved from http://dx.doi.org/10.1287/orsc.1.4.339

Maxwell, J. A. (2012). *A realist approach for qualitative research.* Thousand Oaks, CA: Sage.

Maxwell, J. A. (2013). *Qualitative research design: An interactive approach* (3rd ed.). Thousand Oaks, CA: Sage.

May, K. A. (1986). Writing and evaluating the grounded theory research report. In W. C. Chenitz & J. M. Swanson (Eds.), *From practice to grounded theory* (pp. 146–154). Menlo Park, CA: Addison-Wesley.

McCracken, G. (1988). *The long interview.* Newbury Park, CA: Sage.

McVea, K., Harter, L., McEntarffer, R., & Creswell, J. W. (1999). Phenomenological study of student experiences with tobacco use at City High School. *High School Journal, 82*(4), 209–222.

Merleau-Ponty, M. (1962). *Phenomenology of perception* (C. Smith, Trans.). London, England: Routledge & Kegan Paul.

Merriam, S. (1988). *Case study research in education: A qualitative approach.* San Francisco, CA: Jossey-Bass.

Merriam, S. B. (1998). *Qualitative research and case study applications in education.* San Francisco, CA: Jossey-Bass.

Merriam, S. B., & Tisdell, E. J. (2015). *Qualitative research: A guide to design and implementation* (4th ed.). San Francisco, CA: Jossey-Bass.

Mertens, D. M. (2003). Mixed methods and the politics of human research: The transformative-emancipatory perspective. In A. Tashakkori & C. Teddlie (Eds.), *Handbook of mixed methods in social & behavioral research* (pp. 135–164). Thousand Oaks, CA: Sage.

Mertens, D. M. (2009). *Transformative research and evaluation.* New York, NY: Guilford Press.

Mertens, D. M. (2015). *Research and evaluation in education and psychology: Integrating diversity with quantitative, qualitative, and mixed methods* (4th ed.). Thousand Oaks, CA: Sage.

Mertens, D. M., Cram, F., & Chilisa, B. (Eds.) (2013). *Indigenous pathways into social research*. Walnut Creek, CA: Left Coast Press.

Mertens, D. M., & Ginsberg, P. E. (2009). *The handbook of social research ethics*. Thousand Oaks, CA: Sage.

Mertens, D. M., Sullivan, M., & Stace, H. (2011). Disability communities: Transformative research and social justice. In N. K. Denzin & Y. S. Lincoln (Eds.), *The SAGE handbook of qualitative research* (4th ed., pp. 227–242). Thousand Oaks, CA: Sage.

Mikos, L. (2014). Analysis of film. In U. Flick (Ed.), *The SAGE handbook of qualitative data analysis* (pp. 409–423). Thousand Oaks, CA: Sage.

Miles, M. B., & Huberman, A. M. (1994). *Qualitative data analysis: A sourcebook of new methods* (2nd ed.). Thousand Oaks, CA: Sage.

Miles, M. B., Huberman, A. M., & Saldaña, J. (2014). *Qualitative data analysis: A sourcebook of new methods* (3rd ed.). Thousand Oaks, CA: Sage.

Miller, D. W., Creswell, J. W., & Olander, L. S. (1998). Writing and retelling multiple ethnographic tales of a soup kitchen for the homeless. *Qualitative Inquiry, 4*(4), 469–491. doi:10.1177/107780049800400404

Miller, W. L., & Crabtree, B. F. (1992). Primary care research: A multimethod typology and qualitative road map. In B. F. Crabtree & W. L. Miller (Eds.), *Doing qualitative research* (pp. 3–28). Newbury Park, CA: Sage.

Millhauser, S. (2008). *Dangerous laughter.* New York, NY: Knopf.

Mills, A. J., Durepos, G., & Wiebe, E. (Eds.). (2010). *Encyclopedia of case study research*. Thousand Oaks, CA: Sage.

Mitchell, C. (2011). *Doing visual research*. Thousand Oaks, CA: Sage.

Morgan, D. L. (1997). *Focus groups as qualitative research* (2nd ed). Thousand Oaks, CA: Sage.

Morrow, R. A., & Brown, D. D. (1994). *Critical theory and methodology*. Thousand Oaks, CA: Sage.

Morrow, S. L., & Smith, M. L. (1995). Constructions of survival and coping by women who have survived childhood sexual abuse. *Journal of Counseling Psychology, 42*, 24–33. doi:10.1037/0022-0167.42.1.24

Morse, J. M. (1994). Designing funded qualitative research. In N. K. Denzin & Y. S. Lincoln (Eds.), *Handbook of qualitative research* (pp. 220–235). Thousand Oaks, CA: Sage.

Morse, J. M., & Field, P. A. (1995). *Qualitative research methods for health professionals* (2nd ed.). Thousand Oaks, CA: Sage.

Morse, J. M., & Richards, L. (2002). *README FIRST for a user's guide to qualitative methods.* Thousand Oaks, CA: Sage.

Moss, P. (2007). Emergent methods in feminist research. In S. N. Hesse-Biber (Ed.), *Handbook of feminist research methods* (pp. 371–389). Thousand Oaks, CA: Sage.

Moustakas, C. (1994). *Phenomenological research methods.* Thousand Oaks, CA: Sage.

Muncey, T. (2010). *Creating autoethnographies.* Thousand Oaks, CA: Sage.

Munhall, P. L., & Oiler, C. J. (Eds.). (1986). *Nursing research: A qualitative perspective.* Norwalk, CT: Appleton-Century-Crofts.

Murphy, J. P. (with Rorty, R.). (1990). *Pragmatism: From Peirce to Davidson.* Boulder, CO: Westview Press.

Natanson, M. (Ed.). (1973). *Phenomenology and the social sciences.* Evanston, IL: Northwestern University Press.

Nelson, L. W. (1990). Code-switching in the oral life narratives of African-American women: Challenges to linguistic hegemony. *Journal of Education, 172*, 142–155. Retrieved from http://www.jstor.org/stable/42742191

Neuman, W. L. (2000). *Social research methods: Qualitative and quantitative approaches* (4th ed.). Boston, MA: Allyn & Bacon.

Nicholas, D. B., Lach, L., King, G., Scott, M., Boydell, K., Sawatzky, B., . . . Young, N. L. (2010). Contrasting internet and face-to-face focus groups for children with chronic health conditions: Outcomes and participant experiences. *International Journal of Qualitative Methods, 9*(1), 105–121. doi:10.1177/160940691000900102.

Nieswiadomy, R. M. (1993). *Foundations of nursing research* (2nd ed.). Norwalk, CT: Appleton & Lange.

Nunkoosing, K. (2005). The problems with

interviews. *Qualitative Health Research, 15,* 698–706. doi:10.1177/1049732304273903

Oiler, C. J. (1986). Phenomenology: The method. In P. L. Munhall & C. J. Oiler (Eds.), *Nursing research: A qualitative perspective* (pp. 69–82). Norwalk, CT: Appleton-Century-Crofts.

Olesen, V. (2011). Feminist qualitative research in the Millennium's first decade: Developments, challenges, prospects. In N. K. Denzin & Y. S. Lincoln (Eds.), *The SAGE handbook of qualitative research* (4th ed., pp. 129–146). Thousand Oaks, CA: Sage.

Ollerenshaw, J. A., & Creswell, J. W. (2002). Narrative research: A comparison of two restorying data analysis approaches. *Qualitative Inquiry, 8,* 329–347. doi:10.1177/ 10778004008003008

Orkin, A., & Newbery, S. (2014). Penny Armitage: "I'm the 85th baby born in Marathon," *Canadian Family Physician, 60,* e49–e52. Retrieved from www .cfp.ca/content/60/1/58.full

Padilla, R. (2003). Clara: A phenomenology of disability. *The American Journal of Occupational Therapy, 57*(4), 413–423. doi:10.5014/ajot.57.4.413

Parker, L., & Lynn, M. (2002). What race got to do with it? Critical race theory's conflicts with and connections to qualitative research methodology and epistemology. *Qualitative Inquiry, 8*(1), 7–22. doi:10.1177/ 107780040200800102

Patton, M. Q. (1980). *Qualitative evaluation methods.* Beverly Hills, CA: Sage.

Patton, M. Q. (1990). *Qualitative evaluation and research methods.* Newbury Park, CA: Sage.

Patton, M. Q. (2011). *Essential of utilization-focused evaluation.* Thousand Oaks, CA: Sage.

Patton, M. Q. (2015). *Qualitative evaluation and research methods* (4th ed.). Thousand Oaks, CA: Sage.

Pelias, R. J., (2011). Writing into position: Strategies for composition and evaluation. In N. K. Denzin & Y. S. Lincoln (Eds.), *The SAGE handbook of qualitative research* (4th ed., pp. 659–668). Thousand Oaks, CA: Sage.

Pereira, H. (2012). Rigour in phenomenological research: Reflections of a novice nurse researcher. *Nurse Researcher, 19*(3), 16–19.

Personal Narratives Group. (1989). *Interpreting women's lives.* Bloomington: Indiana University Press.

Phillips, D. C., & Burbules, N. C. (2000). *Postpositivism and educational research.* Lanham, MD: Rowman & Littlefield.

Pink, S. (2001). *Doing visual ethnography.* Thousand Oaks, CA: Sage.

Pinnegar, S., & Daynes, J. G. (2007). Locating narrative inquiry historically: Thematics in the turn to narrative. In D. J. Clandinin (Ed.), *Handbook of narrative inquiry: Mapping a methodology* (pp. 3–34). Thousand Oaks, CA: Sage.

Plummer, K. (1983). *Documents of life: An introduction to the problems and literature of a humanistic method.* London, England: George Allen & Unwin.

Plummer, K. (2011a). Critical humanism and queer theory: Living with the tensions. In N. K. Denzin & Y. S. Lincoln (Eds.), *The SAGE handbook of qualitative research* (4th ed., pp. 195–207). Thousand Oaks, CA: Sage.

Plummer, K. (2011b). Postscript 2011 to living with the contradictions: Moving on: Generations, cultures and methodological cosmopolitanism. In N. K. Denzin & Y. S. Lincoln (Eds.), *The SAGE handbook of qualitative research* (4th ed., pp. 208–211). Thousand Oaks, CA: Sage.

Polkinghorne, D. E. (1989). Phenomenological research methods. In R. S. Valle & S. Halling (Eds.), *Existential-phenomenological perspectives in psychology* (pp. 41–60). New York, NY: Plenum Press.

Polkinghorne, D. E. (1995). Narrative configuration in qualitative analysis. *Qualitative Studies in Education, 8,* 5–23. doi:10.1080/0951839950080103

Poth, C. (2008). *Promoting evaluation use within dynamic organizations: A case study examining evaluator behavior* (Unpublished dissertation). Queen's University, Kingston, Ontario.

Prior, L. (2003). *Using documents in social research.* Thousand Oaks, CA: Sage.

Ravitch, S. M., & Mittenfelner Carl, C. N. (2016). *Qualitative research: Bridging the conceptual, theoretical, and methodological.* Thousand Oaks, CA: Sage.

Ravitch, S. M., & Riggan, M. (2012). *Reason & rigor: How conceptual frameworks guide research.* Thousand Oaks, CA: Sage.

Reinharz, S. (1992). *Feminist methods in social research.* New York, NY: Oxford University Press.

Rhoads, R. A. (1995). Whales tales, dog piles, and beer goggles: An ethnographic case study of fraternity life. *Anthropology and Education Quarterly, 26,* 306–323. Retrieved from http://www.jstor.org/stable/3195675

Richards, L. (2015). *Handling qualitative data: A practical guide* (3rd ed.). Thousand Oaks, CA: Sage.

Richards, L., & Morse, J. M. (2012). *README FIRST for a users guide to qualitative methods* (3rd ed.). Thousand Oaks, CA: Sage.

Richardson, L. (1990). *Writing strategies: Reaching diverse audiences.* Newbury Park, CA: Sage.

Richardson, L. (1994). Writing: A method of inquiry. In N. K. Denzin & Y. S. Lincoln (Eds.), *Handbook of qualitative research* (pp. 516–529). Thousand Oaks, CA: Sage.

Richardson, L. (2000). Evaluating ethnography. *Qualitative Inquiry, 6,* 253–255. doi:10.1177/107780040000600207

Richardson, L., & St. Pierre, E. A. (2005). Writing: A method of inquiry. In N. K. Denzin & Y. S. Lincoln (Eds.), *The SAGE handbook of qualitative research* (3rd ed., pp. 959–978). Thousand Oaks, CA: Sage.

Riemen, D. J. (1986). The essential structure of a caring interaction: Doing phenomenology. In P. M. Munhall & C. J. Oiler (Eds.), *Nursing research: A qualitative perspective* (pp. 85–105). Norwalk, CT: Appleton-Century-Crofts.

Riessman, C. K. (1993). *Narrative analysis.* Newbury Park, CA: Sage.

Riessman, C. K. (2008). *Narrative methods for the human sciences.* Thousand Oaks, CA: Sage.

Rorty, R. (1983). *Consequences of pragmatism.* Minneapolis: University of Minnesota Press.

Rorty, R. (1990). Pragmatism as anti-representationalism. In J. P. Murphy (Ed.), *Pragmatism: From Peirce to Davidson* (pp. 1–6). Boulder, CO: Westview Press.

Rose, G. (2012). *Visual methodologies: An introduction to research with visual materials* (3rd ed.). Thousand Oaks, CA: Sage.

Rossman, G. B., & Wilson, B. L. (1985). Numbers and words: Combining quantitative and qualitative methods in a single large-scale evaluation study. *Evaluation Review, 9*(5), 627–643. doi:10.1177/0193841X8500900505

Roulston, K., deMarrais, K., & Lewis, J. B. (2003). Learning to interview in the social sciences. *Qualitative Inquiry, 9,* 643–668. doi:10.1177/1077800403252736

Rubin, H. J., & Rubin, I. S. (2012). *Qualitative interviewing: The art of hearing data* (3rd ed.). Thousand Oaks, CA: Sage.

Ruohotie-Lyhty, M. (2013). Struggling for a professional identity: Two newly qualified language teachers' identity narratives during the first years at work. *Teaching and Teacher Education, 30,* 120–129. doi:10.1016/j.tate.2012.11.002

Saldaña, J. (2011). *Fundamentals of qualitative research.* Oxford, England: Oxford University Press.

Saldaña, J. (2013). *The coding manual for qualitative researchers* (2nd ed.). Thousand Oaks, CA: Sage.

Sampson, H. (2004). Navigating the waves: The usefulness of a pilot in qualitative research. *Qualitative Research, 4,* 383–402. doi:10.1177/1468794104047236

Sanjek, R. (1990). *Fieldnotes: The makings of anthropology.* Ithaca, NY: Cornell University Press.

Schwandt, T. A. (2007). *The SAGE dictionary of qualitative inquiry* (3rd ed.). Thousand Oaks, CA: Sage.

Sieber, J. E., & Tolich, M. B. (2013). *Planning ethically responsible research* (2nd ed.). Thousand Oaks, CA: Sage.

Silver, C., & Lewins, A. (2014). *Using software in qualitative research: A step-by-step guide* (2nd ed.) Thousand Oaks, CA: Sage.

Silverman, D. (2013). *Doing qualitative research: A practical handbook* (4th ed.). Thousand Oaks, CA: Sage.

Simmonds, S., Roux, C., & ter Avest, I. (2015). Blurring the boundaries between photovoice and narrative inquiry: A narrative-photovoice methodology for gender-based research. *International Journal of Qualitative Methods, 14,* 33–49. doi:10.1177/160940691501400303

Slife, B. D., & Williams, R. N. (1995). *What's behind the research? Discovering hidden assumptions in the behavioral sciences.* Thousand Oaks, CA: Sage.

Smith, J. A., Flowers, P., & Larkin, M. (2009). *Interpretative phenomenological analysis: Theory, method and research.* Thousand Oaks, CA: Sage.

Smith, L. M. (1994). Biographical method. In N. K. Denzin & Y. S. Lincoln (Eds.), *Handbook of qualitative research* (pp. 286–305). Thousand Oaks, CA: Sage.

Solorzano, D. G., & Yosso, T. J. (2002). Critical race methodology: Counter-storytelling as an analytical framework for education research. *Qualitative Inquiry, 8*(1), 23–44. doi:10.1177/107780040200800103

Spiegelberg, H. (1982). *The phenomenological movement* (3rd ed.). The Hague, Netherlands: Martinus Nijhoff.

Spindler, G., & Spindler, L. (1987). Teaching and learning how to do the ethnography of education. In G. Spindler & L. Spindler (Eds.), *Interpretive ethnography of education: At home and abroad* (pp. 17–33). Hillsdale, NJ: Lawrence Erlbaum.

Spradley, J. P. (1979). *The ethnographic interview*. New York, NY: Holt, Rinehart & Winston.

Spradley, J. P. (1980). *Participant observation*. New York, NY: Holt, Rinehart & Winston.

Stake, R. (1995). *The art of case study research*. Thousand Oaks, CA: Sage.

Stake, R. E. (2005). Qualitative case studies. In N. K. Denzin & Y. S. Lincoln (Eds.), *The SAGE handbook of qualitative research* (3rd ed., pp. 443–466). Thousand Oaks, CA: Sage.

Stake, R. E. (2006). *Multiple case study analysis*. New York, NY: Guilford Press.

Stake, R. E. (2010). *Qualitative research: Studying how things work*. New York, NY: Guilford Press.

Stanfield, J. H., II (Ed.) (2011). *Rethinking race and ethnicity in research methods*. Walnut Creek, CA: Left Coast Press.

Staples, A., Pugach, M. C., & Himes, D. J. (2005). Rethinking the technology integration challenge: Cases from three urban elementary schools. *Journal of Research on Technology in Education, 37*(3), 285–311. doi:10.1080/15391523.2005.10782438

Stewart, A. J. (1994). Toward a feminist strategy for studying women's lives. In C. E. Franz & A. J. Stewart (Eds.), *Women creating lives: Identities, resilience and resistance* (pp. 11–35). Boulder, CO: Westview Press.

Stewart, D., & Mickunas, A. (1990). *Exploring phenomenology: A guide to the field and its literature* (2nd ed.). Athens: Ohio University Press.

Stewart, D. W., & Shamdasani, P. N. (1990). *Focus groups: Theory and practice*. Newbury Park, CA: Sage.

Stewart, K., & Williams, M. (2005). Researching online populations: The use of online focus groups for social research. *Qualitative Research, 5*, 395–416. doi:10.1177/1468794105056916

Strauss, A. (1987). *Qualitative analysis for social scientists*. New York, NY: Cambridge University Press.

Strauss, A., & Corbin, J. (1990). *Basics of qualitative research: Grounded theory procedures and techniques*. Newbury Park, CA: Sage.

Strauss, A., & Corbin, J. (1998). *Basics of qualitative research: Techniques and procedures for developing grounded theory* (2nd ed.). Thousand Oaks, CA: Sage.

Stringer, E. T. (1993). Socially responsive educational research: Linking theory and practice. In D. J. Flinders & G. E. Mills (Eds.), *Theory and concept in qualitative research: Perspectives from the field* (pp. 141–162). New York, NY: Teachers College Press.

Strunk, W., & White, E. B. (2000). *The elements of style* (4th ed.). Upper Saddle River, NJ: Pearson.

Sudnow, D. (1978). *Ways of the hand*. New York, NY: Knopf.

Suoninen, E., & Jokinen, A. (2005). Persuasion in social work interviewing. *Qualitative Social Work, 4*, 469–487. doi:10.1177/1473325005058647

Swingewood, A. (1991). *A short history of sociological thought*. New York, NY: St. Martin's Press.

Sword, H. (2012). *Stylish academic writing*. Cambridge, MA: Harvard University Press.

Tashakkori, A., & Teddlie, C. (Eds.). (2003). *SAGE handbook of mixed methods in the social and behavioral sciences*. Thousand Oaks, CA: Sage.

Taylor, S. J., & Bogdan, R. (1998). *Introduction to qualitative research methods: A guidebook and resource* (3rd ed.). New York, NY: John Wiley.

Tesch, R. (1988). *The contribution of a qualitative method: Phenomenological research*. Unpublished manuscript, Qualitative Research Management, Santa Barbara, CA.

Tesch, R. (1990). *Qualitative research: Analysis types and software tools*. Bristol, PA: Falmer Press.

Therberge, N. (1997). "It's part of the game": Physicality and the production of gender in women's hockey. *Gender & Society, 11*(1), 69–87. doi:10.1177/089124397011001005

Thomas, G. (2015). *How to do your case study* (2nd ed.). Thousand Oaks, CA: Sage.

Thomas, J. (1993). *Doing critical ethnography.* Newbury Park, CA: Sage.

Thomas, W. I., & Znaniecki, F. (1958). *The Polish peasant in Europe and America.* New York: Dover. (Original work published 1918–1920)

Tierney, W. G. (1995). (Re)presentation and voice. *Qualitative Inquiry, 1,* 379–390. doi: 10.1177/107780049500100401.

Tierney, W. G. (1997). *Academic outlaws: Queer theory and cultural studies in the academy.* Thousand Oaks, CA: Sage.

Thornton Dill, B., & Kohlman, M. H. (2012). Intersectionality: A transformative paradigm in feminist theory and social justice. In S. Nagy Hesse-Biber (Ed.) *Handbook of feminist research: Theory and praxis* (2nd ed., pp. 154–174). Thousand Oaks, CA: Sage.

Trujillo, N. (1992). Interpreting (the work and the talk of) baseball. *Western Journal of Communication, 56,* 350–371. doi:10.1353/csd.2005.0061

Turner, W. (2000). *A genealogy of queer theory.* Philadelphia, PA: Temple University Press.

van der Hoorn, B. (2015). Playing projects: Identifying flow in the 'lived experience.' *International Journal of Project Management, 33,* 1008–1021. doi:10.1016/j.ijproman.2015.01.009

Van Hout, M. C., & Bingham, T. (2013). "Silk Road," the virtual drug marketplace: A single case study of user experiences. *International Journal of Drug Policy, 23,* 385–391. doi:org/10.1016/j.drugpo.2013.01.005

Van Kaam, A. (1966). *Existential foundations of psychology.* Pittsburgh, PA: Duquesne University Press.

Van Maanen, J. (1988). *Tales of the field: On writing ethnography.* Chicago, IL: University of Chicago Press.

Van Maanen, J. (2011). *Tales of the field: On writing ethnography* (2nd ed.). Chicago, IL: University of Chicago Press.

van Manen, M. (1990). *Researching lived experience: Human science for an action sensitive pedagogy.* Albany: State University of New York Press.

van Manen, M. (2006). Writing qualitatively, or the demands of writing. *Qualitative Health Research, 16,* 713–722.

van Manen, M. (2014). *Phenomenology of practice: Meaning-giving methods in phenomenological research and writing.* Walnut Creek, CA: Left Coast Press.

Wallace, A. F. C. (1970). *Culture and personality* (2nd ed.). New York, NY: Random House.

Warren, C. A., & Xavia Karner, T. (2015). *Discovering qualitative methods: Ethnography, interviews, documents, and images* (3rd ed.). New York, NY: Oxford University Press.

Watson, K. (2005). Queer theory. *Group Analysis, 38*(1), 67–81. doi:10.1177/0533316405049369

Watts, I. E., & Erevelles, N. (2004). These deadly times: Reconceptualizing school violence by using critical race theory and disability studies. *American Journal of Educational Research, 41,* 271–299. doi:10.3102/00028312041002271.

Weiner-Levey, N., & Popper-Giveon, A. (2013). The absent the hidden and the obscured: reflections on "dark matter" in qualitative research. *Quality & Quantity, 47,* 2177–2190. doi:10.1007/s11135-011-9650-7

Weis, L., & Fine, M. (2000). *Speed bumps: A student-friendly guide to qualitative research.* New York, NY: Teachers College Press.

Weitzman, E. A. (2000). Software and qualitative research. In N. K. Denzin & Y. S. Lincoln (Eds.), *The SAGE handbook of qualitative research* (2nd ed., pp. 803–820). Thousand Oaks, CA: Sage.

Weitzman, E. A., & Miles, M. B. (1995). *Computer programs for qualitative data analysis.* Thousand Oaks, CA: Sage.

Wertz, F. J. (2005). Phenomenological research methods for counseling psychology. *Journal of Counseling Psychology, 52,* 167–177. doi:10.1037/0022-0167.52.2.167

Whittemore, R., Chase, S. K., & Mandle, C. L. (2001). Validity in qualitative research. *Qualitative Health Research, 11,* 522–537. doi:10.1177/104973201129119299

Willis, P. (1977). *Learning to labour: How working class kids get working class jobs.* Westmead, England: Saxon House.

Winthrop, R. H. (1991). *Dictionary of concepts in cultural anthropology.* Westport, CT: Greenwood Press.

Wolcott, H. F. (1987). On ethnographic intent. In G. Spindler & L. Spindler (Eds.), *Interpretive ethnography of education: At home and abroad* (pp. 37–57). Hillsdale, NJ: Lawrence Erlbaum.

Wolcott, H. F. (1990). On seeking—and rejecting—validity in qualitative research. In E. W. Eisner & A. Peshkin (Eds.), *Qualitative inquiry in education: The continuing debate* (pp. 121–152). New York, NY: Teachers College Press.

Wolcott, H. F. (1992). Posturing in qualitative research. In M. D. LeCompte, W. L. Millroy, & J. Preissle (Eds.), *The handbook of qualitative research in education* (pp. 3–52). San Diego, CA: Academic Press.

Wolcott, H. F. (1994). *Transforming qualitative data: Description, analysis, and interpretation.* Thousand Oaks, CA: Sage.

Wolcott, H. F. (2008a). *Ethnography: A way of seeing* (2nd ed.). Walnut Creek, CA: AltaMira Press.

Wolcott, H. F. (2008b). *Writing up qualitative research* (3rd ed.). Thousand Oaks, CA: Sage.

Wolcott, H. F. (2010). *Ethnography lessons: A primer.* Walnut Creek, CA: Left Coast Press.

Yin, R. K. (2009). *Case study research: Design and method* (4th ed.). Thousand Oaks, CA: Sage.

Yin, R. K. (2014). *Case study research: Design and method* (5th ed.). Thousand Oaks, CA: Sage.

Yussen, S. R., & Ozcan, N. M. (1997). The development of knowledge about narratives. *Issues in Educational Psychology: Contributions From Educational Psychology, 2,* 1–68.

• Name Index •

• Subject Index •